These essays by leading agricultural economists provide an introduction to California agriculture. Each chapter includes basic data, trends over time, and current issues. The project was supported by the Giannini Foundation of Agricultural Economics, which was established with a 1928 grant to analyze and propose policies to improve California agriculture. We are grateful to the researchers at UC Berkeley, UC Davis, and UC Riverside who contributed to this book, and to Julie McNamara, the Giannini Foundation communications director, and Tiffany Loveridge, outreach coordinator, for editing and laying out the chapters. And special thanks to Julian Alston and Ria DeBiase for providing their expertise and careful review of the manuscripts. Each chapter is self-contained, which means that some basic parameters of the state's agriculture may be found in several chapters. The book is posted online at https://giannini.ucop.edu/publications/cal-ag-book/

Editors

Philip L. Martin
Emeritus Professor
Department of Agricultural and Resource Economics
UC Davis

Rachael E. Goodhue
Professor and Chair
Department of Agricultural and Resource Economics
UC Davis

Brian Wright
Professor and Director of the Giannini Foundation of Agricultural Economics
Department of Agricultural and Resource Economics
UC Berkeley

Managing Editor

Julie McNamara
Communications Director
Giannini Foundation of Agricultural Economics

Production and Design Assistant

Tiffany Loveridge
Outreach Coordinator
Department of Agricultural and Resource Economics
UC Davis

Cover Illustration: Over 44 percent of California's $50 billion in farm sales in 2017 were fruits and nuts, followed by 24 percent for dairy and livestock, 17 percent for vegetables and melons, 14 percent for nursery and other horticultural specialties, and 4 percent for field crops. (Graphic created by Joshua Bingham)

BOOK TABLE OF CONTENTS

Chapter 1. Introduction to California Agriculture

Abstract

California has led the nation in farm sales since 1948, when Los Angeles County had more farm sales than any other U.S. county. The major reason that California's farm sales of $45 billion in 2017, according to the Census of Agriculture, were over $15 billion more than number two Iowa at $29 billion, is the dominance of high-value fruit, nut, and vegetable crops among the state's farm commodities. Over three-fourths of California's farm sales are fruits and nuts, vegetables and melons, and horticultural specialties such as floriculture, nurseries, and mushrooms, so-called FVH crops.

The value of California crops was $33.4 billion in 2017 and the value of livestock was $11.8 billion.[1] California's leading commodities were milk, worth $6.6 billion in 2017; grapes, $5.8 billion; almonds, $5.6 billion; berries, $3.1 billion; cattle, $2.6 billion; and lettuce, $2.4 billion. These six commodities accounted for over half of California's farm sales. California exported farm commodities worth $21 billion (farm value) in 2017, led by almonds $4.5 billion; dairy products, $1.6 billion; and pistachios, $1.5 billion.

The Covid-19 pandemic disrupted California agriculture in 2020. People who stayed home were still eating, but the demand for many California commodities fell as schools and restaurants closed, reducing the farm prices of milk and fresh fruits and vegetables. The demand for fresh flowers evaporated as events were cancelled, while sales of nursery plants rose with more home gardening. Farms were essential businesses and expected their employees to continue to report to work, and most did. There were isolated reports of Covid-19 outbreaks in farm workplaces but, unlike meatpacking plants, farms did not become hotspots for Covid-19.

The longer-term effects of Covid-19 on agriculture are not yet clear. The consolidation of production onto fewer and larger farms is likely to accelerate as, for example, dairies that were already under stress exit. Higher labor costs and labor uncertainties are likely to speed mechanization in raisin grapes, olives, and canning peaches, commodities that can be harvested by machine.

The number of jobs certified to be filled with H-2A guest workers was higher in the first half of FY20 than in the first half of FY19. The U.S. government allowed H-2A workers to enter the United States as essential workers, suggesting that policy makers do not anticipate many jobless U.S. workers filling seasonal farm jobs. California agriculture has always been a dynamic industry capable of adjusting to challenges that range from transportation to water to labor, and will likely adjust to the Covid-19 pandemic as well.

1 These farm sales data exclude cannabis, which is covered in Chapter 13.

About the Editors

Philip L. Martin is an emeritus professor in the Department of Agricultural and Resource Economics at UC Davis, who can be contacted at plmartin@ucdavis.edu. Rachael E. Goodhue is a professor and chair in the Department of Agricultural and Resource Economics at UC Davis. She can be contacted by email at regoodhue@ucdavis.edu. Brian D. Wright is a professor in the Department of Agricultural and Resource Economics at UC Berkeley and director of the Giannini Foundation of Agricultural Economics, who can be contacted at bwright@berkeley.edu. All three authors are members of the Giannini Foundation of Agricultural Economics.

CHAPTER 1. TABLE OF CONTENTS

HISTORY, LAND, LABOR, AND WATER

HISTORY

California's agricultural history differs from that of most states, beginning with the distribution of land. The Spanish and Mexican governments granted large parcels or ranchos of 50,000 or more acres to selected individuals. When California became a U.S. state in 1850, farming consisted largely of cattle grazing and dryland, or non-irrigated wheat farming, on vast ranchos.

There were fewer than 10,000 non-indigenous people in California when gold was discovered in 1848, but over 300,000 settlers arrived over the next decade, increasing local demand for food. The same entrepreneurial spirit animating those who were mechanizing gold mining led to an expansion of wheat production. California developed giant bonanza wheat farms that were much larger than the typical family farms found in the Midwest. California farmers developed a novel cropping system by planting spring-habit wheat varieties in the fall (as opposed to the spring) and harvesting in the summer. They also relied more on hired labor during the harvest than Midwestern operations.

Acreage of wheat and barley peaked at almost 4 million in the late 1880s, and about this time the acreage in fruit production began to expand rapidly. There were an estimated 4 million fruit trees in the state in 1880, and almost seven times more in 1900, reflecting new plantings of oranges, peaches, plums, and pears. Irrigated acreage also expanded quickly. There were fewer than 350,000 irrigated acres in 1880, 1.5 million in 1900, almost 5 million in 1930, and 8 million irrigated acres today.

Many factors helped to transform California agriculture from grains to fruit and other high-value commodities, including the maturation of the transportation system in the 1880s, lower capital costs, biological learning, irrigation, and marketing cooperatives to sell California commodities. California's population rose from a million in 1890 to 5 million in 1930, increasing the demand for a wide range of commodities to feed residents and those outside the state.

Figure 1.1. California Indian Pre-Contact Tribal Territories

California had 100,000 or more Native Americans in at least 70 distinct groups before the arrival of Europeans; they were a third of the indigenous in what is now the United States.

Source: California Indian Library Collections

Biological innovations allowed California farmers to plant the types of grains, fruits, and cotton best suited for the state's Mediterranean climate. Labor-saving machines handled first grain, and later cotton harvests on large-acreage farms. The switch from wheat to perennial fruits in the 1880s was motivated by biological innovations that developed varieties that were optimal for California, and lower interest rates allowed farmers to wait several years for a return on their investment. California farmers were able to produce higher-quality fruit than farmers in Europe's Mediterranean basin, and they expanded fruit production behind U.S. tariffs that protected them from foreign competition despite high transport costs from California to Eastern U.S. markets.

The Depression of the 1930s led to an agricultural crisis marked by low prices for farm commodities, the construction of dams and canals to move water from Northern California to the San Joaquin Valley, and the arrival of Dust Bowl farmers symbolized by John Steinbeck's *The Grapes of Wrath*. California's population expanded to over 10 million by 1950, and California agriculture imported Mexican Bracero workers under a series of agreements between 1942 and 1964.

Since 1960, the state's major agricultural developments include the growing importance of Fruit, Vegetable, and Horticultural (FVH) commodities in the state's farm sales, the rise of the dairy industry, and the expansion and contraction of particular commodities, including the spectacular rise of tree nuts and strawberries and the contraction of cotton and asparagus acreage. California was a pioneer in separating the locations of production from the consumption of fresh commodities, enabling the state to become a leading exporter of high-value fresh fruits and vegetables. California agriculture faces many challenges, from the availability of labor and water to coping with increased competition from other states and countries.

A perennial question is how to view the relationship between the relatively few farmers and the many seasonal farm workers employed in California agriculture. As on Southern plantations, farmers and farm workers in California are from different social classes with different political rights and influence. Unlike family farming in the Midwest, where occasional hired hands hoped to move up the agricultural ladder from worker to farmer, few seasonal

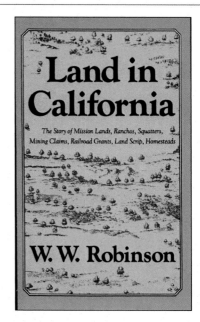

Spain and Mexico granted land to missions and to individuals; these ranchos were often 50,000 to 100,000 acres.

Source: University of California Press

farm workers in California become successful farmers. Instead, most find upward mobility in the nonfarm economy.

LAND

California has over 100 million acres of land, almost half owned by government and a quarter in farms. The United States Department of Agriculture (USDA) considers 9.6 million acres, less than 10 percent, to be cropland. Over 70 percent of this cropland is in the Central Valley between Redding in the north and Bakersfield in the south.

Under Spanish rule, all land was owned by the government. After Mexican independence in 1821, land was granted to private owners in ranchos of 50,000 acres or more; only some of these rancho land grants were honored when California became part of the United States in 1848. Most California land was owned by the federal government, which gave 10.5 million acres in land grants to homesteaders, and awarded 11.6 million acres to private firms that built railroads.

California farmland has always been among the most expensive in the United States. High land prices reflect the high-value commodities that predominate in California and the profits from alternative uses, such as developing land for housing and the related needs of a rapidly growing population. The California chapter of the American Society of Farm Managers and Rural Appraisers in March 2018 reported that prime Napa vineyard acreage was worth $400,000 an acre, while Sonoma vineyards were worth $150,000 an acre, and Fresno vineyards were worth $30,000 an acre. The value of almond orchards ranged from $30,000 to $40,000 an acre, depending on soil quality and access to water. By contrast, the average value of farmland in Iowa is $4,750 an acre.

Policymakers have tried to slow the conversion of farmland to urban uses by allowing California farmers to enroll their land under Williamson Act contracts with local governments. In exchange for continuing to farm their land, farmers pay taxes on the agricultural value of the land rather than its potential nonfarm uses. Governments can also zone land for farm or nonfarm uses, limiting the conversion of farmland into housing.

Table 1.1 shows that between 1997 and 2017, the amount of irrigated crop land decreased by almost a million acres. The acreage of field crops decreased by almost two million acres over the past two decades, led by drops in cotton and grain acreage, while the acreage of tree nuts rose by over a million acres, led by almonds. One effect of fewer field crops and more tree nuts is the need for a reliable supply of water for irrigation: cotton and grain are annual crops that farmers can decide not to plant in dry years, while trees and vines need water each year.

Table 1.1. California Land, Cropland, and Irrigated Land in Farms by Major Crops, 1959–2017

	Census Year						
	1959	**1969**	**1978**	**1987**	**1997**	**2007**	**2017**
	Acres (Thousands)						
Land in Farms	36,887.9	35,722.3	33,130.4	30,598.2	28,795.8	25,364.7	24,522.1
Total Cropland	12,965.6	11,245.1	11,721.1	10,894.5	11,062.8	9,464.6	9,597.4
Harvested Cropland	8,021.8	7,649.0	8,899.4	7,676.3	8,676.2	7,633.2	7,857.5
Irrigated Land	7,395.6	7,240.3	8,603.7	7,596.1	8,886.7	8,016.2	7,833.6
Specialty Crops							
Vegetables	814.3	849.3	1,168.8	1,102.2	1,536.5	1,504.9	1,423.8
Non-Citrus Fruits	472.5	497.3	486.2	538.2	597.3	444.7	365.2
Grapes	469.2	458.3	644.3	707.8	870.5	868.3	935.3
Citrus Fruits	242.5	266.1	248.6	268.8	315.8	303.1	312.2
Nuts	250.6	365.9	540.7	637.9	869.4	1,210.2	2,023.7
Berries	14.3	10.5	14.2	16.6	31.4	42.1	52.9
Total Specialty Crop	2,263.4	2,447.6	3,102.9	3,271.4	4,220.8	4,373.3	5,113.1
Specialty Share of Irrigated Land	30.60%	33.81%	36.06%	43.07%	47.50%	54.56%	65.27%
Field Crops							
Rice	NA	NA	485,416	399.2	514.1	531.1	436.7
Cotton	820.7	659.9	1,520.7	1,083.8	1,036.3	471.4	301.7
Hay, Haylage, Silage	1,369.3	1,286.9	1,204.4	1,279.4	1,465.5	1,554.2	1,344.1
Irrigated Pasture	NA	NA	868.8	631.9	733.5	741.9	484.9
Grain & Other	2,942.1	2,845.8	1,421.5	930.3	916.5	344.3	153.1
Total Field Crops	5,132.2	4,792.6	5,500.8	4,324.6	4,665.9	3,642.9	2,720.5

Source: USDA Census of Agriculture; Carman, H.F. 2019. https://giannini.ucop.edu/publications/are-update/issues/2019/23/2/californias-changing-land-use-patterns-for-crop-pr/

The fertility of the soil in some areas is threatened by farming practices that could reduce the value of the land. On the west side of the San Joaquin Valley, a clay layer under the soil traps salt from irrigation water, eventually reducing yields enough so that some farmers stop planting crops. Excess irrigation water was supposed to drain to the ocean, but instead drained into the Kesterson National Wildlife Refuge and the Tulare Basin, where salty water laced with minerals led to wildlife deformities.

LABOR

There are two major types of workers employed on farms. Farm operators and unpaid family workers have incomes that reflect the difference between farm revenues and costs. Hired workers, on the other hand, are paid wages that are independent of farm revenues and costs. Hired workers can be categorized in many ways, whether they are employed on farms producing crops or animals, whether the workers were hired directly by the farmer where they work or brought to the farm by a nonfarm employer such as a labor contractor, and whether they are legally authorized to work in the United States.

The average annual agricultural employment of hired workers on California farms, a measure of year-round equivalent jobs, was 423,000 in 2018, including over 90 percent on crop farms and less than 10 percent in animal agriculture. There are far more workers than jobs due to seasonality and turnover; the state's agricultural employment peaks in June and is 30 percent lower in January, and many workers are employed in farm jobs for only a few weeks. As a result, there are two unique workers for each year-round job, a total of 850,000. Both the number of year-round equivalent jobs and the number of workers filling them have been increasing.

California is unusual in having more workers brought to crop farms by nonfarm employers known as crop support services than are hired directly by the farms where they work. Most crop support service workers are brought to farms by farm labor contractors (FLCs), the intermediaries who have long been blamed for many farm labor woes. FLCs should improve farm labor market efficiency, assuring farmers that they will have workers when needed and arranging a series of jobs for workers. In practice, FLCs sometimes agree to bring workers to farms for very low commissions, and seek to turn a profit by not paying required payroll taxes or underpaying workers.

Union activities made headlines in the 1960s, when the United Farm Workers led by Cesar Chavez mounted a grape boycott that resulted in most of the state's table grape pickers being represented by the UFW by 1970. Competition between the UFW and the Teamsters, as well as conflicts between unions and growers, persuaded Governor Jerry Brown to sign the Agricultural Labor

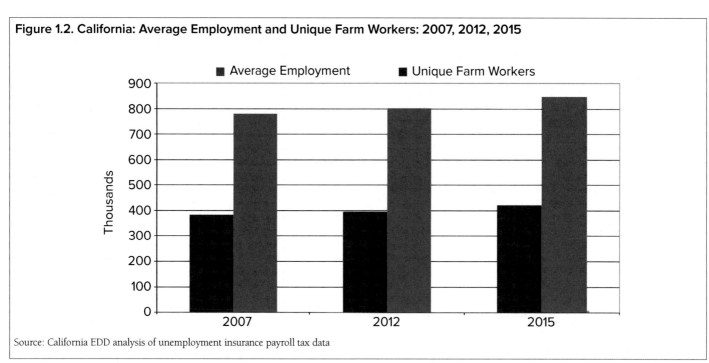

Figure 1.2. California: Average Employment and Unique Farm Workers: 2007, 2012, 2015

Source: California EDD analysis of unemployment insurance payroll tax data

Relations Act of 1975, which gave California farm workers the right to organize and required employers to bargain with the union elected by a farm's employees, including those brought to farms by labor contractors. Intense union activity in the late 1970s was followed by a decline that has left the UFW with fewer than 10,000 members and 50 contracts today.

New entrants to California's farm workforce are mostly legal Mexican guest workers admitted under the H-2A program. California was the major employer of Mexican Bracero guest workers between 1942 and 1964, and the major employer of unauthorized farm workers since. The slowdown in unauthorized Mexico-U.S. migration after the 2008–09 recession has prompted many farmers to turn to the H-2A guest worker program to obtain workers. Many farmers rely on FLCs to recruit, house, and supervise legal Mexican guest workers.

WATER

California farmers normally use about 33 million acre-feet (maf) of water a year to produce crops on 8 million acres of irrigated farmland, an average of 4 acre-feet per irrigated acre. An acre-foot is 43,560 square feet or about a football field covered with one foot of water.

In normal water years, about 60 percent of the water used by farmers is surface water, which is water stored behind dams or in reservoirs and conveyed via canals to farmers.

In dry years, farmers increase the use of groundwater, pumping water from underground aquifers and sometimes fallowing land used to produce lower-value crops such as cotton and buying water to keep high-value crops such as nuts alive. These adjustments helped California's farm sales to rise each year during the 2012–15 drought.

Three factors shape the longer-term outlook for agricultural water. First, most climate-change models predict warmer winters that are less well-suited to California's water storage and transport system. If more winter precipitation falls as rain rather than snow, the capacity of dams and reservoirs to store winter precipitation for summer irrigation is reduced. Agriculture could cope by changing crops and farming practices to use less water, but such changes could lower farm revenues. For example, lower-value forage crops, such as alfalfa for dairy cows, could be grown outside California, raising transport costs to move hay into the state and freeing up water for higher-value crops. However, some dairies may elect to leave California to be closer to feed for their animals.

Second is the hardening of the demand for water, as trees and vines that must be watered for 20 to 30 years replace annual crops on land that in the past could be fallowed in dry years. For example, the acreage of almonds, which requires 3 to 4 acre-feet of water a year, more than doubled over the past three decades to over a million acres, while cotton declined from 1.6 million acres in 1980 to 160,000 acres in 2015.

Figure 1.3. California Water Supply Systems

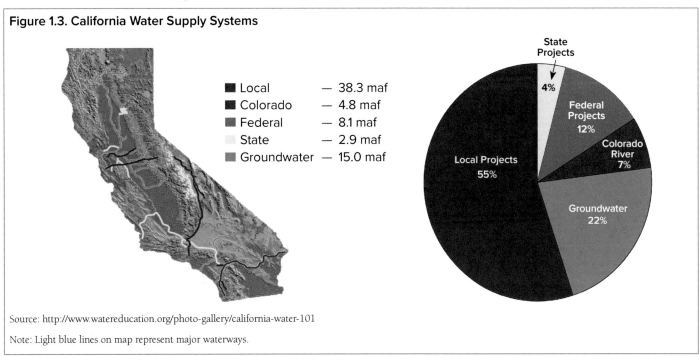

■ Local	— 38.3 maf
■ Colorado	— 4.8 maf
■ Federal	— 8.1 maf
■ State	— 2.9 maf
■ Groundwater	— 15.0 maf

Source: http://www.watereducation.org/photo-gallery/california-water-101

Note: Light blue lines on map represent major waterways.

Third, water marketing could shift water to its highest-value use. Ex-Governor Jerry Brown endorsed twin-tunnels to move fresh water from Northern California 35 miles around the Delta and into reservoirs and groundwater recharge aquifers in the San Joaquin Valley. This so-called WaterFix project could allow farmers who grow rice and other water-intensive crops in the Sacramento Valley to fallow their land and sell water to farmers who grow higher-value crops further south. San Joaquin Valley farmers have been reluctant to contribute to the $17 billion cost of the tunnels, but the Metropolitan Water District of Southern California agreed to contribute $11 billion, reasoning that it could recoup its investment by selling water to farmers and other users. If farmers were to acquire property rights to the ground water under their land, they would have incentives to buy water and recharge aquifers in wet years.

California has a complex federal, state, local, and private system to collect, transport, and distribute water. Several challenges arise with a looming scarcity of water in an arid state with a growing population and irrigated agriculture that produces high-value commodities, including how to move Northern California water through the Sacramento-San Joaquin Delta, how to ensure that groundwater basins are not depleted, and how to make more efficient use of treated wastewater to provide sufficient amounts of water for human, agricultural, and wildlife uses.

MAJOR COMMODITIES

DAIRY

The U.S. had 9.4 million dairy cows in 2018, most on dairies that have 900 or more cows. Dairy farms exemplify the general agricultural trend of fewer and larger operations producing most of the U.S. production of a farm commodity. Most U.S. milk is produced in the northern and western states, led by California, with about 18 percent of milk production and Wisconsin with about 14 percent of milk production.

Milk and cream constitute the most valuable farm commodity produced in California; dairy sales of $6.6 billion in 2017 accounted for almost 60 percent of the total $11.2 billion in the state's animal agriculture sales. Farm milk is about 87 percent water, 9 percent protein and other solids, and 4 percent fat. Across the US, fluid milk consumption has been falling, while cheese and butter consumption has been rising.

California's dairy industry expanded rapidly between 1975 and 2007, when the state accounted for a peak 22 percent of U.S. milk before shrinking to less than 20 percent in 2019. The number of dairy farms is falling, reflecting economies of scale in milk production, but the fewer and larger dairies that remain have a stable number of cows and employees. Tulare county, where the average dairy had 1,800 cows, produced 28 percent of California's milk in 2019. Over 90 percent of the state's milk is produced in the San Joaquin Valley; smaller organic and pasture-based dairies predominate along the Northern California coast where 2 percent of milk is produced.

Raw milk must be processed quickly, and 80 percent of California's milk is processed by farmer-owned cooperatives such as California Dairies Inc., which processes half of the state's milk. Almost 80 percent of California-produced milk is used to make butter, milk powder, or cheese that is sent to other states or exported. A third of the farm quantity of California milk is exported, including to Mexico, China, and Canada.

The major cost of producing milk is feed for cows; feed costs were 55 percent of average milk production costs of $16 per hundredweight in 2017. Labor is the second-largest cost. Some 1,152 California dairies hired an average 18,000 workers in 2018, and paid their employees an average $770 a week. Dairy labor costs are 12 percent of milk production costs and rising with the state's minimum wage, scheduled to reach $15 in 2022, and requirements to pay 1.5 times the usual wage to workers employed more than eight hours a day or 40 hours a week in 2022.

Rising labor costs may lead to more automation on dairy farms. Most dairies hire one employee for each 75 to 100 cows and milk cows around the clock. Robotic milking systems can save on the labor needed for milking, but require significant investments, which many California dairy farmers are reluctant to make at a time of low and uncertain milk prices. Some of the robotic systems entice cows to enter the milking box with food, and cows in such systems are milked as they eat. Cows self-selecting when to eat and be milked average about 2.8 milkings a day.

There are dairy farms in every state, and the federal government has intervened in milk markets since the 1930s to bolster the farm price of milk. Dairy policies require processors to pay farmers a price for milk that reflects the

Milk, cheese, and dairy products are the most valuable commodity group produced in California, worth $6 billion in 2016 or 13 percent of the state's farm sales.
Photo Credit: ViaFilms, www.via-films.com

way their milk was used, whether sold as fluid milk or processed into yogurt, butter or cheese. The current federal Dairy Margin Coverage (DMC) policy makes payments to farmers who buy insurance to protect their margins, the difference between the price of milk and the cost of feed. The DMC benefits mostly smaller dairies in eastern and Midwestern states where a high share of milk is sold as fluid milk.

While the cost of feed is significant for dairy, field and row crops are not significant to California agriculture. Field or row crops are large-acreage annual crops grown for animals or humans, including corn, grains, hay, as well as cotton and rice. California farmers sold field crops worth $2.2 billion in 2017, led by alfalfa hay, $758 million; rice, $678 million; cotton, $475 million; and potatoes (including sweet), $365 million. California produces many of the major grain crops, including corn and wheat, but the value of these mainstays of U.S. agriculture is less than $100 million a year. The major field crop changes over the past quarter century include the sharp decline in cotton and sugar beet acreage as more valuable nut crops expand.

Figure 1.4. Almond Acreage in California

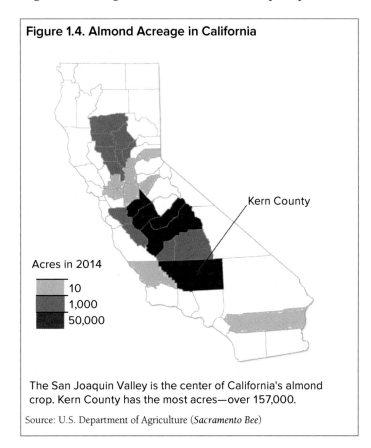

Kern County

Acres in 2014

- 10
- 1,000
- 50,000

The San Joaquin Valley is the center of California's almond crop. Kern County has the most acres—over 157,000.

Source: U.S. Department of Agriculture (*Sacramento Bee*)

FRUITS AND NUTS

Tree fruits and nuts are among the most valuable commodities grown in California: fruit and nut sales of $22 billion were 44 percent of farm sales of $50 billion in 2017. The most valuable include almonds worth $5.6 billion; walnuts, $1.6 billion; and pistachios, $1 billion in 2017. Grapes were worth $5.8 billion in 2017. Berries were worth $3.1 billion, including three-fourths from strawberries, a fifth from raspberries, and 5 percent from blueberries.

The eight-county San Joaquin Valley is California's fruit and nut bowl, with most of the state's citrus, peach, and nectarine orchards as well as most of the almonds, walnuts, and pistachios. The most valuable tree fruits are oranges, worth $934 million in 2017; lemons, $608 million; and tangerines, $535 million. Avocados were worth $383 million in 2017; all types of peaches, $372 million; plums and prunes, $345 million; and cherries, $330 million.

Fresh fruit consumption has been declining as consumers eat fewer oranges, peaches, and nectarines. Many fruit farms are relatively small, and many fruit growers belong to cooperatives such as Sunkist that market their fruit. Fruit farmers often use labor contractors to recruit workers for the most labor-intensive phases of production, which are pruning and harvesting, so that orchards without workers most of the year can have crews of dozens or hundreds during peak seasons. Cherries are an exception to the story of generally declining acreages of fresh fruit, with California's acreage more than tripling, from 10,000 in 1985 to 33,000 acres in 2017.

California produces most U.S. tree nuts and exports many of them. Almonds are the most valuable crop grown in the state, and 80 percent of the state's almonds are exported. The acreage of almonds has been rising rapidly, almost tripling since 2000 to over 1.5 million acres, as land previously planted to raisin grapes and fresh fruit was converted to almonds. A major challenge facing almond growers is water: most nuts are grown south of the Sacramento-San Joaquin Delta, and drought and restrictions on pumping water from the Delta to preserve fish have made water for some nut growers scarce and expensive. Nut growers north of the Delta have much lower irrigation costs.

Labor accounted for half of the top-10 issues identified by the California Fresh Fruit Association each year over the past decade. The state's largest peach grower, Gerawan Farms, was embroiled in a dispute with the United Farm Workers union for five years that resulted in the California Supreme Court upholding the state's 2002 Mandatory Mediation and Conciliation (MMC) law that allows a mediator-turned-arbitrator to develop a contract that the employer must implement. However, Gerawan did not have to implement the MMC contract because Gerawan employees in 2013 voted to de-certify the UFW as their bargaining representative.

The major labor issue facing the fresh fruit industry is that labor represents 30 percent to 40 percent of variable production costs and over half of seasonal fruit pickers are not authorized to work in the U.S. California farmers have been unable to persuade Congress to enact an alternative to the H-2A program that admits Mexican guest workers to harvest most citrus in Florida and apples in Washington, but some are following in the footsteps of the berry and vegetable industries and relying more on H-2A workers.

Farm labor costs are likely to continue to increase, encouraging fruit farmers to adopt labor-saving changes. Nut farming is largely mechanized, but nut farmers face other challenges, including the need to make more efficient use of scarce water, reducing the dust that arises when shaking nuts from trees and sweeping them up, and preventing the spread of invasive species.

GRAPES AND WINE

California grapes were worth $5.8 billion in 2017, including two-thirds from wine grapes, a quarter from table grapes, and less than a tenth from raisins. The state had 840,000 acres of grape vineyards in 2017, with two-thirds devoted to wine grapes, a fifth to raisin grapes, and an eighth to table grapes. Wine grape acreage rose rapidly toward 600,000 acres by 2017, table grape acreage increased slowly to over 100,000 acres, and raisin grape acreage has been decreasing toward 150,000 acres. Most grape vineyards are in the southern San Joaquin Valley, including almost all of the raisin and table grape acreage and a quarter of the wine grape acreage.

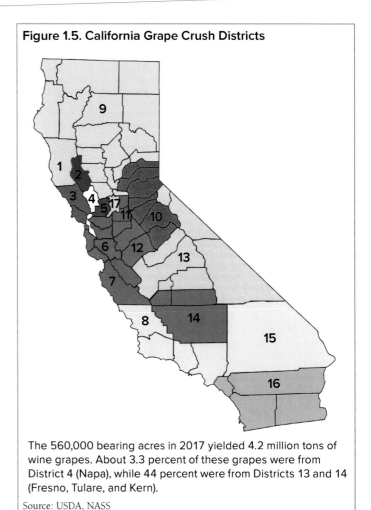

Figure 1.5. California Grape Crush Districts

The 560,000 bearing acres in 2017 yielded 4.2 million tons of wine grapes. About 3.3 percent of these grapes were from District 4 (Napa), while 44 percent were from Districts 13 and 14 (Fresno, Tulare, and Kern).

Source: USDA, NASS

The largest 100 grape growers had a third of the state's grape acreage, and most large vineyards are in the San Joaquin Valley and Central Coast. Over 80 percent of wine grapes are harvested by machine, a third of raisin grapes are machine harvested, but table grapes are hand harvested and packed in bags and other retail packages in the field for retail sale. Labor costs can be 45 percent of variable production costs to produce table grapes.

The value of California's table grapes quadrupled between 1987 and 2017, a period during which table grape production rose by 50 percent. The acreage of raisin grapes is shrinking. Low raisin prices encourage smaller growers with older vineyards to switch from vineyards to tree nuts.

The U.S. produces 10 percent of the world's wine, and California accounts for 85 percent of U.S. wine production. California has 17 crush districts that are grouped into five regions: North Coast, Central Coast, Northern San Joaquin, Southern San Joaquin, and other. The North Coast,

Figure 1.6. Dot Density Plot of California Beef Cattle Inventories by County, January 1, 2017

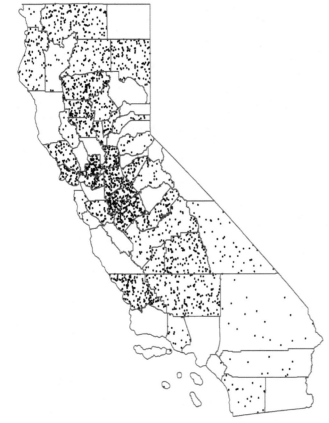

Most of California's beef cattle are in northern and central counties of the state.

Source: California Department of Food and Agriculture

Note: Each dot represents 500 head.

sales, including U.S.-produced wine and imports. Most of the 12,000 U.S. wineries are very small, and some are virtual wineries, meaning that their wine is made for them by another winery.

The U.S. is the world's largest wine market, and a third of U.S. wine is imported, often in bulk to be blended and bottled in the U.S. Most bulk wine is inexpensive, costing about $4 a gallon, equivalent to $0.80 a bottle. The U.S. exports about 10 percent of its wine but imports far more, and is poised to remain a major player in the world of wine.

CATTLE AND SHEEP

U.S. farm sales were $388 billion in 2017, including $193 billion (50%) from crops and $195 billion (50%) from livestock and animal products. Unlike many other states, where animal products have higher gross farm revenue than crops, 80 percent of California's farm sales are from crops. California's $11.2 billion in animal agriculture sales in 2017 were about 6 percent of U.S. animal agriculture revenue. California's cattle and calves sales were $2.6 billion in 2017, and poultry and eggs sales were $1.4 billion.

The beef cattle industry has two distinct subsectors. Some ranches breed cows to produce calves and others fatten cattle before slaughter. The major expense involved in fattening cattle is feed that is often over half of production costs.

California had 2 percent of the 31 million U.S. beef cows in 2017. Three counties, Kern, San Luis Obispo, and Siskiyou, have the largest beef cow herds. California livestock producers rely on public lands to provide forage for cattle, and they move cattle from place to place to access pasture-based forage resources.

Cow-calf operations are the first stage in the beef supply chain, raising calves until they are roughly 7 months old and weigh 600 pounds. Calves are sold to stocker operations that feed them on pasture until they are a year old and weigh 900 pounds. Yearling cattle are sold to feed lots, often in the Midwest, and fattened with grain before slaughter at 1,300 pounds. Almost three-fourths of "cattle on feed" in the U.S. are in Nebraska, Texas, Kansas, Iowa,

including Napa and Sonoma Counties, accounted for an eighth of the state's 4.1 million tons of wine grapes crushed in 2019, but over 40 percent of the $3.2 billion value of the state's wine grapes, due to high per ton prices. The Southern San Joaquin accounts for almost 40 percent of the state's wine grape tonnage but only an eighth of the value of wine grapes. Some wine grapes were not harvested in 2019 because of excess wine in storage, prompting the conversion of more San Joaquin vineyards into almond orchards.

Wine grapes are grown by the winery that uses the grapes to make wine and by independent growers, most of whom have contracts to sell their wine to a particular winery. The largest wineries in 2019, as ranked by 12-bottle cases sold in the U.S., were E&J Gallo, 70 million cases; Wine Group, 53 million cases; and Constellation Brands, 35 million cases; these three wineries accounted for half of U.S. wine

and Colorado, meaning that many yearling cattle leave the state in trucks and return as beef.

California has over 10 percent of the 5.2 million sheep in the U.S., ranking second to Texas in sheep inventory. Like cattle, lambs are raised on grass until they are moved to feed lots for fattening and slaughter. Many California sheep producers rely on H-2A sheepherders from Peru who were paid $2,133 per month in 2020.

Cattle and sheep ranchers need low-cost forage, which is disappearing with increased regulation of grazing on federal lands. There are only a few meat-processing plants in California. Ranchers believe that the big four meatpackers that process 73 percent of U.S. cattle depress cattle prices, although research has not found convincing proof that meatpackers reduce farmers' prices. The use of antibiotics to prevent disease is being restricted in order to slow antibiotic resistance, and new rest requirements for truck drivers may make it more expensive to ship California cattle to Midwest feedlots.

VEGETABLES

U.S. vegetable sales were $14.6 billion in 2017, including $8.3 billion for vegetables and melons from California, 57 percent of the U.S. total. Sales of the state's leading vegetables included $2.2 billion for lettuce, $1.7 billion for tomatoes, and $865 million for broccoli; these three commodities accounted for almost half of the state's vegetable sales. U.S. and California vegetable sales are not strictly comparable because federal data include melons with fruits, while state data include melons with vegetables.

Americans have more vegetables available than ever, about 270 pounds per person per year. Most of these vegetables are consumed fresh, 135 pounds per person in 2017, compared with 110 pounds of vegetables processed by canning or freezing them. The leading fresh vegetables by per capita consumption are head, leaf, and romaine lettuce, 27 pounds per person per year; tomatoes, 22 pounds; onions, 18 pounds; bell peppers, 11 pounds; cucumbers, 8 pounds; and carrots, broccoli, and sweet corn, about 7 pounds each. Processed tomatoes dominate among processed vegetables.

Monterey County is often described as the U.S. salad bowl because it produces the majority of leafy green vegetables in the U.S., including lettuces, broccoli, and celery.
Photo Credit: iStockPhoto

Some 1.4 million U.S. acres of fresh vegetables (excluding potatoes and dry beans) are planted each year, plus another one million acres of processing vegetables. The value of fresh vegetables was $10.8 billion in 2017, and the value of processing vegetables was $2 billion, excluding potatoes and dry beans.

Other important California fresh vegetables were carrots with $368 million in sales in 2017; garlic, $390 million; bell and Chili peppers, $368 million; melons, $367 million; cauliflower, $304 million; celery, $302 million; and onions, $256 million. The production of lettuce and other leafy green vegetables is concentrated in the Salinas Valley, the nation's salad bowl, while melons, garlic, and onions are produced mainly in the San Joaquin Valley.

California's big six fresh vegetables are broccoli, carrots, celery, lettuce, bell peppers, and fresh tomatoes. They are produced by a relative handful of large grower-shippers, that is, businesses that plant and harvest crops to supply fresh vegetables to buyers year-round. Many of the largest grower-shippers are not classified as farms in government statistics, including one of the largest, Dole Fresh Vegetables, which is considered a fruit and vegetable merchant wholesaler (NAICS 424480).

Most fresh vegetables are consumed raw, which makes food safety a major concern. Bagged spinach contaminated with E. coli O157:H7 killed three people and hospitalized over 100 in September 2006, setting in motion efforts to improve food safety practices on farms and packing plants that were codified in the Food Safety Modernization Act (FSMA) of 2011. Later outbreaks in leafy greens, most recently in November 2019, have led to additional changes in food safety practices.

Harvest labor costs for major fresh vegetables range from 15 to 50 percent of production costs, with the higher percentages often including the cost of the container into which produce is packed for sale and marketing expenses. Among the major fresh vegetables, tomatoes are the most unionized, with the United Farm Workers representing workers employed by several major grower-shippers.

The slowdown in unauthorized Mexico-U.S. migration after the 2008-09 recession and the state's rising minimum wage are encouraging efforts to mechanize hand-labor tasks and increasing the employment of guest workers. New varieties of plants that ripen uniformly facilitate once-over machine harvesting, the next step after widespread use of machines to plant and weed vegetable fields. At the same time, some large vegetable growers are building housing for guest workers, suggesting that efforts to mechanize harvesting may not be successful.

Imports of fresh vegetables are rising. A third of the fresh vegetables available to Americans are imported, up from less than 10 percent in the early 1990s. Many California grower-shippers have operations in Mexico to produce

California produces 90 percent of U.S. strawberries, which is the leading crop in Monterey, Ventura, San Luis Obispo, and Santa Cruz counties.

Photo Credit: Jon Bovay, UC Davis, 2013

tomatoes and other vegetables for U.S. consumers. Farmers, who receive an average of 25 percent of the retail price of fresh vegetables, are trying to raise their share of the retail produce dollar by differentiating their produce with labels and convenient packaging, such as ready-to-eat salads and plastic containers of cherry tomatoes.

Mushrooms are fungi but classified with vegetables. California had 70 mushroom farms with 6.2 million square feet of growing space according to the 2017 Census of Agriculture. The 20 largest mushroom farms account for over 85 percent of the state's mushroom-growing space and most of the $255 million in farm revenue from the sale of mushrooms. Santa Clara County had $76 million in mushroom sales, followed by $33 million in San Diego County (data are suppressed for privacy protection for many counties). California's mushroom production is concentrated in Monterey and Santa Clara Counties.

Mushrooms are grown in sealed houses that have wooden beds stacked three to five high. Spawning takes about 12 days, and mushrooms can be harvested 18 days later. Mushrooms are harvested by hand, and California's 35 mushroom farms that paid unemployment insurance taxes (NAICS 111411) had an average 2,200 employees in 2019, when weekly wages averaged $775. The UFW represents workers employed at Monterey Mushrooms and Countryside Mushrooms.

BERRIES

California's berry industry generated five percent of California's farm sales from less than one percent of the state's farm land in 2017. The berry industry includes two subsectors: strawberries planted each year and perennial cane or bush berries: blueberries, raspberries, and blackberries. Demand for berries is rising due to their perceived health benefits, year-round availability, and convenient packaging, making berries the highest-revenue fresh-produce item in U.S. supermarkets.

California produces over 85 percent of U.S. fresh strawberries, and plays a growing role in cane berry production. California's fresh berries were worth $3.7 billion in 2017, including 84 percent from strawberries and 12 percent from raspberries. Four firms market most U.S. fresh strawberries, led by market-leader Driscoll's, which is also the dominant marketer of raspberries. Naturripe

Farms is the leading U.S. marketer of blueberries, and also markets other berries. Most blackberries are imported from Central Mexico and marketed by Driscoll's and Naturripe.

California and Mexico can produce the four major berries almost year-round. Most of the strawberries available to U.S. consumers are produced in California, while most blackberries, blueberries, and raspberries are imported. The share of imports in U.S. strawberry consumption is 14 percent, compared to 53 percent for blueberries and 55 percent for raspberries. Some large Salinas vegetable growers also grow strawberries; the value of strawberries is second only to lettuce in the salad bowl of Monterey County.

Strawberries are a high-value, high-risk, and high-labor-cost crop. Gross revenue per acre can be $60,000 or more, but there are risks of disease and a grower's production may peak during periods of low prices that cover harvesting costs but not the total costs of production. Growers want to plant strawberries in sterile soil, and used methyl bromide to fumigate soil to eliminate pests until 2016, when the use of methyl bromide ended because of its ozone-depleting effects. Strawberries are often picked twice a week during the peak season, and labor costs are half or more of production costs.

U.S. consumption of fresh blueberries, most of which are imported, rose to 2 pounds per person in 2018 (compared to 7 pounds of fresh strawberries). The major U.S. blueberry-producing states are Georgia, Michigan, Oregon, and Washington, accounting for two-thirds of U.S. blueberries. The major sources of blueberry imports are Chile, Canada, and Mexico. California's blueberry production is expanding rapidly, pushing the value of the state's blueberries ($138 million in 2017) to more than the value of the state's nectarines ($133 million).

After expanding rapidly, raspberry prices fell sharply in 2015, prompting reduced acreage. California had 9,000 acres of red raspberries in 2017 that produced 75,200 tons of raspberries worth $452 million. California blackberry production is expanding rapidly, but the state does not publish data on blackberries. Most of the blackberries consumed in the U.S. are imported from Mexico.

Fresh berries are hand-picked, and berries are the state's leading employer of farm workers. Unions have tried and generally failed to organize berry workers, most notably the failure of the UFW's Five Cents for Fairness campaign in the mid-1990s to secure contracts with major growers. Dole had a berry contract with the UFW, but stopped growing strawberries in 2017, leaving organic strawberry grower Swanton Berry Farms with the only UFW contract. The UFW has a contract with Gourmet Blueberry, and struggled to obtain a contract with Premiere Raspberries (previously Dutra Farms).

As U.S. berry consumption continues to rise, will fresh berries be produced in the U.S. or imported? Most fresh strawberries are produced in the US, while most fresh blueberries, blackberries, and raspberries are imported. Marketers who develop proprietary varieties and contract with growers to produce berries for them may elect to move more production to Mexico and other lower-wage countries where there is fresh land to bring into berry production, reducing disease pressures, and lower wages.

Better disease-resistant plant varieties and improved machines to harvest fresh berries could help to maintain or expand U.S. fresh berry production. The fresh berry market may divide into segments that distinguish hand-picked and machine-picked fruit, with different prices for berries picked by hand and machine.

NURSERY AND FLORAL

California's nursery and floriculture sector sales were $3.8 billion in 2017, including $3.4 billion from nursery products. Nurseries are often located in metro areas near their customers. Sales of nursery plants rise with more new housing, while expanding acreages of tree fruits and nuts and grapes boost farm demands for tree and vine seedlings.

San Diego County accounts for a third of the state's nursery and floriculture sales, and most of the other leading nursery counties are in south and central coastal areas with favorable climates and most of the customers for flowers and plants. San Diego, Orange, and Los Angeles counties have almost 16 million or 40 percent of the state's 40 million people.

The Census of Agriculture reported 2,800 nursery and floriculture farms in California with total sales of $2.9 billion in 2017, down from 3,400 farms in 2012. Some of the

Harvest Automation's robot moves plants in nurseries, replacing many workers.

Photo Credit: Dina Rudick / The Boston Globe / Getty Images

Note: https://www.public.harvestai.com

state's nurseries and greenhouses went out of business after the 2008-09 recession.

The fact that nurseries are located near their customers in urban areas also raises labor costs, explaining why the average earnings of full-time nursery workers are $30,000 a year, similar to full-time dairy employees. Land and water costs can also be higher for urban nurseries, which helps to explain why, once nurseries in urban areas are closed during downturns, they rarely reopen.

The floriculture sector is smaller than the nursery sector, with farm-level sales of $414 million in 2017. California florists reported $578 million in sales in 2018, down over half from a peak $1.2 billion in 2007. Most of the cut flowers sold in the U.S. are imported, with Columbia providing 60 percent and Ecuador 20 percent of imported cut flowers. Cut flowers are often flown to Miami and then trucked to customers around the US.

CANNABIS

California was the first state to legalize medical marijuana, after the approval of Proposition 215 in 1996, which gave people diagnosed with cancer and other diseases the "legal right to obtain or grow, and use marijuana for medical purposes when recommended by a doctor." California did not regulate cannabis production for medical marijuana extensively, but federal drug laws continue to classify

marijuana with heroin, calling for a minimum five-year prison sentence for growers with more than 100 plants and prohibiting marijuana from moving legally across state lines. There has been little enforcement of anti-cannabis laws in states such as California where marijuana use is legal, but federal agents enforce laws that prohibit marijuana from moving across state lines.

California voters approved Proposition 64 in November 2016 to legalize recreational marijuana use beginning January 1, 2018. California growers produce about 16 million pounds of raw dried marijuana flowers a year, and sell almost three million pounds in the state, including 20 percent in the legal market and 80 percent in the unlicensed market; 13 million pounds or 80 percent of the state's cannabis is shipped out of California.

The retail price of legal cannabis is higher than the price of illegal cannabis because of state and local taxes and fees. Many cities decided not to allow cannabis retailers to open, although licensed retailers can make home deliveries throughout the state.

The average wholesale price of medical marijuana was $1,200 a pound in 2020, and ranged from $850 a pound for marijuana grown outdoors to $1,800 a pound for marijuana grown indoors; greenhouse-grown marijuana was worth $1,200 a pound. About 60 percent of the state's marijuana is grown outdoors, and over 70 percent is grown north of the Sacramento-San Francisco corridor. Less than 10 percent of the state's marijuana is grown indoors, while a third is grown with mixed natural and artificial light sources in greenhouses. Yields on indoor marijuana farms can be ten times higher than on outdoor farms.

Producing 16 million pounds of marijuana worth $1,200 a pound makes cannabis a $1.9 billion a year commodity. Grower revenue is likely less, because sales in the illegal markets are at lower prices, but costs of production are also relatively low for outdoor cultivation. Taxes, license fees, and other levies can add $300 to $500 a pound, and are most likely to be paid by growers producing indoors and in greenhouses.

Growing marijuana requires farm workers who are granted special rights under Prop 64 and its implementing regulations. Tending and harvesting outdoor marijuana plants takes about 20 hours of labor per pound of dry bud produced, and trimming marijuana flowers to obtain the buds requires 10 hours per pound, for a total of 30 hours per pound. At $15 per hour, labor costs are $450 per pound of dried leaves with an average grower price of $1,200 or almost 38 percent.

Most trimmers are paid piece rate wages per pound of leaves trimmed, and many earn $15 per hour trimming outdoor grown marijuana in Northern California; some growers pay their workers in kind, with marijuana buds. Many Northern California trim workers are family groups from Asia and Eastern Europe whose members aim to earn $200 to $600 a day trimming marijuana leaves. In Coastal California, where more marijuana is grown in greenhouses, wages are typically $20 an hour or more and farm workers are often ex-field workers who were born in Mexico. Up to 100,000 people may be employed in the state's cannabis industry sometime during the year.

Workers who trim cannabis leaves often earn $20 an hour or more.

Photo Credit: Paul Chinn, *SF Chronicle*

Workers on cannabis farms are protected by the state's labor laws, including the Agricultural Labor Relations Act that gives farm workers the right to organize and bargain collectively with farm employers. Under a unique labor peace provision, AB 1291 requires marijuana growers with 20 or more employees to sign a neutrality agreement with a union trying to organize their workers within 60 days of a request. Employers and unions in cannabis, but not in other commodities, may negotiate collective bargaining agreements without an election to determine if workers want to be represented by a particular union.

The 500-member California Cannabis Industry Association (CCIA), which represents legal cannabis growers and distributors, wants the state to lower cannabis taxes, while the United Food and Commercial Workers (UFCW) union wants CCIA members to promote unions and to lower the labor-peace threshold to 10 employees. The UFCW represented 10,000 workers employed in the cannabis industry in 14 states at the end of 2019. Most worked in retail cannabis shops, where workers are protected by the National Labor Relations Act.

DEMAND, MARKETING, AND TRADE

CONSUMER DEMAND

Farmers produce what consumers want to buy, making consumer demand the major factor influencing what farmers produce. People are the ultimate source of the demand for food, but many other factors influence how much and which foods are purchased. Children and the elderly consume different quantities and kinds of foods than working-aged adults, and the demand for foods such as fresh berries rises with income.

The overall demand for food is inelastic, meaning that consumers spend a smaller share of higher incomes on food. Households in the lowest 20 percent of households grouped by income spend a third of their income on food, while those with the highest 20 percent of incomes spend less than a tenth of their income on food. Producers of various commodities often say they are competing for a "share of the stomach," so that successful efforts to promote beef may reduce the demand for pork, since these meats are substitutes. In some cases, commodities may be complements, as with wine and cheese, so that selling more of one commodity increases the demand for the other.

Americans spend relatively little on food, and farmers get a small share of what consumers spend. The U.S. Bureau of Labor Statistics' Consumer Expenditure Survey (https://

www.bls.gov/cex/) measures the spending of the 131 million "consumer units" or households, which in 2018 had an average of 2.5 persons, 1.3 earners, and 1.9 motor vehicles. Average consumer unit income before taxes was $78,635 and average annual expenditures were $61,225.

These expenditures included $7,900 for food, almost 13 percent of expenditures, and food spending was split 57-35 percent, with $4,465 or $86 a week spent for food eaten at home and $3,460 or $66 a week for food bought away from home. Other significant consumer expenditures were $20,100 for housing; $9,760 for transportation; $4,970 for health care; and $3,225 for entertainment.

The cost of food away from home largely reflects convenience, service, atmosphere, and other factors. Food costs are 35 percent of the cost of food purchased in cafeteria-style restaurants, 30 percent of the cost of food purchased at fast food restaurants, and 25 percent in fine dining establishments.

The largest food-at-home expenditures were for meat and poultry, an average of $960 in 2018. Expenditures on cereal and bakery products, $570, exceeded the $450 spent on dairy products. Expenditures on fresh fruits ($320) and fresh vegetables ($285) were $605 a year or $11.60 a week; consumer units spent an additional $115 on processed fruits and $145 on processed vegetables. Consumer units spent almost as much on alcoholic beverages, $585 per year, as on fresh fruits and vegetables, $605.

Most of the value-added in the food system occurs once food leaves the farm. Farmers get less than 20 percent of the average retail food dollar, but slightly more for fresh fruits and vegetables. Farmers received 38 percent of the retail price of fresh fruits in 2015 and 28 percent of the retail price of fresh vegetables.

MARKETING

Agricultural marketing involves the movement of commodities from farm to consumer, including packing and processing, transportation, and retail sales. Most commodities have several "owners" as they move from farm to fork, as when they are sold by farmers to brokers

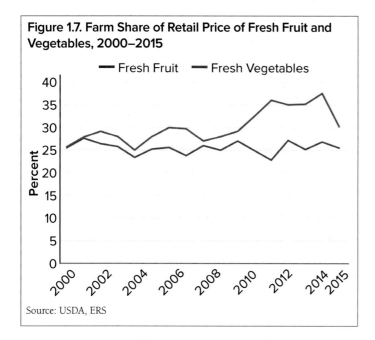

Figure 1.7. Farm Share of Retail Price of Fresh Fruit and Vegetables, 2000–2015

Source: USDA, ERS

and then to supermarkets and other retailers. Farmers receive a relatively small share of retail food spending: less than half of the retail price of fluid milk and meat and only 5 percent of the retail price of cereal and bakery products.

Most California farm commodities are specialty crops such as fruits and nuts, vegetables, and nursery and flower products that present special marketing challenges. Growers of some commodities have formed cooperatives such as Sunkist and Sunmaid to market their products, but the co-op share of sales in many commodities has declined as production expanded and retailers began to purchase directly from large farms that can provide commodities year-round.

California farmers use federal and state marketing programs to sell their commodities, including some that allow marketing boards to specify the quantity and quality of what is offered to consumers. Marketing orders and commodity commissions are approved after most growers representing most of the production of a commodity approve, and packers or first handlers are responsible for submitting small assessments for each box or carton to fund their activities. The number of marketing programs has been increasing, but more are approved under California rather than federal law; the number of commissions has increased faster than the number of

marketing orders. The primary purpose of marketing orders and commodity commissions is to support research that deals with pest and other production problems and to advertise to increase the demand for the commodity.

Do marketing orders and commodity commissions increase grower returns? Volume controls that withhold some of the commodity from the market have been most contentious. The goal is to keep some share of output off the consumer market in order to raise grower prices. However, higher prices can increase production, so that ever more of the commodity must be withheld from the higher-price fresh market, and an ever-increasing share must be diverted to lower-priced processing markets or destroyed. This is what occurred in the fresh lemon industry, where growers agreed to terminate their federal marketing order in 1994.

Cooperative quality-control efforts are less controversial, since their purpose is to increase the demand for the commodity by keeping inferior products off the market; such as preventing the sale of immature peaches or nectarines early in the season so that shoppers do not avoid purchasing them when production peaks later in the season. Quality control has become more important in the fresh vegetable industry after several well-publicized incidents of consumers being sickened by contaminated lettuce and spinach.

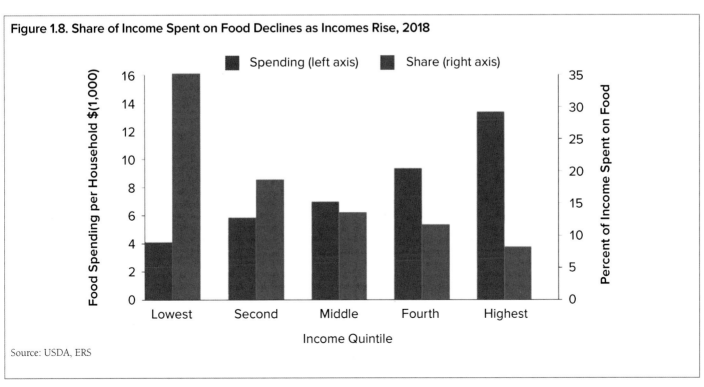

Figure 1.8. Share of Income Spent on Food Declines as Incomes Rise, 2018

Source: USDA, ERS

Most mandatory assessments paid by growers are used for generic advertising and the promotion of particular commodities, such as the Got Milk or Dancing Raisins campaigns. Requiring all producers to pay for such ads reduces free-riding by some farmers who refuse to contribute to advertising campaigns that benefit them. Large growers with their own brand names have sued to avoid making contributions for generic advertising of peaches and other fruits, but the U.S. Supreme Court has upheld USDA regulations that require all growers to contribute.

TRADE

California is a major international exporter of agricultural commodities, with exports worth an average 44 percent of the almost $50 billion a year in farm sales between 2012 and 2016. The U.S. is the world's leading exporter of agricultural commodities, and California exports a higher share of its farm commodities than other major farming states such as Iowa and Texas.

California's three leading agricultural exports in 2017 were almonds, dairy products, and pistachios. Tree nuts are a third of the total value of California farm exports, followed by fruits and vegetables that account for another third. California accounts for a third of U.S. dairy exports, all almond and walnut exports, and over 90 percent of wine exports. The European Union ($3.4 billion), Canada ($3.3 billion), China ($2.3 billion), Japan ($1.5 billion), and Mexico ($1 billion) collectively took over half of California's agricultural exports in 2017.

Most California farmers have more interest in free trade policies than traditional agricultural policies that protect the incomes of farmers. Reducing trade barriers allows California farmers to export more high-value almonds and similar commodities, making farmers interested in the value of the dollar and in non-tariff barriers, as when foreign countries try to block the entry of California commodities in the name of food safety.

California residents consume imported farm commodities, from avocados to zucchini. However, most of the fruits and vegetables for which the state is well known are produced in California, since few foreign competitors can compete when California production is at its peak. For example,

California produces fresh strawberries year-round, but production peaks during the summer months, when imports almost cease.

Trade in fruits and nuts is growing rapidly, posing challenges and opportunities for California agriculture. On the one hand, rising incomes abroad increase the demand for California fruits and nuts, but they also encourage farmers in other countries such as Spain to produce fruits and nuts to export. California and the Netherlands are examples of high-income areas able to compete in global markets despite high wages and extensive regulation.

The North American Free Trade Agreement (NAFTA) divided agriculture, with most farmers seeing new opportunities but some fearing increased competition. However, the example of avocados shows the potential for win-win outcomes: Mexico reduced restrictions on other commodities that California exports and the total U.S. market for avocados expanded, allowing Mexico to export more avocados without reducing prices for U.S. growers. The United States-Mexico-Canada Agreement (USMCA) is expected to promote the continued integration of North American agriculture.

China is the world's largest producer of most fruits and vegetables. There are fears that the world's factory could become the world's farm as Chinese farmers increase production and exports of fruits and vegetables.

China has been a net agricultural importer since 2004, and rising Chinese incomes are increasing the demand for high-value fruits and vegetables, meat, and dairy products. Some Chinese consumers prefer the higher-quality and more attractive packaging of imported fruits and vegetables to local produce. The Trump Administration's trade disputes with China and other countries often result in retaliation that reduces exports of particular California commodities.

California farmers have largely embraced globalization and freer trade because they have more to gain from increased access to more affluent consumers abroad than they would lose in a protectionist U.S. that blocked imports. California farmers successfully competed with other U.S. farmers to become the dominant producers of fruits, nuts, vegetables, and other specialty crops, and they are likely to be able to compete effectively against farmers abroad as well.

CLIMATE AND TECHNOLOGY

CLIMATE CHANGE

The drought of 2013–15 and the enactment of AB 32, a state law to limit greenhouse emissions in 2020 to 1990 levels, have made climate change a central challenge for California agriculture. Rising temperatures could increase tensions between the relatively wetter and sparsely populated northern part of the state and the drier and more populated and agriculture-intensive southern part of the state.

A warming climate could mean that more of the state's precipitation falls as rain rather than snow. The state's water system, which depends on snowmelt to provide surface water for irrigation in summer, would be less viable because dams and reservoirs have limited capacities to store winter rains. Climate change could also increase weather variability, leading to more floods and droughts, and could change the nature and severity of pest and disease infestations.

Rising temperatures affect crops and animals directly. The optimal number of degree days, defined as temperatures between 8°C and 32°C (46°F to 90°F), for many California crops is 2,500 over the growing season. Farm land prices reflect the number of degree days in a particular area, and are lower where there are too many or too few degree days. Average degree days in the Central Valley are currently 2,000, suggesting that global warming could lead to higher farm profits and land prices.

Climate change is expected to reduce the yields of many major field crops, including cotton and wheat, but to have mixed effects on the yields of fruit, nut, and vegetable crops, with some yields rising and others falling. Wine grape yields are less affected by rising temperatures than yields of nut and citrus crops in some models of the likely effects of climate change.

Animals will also be affected by rising temperatures, with milk yields likely declining due to heat stress. Workers also tend to be less productive at low (under 55 degrees) and high (over 100) temperatures. Agriculture could adapt by moving dairy cows to higher elevations, but this could increase the cost of transporting feed. Farm workers could work at night in order to work at lower temperatures, which would necessitate lighting systems and perhaps premium wages.

Figure 1.9. California Drought Years, 2011–2015

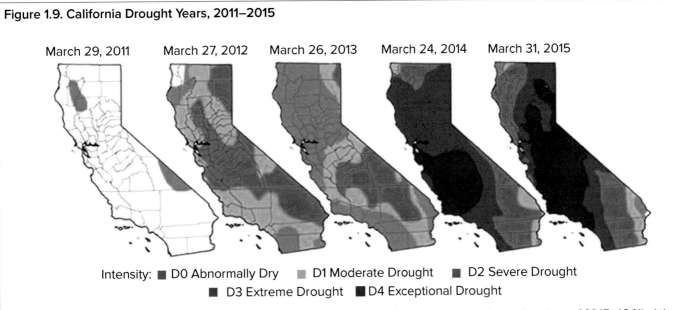

March 29, 2011   March 27, 2012   March 26, 2013   March 24, 2014   March 31, 2015

Intensity: ■ D0 Abnormally Dry   ■ D1 Moderate Drought   ■ D2 Severe Drought   ■ D3 Extreme Drought   ■ D4 Exceptional Drought

California experienced four years of progressively more severe drought until the rain and snow during the winter of 2015–16 filled the state's 154 reservoirs to capacity.

Source: http://www.businessinsider.com/californias-drought-situation-is-worse-than-ever-2015-4

The Agrobot has mechanical arms to pick strawberries that are trained to grow for machine picking.

Source: https://www.cnbc.com/2018/03/08/wave-of-agriculture-robotics-holds-potential-to-ease-farm-labor-crunch.html.

Agriculture accounts for less than 10 percent of the state's greenhouse gas emissions. Agricultural emissions are dominated by methane from dairy cows and other animals, which has prompted efforts to better manage animal manure.

TECHNOLOGY

California's high-tech agriculture is supported by an educational-industrial complex that begins with the education of students, includes research supported by public and private funds, and involves researchers transferring innovations and licensing technologies to commercial users. University of California Cooperative Extension (UCCE) specialists are important intermediaries between researchers and farmers, as are private consultants, and farmer associations.

Innovations are adopted by farmers when they increase profits. Early adopters are often the best-educated farmers, although specific factors also play important roles, as with the high cost of water encouraging San Diego avocado growers to be early adopters of drip irrigation. The continued rising price of water, along with technological improvements, spread drip irrigation throughout the state and across many crops.

California's arid climate reduces pest issues, and the relatively small yield penalty for organic farming encourages organic production in the state; a million acres of the state's cropland is certified as organic. California

farmers are leaders in precision agriculture, using technology to ensure that particular plants and animals receive the optimal amount of water and other inputs. Technology holds more promise; for example, drones that can spray weeds only in the part of a field where they are present.

Precision agriculture depends on information and equipment to deal with particular crops. Harvesting fragile fruits and vegetables presents special challenges, since machines damage more of the crop than hand harvesters. Precision agriculture in animal agriculture includes robotic milking machines that entice cows to enter with feed and record detailed information about the cow.

Prepackaged salads were an innovation motivated by a desire to reduce fluctuations in farm-level lettuce prices and to increase convenience for consumers. Fresh Express adapted technologies that were developed to preserve fresh fruit such as apples by altering the atmosphere and lowering the temperature in order to preserve quality. Vegetable firms learned that food service firms and consumers would pay premium prices for ready-to-eat salads. Some food-related innovations reflect the spread of technology developed for other purposes and adapted for agricultural needs, including sensors in fresh produce trucks that monitor temperature and consumer apps that facilitate purchases at grocery stores and restaurants.

California agriculture is well-positioned to benefit from the technologies developed in Silicon Valley and elsewhere. California has a high-cost and highly-regulated business environment that is offset in part by affluent consumers, a desirable climate and soils, and a robust education and innovation system that can develop, improve, and adapt innovations that keep the state's farmers on the cutting edge of productivity-increasing technologies.

LOOKING FORWARD

The Giannini Foundation of Agricultural Economics was established at the University of California in 1930 to support economic research beneficial to California agriculture. A. P. Giannini, the founder of Bancitaly (later Bank of America) donated $1.5 million to establish the Foundation. In the nine decades since its founding, the Giannini Foundation has supported agricultural economics faculty and graduate students throughout the University of California system, helping to ensure that the departments at UC Berkeley and UC Davis are among the best in the United States.

The Giannini Foundation supports small, innovative research projects regarding the economics of California agriculture led by faculty and graduate students, and communicates its findings to the agricultural industry and policy makers through *ARE Update*, its translational research journal, conferences, and other tools. Giannini Foundation research plays a key role in analyzing the challenges and opportunities facing California agriculture, ranging from land, labor, and water, to marketing commodities at home and abroad.

California agriculture faces the challenge of Covid-19 in 2020, adjusting to the changing demand for the specialty commodities that are the state's hallmark as restaurants and food service outlets close while striving to keep the people involved in agriculture safe. As with past challenges, California agriculture is likely to adjust and adapt, and remain the leading U.S. farm state for the foreseeable future.

The Giannini Foundation was created with a 1928 gift to University of California from A.P. Giannini (1870–1949), who founded the Bank of Italy (later Bank of America).

Painting by Arthur Cahill, 1930;
Photograph by Benjamin Blackwell, 2009

Chapter 2. A History of California Agriculture

Alan L. Olmstead and Paul W. Rhode

Abstract

The history of California agriculture entails a story of innovation and conflict as farmers and their allies repeatedly remolded their environment to create an extraordinarily diverse and productive agricultural-industrial complex. This is not just a story of the triumph of individual entrepreneurial initiative in a largely unfettered competitive economy, because the actual outcomes often depended far more than commonly realized on aggressive government interventions that defined access to land, water, markets, technologies, and labor. These interventions helped, often despite farmer objections, control potentially catastrophic plant and animal diseases.

About the Authors

Alan L. Olmstead is a Distinguished Research Professor in the Department of Economics at the University of California, Davis and a member of the Giannini Foundation of Agricultural Economics. He can be contacted by email at alolmstead@ucdavis.edu. Paul W. Rhode is a professor in the Department of Economics at the University of Michigan and a research associate at the National Bureau of Economic Research.

Fred Lester of San Jose hauling prunes to market with a Yuba crawler, ca. 1916.

Photo Credit: Private collection of Alan L. Olmstead

CHAPTER 2. TABLE OF CONTENTS

INTRODUCTION

In recent years, California has accounted for over one-tenth of the value of the U.S. agricultural output. Perhaps more impressive than the value of farm output is the great diversity of crops, the capital intensity, the high yields, and the special nature of the state's agricultural institutions. California's agriculture evolved differently from what was found in the home states and countries of the immigrants who settled and farmed its soils. These differences were not just an outcome of the state's distinct geoclimatic features; they were molded by the farmers, laborers, researchers, railroad barons, and policymakers who interacted to create one of the most productive and dynamic agricultural-industrial complexes in the world.

Two contrasting legends dominate the telling of California's agricultural history. The first extols California farmers as progressive, highly educated, early adopters of modern technologies, and unusually well organized to use irrigation to make a "desert" bloom. Through cooperation, they prospered as their high-quality products captured markets around the globe. This farmers-do-no-wrong legend is the mainstay of the state's powerful marketing cooperatives, government agencies, and agricultural research establishment, and largely ignores agricultural workers. The second and darker legend sees the California agricultural system as founded by land-grabbers whose descendants continue to exploit migrant workers and abuse the Golden State's natural environment. Even in its mildest form, this view faults California farmers for becoming full-fledged capitalists rather than opting for a more environmentally and labor-friendly system of family farms as in the Midwest. The contest between these competing interpretations of California's farm system has raged for the past one-and-a-half centuries, with each side seldom even talking to the other. Neither legend has engaged in a systematic and objective analysis of the available data nor offered the comparative perspective needed to assess why California agriculture developed as it did.

This chapter analyzes major developments in California's agricultural history to provide a better understanding of how and why the state's current agricultural structure and institutions emerged. We focus on major structural transformations: the rise and fall of the extensive grain-growing economy of the 19th century; the shift to intensive orchard, vine, and row crops; and the emergence of modern livestock operations. Intertwined with our discussion of sectional shifts will be an analysis of some of the special institutional and structural features of California's agricultural development, including farm power and mechanization, irrigation, and the labor market. In these areas, California's farmers responded aggressively to their particular economic and environmental constraints to create unique institutional settings. The results have been remarkable, albeit with significant environmental problems and continuing labor unrest.

THE GRAIN EMPIRE

BONANZA FARMS

Early settlers found an ideal environment for raising wheat: great expanses of fertile soil and flat terrain combined with rainy winters and hot, dry summers. By the mid-1850s, the state's wheat output exceeded local consumption, and California's grain operations began to evolve quite differently from the family farms of the American North. The image is vast tracts of grain grown on huge bonanza ranches in a countryside virtually uninhabited except at harvest and plowing times. California grain farms were very large for the day and used labor-saving and scale-intensive technologies, pioneering the adoption of labor-saving gang plows, large headers, and combines. Californians vigorously pursued the development of technologies and production practices suited to early California's economic and environmental conditions. This search for large-scale, labor-saving technologies culminated in the perfection of the world's first commercially successful combined grain harvesters by the Holt Manufacturing Company and other local manufacturers in the early 1880s. Combines became common in the California grain fields by 1890 (Olmstead and Rhode, 1988), when California was the second largest wheat-producing state, following only Minnesota.

Some bonanza farms planted thousands of acres and were far larger than Midwestern operations. They would establish many precedents. Most of the wheat and barley was shipped to European markets, setting a pattern of integration into world markets that has characterized California agriculture to the present. Their size, the extent of mechanization, and a reliance on hired labor would also become hallmarks of the state's farm sector.

BIOLOGICAL INNOVATION AND FAILURE

In addition, California grain-farmers developed novel biological systems, growing different varieties of wheat and employing fundamentally different cultural techniques than their eastern brethren. When eastern farmers migrated to California, they had to relearn how to grow wheat. In the eastern United States, grain growers planted either winter-habit varieties in the fall to allow the seedlings to emerge before winter, or spring-habit varieties in the spring shortly before the last freeze. The difference was that winter-habit wheat required prolonged exposure to cold temperatures and an accompanying period of dormancy (vernalization) to shift into its reproductive stage. Spring-habit wheat, by contrast, grew continuously without a period of vernalization, but generally could not survive extreme cold. With the mild winters of California, farmers learned it was advantageous to sow spring-habit wheat in the fall.

California's wheat experience exemplifies the importance of biological innovation. After learning to cultivate Sonora and Club wheats in the 1850s, 1860s, and 1870s, California grain growers focused most of their innovative efforts on mechanization, and purportedly did little to improve cultural practices, introduce new varieties, or even maintain the quality of their seed stock. According to contemporary accounts, decades of monocrop grain farming, involving little use of crop rotation, fallowing, fertilizer, or deep plowing, mined the soil of nutrients and promoted the growth of weeds. By the 1890s, there were frequent complaints that what had been prime wheat land would no longer yield paying crops. In addition to declining yields, the grain's quality suffered, becoming starchy and less glutinous, and thus fetched a lower price. Contrary to first impressions, these unsustainable "soil-mining" practices may well have been "economically rational" for individual farmers, given California's high interest rates in the mid-19th century. The result of declining yields and quality was that, in many areas, wheat ceased to be a profitable crop and was virtually abandoned (Rhode, 1995; Olmstead and Rhode, 2008).

INTENSIFICATION AND DIVERSIFICATION

INDICATORS OF CHANGE

Between 1890 and 1914, the California farm economy shifted from large-scale ranching and grain-growing operations to smaller-scale, intensive fruit cultivation. By 1910, the value of intensive crops equaled that of extensive crops, as California emerged as one of the world's principal producers of grapes, citrus, and various deciduous fruits. Tied to this dramatic transformation was the growth of allied industries, including canning, packing, food machinery, and transportation services.

Table 2.1 provides key statistics on the transformation of California agriculture between 1859 and 2007. Almost every aspect of the state's development after 1880 reflected the ongoing process of intensification and diversification. Between 1859 and 1929, the number of farms increased about 700 percent. The average size of farms fell from roughly 475 acres in 1869 to about 220 acres in 1929, and improved land per farm dropped from 260 acres to about 84 acres over the same period. These changes ushered in vastly different production arrangements driven by the differing requirements of extensive grain operations

Table 2.1. California's Agricultural Development

	No. of Farms	Land in Farms	Improved Land	Cropland Harvested	Irrigated Land	No. of Farms Irrigated	Ag. Labor Force
	(1,000)	Acres (Thousands)				(1,000)	(1,000)
1859	19	8,730	–	–	–	–	53
1869	24	11,427	6,218	–	60–100	–	69
1879	36	16,594	10,669	3,321	300–350	–	109
1889	53	21,427	12,223	5,289	1,004	14	145
1899	73	28,829	11,959	6,434	1,446	26	151
1909	88	27,931	11,390	4,924	2,664	39	212
1919	118	29,366	11,878	5,761	4,219	67	261
1929	136	30,443	11,465	6,549	4,747	86	332
1939	133	30,524	–	6,534	5,070	84	278
1949	137	36,613	–	7,957	6,599	91	304
1959	99	36,888	–	8,022	7,396	74	284
1969	78	35,328	–	7,649	7,240	51	240
1978	73	32,727	–	8,804	8,505	56	311
1987	83	30,598	–	7,676	7,596	59	416
1997	74	27,699	–	8,543	8,713	56	260
2007	81	25,364	–	7,633	8,016	52	NA

Sources: Taylor and Vasey, "Historical Background," in Rhode, 1995
    U.S. Bureau of the Census: Fifteenth Census 1930, Vol. 4
    Census of Agriculture 1959, California, Vol. 1, Part 48
    1980 Census of Population, California, Vol. 1, Part 6
    Census of Agriculture 1997, California, available at: http://www.nass.usda.gov/census/census97/volume1/ca-5/ca1_01.pdf
    1990 Census of Population, California, Section 1
    2000 Census, available at: https://www2.census.gov/library/publications/decennial/1990/cp-2/cp-2-6-1.pdf
    "Industry by Sex : 2000 Data Set: Census 2000 Summary File 3 (SF 3)—Sample Data," available at: http://factfinder.census.gov
    USDA, Census of Agriculture 2007 Census, Volume 1, Chapter 2: State Level Data, available at:
    https://www.agcensus.usda.gov/Publications/2007/Full_Report/Volume_1,_Chapter_2_US_State_Level/
    Thomas Weiss, Unpublished data

Figure 2.1. Distribution of California Cropland Harvested, 1879–2007

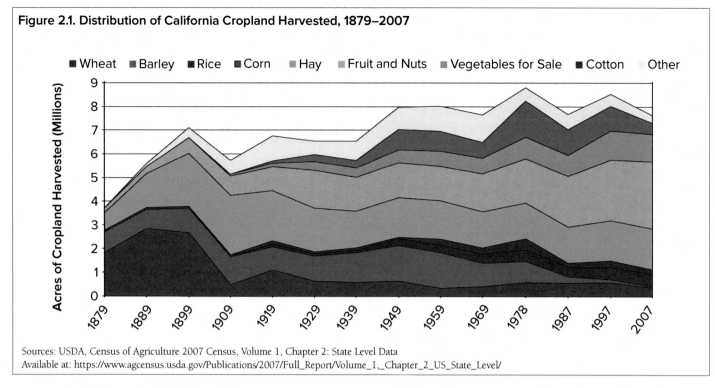

Sources: USDA, Census of Agriculture 2007 Census, Volume 1, Chapter 2: State Level Data
Available at: https://www.agcensus.usda.gov/Publications/2007/Full_Report/Volume_1,_Chapter_2_US_State_Level/

compared with intensive fruit farms. Movements in cropland harvested per worker also point to increased intensification after the turn of the century. The statewide land-to-labor ratio fell from about 43 acres harvested per worker in 1899 to 20 acres per worker in 1929. The spread of irrigation broadly paralleled the intensification movement. Between 1869 and 1889, the share of California farmland receiving water through artificial means increased from less than one percent to five percent. Growth was relatively slow in the 1890s, but expansion resumed over the 1900s and 1910s. By 1929, irrigated land accounted for nearly 16 percent of the farmland.

Data on the value and composition of crop output place California's agricultural transformation into sharper relief. Between 1859 and 1929, the real value of the state's crop output increased over 25 times. Growth was especially rapid during the grain boom of the 1860s and 1870s, associated primarily with the expansion of the state's agricultural land base. But improved acreage in the state peaked in 1889, and cropland harvested peaked in 1899. Subsequent growth in crop production was mainly due to increasing output per acre and was closely tied to a dramatic shift in the state's crop mix. After falling in the 1860s and 1870s, the share of intensive crops in the value of total output climbed from less than 4 percent in 1879 to over 20 percent in 1889. By 1909, the intensive share reached nearly

one-half, and by 1929, it was almost four-fifths of the total. In terms of the crops produced—the scale of operations, the quantity and seasonality of the labor demanded, and the types of equipment needed—California agriculture was a very different place than it had been 50 years earlier.

Figure 2.1, which shows how cropland harvested was distributed across selected major crops over the 1879–2007 period, displays the transformation in further detail. In 1879 wheat and barley occupied over 75 percent of the state's cropland, whereas the combined total for the intensive crops (fruit, nuts, vegetables, and cotton) was around five percent. By 1929, the picture had changed dramatically. Wheat and barley then accounted for about 26 percent of the cropland harvested and the intensive crop share stood around 35 percent. In absolute terms, the acreage in the intensive crops expanded more than ten times over this half-century, while that for wheat and barley fell by more than one-third.

EXPLAINING THE TRANSITION

Many of the commonly accepted explanations for the causes and timing of California's structural transformation—such as the advent of the transcontinental railroad, the spread of irrigation, and the slump in world grain prices—fail under close inspection. The transcontinental railroad was completed in 1869, and one of the first effects was an increase in the importation of fruits from the East. At that time, California was not yet self-sufficient in fruit production. Monopoly railroad pricing limited exports from California, and shippers of canned and dried fruits found ocean transport preferable. In the 1880s, the Santa Fe Railroad connected to California, creating more competition. In addition, during roughly the first 15 years of railroad availability, the rudimentary Southern Pacific service was not well suited to handling perishable commodities. Key changes occurred in the mid-1880s, when the Southern Pacific began express shipments of entire trains carrying fruit in ventilated cars, and refrigerator cars were introduced in 1888. These changes in handling and shipping were facilitated by cooperatives that helped to assemble large quantities of fruit, which received preferential service from the railroads. So, the transcontinental rail service played little role in the initial spurt in the California fruit industry, but eventually became important for the fresh fruit trade. At first, most canned and dried fruit and wines still traveled via ship.

A second explanation argues that irrigation was essential for the transition to intensive agriculture. However, a close look at the data shows that irrigation lagged intensification. As late as 1899, irrigated land accounted for only 12 percent of California's improved farmland and less that 25 percent of all cropland harvested; over 70 percent of the state's grape acreage and about 60 percent of its orchard-fruit acreage was not irrigated. Thus, as with railroads, irrigation would become important, but it was not a causal necessity for the growth of the California fruit economy.

Another explanation points to the slump in world grain prices stimulating farmers to transition to orchard and vine crops. This story depicts intensive fruit farmers in direct competition with extensive wheat farmers: a decline in world wheat prices would reduce California wheat production, thereby freeing land and labor for fruit production. However, the real price of wheat fell by about 28 percent from 1870 to 1900; but in the late 1800s and the early decades of the 1900s, real wheat prices recovered, rising at about one percent a year, precisely when California wheat production shrank most. Further evidence discrediting the hypothesis that the rise in fruit production was tied to the fall in wheat prices is that real fruit prices fell far more rapidly than grain prices, so movement in the ratio of wheat and grain prices to fruit prices favored

wheat production. In addition, very little of the land taken out of wheat production was replanted in fruit trees and vines. Finally, the peak labor demands for wheat were much earlier in the year than for fruits. If anything, the two types of crops complemented each other by providing workers with steadier employment.

HITHERTO NEGLECTED FACTORS

If the usual explanations for the movement from extensive to intensive crops all fail, how do we account for the shift? The surprising result is that exogenous declines in real interest rates and "biological" learning deserve much of the credit for the transformation (Rhode, 1995; and Olmstead and Rhode, 2008).

THE COST OF CAPITAL

Isolated from America's financial markets, California farmers faced high—even astronomical—interest rates, which discouraged capital investments in activities such as tree crops that would not begin yielding an income for many years. Rates fell from well over 100 percent during the Gold Rush to about 30 percent circa 1860, and the downward trend continued with real rural mortgage rates approaching 8 to 12 percent by 1890. The implications of falling interest rates for a long-term investment such as an orchard were enormous. As one Bay Area observer noted in the mid-1880s, the conversion of grain fields to orchards "has naturally been retarded in a community where there is little capital, by the cost of getting land into orchard, and waiting several years for returns (Burns, 1888)." The break-even interest rate for the wheat-to-orchard transition was about 10 to 13 percent; at rates above 15 percent, the value of investments in orchards started to turn negative. These estimates conform closely to the interest rate levels prevailing in California when horticulture began its ascent.

BIOLOGICAL LEARNING

A second key supply-side force was the increase in horticultural productivity associated with biological learning, as farmers gradually gained the knowledge of how to grow new crops in the California environment. Yields for leading tree crops nearly doubled between 1889 and 1919. When the Gold Rush began, the American occupiers knew little about the region's soils and climate. As settlement continued, would-be farmers learned to distinguish the better soils from poorer soils, the more amply watered land from the more arid, the areas with moderate climates from those suffering greater extremes. Occasionally overcoming deep-seated prejudices, farmers learned which soils were comparatively more productive for specific crops (U.S. Weather Bureau 1903; U.S. Bureau of the Census, *Tenth Census 1880, Vol. 6, Cotton Production, Part 2,* 1884).

California fruit growers engaged in a similar process of experimentation to find the most appropriate plant stocks and cultural practices. Varieties were introduced from around the world, and new varieties were created. In the early 1870s, USDA plant specialists established the foundation for the state's citrus industry with navel orange budwood imported from Bahia, Brazil. Prune and plum trees were imported from France and Japan; grape vines from France, Italy, Spain, and Germany; and figs (eventually together with the wasps that facilitated pollination) from Greece and Turkey. Plant breeders also got in on the act. The legendary Luther Burbank, who settled in California in 1875, developed hundreds of new varieties of plums and other fruits over his long career (Tufts, 1946; Hodgson, 1993).

In part, the growth of horticultural knowledge occurred through the informal "folk process" but, over time, the process of research and diffusion became increasingly formalized and institutionalized. Agricultural fairs served to demonstrate new practices and plants. As an example, a series of major citrus expositions, held annually in Riverside from the late 1870s, helped popularize the new Bahia orange variety. An emerging group of specialty farm journals, such as the *Southern California Horticulturist, California Citrograph,* and *California Fruit Grower,* supplemented the stalwart *Pacific Rural Press* to spread information about fruit growing (Teague, 1944; Cleland and Hardy, 1929). The California State Board of Horticulture, formed in 1881, provided an active forum for discussion of production and marketing practices, especially through its annual convention of fruit growers.

The Agricultural College of the University of California, under the leadership of Eugene Hilgard and Edward Wickson, intensified its research efforts on horticultural and viticultural problems after the mid-1880s. By the early 1900s, the USDA, the state agricultural research system, and local cooperatives formed an effective working arrangement to

acquire and spread knowledge about fruit quality and the effects of packing, shipping, and marketing on spoilage and fruit appearance. These efforts led to the development of pre-cooling and other improved handling techniques, contributing to the emergence of California's reputation for offering high-quality horticultural products. This learning process eventually propelled California's horticultural sector to a position of global leadership. More generally, the example of the state's horticultural industry highlights the important, if relatively neglected, contribution of biological learning to American agricultural development before the 1930s (Olmstead and Rhode, 2008).

The application of science, strict quality control in the fields and packing houses (often via policies supported by cooperatives), and a rapid and quality-conscious transportation system to bring fruits to the market, all supported by a commercial financial network, was the landmark creation of California's agribusiness community. This integrated system became known as the "California Model," and was the envy of fruit producers around the world. It allowed California producers to capture the high-price end of markets across Europe.

A second major transformation took place before 1930, with the increased cultivation of row crops including sugar beets, vegetables and, most notably, cotton (see Figure 2.1). These changes represented an intensification of farming, requiring significant capital investments and significant increases in labor. The rise of row crops often led to a vast increase in productivity on what had been marginal or under-utilized lands. The advent of cotton, which by 1950 had become the state's most valuable crop, offers another important case study in the continuing evolution of California agriculture. As with the shift to fruit crops, the shift to cotton was also associated with significant scientific and institutional innovations.

CALIFORNIA'S WHITE GOLD

THE INTRODUCTION OF COTTON

From Spanish times, visionaries attempted to introduce cotton into California on a commercial basis. A variety of factors—including the high cost of labor, the distance from markets and gins, and inadequate knowledge about appropriate varieties, soils, etc.—doomed these early efforts. The real breakthrough came during World War I when high prices, coupled with government research and promotional campaigns, encouraged farmers in the Imperial, Coachella, and San Joaquin valleys to adopt the crop. Figure 2.2 illustrates acres harvested, bales produced, and yields per acre from 1910 to 2017. The tremendous absolute increase in California's cotton acreage from the 1920s to 1980 contrasts with the absolute decline nationally. California's acreage in cotton ranked 14th out of 15 cotton-producing states in 1919; by 1959 it ranked only behind Texas.

Several factors distinguished California's cotton industry from other regions. First, cotton yields were typically more than double the national average. High yields resulted from the favorable climate, rich soils, controlled application of irrigation water, use of the best agricultural practices and fertilizer, adoption of high-quality seeds, and a relative freedom from pests. Second, the scale and structure of cotton farms was remarkably different in California. From the mid-1920s through the 1950s, the acreage of a California cotton farm was about five times that of farms in the Deep South.[1] As an example of the structural differences between California and other important cotton states, in 1939 farms producing 50 or fewer bales grew about 17 percent of the output in California, but in other leading cotton states, farms in this class produced at least 80 percent of all cotton output. Thus, it is not surprising that California's gross income per cotton farm was almost nine times the national average (Musoke and Olmstead, 1982).

MECHANIZATION

Other distinctive features of California cotton farms were their more intensive use of power and their earlier mechanization of pre-harvest activities. In 1929, a California farm

---

1   Some of these San Joaquin Valley farms would grow into immense holdings. The J.G. Boswell company is purportedly the world's largest private farm and cotton farm, credited with owning over 135 million acres (Arax and Wartzman, 2005).

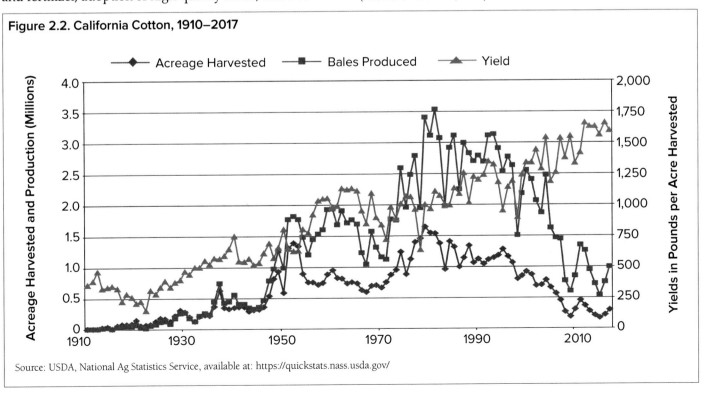

Figure 2.2. California Cotton, 1910–2017

Source: USDA, National Ag Statistics Service, available at: https://quickstats.nass.usda.gov/

was almost 20 times more likely to have a tractor than a Mississippi farm (U.S. Bureau of the Census, *U.S. Census of Agriculture: 1959, General Report: Statistics by Subjects*, Vol. II). The *Pacific Rural Press* in 1927 offered a description of the highly mechanized state of many California cotton farms: "men farm in sections.... By the most efficient use of tractor power and tools, one outfit with a two-man daylight shift plants 100 acres per day, six rows at a time, and cultivates 70 acres, four rows at a time (April 2, 1927)." The more rapid adoption of tractors created a setting favorable to further modernization. When picking machines became available, farmers already possessed the mechanical skills and aptitudes needed for machine-based production.

The larger size of cotton operations in California and the more intensive use of tractors reflected a fundamentally different form of labor organization than existed in the South. By the 1940s, on the eve of cotton harvesting mechanization, most cotton in California was picked on a piece-rate basis by seasonal laborers under a contract system (California Committee to ... March 15, 1951; Fisher, 1953). Although conditions varied, a key ingredient was that a labor contractor recruited and supervised the workers, and dealt directly with the farmer, who might have had little or no personal contact with his laborers. This type of arrangement implied different class and social relationships from those that prevailed in much of the South. The California farm worker was more akin to an agricultural proletarian than to a peasant. The proverbial paternalism of Southern planters toward their tenants had few parallels in California. Tenants remained on their allotted plots year-round, while many California farmworkers followed the harvest cycle, migrating from crop to crop.

As with many crops, California cotton growers also led the way in harvest mechanization. Many of the factors discussed above—including pre-harvest mechanization (and familiarity with machines), relatively high wages, large-scale operations, high yields, a flat landscape, and a relative absence of rain during the harvest season—all aided in the adoption of the mechanical harvester. Spindle picking machines first appeared on a commercial basis following World War II. In 1951, over 50 percent of the California crop was mechanically harvested compared to about 10 percent for the rest of the nation. Roughly one-half of the country's machines were in California (Musoke and Olmstead, 1982).

ONE-VARIETY COMMUNITY

California was also home to the largest one-variety cotton community. In the first decades of the 20th century, USDA cotton specialists became increasingly alarmed by the declining quality of American cotton due to the effects of the boll weevil, which prompted farmers to switch to earlier-maturing but lower-quality cottons. In addition, smaller production units in the South, seed mixing at gins, and market failures in cotton grading and marketing, contributed to the quality problem. After about a decade of one-variety experiences in the Southwest, the California Legislature declared eight San Joaquin Valley counties and Riverside County as a one-variety community. The 1925 legislation stipulated that only Acala cotton, bred by an association research facility, could be planted, harvested, or ginned in an area of more than four million acres. In the early years, the California one-variety system probably had the desired effects of increasing quality and prices of the state's cotton. However, Constantine, Alston, and Smith demonstrated that by the late 1970s, this system was becoming increasingly inefficient, costing the state's cotton farmers about $180 million a year. In the rest of the nation, one-variety communities had faded away in the 1950s, but in California the system lingered on far too long (Constantine, Alston, and Smith, 1994; Olmstead and Rhode, 2008).[2]

As Figure 2.2 makes clear, after reaching a peak circa 1980, California's cotton acreage and production declined rapidly. Yields continued their upward march, and over the 2007–2011 period were still nearly double the national average. The dramatic fall in cotton's importance once again reflects the dynamism of California agriculture as growers responded to changing environmental conditions and opportunities. Rising water cost and growing pest problems made cotton production less lucrative while, especially in Fresno County, farmers converted considerable acreage to more lucrative crops such as almonds, grapes, and tomatoes. Another change not evident in Figure 2.2 is that since the 1980s, there has been a marked increase in the importance of high-quality, extra-long staple, Pima cotton, which was planted on about one-half of the state's cotton acreage (Geisseler and Horwath, 2016).

---

2 For more traditional accounts see Turner, 1981; Weber, 1994; and Briggs and Cauthen, 1983.

LIVESTOCK PRODUCTION

RANCHING

Similar forces—early adoption of large-scale operations and advanced technologies—characterized California's livestock economy. The broad trends in livestock production in California since 1850 are reflected in Figure 2.3, which graphs the number of head of various types of livestock as aggregated into a measure of animal units fed.[3] California emerged from the Mexican period primarily as a cattle producer. A series of droughts and floods in the 1860s devastated many herds, and in the 1870s, sheep-raising had largely replaced cattle-ranching (U.S. Bureau of the Census, *Census of Agriculture 1959, General Report*, Vol. II).

Many of the livestock ranches of the nineteenth century, including Miller-Lux, Tejon, Kern County Land Company,

Flint-Bixby, Irvine, Stearns, and Hearst, operated on extremely large scales. For example, Henry Miller and Charles Lux amassed more than 1.25 million acres of land, often with valuable water rights (Igler, 2001). With the intensification of crop production in California, aggregate livestock activities tended to grow slowly. Although the smaller, family-sized fruit farms began to replace the large bonanza grain farms and livestock ranches, "general" farms, modeled on Midwestern prototypes, remained rare. This is reflected in the relatively small role of swine production in Figure 2.3. Largely as a result, over the 20th century, livestock production has been relatively less important in California than in the rest of the country. The market value of livestock and livestock products sales as a share of the sales of crops, livestock, and livestock products has generally exceeded one-half nationally but usually hovered around a third in California.

3   This measure combines livestock into dairy-cow-equivalents using the following weights: dairy cows=1; non-dairy cows=0.73; sheep=0.15; goats=0.15; hogs=0.18; horses and mules=0.88; chickens=0.0043.

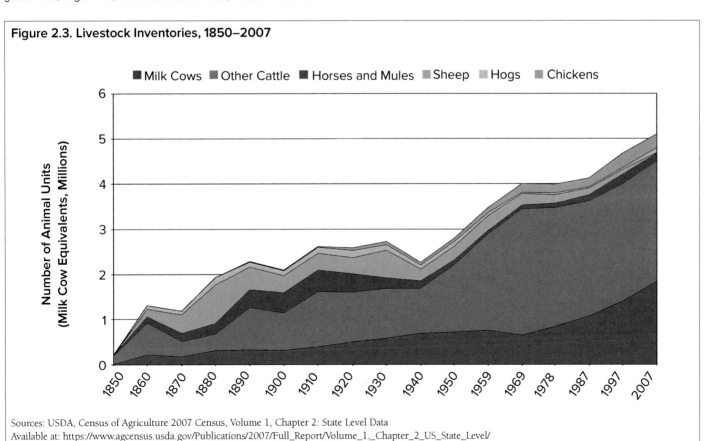

Figure 2.3. Livestock Inventories, 1850–2007

■ Milk Cows   ■ Other Cattle   ■ Horses and Mules   ■ Sheep   ■ Hogs   ■ Chickens

Sources: USDA, Census of Agriculture 2007 Census, Volume 1, Chapter 2: State Level Data
Available at: https://www.agcensus.usda.gov/Publications/2007/Full_Report/Volume_1,_Chapter_2_US_State_Level/

Dairy Herds

Dairy and poultry operations represent exceptions to the general pattern of slow growth of livestock farming in the first decades of the 20th century. These activities steadily expanded, primarily to serve the state's rapidly growing urban markets. In 1993, California replaced Wisconsin as the nation's No. 1 milk producer (USDA, *Agricultural Statistics*, 1995). Between 1900 and 1960, the number of milk cows grew at a rate of 1.5 percent per annum and the number of chickens at a 3.3 percent rate. Output grew much faster as productivity per animal unit increased enormously, especially in the post-1940 period. From the 1920s to 2000, California was a leader in milk output per dairy cow in most years. For example, in 1924 milk production per dairy cow in California was 5,870 pounds, while similar figures for Wisconsin and the United States were 5,280 and 4,167 pounds, respectively (USDA, *Statistics Bulletin* 218, 1957). Revolutionary productivity changes have occurred in recent decades. In 2015, California remained the nation's largest milk producer with almost 41 billion pounds, Wisconsin was a distant second with 29 billion pounds, and no other state exceeded 15 billion pounds But by this latter date, the breeding, feeding, and maintenance technologies that had propelled the increase in yields had diffused more widely. In 2015, California's 23,002 pounds per cow ranked ninth in the nation, with Colorado's average of 25,685 topping the list (USDA, *Agricultural Statistics*, 2016).

The post-1940 period also witnessed a dramatic revival of the state's cattle sector outside dairying. The number of non-milk cows in California increased from about 1.4 million head in 1940 (roughly the level prevailing since 1900) to 3.8 million in 1969. This growth was associated with a significant structural change that was pioneered in California and Arizona—the introduction of large-scale, commercial feed-lot operations (Committee on Agriculture, Nutrition, and Forestry, 1980). By 1963, almost 70 percent of the cattle on feed were in mega-lots of 10,000 or more head. A comparison with other areas provides perspective. In 1963, there were 613 feed lots in California with an average of about 3,100 head per lot. By contrast, Iowa had 45,000 feedlots with an average of less than 63 head per lot; Texas had 1,753 feed lots with an average of 511 head per lot. Employment of state-of-the-art feed lots and modern science and veterinary medicine, along with favorable

climatic conditions, allowed ranchers in California and Arizona to achieve significant efficiencies in converting feed to cattle weight. After the 1960s, larger commercial feedlots started to become more prevalent in the Southwest and in the Corn Belt (Hopkin and Kramer, 1965). Again, technologies and organizational strategies developed in California spread to reshape agricultural practices in other regions.

Government Interventions to Control Diseases

Few observers appreciate how vitally important federal government animal-health policies were in the development of California's livestock industry. The state faced many severe disease outbreaks that farmers, state and local officials, and private veterinarians were incapable of combating effectively. Two of the most destructive diseases were foot and mouth disease (FMD) and bovine tuberculosis (BTB). FMD hit California twice in the 1920s, with the most serious outbreak erupting in February 1924, when the affliction appeared in a Berkeley dairy herd. As officials raced to stamp out infected herds, the disease stayed one jump ahead, eventually spreading to 16 counties. At its peak, the USDA's Bureau of Animal Industry (BAI) quarantined parts or all of 23 California counties. The BAI sent 204 agents to California and hired numerous laborers, private veterinarians, and others to help in the fight. By the end of August, officials destroyed more than 100,000 animals.

The FDM crisis was a catastrophe for California's agricultural and tourist industries. Shortly after the crisis began, 37 U.S. states and territories and several foreign countries embargoed California products, barring livestock and poultry (and their products), straw, grain, grasses, fruit (including canned and dried fruit), vegetables, nursery stock, and more. Oregon and Arizona raised especially severe barriers, blocking roads, and stopping trains. Tourist traffic was diverted through Utah and Nevada. Civic and sporting events were canceled, and parks, hiking trails, and hunting and fishing areas were closed.

The problem was amplified because California's legal and constitutional provisions made it difficult, if not impossible, for state officials to efficiently cull animals, to pay compensation, and to cooperate fully with federal officials. This same class of problems also impaired to the state's fight against BTB. By the 1930s, California dairy cattle had become the talk of the nation because of the high incidence of BTB, a disease easily transmitted from cattle to other livestock and from livestock to humans, either by direct contact or through animal products. The most likely path of transmission was in cows' milk and milk products.

Around 1910, about 15,000 Americans, mostly children, were dying from tuberculosis contracted from animals and animal products every year, and many more suffered painful and debilitating illnesses. The BAI undertook the first steps in what would become a successful national eradication program in 1917. County-by-county and state-by-state, BAI-approved veterinarians entered farms with or without the farmers' permission, tested animals, and ordered the destruction of animals that tested positive. Where needed, armed guards accompanied the veterinarians. This was an enormously controversial campaign that witnessed countless confrontations, some gun play, and the declaration of martial law in Iowa.

Contrary to California's image as a pacesetter, it was the last state in the Union to eradicate BTB due to exceptionally poor state leadership, corruption, funding pressures, state constitutional limitations, and vigorous opposition—including by mobs of farmers. The campaign pitted urban interests against dairy interests, dairymen with clean herds against those with suspect cattle, and reputable scientists against popular quacks. Only when other states and the federal government threatened to quarantine California cattle and cattle products, did the state enact the life-saving policies that allowed it to cooperate fully with federal officials and pay indemnities that were needed to gain farmer cooperation (Olmstead and Rhode, 2015).

MECHANIZATION AND FARM POWER

INDUCED INNOVATION, PATH DEPENDENCY, AND SUPPLY-SIDE FORCES

A hallmark of California agriculture since the wheat era has been its highly mechanized farms. Nineteenth-century observers watched in awe as cumbersome steam tractors and giant combines worked their way across vast fields. In the twentieth century, California farmers led the nation in the adoption of gasoline tractors, mechanical cotton pickers, sugar beet harvesters, tomato harvesters, electric pumps, and dozens of less well-known machines.

The story of agricultural mechanization in California illustrates the cumulative and reinforcing character of the invention and diffusion processes. Mechanization of one activity set in motion strong economic and cultural forces that encouraged further mechanization of other, sometimes quite different, activities. On-farm mechanization was closely tied to the inventive efforts of local mechanics. Specialized crops and growing conditions created niche demands for new types of equipment. Protected by high transportation costs from large firms located in the Midwest, a local farm implement industry flourished by providing Pacific Coast farmers with equipment especially suited to their requirements. In many instances, the inventors designed and perfected prototypes that later captured national and international markets. Grain combines, track-laying tractors, giant land planes, tomato pickers, and sugar beet harvesters, to name but a few, emerged from California's shops.

Several factors contributed to mechanization. In general, California farmers were more educated and more prosperous than farmers elsewhere. These advantages gave them the insight, skills, and financial wherewithal to support their penchant for tinkering. Nowhere was this more evident than on the bonanza ranches that often served as the design and testing grounds for harvester prototypes. The large scale of many California farms allowed growers to spread the fixed cost of expensive equipment. The scarcity of labor in California meant relatively high-wage rates and periods of uncertain labor supply that further stimulated the incentive to find labor-saving alternatives.

The climate and terrain were also favorable. Extensive dry seasons allowed machines to work long hours in near-ideal conditions, and the flat Central Valley offered few obstacles to wheeled equipment. In the cases of small grains and cotton, mechanization was delayed in other regions of the country because free-standing moisture damaged the crops. Such problems were minimal in California. All things considered, the state's climatic and economic conditions were exceptionally conducive to mechanization.

FARM POWER

Over the years 1870 to 1930, the average value of implements per California farm was about double the national average. The new generation of farm equipment of the 19th century relied increasingly on horses and mules for power. Horses on any one farm were essentially a fixed asset. A stock of horses accumulated for a given task was potentially available at a relatively low variable cost to perform other tasks. For these reasons, an examination of horses on California farms offers important insights into the course of mechanization. In 1870, the average number of horses and mules per male worker was more than twice the national average. Throughout the 19th century, California farmers were using an enormous amount of horsepower (Olmstead and Rhode, 1988).

California was a leader in the early adoption of tractors. By 1920, over 10 percent of California farms had tractors compared with 3.6 percent for the nation as a whole. In 1925, nearly one-fifth of California farms reported tractors, proportionally more than in Illinois or Iowa, and just behind the nation-leading Dakotas. These figures understate the power available in California, because the tractors adopted in the West were typically larger than those found elsewhere. Western farmers were the predominant users of large track-laying tractors.

The state's farmers were also the nation's pioneers in the utilization of electric power. The world's first purported use of electricity for irrigation pumping took place in the Central Valley just before the turn of the century. In 1929, over one-half of California farms purchased electric power compared with about one-tenth for the United States (U.S. Bureau of the Census, *Sixteenth Census of the United States, 1940, Agriculture* Vol. 1, Pt. 6).

The abundant supply of power on California farms encouraged local manufacturers to produce new types of equipment and, in turn, the development of new and larger implements often created the need for new sources of power. This process of responding to the opportunities and bottlenecks created by previous technological changes provided a continuing stimulation to innovators. Tracing the changes in wheat-farming technology illustrates how the cumulative technological changes led to a markedly different path of mechanical development in the West.

Almost immediately after wheat cultivation began in California, farmers developed a distinctive set of cultural practices. Plowing the fertile California soil was nothing like working the rocky soils in the East or the dense sod of the Midwest. In California, ranchers used two, four, and even eight-bottomed gang plows, cutting just a few inches deep. In the East, plowing 1.5 acres was a good day's work in 1880. In most of the prairie regions, 2.5 was the norm. In California, it was common for one man with a gang plow and a team of eight horses to complete six to ten acres per day. The tendency of California's farmers to use larger plows continued into the 20th century. After tractors came on line, the state's farmers were also noted for using both larger models and larger equipment in tow. This pattern influenced subsequent manufacturing and farming decisions (U.S. Bureau of the Census, *Tenth Census of the United States, 1880, Agriculture* Vol. 3; USDA, *Monthly Crop Report*, 1918).

The preference for large plows in California stimulated local investors and manufacturers: the U.S. Commissioner of Agriculture noted that "patents granted on wheel plows in 1869 to residents of California and Oregon largely exceed in number those granted for inventions of a like character from all the other states of the Union" (USDA, *Agricultural Report, 1869*)." Between 1859 and 1873, California accounted for one-quarter of the nation's patenting activity for multi-bottom plows, while the state's contribution to the development of small, single-bottom plows was insignificant (U.S. Patent Office, 1874). The experience with large plows directly contributed to important developments in the perfection and use of listers, harrows, levelers, and earth-moving equipment.

THE GRAIN HARVEST

The adoption of distinctive labor-saving techniques carried over to grain sowing and harvest activities. An 1875 USDA survey showed that over one-half of Midwestern farmers used grain drills, but that virtually all California farmers sowed their grain (USDA, Agricultural Report, 1875). California farmers were sometimes accused of being slovenly for sowing, a technique which was also common to the more backward American South. However, the use of broadcast sowers in California reflected a rational response to the state's own factor price environment, and bore little resemblance to the hand-sowing techniques practiced in the South. Advanced, high-capacity endgate seeders of local design were among the broadcasting equipment used in California. By the 1880s, improved models could seed up to 60 acres in one day. By contrast, a standard drill could seed about 15 acres per day and a man broadcasting by hand could seed roughly 7 acres per day (Rogin, 1931; Adams, 1921). The use of labor-saving techniques was most evident on the state's bonanza wheat ranches, where some farmers attached a broadcast sower to the back of a gang plow and then attached a harrow behind the sower, thereby accomplishing the plowing, sowing, and harrowing with a single operation.

California wheat growers also followed a different technological path in their harvest operations by relying primarily on headers instead of reapers. This practice would have important implications for the subsequent development of combines in California. The header cut only the top of the straw. The cut grain was then transported on a continuous apron to an accompanying wagon. Headers typically had longer cutting bars and, hence, greater capacity than reapers, but the most significant advantage was that headers eliminated the need for binding. The initial cost of the header was about 50 to 100 percent more than the reaper, but its real drawback was in humid areas where the grain was not dry enough to harvest unless it was dead ripe. This involved huge crop risks in the climate of the Midwest; risks that were virtually nonexistent in the dry California summers. For these reasons, California became the only substantial market for the header technology.

Header technology evolved in an entirely different direction from the reaper, leading directly to the development in California of a commercial combined harvester. From the starting point of the header, it was quite simple and natural to add a thresher pulled along its side. There had been numerous attempts in the East and Midwest to perfect a machine that reaped and threshed in one operation. Among those that came closest to succeeding was Hiram Moore's combine built in Kalamazoo, Michigan, in 1835. But in the humid Midwest, combining suffered from the same problems with moisture that had plagued heading. In 1853, Moore's invention was given new life when a model was sent to California, where it served as a prototype for combine development (Higgins, 1958). After several decades of experimentation in California, workable designs were available by the mid-1880s and the period of large-scale production and adoption began. Most of the innovating firms, including the two leading enterprises—the Stockton Combined Harvester and Agricultural Works and the Holt Manufacturing Company—located in Stockton, which became an important equipment-manufacturing center.

During the harvest of 1880, "comparatively few" machines operated in California, and agricultural authorities, such as Brewer and Hilgard, clearly suggest that even those machines were experimental. In 1881, about 20 combines were being built in Stockton (U.S. Bureau of the Census, 1883). By 1888, between 500 and 600 were in use. The first truly popular model was the Houser, built by the Stockton Combined Harvester and Agricultural Works. In 1889, its advertisements claimed that there were 500 Houser machines in use, and that they outnumbered all other competitors combined (Rogin, 1931; Brewer, 1883). Soon thereafter, machines in the Holt line overtook the Houser. The innovative products of the Holt company, which included in 1893 the first successful hillside combine, became dominant on the West Coast. By 1915, Holt's advertisements boasted that over 90 percent of California's wheat crop was harvested by the 3,000 Holt combines (*Economist*, Nov. 28, 1914). These machines were powered by teams of 20 or more equines. At this date, the adoption of combine-harvesters east of the Rockies was still in its infancy.

Combine models that eventually were adopted in the Midwest and Great Plains were considerably smaller than West Coast machines. The primary reasons for the differences were undoubtedly cost and scale considerations. In addition, eastern farmers generally lacked the horses needed to pull the large western machines and they often lacked the know-how and will to manage such large teams. California

farmers had gradually developed their ability to manage large teams because of their experience with gang plows and headers (Olmstead and Rhode, 1988).

The difficulties associated with controlling large teams induced Holt and others to perfect huge steam tractors to pull their even larger harvesters. While steam-driven combines never came into vogue, these innovative efforts did have one highly important by-product—the track-laying tractor. The first practical track-laying farm tractors (identified with Holt's first test in 1904) were initially developed for the soft soil of the Sacramento-San Joaquin Delta. Although the crawlers were first designed to solve a local problem, this innovation was of global significance. The Caterpillar Tractor Company (formed by the merger of the Holt and Best enterprises) would build larger, more powerful equipment that rapidly spread throughout the world.

The reoccurring pattern of one invention creating new needs and opportunities that led to yet another invention offers important lessons for understanding the lack of development in other times and places. One key to explaining the progression of innovations in California was the close link between manufacturers and farmers that facilitated constant feedback between the two groups and the keen competition among producers that spurred inventive activity and production efficiencies. Entrepreneurs seeking their fortunes were in close tune with their potential customers' needs and vied with one another to perfect equipment that would satisfy those needs. Where these forces were not at work, the burdens of history severed the potential backward linkages that are so critical for economic development.

IRRIGATION

RESHAPING THE LANDSCAPE

Just as there were major investments in mechanical technologies to increase the productivity of labor, there were also substantial investments to increase the productivity of California's land. These included agro-chemical research, biological learning concerning appropriate crops and cultural practices, and land clearing and preparation; but the most notable were investments in water control and provision. These took two related forms. The first consisted of measures primarily intended to drain and protect agricultural land from flooding. In this realm, Californians literally re-shaped their landscape as individual farms leveled the fields and constructed thousands of miles of ditches. In addition, individual farms, reclamation districts, and the Army Corps of Engineers built several thousand miles of major levees to tame the state's inland waterways. Without these investments, much of the Central Valley's land could not have been planted in intensive crops (Kelley, 1998).

The second form consisted of a variety of measures to supply the state's farms with irrigation water. Table 2.1 details the growth in the state's irrigated acreage between 1890 and 2007. Expansion occurred in two main waves: the first lasting from 1900 through the 1920s and the second, linked to the Central Valley Project, during the decade after World War II. Much of the historical growth of irrigation was the result of small-scale, private initiatives rather than large-scale, public projects that have attracted so much scholarly attention. Up until the 1960s, individuals and partnerships were the leading suppliers of irrigation water. These two types of suppliers accounted for roughly one-third of irrigated acres between 1910 and 1930, and over one-half by 1950.

These small-scale irrigation efforts were closely associated with the rising use of groundwater in California over the first half of the 20th century. Between 1902 and 1950, the acreage irrigated by groundwater sources increased more than thirty-fold, whereas that watered by surface sources only tripled. Groundwater, which had supplied less than 10 percent of irrigated acreage in 1902, accounted for over 50 percent of the acreage by 1950. This great expansion was reflected in the growing stock of pumping equipment

in the state. Significant technological changes in pumping technology and declining power costs underscored this growth. During the 1910s and 1920s, the number of pumps, pumping plants, and pumped wells doubled each decade, rising from roughly 10,000 units in 1910 to just below 50,000 units in 1930. Pumping capacity increased two-and-one-half to three times per decade over this period. Expansion stalled during the Great Depression but resumed in the 1940s, with the number of pumps, plants, and wells rising to roughly 75,000 units by 1950. Individuals and partnerships dominated pumping, accounting for about 95 percent of total units and approximately 80 percent of capacity over the 1920–1950 period.

IRRIGATION DISTRICTS

Since the 1950s, there has been a shift away from individuals and partnerships, as well as from groundwater sources. By the 1970s, irrigation districts—public corporations run by local landowners and empowered to tax and issue bonds to purchase or construct, maintain, and operate irrigation works—had become the leading suppliers. The irrigation district as an organizational structure rapidly rose in importance over two periods. In the first, lasting from 1910 to 1930, acreage supplied by irrigation districts increased from one-in-fifteen to approximately one-in-three. Much of this growth came at the expense of cooperative and commercial irrigation enterprises. Between 1930 and 1960, the district share changed little. During the 1960s, the irrigation district form experienced a second surge of growth. This was due in part to the rising importance of large-scale federal and state projects, which distributed water through these organizations. By 1969, irrigation districts supplied more than 55 percent of all irrigated acreage.

As with so many other areas of California agriculture, success in managing water heavily depended on cooperative action, rather than just individual initiative. Water access has often been contentious, pitting farmers against urban interests and farmers against farmers. Everyone involved attempted to capture government to gain an advantage. Part of the problem is that historically, property rights in water were less well defined than in most private goods and assets, and rights based on location or historic conditions invariably led to inefficient patterns of use.[4]

ADVERSE CONSEQUENCES

Moreover, with few restraints on farmers' use of private pumps, individual farmers have predictably depleted aquifers, leading to deeper and more expensive wells and higher energy costs. In addition, decades of irrigation, along with the use of fertilizers and chemicals to control weeds and pests, have contaminated the soil with salts, selenium, and other chemicals. As one sign of the problem in the 1980s, the drainage of farm water into the Kesterson National Wildlife Refuge, located in the San Joaquin Valley, resulted in widespread birth defects in birds and fish from selenium poisoning. More troubling, many have noted high incidents of environmentally-related health problems of agricultural workers. The long-run survival of the current agricultural system is now being questioned (Leslie, 2010). One thing seems certain, especially in light of global warming ushering in an era of hotter and more variable climatic conditions: dealing effectively with these problems will require more regulation to preserve aquifers, use water wisely, and limit harmful practices.

---

4   Many books deal with this complicated history, including Hundley, 1992; Pisani, 1984; and Reisner, 1986.

LABOR

A HISTORY OF STRIFE

Few issues have invoked more controversy in California than recurrent problems associated with agricultural labor. Steinbeck's portrayal of the clash of cultures in *The Grapes of Wrath* represents the tip of a gigantic iceberg. The Chinese Exclusion Act, the Gentlemen's Agreement aimed at Japanese immigrants, the forced repatriation of Mexicans during the Great Depression, the Great Cotton Strikes of 1933, 1938, and 1939, the Bracero Program (1942–64), the United Farm Worker (UFW) and Teamsters' organizing campaigns and national boycotts, the state's Agricultural Relations Act, the legal controversy over the mechanization of the tomato harvest, the current battles over illegal immigration, and now the growing concerns over the health of agricultural laborers are all part of a reoccurring pattern of turmoil deeply rooted in California's agricultural labor market. There are few, if any, parallels in other northern states.

Historians often concentrate on past labor-management conflicts. Just as farmers attempted to gain advantages through collective action (cooperatives, water projects, pest control, labor relations, capturing governments, etc.), workers attempted collective action in the form of labor unions. The strikes and unrest associated with Cesar Chavez's UFW organizing drives in the 1960s and 1970s are probably the best remembered labor-management confrontations, but these events were dwarfed in scale by the agricultural strikes in the 1930s. In 1933, 50,000 agricultural laborers walked out of the harvests. The largest of these many strikes saw nearly 20,000 cotton pickers in the San Joaquin Valley refuse to work. Hired thugs and police tear-gassed, arrested, and sometimes beat strikers. It is useful to contrast the experience of workers in the agricultural and non-agricultural sectors.

The National Labor Relations Act of 1935 granted most private sector non-agricultural workers the right to collective bargaining, but agricultural laborers in California did not receive this legal right until 40 years later with the passage of the California Agricultural Relations Act. Violence was most common during organizing strikes, when the very legitimacy of a union was in question, so the delay in granting a legal basis for agricultural unions enhanced the likelihood of conflict. In addition, agricultural strikes invariably occurred during the peak-harvest season, when the absence of labor could mean the loss of an entire year's crop for the farmer. In most mining and industrial enterprises, strikes could be disruptive, but they would not threaten an entire year's output. The fact that agricultural workers were often migrant minorities with little power in the community contributed to social differences and the possibility of violence, including by local police (McWilliams, 1939; Flores, 2016; and Olmsted, 2015).

A Comparative Perspective

For all the controversy, however, the state's farms have remained a magnet attracting large voluntary movements of workers seeking opportunity. Chinese, Japanese, Sikhs, Filipinos, Southern Europeans, Mexicans, Okies, and then Mexicans again have all taken a turn in California's fields. Each group has its own story, but in the space allotted here we attempt to provide an aggregate perspective on some of the distinguishing characteristics of California's volatile agricultural labor market. The essential characteristics of today's labor market date back to the beginning of the American period.

Table 2.2 offers a view of the role of hired labor in California compared to the national situation. Expenditures on hired labor relative to farm production and sales have generally been two-to-three times higher in California than for the United States. Within California, the trend shows some decline. Another important perspective is to assess the importance of agricultural employment in the economy's total labor force. Here, the evidence is somewhat surprising. Both agriculture and agricultural labor play a relatively prominent role in most renderings of the state's history. But as Table 2.2 indicates, until the last two decades, agricultural employment as a percent of total employment in California has generally been less important to the state than for the country. Agricultural labor is two percent of the state's total labor force, but it generates a larger share of news and legislative interest due to the special nature of the state's labor institutions.

From the beginning of the American period, California farms have relied more extensively on hired labor than their counterparts in the East. At the same time, Californians never fully developed the institutions of slavery or widespread share-cropping as in the South. The parade of migrants who have toiled in California's fields have often been described as "cheap labor," and indeed they were near the bottom of the state's labor hierarchy. But the "cheap" appellation is something of a misnomer, because the daily wage rate in California was typically higher than in other regions of the United States, and the United States was one of the world's highest-wage countries.

Labor Mobility

In an important sense, the "cheap labor" in California agriculture was among the highest wage labor on the globe. In addition, one of the remarkable features of California agriculture is that the so-called "development" or "sectoral-productivity" gap—the ratio of income per worker in agriculture to income per worker outside agriculture—has been relatively narrow[5] due to the relatively high productivity of the state's agricultural sector. In addition, because workers "followed the harvest," moving from crop to crop, they worked more days in the high-productivity season than Southern sharecroppers who experienced long periods of relatively low productivity, non-harvest work.

Due to low rates of natural increase, California's farm sector never generated a large, home-born surplus population that put downward pressure on rural living standards. Instead, the sector attracted migrants from the surplus populations of other impoverished regions of the world. For these migrants, many with little facility in English, agricultural labor offered a stepping stone into the robust, high-wage California economy. Hard work, high savings rates, and the availability of public education worked wonders: few of the descendants of the earlier generations of agricultural laborers toil in the fields today. Some of those separated by only a few generations from the original immigrants are in fact landowners, but most (who remained in the United States) have moved into urban blue- and white-collar professions with skills, educational levels, and incomes on par with citizens who are descendants from earlier waves of Northern European migrants. Over the span of decades, agricultural labor in California has not been a dead-end pursuit creating a permanent class

---

5   The "development" gap is measured as (Yag/Lag)/(1-Yag)/(1-Lag) where Yag is the share of income generated in the agricultural sector and Lag is the share of the labor force employed there.

Table 2.2. Agricultural Labor in California and the United States

	Farm Labor Force as a Share of: Total Labor Force		Hired Labor Expenditures as a Share of:			
			Gross Value of Farm Production		Market Value of Farm Products Sold	
	California	U.S	California	U.S.	California	U.S.
	Percent		Percent			
1870	29.3	52.3	20.8	12.7	–	–
1880	28.6	49.4	–	–	–	–
1890	29.0	41.2	–	–	–	–
1900	25.0	37.6	19.6	7.6	–	–
1910	17.9	31.1	22.2	7.7	–	–
1920	17.3	27.0	16.4	6.3	–	–
1930	13.3	21.4	–	–	21.4	9.9
1940	11.0	18.9	–	–	25.3	11.7
1950	7.5	12.3	–	–	21.8	11.0
1960	4.7	6.7	–	–	17.7	8.5
1970	3.0	3.5	–	–	16.2	7.4
1980	2.9	3.0	–	–	14.7	6.4
1990	3.0	2.5	–	–	17.1	8.0
2000	1.8	1.5	–	–	14.7	7.7
2010	2.3	1.6	–	–	14.8	7.4

Sources: Margaret Gordon, *Employment Expansion and Population Growth,* UC Press, Berkeley, 1954
U.S. Dept. of Commerce, Regional Employment by Industry, 1940-1970
U.S. Census Office: Compendium of the Ninth Census 1870
U.S. Bureau of the Census: Twelfth Census 1900, Agriculture; Fourteenth Census 1920, Agriculture, Vol. 5
Census of Agriculture 1959, California, Vol. 1, Part 48
1980 Census, Population, Vol. 1
1990 Census, "Labor Force Status and Employment Characteristics: 1990 Data Set: 1990 Summary Tape File 3 (STF 3)—Sample data," and 2000 Census, "Industry by Sex—Percent Distribution: 2000 Data Set: Census 2000 Summary File 3 (SF 3) —Sample Data," available at: http://factfinder.census.gov
USDA, Census of Agriculture 1997, Table 1 on "Historical Highlights" for United States and California, available at:: http://www.nass.usda.gov/census/census97/volume1/us-51/us1_01.pdf and http://www.nass.usda.gov/census/census97/volume1/ca-5/ca1_01.pdf
USDA, Census of Agriculture 2007 Census, Volume 1, Chapter 2: State Level Data. https://www.agcensus.usda.gov/Publications/2007/Full_Report/Volume_1,_Chapter_2_US_State_Level/

of peasant laborers, but this result has been dependent on the existence of a growing non-agricultural economy.

The agricultural history literature often laments the end of the "agricultural ladder," whereby workers start off as laborers or sharecroppers and work their way up to cash tenants and then owners of their own farms. According to the traditional literature, ending this process represented one of the great failings of 19th century American society. The literature is particularly critical of California because of its large farms and high ratio of hired workers to farm owners. However, Engel's Law tells us that, as income per capita grows, a smaller percentage of income will be spent on food, so in a growing economy the agricultural sector shrinks relative to the non-agricultural sector. This is precisely what transpired. At the same time, the closing of the frontier meant that the total supply of agricultural land could not continue to grow as it did for most of the 19th century. Thus, unless farms were Balkanized (divided) into smaller and smaller units, there was no possible way for the 19th century ideal to have continued.

THE DOMAR MODEL

Economic historians often explain the prevalence of the family farm in the northern United States by the workings of the Domar model—if there is free land, and crop production technology offers few economies of scale and requires little capital, then anyone can earn as much working for themselves as for anyone else (Domar, 1970). There will be no free hired labor, and if bound labor (slavery) is illegal, farms will be family-sized. Like many simple abstract models, the implications of the Domar hypothesis are starker than the realities, but its fundamental logic explains many features of the development of northern agriculture.

California's so-called "exceptionalism" also follows from the Domar model. In California, very large estates emerged from the legacy of Mexican and Spanish land grants, railroad land grants, and control of water. Gradually, many of the large estates were broken up by market forces as California's agriculture intensified, but many remained—especially in parts of the Central Valley and the Salinas Valley. A snapshot taken at any number of historical dates would show a handful of wealthy landowners and a multitude of itinerant laborers and their families. The legacy of this unequal "initial" distribution of property rights was that especially land with good access to water was not free in California. In part because of the initial distribution of land and in part due to environmental conditions, production tended to involve larger scale and greater quantities of capital (for machinery, irrigation, and orchards). Hence, the gap between the assumptions of the Domar model and reality was greater in California than in the Midwest. It proved possible for farmers to pay workers more than they could earn working for themselves and still earn a profit. From the mid-19th century on, California was characterized by "factories in the fields" or "industrial agriculture" or, in more modern terms, "agribusiness."

However, it is important to note that agriculture based on profit-oriented commodity production employing a substantial amount of hired labor was a widespread phenomenon in the period, and by no means limited to California. This organizational form was common to the agriculture of many capitalist countries (e.g., Britain, Germany) in the late-19th century, and it has arguably become increasingly common throughout the United States over the 20th century. From a global historical perspective, the stereotypical Midwestern commercially-oriented family farm employing little or no hired labor is probably a greater exception than what prevailed in California.

THE PUZZLE OF LABOR-INTENSIVE CROPS
IN A HIGH-WAGE ECONOMY

Today, California farmers often complain about the high cost of labor relative to what their international competitors must pay. But when the state first moved into the production of specialty crops, California producers of fruit and nuts also faced labor costs that were several times higher than their competitors in the Mediterranean Basin. Given these conditions, how did the early Californian producers not only survive, but in many cases, drive European producers out of markets in their own backyards?

WAGES, LAND, AND TRANSPORTATION

There is no doubt that California was a high-wage economy in the national, not to mention global, context. For example, in 1910, California farmers paid monthly agricultural laborers 71 percent more than did their counterparts nationally; day harvest labor was paid a 36 percent premium. The wage differentials with traditional producing countries in the Mediterranean Basin were much larger, with California farmers paying roughly four to eight times more. Moreover, most fruit and nut crops were characterized by high labor-to-land ratios. For example, the U.S. Department of Agriculture estimated that in 1939, producing almonds on the Pacific Coast required 96 hours per bearing acre; dates, 275; figs, 155; grapes, 200; prunes, 130; and walnuts, 81 hours; this compared with only 6.6 hours of labor per acre of wheat (Hecht and Barton, 1950).

One important question is whether grain and fruit actually competed for the same land and labor. On the Pacific Coast, the labor requirements of both activities were highly seasonal and their peak harvest demands did not fully overlap. In California, for example, the wheat harvest was typically complete by early July whereas the raisin and wine grape harvest did not commence until September and continued through late October. Hence, a worker could, in principle, participate fully both in the grain and grape harvests. Rather than conceiving of the different crops as being competitive in labor, we might be better served by considering them as complimentary. As an example, in the lush Santa Clara Valley, harvest workers would migrate from cherries to apricots to prunes to walnuts and almonds

over a roughly six-month season. Adding other semi-tropical crops, such as cotton and navel oranges, stretched the harvest season into large sections of California into the winter months. By filling out the work year and reducing seasonal underemployment, the cultivation of a range of crops in close proximity increased the attractiveness to laborers of working in Pacific Coast agriculture. The succession of peak-load, high-wage periods allowed California workers more days of high-intensity and high-pay work in a year than was possible in most other regions.[6]

It is also important to recognize that the land used for grain and fruit crops was largely "non-competing." Prime-quality fruit lands, with the accompanying climatic conditions, were so different from the lands that remained in grain production that they constituted a "specific input." Differences in the land values help bring these points home. According to R. L. Adams' 1921 California farm manual, the market value of "good" wheat land in the state was approximately $100 per acre in the period immediately before the First World War. "Good" land for prune production was worth $350 even before planting and valued at $800 when bearing. The "best" land for prunes had a market value of $500 not planted and $1,000 in bearing trees. Similarly, "good" land for raisin grape production was worth $150 raw and $300 in bearing vines; the "best" sold for $250 not planted and $400 bearing. Focusing on physical labor-to-land ratios in comparing wheat and fruit production can be seriously misleading because the acreage used for fruit cultivation was of a different quality (and ultimately higher market value) than that used for grains (Rhode, 1995; Adams, 1921; Sackman, 2005).

---

6   This argument also draws attention to the important role of labor mobility in the region's agricultural development, and in particular to the many and often conflicting efforts of local authorities to control the migrant flows of specific ethnic groups. By focusing on the political economy of migration, this literature helps to undermine the notion that labor scarcity was a "natural" immutable feature of the region. Rather, it was in part an outcome of collective political decisions. The migrant flows presumably would have been far larger but for exclusionary agitation and legislation.

A further reason why horticultural crops could compete was that, unlike the key agricultural staples, many fruit and nut products enjoyed effective tariff protection during the late-19th and early-20th centuries. Tariffs almost surely sped up the growth of Mediterranean agriculture in the United States and were strongly supported by domestic producers, railroads, and packers. One of the recurrent justifications for tariffs offered by domestic growers was to help offset high transportation differentials. Almost across the board, Mediterranean producers enjoyed lower freight rates to the key markets of the Northeastern United States (not to mention Northern Europe) than their American rivals did. For example, circa 1909, shipping currants from Greece for New York cost 17 cents per hundred weight while the freight on an equivalent quantity of California dried fruit averaged about one dollar.

An Emphasis on Quality

For the Pacific Coast fruit industry, the cost of transportation remained an important factor, shaping production and processing practices. This is reflected in an observation that has entered textbook economics: that the best apples are exported because they can bear the cost of shipping. It also helps explain one of the defining characteristics of the region's fruit industry: its emphasis of quality. Local producers and packers devoted exceptional efforts to improving grading and quality control, removing culls, stems and dirt, reducing spoilage in shipment, and developing brand-names/high-quality reputations. This focus makes sense given the high transportation cost that western producers faced in reaching the markets of the U.S. Atlantic Coast and Europe.

To a large extent, the ability of Californians to compete with the growers in Southern Europe depended on capturing the higher end of the market. With only a few exceptions, California dried fruits earned higher prices than their European competition because the state's growers gained a reputation for quality and consistency. As an example, the United States produced far higher-quality prunes than Serbia and Bosnia, the major competitors, and as a result, American prunes sold for roughly twice the price of the Balkan product in European markets. Not only were California prunes larger, they also enjoyed other significant quality advantages stemming from the state's better dehydrating, packing, and shipping methods (Morilla Critz,

Olmstead, and Rhode, 1999). Similar quality advantages applied virtually across the board for California's horticultural crops.

It is interesting to note that at least some of California's current problems with foreign competition stem directly from the ability of others to copy the state's methods. After the California horticultural industry established its strong market presence, the message eventually got through to other producers. The extensive efforts that producers in other new areas (such as South Africa, Chile, and Australia) and in Europe made to copy the California model provide another indicator of the importance of superior technology and organization in establishing California's comparative advantage.

CONCLUSION

This essay should provide a historical context for other chapters in this volume.[7] Responding to market forces, the state has witnessed numerous transformations in cropping patterns, labor sources, and technologies. Despite these changes, many fundamental characteristics have endured; many of the institutional and structural features found today have deep roots in the state's past.

Two issues of interest in the literature on agricultural development warrant mention. First, the history of agricultural mechanization in California conforms nicely with the familiar predictions of the induced innovation model: mechanization represented a rational response by the state's farmers and mechanics to factor scarcities and the state's environmental conditions. But to fully capture the reality of the state's development, it is useful to supplement the induced innovation model with three additional insights: the importance of path dependency (whereby early investment decisions paved the way for subsequent developments); the importance of learning by doing; and the close, ongoing interactions between farmers and inventor-manufacturers.

Secondly, California's history does not conform to the standard paradigm that treats biological productivity changes (in the context of the literature, this means non-mechanical innovations) as primarily a post-1930 phenomenon in American agriculture. The settlement process, the worldwide search for appropriate crops and cultural practices, the wholesale shift in crop mixes, and the massive investments in water control and irrigation, along with numerous other measures, are fundamentally stories of biological investment in a labor-scarce, land-abundant environment. These biological investments transformed the state's agriculture, vastly increasing productivity per acre and per worker (Olmstead and Rhode, 2008).

---

7   Our account has neglected many important crops and activities. More so than most states, California's agricultural economy is really many economies. The grape and wine industries, the specialized citrus economy, the growers of vegetables, and many others have stories of their own that deserve detailed analysis. In a similar vein, our treatment of mechanization represents only a fraction of the more general category of science, technology, and productivity change.

REFERENCES

Adams, R.L. 1921. Farm Management Notes for California. Berkeley CA: University of California Associated Students' Store.

Andrews, F. 1911. "Marketing Grain and Livestock in the Pacific Region." Bulletin 89. Washington DC: U.S. Department of Agriculture, Bureau of Statistics.

Arax, M. and Wartzman, R. 2005. *The King of California: J.G. Boswell and the Making of a Secret American Empire.* New York NY: Public Affairs.

Blanchard, H.F. 1910. "Improvement of the Wheat Crop in California." Bulletin 178. Washington DC: U.S. Department of Agriculture.

Brewer, W.H. 1883. "Cereal Report." *Tenth Census of the United States 1880, Vol. 3: Agriculture.* Washington DC: U.S. Department of the Interior.

Briggs, W.J. and H. Cauthen. 1983. *The Cotton Man: Notes on the Life and Times of Wofford B. (Bill) Camp.* Columbia SC: University of South Carolina.

Burns, J. 1888. "A Pioneer Fruit Region." *Overland Monthly* 12(67): 2nd Series.

California Committee to Survey the Agricultural Labor Resources. 1951. *Agricultural Labor in the San Joaquin Valley: Final Report and Recommendations.* Sacramento CA: March.

Cleland, R.G. and O. Hardy. 1929. *March of Industry.* Los Angeles CA: Powell.

Committee on Agriculture, Nutrition, and Forestry, U.S. Senate. 1980. Farm Structure: A Historical Perspective on Changes in the Number and Size of Farms. Washington DC: U.S. Government Printing Office, April.

Constantine, J.H., J.M. Alston, and V.H. Smith. 1994. "Economic Impacts of the California One-Variety Cotton Law." *Journal of Political Economy* 102(5): 951-74.

Domar, E. 1970. "The Causes of Slavery or Serfdom: A Hypothesis." *Journal of Economic History* 30(1): 18-32.

Economist. 1914. November 28.

Fisher, L.H. 1953. *The Harvest Labor Market in California.* Cambridge MA: Harvard University Press.

Flores, L.A. 2016. *Grounds for Dreaming: Mexican Americans, Mexican Immigrants, and the California Farmworker Movement.* New Haven CT: Yale University Press.

Geisseler, D. and W.R. Horwath. 2016. "Cotton Production in California." Davis CA: University of California, Davis, California Department of Food and Agriculture Fertilizer Research and Education Program (FREP), June. Available at: https://apps1.cdfa.ca.gov/Fertilizer-Research/docs/Cotton_Production_CA.pdf.

Hecht, R.W. and G.T. Barton. 1950. "Gains in Productivity of Labor." *USDA Technical Bulletin No. 1020.* Washington DC: U.S. Department of Agriculture, December.

Higgins, F.H. 1958. "John M. Horner and the Development of the Combine Harvester." *Agricultural History* 32: 14-24.

Hodgson, R. 1993. "California Fruit Industry." *Economic Geography* 9(4): 337-355.

Hopkin, J.A. and R.C. Kramer. 1965. *Cattle Feeding in America.* San Francisco CA: Bank of America, February.

Hundley Jr., N. 1992. *The Great Thirst: Californians and Water-A History.* Berkeley CA: University of California Press.

Igler, D. 2001. *Industrial Cowboys: Miller & Lux and the Transformation of the Far West, 1850–1920.* Berkeley CA: University of California Press.

Kelley, R. 1998. *Battling the Inland Sea: Floods, Public Policy and the Sacramento Valley.* Berkeley CA: University of California Press.

Leslie, J. 2010. "How Gross Is My Valley." *The New Republic,* June 29.

Los Angeles Times. 1921. "Farm and Tractor Section." May 8.

McWilliams, C. 1939. *Factories in the Field: The Story of Migratory Farm Labor in California.* Boston MA: Little-Brow.

Morilla Critz, J., A.L. Olmstead, and P.W. Rhode. 1999. "'Horn of Plenty': The Globalization of Mediterranean Horticulture and the Economic Development of Southern Europe, 1880–1930." *Journal of Economic History* 59(2): 316-352.

Musoke, M.S. and A.L. Olmstead. 1982. "The Rise of the Cotton Industry in California: A Comparative Perspective." *Journal of Economic History* 42(2): 385-412.

Olmstead, A.L. and P.W. Rhode. 1988. "An Overview of California Agricultural Mechanization, 1870–1930." *Agricultural History* 62(3): 86-112.

———. 2003. "The Evolution of California Agriculture, 1850-2000." In Jerome B. Siebert, ed. *California Agriculture: Dimensions and Issues.* Berkeley CA: University of California Press, pp. 1-28. Available at: https://s.giannini.ucop.edu/uploads/giannini_public/4e/a8/4ea8b9cc-df88-4146-b1ae-e5467736e104/escholarship_uc_item_9145n8m1.pdf.

———. 2015. *Arresting Contagion: Science, Policy, and Conflicts over Animal Disease Control.* Cambridge MA: Harvard University Press.

———. 2008. *Creating Abundance: Biological Innovation in American Agricultural Development.* New York NY: Cambridge University Press.

Olmsted, K.S. 2015. *Right Out of California: The 1930s and the Big Business Roots of Modern Conservatism.* New York NY: New Press.

Pacific Rural Press. 1927. April 2.

Pisani, D. 1984. *From the Family Farm to Agribusiness: The Irrigation Crusade in California, 1850–1931.* Berkeley CA: University of California Press.

Reisner, M. 1986. *Cadillac Desert: The American West and Its Disappearing Water.* New York NY: Penguin.

Rhode, P.W. 1995. "Learning, Capital Accumulation, and the Transformation of California Agriculture." *Journal of Economic History* 55(4): 773-800.

Rogin, L. 1931. *The Introduction of Farm Machinery in its Relation to the Productivity of Labor in the Agriculture of the United States During the Nineteenth Century.* Berkeley CA: University of California Press.

Sackman, D.C. 2005. *Orange Empire: California and the Fruits of Eden.* Berkeley CA: University of California Press.

Shaw, G.W. 1911. "How to Increase the Yield of Wheat in California." *California Agricultural Experiment Station Bulletin No. 211.* Berkeley CA: Agricultural Experiment Station, University of California.

Teague, C. 1944. *Fifty Years A Rancher: The Recollections of Half a Century Devoted to the Citrus and Walnut Industries of California and to Furthering the Cooperative Movement in Agriculture.* Los Angeles CA: Ward Ritchie.

Turner, J. 1981. *White Gold Comes to California.* Bakersfield CA: California Planting Cotton Seed Distributors.

Tufts, W. 1946. "Rich Pattern of California Crops." In Claude B. Hutchison, ed. *California Agriculture.* Berkeley CA: University of California Press.

U.S. Bureau of the Census. 1872. *Compendium of the Ninth Census 1870.* Washington DC: Government Printing Office.

———. 1884. *Tenth Census of the United States 1880, Vol. VI. Cotton Production, Part 2–Eastern, Gulf, Atlantic, and Pacific States.* Washington DC: Government Printing Office.

———. 1902. *Twelfth Census of the United States 1900. Agriculture.* Washington DC: Government Printing Office.

———. 1922. *Fourteenth Census of the United States 1920, Agriculture, Vol. V.* Washington DC: Government Printing Office.

———.1932. *Fifteenth Census of the United States 1930, Agriculture, Vol. II, Part 3–The Western State.* Washington DC: Government Printing Office.

———. 1932. *Fifteenth Census of the United States 1930, Agriculture, Vol. IV.* Washington DC: Government Printing Office.

———. 1942. *Sixteenth Census of the United States 1940, Agriculture, Vol. I, Part 6.* Washington DC: Government Printing Office.

U.S. Department of Agriculture. 1870. *Report of the Commissioner of Agriculture for the Year 1869.* Washington DC: Government Printing Office.

———. 1876. *Report of the Commissioner of Agriculture for the Year 1875.* Washington DC: Government Printing Office.

———. 1995. *Agricultural Statistics 1995-96.* Washington DC: United States Government Printing Office.

———. 2016. *Agricultural Statistics 2016.* Washington DC: United States Government Printing Office.

U.S. Patent Office. 1874. Subject-matter Index of Patents for Inventions Issued by the United States Patent Office from 1790 to 1873, inclusive 1874. Washington DC: Government Printing Office.

Weber, Devra. 1994. *Dark Sweat, White Gold California Farm Workers, Cotton, and the New Deal.* Berkeley CA: University of California Press.

CHAPTER 3. CALIFORNIA'S EVOLVING LANDSCAPE

KEVIN NOVAN

ABSTRACT

California's footprint covers 101.5 million acres, approximately 26 million of which are classified as farmland by the U.S. Department of Agriculture. Farmland values vary substantially across the state, with some of the most valuable land concentrated in the state's fertile Central Valley. While the Central Valley has served as the engine driving the state's agricultural sector for much of the last century, farmland in the region is facing a number of threats. In particular, population growth, soil salinity, and water scarcity are spurring the conversion of farmland to non-agricultural uses.

ABOUT THE AUTHOR

Kevin Novan is an associate professor in the Department of Agricultural and Resource Economics at the University of California, Davis, and a member of the Giannini Foundation of Agricultural Economics. He can be contacted by email at knovan@ucdavis.edu.

Aerial view of farmland and waterways in the Sacramento-San Joaquin Delta, which includes five counties in Northern California.

Photo Credit: California Department of Water Resources

Chapter 3. Table of Contents

INTRODUCTION

California's 101.5 million-acre footprint covers an incredibly diverse landscape (Figure 3.1). The Mojave Desert in the barren southeast is home to Death Valley, the hottest and lowest location in the United States. Roughly 80 miles away in the Sierra Nevada Range sits Mount Whitney, the highest point in the contiguous United States. The far northern reaches of the state are dominated by woodlands, while the south coast alternates between grasslands and heavily developed urban space.

Running through the middle of the state lies the state's key agricultural region, the 11 million-acre Central Valley. The valley's natural endowments—e.g., fertile soil and excellent growing conditions—combined with past human interventions—e.g., the construction of a vast irrigation infrastructure—have made the land one of the most productive agricultural regions the world has ever seen. By itself, output from the Central Valley accounted for 84 percent of the $47 billion in annual sales generated by the state's agricultural sector in 2015 (CDFA, 2016).

While the Central Valley has been the dependable engine driving the state's agricultural sector for much of the last century, farmland in the valley is facing a variety of threats. As California's population grows, some of the state's most productive farmland is being converted to non-agricultural uses (e.g., suburban developments). Past irrigation investments and practices have caused soil quality problems throughout large swathes of the Central Valley, resulting in productivity declines and, in many cases, abandonment of farmland. Moreover, prolonged droughts, environmental regulations, and looming groundwater restrictions will continue to affect water availability, potentially resulting in a variety of land-use changes.

This chapter provides an overview of land use in California. It begins with a summary of the data characterizing the current state of land use and land values in California. Next, looking back over the last century and a half, the patterns in land use and land values are explored. We pay particular attention to understanding how the footprint of California's agricultural sector changed over time in response to two key factors—the movement of people and the movement of water.

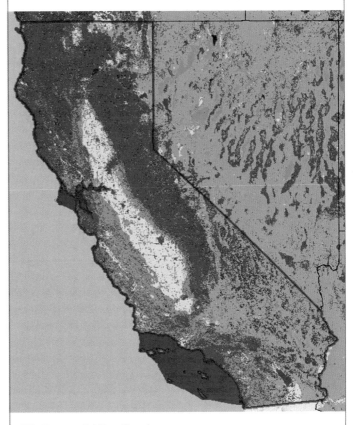

Figure 3.1. California Land Cover, 2011

- ■ Forest & Woodland
- ■ Shrub & Herb Vegetation
- □ Desert & Semi-Desert
-   Polar & High Montane Scrub, Grassland & Barrens
- ■ Aquatic Vegetation
- ■ Open Rock Vegetation
- ■ Nonvascular & Sparse Vascular Rock Vegetation
-   Agricultural & Developed Vegetation
- ■ Introduced & Semi Natural Vegetation
- ■ Recently Disturbed or Modified
- ■ Open Water
- ■ Developed & Other Human Use

Source: United States Geological Survey, National GAP Analysis Project

A Snapshot of Land Use in California

Federal Lands

To understand land use, it is important first to consider who owns the land. Across the entire U.S., 21 percent of the surface area is publicly owned land managed by the federal government. Like many states in the Western U.S., this share is much larger in California. Data from the United States Department of Agriculture's (USDA) National Resources Inventory (NRI) reveals that the federal government manages nearly 47 percent of California land (Figure 3.2). Federal land within California falls almost exclusively under the management of three agencies—the U.S. Forest Service (USFS), the U.S. National Park Service, and the U.S. Bureau of Land Management (BLM).

As of 2017, the USFS oversaw 20.76 million acres within California (CPAD, 2017). This ranges in size from the 2.2 million-acre Shasta-Trinity National Forest to the 150,000 acres of the Lake Tahoe Basin Management Unit inside California. Within the National Forests and Management Units, the USFS actively management of watersheds and forests (e.g., fire management). The U.S. National Park Service oversees an additional 7.6 million acres of national parks, monuments, and other areas (e.g., recreational areas) within California.

As of 2017, the BLM oversaw 15 million acres within California, a large share of which is located in the arid southeast. Ultimately, the BLM is responsible for protecting and managing a wide array of natural resources and services provided by the land. For example, BLM land is used for recreation—e.g., trails, campgrounds, and off-road open areas. In addition, livestock uses approximately 6.1 million acres of BLM land in the state for grazing. As of March 2017, individuals can pay $1.87 to allow a cow and her calf, a horse, or five sheep or goats to graze on the public land for a month. In addition, the BLM manages the rights to extract timber, minerals, oil, and gas from the land it manages.

Often, the extraction or use of valuable resources (e.g., timber) found on the public lands directly reduces the ability of the land to provide important non-market services (e.g., habitat preservation). As a result, management of federal land is often quite contentious. For example, through the early 1980s, thriving mill towns (e.g., Happy Camp, CA) throughout Northern California were heavily dependent on timber harvested from federal lands. However, several species protected by the federal Endangered Species Act, including the spotted owl, are also dependent on the old-growth forests that were being logged as their habitat. Beginning in 1991, legal battles resulted in dramatic reductions in the amount of timber available for harvest from the USFS lands. Mill towns throughout the state are still reeling economically as a result of these logging restrictions.

Ongoing political debates involve proposed increases in wind and solar electricity generation capacity on BLM land in southeastern California. This region has some of the best solar potential in the state and numerous locations with excellent wind resources. However, the desert also serves as a vital ecosystem safeguarding several at-risk species, including the golden eagle and the desert tortoise. In 2016, conservationists scored a key victory at the expense of energy firms with the passage of the Desert Renewable Energy Conservation Plan. The plan set aside 6.5 million desert acres for conservation and 3.6 million acres for recreation, restricting potential future desert renewable energy sites to less than 400,000 acres.

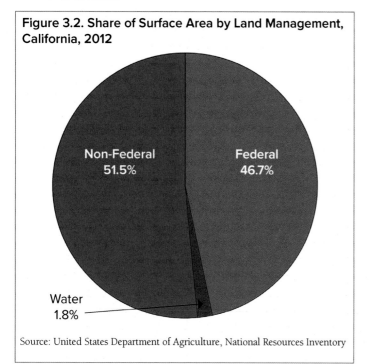

Figure 3.2. Share of Surface Area by Land Management, California, 2012

Non-Federal 51.5%

Federal 46.7%

Water 1.8%

Source: United States Department of Agriculture, National Resources Inventory

NON-FEDERAL LAND

The remaining half of the state—approximately 52 million acres of non-federally managed lands—includes privately owned land, tribal and trust land, and land controlled by the state and local governments. This non-federal land is divided across a variety of land types and uses. The USDA National Resources Inventory data from 2012 (Figure 3.3) reveals that pasture and rangeland (38.4 percent) and forestland (27.1 percent) accounted for nearly two-thirds of the non-federal land. The "Other" land category, which made up 5.1 percent of the non-federal land in California in 2012, includes farmsteads, barren land, marshland, and land in the Conservation Reserve Program (CRP).

The CRP is a federal program that offers landowners an annual payment for voluntarily removing environmentally sensitive land from agricultural production and planting native species that improve environmental quality. The CRP has had a substantial impact on land use across the country. As of January 2017, landowners enrolled 23.5 million U.S. acres in the CRP (Farm Service Agency, 2018). However, in California, only 74,338 acres were in the CRP.

Ultimately, the CRP has not had a dramatic impact within California. Instead, California policymakers have focused on preventing the conversion of the state's productive cropland into developed, built-up space. The USDA's National Resources Inventory data show that 30 percent of the non-federal land in California in 2012 was split between cropland (9.14 million acres) and developed land (6.26 million acres). The NRI's definition of cropland includes land used for cultivated crops (e.g., row crops) as well as non-cultivated crops (e.g., horticultural crops). Developed land includes urban and rural tracts of land that have been built up, as well as land outside of built-up tracts in rural transportation corridors (e.g., roads, railroads). Cropland and developed land account for a relatively small share of the state's total area (approximately 15 percent), but are tightly linked. As developed land has grown since the 1950s, cropland has steadily shrunk.

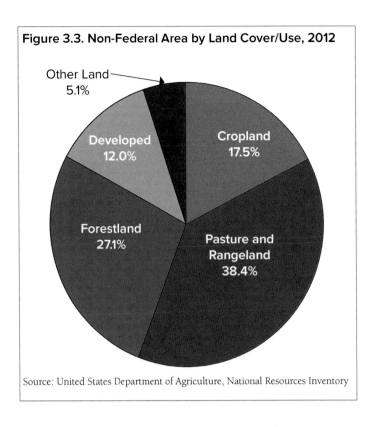

Figure 3.3. Non-Federal Area by Land Cover/Use, 2012

Source: United States Department of Agriculture, National Resources Inventory

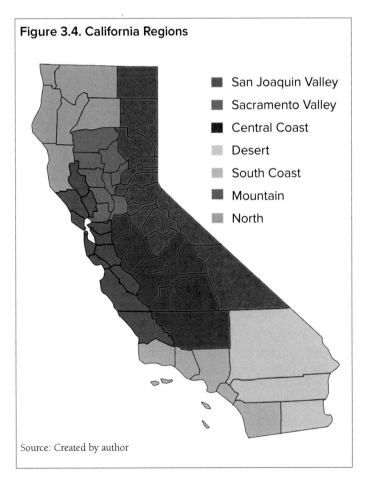

Figure 3.4. California Regions

- San Joaquin Valley
- Sacramento Valley
- Central Coast
- Desert
- South Coast
- Mountain
- North

Source: Created by author

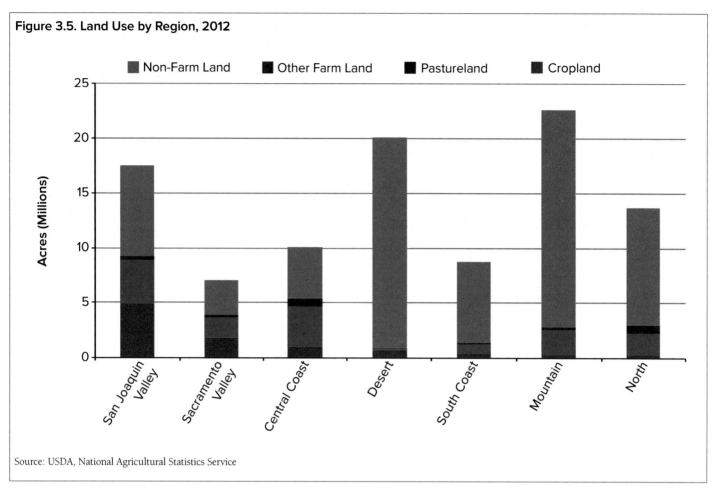

Figure 3.5. Land Use by Region, 2012

Legend: Non-Farm Land | Other Farm Land | Pastureland | Cropland

Y-axis: Acres (Millions)

X-axis categories: San Joaquin Valley, Sacramento Valley, Central Coast, Desert, South Coast, Mountain, North

Source: USDA, National Agricultural Statistics Service

VARIATION IN LAND USE ACROSS CALIFORNIA

To explore how land use varies throughout California, the state's 58 counties have been broken up into seven regions with similar climates and geologies. The regions displayed in Figure 3.4 include the San Joaquin and Sacramento valleys; the Central and South coasts; and finally, the North, Mountain, and Desert regions.

The USDA's National Agricultural Statistics Service (NASS) quantifies the amount of farmland and non-farm land by county. As of 2012, 26.8 million acres of California were classified by the NASS data as farmland. Of this, 17.2 million acres were in pastureland, rangeland, and other farmed forestland—which includes wooded grazing land. Figure 3.5 highlights a fairly even distribution of these 17.2 million acres across each region in the state.

In total, 2012 NASS data classified 9.6 million acres of California farmland as cropland. Figure 3.5 highlights that, combined, the counties in the San Joaquin and Sacramento valleys—which together, make up the Central

Valley—account for over 70 percent of the state's cropland. In contrast, in the heavily populated South Coast counties, agriculture has very little presence. Only 16 percent of the South Coast region's 8.73 million acres were classified as land in farms in 2012—with only 371,000 acres in cropland (4 percent of the state's total cropland). However, this was not always the case. Data from the 1950 USDA Census of Agriculture reveals that, in 1949, agricultural production in Los Angeles County generated nearly $157 million in revenue, more than any other county in the nation.

Ultimately, market forces and changes in the value of land across competing uses (i.e., agriculture vs. development) drove the dramatic land-use transition in locations like Los Angeles County. To understand how these land-use transitions occur, it is important first to consider how the value of land is determined.

AGRICULTURAL LAND VALUE

The value of California's farmland varies considerably across the state. Figure 3.6 displays the average value of an acre of agricultural land during 2012 within each county. The spatial variation in agricultural land value is driven in part by differences in how profitable agricultural production is expected to be in different locations. All else equal, land that generates greater profits will be in higher demand and have a higher market value.

The profitability of agricultural production on a given piece of land depends on the combination of several factors. For one, the natural endowments of the land—e.g., the soil quality and the climate—will dramatically affect not only the productivity of the land, but also what crops will grow. For example, agricultural land in Napa County, which has a climate that is uniquely well suited for growing very high-value wine grapes, had an average value of $21,801 per acre in 2012—the third highest across the state's 58 counties.

The productivity of agricultural land, and therefore its profitability, also depends heavily on whether the land is irrigated or not. Precipitation in California occurs almost entirely during the late fall and winter months (October through March). In contrast, agricultural demand for water typically peaks during the spring and summer months (April through September). Without access to irrigation, the types of crops that will grow, and the productivity of agricultural land in California, would be dramatically reduced.

Figure 3.7 shows the average value of an acre of California cropland from 1997 through 2017 (inflated to 2017 dollars using the Consumer Price Index), and the average values of an acre of irrigated cropland and an acre of non-irrigated cropland. Over the past 20 years, the average value of irrigated cropland was approximately three times higher than the average value of non-irrigated cropland.

It is important to note, however, that a simple comparison of the average value of irrigated land to non-irrigated land fails to accurately uncover the impact of access to irrigation on land values. In particular, irrigated land can differ from non-irrigated land in a variety of ways that also affect land values. For example, low-value land with poor soil quality

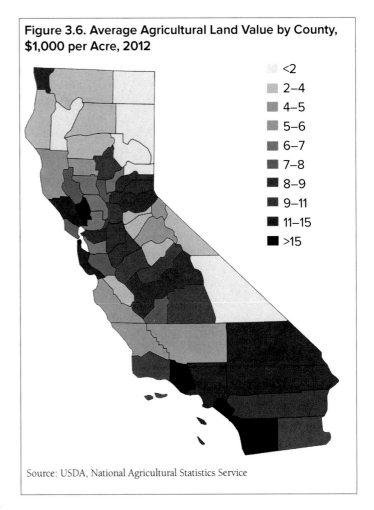

Figure 3.6. Average Agricultural Land Value by County, $1,000 per Acre, 2012

Legend:
<2
2–4
4–5
5–6
6–7
7–8
8–9
9–11
11–15
>15

Source: USDA, National Agricultural Statistics Service

may be less likely to be irrigated, resulting in a larger average gap between the value of irrigated and non-irrigated land.

Previous research examines how land values at the farm-level vary across space (Schlenker et al., 2007) and across time (Buck et al., 2014) as a function of the average surface water delivered (acre-feet/acre) to each regional irrigation district. Importantly, the studies also control for differences across space and time that could also affect farmland values (e.g., climate, soil quality) and may be correlated with surface water deliveries. These studies estimate that access to an additional acre-foot of surface water increases the value of California farmland by $880/acre to $3,723/acre (in 2012 dollars). To get a sense of the magnitude of this impact, from 2001–2008, an estimated average of 0.47 acre-feet/acre of surface water was delivered to California counties (Buck et al., 2014), so an additional acre-foot of surface water increases the value of an acre of California farmland by roughly $414 to $1,750 (in 2012 dollars).

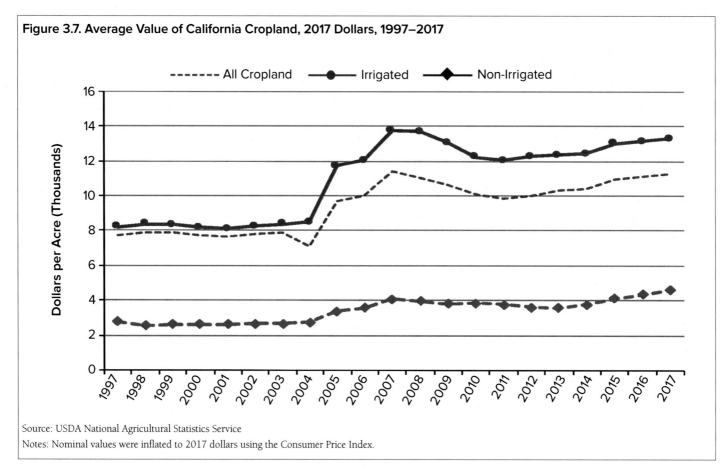

Figure 3.7. Average Value of California Cropland, 2017 Dollars, 1997–2017

Source: USDA National Agricultural Statistics Service

Notes: Nominal values were inflated to 2017 dollars using the Consumer Price Index.

Importantly, the value of agricultural land is also heavily influenced by non-agricultural factors. In particular, if, at some point in the future a given piece of farmland would be more valuable when used for something other than agricultural production (e.g., residential or commercial space, part of a transportation corridor), then this non-agricultural value will be capitalized into the present value of the land.

Figure 3.6 highlights a couple of extreme cases where urban influences have driven up agricultural land values. According to NASS data, San Francisco County, which encompasses 30,011 acres, had only 12 acres of farmland in 2012. The estimated value of this farmland was $126,111 per acre—dramatically above California's 2012 average value of $6,880 per acre of farmland. Similarly, heavily developed Orange County encompasses 505,994 acres, of which 55,775 acres were in farmland in 2012. This farmland had an average value of $21,854 per acre. Ultimately, San Francisco County and Orange County were the only two counties with higher average farmland values than Napa in 2012. This does not imply that agricultural production from an acre of farmland in San Francisco or Orange County generates a greater profit than an acre of wine grapes grown in Napa. Instead, the inflated land values reflect urban pressure driving up land values.

LAND USE OVER TIME

Land use is constantly evolving. The USDA performs a comprehensive survey of the nation's agricultural sector—the Census of Agriculture. Figure 3.8, which displays data from the USDA's Census of Agriculture for California from 1850 through 2012, shows the number of acres devoted to some type of farmland during each census. In addition, from 1925 and on, the plot displays the acreage of farmland that was cropland, pasture and rangeland, and wooded farmland.

There are two clear patterns displayed in Figure 3.8. First, from 1850 until the 1950s, the total area in farmland steadily increased from approximately 4 million acres to nearly 38 million acres. Beginning in the 1950s, the trend reversed—the total area in farmland has consistently fallen. In 2012, there were approximately 26 million acres of farmland in the state, a 32 percent decline from the peak observed in the 1950s. Figure 3.8 illustrates the decline in farmland over the 50-plus years within each category. In particular, cropland declined by 30 percent from 1950 to 2012. This section highlights the key factors that spurred the initial growth in agriculture's footprint and the subsequent decline in agricultural land.

EARLY SETTLEMENT (PRE-1850)

Western settlement of California began in earnest in 1769. Spain's effort to colonize present-day California focused not only on establishing forts (presidios) in the region, but also on supporting the establishment of a chain of 21 religious outposts (missions) stretching from modern-day San Diego (San Diego de Acala) to Sonoma (San Francisco de Solano). During the period of Spanish control, there was effectively no private ownership of land (Robinson, 1948). The missionaries were simply caretakers of the land. In some cases, individuals were granted concessions to use land for grazing or agriculture. However, these concessions were simply use rights—the Spanish government owned the land.

This changed when Mexico gained independence from Spain in 1821 and took control of Alta California. To encourage settlement, the Mexican government began granting land rights to individuals. By 1846, over 500 ranchos were scattered throughout Mexican-controlled Alta California (Robinson, 1948). Located on lands along the coast and coastal rivers, these ranchos were originally

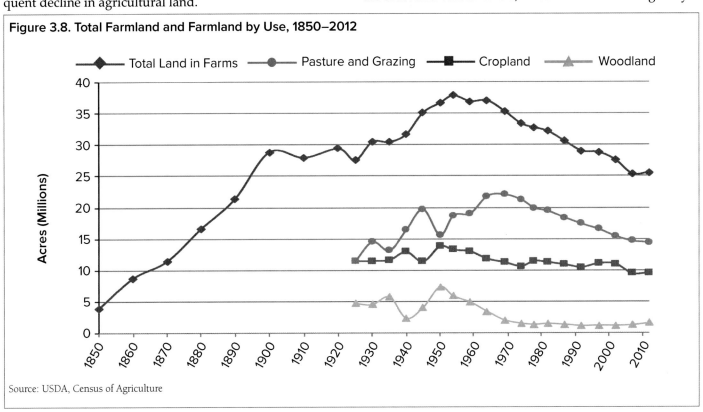

Figure 3.8. Total Farmland and Farmland by Use, 1850–2012

Source: USDA, Census of Agriculture

overseen by the Spanish missions. In addition, ranchos were found throughout the San Joaquin and Sacramento valleys. Ultimately, the privately held ranchos encompassed most of the best grazing and agricultural land in Alta California.

EARLY STATEHOOD

With the signing of the Treaty of Guadalupe Hidalgo in 1848, the Mexican-American War ended. With the U.S. assuming control of California, the new government honored the pre-existing rights to the majority of rancho land grants. As a result, when California officially became the 31st state in the nation in 1850, approximately 9 million acres of large (15,000 plus-acres per grant) tracts of rancho land—which included much of the best grazing land along the coast—were already privately "owned."

Ultimately, proving ownership of lands granted by the Spanish and Mexican governments was challenging. With the 1848 discovery of gold and the subsequent Gold Rush, the population in California increased. Homesteaders and squatters inundated the regions surrounding cities like San Francisco and Sacramento—often residing on the prime rancho lands. The U.S. Federal Government established the Public Land Commission in 1851 to determine the validity of the original rancho land grants. Ultimately, the commission reviewed 813 cases, and upheld 604 of the original rancho land claims (Robinson, 1948). However, the legal process was so long and costly that the majority of Spanish Californian landowners were forced to sell their claims to speculators prior to the resolution of the cases.

While private ownership disputes over the highly desirable rancho lands were being settled, the vast majority of the new state of California (nearly 90 percent) was newly owned federal land. Much of the federal land was transferred from public to private ownership in the early decades of statehood via a variety of federal land-disposal policies.

One of the most well-known policies was the 1862 Homestead Act. The act offered any head of household 160 acres of public land for $1.25 per acre after six months of continuous residence, or free after five years of residence. Overall, 10,476,665 acres of California, approximately 10 percent of the surface area, were distributed through the Homestead Act (National Park Service, 2018). Other important land-disposal policies included the 1877 Desert Land Act, which allowed individuals to purchase 640 acres of dry land at 25 cents per acre under the condition that the land was irrigated within three years. In addition, the 1878 Timber and Stone Act provided public timber and stone lands that were unfit for cultivation to individuals for $2.50 per acre.

Perhaps the most important land-disposal policies were the railroad land grants that began with the Pacific Railway Acts of 1862 and 1864. From a military and economic standpoint, it was viewed as absolutely vital to create a transcontinental railway linking the newly acquired Pacific Coast to the eastern half of the country. To achieve this objective, the federal government incentivized railroad companies to construct the railways using two forms of payment. First, direct payments were made for each mile of track laid. Second, the railroad companies were given land. Extending out 10 miles on either side of the newly constructed track, the railroad companies were given every other 640-acre (1 square mile) section of land. Therefore, for every mile of track laid, the railroad company received 6,400 acres of public land (10 square miles). By receiving the rights to the land, the railroad companies had access to resources required to construct the railways (e.g., timber) and they could sell the land to raise additional funds to pay for the construction. If the granted lands were not subsequently sold within three years, the land was to be made open to settlement at the regular $1.25 per acre.

In 1869 the Central Pacific railway, which began in Sacramento, was linked with the Union Pacific track in Promontory Point, Utah, completing construction of the transcontinental railroad. Subsequent land grants funded the construction of additional railways throughout California—e.g., Los Angeles towards Texas, Sacramento to San Francisco, Sacramento to Oregon, and Sacramento to Los Angeles. In total, the federal government granted 11,585,534 acres of California to the railroads (Robinson, 1948).

The railroad land grants had a substantial impact on the state's agricultural sector. First, as the granted lands were sold off to settlers pouring into the region, the amount of privately held acreage in farmland steadily increased. Recognizing that transporting produce would be an

Figure 3.9. Total Number of Irrigated Acres of Farmland, 1889–2012

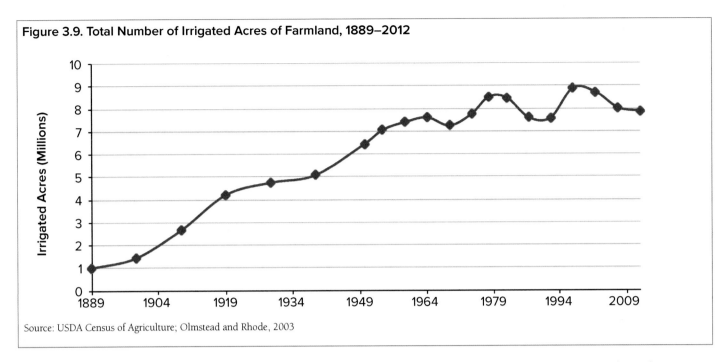

Source: USDA Census of Agriculture; Olmstead and Rhode, 2003

integral part of their business, the railroads encouraged farming by constructing shops, warehouses, loading docks, etc. in market towns up and down the Central Valley. The railroads put up capital to finance the construction of local irrigation projects. The railroads also ran special refrigerated fruit trains to move the specialty produce grown in the valley to eastern markets.

Data from the U.S. Census of Agriculture reveals that, in 1870, there were 35,934 farms in California. By 1900, this number was up to 72,542 farms, including 28,000 growing specialty crops like fruits and vegetables.

IRRIGATING THE VALLEY

While much of the initial growth in California's farmland was driven by population growth and the redistribution of land from public to private ownership, the dramatic expansion in agriculture's footprint into the Central Valley from the early 1900s through the 1950s would not have been possible without substantial investment in flood control and irrigation.

Prior to human intervention, runoff from the Sierra Nevada made its way to the San Francisco Delta and the Tulare Basin and inundated the Sacramento and San Joaquin valleys, resulting in vast, flooded wetlands. During the 1850s, approximately 4 million acres of the valley floor

were seasonal wetlands (Frayer et al., 1989). At the same time, vast amounts of arable land in the Central Valley that were not adjacent to reliable sources of surface water relied on spring flooding or scarce rainfall.

As demand for farmland grew, farmers in some areas began to pool their resources to purchase the rights to surface water and fund the construction of small-scale dams and irrigation ditches (Hanak et al., 2011). This strategy was formalized with the 1887 passage of the Wright Act, which allowed for the formation of local irrigation districts with two-thirds support from the local landowners. The irrigation districts could raise funds through taxes and bonds to acquire water rights and construct water-distribution infrastructure (Pincet, 1999). By the early 1900s, irrigation districts had been established throughout much of the state (Pisani, 1984).

While irrigation districts made headway in irrigating the valley's fertile land, the localized strategy was ultimately insufficient given the huge demand for irrigation. Simply put, there was not enough local surface water to go around. Initially, farmers went underground for extra water. With improvements in drilling and pumping technology, the early 1900s saw a dramatic increase in groundwater extraction from aquifers. In 1910, there were around 10,000 pumping units (Olmstead and Rhode, 2003). By 1930, there were nearly 50,000 units, and 75,000 units by 1950.

Figure 3.9 displays the number of acres of irrigated farmland in California by year. At the turn of the century, there were 1 million acres of irrigated farmland. With the growth in local irrigation districts and groundwater extraction, this number reached 4.7 million acres by 1930. Interestingly, total farmland increased by only 2 million acres over the same 30-year window (Figure 3.8). Perhaps the most dramatic impact this initial wave of irrigation had on the agriculture sector came in terms of what was grown, rather than on how much land was in production. Comparing the 1900 and 1930 agricultural censuses reveals a shift away from low-value crops—e.g., wheat acreage fell from 2,683,405 acres in 1899 to 632,779 acres in 1929—in favor of much higher-value, specialty crops (Olmstead and Rhode, 2003). For example, California lettuce crops, which only covered 46 acres in 1899, grew to cover 60,564 acres in 1929 and had a total value of over $11 million. Cantaloupes and melons, valued at over $9 million in 1929, increased from 764 acres in 1899 to 46,365 acres in 1929.

In Southern California and the southern San Joaquin Basin, the regions with the greatest reliance on groundwater extraction, groundwater withdrawals dramatically exceeded the amount of surface water that replenished the aquifers (Hanak et al., 2011). Instead of managing groundwater withdrawals, farmers and policymakers simply sought to increase the amount of surface water being diverted to the region, both for irrigation and to supply the growing urban demand in the booming coastal cities. This required going beyond small-scale, local irrigation districts and instead required large infrastructure investments that could store and move water over vast distances.

Initially, very contentious inter-basin water projects supplied urban demand centers in San Francisco (via Hetch Hetchy) and Los Angeles (via Owens Valley). In the 1940s, the Boulder Canyon Project began delivering water from the Colorado River to the Coachella Valley in Southern California, driving an expansion in agriculture in the region. The first steps of the Central Valley Project (CVP) began in 1937, with the construction of the Shasta Dam on the Sacramento River. The CVP would ultimately include a series of dams, reservoirs, and canals that would store and divert waters from the Sacramento, Trinity, American, Stanislaus, and San Joaquin rivers as well as pump water from the San Francisco Delta. The CVP ultimately provided roughly 7 million acre-feet of water annually, with

approximately 90 percent used for irrigation in the Central Valley (Hanak et al., 2011).

However, 7 million acre-feet was not enough to meet the state's growing agricultural and urban water demand. In 1961, construction on the State Water Project (SWP) began with the massive Oroville Dam on the Feather River, northeast of Sacramento. Water stored behind the dam would be released throughout the year and allowed to flow towards the Delta. Ultimately, it would be pumped from the Delta and delivered south via the California Aqueduct to farmers in the San Joaquin Valley and, finally, lifted over the Tehachapi Mountains and delivered to Southern California.

The investment in irrigation and flood control over the last century and a half has dramatically reshaped the Central Valley. Most notably, the valley's wetlands have largely been erased by the construction of over 100 dams, an extensive network of levees, and thousands of miles of water-delivery canals. By the 1980s, the valley's 4 million-plus acres of wetlands had been reduced to less than 400,000 acres (Frayer et al., 1989). Not only did the water projects dry up the wetlands, they transformed the center of California from a dry valley to the agricultural engine of the state. By the 1950s, the number of irrigated acres of farmland eclipsed 7 million acres. Ultimately, the increased access to irrigation made it possible for California's farmland to steadily increase to its peak acreage in the 1950s (see Figure 3.8).

POST-WAR SUBURBANIZATION

From 1920 through 1940, California's population steadily grew from 3.4 million to 6.9 million—roughly adding 174,000 people per year. After the end of WWII, the population exploded. In 1950, there were 10.6 million residents, and by 1960, there were over 15.7 million.

To understand how this growth affected land in California, it is crucial to observe where the population expanded. Figure 3.10a displays the population in San Francisco County and several of the neighboring counties from 1860 through 2010. In 1940, the population of San Francisco County had reached 634,536—nearly twice as much as the sum of the populations of Contra Costa, San Mateo, and Santa Clara counties, all neighboring San Francisco. By 1950, the population of the three neighboring counties

Figure 3.10a. Population by County, 1860–2010

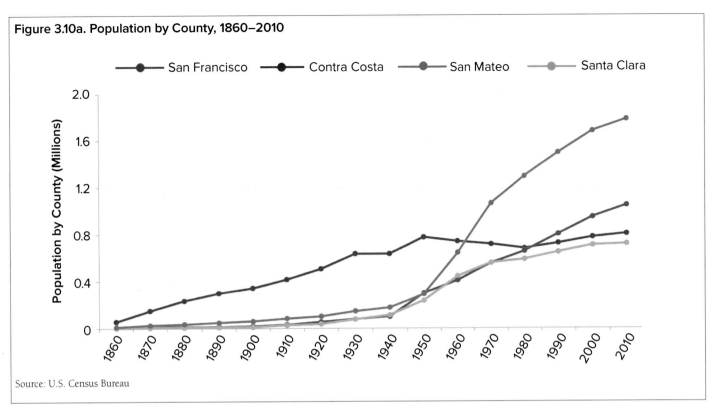

Source: U.S. Census Bureau

Figure 3.10b. Population by County, 1860–2010

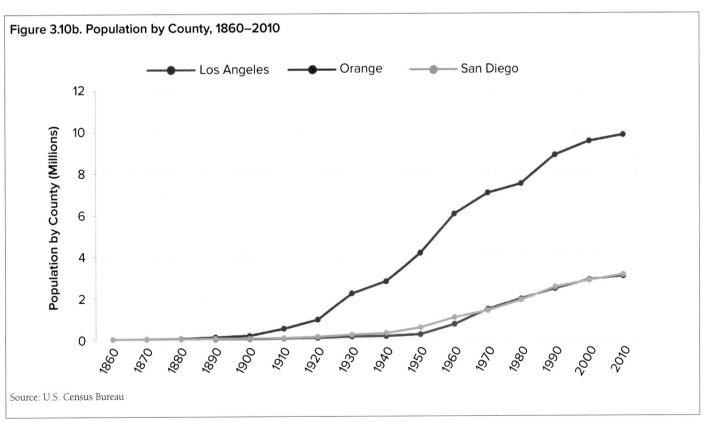

Source: U.S. Census Bureau

Figure 3.11. Real Farmland Values by Acre, 2017 Dollars, 1910–2017

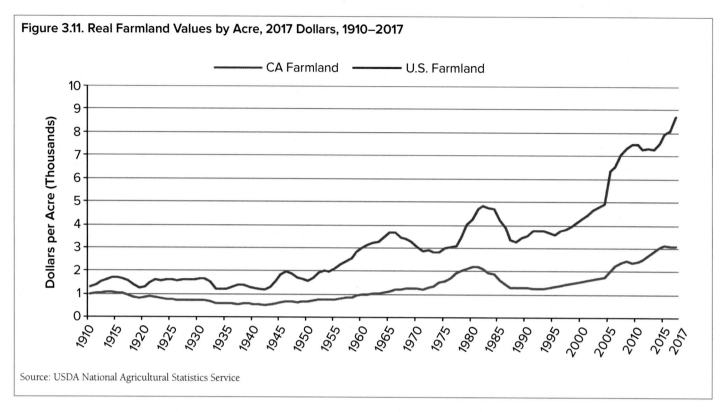

Source: USDA National Agricultural Statistics Service

exceeded San Francisco's population by nearly 50,000 residents. Even more striking, from 1950 through 1980, San Francisco's population shrunk while the surrounding counties continued to see rapid growth.

Figure 3.10b paints a similar picture of growth in Southern California. While Los Angeles County continued to rapidly grow from 1900 and onwards, the other southern counties (Orange and San Diego) began to experience rapid growth beginning in the post-War period.

This suburban expansion had a dramatic impact on the value of farmland. Figure 3.11 displays the average real value (in 2017 dollars) of an acre of farmland in California and the U.S. as a whole from 1910 through 2017. From 1910 through 1940, the real value of California farmland hovered around $700 per acre more than the national average. We attribute this difference to the fact that California farmland was very productive and amenable to producing high-value crops. Coinciding with the substantial growth in suburbanization, California farmland values exceeded the national average by nearly $2,000 per acre from 1955 through 1965.

As demand for land grew throughout Southern California and around the Bay Area, much of early rancho land—the earliest land in agricultural production, and some of

the most productive farmland—was steadily sold off to large developers. This process was also accelerated by the system of property taxes. Landowners paid taxes based on the assessed market value of their property. As farmland values increased, so did farmers' property tax bills. Financial pressure from growing tax bills, combined with lucrative offers from developers, lead to large reductions in farmland. From 1945 through 1968, over 1 million acres of prime agricultural land was developed (Pincetl, 1999).

To mitigate the loss of farmland to urban and suburban development, the state passed the Williamson Act in 1965. Agricultural land owners could voluntarily sign 10- to 20-year contracts with their local government guaranteeing that their land would remain undeveloped during the contract period. In exchange, the landowners paid property taxes based on an estimate of their land's value that only reflected the income that would be earned through agricultural production, not based on the market value of their land, which was being driven up in many regions by demand for non-agricultural uses.

Participating in the program was not only voluntary on the part of the landowners, but also the local governments. To incentivize counties and cities to participate in the program, and to compensate them for the reduction in

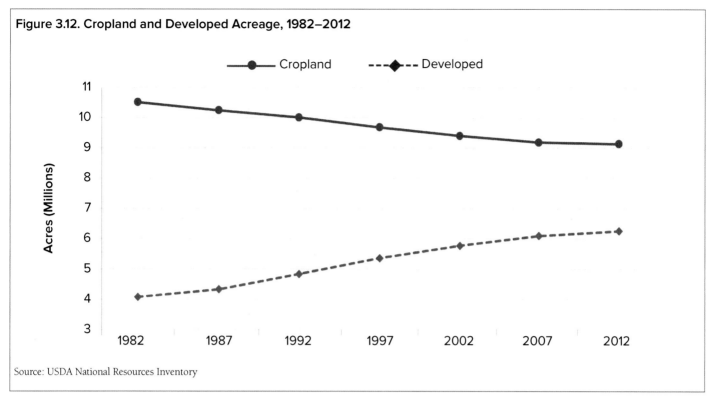

Figure 3.12. Cropland and Developed Acreage, 1982–2012

Source: USDA National Resources Inventory

their stream of property tax revenues, the state government would make payments to the local governments based on the acres of land enrolled in the program and the type of land (e.g., prime farmland, prime farmland bordering urban land, and non-prime farmland).

The Williamson Act has been very successful in enrolling acreage. By 1968, 23 counties were participating in the program with over 2 million acres of farmland contracted to remain out of development (Sokolow, 1990). By 1978, 48 counties were participating and over 16 million acres of farmland were under contract. As of 2015, an estimated 16.1 million acres remain under contract (California Department of Conservation, 2016). However, it is not clear whether the Williamson Act meaningfully slowed the rate of farmland conversion to developed land. Ultimately, very little farmland in the immediate path of development was enrolled in the program (Sokolow, 1990). Research from the 1970s suggests that landowners expecting lucrative and imminent development opportunities were unlikely to participate (Hansen and Schwartz, 1975; Carman, 1977).

Ultimately, suburban growth and development through the second half of the 1900s resulted in the loss of a substantial amount of farmland in Southern California and throughout the Bay Area. This land included much of the Spanish

and Mexican rancho land grants and represented some of the most productive farmland in the state. Over the most recent decades, the trend of urban development and farmland conversion has continued. Figure 3.12 reveals that, from 1982 to 2012, the number of acres in built-up land in California increased from 4.1 million acres to 6.3 million acres. Over the same period, total cropland in the state fell from 10.5 million acres to 9.1 million acres.

ONGOING ISSUES FACING CALIFORNIA'S FARMLAND

PAVING OVER THE VALLEY?

While much of the initial urbanization occurred in the coastal regions of California, the Central Valley has not been immune to the issue of development and farmland conversion. The California Department of Conservation's Farmland Mapping and Monitoring Program (FMMP) began tracking changes in land usage throughout California's key agricultural regions. Every two years, the FMMP quantified the amount of land that changed between uses—for example, farmland to grazing land or farmland to developed land.

The agricultural land surveyed by the FMMP is classified into different categories based on the USDA Natural Resource Conservation Service's (NRCS) evaluation of the land's suitability for agricultural production (e.g., physical and chemical properties of the soil and climate). The best agricultural land is classified as Prime Farmland. Land with minor shortcomings (e.g., not perfectly flat terrain) is classified as Statewide Important Farmland. Both Prime and Statewide Important Farmland are restricted to land that was used to grow irrigated crops at some point during the four years preceding the survey year. Unique Farmland contains lower-quality soil but is still largely irrigated cropland or used for non-irrigated orchards or vineyards. The definition of Local Important Farmland varies by

county but largely includes farmland that does not meet the standards of Prime, Statewide Important, or Unique Land. Finally, the FMMP includes Grazing Land, Urban or Built-up Land (e.g., residential, industrial, commercial, landfills, golf courses, etc.), and Other Land. The Other category importantly includes vacant, non-agricultural land that is bordered by developed land—a point which will be discussed in more detail below.

By 1994, 44.1 million acres—roughly 90 percent of the privately held land in the state—was being surveyed by the FMMP. The top panel of Table 3.1 displays the total acreage of FMMP-surveyed land that was converted to urban or built-up space between 1992 and 2012. In total, 893,930 surveyed acres were converted to urban space. Of this total, 512,007 acres came from agricultural land—223,984 being Prime, Statewide Important, and Unique Farmland acres.

The bottom panel of Table 3.1 focuses on the FMMP-surveyed land specifically in the counties that make up the Central Valley—the Sacramento and San Joaquin Valley regions displayed in Figure 3.4. Over the 20-year period, 243,665 acres of valley's land was converted to urban space. From 1992–2002, 45 percent of the state's Prime, Statewide Important, and Unique Farmland converted to Built-up Land came from the Central Valley. From 2002–2012, this share had increased to 60 percent.

Table 3.1. Acres Converted to Urban and Built-up Land by Source

California					
	Prime Farmland	Statewide Important & Unique Farmland	Grazing & Local Important	Other Land	Total
1992–2002	85,961	37,123	158,737	219,385	501,206
2002–2012	67,763	33,137	129,286	162,538	392,724
Total Acres	153,724	70,260	288,023	381,923	893,930
Central Valley					
	Prime Farmland	Statewide Important & Unique Farmland	Grazing & Local Important	Other Land	Total
1992–2002	37,500	18,432	31,181	25,332	112,445
2002–2012	41,671	18,004	39,669	31,876	131,220
Total Acres	79,171	36,436	70,850	57,208	243,665

Source: Farmland Monitoring and Mapping Program

Table 3.2. Actual and Projected Population by Region, 1970–2060

	Total California Population	Central Coast	Desert	Mountain	North	Sacramento Valley	San Joaquin Valley	South Coast
Population By Region								
U.S. Census								
1970	19,971,069	4,973,291	1,213,641	259,809	283,853	1,146,258	1,630,329	10,463,888
1980	23,667,764	5,639,947	1,650,325	418,017	360,683	1,450,817	2,048,102	12,099,873
1990	29,760,021	6,573,040	2,698,096	591,779	426,553	1,918,193	2,742,000	14,810,360
2000	33,871,653	7,404,808	3,397,182	743,681	460,869	2,230,317	3,302,792	16,332,004
2010	37,253,956	7,804,405	4,399,379	887,290	486,983	2,532,877	3,971,659	17,171,363
Projected								
2020	40,748,172	8,659,967	4,938,561	936,655	493,711	2,856,369	4,410,489	18,452,420
2030	44,031,155	9,433,021	5,567,287	1,022,005	509,577	3,154,574	4,972,092	19,372,599
2040	46,873,884	10,115,513	6,144,984	1,100,396	519,806	3,436,193	5,528,504	20,028,488
2050	49,118,640	10,670,040	6,655,039	1,160,209	525,726	3,681,988	6,026,361	20,399,277
2060	50,985,273	11,147,001	7,129,550	1,229,036	535,519	3,919,560	6,494,076	20,530,531
Share of Growth								
Observed: 1970–2010		16.4%	18.4%	3.6%	1.2%	8.0%	13.5%	38.8%
Projected: 2020–2060		24.3%	21.4%	2.9%	0.4%	10.4%	20.4%	20.3%

Source: U.S. Census Bureau and California Department of Finance

Previous research also notes that the FMMP farmland-to-urban conversion statistics could understate the true amount of farmland being developed (Kuminoff et al., 2001). In particular, the Other Land category can mask important dynamics in land use. While Other Land includes a variety of undeveloped land types (e.g., brush, timber, and wetlands), not all Other Land is truly undeveloped. For example, Other Land includes low-density, rural developments—e.g., large rural residences, or "ranchettes," that are likely not used for commercial agriculture. In addition, Other Land includes farmland that has been idled for at least four years. In many cases, this land may simply be awaiting development.

FMMP statistics reveal that, from 1992–2012, 611,848 acres of California's Prime, Statewide Important, Unique, and Local Important land was converted to Other Land. Much of this represents cropland being taken out of agricultural production. Over the same 20-year period, Table 3.1 highlights that 43 percent of the FMMP-surveyed land converted to urban built-up space came from the Other Land category. Combined, this suggests that the impact of urban expansion on farmland acreage is larger than the FMMP statistics initially revealed.

THE CHALLENGE OF SLOWING DEVELOPMENT

Looking forward, the conversion of Central Valley farmland to built-up space will continue to be an important issue. Table 3.2 shows the historical population by region during each census from 1970 through 2010. In addition, the table includes projected population to 2060 from the California Department of Finance. From 1970 through 2010, the South Coast region accounted for 38.3 percent of the growth in the state's population, more than any other region. From 2020 through 2060, however, the San Joaquin Valley's population is expected to grow by nearly 2.1 million residents—an absolute increase that exceeds the expected growth in the South Coast.

This population growth will continue to exert development pressure on the valley's farmland, and particularly the farmland located on the urban fringe of the main population centers up and down the Highway 99 corridor in the Central Valley. A prime example is Fresno, CA—the state's fifth-most-populated city. Between the 2000 and 2010 censuses, Fresno's population grew by 15 percent. Over the same period of time, the area encompassed by the city grew by 7 percent.

Reducing the conversion of farmland to developed land is a major focus of policymakers, but is difficult to accomplish. Aside from the Williamson Act, which differentially assessed agricultural and non-agricultural land values, a number of other strategies are being actively used in an attempt to conserve farmland (e.g., land trusts, development rights purchase or transfer programs). Perhaps the most impactful policy tools are zoning regulations. Local governments use zoning restrictions to prevent agricultural land from being used for other purposes. Of course, the fact that zoning can be changed over time reduces the efficacy of the policy.

Moreover, local land-use policies can often work at odds with one another. For example, local governments often simultaneously impose growth (zoning) restrictions—which prevent a city's footprint from expanding into neighboring agricultural land or open-space—along with building restrictions preventing densification (e.g., height limits on new structures). Other examples of land-use policies with competing effects include transportation projects. For example, as part of the 2005 SAFETEA-LU federal transportation legislation, funding was approved for the California Farm-to-Market Corridor, which aimed at converting Highway 99 into a four-lane expressway running from the southern end of the Central Valley all the way to Sacramento. While this investment in infrastructure was, in part, motivated by the benefits that would accrue to the agricultural sector from the more efficient movement of products, the highway improvements—which were completed in 2014—will also inevitably speed the rate of urban expansion and sprawl along the Highway 99 corridor.

ENVIRONMENTAL AND WATER ISSUES

While population growth in key agricultural regions will continue to increase the revenue that can be earned by converting farmland to non-agricultural uses, other factors are simultaneously affecting the profits that can be earned by continuing to use the land for agricultural production. One particularly acute threat affecting the productivity of agricultural land in the western San Joaquin Valley is the issue of soil salinity (Schoups, 2005).

Throughout much of the San Joaquin Valley, groundwater was the chief source of irrigation water from the 1920s up through 1950. The reliance on pumping was reduced substantially by 1951 as the CVP began delivering surface water to the northern San Joaquin Valley and farther south through the San Luis Unit by 1968. However, more than just water has been delivered to the region. While the surface water has relatively low salt content, given the sheer volume of water delivered to the San Joaquin Valley, an estimated 1.6 million tons of salt are applied to the land annually (SJVDP, 1990). Ultimately, the salt from surface water and the soil, as well as other naturally occurring minerals and heavy metals, leach into the groundwater that is largely confined by a layer of clay.

It was always well understood that the water applied to the land would need to be drained from the region or else there would be serious issues with soil salinity as the water tables steadily rose (Letey, 2000). Initially, there were plans for the Bureau of Reclamation to construct a system of tile drains to return the water to the Delta (Hanak et al., 2011). However, the San Luis Drain was never completed. Instead, drainage water was diverted to the northwest portion of the San Joaquin Valley where it pooled at the Kesterson National Wildlife Refuge. Once the drainwater evaporated, high levels of salt, selenium, and a range of other heavy metals from the soil steadily accumulated and, by the early 1980s, large numbers of fish and waterfowl were dying or being found with severe deformities. Similar levels of contamination and wildlife deformities and deaths also were observed in the Tulare Basin, in the southern half of the San Joaquin Valley (SJVDP, 1990).

In 1986, drainage into Kesterson was halted and no drainage infrastructure has been constructed. As the water table has risen, high levels of salt have been drawn up into the top layer of soil, resulting in severe productivity issues for large swathes of farmland. Estimates from the San Joaquin Valley Drainage Report suggest that 460,000 acres of San Joaquin farmland will be abandoned by 2040 at the current rate of salt accumulation (SJVDP, 1990). These impacts are already being observed in the Westlands Water District, where over 100,000 acres of drainage-impacted land has been abandoned or is being converted to alternative uses—e.g., the Westlands Solar Park, a 2.4-GW solar farm to be in operation in 2025.

Drainage issues are not unique to the Central Valley. To the south, cropland in the Coachella and Imperial Valleys receive surface water diverted from the Colorado River, which has relatively high saline levels. This water, along with salt and minerals (e.g., selenium), ultimately drains into the Salton Sea—a 350-square mile lake southeast of Palm Springs. Over time, the saline levels in the Salton Sea have been steadily climbing, resulting in the collapse of the wildlife ecosystem. Moreover, the Salton Sea is steadily drying up. As a result, the surrounding farming communities face serious health threats posed by the toxic dust from the dry lakebed being swept into the air.

Cropland along the coast also must also confront salinity issues. For example, farms in the Salinas Valley, located west of the San Joaquin Valley in Monterey County, rely heavily on groundwater for irrigation. Over time, as the rate of groundwater extraction has outstripped the rate of freshwater recharge, seawater has steadily been pulled under the coastal Salinas Valley. To become less reliant on the salt-tainted groundwater, and to slow the rate of seawater incursion into the underlying groundwater, there have been steady efforts to reduced groundwater extraction and to instead irrigate with recycled water as well as surface water stored during wet periods.

The profitability of agricultural production is also affected by growing scarcity of the chief complement to land—water for irrigation. A wide range of factors have and continue to impact water availability, including environmental regulations surrounding water flows required for habitat preservation in the San Francisco Bay-Delta; growth in urban-water demand; variability in snow and rainfall induced by climate change; and the looming regulation of groundwater withdrawals following the Sustainable Groundwater Management Act (SGMA). The steady growth in water scarcity has had a clear impact on the amount of irrigated acreage in California over recent decades. Data from the USDA National Resources Inventory reveals that irrigated cropland in California fell from 9 million acres in 1982 to 8 million acres in 2012.

Ultimately, water scarcity has dramatic impacts on how farmland is used in California. For one, a lack of access to water can alter whether land is even used for agricultural production. For example, USDA and NASA estimates based on satellite imagery suggest that in 2015, during the prolonged drought California faced, 1.03 million acres of Central Valley cropland were fallowed. In contrast, in 2011, prior to the drought, approximately 400,000 acres of cropland were fallowed (Melton et al., 2015). Of course, these represent short-run changes in response to extreme drought conditions. In response to longer-run changes in water supply, there can also be changes in the composition of crops being grown, with a movement away from water-intensive crops to less water-intensive crops.

There are important interactions between the set of issues facing farmland in the Central Valley. For example, population growth will continue to create a financial incentive for farmland to be converted to developed land. At the same time, as water becomes scarce and more expensive, the profitability of agricultural production will fall, potentially accelerating the rate of farmland conversion. In contrast, if water scarcity results in lower levels of surface water being applied to farmland in the San Joaquin Valley, the loss of productive farmland stemming from rising water tables and soil salinity will be mitigated.

CONCLUSION

In 1850, California's population was just over 90,000. By 2017, the population had risen to 40 million. In many regions in California, the landscape has been largely unaffected by the swelling population. Federally owned lands in the arid southeast, throughout the rugged Sierras, and scattered across the wooded northern reaches remain sparsely populated and relatively untouched. In contrast, the coastal regions and the Central Valley have undergone dramatic changes over the last decade and a half.

Following WWII, suburbanization swept through the Bay Area and Southern California. The state's oldest and most productive farmlands, the initial Spanish and Mexican ranchos, were largely paved over. The South Coast and Bay Area now account for a large share of the state's roughly 7 million acres of developed land. Moving inland from the coast, the construction of over 100 dams, an extensive network of levees, and thousands of miles of water-delivery canals have permanently reshaped the landscape in the Central Valley. Millions of acres of wetlands have been erased and the once dry Central Valley has been transformed into the most productive agricultural region in the country.

Looking forward, California's lands will continue to evolve. Much of the future growth in population is projected to occur in the Central Valley. As the population expands, there will be pressure to convert Central Valley farmland into developed land. As this chapter highlights, slowing this process is challenging, and even more so when the profitability of agricultural production is threatened by soil-quality problems and water scarcity. Ultimately, the state's very diverse agricultural sector will continue to evolve and adjust to the reality of a shrinking footprint on the land.

REFERENCES

Buck, S., M. Auffhammer, and D. Sunding. 2014. "Land Markets and the Value of Water: Hedonic Analysis Using Repeat Sales of Farmland." *American Journal of Agricultural Economics* 96(4): 953-969.

California Department of Conservation. 2015. *California Farmland Conservation Report, 2015.* Sacramento CA: Division of Land Resource Protection, September.

California Department of Conservation. 2016. *The California Land Conservation Act of 1965, 2016 Status Report.* Sacramento CA: Division of Land Resource Protection, December.

California Department of Food and Agriculture. 2016. *California Agricultural Statistics Review 2015-2016.* Sacramento, CA.

California Protected Areas Database. 2017. "CPAD Statistics." CPAD Project Working Paper, August.

Carman, H.F. 1977. "California Landowners' Adoption of a Use-Value Assessment Program." *Land Economics* 53(3): 275-287.

Farm Service Agency. 2018. "Conservation Reserve Program Statistics." Washington DC: U.S. Department of Agriculture. Available at: https://www.fsa.usda.gov/programs-and-services/conservation-programs/reports-and-statistics/conservation-reserve-program-statistics/index.

Frayer, W. E., D. Peters, and H.R. Pywell. 1989. *Wetlands of the California Central Valley: Status and Trends – 1939 to mid-1980s.* Portland, OR: U.S. Fish and Wildlife Service.

Hanak, E., J. Lund, A. Dinar, B. Gray, R. Howitt, J. Mount, P. Moyle, and B. Thompson. 2011. "Floods, Droughts, and Lawsuits: A Brief History of California's Water Policy." In *Managing California's Water: from Conflict to Reconciliation*: 19-69. San Francisco CA: Public Policy Institute of California.

Hansen, D. E. and S.I. Schwartz. 1975. "Landowner Behavior at the Rural-Urban Fringe in Response to Preferential Property Taxation." *Land Economics* 51(4): 341-354.

Kuminoff, N., A. Sokolow, and D. Sumner. 2011. "Farmland Conversion: Perceptions and Realities." *AIC Issues Brief Number 16*, May. Davis CA: University of California, Agricultural Issues Center.

Letey, J. 2000. "Soil Salinity Poses Challenges for Sustainable Agriculture and Wildlife." *California Agriculture* 54(2): 43-48.

National Park Service. 2018. "Homestead Act, State by State Numbers." *U.S. Department of Interior.* Available at: https://www.nps.gov/home/learn/historyculture/bynumbers.htm.

Melton, F., C. Rosevelt, A. Guzman, L. Johnson, I. Zaragoza, J. Verdin, P. Thenkabail, C. Wallace, R. Mueller, P. Willis, and J. Jones. 2015. *Fallowed Area Mapping for Drought Impact Reporting: 2015 Assessment of Conditions in the California Central Valley.* NASA Ames Research Center Cooperative for Research in Earth Science Technology and Education & CSU Monterey Bay, USGS, USDA, California Department of Water Resources, October 14.

Olmstead, A. and P. Rhode. 2003. "The Evolution of California Agriculture 1850-2000." In J. Siebert, ed *California Agriculture Dimensions and Issues.* Berkeley CA: University of California Giannini Foundation of Agricultural Economics, Division of Agriculture and Natural Resources. Avalable at: https://s.giannini.ucop.edu/uploads/giannini_public/4e/a8/4ea8b9cc-df88-4146-b1ae-e5467736e104/escholarship_uc_item_9145n8m1.pdf.

Pincetl, S. 1999/ *Transforming California: A Political History of Land Use and Development.* Baltimore MD: The Johns Hopkins University Press.

Robinson, W.W. 1948. *Land in California.* Berkeley CA: University of California Press.

San Juan Valley Drainage Program. 1990. *A Management Plan for Agricultural Subsurface Drainage and Related Problems on the Westside San Joaquin Valley.* U.S. Department of the Interior, California Resources Agency, September.

Schlenker, W., W.M. Hanemann, and A. Fisher. 2007. "Water Availability, Degree Days, and the Potential Impact of Climate Change on Irrigated Agriculture in California." *Climatic Change* 81: 19-38.

Schoups, G., J. Hopmans, C. Young, J. Vrugt, W. Wallender, K. Tanji, and S. Panday. 2005. "Sustainability of Irrigated Agriculture in the San Joaquin Valley, California." *Proceedings of the National Academy of Sciences* 102(43): 15352-15356.

Sokolow, A. 1990. *The Williamson Act, 25 Years of Land Conservation.* The Resources Agency of California, December.

U.S. Department of Agriculture. 2015. *2012 National Resources Inventory, Summary Report.* Washington DC: Natural Resources Conservation Service, August.

U.S. Environmental Protection Agency (EPA). 2007. "Tulare Lake Basin Hydrology and Hydrography: A Summary of the Movement of Water and Aquatic Species." *U.S. EPA Document Number 909R07002.*

CHAPTER 4. IMMIGRATION AND FARM LABOR: CHALLENGES AND OPPORTUNITIES

PHILIP L. MARTIN

ABSTRACT

Hired workers do most of the work on U.S. farms, three-fourths were born abroad, and about half are unauthorized. Hired farm workers are most closely associated with the production of fruits and vegetables, and most are employed on 10,000 large farms across the United States. Farm employers are adjusting to the slowdown in Mexico-U.S. migration with the 4-S strategies of satisfying current workers to retain them, stretching them by providing them with productivity-increasing aids, substituting machines for workers, and supplementing current workers with H-2A guest workers. Immigration policy is the major determinant of which 4-S strategy will dominate.

ABOUT THE AUTHOR

Philip L. Martin is an emeritus professor in the Department of Agricultural and Resource Economics at the University of California, Davis and a member of the Giannini Foundation of Agricultural Economics. He can be contacted at plmartin@ucdavis.edu.

Many of California's fruit and vegetable crops are labor-intensive, requiring a steady farmworker labor force.

Photo Credit: Rachael Goodhue, UC Davis

Chapter 4. Table of Contents

FRUIT AND VEGETABLE AGRICULTURE

Agriculture is the production of food and fiber on farms, and serves as the keystone of the larger food system that includes input industries such as seed, fertilizer, and equipment firms, as well as the output sector that packs, processes, and distributes food and fiber to consumers in the U.S. and abroad via grocery stores and restaurants. Relatively few food-system jobs are on farms, about a sixth, while two-thirds are in food services and restaurants.

Food-system jobs are shifting from farming and food manufacturing to services that distribute, prepare, and serve food (Figure 4.1). The average number of jobs for hired workers on farms has been relatively stable at about 1.3 million over the past several decades, as the expansion of labor-intensive commodities such as strawberries creates new jobs to replace those lost as labor-saving mechanization eliminates jobs in commodities such as raisin grapes. Some jobs that nonfarm workers previously did in packing houses, farm workers now perform in the field, such as the preparation of lettuce and melons for the market.

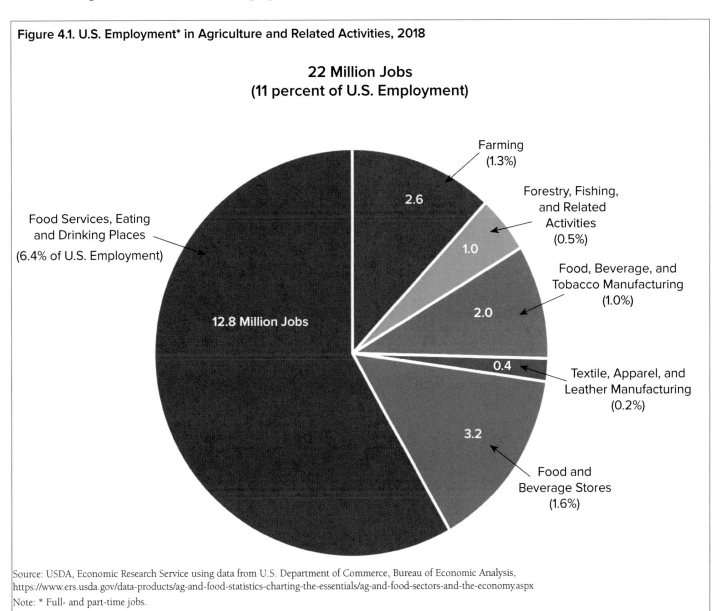

Figure 4.1. U.S. Employment* in Agriculture and Related Activities, 2018

**22 Million Jobs
(11 percent of U.S. Employment)**

Farming (1.3%) — 2.6

Forestry, Fishing, and Related Activities (0.5%) — 1.0

Food, Beverage, and Tobacco Manufacturing (1.0%) — 2.0

Textile, Apparel, and Leather Manufacturing (0.2%) — 0.4

Food and Beverage Stores (1.6%) — 3.2

Food Services, Eating and Drinking Places (6.4% of U.S. Employment) — 12.8 Million Jobs

Source: USDA, Economic Research Service using data from U.S. Department of Commerce, Bureau of Economic Analysis, https://www.ers.usda.gov/data-products/ag-and-food-statistics-charting-the-essentials/ag-and-food-sectors-and-the-economy.aspx
Note: * Full- and part-time jobs.

Table 4.1. U.S. Average Agricultural Employment (Thousands)					
	2006	**2016**	**2026**	**2006–2016**	**2016–2026**
Sector	Thousands of Workers			Percent Change	
Ag Wage and Salary	1,219	1,501	1,518	23	1
Ag Self-Employed	893	850	828	-5	-3
Total Ag	2,112	2,351	2,346	11	0
Hired Share of Total Employment	58%	64%	65%		

Source: U.S. Bureau of Labor Statistics, Table 1, https://www.bls.gov/opub/mlr/2017/article/projections-overview-and-highlights-2016-26.htm

Note: BLS projections based on CPS; agricultural sector, including forestry, fishing, and logging.

The U.S. Department of Labor projects stable farm employment. Hired workers did almost two-thirds of U.S. farm work in 2016, that is, wage and salary workers were two-thirds of average employment, reflecting the fact that many farmers also have nonfarm jobs. The number of farmers and unpaid family members has been falling, while average farm worker employment is rising slightly, so that the share of hired workers in agricultural employment is rising (Table 4.1).

THREE FARMING SYSTEMS

The major farm labor issue is seasonality: agriculture's biological production process requires more workers at some times of the year than others. There are many seasonal jobs, from teaching to professional sports, and most offer some type of monetary or other benefits to compensate for seasonality. Seasonal farm jobs are unusual because they offer few monetary or other benefits to compensate for the fact that seasonal workers are employed less than full time in agriculture; that is, farmers expect workers to be available when they are needed to work at the minimum wage or slightly more.

The U.S. developed three major types of farms, and each obtained workers to meet seasonal labor demands in a different way. Diversified family farms in the northeastern and midwestern states relied on large farm families and an occasional hired hand to produce crops and livestock, and family farms became fewer and larger as labor-saving technology spread and more family members worked off the farm.

In the southeastern states, plantations relied on slaves to produce non-perishable and long-season cotton and tobacco for export to Europe. Most plantations had at least 400 acres and 20 slaves, and the price of slaves fluctuated with the prices of the commodities they helped to produce.[1] Slaves were replaced by sharecroppers until cotton harvesting machines in the 1940s and 1950s prompted the migration of many sharecroppers to northern and midwestern cities.

In western states such as California, first the Spanish and later the Mexican government made large land grants of 50,000 acres or more to individuals for cattle grazing and dryland wheat farming.[2] California became a state in 1850, and after the transcontinental railroad in 1869 lowered transportation costs and interest rates, fruit production became more profitable than cattle and wheat. California in the 1870s was expected to become an Iowa of family fruit farms, relying on large families to meet peak seasonal labor demands.

Large ranchos were not broken up into family farms for two interconnected reasons. First, Chinese workers who had been imported to help build the transcontinental railroad were laid off, driven out of San Francisco and other cities, and became seasonal farm workers who "came with the wind and went with the dust"—that is, they were paid only when they worked. Second, the low wages paid to Chinese workers were capitalized or incorporated into the price of farm land, giving California some of the most expensive U.S. farm land despite its distance from most

---

1 For more details on these farming systems, see Martin, 2003 (Chapter 2).

2 Dryland wheat farming meant planting in the fall and, if there was sufficient rain, harvesting in the spring.

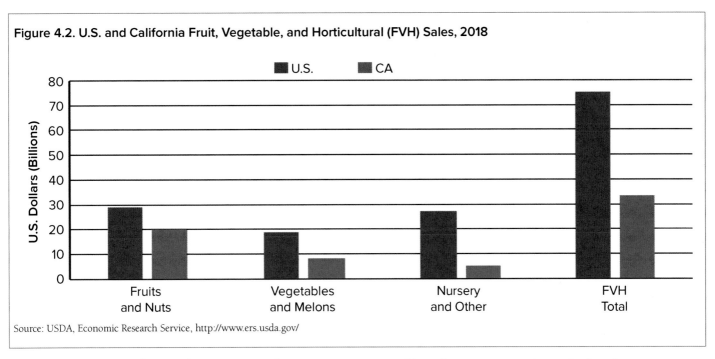

Figure 4.2. U.S. and California Fruit, Vegetable, and Horticultural (FVH) Sales, 2018

Source: USDA, Economic Research Service, http://www.ers.usda.gov/

consumers.[3] Families who did their own work had to pay high prices to buy farm land but earned the equivalent of the low wages paid to Chinese workers, explaining why few family farms developed (Fuller, 1991).

The Chinese Exclusion Act of 1882 suspended Chinese immigration, but Japan legalized emigration in 1885, and Japanese newcomers soon replaced the Chinese as the core of the seasonal farm work force. They were followed by Punjabis and other South Asians early in the 20th century, Mexicans during World War I, Filipinos in the 1920s, Dust Bowl migrants in the 1930s, and Mexicans since. These waves of immigrants made it unnecessary to break up the large farms that developed from land grants and entrepreneurs who assembled large farms,[4] resulting in a system of factories in the fields that rely on hired workers born elsewhere.

FVH COMMODITIES

California looms large in farm labor discussions because the state produces many labor-intensive fruits and

vegetables. There are two major agricultural sectors, crops and animal products, and each accounted for about half of U.S. farm sales of $372 billion in 2018, when crops were worth $196 billion and animal products $176 billion.

Many U.S. states mirror this 50–50 split between crop and livestock agriculture,[5] but not California, a state where crops predominate. California has been the leading farm state since 1950 because of its production of high-value fruit and vegetable crops. California's farm sales of $50 billion in 2018 included $39 billion worth of crops and $11 billion worth of animal products.

The U.S. produced about $64 billion worth of fruits and nuts, vegetables and melons, and other horticultural crops, including nursery crops and flowers in 2017 (Figure 4.2). These so-called FVH crops included $29 billion worth of fruits and nuts, $20 billion worth of vegetables and melons, and $16 billion worth of other horticultural crops. California produced $31 billion worth of FVH crops in 2017, including $20 billion worth of fruits and nuts, $8 billion worth of vegetables and melons, and $3 billion worth of other horticultural crops; that is, California accounted for 68 percent of the value of U.S. fruits and nuts, 42 percent of vegetables and melons, and 18 percent of other horticultural crops.

---

3 In 1888, for example, California orchard land was worth $200 to $300 an acre, while land used to produce wheat was worth $25 to $50 an acre. Fruit generated more revenue per acre, but also had higher production costs.

4 The Tejon Ranch (http://tejonranch.com) in the southern San Joaquin Valley, with 270,000 acres that were originally four Mexican land grants, is an example of a large farm that has persisted.

5 For example, in the state second to California in farm sales, Iowa, farm sales of $31 billion were divided 55-45 percent between crops and animal products in the 2012 Census of Agriculture.

STRAWBERRIES

Strawberries are an example of a labor-intensive commodity produced mostly in California whose production expanded to meet consumer demand. For most of the 20th century, fresh strawberries were a seasonal commodity produced locally. New varieties, shippers who made contracts with berry farmers around the state so that they could supply fresh berries year-round, and the availability of berry pickers encouraged a near tripling of U.S. strawberry production over the past quarter-century.

The California climate is ideal for strawberries, and few foreign suppliers can deliver fragile and perishable strawberries to U.S. consumers at competitive prices, explaining why California produces over 90 percent of U.S. strawberries. Strawberries must be picked once a week or more, and a normal strategy is to have 1.5 pickers per acre, so that the 40,000 acres of California strawberries require 60,000 workers.

Strawberries are picked directly into the pint or pound clamshells in which they are sold. Farmers typically receive about 40 percent of the average retail price, and labor is 30 to 40 percent of production costs, so that a $2 pound of strawberries in a retail store means 80 cents for the farmer and 28 cents for the worker.[6]

There are many wage payment systems, such as $5 an hour plus $1 per 12-pint or 9-pound flat, or simply $1.75 per flat. All workers are guaranteed the state's $13 an hour minimum wage in 2020, and most pick six or more flats per hour, earning more than the minimum wage. Few strawberry workers migrate around California. Instead, most live in the coastal valleys where strawberry production is concentrated, and many 60-person picking crews include several family members and their relatives.

The strawberry industry is unusual in several respects. The majority of growers (but not most producers) are of Hispanic or Japanese ancestry. Many of the Hispanics moved up from farm worker to farmer with the help of berry marketers such as Driscoll's or Naturipe that contract with farmers to produce berries from varieties patented by these marketers. Farmers use these shipper contracts to rent land and equipment, receive advice from marketers on how to farm, and deliver the berries to the marketer, who deducts any loans and marketing charges and sends the balance to the grower. The California Supreme Court's Borello 1989 decision found that some smaller growers were employees of the marketers rather than independent farmers, forcing changes in how marketers interact with the growers who grow, pick, and deliver berries.[7]

The second feature of the strawberry industry is its response to the slowdown in Mexico-U.S. migration. With many family groups among strawberry pickers, workers normally carpool to work. They wheel small carts with a flat or tray of clamshells between two elevated rows of plants that develop through plastic and send out vines with berries, so that one worker picks from two rows.

---

6 Price spreads from farm to consumer are at: www.ers.usda.gov/data-products/price-spreads-from-farm-to-consumer.aspx#25657.

Costs of production studies are at:
http://coststudies.ucdavis.edu/current/commodity/strawberries/.

University of California put total costs of production at $44,000 an acre, with labor about $14,000. Harvesting accounted for 83 percent of labor costs.

---

7 The California Supreme Court developed a six-factor test to distinguish employees from independent contractors, that is, who controls the work, what is the opportunity for profit or loss, what investment does the individual make in equipment, what skills are required, how permanent is the relationship, and is the service integral to the employer's business. In share-farming, the California Supreme Court said that harvesters are employees even if they sign contracts saying they are independent contractors because growers retain control over the production and sale of the crop. S. G. Borello & Sons, Inc. v. Department of Industrial Relations (1989). Available at:
http://law.justia.com/cases/california/supreme-court/3d/48/341.html.

California produces over 90 percent of U.S. strawberries.
Photo Credit: UC Davis ARE

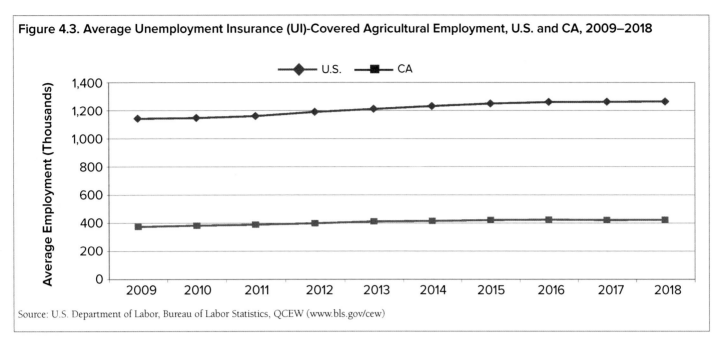

Figure 4.3. Average Unemployment Insurance (UI)-Covered Agricultural Employment, U.S. and CA, 2009–2018

Source: U.S. Department of Labor, Bureau of Labor Statistics, QCEW (www.bls.gov/cew)

Workers take full flats to checkers to receive credit, get an empty flat, and resume picking. Many larger growers put conveyor belts in the field on which pickers can place trays of berries to reduce the amount of time spent walking to receive credit for their work—increasing worker productivity. There are experiments underway to use machines to harvest strawberries.

The strawberry industry illustrates the immigration and farm labor conundrum. The industry responded to rising consumer demand by expanding production and supplying berries year-round. Workers settled in areas that offered berry jobs for up to eight months a year and, with two earners, many berry-picking families have annual incomes of $15,000 to $25,000 a year. However, berry picking remains a one or two decade-long job rather than a lifetime career for most pickers, and the children of strawberry workers educated in the U.S. generally shun their parents' jobs, explaining why the arrival of newcomers from poorer countries eager to work is of keen interest to farmers.

FARM WORKER EMPLOYMENT

Farm worker employment involves several concepts. First is average employment, the number of workers employed each month, summed, and divided by 12 months.[8] Average

U.S. farm employment, as measured by employer reports when paying unemployment insurance (UI) taxes, was over 1.2 million in 2015. Some states do not require smaller farmers to pay UI taxes on farm worker wages, so UI covers an estimated 86 percent of U.S. hired farm workers, making average total employment 1.4 million.[9]

California requires all employers to participate in UI, and its average agricultural employment was 423.000 in 2018, a third of average U.S. agricultural employment. Over the past decade, average farm worker employment increased in both the U.S. and California (Figure 4.3).

There are more farm workers than average employment because of seasonality that generates peaks and troughs. UI-covered farm worker employment across the U.S. ranged from a high of 1.4 million in July 2018 to a low of 1.1 million in January, for a peak-trough ratio of 1.3. California had a peak 475,500 in August 2018 and 344,900 in January 2018, for a ratio of 1.4. The peak-trough ratio increases as the geographic unit decreases. At the county level, the peak-trough ratio may be two to one, and on an individual farm as high as 100 to one, as when 200 workers are hired for harvesting but only two during the winter.

---

8 Average employment data are from the Quarterly Census of Employment and Wages (www.bls.gov/cew), and include workers on the payroll for the period that includes the 12th of the month.

9 Federal law requires farm employers to provide UI coverage to wage and salary farm workers if they paid $20,000 or more in wages in a calendar quarter or employed at least ten farm workers on each of 20 days in 20 different weeks during the current or preceding calendar year.

Table 4.2. California Farm Workers and Earnings, 2014

NAICS		Primary Workers	CA Earnings ($ Millions)	Avg. Earnings per Worker ($)	Only Job	Percent Share[1]
11	Agriculture	691,615	11,430	16,527	499,440	72
1111	Oilseed and Grain Farming	4,587	116	25,363	3,144	69
1112	Vegetable and Melon Farming	44,878	1,068	23,789	30,760	69
1113	Fruit and Tree Nut Farming	153,999	2,710	17,600	102,805	67
1114	Greenhouse & Nursery Production	34,715	884	25,452	26,530	76
1119	Other Crop Farming	19,052	446	23,414	14,244	75
1121	Cattle Ranching and Farming	25,224	737	29,223	19,817	79
1122	Hog and Pig Farming	132	4	26,804	109	83
1123	Poultry and Egg Production	2,851	83	29,143	2,123	74
1124	Sheep and Goat Farming	543	12	21,759	465	86
1125	Animal Aquaculture	441	13	30,104	324	73
1129	Other Animal Production	3,069	77	25,144	2,308	75
1151	Support Activities for Crop Production	391,711	4,982	12,719	288,435	74
1152	Support Activities for Animal Production	3,156	81	25,765	2,585	82
1153	Support Activities for Forestry	2,589	76	29,217	2,012	78
Nonfarm[2]		137,711	4,548	33,025	--	--
All Workers with at Least One Ag Job		829,326	15,978	19,266	--	--

Source: Employment Development Department, special data tabulations

Notes: The North American Industry Classification System or NAICS classifies business establishments according to type of economic activity. NAICS 11 is Agriculture, Forestry, Fishing and Hunting.
[1] Share of primary farm workers who were only employed in this NAICS.
[2] Nonfarm are workers with at least one farm and one nonfarm job, and their highest earning job was a nonfarm job.

JOBS VERSUS WORKERS

Average employment and peak-trough ratios are measures of jobs, not the number of unique workers who fill them. There are more farms than full-time equivalent farmers,[10] and more farm workers than full-time equivalent jobs for hired workers.

The question of how many more workers than jobs is hard to answer. During the 1980s, when the Current Population Survey included questions in December asking whether anyone in the household worked for wages on a farm during the year, it found 2.6 million unique farm workers when average farm employment was 1.3 million, suggesting two unique workers per job. These workers were grouped at the ends of the days-of-farm work spectrum. One-third did fewer than 25 days of farm work during the year, while 20 percent worked year-round.[11]

There are no national data on the number of individuals who work for wages on farms sometime during the year. California extracted the social security numbers (SSNs) of all workers reported by farmers sometime during the year, allowing a comparison between unique farm workers and

10 There are 2.2 million U.S. farms but only 750,000 full-time equivalent farmers. Many farmers work off the farm full- or part-time.

11 For an example of the 1980s CPS reports, see http://naldc.nal.usda.gov/download/IND20402024/

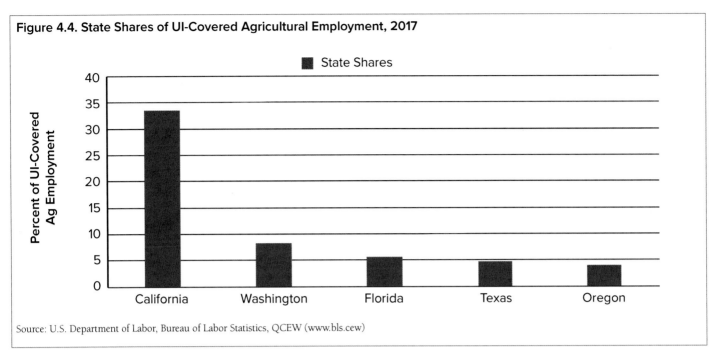

Figure 4.4. State Shares of UI-Covered Agricultural Employment, 2017

Source: U.S. Department of Labor, Bureau of Labor Statistics, QCEW (www.bls.cew)

average employment. In 2014, when average agricultural employment was 411,000, some 829,000 unique SSNs were reported by California farm employers, suggesting the same two workers for each average job as in the 1980s.

The 829,000 farm workers in California earned a total of $16 billion, including $11.4 billion or over 70 percent from agricultural employers (NAICS code 11).[12] Average earnings for all workers with at least one farm employer were over $19,000 in 2014, while average earnings for primary farm workers, those who had their maximum earnings in agriculture, were $16,500.

One sector stands out as employing the most primary farm workers, crop support employers (NAICS 1151), many of whom are farm labor contractors. Almost 392,000 or 57 percent of primary farm workers were employed by crop support employers, followed by 22 percent who were employed by fruit and nut farming establishments (NAICS 1113). Crop support workers had the lowest average earnings, $12,700, explaining why the overall average earnings of primary farm workers were only $16,500 even though all commodities except crop support and fruit and nut farming had higher average earnings (Table 4.2).

---

12 The North American Industry Classification System or NAICS classifies business establishments according to type of economic activity. NAICS 11 is Agriculture, Forestry, Fishing, and Hunting.

CONCENTRATION BY STATE AND COMMODITY

Average employment, peak-trough ratios, and unique farm workers are three ways to study who works for wages on U.S. farms. There are other windows into farm work, including which states and commodities have the most farm workers.

Figure 4.4 shows that five states accounted for 55 percent of average agricultural employment covered by unemployment insurance in 2017, including 33 percent in California.

The Census of Agriculture, which collected data from farm employers on their expenses for hired farm labor in 2017, including workers hired directly and expenses for contract labor, shows a similar concentration of farm labor in a few states. Nine states accounted for 57 percent of direct hire and contract farm labor expenses in 2017. California had $10.8 billion in direct hire and contract farm labor expenses in 2017, followed by Washington, $2.4 billion; Texas, $2 billion; Florida, $1.8 billion; and Oregon, $1.2 billion. Wisconsin, North Carolina, and Michigan each had about $1.1 billion in farm labor expenses, and Iowa had $1 billion. In California, Washington, Florida, and Oregon, crop direct hire and contract farm labor expenses were over 80 percent of farm labor expenses, while in Texas, Wisconsin, and Iowa, over half of farm labor expenses were for direct hire and contract labor on livestock farms.

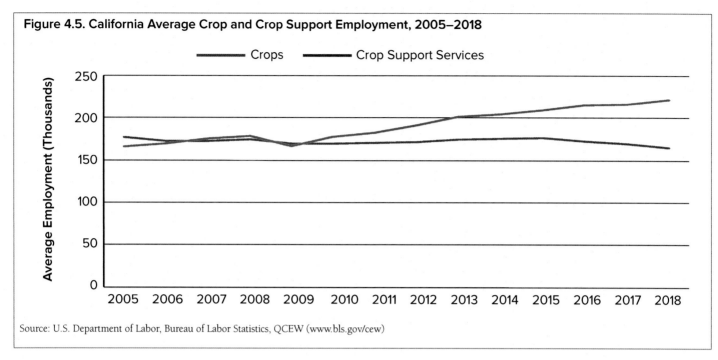

Figure 4.5. California Average Crop and Crop Support Employment, 2005–2018

Source: U.S. Department of Labor, Bureau of Labor Statistics, QCEW (www.bls.gov/cew)

Within California, five counties accounted for 43 percent of the state's direct hire and contract farm labor expenses. Fresno had $1.2 billion in total farm labor expenses; Monterey, $1.1 billion; Kern, $867 million; Tulare, $852 million; and Santa Barbara, $595 million.

Farm worker employment is concentrated by commodity. U.S. crop employment averaged 550,000 in 2018, including almost 184,000 in fruits and nuts, 93,000 in vegetables and melons, and 155,000 in greenhouse and nursery production, so that 80 percent of average crop employment was in FVH crops.[13]

The UI data do not specify the commodity in which the average 325,000 workers brought to farms by crop support services, mostly farm labor contractors, worked. This makes it very hard to determine exactly which commodities employed the most farm workers in a state like California, where Figure 4.5 shows that over half of average employment on crop farms is with crop support services.

Farm worker employment is complicated because the seasonal nature of production upends normal assumptions about average employment and unique workers, as when 100 jobs means 110 workers, indicating 10 percent turnover.

Turnover is much higher in agriculture, an industry that has long relied on a reserve of workers who had few other job options so that they would be available when they were needed but do not have to be paid when there is no work. In the words of economist Varden Fuller, agriculture relies on "poverty at home and misery abroad" to ensure that a supply of seasonal workers is "on tap."[14]

The U.S. Department of Labor's National Agricultural Worker Survey (NAWS) finds that farm workers are mostly Mexican-born men.[15] The NAWS, launched in 1989 to detect farm-labor shortages due to immigration reforms, found that the foreign-born share of U.S. crop workers was 55 percent in 1989–90, peaked at 83 percent in 1999–2000, and is now 70 percent. About 30 percent of U.S. crop workers were born in the United States.

---

14 See: https://gifford.ucdavis.edu/events/#agenda

15 NAWS data are available at: https://www.dol.gov/agencies/eta/national-agricultural-workers-survey/research/data-tables

---

13 By commodity, average employment was 40,000 in apples, 32,000 in strawberries, 30,000 in grapes, 22,000 in other berries such as blueberries, and 20,000 in nuts.

HIRED FARM WORKERS

1990, 2000, AND TODAY

Many crop worker characteristics have V- or inverted V-shapes, with peaks or troughs around 2000. The share of unauthorized workers was less than 10 percent in 1990 due to legalizations in 1987–88, peaked at almost 60 percent in 2000, and is now less than 50 percent.

This inverted V-shape of unauthorized farm workers reflects changing patterns of Mexico–U.S. migration. Newcomers are persons in the U.S. less than a year before being interviewed, and they are almost always unauthorized. The newcomer share of crop workers was less than 5 percent in 1990, peaked at 25 percent in 2000, and is less than 5 percent today.

Most crop workers are not migrants, persons who cross borders to work for wages. There is no single federal definition of a migrant farm worker. The NAWS, which considers a worker to be a migrant if he moved at least 75 miles from his usual home for a farm job, finds a declining share of migrants—about 15 percent in both the U.S. and California.

Of those who migrate to do crop work, a quarter follow the crops by having at least two farm jobs 75 miles apart, while three-fourths shuttle between homes in Mexico and jobs in the U.S. This means that fewer than 5 percent of U.S. crop workers are follow-the-crop migrants who move with the ripening crops from Florida up the Eastern Seaboard or who move from Texas to Michigan.

With fewer young newcomers arriving, the crop workforce is aging. The average age of crop workers is 39, compared with a median of 42 for all U.S. workers.[16] In 1990 and 2000, over half of U.S. crop workers were in the 20 to 34 age group. Today, the share of workers in this age group is below 40 percent (Figure 4.6).

Average years of schooling for U.S. crop workers were eight in 1990, seven in 2000, and nine today. California crop workers are less educated, with an average seven years of schooling. The share of U.S. workers who speak English well fell from a quarter in 1990 to less than 20 percent in 2000, and is now a third. In California, the share of workers speaking English well has always been less than 15 percent.

---

16 One-seventh of crop workers are 55 or older, compared with about 20 percent of all U.S. workers, http://www.bls.gov/emp/ep_table_306.htm.

Figure 4.6. U.S. Crop Worker Characteristics, 1990, 2000, 2015–2016 (Share of Workers)

■ 1990　■ 2000　■ 2015—2016

Source: National Agricultural Workers Survey; Available at: https://www.dol.gov/agencies/eta/national-agricultural-workers-survey/research/data-tables.

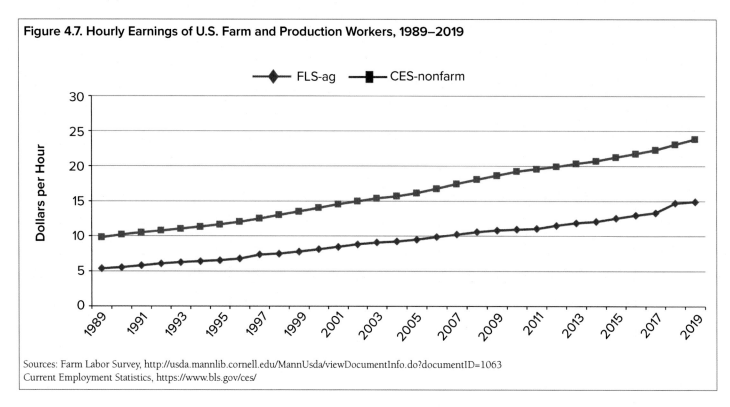

Figure 4.7. Hourly Earnings of U.S. Farm and Production Workers, 1989–2019

Sources: Farm Labor Survey, http://usda.mannlib.cornell.edu/MannUsda/viewDocumentInfo.do?documentID=1063
Current Employment Statistics, https://www.bls.gov/ces/

Almost 60 percent of U.S. and California crop workers are married parents; only a quarter are single with no children. Median family income has risen to the $20,000 to $25,000 range for U.S. and California crop workers over the past two decades; many families have two earners. A rising share of U.S. and California crop worker families, about half, receive some type of means-tested assistance such as Medicaid or SNAP (Food Stamps), a sharp jump from less than a quarter in 1990 and 2000. Rising benefit usage reflects low-income and "mixed-status" farm worker families that have unauthorized parents and U.S.-citizen children eligible for health and other benefits.[17]

EMPLOYERS AND EARNINGS

Workers can be hired directly by farm operators or brought to farms by nonfarm entities such as custom harvesters and farm labor contractors. Type-of-employer data follow a V-shaped trajectory, starting high, dipping in 2000, and rebounding since. About 86 percent of U.S. crop workers were hired directly by farmers in 1990, 73 percent in 2000,

and 85 percent today; the California direct-hire shares were 73, 55, and 66 percent, respectively; that is, the California direct-hire share has not yet returned to 1990 levels[18] (Figure 4.5).

When newcomers were pouring into the U.S. in the 1990s, the average years of U.S. farm work experience fell from ten years in 1990 to eight years in 2000. However, the slowdown in Mexico-U.S. migration after the 2008–09 recession contributed to rising farm work experience, which is now 14 years across the U.S. In California, the average farm work experience fell from 11 to 9 years, and is now 16 years. U.S. and California crop workers have been employed an average of seven years by their current farm employer.

Crop workers across the U.S. reported that they earned an average $5.25 an hour in the early 1990s, when the federal minimum wage was $4.25. They earned $6.50 an hour in 2000, when the federal minimum wage was $5.15, and $10 an hour today, when the federal minimum wage is $7.25. In California, workers reported average earnings of $5.55 in

---

17 In 2016, California made all unauthorized poor children eligible for Medicaid, called Medi-Cal in California. Since a third of NAWS workers are interviewed in California, the share of farm worker families receiving some type of assistance is likely to rise.

18 The UI data find that 55 percent of average employment on California farms is comprised of workers brought to farms by crop support services, suggesting that the NAWS sample in California includes a higher share of directly hired workers.

the early 1990s, when the state's minimum wage was $4.25, $6.55 in 2000, when the state's minimum wage was $5.75, and $11.83 in 2015–16, when the state's minimum wage was $9 an hour. The NAWS finds that the California wage premium of earlier years has disappeared.

Farm employers also report the average hourly earnings of their non-supervisory employees; U.S. farm workers earned an average of almost $15 in 2019, almost triple their 1989 nominal wage (Figure 4.7). The earnings of U.S. nonfarm workers, which were $24 an hour in 2019, rose from almost $10 an hour in 1989. The ratio of average farm to nonfarm earnings rose from 55 percent in 1989 to 63 percent in 2019, narrowing the farm-nonfarm wage gap. Farm employers report higher earnings to USDA than workers report to the NAWS.[19]

U.S. crop workers averaged over 190 days in 35 weeks of farm work in 2015–16, suggesting 5.4 days of work a week. California crop workers had even more days of farm work, an average 205 days in 36 weeks in recent years, or an average 5.7 days a week. The share of U.S. crop workers with at least one nonfarm job was over 30 percent in 1990, 15 percent in 2000, and 25 percent today. The California shares are 16, 6, and 17 percent, respectively; that is, California crop workers are less likely to have nonfarm jobs.

About 80 percent of U.S. crop workers interviewed in the NAWS are employed in FVH commodities, as are 90 percent of California crop workers. However, the interviewed U.S. workers have switched from mostly vegetable workers in 1990 to mostly fruit workers today; California has always had a much higher share of fruit workers.

The share of U.S. crop workers in harvesting jobs has been falling, from 40 percent in 1990 to 30 percent in 2000, to less than a quarter today. For California, the harvesting share fell from almost half to 30 percent to 25 percent in the same time frame. The most common job today is semi-skilled, such as equipment operator: a third of U.S. workers, and 37 percent of California workers, had such jobs when interviewed.

Most crop workers plan to continue to do farm work for at least five more years. In 1990, two-thirds of U.S. workers said they would continue to do farm work as long as they could; in 2000 this dipped to 56 percent, and today over 75 percent of workers plan to continue to do farm work indefinitely. The California shares are 75 percent, 65 percent, and 80 percent, respectively. A declining share, about a third of U.S. workers and a quarter of California workers, say they could find a nonfarm job within a month.

The NAWS portrays a Mexican-born crop workforce that has settled in the U.S., formed or united families, and found employment with one fruit or vegetable farmer during the year. By working about 200 days or 1,600 hours a year at $10 an hour, long-season and full-year farm workers can earn $15,000 to $20,000 a year.

Working on farms is much like working in any other job. Most workers live away from the farm where they work, drive or carpool to work, and return to nonfarm homes when they finish work. Many farm workers would like to keep working in agriculture, but their capacity to do so may depend on the pace of the introduction of back-saving mechanical aids.

---

19 NAWS question D12 asks the hourly wage of workers who are paid hourly, and D13–D18 ask about piece-rate wages, including how many hours per day piece-rate workers were employed.

FARM LABOR MARKETS

Work is the exchange of effort for reward, and labor markets perform 3-R functions: recruitment or matching workers with jobs, remuneration or paying wages and benefits to motivate workers to work, and retention to keep experienced and productive workers. Each of these 3 Rs operates differently in agriculture.

RECRUITMENT

Recruitment normally involves developing job descriptions that lay out the minimum qualifications required to fill a job, advertising for candidates, and screening and interviewing applicants to find the best worker. Some farmers use formal procedures to hire skilled and professional workers, but most hiring of farm workers is informal.

Since most farm workers do not speak English, and most farmers do not speak Spanish, the key job matcher is a bilingual intermediary, a directly hired crew boss or a farm labor contractor who recruits a crew of workers by asking current workers to refer qualified friends and relatives. Some growers place signs along roads advertising for workers or pickers, assuming that workers drive around looking for work.

There are sometimes job vacancies posted in employment service offices or advertised in newspapers, but many advertised farm jobs reflect farmers who are seeking certification to hire guest workers; farmers must advertise for U.S. workers to be certified to hire guest workers. Fewer than 5 percent of farm job vacancy postings result in the employment of U.S. workers to fill jobs.

The key work unit in agriculture is the crew, which ranges from 10 to 60 depending on the commodity and task. A hoeing and weeding crew may consist of 10 or 20 workers accompanied by a working supervisor who sets the pace of work, while a fruit harvesting crew may include 40 to 60 workers, a quality checker to record each worker's production, and a non-working crew boss.

Supervisors and crew bosses, many of whom climbed the job ladder from hoeing or harvesting to foreman, are expected to maintain their crews at full-strength and monitor the pace and quality of work. The often close relationships between supervisors and crews, which may include the foreman's relatives and workers from the same Mexican community, minimizes complaints. Instead of voicing disagreement, farm workers often move on to another crew when there are disputes or they perceive that bosses are favoring particular workers, since they can do the same work for similar wages with another employer. Most farm workers have access to cell phones, making it easy to learn about wages and earnings on nearby farms.

Very few farm labor supervisors have formal training in managing workers, an omission that attracts little attention as long as supervisors ensure that farm work gets done. Union contracts impose restrictions on supervisors by allowing workers to file grievances, and labor compliance systems imposed by produce buyers restrict the freedom of supervisors. For example, the Fair Food Program (FFP) of the Coalition of Immokalee Workers calls for firing supervisors who commit or tolerate sexual harassment in tomato-picking crews in Florida, while the Equitable Food Initiative (EFI) in California creates teams of supervisors and workers on the strawberry and vegetable farms it has certified to monitor recruitment and supervision.[20]

There are public and private efforts to train farm supervisors and improve the quality of recruitment, including California requirements that labor contractors receive eight hours of training each year on protective labor laws and regulations. The California Farm Labor Contractor Association provides training for supervisors employed by farmers and contractors, teaching them about their responsibilities under federal and state labor laws. The University of Florida operates a Farm Labor Supervisor Training Program that issues certificates to supervisors who volunteer to complete training on labor, health, and safety laws. Many farm managers take little interest in why workers quit, turning recruitment over to supervisors and not questioning how they treat workers.

---

20 For details on the FFP and EFI, see Martin, 2016.

REMUNERATION

Remuneration or motivation to perform the job is encouraged by the wage or reward system. Most farm and nonfarm jobs pay hourly wages or monthly salaries, and managers monitor the speed and quality of the work performed to ensure "an honest day's work for an honest wage." The labor market is unusual because of this continuous bargaining between employers and employees, with some workers being fired for poor performance and others quitting for other options.

The share of farm jobs paid hourly wages has been rising, reflecting a more homogenous workforce (mostly Mexican-born men) with similar productivity, new ways to monitor the pace of work, as when conveyor belts move in front of harvest workers and the employer controls the speed of the machine. Laws and court decisions require farm employers to keep detailed records of hours and units of work accomplished for workers paid on an incentive or piece-rate basis.

When workers harvest fruit in trees, making them difficult to monitor, many employers pay incentive or piece-rate wages, such as $20 to pick a 1,000-pound bin of apples, to give workers an incentive to work fast without close monitoring. Piece rates have other advantages as well, such as keeping the cost of getting work done predictable without screening workers, since slower workers earn less. As child labor laws tightened and minimum wage laws were applied to farm work, the workforce became more uniformly young, Mexican-born men, allowing farmers to pay hourly wages and expect workers to pick at similar rates. Court decisions have also encouraged a switch from piece to hourly wages.[21]

Piece-rate wage systems create an iron triangle between three elements of farm jobs: the government-set minimum hourly wage, the employer-set piece rate, and the productivity standard or the units of work per hour or day that a worker must accomplish to earn at least the minimum wage. A worker's earnings are the higher of the minimum hourly wage or his or her piece-rate earnings.

Piece rates are set so that the average worker earns more than the minimum wage to give him or her an incentive to work fast. However, employers do not have to retain workers who cannot earn at least the minimum hourly wage at the employer-set piece rate, so the combination of the minimum wage and the piece rate creates a minimum productivity standard. For example, if the piece rate is $20 to pick a bin of apples and the minimum wage is $10 an hour, workers must pick at least four bins in an 8-hour day to earn the $80 minimum wage. Employers may fire workers who are not able to earn the minimum wage.

The iron triangle between minimum wages, piece rates, and productivity standards is important because of the aging crop workforce. Minimum wages are rising in many states, such as to $15 an hour in California by 2022. If piece rates do not rise, workers must work faster to earn the minimum wage. For example, if the minimum wage is $15 an hour and the piece rate stays at $20 a bin, workers must pick six rather than four bins to earn the higher minimum wage of $120 in an eight-hour day.

If the piece rate does not rise with the minimum wage, the composition of the labor force may change to include only those who can pick fast enough to earn the higher minimum wage at the old piece rate. Piece rates should rise with minimum wages so that workers do not have to do more work to earn the higher wage. However, there is no database of piece-rate wages and productivity standards.

The basic federal labor law—the Fair Labor Standards Act—that sets minimum wages, child labor rules, and overtime requirements, has different provisions for agriculture. Youth 16 and older may work in any farm job anytime, and those 12 and older may work in non-hazardous farm jobs outside of school hours with the consent of their parents. Farm workers employed on farms that used fewer than 500 man-days of labor in any quarter of the preceding year are exempt from the federal minimum wage, and all farm workers are exempt from federal overtime pay requirements.[22]

---

21 Two 2013 California appellate court decisions, Gonzalez v. Downtown LA Motors and Bluford v. Safeway Stores, encouraged the switch. Gonzalez held that workers who are paid piece-rate wages must be paid at least the minimum wage when not doing piece-rate work, while Bluford held that piece-rate employees must be paid for rest periods required by law. Most piece-rate workers earn more than the minimum wage, so before these decisions, many employers did not pay piece-rate workers for waiting and rest time. See https://migration.ucdavis.edu/rmn/more.php?id=1939.

22 See https://www.dol.gov/whd/ag/ag_flsa.htm.

Some growers place roadside signs looking for workers.
Photo Credit: *The Rural Blog*,
http://irjci.blogspot.com/2011_11_13_archive.html

California and some other states adopted tighter standards, requiring that all farm workers receive at least the state's minimum wage and that farm workers employed more than 10 hours a day and 60 hours a week receive overtime pay of 1.5 times their usual wage. In 2016, California enacted legislation requiring overtime pay for farm workers after eight hours a day or 40 per week, treating farm workers the same as nonfarm workers.[23]

RETENTION

Most workers are employed less than a full year on a farm, which creates a retention issue of how to keep them during the season and induce them to return next season. Farmers often stress that farm work requires skills, emphasizing that workers must learn how to distinguish ripe and unripe produce and work quickly, so that two or more seasons may be required to be fully proficient.

Experienced workers may be more productive, but most farmers do remarkably little to retain them and to maintain contact with them during the off-season. One model employer, the Coastal Growers Association, gave letters to employees as they were laid off at the end of the season thanking them for their work, and sent them letters at Christmas advising them when seasonal work was likely to begin in the spring. Such written communications with employees are rare.

Crew bosses who hire workers also tell them when they are no longer needed. Even though many farms have payroll systems that would make it easy to identify the most productive workers, few acknowledge such workers in any public way at the end of the season, leaving even productive workers unsure if they will be recalled.

The usual attitude to labor supply and retention is similar to that toward water. Commercial fruit and vegetable farms in California rely on irrigation, and farmers in the past worked collectively to maximize supplies of available water rather than investing stretching water supplies on their particular farms. That is, they urged the construction of more dams and canals rather than investing in drip irrigation systems that provide water to each plant or vine. More expensive water has encouraged a shift from the collective to individual strategies to use less water, and drip irrigation is now common.

There may be a similar evolution toward the retention of experienced workers as wages rise. With fewer newcomers, many farmers are introducing bonus systems to retain workers for the season, and some are offering bonuses to experienced workers who return next season. Reliance on guest workers reduces uncertainty, as most arrive on the date specified by the employer and depart at the end of the season. Most first-time guest workers have no experience doing the work they are expected to perform in the U.S., but by returning year-after-year, their productivity rises.

---

23 See https://migration.ucdavis.edu/rmn/more.php?id=1995.

UNIONS

Farm worker unions were once described as "much ado about nothing."[24] Hired farm workers often receive low wages and find work only seasonally, but they have been hard to organize into unions for three major reasons: exits, contractors, and dispersion.

The most able farm workers who could be effective local union leaders are typically the first to leave for better nonfarm jobs, so that unions must constantly organize and educate the new workers who join the farm workforce to maintain their ranks. Second, farm worker unions have found it hard to raise wages and benefits for the workers they represent because the contractors who bring workers to farms make it hard to determine the reason for low wages; is it the Mexican-born contractor or the white employer with whom most workers cannot communicate? Third, farm workers are dispersed across many farms, making it costly to organize and serve farm workers.

There were major efforts to organize farm workers in the past, but there are no links between past and present farm labor unions. The first California farm worker unions had radical leaders who wanted to replace the employer-employee system with cooperatives (Industrial Workers of the World or Wobblies), or were Communists (Cannery and Agricultural Workers Industrial Union) who wanted to eliminate capitalist employers. In this clash of extremes between radical unions and conservative growers, there was often violence, and farm employers were able to rally local law enforcement against "outsider" union leaders, who were often arrested and jailed.

The AFL-CIO tried to organize farm workers in the 1950s, but this effort failed because English-speaking organizers signed up workers in a top-down fashion via contractors. Unions relied on strikes that could boomerang and help growers by only partially stopping production and increasing grower prices, and many unions were anti-immigrant and anti-minority. Cesar Chavez and the United Farm Workers were successful in the 1960s for reasons that

included charismatic leadership and a nonviolence philosophy that won the support of churches and other unions, tight labor markets due to the demise of the Bracero program in 1964, and boycotts that won widespread consumer support during the Civil Rights movement.

The UFW won a 40 percent wage increase for table grape workers in 1966, raising the usual wage from $1.25 to $1.75 an hour at a time when the California minimum wage was $1.65. Farm workers were not covered by labor laws that required government agencies to hold elections to determine whether workers wanted to be represented by unions, so the UFW sent letters to grape growers, asking them to sign contracts or negotiate. They refused, prompting the 1968–1970 grape boycott, one of the most successful union boycotts, as over 12 percent of American adults avoided grapes. By 1970, the UFW had contracts with most grape growers.

The UFW next turned to lettuce, bringing it into conflict with the Teamsters who represented the nonfarm workers who packed and transported lettuce and other vegetables. Instead of dealing with the UFW, many growers signed contracts with the Teamsters, which was lawful as labor relations laws excluded farm workers. The UFW soldiered on and in March 1973, claimed 67,000 members and contracts with 180 farms. However, many of the grape farmers who signed contracts with the UFW switched to the Teamsters as their contracts expired, so that the UFW ended 1973 with 12 contracts and the Teamsters with over 300.

The UFW battled the Teamsters and growers in agricultural areas, leading to thousands of arrests and convincing most Californians that a farm labor law was necessary to resolve farm labor conflicts. The UFW supported Democrat Jerry Brown, who became governor in 1975 and made the enactment of the Agricultural Labor Relations Act (ALRA) his top priority. Outgoing Governor Ronald Reagan supported a farm labor law that would have banned harvest time strikes and boycotts, but the ALRA allowed both, and extended more rights to farm workers than are available under the federal National Labor Relations Act to nonfarm workers.

---

24 Jamieson, Stuart. 1945. "Labor Unionism in American Agriculture." Washington. Bureau of Labor Statistics. Bulletin 836.
https://fraser.stlouisfed.org/docs/publications/bls/bls_0836_1945.pdf.

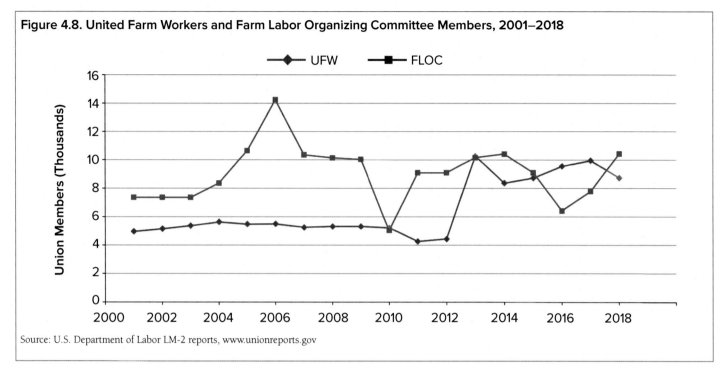

Figure 4.8. United Farm Workers and Farm Labor Organizing Committee Members, 2001–2018

Source: U.S. Department of Labor LM-2 reports, www.unionreports.gov

The paradox of the ALRA is that, after an initial flurry of state-supervised elections and perhaps 200 contracts, the number of unionized farm workers and contracts has trended downward. There have been many books and articles on the failure of Cesar Chavez and the UFW to transform the farm labor market, which they ascribe to four major factors. First, many blame Chavez, a charismatic leader who preferred idealism to administering contracts and was unwilling to tolerate dissent, as evidenced by the fact that the UFW has no locals to train farm workers as leaders.

Second, the Agricultural Labor Relations Board (ALRB), courts, and growers are blamed for frustrating the desires of workers to form and join unions; the UFW often enlists its supporters in the Legislature to disagree loudly with particular ALRB decisions.

Third, the structure of agriculture changed to make organizing more difficult. The UFW's first contracts were with conglomerates that also had farming operations, making them vulnerable to boycotts of their nonfarm products. Many conglomerates sold their farming operations in the 1980s, and the independent growers who replaced them often obtained farm workers via contractors.

Fourth, illegal immigration surged in the late 1970s and 1980s, and again after immigration reforms in 1986. New

workers streaming into the U.S. sometimes assumed that Cesar Chavez was the Mexican boxer[25] rather than the UFW leader. With more workers than jobs, it proved hard for unions to win wage increases.

There are two major farm worker unions today, the UFW in California and the Farm Labor Organizing Committee (FLOC) in Ohio and North Carolina. The UFW reported 5,000 members to the Department of Labor (DOL) for most of the past decade, but jumped to 10,000 in 2013 before dipping to 9,000 in 2014 and 2015 (Figure 4.8). FLOC's membership rose from about 7,500 to a peak of over 14,000 in 2006, and was 9,100 in 2015. Many FLOC members are guest workers brought into the U.S. by the North Carolina Growers Association.

Even though FLOC has the same number of members as the UFW, the UFW has receipts and disbursements much higher than FLOC (Table 4.3). One reason is that almost all FLOC receipts are the dues and fees paid by members, while some UFW receipts are from contributions and other businesses. The UFW, which requires 3 percent dues on the earnings of members, reported $4 million in member dues and fees in 2018, while the FLOC, which charges 2 percent, reported $600,000 in dues and fees. The UFW

---

25 Julio César Chávez, a six-time world champion boxer in the 1980s, is considered the greatest Mexican fighter of all time.

Table 4.3. UFW and FLOC Receipts and Disbursements, Dollars, 2001–2018

Year	UFW Receipts	UFW Disbursements	FLOC Receipts	FLOC Disbursements
		U.S. Dollars		
2001	6,629,050	7,160,500	254,232	204,549
2002	6,881,772	7,431,927	164,803	153,351
2003	6,716,966	6,608,412	187,094	157,989
2004	6,668,763	7,247,636	272,465	216,599
2005	6,710,469	6,774,191	490,343	445,295
2006	6,373,269	6,624,551	781,726	646,770
2007	6,196,231	6,073,440	514,507	681,084
2008	6,446,247	5,683,478	337,509	418,998
2009	6,446,247	5,683,478	613,712	514,974
2010	6,932,943	7,170,861	523,059	532,640
2011	7,221,571	6,620,104	439,451	442,573
2012	7,470,884	8,709,953	499,283	520,294
2013	7,119,904	7,396,471	528,081	588,295
2014	6,956,943	6,857,503	600,556	486,812
2015	7,191,804	7,270,396	509,136	461,029
2016	7,844,003	7,491,906	546,581	431,584
2017	8,535,023	8,399,684	785,973	624,120
2018	8,203,082	8,210,166	607,843	623,415

Source: U.S. Department of Labor LM-2 reports, www.unionreports.gov

in 2018 reported 7,500 members and 370 agency payers, while FLOC reported 10,400 members .Other unions also represent farm workers. The Chino, CA-based Christian Labor Association's Local 16 had 50 dairy worker members in 2015, down from over 300 in 2000. San Jose-based UFCW Local 5 reported 29,000 members in 2015, including 1,000 farm workers, while Salinas-based Teamsters Local 890 reported 5,400 members in 2015, including 500 farm workers.[26]

The Coalition of Immokalee Workers is a workers' organization, not a union, that negotiates agreements with the buyers of Florida tomatoes and other commodities. These agreements require the growers who produce these commodities to abide by the terms of a Fair Food Program that lays out worker rights, including making the grower responsible for compliance with all labor laws. Buyers such as McDonald's pay a "penny-a-pound" premium for the Florida tomatoes they buy, and growers pass this premium on to their workers. The Equitable Food Initiative (EFI) is an NGO that certifies farms as in compliance with its standards, including compliance with labor laws as well as food safety and environmental sustainability. The EFI operates in conjunction with the UFW, which says that unions cannot rely only on "collective bargaining to improve the lives of farm workers."[27]

Three major scenarios could unfold in farm labor over the next decade: status quo, immigration enforcement only, and an immigration reform that includes legalization for unauthorized workers, requires farmers to check the legal status of new hires, and makes it easier for farmers to hire guest workers. While consumer demand and trade affect the volume of FVH production, immigration is likely to determine how they are grown and harvested.

---

26 UFCW Local 5 has another 1,800 members in nonfarm fresh produce packing plants, and Teamsters Local 890 has another 200 drivers who haul produce from the fields to plants and are considered nonfarm workers.

27 See https://migration.ucdavis.edu/rmn/more.php?id=1978.

WHAT'S NEXT?

STATUS QUO

The status quo would see FVH agriculture continuing to expand in ways that create enough new jobs to offset those lost to mechanization and imports, so that average farm worker employment remains stable. The dynamic factors in the status quo scenario are the aging of the current farm work force and the absence of new farm workers except via guest worker programs.

Agriculture is akin to a canary in a coal mine in adjusting to fewer newcomers from abroad. After two decades of large-scale unauthorized Mexico-U.S. migration, farm employers became accustomed to workers appearing when they were needed. In California, many farmers turned to labor contractors to bring workers to their farms, and competition between contractors kept wages near the minimum and meant that there were few work-related benefits beyond those such as social security and workers compensation insurance required by law.

In response to fewer newcomers from Mexico, farm employers are pursuing four strategies: satisfy, stretch, substitute, and supplement. The first strategy is to satisfy current workers to retain them longer. This strategy seems to be working, as the NAWS finds an aging crop workforce employed by one farm employer for an average seven years. However, there may be physical limits to how long farm workers can continue to lift and carry heavy bags of fruits and vegetables in 100-degree heat as their average age approaches 40. A familiar aphorism says that it is hard to find a farmer under 40 because of the capital required to farm and hard to find a farm worker over 40 because of the physical demands of farm work.

Most farmers believe that the supply of labor inside U.S. borders is fixed or inelastic, so that higher wages will not attract or retain more farm workers. Instead, some are improving the training of first-level supervisors to reduce favoritism and harassment. Others are offering benefits and bonuses, such as low-cost health care to employees and their families or bonuses for staying until the end of the season.[28]

The second strategy is to stretch the current workforce with mechanical aids that increase productivity and make farm work easier. Most fruits and vegetables are over 90 percent water, and hand harvesters spend much of their time carrying harvested produce down ladders to bins or to the end of rows to receive credit for their work. Smaller trees mean fewer ladders and faster picking, and hydraulic platforms reduce the need to fill 50- to 60-pound bags of apples and oranges from ladders. Slow-moving conveyor belts that travel ahead of workers harvesting berries, broccoli, and other vegetables reduce the need to carry harvested produce, making workers more productive and harvesting jobs more appealing to older workers and women.

Under the 1942–64 Bracero program, most fruits and vegetables were picked into 50- or 60-pound field boxes, lifted onto trucks, and taken to packing sheds for nonfarm workers to prepare for marketing. Fewer workers and higher wages in the 1960s led to bulk bins that hold 1,000 pounds of apples or oranges and forklifts to move the bins. Conveyor belts for harvested produce and packing for market in the fields means higher productivity for workers and less handling of produce.

More can be done to raise the productivity of hand-harvesters. Trees and plants have been designed for maximum yields, not maximum worker productivity. Dwarf trees, talk-stalk broccoli that requires less bending to cut, and table-top production of strawberries, as in some European countries, could stretch a smaller farm workforce by increasing worker productivity. The time between development of new plants and their widespread diffusion is measured in decades. However, scheduled increases in minimum wages in major farming states have accelerated efforts to add worker productivity to the usual yield and eye-appeal characteristics desired in fruits and vegetables.

---

28 Bonuses of 5–10 percent to earnings for workers who stay through the season can be cheaper than raising wages to enhance retention, since they can be ended when not needed, while it is difficult to reduce wages.

The third strategy is substitution, or replacing workers with machines. Labor-saving mechanization is the story of agriculture, as the U.S. went from 95 percent of U.S. residents in agriculture in 1790 to less than 2 percent today. The production of the big-five crops—corn, soybeans, wheat, cotton, and rice—has been mechanized. There have been enormous labor-saving changes in livestock production as well, including robotic milking systems. Most nuts are harvested mechanically, with machines shaking them from trees and sweeping them into rows for collection.

Fresh fruits and vegetables have defied mechanization for several reasons. Many are fragile, and human hands are far gentler than mechanical fingers to harvest grapes or peaches. Machines that shake apples or pears from trees damage a higher share of the fruit than hand-harvesters, meaning a smaller share goes to market. Finally, machines are fixed costs and workers are variable costs—farmers must pay for a $200,000 harvesting machine whether there are apples to pick or not, while they do not pay wages to workers if storms or disease destroy the apple crop.

Raisin grapes provide an example of the difficulties of mechanizing a harvest even when technology is available. For most of the past half-century, some 50,000 workers harvested raisin grapes around Fresno each August and September, cutting bunches of green grapes and laying 25 pounds on paper trays to dry into raisins in the sun, earning about $0.25 a tray or a penny a pound.

Grapes are sugar balls, with 20 to 25 percent sugar, and harvesting raisins is a race between sugar and rain. Allowing grapes to stay on the vine increases sugar levels but raises the risk that September rains will damage the drying raisins. The longer growers wait until they begin to harvest, the more workers will be needed to pick the grapes so that they can dry into raisins before suffering rain damage.

There are new grape varieties that reach optimal sugar levels earlier in August, and allow the canes holding bunches of green grapes to be cut and the grapes dried partially or fully into raisins while they are on the vine. Harvesting machines use rotating fingers to knock the partially dried raisins onto a continuous paper tray in the vineyard until they dry into raisins or harvest fully dried-on-the-vine (DOV) raisins.

The harvesting of one-third of California raisin grapes uses some type of DOV mechanization, and the question is: why not more? Most raisin growers are over 60, have fully paid for their 20-to 40-acre vineyards, and are reluctant to make up-front investments to retrofit vineyards for DOV mechanization when China, Iran, and Turkey can produce raisins cheaper. Switching to DOV methods locks in costs, while hand-harvesting maximizes flexibility. Depending on the relative prices of wine and raisin grapes, farmers can wait until shortly before harvest to decide whether their Thompson Seedless grapes will be sold to wine makers or harvested mechanically or hand-harvested for raisins.

The fourth adjustment is to supplement current workers with guest workers. The H-2A program was created in 1952 to provide foreign workers for U.S. farmers and was used primarily by sugar cane growers in Florida and apple growers along the East Coast until the mid-1990s. North Carolina tobacco farmers became the largest users after ex-government officials created an association that, for a fee, recruits guest workers in Mexico, brings them to North Carolina, and deploys them to farmers. Turn-key and loyal H-2A guest workers proved very attractive to farmers, especially as the workers gained experience by returning year after year.

Receiving government certification to employ H-2A guest workers requires employers to satisfy three major criteria. First, farmers must try to recruit U.S. workers and provide reasons why U.S. workers who applied for jobs were not hired. Farmers convinced that most U.S. workers will not remain for the entire season often try to discourage U.S. workers from applying. For example, U.S. workers applying for jobs with the North Carolina association must be willing to accept a farm job anywhere in the state rather than near their homes, and some U.S. workers say they are deliberately assigned jobs far away from home to discourage them.

Second, farmers must provide free housing to H-2A guest workers and out-of-area U.S. workers. Housing is a special concern in California, where most labor-intensive agriculture is in metro counties that often have shortages of affordable housing and restrictions on building more. Third, the law requires that H-2A guest workers should not "adversely affect" U.S. workers. The government enforces this no-adverse-effect requirement by setting a

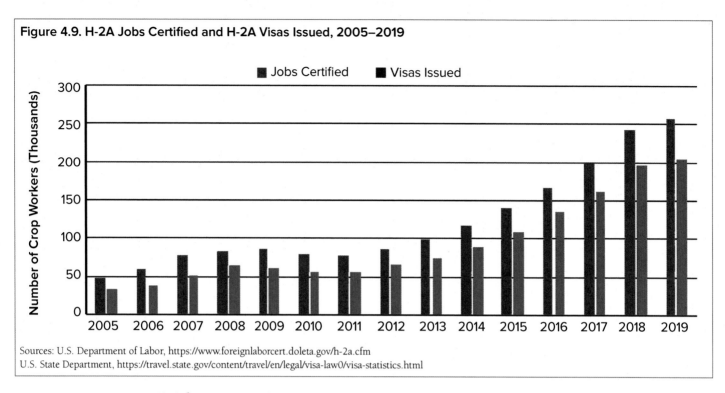

Figure 4.9. H-2A Jobs Certified and H-2A Visas Issued, 2005–2019

Sources: U.S. Department of Labor, https://www.foreignlaborcert.doleta.gov/h-2a.cfm
U.S. State Department, https://travel.state.gov/content/travel/en/legal/visa-law0/visa-statistics.html

super-minimum wage called the Adverse Effect Wage Rate (AEWR), which is $14.77 an hour in California in 2020, when the state's minimum wage is $13 an hour.

The H-2A program is expanding. Some 258,000 farm jobs were certified by DOL to be filled with H-2A workers in FY19, a tripling over the past decade. The top five H-2A states, FL, GA, WA, CA, and NC, accounted for half of the jobs certified to be filled with H-2A workers and doubled over the past decade to over 140,000 farm jobs certified by DOL to be filled by guest workers in FY15 on about 7,500 U.S. farms (Figure 4.9). The largest 300 farm employers with H-2A workers each requested certification to fill 100 or more jobs, and accounted for almost half of all certifications. H-2A workers are in the U.S. for an average six months, so the 205,000 H-2A workers in FY19 contributed the equivalent of 100,000 full time workers, about 11 percent of the 900,000 full-time equivalent jobs in U.S. crop agriculture. At its peak in the mid-1950s, Braceros were an average of 20 percent of U.S. farm workers. If H-2A workers fill the equivalent of 180,000 U.S. crop jobs, they would be 20 percent of U.S. crop employment.

Many of the largest employers of H-2A workers are associations and farm labor contractors that recruit workers in Mexico and move them from farm to farm. The North Carolina Growers Association is the largest association, bringing over 10,000 Mexican workers into the state to work on tobacco and vegetable farms. The Washington Farm Labor Association (WAFLA) is second, bringing almost 10,000 Mexican guest workers to the state that leads in fresh apple and cherry production. Many of the other large requesters of H-2A workers are labor contractors, including Fresh Harvest in California and Rodrigo Gutierrez-Tapia in Florida. Contractors must submit documentation to DOL of their arrangements to provide workers to farmers, but FLC-farmer contracts are not made public.

Some H-2A workers fill more than one job, so that there are more certified jobs than visas issued to H-2A workers. In recent years, for every 130 farm jobs certified, DOS issued 100 H-2A visas. H-2A admissions data published by the U.S. Department of Homeland Security are not useful because they record each entry, so that an H-2A worker living in Mexico and working in the Yuma, Arizona area creates an admission each day he enters the U.S., so that one worker entering daily for 60 days becomes 60 admissions.

ENFORCEMENT ONLY

Almost half of U.S. crop workers are unauthorized. An enforcement-only strategy of building a wall on the Mexico-U.S. border, requiring employers to verify the legal status of new hires, and aggressively trying to remove unauthorized foreigners from the U.S. would squeeze a farm workforce that is growing primarily via H-2A guest workers.

A combination of tougher border enforcement and better conditions in Mexico reduced the inflow of unauthorized Mexicans joining the farm workforce to a trickle, and it is not clear how much more a border surge or wall would prevent the entry of unauthorized newcomers. However, requiring all employers to use E-Verify, the internet database that verifies the legal status of all newly hired workers, could make it harder for farm employers to hire and rehire unauthorized workers.

Audits of the I-9 forms that newly hired workers and their employers complete illustrate the potential of more enforcement to disrupt the hiring of unauthorized farm workers. In June 2015, Broetje Orchards, a 6,000-acre apple and cherry grower in Eastern Washington, agreed to pay a $2.25 million fine for employing 950 unauthorized workers in 2014. Broetje is considered a model farm employer in the relatively remote area where its orchards are located, providing housing for many of its 2,000-plus workers.[29] The Department of Homeland Security (DHS) said that it wants to hold Broetje "accountable but not cripple its ability to provide jobs to lawful workers."

Many employers terminate unauthorized workers after I-9 audits and hire workers via the H-2A guest worker program. Gebbers Farms, a 5,000-acre apple and cherry operation north of Wenatchee, Washington, fired 550 workers after a 2009 audit. A year later, Gebbers was certified to hire 1,200 H-2A guest workers. School enrollment and population did not go down as predicted, suggesting that many of those who lost their jobs at Gebbers found other jobs in the area. Grocery store owner Esteban Camacho said: "Everything is back to normal. I think most of the people who stayed here wound up working somewhere else. There are a lot of the same people around."[30]

The third prong of an enforcement-only approach is to make it difficult for unauthorized foreigners to live in a particular place. Alabama (HB 56), Arizona (SB 1070), Georgia (HB 87), and South Carolina (HB 4400) enacted laws beginning in 2010 that required all employers to use E-Verify to check new hires and to have state and local police determine the legal status of persons they encounter. These laws were challenged as promoting racial profiling, and some provisions did not go into effect.

Unauthorized foreigners were expected to leave enforcement-only states and leave crops unpicked. For example, Georgia farmers led the opposition to HB 87, and complained of labor shortages when it was enacted. However, they continued to plant blueberries, a very labor-intensive crop whose acreage rose 40 percent from 12,000 in 2011 when HB 87 was enacted to over 17,000 by 2016.

LEGALIZATION

The U.S. has dealt with unauthorized farm workers before. In the early 1980s, as farm labor unions were weakening in California and farm wages were falling, the share of unauthorized workers was about 20 percent. Migrant advocates complained that unauthorized status made workers vulnerable, and growers said they preferred to hire legal workers, leading to the farm labor compromise included in the Immigration Reform and Control Act of 1986. IRCA's Special Agricultural Worker (SAW) program allowed unauthorized foreigners who did at least 90 days of farm work in 1985–86 to become legal immigrants, and the H-2A guest worker program was modified to make it easier for farmers to hire foreign guest workers.

IRCA did not work out as anticipated for several reasons. First, the SAW program's easy application requirements legalized far too many unauthorized foreigners. Once a worker presented a letter from a farm employer saying he had done 90 days of farm work in 1985-86, the burden of proof shifted to the government to show that the applicant was lying. In part because the government lacked investigators with expertise to detect false claims, over 1.2 million unauthorized foreigners became immigrants under the

---

29 Broetje opened a $6.7 million, 48-unit complex near Prescott in 2013. Each 1,400-square-foot unit can house up to eight people, with rent set at up to 23 percent of gross wages. Available at: https://migration.ucdavis.edu/rmn/more.php?id=1766.

30 See https://migration.ucdavis.edu/rmn/more.php?id=1550_0_4_0.

SAW program—perhaps the largest immigration fraud ever perpetrated on the U.S. government.[31]

Second, illegal immigration increased rather than decreased. There was relatively little border or interior enforcement after the enactment of IRCA, and Mexicans found it easy to cross the border illegally and obtain false documents to present to employers. With IRCA's general and SAW legalization programs granting immigrant status to 2.7 million unauthorized foreigners, 85 percent Mexicans, Mexican-born workers spread throughout the U.S. from bases in California and the Southwest. Farm, construction, and meatpacking employers asked these pioneering migrants to recruit friends and relatives, and both legal and unauthorized Mexican workers were soon a familiar presence in most states.

Third, the H-2A program shrank rather than expanded, as farmers found it easier to hire unauthorized workers, to whom they did not have to provide housing and pay a special minimum wage, than to hire H-2A guest workers. As the Florida sugarcane harvest mechanized in the early 1990s, the number of H-2A guest workers dropped below 15,000, and most were employed to pick apples in New England and herd sheep in the western states.

Farmers knew that half of their workers were unauthorized by the mid-1990s, a higher share than before IRCA was enacted, and tried to get Congress to enact an easy guest worker alternative to the H-2A program. Congress considered several proposals, but President Clinton threatened to veto any new guest worker program for agriculture and none was enacted. Instead, the election in 2000 of Presidents Fox in Mexico and Bush in the U.S. spurred farm employers and worker advocates to negotiate the Agricultural Job Opportunities, Benefits and Security Act (AgJOBS), an IRCA-like effort to legalize unauthorized farm workers and make it easier to hire guest workers.

AgJOBS differs from IRCA in two important respects. First, instead of the IRCA legalization that moved workers directly from unauthorized to immigrant status, AgJOBS would have given unauthorized farm workers a temporary legal status that could be converted to immigrant status only if the temporary legal worker continued to do farm work for three to five years, an effort to slow exits from farm work. Second, AgJOBS would have given farm employers what they want in a guest worker program, viz, an end to the requirement to try to recruit U.S. workers, an option to pay a $1 to $2 an hour housing allowance instead of providing housing, and a reduction in the AEWR to offset the cost of the housing allowance.

AgJOBS was not enacted, but in November 2014, President Obama issued an executive order to create the Deferred Action for Parents of Americans and Lawful Permanent Residents (DAPA) program. DAPA would have provided 4 million unauthorized parents with legal U.S. children temporary work permits, including up to 500,000 farm workers. However, Texas and 25 other states sued to block DAPA's implementation, arguing that DAPA was an unconstitutional overreach of executive power. Federal courts agreed, and the U.S. Supreme Court on a 4–4 vote in June 2016, allowed lower court injunctions blocking the implementation of DAPA to remain in effect.

Immigration provided one of the sharpest contrasts between Republicans and Democrats in the 2016 elections. Donald Trump called for a wall on the Mexico-U.S. border and the removal of "illegal aliens" from the U.S., while Hillary Clinton promised comprehensive immigration reform with a path to U.S. citizenship for unauthorized foreigners. The Republican platform opposed "any form of amnesty for those who, by breaking the law, have disadvantaged those who have obeyed it," while the Democrats asserted that "DAPA is squarely within the President's authority" and should be expanded.

Many farm and nonfarm employers expected Trump to make it easier to recruit and employ guest workers under the H-2A and H-2B programs, since Trump's businesses use these programs to obtain farm and nonfarm workers. However, there have been no major changes to the H-2A and H-2B programs as of Fall 2020. The H-2A program continued to grow as growers found the housing they must provide to H-2A workers, and employers requested two or three times more than the 66,000 H-2B visas available each year. Despite record unemployment rates, H-2A workers were deemed essential and allowed to enter the U.S. despite otherwise closed borders in Spring 2020.

---

31 Roberto Suro, "Migrants' False Claims: Fraud on a Huge Scale," New York Times, November 12, 1989. www.nytimes.com/1989/11/12/us/migrants-false-claims-fraud-on-a-huge-scale.html. Almost 300,000 applicants for SAW status were rejected, that is, they did not become immigrants.

CONCLUSION

The farm labor market is changing as fewer new workers arrive to replace those who age out of farm work or find nonfarm jobs. Amidst uncertainty over the future direction of U.S. immigration policy, farmers are pursuing 4-S strategies to: satisfy current workers, stretch them by increasing their productivity with mechanical aids, substitute machines for workers where possible, and supplement current workers with H-2A guest workers.

In this time of farm labor change, there are four recommendations for government action: better data, support for mechanical aid and mechanization research, a focus on worker-to-farmer mobility, and a strategy for FVH agriculture in a globalizing world. There are also perennial recommendations such as improved enforcement of labor, safety, tax, and other laws to protect farm workers, and more efficient spending of the over $1 billion the federal government devotes to improving the education, health, housing, and training of farm workers.

DATA

Farm workers are often seen through hazy windows. The various data sources are like windows into a room whose size and shape is not completely known. Some of the windows are large and clear, while others are small and scratched.

The NAWS provides the clearest window on who farm workers are, but covers only non-H-2A crop workers. With H-2A guest workers now filling 10 percent of long-season crop jobs, the NAWS window is shrinking. The NAWS portrays directly hired workers employed in non-harvesting jobs in fruit and vegetable agriculture who are settled and aging, but provides less information on harvest workers brought to farms by farm labor contractors. Expanding the NAWS to include H-2A and livestock workers, and redoubling efforts to interview harvest workers brought to farms by contractors, could improve the database for evidence-based policies.

More could be done with employer-reported administrative data. Much of the detail on earnings that is released each month along with the unemployment rate comes from employers who are paying their unemployment insurance taxes. Since farm employment is concentrated on large farms that must pay UI taxes, and major farming states such as California require all farmers to pay UI taxes, more could be done to study all workers employed on farms for wages, as was done to show that there were two unique workers for each full-time equivalent job in California.

RESEARCH

Federal and state governments spend over $4.5 billion a year on agricultural and food-related research, much of which is conducted at land-grant universities to raise yields and to make crops and livestock more resilient to diseases and pests. During the 1960s and 1970s, government funds were also used to develop machines to replace farm workers. A combination of rising illegal immigration that reduced employer interest in labor-saving mechanization and union-filed lawsuits charging that taxpayer monies were being used to develop machines to displace farm workers eliminated government support for mechanization research in the 1980s.[32]

Research is a long-term investment with an uncertain payoff. To develop crops that ripen uniformly so that they can be picked by machine, or trees that are shorter and vegetables that are taller to make picking easier, may require a decade or more. With newcomers pouring into the U.S. over the past two decades, there was little economic incentive to research crops that could be harvested mechanically or are easier to harvest by hand.

Incentives are changing to favor more agricultural research that considers the availability and cost of labor. The clearest signal comes from state laws that will raise the minimum wage to $15 an hour in less than a decade, so that employers can expect a 50 percent increase in the wages of hand workers. The immigration signals are less clear, and raise questions about how farmers should weigh trade-offs between investing in housing for guest workers versus investing in machines to replace hand workers.

---

32 In 2006, public-sector investment in farm machinery and engineering was less than $200 million, versus $1.5 billion spent on crops, $1.3 billion on animals, and almost $1 billion on environmental issues (Fuglie and Toole, 2014).

THE FUTURE

Almost all farm workers are Hispanic, and almost all farmers are white, making agriculture the closest to a U.S. "apartheid industry." Both farmers and farm workers are aging, and there are fears about the source of the next generation of farmers and farm workers.

American folklore imagined hired hands on family farms marrying the farmer's daughter and moving up the job ladder from farm worker to farmer. Such mobility was more myth than reality, but if the U.S. is to avoid having an agriculture dominated by landowners who rely on hired managers and hired workers, more could be done to help workers make the transition to farmer. Many workers with the expertise to grow crops lack the capital needed to become farmers, opening the possibility of farmers financing the sale of their farms to trusted workers and changing the face of farming. Governments could support projects that minimize the risks involved in such worker-to-farmer transitions.

THINKING STRATEGICALLY

China and India, with 40 percent of the world's people, are also the largest producers of many crops, including most fresh fruits and vegetables. However, the U.S. is the major exporter of farm commodities, selling twice as much to other countries as the No. 2 farm exporter, Brazil. The leading U.S. farm exports reflect comparative advantage, with soybeans, corn, and wheat leading the list, followed by meat-animals that is fed these U.S.-produced grains. Although the U.S. exports some fresh fruits and vegetables, primarily to Canada, none are among the top 25 U.S. farm exports.

The U.S. is likely to continue to produce most of the fresh fruits and vegetables consumed by Americans for reasons that range from high productivity to lower transportation costs. However, the production of some very labor-intensive commodities may shift toward lower-wage countries. Almost all bananas, most fresh asparagus, and many winter fresh fruits are imported, raising the question posed by Mexican President Carlos Salinas in urging the approval of NAFTA, "Does the U.S. prefer Mexican tomatoes or Mexican tomato pickers? Should the U.S. government continue to admit foreign workers so that labor-intensive commodities are produced in the U.S., or should the U.S. make it easier to import such commodities from abroad?"

REFERENCES

Calvin, L., and P. Martin. 2010. *The U.S. Produce Industry and Labor: Facing the Future in a Global Economy*. Washington DC: U.S. Department of Agriculture, Economic Research Report No. (ERR-106), November. Available at: https://www.ers.usda.gov/webdocs/publications/44764/err-106.pdf?v=41056.

Fuglie, K., and A. Toole. 2014. "The Evolving Institutional Structure of Public and Private Agricultural Research." *American Journal of Agricultural Economics* 96(3):862-883. Available at: https://doi.org/10.1093/ajae/aat107.

Fuller, V. 1991. "Hired Hands in California's Fields." *Giannini Foundation Special Report 91-1*. University of California Giannini Foundation of Agricultural Economics.

Martin, P. 2019. "The Role of the H-2A Program in California Agriculture." *Choices*. Qtr. 1. Available at: www.choicesmagazine.org/choices-magazine/theme-articles/the-role-of-guest-workers-in-us-agriculture/the-role-of-the-h-2a-program-in-california-agriculture.

Martin, P. 2009. *Importing Poverty? Immigration and the Changing Face of Rural America*. New Haven CT: Yale University Press.

Martin, P. 2003. *Promise Unfulfilled: Unions, Immigration, and Farm Workers*. Ithaca NY: Cornell University Press.

Rural Migration News. Quarterly. Available at: https://migration.ucdavis.edu/rmn/.

U.S. Department of Agriculture, Economic Research Service. 2018. "Farm Labor." Available at: https://www.ers.usda.gov/topics/farm-economy/farm-labor/.

U.S. Department of Labor. (n.d.). "National Agricultural Workers Survey." Available at: https://www.dol.gov/agencies/eta/national-agricultural-workers-survey.

APPENDIX: FARM WAGES AND PRICES

The U.S. Bureau of Labor Statistic's Consumer Expenditure Survey (www.bls.gov/cex) reported a total of 132 million U.S. "consumer units" or households in 2019. They had an average of 2.5 persons, 1.3 earners and 1.9 motor vehicles; 63 percent were homeowners and the average age of the reference person in the household was 51. Average consumer unit income before taxes was $82,850, and average annual expenditures were $63,000.

These expenditures included $8,200 a year for food, 13 percent of total expenditures. Food spending was divided between 56 percent or $4,600 a year—an average of $88 per week for food eaten at home, and 46 percent or $3,509 a year—an average of $67 a week for food bought away from home. The cost of food away from home largely reflects convenience, service, atmosphere and other factors, since the cost of food is a relatively small share of away-from-home food spending. The cost of food represents 35 percent of what is spent in cafeteria-style restaurants, 30 percent of spending on fast food, and 25 percent of spending in fine dining restaurants.

Figure 4.1A shows that other significant consumer-unit expenditures were $20,700 for housing, $10,700 for transportation, $5,200 for health care, $1,900 for apparel, and $3,000 for entertainment.

The largest food-at-home expenditures were for meat and poultry, an average of $980 in 2019. Expenditures on cereal and bakery products, $585, exceeded the $455 spent on dairy products. Expenditures on fresh fruits ($320) and fresh vegetables ($295) were $615 a year or $11.80 a week in 2019, and consumer units spent an additional $110 on processed fruits and $145 on processed vegetables. Consumer units spent almost as much on alcoholic beverages, $580 in 2019, as on fresh fruits and vegetables, $615.

Data on food spending by pre-tax income are available only for 2018; the 13 percent of consumer units with incomes of less than $15,000 spent 54 percent of their pre-tax incomes on food, while the 7 percent with incomes of $200,000 or more spent 5 percent of their income on food. Lower-income consumer units spent a higher share of their incomes on food at home.

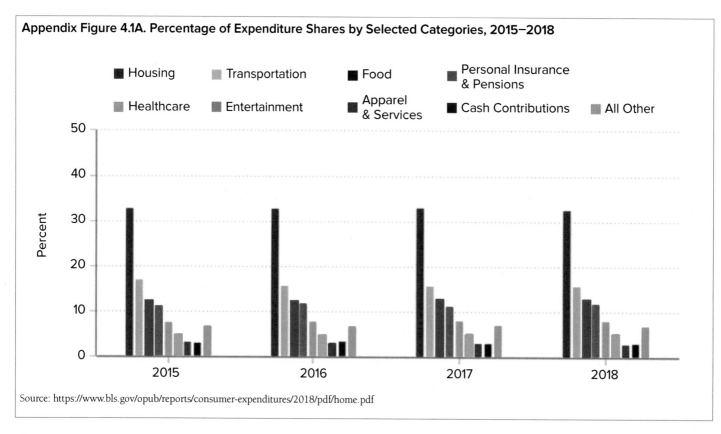

Appendix Figure 4.1A. Percentage of Expenditure Shares by Selected Categories, 2015–2018

Source: https://www.bls.gov/opub/reports/consumer-expenditures/2018/pdf/home.pdf

Appendix Table 4.1A. Consumer Unit Spending on Food and Fruits and Vegetables by Income, 2018

	All Consumer Units	<$15,000	$15,000 – $29,999	$30,000 – $39,999	$40,000 – $49,999	$50,000 – $69,999	$70,000 – $99,999	$100,000 – $149,999	$150,000 – $199,999	$200,000 and more
Number of Consumer Units	131,439	17,156	20,575	13,022	10,683	17,003	19,074	17,243	8,118	8,566
Share of Units (%)	100%	13%	16%	10%	8%	13%	15%	13%	6%	7%
Pre-tax Income ($)	78,635	7,604	22,316	34,729	44,763	59,313	83,370	120,778	171,314	320,317
Food ($)	7,923	4,130	4,628	6,077	6,286	7,168	8,753	10,854	13,195	16,392
Food Share (%)	10%	54%	21%	17%	14%	12%	10%	9%	8%	5%
Food at Home ($)	4,464	2,690	3,011	3,744	3,633	4,228	4,900	5,759	6,764	8,002
Food at Home Share (%)	56%	65%	65%	62%	58%	59%	56%	53%	51%	49%
Alcohol ($)	583	201	190	326	383	512	569	854	1,108	2,052
Fruits & Vegetables ($)	858	485	589	700	690	817	933	1,111	1,344	1,567
Fresh Fruits ($)	322	156	214	246	310	301	334	400	500	606
Fresh Vegetables ($)	112	61	86	82	103	102	113	143	174	196
Spending on Fruit ($ million)	42.3	2.7	4.4	3.2	3.3	5.1	6.4	6.9	4.1	5.2
Spending on Vegetables ($ million)	14.7	1.0	1.8	1.1	1.1	1.7	2.2	2.5	1.4	1.7

Source: Table 3 https://www.bls.gov/opub/reports/consumer-expenditures/2018/home.htm

Note: Spending on fruits and vegetables is for fresh produce.

Appendix Figure 4.2A. Share of Consumer Units and Share of Spending on Fresh Fruits and Vegetables by Pre-tax Income, 2018

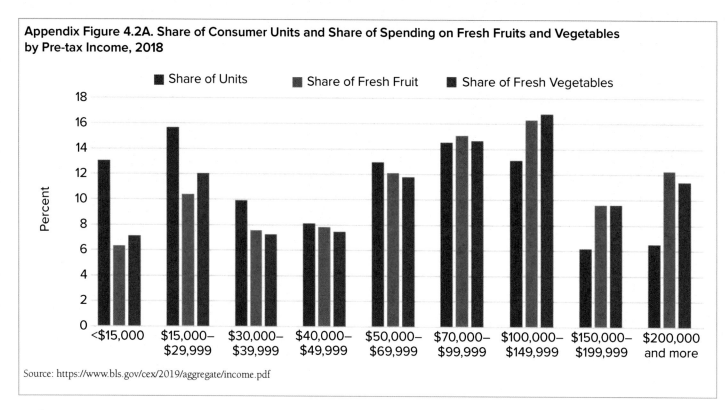

Source: https://www.bls.gov/cex/2019/aggregate/income.pdf

Higher income units spent more on fruits and vegetables, about three times more for those with incomes of $200,000 or more compared with those earning less than $30,000. Spending on alcoholic beverages rose with income as well; those earning $200,000 or more were the only group to spend more on alcoholic beverages than on fruits and vegetables.

Half of spending on fruits and vegetables was on fresh fruits and fresh vegetables. The leading fresh fruits by expenditure were fresh apples, an average $44 spent per consumer unit in 2018; bananas, $44; oranges, $32; other fresh citrus, $5;, and other fresh fruits, $149. The leading fresh vegetables were potatoes, with $45 spent per consumer unit in 2018, followed by lettuce, $30; tomatoes, $48; and other fresh vegetables, $172.

Figure 4.2A shows that in 2018, the quarter of consumer units with incomes of $100,000 or more, accounted for 38 percent of total spending on fresh fruits and vegetables. By contrast, almost half of consumer units had incomes of less than $50,000 in 2018, and they accounted for a third of total spending on fresh fruits and vegetables.

Farmers get less than 20 percent of the average retail food dollar, but slightly more for fresh fruits and vegetables.[33] Farmers received an average 38 percent of the average retail price of fresh fruits and 28 percent of the average retail price of fresh vegetables in 2015, the most recent data available. This means that average consumer expenditures on these items include $203 a year for farmers (0.38 x 320 = $120 + 0.28 x 295 = $83).

Farm labor costs are less than a third of farm revenue for fresh fruits and vegetables, so farm worker wages and benefits for fresh fruits and vegetables cost the average consumer unit $67 a year (0.33x $203 = $67). In fact, farm labor costs are less than $67 because over half of US fresh fruits, and a third of U.S. fresh vegetables, are imported.

Even though strawberries are picked directly into the containers in which they are sold, and iceberg lettuce is wrapped in the field, farmers and farm workers get a very small share of retail spending on fruits and vegetables. Consumers who pay $2 for a pound of strawberries are paying about 70 cents to the farmer and 30 cents to farm workers. For $2 worth of fresh field-grown tomatoes, farmers receive 50 cents and workers 15 cents.

---

33 www.ers.usda.gov/data-products/price-spreads-from-farm-to-consumer/price-spreads-from-farm-to-consumer/#Fresh%20fruit.

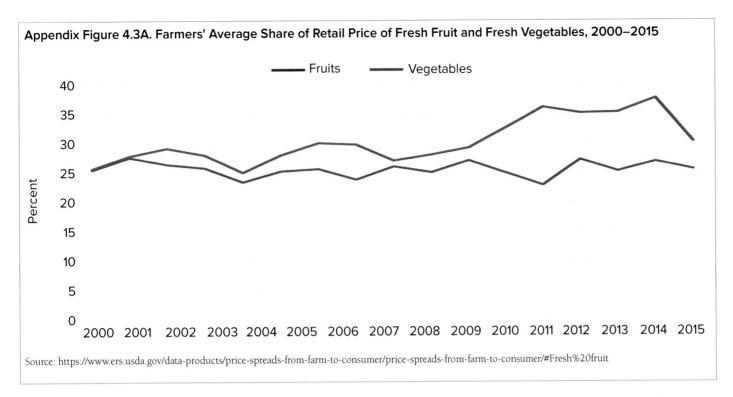

Appendix Figure 4.3A. Farmers' Average Share of Retail Price of Fresh Fruit and Fresh Vegetables, 2000–2015

Source: https://www.ers.usda.gov/data-products/price-spreads-from-farm-to-consumer/price-spreads-from-farm-to-consumer/#Fresh%20fruit

About half of the workers employed on U.S. crop farms are unauthorized. These unauthorized crop workers are aging and settling, making them less mobile and flexible. Farmers are adjusting to fewer unauthorized newcomers by substituting machines for workers and supplementing the current workforce with legal H-2A guest workers.

What would happen to consumer expenditures on fresh fruits and vegetables if farm labor costs rose, perhaps due to the introduction of E-Verify, the internet-based system that allows employers to check the work authorization of newly hired workers?

The closest natural experiment occurred after the Bracero program ended in 1964. Mexican Braceros were guaranteed a minimum wage of $1.40 an hour at a time when U.S. farm workers were not covered by the minimum wage. Some table grape harvesters, who were paid $1.40 when they worked alongside Braceros in 1964, were offered $1.25 in 1965, prompting a strike. Cesar Chavez became the leader of the strike and won a 40 percent wage increase in the first UFW table grape contract in 1966, raising workers' wages to $1.75 an hour.

What would happen to consumer expenditures if there were a similar 40 percent wage increase today? The average hourly earnings of U.S. field and livestock workers was $14 an hour in 2019, so a 40 percent increase would raise them to $19.60 an hour.

For a typical household or consumer unit, a 40 percent increase in farm labor costs translates into a 4 percent increase in the retail price of fresh fruits and vegetables (0.30 farm share of retail prices x 0.33 farm labor share of farm revenue = 10 percent; if farm labor costs rise 40 percent, retail spending rises 0.4 x 10 = 4 percent). If average farm worker earnings rose by 40 percent, and the increase were passed on fully to consumers, average spending on fresh fruits and vegetables for a typical household would rise by less than $25 a year (4 percent x $615 = $24.60).

A 40 percent wage increase, on the other hand, would raise the average earnings of seasonal farm workers from $14,000 for 1,000 hours of work to $19,600, lifting the earnings of a farm worker household of four from half of the federal poverty line of $25,750 in 2019 to three-fourths of the poverty line.

CHAPTER 5. THE EVOLVING NATURE OF CALIFORNIA'S WATER ECONOMY

ARIEL DINAR, DOUG PARKER, HELEN HUYNH, AND AMANDA TIEU

ABSTRACT

The California water sector faces many challenges and demonstrates the ability to adapt. With a water-dependent economy, the state of California's water sector is very vulnerable to external climatic shocks as well as changes in demands by an ever-growing population and dynamic agricultural sector. In response to these challenges, the California water sector continues to reform itself by introducing various types of waters, and developing regulatory tools to protect sustainable water use, water quality, and water-dependent ecosystems. In addition to the evolution of the technological, institutional, and agronomic capacities of the water-using framework, the state has seen changes in the perceptions and behaviors of its water consumers and decision-makers.

ABOUT THE AUTHORS

Ariel Dinar is a Distinguished Professor in the School of Public Policy at University of California, Riverside. Doug Parker is director of the California Institute for Water Resources, University of California Agriculture and Natural Resources. Both are members of the Giannini Foundation of Agricultural Economics. They can be contacted by email at adinar@ucr.edu and Doug.Parker@ucop.edu, respectively. Helen Huynh and Amanda Tieu are both undergraduate student researchers in the School of Public Policy at University of California, Riverside.

The California Aqueduct bifurcates to the East Branch (left) and West Branch (right) as it travels into Southern California at the border of Kern and Los Angeles Counties.

Photo Credit: California Department of Water Resources

CHAPTER 5. TABLE OF CONTENTS

INTRODUCTION

California has an advanced water economy. A comprehensive water distribution network connects its significant surface water and groundwater resources. California has complex institutional arrangements to regulate the amount of water used in each sector, with unique quantity and quality requirements that make it hard to maximize the benefits of water resources. Challenges such as population growth, rural to urban migration, and climate change are manifested in frequent, severe and prolonged droughts and the reciprocal relationship between precipitation (north) and population concentration and demand for water (south).

Figure 5.1 presents available renewable water per capita in California, using data on water availability and population from 1950 through 2050 (population projections for 2015–2050). This is a crude measure of water scarcity that assumes the amount of available renewed water in the state is more or less fixed (between 74,000 and 123,500 million cubic meters—60 million and 100 million-acre feet—per year, depending on the year (PPIC, 2016). A fixed quantity of available water for a growing population suggests declining available renewable water per capita. Using the simple mean of 98,400 million cubic meters suggests that California enters the zone of water scarcity around 2020.

Declining water availability makes water a subject for public policy debate (Hanak et al., 2011). This chapter explains the external forces shaping water availability and usage, including historical trends in water availability and consumption by sectors and regions, the effects of climate change, and changes in the socioeconomic conditions of the demand side. Policy reforms and external shocks have led to changes in perceptions regarding various types of water that were undesirable in the past—such as recycled wastewater. The chapter will conclude with a futuristic set of possible scenarios with implications for California.

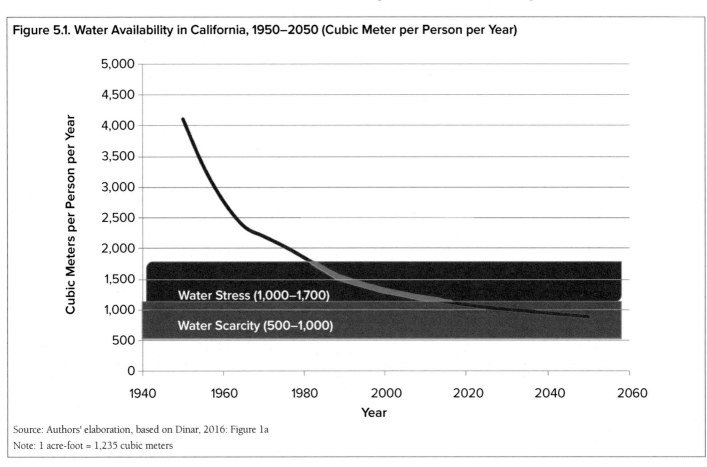

Figure 5.1. Water Availability in California, 1950–2050 (Cubic Meter per Person per Year)

Source: Authors' elaboration, based on Dinar, 2016: Figure 1a

Note: 1 acre-foot = 1,235 cubic meters

WATER SUPPLY/SOURCES AND CONSUMPTION BY MAIN SECTORS

California receives almost two-thirds of its water supply in the northern one-third of the state, primarily in the coastal areas and in the Sierra Nevada (Figure 5.2). However, most water is consumed in the southern two-thirds of the state. The major regions of water use include the fertile Central Valley, which has large agricultural lands, the urban areas of San Francisco, Los Angeles and other coastal regions, as well as the southern deserts. The water balance of the state consists of 246.7 cubic kilometers (km³) of precipitation and 154.2 km³ of evapotranspiration, which leaves about 92.5 km³ of available runoff for use. California also has 18.5 km³ of snow storage, 53 km³ of reservoir storage and more than 185 km³ of groundwater storage (California Department of Water Resources, 2016).

California's precipitation varies geographically and within and across seasons. Most precipitation occurs between November and April, concentrated from December through February, as demonstrated, using main water supply watersheds. The months of May through September see very little, if any, precipitation (Figure 5.3). In addition to seasonal variations in precipitation, there are significant variations across years (Figure 5.4), ranging from critically dry years to wet years.

Figure 5.2. Precipitation in California

Water Resources of California

Streams, Lakes, and Reservoirs

100 miles

Average Annual Precipitation in Inches: 1961–1990

- 180.1–200.0
- 140.1–180.0
- 120.1–140.0
- 100.1–120.0
- 80.1–100.0
- 70.1–80.0
- 60.1–70.0
- 50.1–60.0
- 40.1–50.0
- 35.1–40.0
- 30.1–35.0
- 25.1–30.0
- 20.1–25.0
- 15.1–20.0
- 10.1–15.0
- 5.1–10.0
- < 5.0

Source: Geology Café, 2014

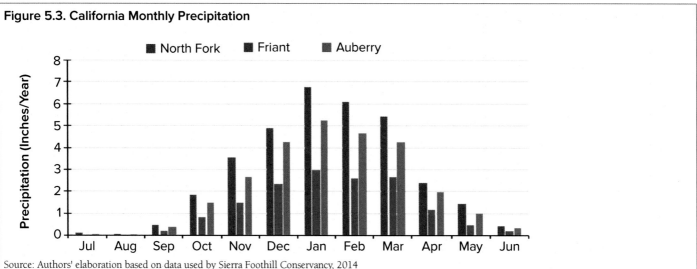

Figure 5.3. California Monthly Precipitation

Source: Authors' elaboration based on data used by Sierra Foothill Conservancy, 2014

Note: North Fork, Friant, and Auberry are locations of meteorological stations on a water reservoir/dam. North Fork is in Madera County, Friant and Auberry are in Fresno County.

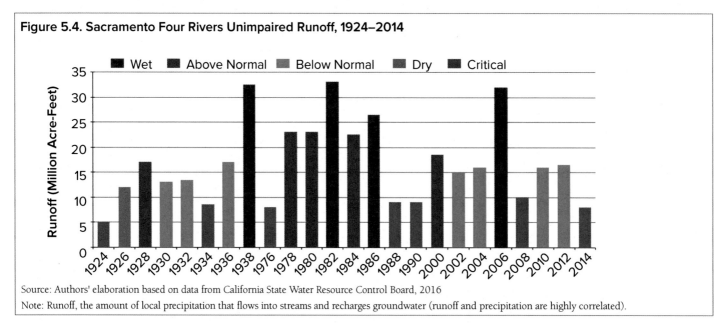

Figure 5.4. Sacramento Four Rivers Unimpaired Runoff, 1924–2014

Source: Authors' elaboration based on data from California State Water Resource Control Board, 2016

Note: Runoff, the amount of local precipitation that flows into streams and recharges groundwater (runoff and precipitation are highly correlated).

Dettinger et al. (2011) provide another illustrative measure of variability of water supply. They calculate the coefficient of variation (CV) of annual precipitation (Standard deviation /mean) for all measuring stations in the U.S. for the period 1951–2008. The eastern and central regions experience a low range of precipitation variability (CV ranging between 10–30 percent) while California experiences a wide range with levels of variability ranging from 10–30 percent in the northwest regions of the state to 30–70 percent in the southern regions of the state.

WATER RESOURCES

Due to the large spatial and inter-annual variations in precipitation (Figures 5.2, 5.3, and 5.4), California has developed a diverse portfolio of water sources. During a normal year, the state gets 47 percent of its water from local projects, 6 percent from Colorado River deliveries, 8 percent from federal projects, 3 percent from the state water project (SWP), 18 percent from groundwater sources, and 18 percent from surface water reuse (Figure 5.5). This diverse portfolio of water resources helps California to be resilient in dry years, particularly in areas of the state that have multiple water sources supplied by federal, state, and local projects.

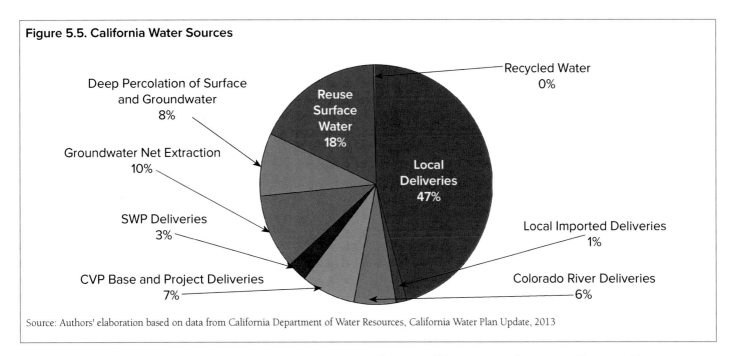

Figure 5.5. California Water Sources

Deep Percolation of Surface and Groundwater 8%

Groundwater Net Extraction 10%

SWP Deliveries 3%

CVP Base and Project Deliveries 7%

Reuse Surface Water 18%

Recycled Water 0%

Local Deliveries 47%

Local Imported Deliveries 1%

Colorado River Deliveries 6%

Source: Authors' elaboration based on data from California Department of Water Resources, California Water Plan Update, 2013

Water supply projects have created significant water storage capacity. The state currently has about 53 km³ of surface water storage, primarily in reservoirs along the Sierra Nevada and northern coastal regions of California (Figure 5.6). In addition, California has over 185 km³ of groundwater storage in the Central Valley, the Salinas Valley, the Santa Maria Valley, the Ventura Coastal Plain and aquifers in the desert regions. California also receives annual snowpack storage in the Sierra Nevada of about 18.5 km³ (California Natural Resources Agency, Department of Water Resources, 2014), which provides additional in-place storage in winter months. Many California dams are used for flood control purposes in the winter and early to mid-spring seasons, so reservoirs are often kept low to allow room for flood control, sometimes forcing operators to release water they would otherwise store. In the late spring and summer, reservoirs capture and utilize the melting snowpack in the months between May and August. One issue of significant concern to California is that increases in temperatures from global climate change are expected to lead to a shift in precipitation from snow to rain, and to early melt of the snowpack. Current models estimate that the snowpack will decrease by 30 percent, from 18.5 km³ per year to around 12 km³ per year (California Natural Resources Agency, Department of Water Resources, 2007).

SURFACE WATER FROM STATE AND FEDERAL PROJECTS

Due to the spatial and temporal variability in water supply, California has created one of the most complex water supply systems in the world. Local, state, and federal water projects are spread throughout the state, collecting, storing, and conveying water to demand centers.

The major local projects belong to the larger cities of the state and to some of the older agricultural regions. The urban projects include: the Hetch Hetchy water project that supplies water to San Francisco and parts of the Bay Area; the Mokelumne River project that supplies water to the East Bay cities in the San Francisco Bay Area; the Los Angeles Aqueduct that takes water from the east side of the Sierra Nevada to the city of Los Angeles; the Colorado River Aqueduct that moves water from the Colorado River to Southern California cities and coastal communities.

The State Water Project (SWP) delivers water from Northern California to farms in the Central Valley, cities in the Bay Area, and cities and farms in Southern California. The Oroville Dam on the Feather River, the tallest U.S. dam, anchors the SWP. Water flows from this reservoir into the Sacramento River and travels south to the Sacramento-San Joaquin Delta. Pumps move the water into the California Aqueduct, which carries the water over 710 kilometers south along the west-side of the San Joaquin Valley. It supplies water to several coastal communities through branch aqueducts and delivers water to farmers in the

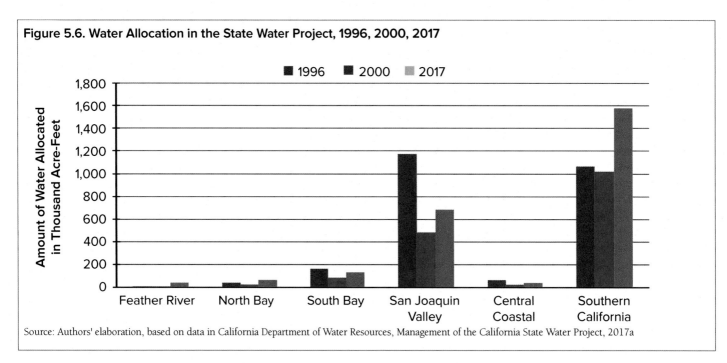

Figure 5.6. Water Allocation in the State Water Project, 1996, 2000, 2017

Source: Authors' elaboration, based on data in California Department of Water Resources, Management of the California State Water Project, 2017a

southern portion of the San Joaquin Valley; the remaining water is then pumped up 610 meters over the Tehachapi Mountains to Southern California agricultural and urban water users. The SWP distributes water to 29 locations. The project provides water for 25 million California residents and 750,000 acres of irrigated farmland; 70 percent of the allocated water goes to urban areas and 30 percent goes to agricultural areas in various regions of the state.

The Central Valley Project (CVP) is a federal project that collects water in Northern California's Trinity and Shasta reservoirs, as well as a series of reservoirs along the west side of the Sierra Nevada. The CVP also uses the Sacramento River and the Sacramento-San Joaquin Delta to deliver water to the pumps of the Delta-Mendota Canal, which also runs down the western side of the San Joaquin Valley parallel to the California Water Aqueduct. The Delta-Mendota Canal is much shorter than the California Water Aqueduct and ends at the Mendota Pool on the San Joaquin River, where the water enters the San Joaquin River and flows north back towards the Sacramento-San Joaquin Delta, essentially creating a loop. This allows the federal CVP to distribute water to many different places, mostly to farmers, towns along its route, and for wildlife preserves in the central part of the state. The CVP includes the Friant-Kern Canal, which moves water from the southern Sierra Nevada southward to Bakersfield, supplying communities and agricultural lands on the eastern side of the San Joaquin Valley.

Both the CVP and the SWP rely on the Sacramento-San Joaquin Delta to move water from north to south. This delta has become the linchpin of California's water system: the water projects move water from north to south in an ecosystem where water would normally be moving from east to west. Parts of the Delta are influenced by tidal forces, forcing the projects to release extra water in order to maintain low salinity levels in the water. Due to reduced flows, pumping, and changes in flow direction, there are several endangered species in the Sacramento-San Joaquin Delta ecosystem. In an effort to alleviate this problem, the state of California proposed a controversial plan to move water from the Sacramento River under the Delta to the pumping stations through a series of massive tunnels. If implemented, this plan would reduce the amount of water flowing in the Delta, but allow for more natural flows of Delta water in the east to west direction. It would also allow more tidal influences in the Delta, which might help to restore and improve the Delta ecosystem.

The Colorado River collects water from seven states as it flows from Wyoming to the Sea of Cortez. Allocation of the Colorado River took place through an interstate pact in 1922 and an international treaty with Mexico in 1944. The international Colorado River Treaty allocates the 20 km³ of water estimated to be available annually in the basin as follows: 1.85 km³ to Mexico and 18.5 km³ allocated among the five states in the U.S. side of the basin. California's allocation is 5.4 km³ of water (U.S. Bureau of Reclamation, 2016).

When first allocated, historic data showed higher flows in the river basin than current flows, meaning that the river is over-allocated and rarely flows through its natural course to the Sea of Cortez in Mexico.

The federal government operates several dams on the Colorado River, the Coachella Canal, and the All-American Canal to supply water to farmers in the Imperial and Coachella valleys. Through the Colorado River Aqueduct, Colorado River water is distributed by the Metropolitan Water District of Southern California to Southern California cities from Los Angeles to San Diego (Glenn Canyon Dam Adaptive Management Program, 2012).

California's water systems are intertwined. The California Aqueduct, the Delta-Mendota Canal, the Los Angeles Aqueduct, and the Colorado River Aqueduct share certain facilities where water is exchanged, adding to the resiliency of the system.

LOCAL PROJECTS

In addition to the massive federal and state projects, many cities developed local water projects for all or a portion of their supplies. These local projects supply water to coastal and Central Valley agricultural regions. We briefly describe a couple of these projects below.

THE LOS ANGELES AQUEDUCT (OWENS VALLEY AQUEDUCTS)

The city of Los Angeles developed a water supply plan to utilize both the SWP water and amend it with its own water projects, such as local groundwater supplies and the Los Angeles Owens Valley Aqueducts (Los Angeles Department of Water and Power, 2015).

There is a wide variation in total water supply and water sources to Los Angeles. Starting in 1992, recycled water has been increasingly used as a source for water supply to the city, although still a minute quantity.

THE HETCH HETCHY AQUEDUCT

Snowmelt from the high Sierra Nevada and water from the Tuolumne River at the Hetch Hetchy Valley in the Yosemite National Park serve as the primary water source for the City of San Francisco and several municipalities in the greater San Francisco Bay Area via the Hetch Hetchy Project, operated by the San Francisco Public Utilities Commission (SFPUC). The project provides annually 330

million cubic meters of water, which is nearly 80 percent of the water supply for nearly 3 million people in the region (San Francisco Public Utilities Commission, 2005). A map of the Hetch Hetchy Aqueduct and Water Supply System can be found in *Maven's Notebook*, Hetch Hetchy Water and Power System, (n.d.).

THE MOKELUMNE AQUEDUCT

The Mokelumne Aqueduct is a 95-mile water conveyance system that collects 450 million cubic meters of water a year from the Mokelumne River watershed for 1.5 million people in 35 municipalities in the East Bay of the San Francisco Bay Area. The entire infrastructure of dams, canals, pipes, and reservoirs is owned and operated by the East Bay Municipal Utility District (EBMUD) and provides over 90 percent of the water delivered by the agency (East Bay Municipal Utility District, 2015). A map of the Mokelumne Water Supply Project can be found in *Maven's Notebook*, Mokelumne Aqueduct, (n.d.).

GROUNDWATER SUPPLIES

California has 515 groundwater basins. Groundwater is an important source of water: nearly one-third of water originates from groundwater sources under normal conditions, and up to 60 percent during drought and severe drought years (California Natural Resources Agency, Department of Water Resources, 2015).

Groundwater levels in many regions of the state have been declining for many years (Figure 5.7). At the end of 2017, 21 groundwater basins were critically depleted, reflecting intensified pumping during the recent drought. Major groundwater declines occurred in the Central Valley—especially the San Joaquin Valley—and in the Salinas Valley and areas of the South Coast. (www. water.ca.gov/Programs/Groundwater-Management/ Groundwater-Elevation-Monitoring--CASGEM).

The Central Valley's aquifers are the source of irrigation water to many farmers. As can be seen in Figure 5.8, groundwater stocks decrease during dry years (white and gray areas) and increase during wet years (blue areas). Figure 5.8 presents a reciprocal correlation between surface water deliveries and groundwater-storage change in that aquifer system.

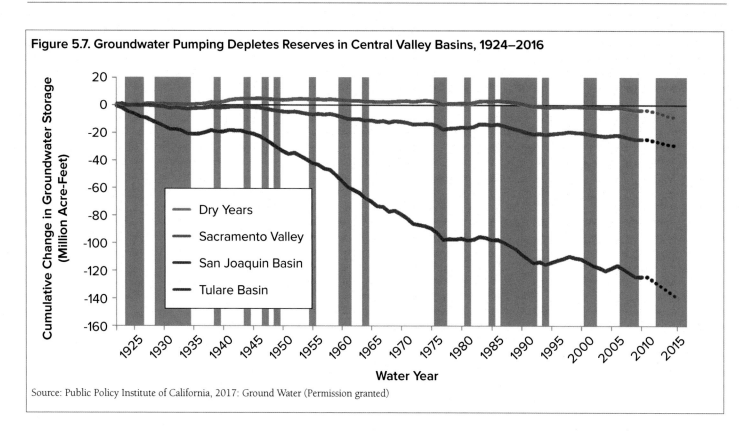

Figure 5.7. Groundwater Pumping Depletes Reserves in Central Valley Basins, 1924–2016

Source: Public Policy Institute of California, 2017: Ground Water (Permission granted)

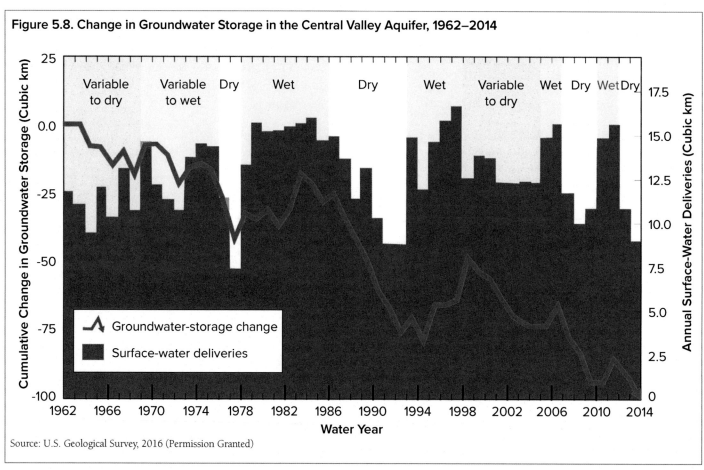

Figure 5.8. Change in Groundwater Storage in the Central Valley Aquifer, 1962–2014

Source: U.S. Geological Survey, 2016 (Permission Granted)

Table 5.1. Recycled Wastewater Reuse for Various Purposes in California, 2001, 2009, 2015

Year	2001		2009		2015	
BENEFICIAL REUSE	Acre-Feet/Year (Thousands)	Percent Total	Acre-Feet/Year (Thousands)	Percent Total	Acre-Feet/Year (Thousands)	Percent Total
Golf Course Irrigation	115	22	44	7	56	8
Landscape Irrigation			112	17	126	18
Agriculture Irrigation	239	45	245	37	219	31
Commercial	22	4	6	1	5	1
Industrial			50	7	67	9
Geothermal Energy Production	1	<<1	15	2	18	3
Seawater Intrusion Barrier	22	4	49	7	54	8
Groundwater Recharge	49	9	80	12	115	16
Recreational Impoundment	35	7	26	4	28	4
Natural Systems: Restoration, Wetlands, Wildlife Habitat	22	4	30	4	24	3
Other (Sewer flushing, misc. wash-down etc.)	20	4	12	2	2	<<1
Grand Total	525		669		714	

Source: California State Water Resources Control Board (n.d.)

Notes: Acre-feet (in thousands) are rounded values.

In 2001, Golf Course and Landscape Irrigation were grouped in a single category; Commercial and Industrial were also grouped as one category.

The declining water levels in the Central Valley's aquifers are severe but not unique. For example, as measured in nearly 3000 wells, changes in groundwater levels between spring 2010 and spring 2014 (California Department of Water Resource, 2015) suggest that water levels in most California aquifers declined during the drought years of 2010–2014. Sixty percent of the wells experienced a decline of more than 2.5 feet during this period, while nearly 15 percent of the wells, mostly in Southern California, experienced an increase in water levels (many wells in this category are in adjudicated aquifers).

ALTERNATIVE WATER SOURCES

In addition to the 'traditional' fresh water resources from surface water and groundwater, California also utilizes alternative water sources that are growing in importance.

California regulations require sewage treatment prior to disposal. The majority of the treated wastewater is disposed of into the ocean and other inland waterways with only a small fraction reused, 714,000 acre-feet in 2015

(Table 5.1). This volume of wastewater reuse represents a steady increase from previous years, but it is only 13 percent of all treated wastewater in the state.

Analyzing the use of recycled wastewater over time sheds light on the changing role this resource plays in California's water economy. Table 5.1 shows that between 2001 and 2015, agriculture's percent total use of recycled water is declining as other uses such as recharge of groundwater and irrigation of urban landscapes are rising.

California has developed limited desalinated ocean water capacity as an alternative source for residential consumption. Costs and environmental regulations challenge plans for expanding the desalination capacity in California. At present, there are a handful of desalination plants, most with a small overall capacity. The exception to this is the recently built desalination facility in Carlsbad, California. This plant has a capacity of 50 million gallons per day (mgd)—the largest desalination facility in the Western Hemisphere—enough to meet 7 percent of San Diego County's current needs. Many new plants are proposed

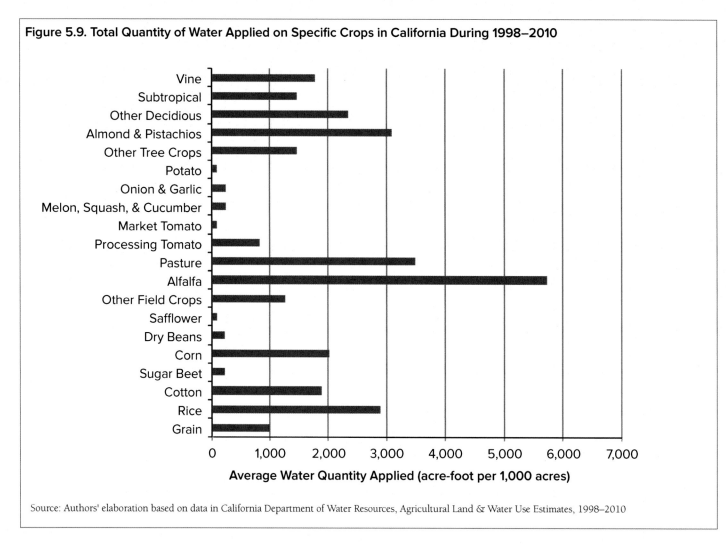

Figure 5.9. Total Quantity of Water Applied on Specific Crops in California During 1998–2010

Average Water Quantity Applied (acre-foot per 1,000 acres)

Source: Authors' elaboration based on data in California Department of Water Resources, Agricultural Land & Water Use Estimates, 1998–2010

and likely will be operational in the future. This information can be found in a map of existing and proposed seawater desalination plants in California (Seawater Desalination, Huntington Beach Facility, n.d.).

Desalination technologies are also being used to treat brackish groundwater for use in agriculture. Experimentation with solar desalination technologies demonstrated promising results for brackish water. There are significant brackish groundwater supplies in several areas of the state.

WATER CONSUMPTION

The allocation of California's water supplies are as follows: environmental flows take 49 percent (31 percent for wild and scenic rivers, 9 percent for to instream flows, 7 percent for Sacramento-San Joaquin Delta outflows, and 2 percent for managed wetlands), irrigated agriculture takes 41 percent and urban water use takes 10 percent.

AGRICULTURE

Agriculture is the largest user of water. California has over 80,000 farms with agricultural sales of nearly $50 billion per year ($53.5 billion in 2014). There are over 25.5 million acres of agricultural lands in California, including half in pasture and rangeland, and 9 million acres of irrigated cropland. About two-thirds of that cropland is in annual crops and about one-third of it is in permanent crops such as orchards and vineyards (California Department of Food and Agriculture, 2015).

Figure 5.9 presents the quantity of water applied on major crops between 1998 and 2010. Alfalfa, to highlight the most water-intensive crop, used 5,727 acre-foot of water per 1,000 acres of land during that period. Water scarcity has encouraged farmers to (1) adopt more efficient irrigation technologies, and (2) alter the mix of crops grown in response to changes in markets, climate, and water availability.

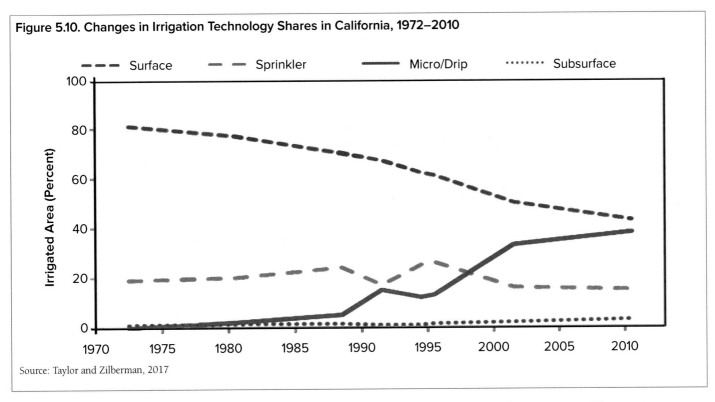

Figure 5.10. Changes in Irrigation Technology Shares in California, 1972–2010

Source: Taylor and Zilberman, 2017

In addition to changes in crop mix, between 1972 and 2010, micro and drip irrigation technologies usage increased from 0 to nearly 40 percent of the irrigated area. By contrast, surface irrigation fell from 80 to 40 percent of the irrigated area (Figure 5.10).

URBAN

Urban water consumption in California accounts for about 10 percent of water usage in the state (Figure 5.11). In recent years, agricultural and urban water consumption are declining, likely due to increased water prices, conservation efforts, public media impacts, and drought-related policies.

ENVIRONMENT

Environmental water usage includes four categories: water in rivers that are protected as "Wild and Scenic" under federal and state law, water required to maintain habitat within streams, water that supports wetlands within wildlife preserves, and water that is needed to maintain water quality for agricultural and urban use. Water use for the environment varies across California's regions, with variation between dry and wet years. Between wet years (2006) and dry years (2001), the share of water for the environment is reduced from 62 percent to 36 percent, while the shares of urban use and agricultural use increase from 8

percent to 13 percent and 29 percent to 50 percent, respectively (Public Policy Institute of California, Water Use in California, 2016).

HYDROPOWER

California has 287 hydroelectric generation plants (California Energy Commission 2008), mostly located in the eastern mountain ranges with a total capacity of about 21,000 megawatts (MW) (California Energy Commission, 2017).Hydroelectric generation is subject to variation depending on the year (wet versus dry) (California Energy Commission, 2017). It is hard to estimate the volume of water that runs annually through these power plants because their production relies on water in rivers and reservoirs that are subject to variation, depending on the water situation in that year. With warming climate and frequent droughts, the loss of snowpack and increased winter runoff diminish the high-elevation hydropower generation during summer months (PPIC, 2016).

Figure 5.11. California Dedicated Water Uses

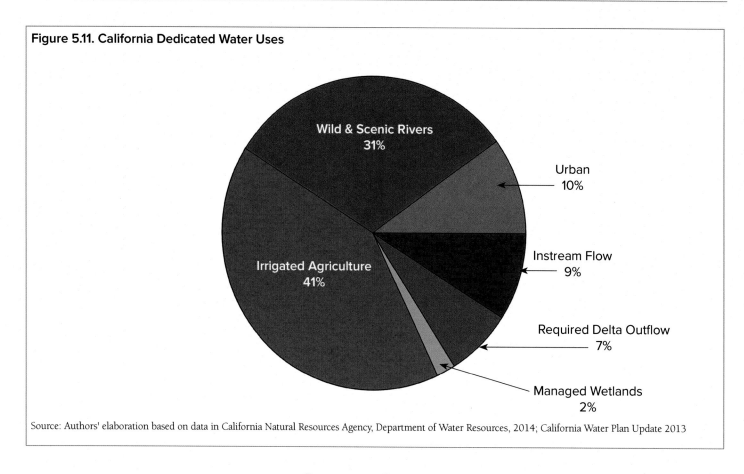

Source: Authors' elaboration based on data in California Natural Resources Agency, Department of Water Resources, 2014; California Water Plan Update 2013

CLIMATE CHANGE

Climate change will have a profound effect on California's water resources by changing precipitation patterns (California Department of Water Resources, Climate Change, n.d.) due to increased variability in 'atmospheric river flows' that affect snowpack and river flows (Scripps Institute of Oceanography, 2015). Such changes are expected to intensify in the future, leading to shifts in patterns of precipitation (more rain than snow), which are expected to increase risk of flooding, and pose challenges for a reliable water supply.

Climate change has already resulted in more variable weather patterns throughout California. Higher variability can lead to longer and more extreme droughts. The sea level is expected to continue rising, adversely affecting the Sacramento-San Joaquin Delta, the hub of the California water supply system and the source of water for 25 million Southern Californians and millions of acres of prime irrigated farmland. California is also expected to face warmer temperatures in the future. The increase in temperatures will cause snowpack to melt faster and earlier and increase

evaporation from reservoirs and from open water conveyance systems (California Department of Water Resources, Climate Change, n.d.).

CLIMATE CHANGE IMPACTS

California faces several climate-warming scenarios (California Energy Commission, 2006) that will affect precipitation, snowpack, and temperature. An increase in temperatures will: reduce the amount of precipitation that falls as snow; increase the amount that falls as rain; melt the snowpack earlier in the year; and, increase evapotranspiration in natural and agricultural lands, thus increasing statewide water usage by plants.

Precipitation is expected to change over this century. Climate models vary in precipitation estimates but the four most used models show a slight decrease in average precipitation between 1950 and 2090 (Cal-Adapt Data, Precipitation, n.d.). While the decadal changes in precipitation between 1950 and 2090 may be small, changes to

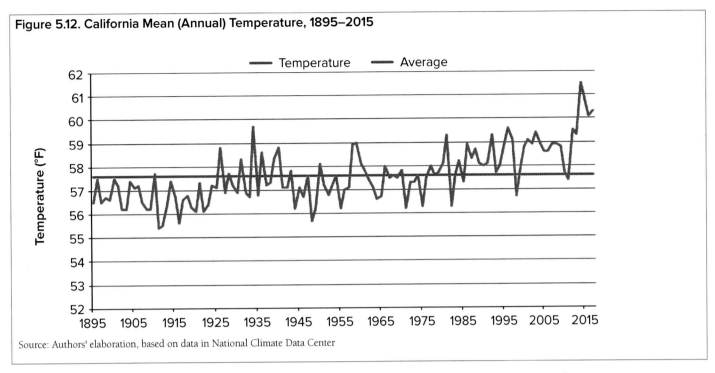

Figure 5.12. California Mean (Annual) Temperature, 1895–2015

Source: Authors' elaboration, based on data in National Climate Data Center

snowpack are expected to be significant (Cal-Adapt Data, Snowpack, n.d.). Change in snowpack above the state's key reservoirs will necessitate changes in reservoir operations and changes in surface and groundwater storage strategies.

The temperature in California has been steadily increasing since the 1970s (Figure 5.12). In addition to the increasing trend in temperatures, the spatial distribution of the temperature increases is also important. The greatest increases in temperatures are expected at higher elevations, where it exacerbates the reduction in snowpack and increases snowmelt earlier in the season (Cal-Adapt, Annual Temperature, n.d.). Increased temperatures in these elevations will increase water demand from mountain ecosystems (predominantly forests), which will further reduce stream flow and recharge to surface and groundwater storage systems.

The Sierra Nevada snowpack contributes a third of California's water. Drought reduces the snowpack, while wet and cold winters increase it (Figure 5.13).

Increases in temperatures can increase the frequency and severity of droughts. Figure 5.14 shows how the most recent drought in California intensified over time in terms of duration and geographic extent.

Impacts of the 2011–2016 drought in California were mirrored in depletion of both groundwater aquifers (see section on groundwater) and major surface water reservoirs

across the state. During this drought, precipitation was at a record low. Annual precipitation data from the 8-station index in the northern Sierra Nevada (California Department of Water Resources, California Data Exchange Center, 2017) shows the accumulated decrease in precipitation in California during the 2011–2016 drought. This prolonged catastrophic drought situation led California water policy makers to implement several regulatory interventions aiming to conserve water. These will be discussed in the next sections.

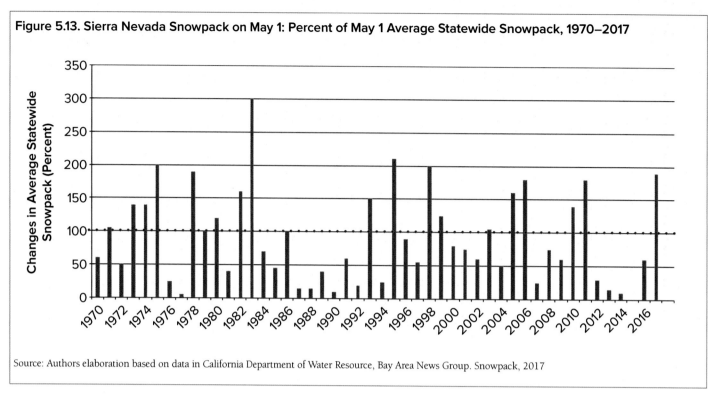

Figure 5.13. Sierra Nevada Snowpack on May 1: Percent of May 1 Average Statewide Snowpack, 1970–2017

Source: Authors elaboration based on data in California Department of Water Resource, Bay Area News Group. Snowpack, 2017

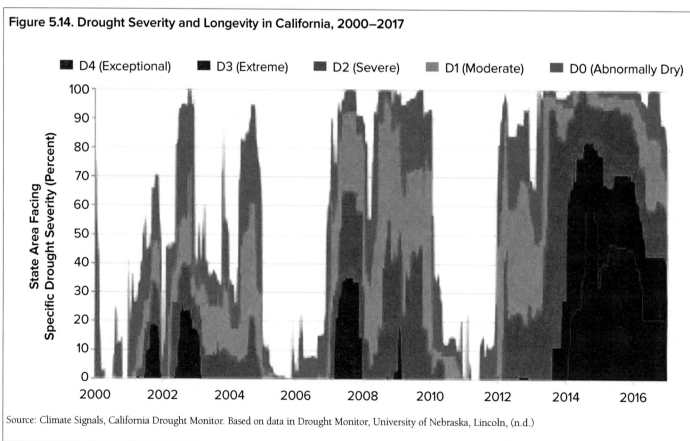

Figure 5.14. Drought Severity and Longevity in California, 2000–2017

Source: Climate Signals, California Drought Monitor. Based on data in Drought Monitor, University of Nebraska, Lincoln, (n.d.)

CHANGES IN DEMANDS FOR WATER

Several factors and processes are associated with changes in the water sector in California. First, California had a surge in population growth due to its relatively pleasant climate and increased job opportunities. Second, a rural to urban migration intensified over time, affecting demand for drinking water, need for treating sewage, and opportunities for use of recycled water. Third, there is a change to the crop mix, especially in regions facing higher levels of water scarcity. Lastly, attitudes are changing regarding (1) the importance of environmental amenities, (2) the sources and impact of climate change, and (3) the use of recycled water for irrigation of crops, of open spaces, and for recharge to groundwater.

POPULATION GROWTH

California's population doubled from 20 million to 40 million between 1965 and 2020. Due to population growth, water demand increases and availability per capita decreases. It also means that more sewage treatment is necessary, which implies a new water source in the form of recycled wastewater.

URBAN EXPANSION

The urban share of population has been increasing. Competition between rural/agricultural water users and urban users increases the need to invest in infrastructure to convey additional water and distribute it to new urban developments. Cities will also need to spend more on constructing and operating wastewater treatment plants.

Urbanization affects the environment and the hydrologic cycle. Urban areas affect the water cycle because paved surface areas (streets, driveways, parking lots) pick up pollutants and prevent rainwater from percolating naturally to the aquifer. Urbanization also has positive consequences, such as a concentration of sewage and economies of scale for using treated wastewater in the agricultural sector surrounding the city. Agricultural water users may give up freshwater to the city for treated wastewater from the city, a possible win-win arrangement.

In the case of California, urban populations increased from 50 percent of total population in 1900 to nearly 95 percent in 2010 (U.S. Census Bureau, Decennial Censuses Urban and Rural Definitions and Data United States, Regions, Divisions, and States, Table 5.1, 2010). This increase in urban population has significant impacts on the state's water systems. With appropriate policy interventions, the production of recycled water can reduce the demands on freshwater in the state.

CHANGING CROPPING PATTERNS

Market forces and water availability are major factors affecting planting decisions of agriculture growers. Droughts in California affect cropping-pattern decisions. Growers' perception and fear about future water availability makes them change their cropping patterns. Figure 5.15 presents changes in cropping patterns over time in three major agricultural counties of California. While all three counties saw an increase in fruit and nut acreage, Kern County witnessed the largest decline in field crops, while San Joaquin and Fresno counties experienced a decline in both vegetables and field crops.

PERCEPTIONS

California citizens have been involved in setting water policy priorities. A major component of the public support for, or objection to, certain policies is public attitudes, which change with exposure to scientific-based dialogue (education), and from environmental shocks (e.g., droughts).

One change in perception is the attitude towards reuse of treated recycled wastewater. A 2014 poll found that 62 percent of Californians are confident that it is possible to treat recycled water to drinking water quality standards. While this does not suggest an implicit agreement to use recycled treated wastewater for drinking purposes, such confidence indicates an easier path to household reuse in the future. Change in climate, having direct impacts on agriculture and water resources, is a concern to

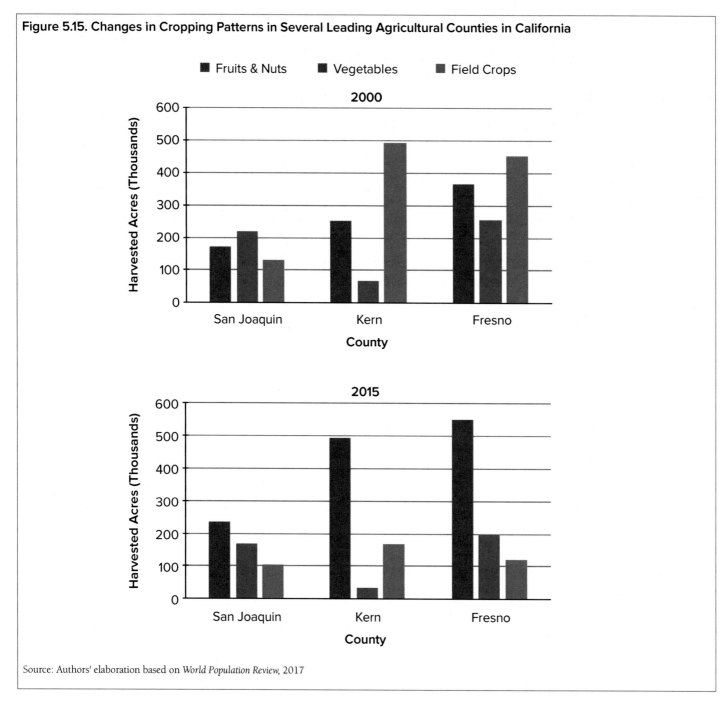

Figure 5.15. Changes in Cropping Patterns in Several Leading Agricultural Counties in California

Source: Authors' elaboration based on *World Population Review,* 2017

agricultural growers. A study (Niles et al., 2013) focusing on Yolo County growers suggests a range of responses regarding climate change interactions with agricultural production. The main findings suggest that 60 percent of farmers believe that the climate is changing and that it poses risks to agricultural production. These perceptions are expected to lead to behavioral changes regarding water consumption and technology adoption as part of the adaptation efforts of the farming community.

REGULATIONS TO REDUCE WATER USE

When facing severe water scarcity, California has had to consider changes to the way water is managed and allocated. During the 1986–1991 drought, an institution defined as the Water Bank was established to act as a water broker, buying and selling water-use rights from willing sellers to interested buyers (California Department of Water Resources, 1991). The Water Bank gave rise to water trading among buyers and sellers. The 2011–2016 drought led to institutional changes such as water pricing reforms, mandatory water-use restrictions (that are expected to be renewed independently of removal of the drought emergency), and the Sustainable Groundwater Management Act (SGMA) of 2014. These reforms are discussed in this section.

GOVERNOR'S DECREE TO CUT WATER USE (URBAN AND AGRICULTURAL)

"In January 2014, Governor Jerry Brown urged Californians to voluntarily cut their water usage by 20 percent to help preserve the state's already limited supply during this severe drought. But sometimes, asking nicely doesn't work. Between January and May, water use was reduced by a measly percent. Clearly, the voluntary approach isn't enough—water use is even up in some communities—and the state needs to take a harder line."
(*Los Angeles Times*, July 14, 2014)

Data on how Californians responded in the short-run (May 2014) suggest (*LA Times*, July 14, 2014) that water users in Northern California were more effective than water users in Southern California in meeting the Governor's decree. Analysis of the water districts' performance in May 2014 (compared to previous water years' use) suggests a range of performances contingent on the set of measures water districts had in place in addition to the mandatory water reduction, as follows:

- Districts with only mandatory water restrictions: –5 percent;
- Mix of mandatory and voluntary water restrictions: +2 percent;
- Voluntary water restrictions: +4 percent;

- Lawn watering limited to fewer than three days per week: –9 percent;
- Lawn watering allowed for three or more days a week: +3 percent.

Results for the longer run (November 2014) suggest (California State Water Resources Control Board, Bay Area News Group, 2014b) a statewide reduction of 9.8 percent in water consumption, with northern coastal regions reaching nearly 20 percent reduction, Central Valley regions reaching 15–25 percent reduction, and Southern California and desert regions reaching 1–7 percent reduction.

THE 2014 SUSTAINABLE GROUNDWATER MANAGEMENT ACT

During the record-breaking drought of 2011–2016, agriculture increased groundwater pumping by over 100 percent. In response to the increase in pumping, along with the recognition that for many areas of the state groundwater aquifers had been over-pumped for years, the state passed the Sustainable Groundwater Management Act (SGMA) of 2014.

SGMA requires local agencies to assess and manage groundwater use in a sustainable manner or the state will step in and improve groundwater management in the basin until local agencies can demonstrate an ability to do so themselves. SGMA requires local governments (including water districts) to work together to form Groundwater Sustainability Agencies (GSAs). These agencies were supposed to have been formed by June 30, 2017 (Table 5.2). Failure to form single or multiple GSAs that cover each groundwater basin forces the state to place basins on probation and require extraction reporting within the basin.

Once formed, the GSAs have differential deadlines to create Groundwater Sustainability Plans (GSPs). Critically overdrafted basins have until January 31, 2020, while high and medium over-drafted basins have until January 31, 2022, to create GSPs. Each GSP has 20 years from their submission deadline to achieve sustainability. Sustainability in the SGMA legislation is defined by the avoidance of six undesirable states:

Table 5.2. Sustainable Groundwater Management Act Timeline

Date	Deadlines
September 16, 2014	Groundwater management legislation become laws
January 1, 2015	Legislation goes into effect
January 31, 2015	California Department of Water Resources (DWR) establishes initial groundwater basin priority
December 31, 2016	DWR estimate of water available for groundwater replenishment due
June 30, 2017	Deadline to form Groundwater Sustainability Agencies (GSAs)
July 1, 2017	Pumpers in probationary basins must report extractions
January 31, 2020	Groundwater Sustainability Plans (GSPs) required for all high and medium priority groundwater basins in designated critically over-drafted basins
January 31, 2022	GSPs required for all remaining high and medium-priority groundwater basins
January 31, 2040–42	Basins must achieve sustainability

Source: Buena Vista Water Storage District, 2014

(1) Chronic lowering of groundwater levels indicating a significant and unreasonable depletion of supply if continued over the planning and implementation horizon. Overdraft during a period of drought is not sufficient to establish a chronic lowering of groundwater levels if extractions and groundwater recharge are managed as necessary to ensure that reductions in groundwater levels or storage during a period of drought are offset by increases in groundwater levels or storage during other periods.

(2) Significant and unreasonable reduction of groundwater storage.

(3) Significant and unreasonable seawater intrusion.

(4) Significant and unreasonable degraded water quality, including the migration of contaminant plumes that impair water supplies.

(5) Significant and unreasonable land subsidence that substantially interferes with surface land uses.

(6) Depletions of interconnected surface water that have significant and unreasonable adverse impacts on beneficial uses of the surface water.

Bringing basins into balance will require GSAs to raise fees, create reporting requirements, assess potential groundwater enhancement opportunities, and manage withdrawals. The GSPs that incorporate all of the above components must have measurable milestones and are subject to review and approval by the California State Water Resources Control Board.

WATER QUALITY

The Porter-Cologne Act of 1969 empowers the State Water Resources Control Board as well as the nine Regional Water Quality Control Boards to protect the state's water from degradation. Each board enforces water quality controls through Waste Discharge Requirements (WDR).

For the Central Valley, agricultural impacts on water quality are regulated under the Irrigated Lands Regulatory Program (ILRP), which was created in 1999 and expanded in 2012. Growers in the Central Valley are required to file individual permits for their operation or may join coalitions that pool permits and reduce filing requirements. There are 13 geographic coalitions across the Central

Valley, and one coalition entirely for rice production, that monitor surface water and groundwater quality and work with their members to avoid contamination.

The regional and state water boards are in the process of requiring growers to report nutrient applications to their respective coalitions. These coalitions will be responsible for collecting and summarizing this information. Ultimately, many believe that this reporting will improve nutrient use efficiency and reduce nutrient pollution. It is unclear whether additional nutrient-based regulatory restrictions will be imposed on agriculture.

WATER PRICING REFORMS

As the drought intensified and following the Governor's 2014 decree, many urban water districts revised their water pricing policies to signal the scarcity of water to consumers. A survey of 217 water utilities in California (American Water Works Association, 2005–2013) in odd years, suggests that the water pricing method used, in order of increasing efficiency and effectiveness, are:

(1) Other (non-volumetric such as per-household fee);

(2) Uniform pricing (same per-unit price for any volume consumed);

(3) Declining pricing (price per-unit of water declines with consumption);

(4) Inclining pricing (price per-unit of water increases with consumption);

(5) Budget pricing (households face inclining tiers, but first two tiers take into account the household circumstances and varies between households).

The results presented are quite interesting. First, more than 90 percent of the urban water utilities adopted more advanced water pricing structures starting in 2010. Second, a majority of adopted pricing schemes are inclining prices (Figure 5.16).

The severe drought, combined with the financial crises that hit California in 2008, led to re-introduction of "Water Budget Rate Structures" (WBRS) that allow utilities to achieve two important objectives: (1) send the scarcity signal to consumers, and (2) secure a steady and acceptable flow of revenue to cover the fixed costs of the utility (Dinar and Ash, 2015). WBRS were initially implemented by Irvine Ranch Water District in 1991, two more water districts in 1992 and 1993, and then none until 2008. When the financial crisis combined with the drought crisis hit California, the adoption of the WBRS began to surge and in 2011 there were 12 utilities using WBRS.

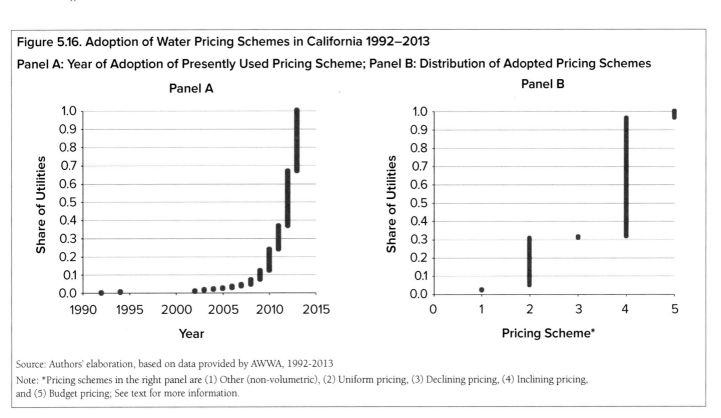

Figure 5.16. Adoption of Water Pricing Schemes in California 1992–2013

Panel A: Year of Adoption of Presently Used Pricing Scheme; Panel B: Distribution of Adopted Pricing Schemes

Source: Authors' elaboration, based on data provided by AWWA, 1992-2013

Note: *Pricing schemes in the right panel are (1) Other (non-volumetric), (2) Uniform pricing, (3) Declining pricing, (4) Inclining pricing, and (5) Budget pricing; See text for more information.

GROUNDWATER

Groundwater provides up to 100 percent of the water supply for some municipal, agricultural, and disadvantaged communities in California. Groundwater is the main source of water supply during drought years, reaching as much as 60 percent of the state's water supply (California Department of Water Resources, 2016a).

SGMA vests authority in local basin agencies to manage groundwater in a sustainable manner. However, SGMA does not modify water rights; it maintains the authority of cities and counties to manage groundwater according to their policies and ordinances.

Local groundwater ordinances are yet another regulation used for managing groundwater resources in California. Counties can develop ordinances to regulate groundwater management and groundwater transfers to destinations outside of that county (Milanes-Murcia, 2017).

With the intensification of the 2011–2016 drought, 30 of the 58 counties in California had ordinances in place to prevent water from leaving the county. The county ordinances have been identified and quantified as contributing to the impediments associated with water transfers in California, and could be one of the explanations to the question why there are so few water transactions in California (Regnacq et al., 2016).

WATER TRADING

Water trading is often touted as a potential solution to California's water supply challenges. Given current water allocation systems in California—a combination of riparian and appropriative rights—trading allows water to flow to its highest-valued use. Through a system of voluntary trades (markets), buyers and sellers exchange water. Market signals—prices—would ensure that water moves from lower-valued uses to a higher-valued one.

There are many complexities that must be overcome to create efficient water markets. Water itself is not an easily transported and measured commodity. There are externalities that markets can create. When water is traded, there may be local economic consequences (unemployment) as well as environmental impacts such as land subsidence and air quality impairments (from dust). This led California counties to introduce impediments that would prevent or reduce trades out of certain counties (see previous sections).

Water trade data between 1982 and 2014 (Public Policy Institute of California, California Water Market, 2016) suggest that permanent sales transactions were initiated in 1998 and remain more or less constant over time; short-term leases have decreased and long-term leases have increased over time. However, the total volume of water traded doesn't increase during dry years, suggesting that water markets in California have not emerged as a major

Table 5.3. Average Spot Market Prices During Drought and Non-Drought Years

Drought Years		Non-Drought Years	
Year	Average Price ($/Acre-Foot)*	Year	Average Price ($/Acre-Foot)*
2007	150	2006	80
2008	220	2010	180
2009	265	2011	80
2012	150		
2013	170		

Source: Based on data in WestWater Research, 2014: Figure 1
Note: * Calculations for $/Acre-Foot are rounded.

reallocation mechanism. While legislation was developed to boost water trading in the 1980s, it was not until the 1986–1991 drought that the drought water bank was established and 820,000 acre-feet were traded from northern to southern users. However, the quantities of water that were traded never exceeded 3–5 percent of the total water use in agricultural and urban sectors (Hanak, 2015, Regnacq et al., 2016).

Water sector institutions and local impediments are the main reasons for the inflexibility of the water market, especially during drought periods. Another factor affecting trade is the physical and institutional difficulties of moving water across different water projects. Therefore, the majority of the transactions occur between agricultural users in same project or projects in close proximity. Only in periods of severe shortage do trades occur over longer distances and between agricultural and urban users.

In an analysis of the distribution of short-term leases during 1995–2011, Regnacq et al. (2016) identify trades by proximity. The majority of contracts and volumes leased were between sellers and buyers in the same county, followed by buyers and sellers in a given region, and a relatively small number of contracts and volumes statewide.

A comparison of short-term trades (spot market water transfers) in California suggests that this trading mechanism has become one of the most important adaptation measures to address drought for users in the agricultural, urban, and environmental sectors (WestWater Research, 2014). Comparing the drought years to non-drought years (Table 5.3) suggests that market prices increased during drought periods and declined during non-drought periods.

CONCLUSION: DIFFERENT WATERS

The endemic water scarcity situation facing California has led to recognition of the importance of different types of water in the water equation of the state and of the importance of managing these waters conjunctively. This recognition is amplified during drought and water-scarce years.

Groundwater is valuable as a resource that is subject to natural recharge and a resource that can be artificially recharged and managed. The Arvin-Edison Water Storage District is probably one of the earliest groundwater management agencies in California (Arvin-Adison Water Storage District, 2003; Dinar and Xepapadeas, 1998).

Recently, with the increased duration and impact of drought in California, the state initiated several programs to promote management of aquifer recharge with various types of water. This management recognizes the value of groundwater that can be recharged during years of abundant water supply and then pumped in years with scarce supply. Wastewater is now considered a valuable resource rather than a public nuisance. Finally, desalinated water, as was discussed in earlier sections, has seen an increase in interest. All these types of water are discussed in this section.

GROUNDWATER

Groundwater is extremely important to California because agriculture and urban cities depend on it for their water supply. In an average year, 30–40 percent of California's water supply comes from groundwater, increasing to around 60 percent in dry years. However, groundwater is hard to manage because over-pumping can lead to groundwater quality degradation by allowing intrusion of poor-quality water from adjacent aquifers and/or from ocean water intrusion in aquifers close to the Pacific Ocean. The importance of groundwater will continue to grow in California as urban and agricultural demands increase.

Between 2000–2006, 248 managed aquifer recharge projects were submitted for funding to the State of California via funding propositions. One hundred and two proposed projects were awarded funding of $879.2 million (in 2015 dollars) (Perrone and Rohde, 2016). Data in Perrone and

Rohde (2016) suggest that, of the approved and presently managed aquifer recharge projects in California, a majority are from surface water, some are from storm water, and many are from wastewater and a blend of surface water, storm water, and wastewater. Two regions with major managed aquifer recharge projects are the Central Valley and Southern California.

WASTEWATER

As an increase in demand for water ensues, recycled water is becoming significant to the water supply of California. In some regions of California, recycled water is 7–13 percent of water used. In future years, California is planning to increase the use of recycled water. This will reduce the need for long-distance water conveyance, provide local water supplies, and be a drought-resistant resource.

BRACKISH WATER

Brackish groundwater can be used as cooling water for power generation, for aquaculture, for mixing with freshwater, and for other uses. The use of brackish water in California rose between 2000–2010 (U.S. Geological Survey, 1950-2010. Brackish Water, National Brackish Groundwater Assessment, n.d.). Although 1950–2010 data from the U.S. Geological Survey, cited above, reports brackish water use in few sectors (not including agriculture), brackish water is used by the agricultural sector through mixing with freshwater for irrigation of traditional crops, and for direct use in irrigation of biofuel plants (Levers and Schwabe, 2017).

DESALINATED WATER

Desalination is seeing increased interest as a potential water supply. Due to the high cost of desalination of seawater and brackish water, this process is used infrequently. However, with population growth in California, the likely effects of climate change on severity and duration of drought, and projections of reductions in the cost of desalination (Water Reuse Association, 2012), this technology could become a more attractive option for California in the not too distant future.

FUTURE WATER RESOURCES

There is no single silver bullet to meet California's current and future water challenges. Instead, we must move forward with the existing set of institutions, infrastructure, management choices, and technologies while investing in innovative approaches to meet future needs. California's water challenges span the four major areas of water management and use: surface water supplies, groundwater supplies, surface water quality, and groundwater quality. While each challenge has unique features, they all have overlapping interactions that require managers to address water from a holistic perspective.

REFERENCES

American Water Works Association. 2005-2013. *Dataset of Water Rate Survey*. Personal Communication with Mr. Sudhir Pardiwala on 8/6/14.

Arvin-Edison Water Storage District and Provost & Pritchard Inc. 2003. *Arvin-Edison Water Storage District Groundwater Management Plan*. Available at: http://www.water.ca.gov/groundwater/docs/GWMP/TL-2_Arvin-EdisonWSD_GWMP_2003.pdf.

Buena Vista Water Storage District. 2014. *Sustainable Groundwater Management Act Timeline*. Available at: http://www.bvh2o.com/SGMA/SGMA%20Timeline.pdf.

Cal-Adapt. (n.d.). "Snowpack: Decadal Averages Map." Available at: http://v1.cal-adapt.org/snowpack/decadal/.

———. (n.d.). "Precipitation Decadal Averages Map." Available at: http://v1.cal-adapt.org/precip/decadal/.

———. (n.d.). "Annual Temperature: Decadal Averages Map." Available at: http://v1.cal-adapt.org/temperature/decadal/.

California Department of Food and Agriculture. 2015. *California Agricultural Statistics Review 2014-2015*. Available at: https://www.cdfa.ca.gov/statistics/PDFs/2015Report.pdf.

California Department of Water Resources. 1991. "The 1991 Drought Water Bank." *DWR Report 10_1991*. Available at: http://www.water.ca.gov/waterconditions/docs/10_1991-water_bank.pdf.

California Department of Water Resources. 2014. *CASGEM Groundwater Basin Prioritization*. Available at: http://www.water.ca.gov/groundwater/casgem/pdfs/CASGEM_BasinPrioritization_Statewide.pdf.

———. 1998-2010. "Agricultural Land & Water Use Estimates." Available at: https://www.water.ca.gov/Programs/Water-Use-And-Efficiency/Land-And-Water-Use/Agricultural-Land-And-Water-Use-Estimates.

———. 2015. *Sustainable Groundwater Management Program, Draft Strategic Plan, March 9, 2015*. Available at: https://www.water.ca.gov/LegacyFiles/groundwater/sgm/pdfs/DWR_GSP_DraftStrategicPlanMarch2015.pdf.

———. 2016. *Bulletin 118 Interim Update 2016*. Available at: https://www.water.ca.gov/Programs/Groundwater-Management/Bulletin-118.

———. 2017. "Biggest May 1 Sierra Nevada Snowpack Since 1998 Raises Flood Risk." *The Mercury News*, May 1. Available at: http://www.mercurynews.com/2017/05/01/may-1-sierra-nevada-snowpack-is-biggest-since-1998/.

———. 2017a. *Management of the California State Water Project, Bulletin 132-16, June 2017*. Available at: https://www.water.ca.gov/LegacyFiles/swpao/docs/bulletins/bulletin132/Bulletin132-16.pdf.

———. 2017b. "North Sierra Precipitation: 8-Station Index." *California Data Exchange Center*. Available at: http://cdec.water.ca.gov/cgi-progs/products/PLOT_ESI.pdf.

———. (n.d.). "Climate Change." Available at: https://www.water.ca.gov/Programs/All-Programs/Climate-Change-Program/Climate-Change-and-Water.

California Energy Commission. 2006. *Scenarios of Climate Change in California: An Overview*. White Paper. Available at: http://www.energy.ca.gov/2005publications/CEC-500-2005-186/CEC-500-2005-186-SF.PDF.

———. 2008. "California Hydroelectric Power Projects." Available at: http://animalsciencey.ucdavis.edu/PulsedFlow/hydro.htm.

———. 2017. Hydroelectric Power in California. Available at: http://www.energy.ca.gov/hydroelectric/.

California Natural Resources Agency: Department of Water Resources. 2007. *Climate Change in California*. Available at: www.water.ca.gov/climatechange/docs/062807factsheet.pdf.

———. 2014. "California Water Plan Update 2013." Available at: https://www.water.ca.gov/Programs/California-Water-Plan.

———. 2014. *California Water Plan Update 2013: Investing in Innovation and Infrastructure*. Available at: https://www.water.ca.gov/-/media/DWR-Website/Web-Pages/Programs/California-Water-Plan/Water-Plan-Updates/Files/Update-2013/Water-Plan-Update-2013-Highlights.pdf.

———. 2015. *California's Groundwater Update 2013: A Compilation of Enhanced Content for California Water Plan Update*. Available at: https://www.water.ca.gov/LegacyFiles/waterplan/docs/groundwater/update2013/GWU2013_FrontMatter_TOC_Final.pdf.

California Public Utilities Commission. 2016. *What Will Be the Cost of Future Sources of Water for California?* Available at: http://www.cpuc.ca.gov/uploadedFiles/CPUC_Public_Website/Content/About_Us/Organization/Divisions/Policy_and_Planning/PPD_Work/PPD_Work_Products_(2014_forward)/PPD%20-%20Production%20costs%20for%20new%20water.pdf.

California Water Resources Control Board. 2014a. *Financial, Environmental, and Social Factors of Water Reuse.* Available at: https://www.waterboards.ca.gov/water_issues/programs/water_recycling_policy/docs/wr_research/minton_triple_bottom_line.pdf.

———. 2014b. "Who Saved the Most Water?" *The Mercury News.*

———. 2015. *California Recycled Water Use in 2015.* Available at: http://www.water.ca.gov/recycling/docs/2015RecycledWaterSurveySummary_SIunits.pdf.

———. 2016. *Sacramento Four River Unpaired Runoff 1906 Thru 2015 Water-Years.* Available at: https://www.waterboards.ca.gov/waterrights/water_issues/programs/bay_delta/california_waterfix/exhibits/docs/PPorgans/porgans_104.pdf.

———. (n.d.). "Municipal Wastewater Recycling Survey." Available at: https://www.waterboards.ca.gov/water_issues/programs/grants_loans/water_recycling/munirec.shtml.

Climate Signals. (n.d.). "California Drought Monitor." Based on data in Drought Monitor, University of Nebraska, Lincoln. Available at: http://droughtmonitor.unl.edu/Data/DataTables.aspx. http://www.climatesignals.org/resources/graph-california-drought-monitor-statistics-graph-2011-2016.

Dettinger, M., D., F.M. Ralph, T. Das, P.J. Neiman, and D.R. Cayan. 2011. "Atmospheric Rivers, Floods and the Water Resources of California." *Water*, 2011(3): 445-478; doi:10.3390/w3020445.

Dinar, A. and A. Xepapadeas. 1998. "Regulating Water Quantity and Quality in Irrigated Agriculture." *Journal of Environmental Management* 54(4): 273-289.

Dinar, A. and T. Ash. 2015. "Water Budget Rate Structure: Experiences from Several Urban Utilities in Southern California." In Lago, M., J. Mysiak, C. Mario Gómez, G. Delacámara and A. Maziotis (eds.), *Use of Economic Instruments in Water Policy: Insights from International Experience*, Berlin: Springer, 2015, pp. 147-170.

Dinar, A. 2016. "Dealing with Water Scarcity: Need for Economy-Wide Considerations and Institutions." *Choices* 31(3). Available at: http://www.choicesmagazine.org/choices-magazine/theme-articles/theme-overview-water-scarcity-food-production-and-environmental-sustainabilitycan-policy-make-sense/dealing-with-water-scarcity-need-for-economy-wide-considerations-and-institutions.

East Bay Municipal Water District. 2015. *Biennial Budget Fiscal Years 2016 & 2017, District Overview, Water System Budget, Wastewater System Budget.* Available at: http://www.mwdh2o.com/PDF%202016%20Background%20Materials/East%20Bay%20Municipal%20Utility%20District%202016-17.pdf.

Geology Café. 2014. "California Precipitation Map." Available at: http://geologycafe.com/california/maps/california_precipitation&relief2.htm.

Glenn Canyon Dam Adaptive Management Program. 2012. "Colorado River Basin Map." Available at: http://gcdamp.com/index.php?title=File:Colorado_River_Basin-_MAP-_CRBC-_Chris_Harris.jpg.

Hanak, E., J. Lund, A. Dinar, B. Gray, R. Howitt, J. Mount, P. Moyle, B. Thompson. 2011. *Managing California's Water: From Conflict to Reconciliation.* San Francisco: Public Policy Institute of California.

Hanak, E. 2015. "A Californian Postcard: Lessons for a Maturing Water Market." In K. Burnett, R.E. Howitt, J. Roumasset and C.Wada (eds.), Routledge *Handbook of Water Economics and Institutions.* New York: Routledge, pp. 253-280.

Los Angeles Department of Water and Power. 2015. *2015 Urban Water Management Plan.* Los Angeles, CA, June. Available at: https://www.ladwp.com/ladwp/faces/wcnav_externalId/a-w-sos-uwmp;jsessionid=fHdhhf4N1byLd4QnT2Rbh0knRKDs3ByDPxJq4DKT9cM3cY2DMQhK!-900998625?_afrLoop=918125337433954&_afrWindowMode=0&_afrWindowId=null#%40%3F_afrWindowId%3Dnull%26afrLoop%3D918125337433954%26afrWindowMode%3D0%26_adf.ctrl-state%3Ddmxwq8w4d_4.

Los Angeles Times. 2014. *Water Conservation in California.* Available at: http://www.latimes.com/opinion/editorials/la-ed-water-conservation-20140711-story.html.

Levers, L. and K. Schwabe. 2017. "Biofuel as an Integrated Farm Drainage Management Crop: A Bioeconomic Analysis." *Water Resources Research* 53:2940-2955, DOI: 10.1002/2016WR019773.

Maven's Notebook, (n.d.). "Hetch Hetchy Water and Power System." Available at: https://mavensnotebook.com/the-notebook-file-cabinet/californias-water-systems/hetch-hetchy-aqueduct/.

———. (n.d.). "Ebmud Water Supply: Ebmud Mokelumne Aqueducts." Available at: https://mavensnotebook.com/wp-content/uploads/2014/08/EBMUD-Map.jpg.

Milanes-Murcia, M. 2017. "Transferring Groundwater among Counties in California: A Legal Approach." Unpublished, draft mimeo, under review. Permission to use granted by author on November 24, 2017.

National Climate Data Center. 2015. "State Annual and Seasonal Time Series." Available at: https://www.ncdc.noaa.gov/temp-and-precip/state-temps/.

Niles, T. Meredith, M. Lubell, and V.R. Haden. 2013. "Perceptions and Responses to Climate Policy Risks Among California Farmers. "*Global Environmental Change* 23(6): 1752-1760.

Perrone, D., and M.M. Rohde. 2016. "Benefits and Economic Costs of Managed Aquifer Recharge in California." *San Francisco Estuary and Watershed Science,* 14(2, Article 4). Available at: http://dx.doi.org/10.15447/sfews.2016v14iss2art4.

PPIC (Public Policy Institute of California). 2016. "California Water Market." Available at: http://www.ppic.org/publication/californias-water-market/.

———. 2016. "Energy and Water." Available at: http://www.ppic.org/content/pubs/report/R_1016AER.pdf.

———. 2016. "Water Use in California." Available at: http://www.ppic.org/publication/water-use-in-california/.

———. 2017. "Groundwater in California." Available at: http://www.ppic.org/publication/groundwater-in-california/.

Regnacq, C., A. Dinar, and E. Hanak. 2016. "The Gravity of Water: Water Trade Frictions in California." *American Journal of Agricultural Economics.* 98(5): 1273-1294.

San Francisco Public Utilities Commission. 2005. *A History of the Municipal Water Department & Hetch Hetchy System.* Available at: http://sfwater.org/Modules/ShowDocument.aspx?documentID=5224.

Scripps Institute of Oceanograph. 2015. "Atmospheric Rivers, Cloud-Creating Aerosol Particles, and California Reservoirs." San Diego CA: University of California, San Diego, January. Available at: https://scripps.ucsd.edu/news/atmospheric-rivers-cloud-creating-aerosol-particles-and-california-reservoirs.

Seawater Desalination, Huntington Beach Facility. 2014. "Is Desal the Future for California?" Huntington Beach CA: June. Available at: http://hbfreshwater.com/news/is-desal-the-future-for-california.

Sierra Foothill Conservancy. 2014. "California Average Monthly Precipitation." Available at: http://www.sierrafoothill.org/.

Taylor, R. and D. Zilberman. 2017. "Diffusion of Drip Irrigation: The Case of California." *Applied Economic Perspectives and Policy* 39(1): 16-40.

U.S. Census Bureau. 2010. Urban and Rural Population for the U.S and All States: 1900–2000. Available at: http://www.iowadatacenter.org/datatables/UnitedStates/urusstpop19002000.pdf.

U.S. Department of the Interior, Bureau of Reclamation, Lower Colorado Region. 2016. "Law of the River." Available at: http://www.usbr.gov/lc/region/g1000/lawofrvr.html.

U.S. Drought Monitor 2000–2017. "Percent Area in U.S. Drought Monitor Categories." Available at: http://droughtmonitor.unl.edu/Data/DataTables.aspx.

U.S. Geological Survey. (n.d.). Water-use Data Available from USGS: 1950–2010 Publication Data for Counties and States. Available at: https://water.usgs.gov/watuse/data/index.html.

———. 1950–2010. "Brackish Water." National Brackish Groundwater Assessment. Available at: https://water.usgs.gov/ogw/gwrp/brackishgw/use.html.

———. 2016. *Sustainable Water Management.* Sacramento CA: California Water Science Center, Fact Sheet 2015-3084, version 2.0, February. Available at: https://pubs.usgs.gov/fs/2015/3084/fs20153084.pdf.

United States Bureau of Reclamation. 2016. "Law of the River." Available at: http://www.usbr.gov/lc/region/g1000/lawofrvr.html.

U.S. Department of Agriculture, National Agricultural Statistics Service. (n.s.). "USDA's National Agricultural Statistics Service California Field Office: County Ag Commissioner's Data Listing. Available at: https://www.nass.usda.gov/Statistics_by_State/California/Publications/AgComm/Detail/.

Water Reuse Association. 2012. "Seawater Desalination Costs." White Paper, The WaterReuse Desalination Committee, September 2011, Revised January 2012. Available at: https://watereuse.org/wp-content/uploads/2015/10/WateReuse_Desal_Cost_White_Paper.pdf.

WestWater Research. 2014."Drought Intensity Highlights Importance of Spot Market Water Transfers in California." *WaterMarket Insider California* Q2:1-4. Available at: http://www.waterexchange.com/wp-content/uploads/2015/02/California_q2_2014.pdf.

World Population Review. 2017. "California Population." Available at: http://worldpopulation review.com/states/california-population/.

Chapter 6. California Dairy: Resilience in a Challenging Environment

Daniel A. Sumner

Abstract

Milk is the top farm commodity (by farm revenue) in California, and California is the top dairy producer in the United States. The California dairy industry is central to the agricultural economy and environment in California. The California dairy industry had a record of remarkable expansion that lasted many decades before ending abruptly 2007. For these earlier decades, California dairy had some remarkable advantages relative to farms and processors in the rest of the United States. Dairy farms capitalized on California's climate, topography, and economic openness to create large dairies that provided opportunities for the best farms to thrive by accessing capital, advanced genetics, and exceptional managerial practices. Processors also captured scale economies and new technology to lower processing costs, improve returns for further innovation, and to incentivize the expansion of raw milk production. In the more recent period, growth has stopped as other regions in the United States adopted much of what had made California distinctive while California farms and processors have grappled with costs of increased environmental, farm labor, and other cost-side pressures. This chapter explains the recent history and the current situation and outlook for California dairy.

About the Author

Daniel A. Sumner is the Frank H. Buck, Jr. Distinguished Professor in the Department of Agricultural and Resource Economics at University of California, Davis; the director of the University of California Agricultural Issues Center; and a member of the Giannini Foundation of Agricultural Economics. He can be contacted by email at dasumner@ucdavis.edu.

Acknowledgements

The author appreciates the assistance and collaboration from many individuals during the course of preparing this chapter, which draws on research reported in several recent reports and articles. In addition to the editors, he would like to thank especially Joseph Balagtas, Antoine Champetier, Michaela Elder, Elizabeth Fraysse, Georgi Gabrielian, Tristan Hanon, Hanbin Lee, William Matthews, Dustin Messner, Quaid Moore, Qianyao Pan, Scott Somerville, Pablo Valdes Donoso, and Jisang Yu.

The California dairy industry emerged as the largest milk producer in the U.S. in the early 1990s and continues as the largest dairy industry among the states and the largest farm industry by revenue in California.

Photo Credit: Karen Higgins, UC Davis

CHAPTER 6. TABLE OF CONTENTS

INTRODUCTION

Milk has long been significant in California agriculture, and the California dairy industry has a unique place in U.S. dairy history. The California dairy industry emerged as the largest milk producer in the United States in the 1990s after a remarkable period of transformation. It continues to be the largest dairy industry among the states and the largest farm industry by revenue in California.

In the late 1940s and early 1950s, when most U.S. farms had at least one milk cow, California milk production held a significant but moderate place in the national totals. In 1949, California accounted for about 4.5 percent of U.S. milk production, compared to California's 7.9 percent of the U.S. value of all farm products. By 1954, California's shares had grown to 7.5 percent of U.S. milk production and 9.2 percent of U.S. value of all farm products. During this period, milk accounted for about 12 percent of the value of California farm products.

The late 1940s through 2008 was a period of incredibly rapid growth for the California dairy industry. By 1975, California had grown to No. 2 among dairy states, behind Wisconsin, with about 9.4 percent of U.S. milk output. In the next 25 years to 2000, California milk output tripled again, so California produced 50 percent more milk than Wisconsin and about 19 percent of all milk in the United States. In the next seven years, California milk production grew by one-third to hit its peak, in 2007 and 2008, of about 41 billion pounds of milk and about 22 percent of the U.S. total. Since then, California milk production has bounced up and down a little, while the share of U.S. production has declined to about 18.6 percent in 2019.

The California dairy industry continues to be large, dynamic and closely linked to other parts of agriculture and the California economy. Almost all of the milk produced in California is processed in California, and almost all of the milk processed in California is produced on dairy farms in the state. Much of California's processed dairy product (about half) leaves California in the form of cheese, whey, lactose, milk powders, butter, and other processed products.

California milk production depends on feed, mostly hay and silage, produced in California or shipped in from other western states, such as Utah or Idaho. The economic health of the California dairy industry depends crucially on a healthy local forage industry to supply much of its silage, hay, and other forages that are expensive to haul long distances. Concentrate feeds, based on grains and oilseeds, are mostly shipped in from other states and Canadian provinces. California cows also consume a wide variety of feed by-products, from almond hulls to tomato pumice, from the huge diversity of California crop agriculture. California dairy farming depends on a viable local milk-processing industry because raw milk is costly to move long distances. Likewise, although the California dairy-processing industry ships cheese, milk powders, and other products across the country and around the world, its viability requires milk production on nearby farms.

This chapter reviews the recent economic history, situation, and outlook of the California dairy industry. The chapter begins with on-farm milk production and illustrates the size, productivity, and growth of the industry. It compares recent trends in California milk production and productivity with data from other states.

Dairy farm consolidation has proceeded rapidly in California and elsewhere. Dairy farm numbers have dropped, and herd size has grown. This chapter reviews data from successive U.S. Censuses of Agriculture to document the evolution over time of the size distribution of California dairy farms. They show that fewer farms are in small farm categories, and more are in the larger size categories over time. This evolution has accompanied more concentration of the industry into the San Joaquin Valley.

Feed inputs dominate farm costs of milk production—concentrates and some hay are shipped into California, while much hay and silage are grown locally. These forage crops compete with tree and vine crops in the Central Valley for land, and increasingly, scarce irrigation water, which places pressure on the production cost of milk. Other challenges for farm costs relate to regulatory compliance with local air and water quality regulations, as well as California labor and greenhouse gas regulations.

Demand for milk comes from processors, the largest of which are farm-owned cooperatives. The milk products comprise the full range from milk beverages through soft and frozen products to butter, dry milk powder, and cheese. Most of California milk output ships to the rest of the United States and world markets, with beverage milk and 15 percent or so of other milk products remaining in California. Exports are an important part of demand for California dairy production.

Milk price policy is complicated and pervasive. In November 2018, California ended more than 80 years of state milk price regulations and joined the Federal Milk Marketing Order (FMMO) system. The FMMO system is similar to the old California marketing order in continuing to set minimum prices for farm milk based on the product made from that milk. The FMMO system also continues to require pooling the minimum payments before distributing revenue to farms as a weighted average "pooled price." This chapter explains the consequences of federal milk price policy, the federal Dairy Margin Coverage program—which is a kind of net revenue insurance available to dairy farms—and recent ad hoc policy designed to support dairy farm income. This chapter also explains a unique California "quota" policy, that redistributes milk revenue among farms.

This chapter concludes with a look at the future prospects for the California dairy industry, given a set of significant challenges but, at the same time, a legacy of innovation and resilience.

The current COVID-19 pandemic put immediate pressure on the industry in 2020 from low prices and then price variability. Milk prices collapsed, then price of milk used for cheese jumped, fell again, and rose again. Overall, dairy prices have risen from their springtime lows and are likely to be above recent year averages in 2020. After the U.S. and global recession pass, the California dairy industry is likely to return to its long-term outlook.

CALIFORNIA MILK PRODUCTION, PRODUCTIVITY, AND COSTS

Technology, management, the underlying economics that determine expected input prices and milk prices drive milk production in California. A later section of this chapter will provide details on the demand side. This section focuses on California milk supply, including how dairy farm economics in California has changed and changed relative to competitive regions and U.S. states (Matthews and Sumner, 2019). Increasing dairy farm size, typically measured by numbers of cows per herd, has long been important in California and elsewhere. California continues to have relatively large herd sizes, but herd size in other regions has grown relative to California. As the dairy industry expanded, it also concentrated geographically into the San Joaquin Valley, where dairy farms are larger and costs are lower. Exceptions are a specialized and heavily organic dairy industry in the coastal counties north of San Francisco and a remaining concentration of dairies east of Los Angles.

Milk production costs rise gradually with increases in wages and input prices but fluctuate from month-to-month with feed prices. Dairy cow feed accounts for more than half of total costs and affect dairy farm margins, returns to invested capital, and farm family labor. In particular, periods of high feed costs that are not matched by high milk prices cause severe financial pressures.

OVERVIEW OF CALIFORNIA AND U.S. PRODUCTION TRENDS

Figure 6.1 illustrates well the recent production history and situation of the California dairy industry. The vertical axis represents an index where the value 100 represents statewide milk production, number of cows, and production per cow in 1987. In 1987, California produced 17.9 billion pounds of milk from 1.06 million cows for an average of 16,881 pounds per cow. By 2018, milk production had risen by 120 percent to 40.4 billion pounds, while the number of cows had risen by about 64 percent to 1.74 billion, and milk per cows had risen by about 37 percent, to 23,239 pounds per cow. These are impressive growth rates, but the three-decade change hides that there has been little or no growth

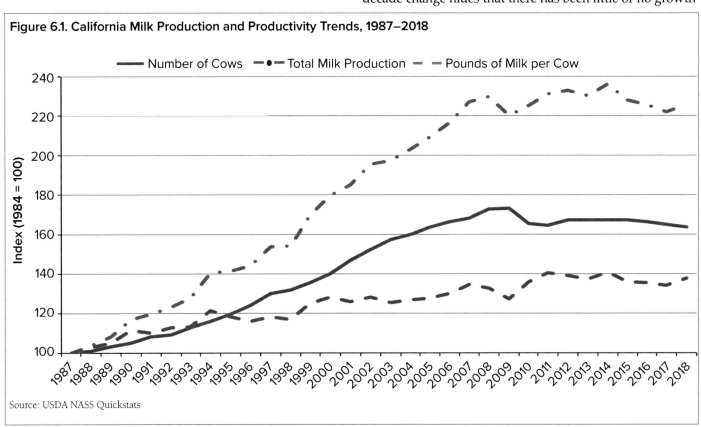

Figure 6.1. California Milk Production and Productivity Trends, 1987–2018

Source: USDA NASS Quickstats

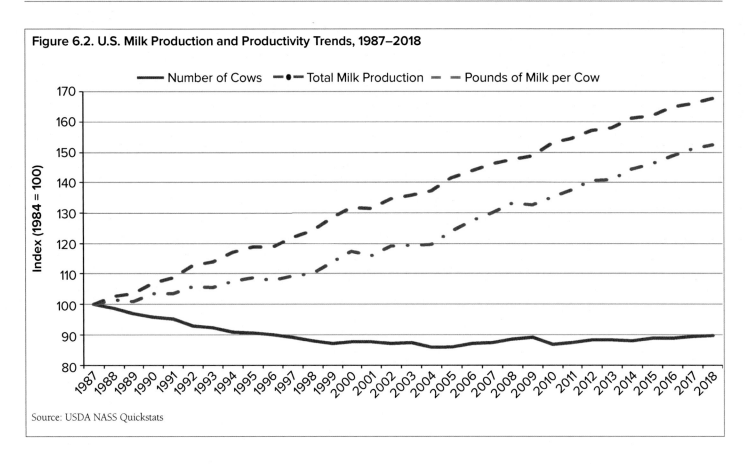

Figure 6.2. U.S. Milk Production and Productivity Trends, 1987–2018

Source: USDA NASS Quickstats

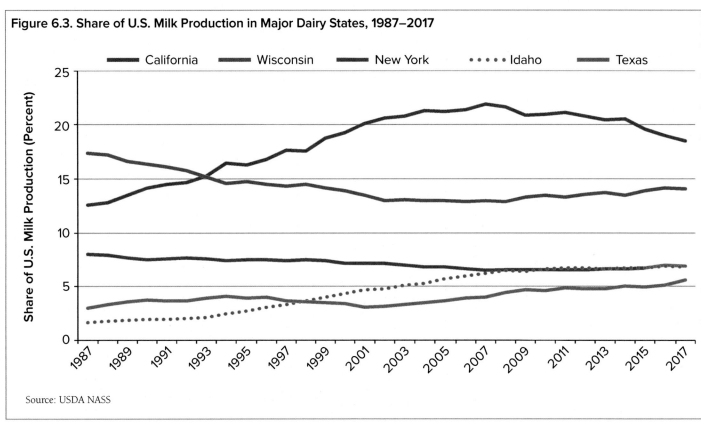

Figure 6.3. Share of U.S. Milk Production in Major Dairy States, 1987–2017

Source: USDA NASS

for a decade or more. The number of cows peaked in 2007–2008 and has fallen gradually by about 1 percent per year since then. Milk per cow fell from 2007 to 2009 as milk prices and profitability collapsed. It reached a high in 2014, when dairy profits were exceptional, and then has fallen by a few percent since then. The result for milk production has been some small ups and downs, with total milk production a couple of percent below where it stood more than a decade ago. The industry expected milk production to rise in 2020, but now may be lower than any year since 2009.

It is important to compare these California trends to the national trends. Figure 6.2 shows that national growth in the number of cows, production per cow, and milk production were all below California growth in the first 20 years; yet, all three have grown relative to California in the most recent decade. Indeed, national cow numbers declined rapidly and were 13 percent below 1987 in 2007, but have grown by about 3 percent in the past decade. Production per cow has grown steadily by almost 70 percent over the three decades, and after starting about 18 percent below California, it has caught up. After having a growing share of U.S. milk production, California's share of the national total has gradually declined for a decade as national production, and especially production in a few other major dairy states, has continued to grow rapidly.

Table 6.1 displays cow numbers in five major dairy states in 2004, when U.S. cow numbers bottomed out, and in 2018. The national milk cow herd grew about 2 percent over these 15 years, as did the Wisconsin and California herds. New York, had fewer cows, whereas Idaho and especially Texas added cows rapidly during this period. Several other states, such as New Mexico, also added to their milk cow herds.

Table 6.2 compares milk per cow in California to other major dairy states. California's milk per cow increased gradually. In contrast, it grew at a rapid pace in all other major states such that now California is at the bottom of this productivity metric. Of course, milk per cow depends on many contributing factors. For example, the increase in the share of Jersey cows in California, which produce higher solid content per pound of milk but less milk per cow, is one reason growth in average milk per cow has slowed in California. Nonetheless, the relative changes in milk per cow over the past 15 years indicates that dairies in other states have improved on this productivity metric.

Table 6.1. Cow Numbers in California and Major Dairy States

| | Number of Cows (Thousands) | | Change |
	2004	2018	Percent
California	1,700	1,740	2
Wisconsin	1,245	1,275	2
New York	658	625	-5
Idaho	412	600	46
Texas	317	515	62
U.S. Total	8,988	9,400	2

Source: USDA NASS Quickstats; https://quickstats.nass.usda.gov/results/B7B4F72F-BB67-31C9-A3C7-F9BFC3767580; https://quickstats.nass.usda.gov/results/84179ADF-E4F8-3210-88F4-9776C31C6F31

Table 6.2. Milk per Cow in California and Major Dairy States

| | Milk per Cow (in pounds) | |
	2004	2018
California	21,450	23,239
Wisconsin	17,739	23,974
New York	17,705	23,842
Idaho	22,070	25,077
Texas	18,956	24,955
U.S. Average	19,008	23,137

Source: USDA NASS Quickstats, See Table 6.1 above.

California's share of national milk production matched Wisconsin in 1993 at about 15 percent and reached 21.9 percent in 2007, by which time the Wisconsin share had slid to 13 percent (Figure 6.3). From 2007 forward, the national shares of Texas, Idaho, and Wisconsin have grown, and that of New York has stabilized. The decline in California's share exceeds the gains in the other listed states, indicating gains in states such as Michigan and New Mexico.

DAIRY FARM CONSOLIDATION

The number of dairy farms has been falling rapidly in California and throughout the United States for many decades—in good times and bad (MacDonald et al., 2016). For example, California had rapidly declining farm numbers even as the aggregate number of milk cows and milk

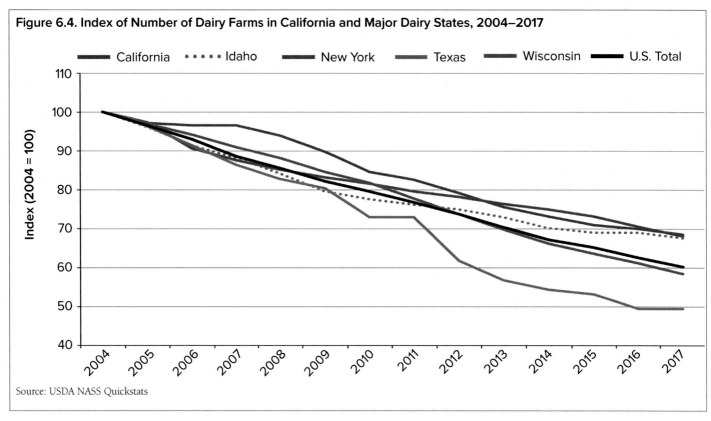

Figure 6.4. Index of Number of Dairy Farms in California and Major Dairy States, 2004–2017

Source: USDA NASS Quickstats

production was growing rapidly. On a year-to-year basis, farm numbers decline more in years with low milk prices. However, even high milk prices do not stop the farm consolidation process, in which more farms exit the industry than enter, and farms that remain increase in both numbers of cows and milk production. Figure 6.4, which sets 2004 data equal to 100, shows that the number of dairy farms in California fell by about 30 percent from 2004 to 2017, with a similar decline for Idaho and New York. Farm numbers

declined by 40 percent in Wisconsin and the United States as a whole, and by 50 percent in Texas. And as we saw in Tables 6.1 and 6.2, milk production rose in Texas at the most rapid rate among the top dairy states.

Table 6.3 shows the number of dairies in 2004 and 2017 for major U.S. dairy states and the U.S. average. California had the largest average herd size in 2004. But, herd size in Idaho and Texas almost equaled California by 2017. Herd size in New York, and especially Wisconsin, also grew rapidly in percentage terms but still lagged far behind the western states. These data, together with those in Figure 6.4, show how dairy industries in other states have become more like those in California.

Dairy farm consolidation has been underway for decades, and there are many drivers of this pattern. In addition to scale economies in production and input purchases, the high degree of human capital demands of dairy farm management seems to be important (Sumner and Leiby, 1987). Operating a modern dairy farm demands substantial managerial ability, and individuals with these talents command relatively high salaries. Therefore, to attract those with sufficient human capital requires a competitive return to human capital (Sumner, 2014).

Table 6.3. Average Number of Cows per Dairy in California and Major Dairy States

	Number of Cows per Dairy		Change
	2004	2017	Percent
California	837	1,263	51
Wisconsin	80	141	76
New York	100	138	38
Idaho	546	1,176	116
Texas	391	1,225	213
U.S. Average	134	232	73

Sources: USDA NASS Quickstats; https://quickstats.nass.usda.gov/results/B7B4F72F-BB67-31C9-A3C7-F9BFC3767580; https://quickstats.nass.usda.gov/results/84179ADF-E4F8-3210-88F4-9776C31C6F31.

Figures 6.5a – 5d. Dairy Size Trends

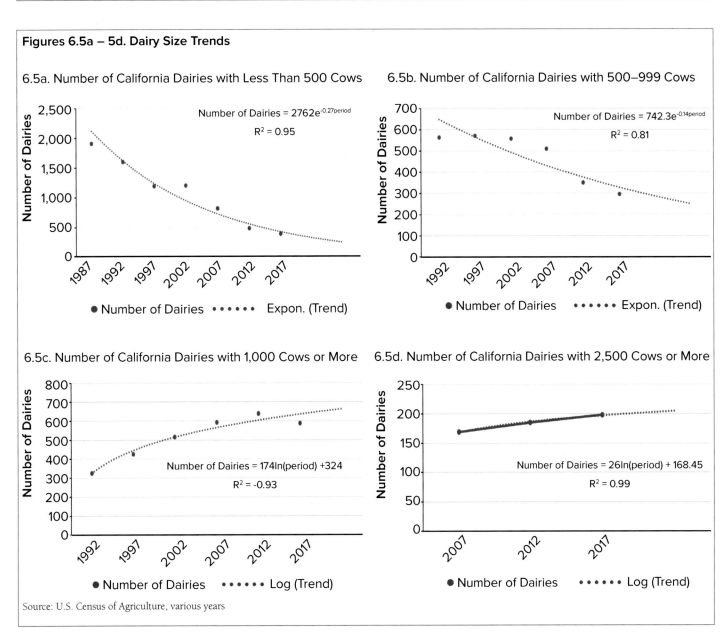

6.5a. Number of California Dairies with Less Than 500 Cows

Number of Dairies = $2762e^{-0.27period}$

$R^2 = 0.95$

• Number of Dairies ······ Expon. (Trend)

6.5b. Number of California Dairies with 500–999 Cows

Number of Dairies = $742.3e^{-0.14period}$

$R^2 = 0.81$

• Number of Dairies ······ Expon. (Trend)

6.5c. Number of California Dairies with 1,000 Cows or More

Number of Dairies = 174ln(period) +324

$R^2 = -0.93$

• Number of Dairies ······ Log (Trend)

6.5d. Number of California Dairies with 2,500 Cows or More

Number of Dairies = 26ln(period) + 168.45

$R^2 = 0.99$

• Number of Dairies ······ Log (Trend)

Source: U.S. Census of Agriculture, various years

Figures 6.5a through 6.5d display herd size trends for the California dairy industry over a three-decade period using data at five-year intervals from each Census of Agriculture 1987 through 2017 (NASS, 2017). Herd size is the most common measure of dairy farm size, but does not capture some interesting patterns (Sumner and Wolf, 2002). For example, a vertically integrated dairy farm that produces much of its own feed may have fewer cows but generates more profit within the farm than a farm with more cows that does not produce feed. Vertical integration into value-added marketing, as practiced by some of the small-herd dairies in the North Coast region, may indicate a larger dairy business even with fewer cows. Similarly, a farm that operates intensely to produce more milk or higher-quality milk may have more farm revenue than a farm with more

cows. In California, dairy farms tend to be specialized in milk production more than those in most of the United States, which is one reason California herd sizes are relatively large.

Figures 6.5a through 6.5d use data on cows per herd for those farms that report milk sales during the year. This sample choice eliminates many farms that have a few milk cows; for example, milk cows used to nurse calves, but are not in the commercial dairy business. Figure 6.5a demonstrates that there were almost 2,000 herds with fewer than 500 cows in 1987 but less than 400 herds in this category by 2017. The rate of decline is about 27 percent every five years, and this trend alone accounts for 95 percent of the variation over the thirty years. If this trend continues,

Table 6.4. Distributions of Farms, Revenue, and Cows by Herd Size, 2017

Cows/Farm	Dairy Farms		Milk Revenue		Milk Cows	
	Number	Percent	$ (Millions)	Percent	Thousands	Percent
1 to 499	395	30.9	364	5.6	94	5.4
500 to 999	296	23.1	829	12.8	210	12.0
1,000 to 2,499	390	30.5	2,385	36.8	638	36.5
2,500 to 4,999	163	12.7	1,968	30.4	547	31.2
5,000 or more	35	2.7	931	14.4	262	15.0
Total	1,279	100	6,477	100	1,750	100

Source: NASS, USDA. U.S. Census of Agriculture 2017. https://www.nass.usda.gov/Publications/AgCensus/2017/Full_Report/Census_by_State/California/

California would have about 250 herds with fewer than 500 cows by 2027.

Figure 6.5b shows the trend in the next size category of 500 to 999 cows, starting in 1992—the first year the data were available. Prior to this date, the census provided no breakdown of herds larger than 500 cows. This trend shows a gradual decline of about 14 percent per five-year interval, starting with about 550 herds with between 500 and 999 cows in 1992 and declining to 300 herds 25 years later. For herds with 1,000 cows or more, the number doubled in 25 years from about 300 herds in 1992 to about 600 herds in 2017. For this size category, a logarithmic trend fits the data to reflect a rise at a declining rate over time. Finally, for the last three censuses, we only have data for the larger category of dairies with 2,500 cows or more. Clearly, the trend is upward.

Table 6.4 documents the California dairy farm size distribution using census categories in 2017. There were 395 dairies, accounting for about 31 percent of all dairy farms, with fewer than 500 cows. These farms represented only 5.6 percent of milk revenue. The next larger category included 23.1 percent of farms and 12.8 percent of the milk revenue. What is now the mid-size category, 1,000 to 2,499 cows per farm, had 30.5 percent of the farms and 36.8 percent of the milk revenue. The category of herd sizes between 2,500 and 4,999 had 12.7 percent of the farms and about 30.4 percent of the milk revenue. Finally, the category with more than 5,000 cows comprised only 35 farms—about 2.7 percent of the total— but generated about 14.4 percent of milk revenue.

The distribution of milk cows, shown in Table 6.4, closely matches the distribution of revenue but shows slightly more average revenue per cows for the smaller dairies. Milk revenue per cow in 2017 was about $3,705 for the statewide average. Milk revenue averaged about $3,952 per cow for herds with 500 to 999 cows and only $3,557 for herds with more than 5,000 cows. Some of the higher revenue per cows for small herds is due to a significant number of organic herds that receive an average farm price that is almost double the price of conventional milk. For conventional dairies, the milk per cow and market price of milk tend to be slightly higher for mid-sized dairies. The larger dairies benefit from lower fixed cost and less management time per dollar of revenue.

Some observers have suggested that mid-sized dairies have been especially vulnerable to trends of fewer and larger farms. These census trends do not support that hypothesis. The number of herds in the smallest category of farms has been declining fastest in both absolute and percentage terms, which is consistent with the econometric tests for bimodal distributions of Wolf and Sumner (2001). They reject the hypothesis of bimodal distributions. An emerging exception may be in the continued presence of organic dairies with relatively small herd sizes in California, but even among organic farms, average herd size is growing.

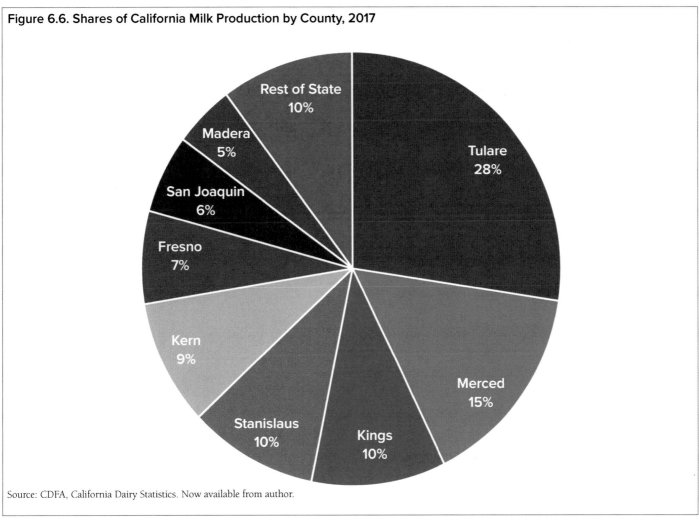

Figure 6.6. Shares of California Milk Production by County, 2017

- Rest of State 10%
- Madera 5%
- San Joaquin 6%
- Fresno 7%
- Kern 9%
- Stanislaus 10%
- Kings 10%
- Merced 15%
- Tulare 28%

Source: CDFA, California Dairy Statistics. Now available from author.

LOCATION, COST, AND SEASONALITY OF MILK PRODUCTION

The San Joaquin Valley has been the major milk-producing region in California for decades, and about 90 percent of milk output and dairy revenue come from that large region, from Kern County to the south and San Joaquin County to the north (Figure 6.6). The dairy farms in this region are almost all confinement-style dairies. Figure 6.6 documents that more than 40 percent of milk production comes from Tulare and Merced counties.

Beyond the San Joaquin Valley, two areas account for almost all the rest of California's milk production. First, a few large dairies remain in western San Bernardino and Riverside counties. The number of farms and the amount of milk production in this small region have declined steadily in the face of suburban population growth. Remaining dairies have a transport cost advantage to serve some of the demand for fluid milk use in the Southern

California region. Second, the coastal area north of San Francisco continues to support a significant dairy industry that focuses on pasture-based and organic dairies in Marin, Sonoma, and Humboldt counties. Organic and other pasture-based dairies in this region yield less milk per cow (about two-thirds the state average), but receive much higher prices per pound of milk. They also tend to have herd sizes about one-quarter of the state average.

After growing rapidly until 2007, the number of cows in the San Joaquin Valley has remained constant for more than a decade. In Tulare County, cow numbers have fallen by about 10 percent since a peak in 2010, offset by slight growth in some of the less dairy-intensive counties. The number of dairy farms continued to decline in all counties except Kern County. Herd size differs by county, with larger herds in the Southern San Joaquin Valley. Figure 6.7 shows that the average herd size in Kern County has been about 3,500 for more than a decade. The average herd size in Kings and Tulare counties has steadily grown and now

143

Figure 6.7. Average Cows per Farm for Top Five Counties and State, 2004–2017

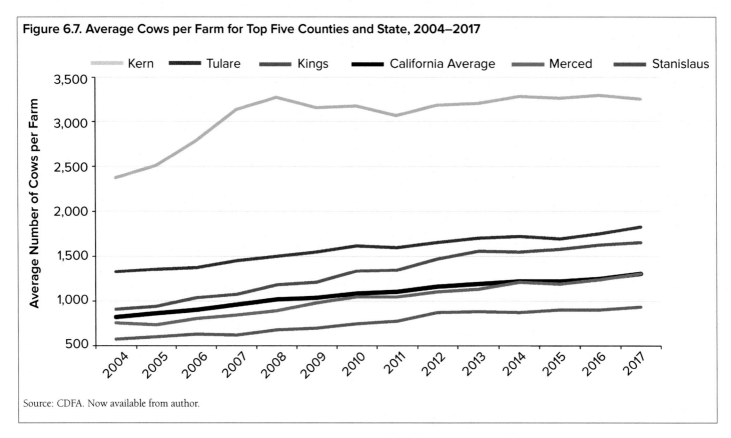

Source: CDFA. Now available from author.

exceeds 1,600 cows per farm. Herd size is also growing rapidly in the Northern San Joaquin Valley, but it remains below 1,000 cows per farm as shown by Stanislaus County data in Figure 6.7.

Dairy production costs vary from year to year, largely depending on the cost of feed, which accounts for more than half of total costs (Table 6.5). In 2014, grain, oilseed, and other livestock feed prices were very high, as were milk prices. Feed accounted for 63 percent of costs in that year, but despite high feed costs, the milk price margin over the production costs was almost $5 per hundredweight (cwt). In subsequent years, milk prices and feed prices were lower, but other costs rose. In 2017, the last complete year for which data is available, feed costs had fallen and were 54 percent of total costs, but because of low milk prices, the margin of milk revenue over costs was only $0.86 per cwt.

Dairy feed rations are comprised of a mixture of forages, such as hay and silage; concentrates, such as corn and other grains, and high-protein oilseed meals. Farms produce corn silage and small grain silage near the dairies where it is fed because hauling costs are high relative to the value of the feed. Much California-fed grain and oilseed meal comes from the Midwest. But significant amounts are by-products such as cottonseed. By-products, especially almond hulls, are also important forages.

California farms produce most of the hay and silage used on California dairies, but some is shipped in from other western states such as Idaho, Nevada, and Utah. A challenge for California dairies is the high cost of forage feeds. Competition with tree nuts and other crops for land and irrigation water has reduced the production and raised the cost of hay and silage in the San Joaquin Valley (Sumner and Pan, 2019).

Hired labor rates account for about 12 percent of milk production costs and have been rising for two reasons. As farms get larger, the share of labor on the farm that can be performed by unpaid family labor declines and, therefore, the ratio of hired labor to revenue rises. More important in recent years is the increase in wages of hired farm workers, who may have opportunities at non-farm jobs. Dairy farm work, mainly feeding and milking cows, is a relatively low-wage occupation and dairy farms are sensitive to having workers who treat animals well, while also having the ability to use increasingly sophisticated technology.

Table 6.5. Farm Costs of California Milk Production

Dairy Input	2014		2017	
	$/cwt	Percent Share	$/cwt	Percent Share
Feed	11.05	63	8.77	54
Hired Labor	1.56	9	1.87	12
Herd Replacement	1.37	8	1.88	12
Other Operating Costs	2.88	17	3.06	19
Milk Marketing	0.56	3	0.55	3
Total Costs	17.42	100	16.13	100
Average Mailbox Price	22.37		16.99	
Price – Costs (Residual)	4.95		0.86	

Source: CDFA California Dairy Statistics, available from the author

Note: Operating costs include utilities, supplies, veterinary and medicine, outside services, repairs and maintenance, bedding and manure hauling, fuel and oil, miscellaneous expenses, interest, lease expense, depreciation, taxes and insurance. Milk marketing costs include hauling milk from farm to plant, State of California assessments, Federal assessments and miscellaneous deductions.

Automation is growing, but technologies such as robotic milking are not yet dominant in the industry.

Dairy farms produce milk every day and receive their revenue in a monthly milk check. The individual cows are typically milked twice a day (three times per day on some farms) about 305 days per year. The cows are "dry" about two months per year during the last two months of a nine-month pregnancy. They re-enter the lactating herd shortly after giving birth. The typical cow lasts about two lactations with some healthy, high-productivity cows lasting longer.

Although farms produce milk every day, production does vary seasonally. The milk production in California is about 10 percent higher in the spring than in the later summer and fall, when it reaches a season-low, before gradually climbing in the winter. Milk prices tend to be lower in the spring because of the peak supply during this period. Milk production declines in periods of extreme heat. Many California dairies have installed misters and other technology to reduce cow discomfort during high-temperature days. Generally, cows are more productive where humidity is low, which is not an issue in California. So far, there is little evidence of climate change reducing milk cow productivity enough to cause problems for dairies in the San Joaquin Valley (Key and Sneeringer, 2014).

REGULATIONS THAT AFFECT FARM PRODUCTION AND COSTS

California has many environmental, labor, zoning, and other business regulations that affect dairy farm operations as well as milk transport and processing. Among the most prominent of the environmental regulations are those related to methane emissions in the context of greenhouse gas programs, local air quality concerns, and groundwater quality and quantity.

California regulations designed to improve air quality in the San Joaquin Valley specify practices on dairy farms that limit local air pollutants from manure, animal feed storage, and other potential sources such as dust. Zhang (2018) conducted a detailed evaluation of changes in farm practices indicated by some specific California air quality regulations, and used econometric estimation of data from the farm cost surveys that are summarized above. Her empirical investigation finds little or no measurable cost impact of the regulations she studies. Of course, some potential costs, such as the demands on the time and attention of the farm operators, are difficult to measure.

Regulations related to groundwater quality have required changes in manure handling to reduce the seepage of pollutants that affect the water in residential wells, among other concerns. Nitrate pollution of groundwater has been a particular concern for rural towns that do not have access

145

to costly water treatment. Dairy manure has been a source of some of that pollution. Regulations now require sealing the bottoms of manure lagoons and controlling when, where, and how manure is spread on fields.

The issue of dairy manure handling impacts on methane emissions as a short-lived greenhouse gas has become prominent in California in the last decade (Kaffka et al., 2016; Lee and Sumner, 2018). With legislation in 2016 (Senate Bill 1383), California began an effort to achieve a 40 percent reduction in short-lived greenhouse gas emissions by 2030. Because dairy farms contribute significantly to the state methane emission total, reduction of methane emissions from dairy farm manure is a prominent component of that effort. For several years, the California Department of Food and Agriculture has been subsidizing efforts to reduce methane emission with methane digesters and alternative manure management practices. If considered feasible, regulations would begin in 2024.

Manure flushed from dairy barns into lagoons decomposes anaerobically and generates methane in the process. One strategy to reduce methane emissions uses alternatives that move less manure into lagoons and facilitates drying and

aerobic decomposition. These are considered more appropriate on farms with smaller herd sizes. Another strategy is to allow the anaerobic digestion of manure in covered lagoons that seal in methane before it is emitted. Then the methane, which is the energy component of natural gas, can be cleaned and used to generate electricity, or what is now more common in California, piped to substitute as a motor fuel. With sufficient subsidy for digestion, piping, and cleaning, biogas as it is sometimes called, can compete with natural gas, so long as there are subsidies for "renewable fuels" in general (Lee and Sumner, 2018)."

Substantial investment, subsidized by the California state government, has recently developed a series of centralized facilities to produce and sell renewable fuel from clusters of large dairies in the San Joaquin Valley. This fuel has qualified for both the federal renewable fuels subsidies and the California Low Carbon Fuels subsidy. If fuel subsidy rates continue, the investments will likely be profitable (Lee and Sumner, 2018). However, the Spring 2020 collapse in petroleum and other energy prices, severe recession with reduced fuel demand, and the new challenges for the California state government budget may make such investments more difficult to sustain.

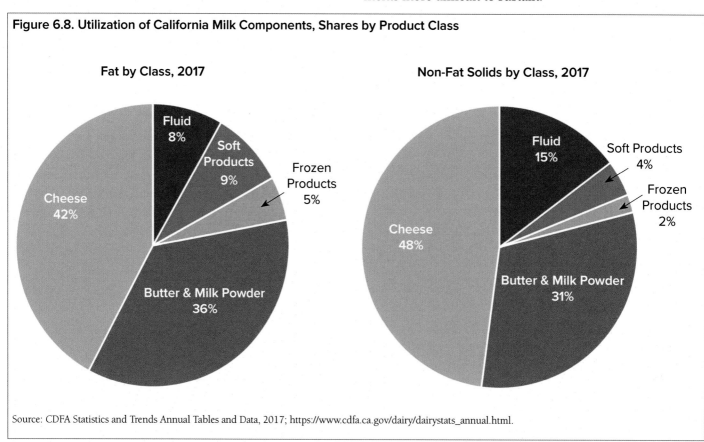

Figure 6.8. Utilization of California Milk Components, Shares by Product Class

Source: CDFA Statistics and Trends Annual Tables and Data, 2017; https://www.cdfa.ca.gov/dairy/dairystats_annual.html.

PROCESSING ISSUES AND COSTS

Almost all milk produced on California farms is processed in California and almost all milk processed in the state is produced in California. Transport costs are high relative to the unit value of milk. Therefore, before shipping, most milk in California is transformed into cheese, whey, milk powder, and butter. Such processing removes most of the water, reduces perishability, and increases the value of the product to be shipped. Fluid milk products processed in California tend to be used near to where the products are produced, again because of perishability and transport costs. Soft products, such as yogurt and cottage cheese, and frozen products such as ice cream, are intermediate in terms of perishability and transport costs relative to product value and tend to be shipped further than fluid milk products. These practical considerations about milk transport costs are key to understanding the relationship between farm production and milk processing in California.

More than 80 percent of California milk is produced by members of farmer-owned cooperatives that represent their members in bargaining, and process much of their members' milk as well. Members of California Dairies, Inc. (CDI) produce just under half of all milk in California and members of two large national cooperatives, Dairy Farmers of America and Land O' Lakes, each produce about twenty percent.

In California, cooperatives mainly process milk into dry milk powder and butter, while proprietary firms produce fluid milk, soft and frozen products, and cheese. This may be changing in 2020 as Dairy Farmers of America is acquiring California fluid milk processing plants owned by the now-bankrupt Dean Foods. Cheese processing in California continues to be mainly by larger proprietary firms such as Hilmar, Leprino, and Saputo, and many smaller cheese makers.

THE USE OF CALIFORNIA COMPONENTS

There are four major components in raw milk from the farm: fat (about 3.9 percent), protein (about 3.2 percent), other solids (about 5.8 percent), and fluid (about 87.1 percent). The milk's value is mainly in the fat and protein with some marketable value associated with the other solids, which are mostly lactose and minerals. The subsequent section discusses milk pricing regulations; here, we discuss the use of these milk components in California. The regulatory framework groups milk products into "classes." Products use milk components differently.

Figure 6.8 shows the 2017 utilization of California milk fat and nonfat solids by product class. Fluid products used about 15 percent of the nonfat solid component, and soft and frozen products used about 6 percent. In contrast, fluid products used only 8 percent of milk fat whereas soft and frozen products used 14 percent. Cheese plants use about 48 percent of the nonfat solids and 42 percent of the fat. Cheese making also produces whey products, including whey protein powders used as a food ingredient and an important export product. Butter and milk powder are listed together as a product class because they are processed together. A butter-powder processing plant uses most of the fat component in raw milk to produce butter and butter oils and uses the nonfat solids to make nonfat dry milk and similar products. Some plants also make whole milk powders.

Milk is delivered from farms to the manufacturing plant that is expected to use most of the milk. Except in the case of fluid milk, plants remove most of the fluid. Processing plants, including fluid milk plants, use components required for their product and send excess components to processing plants that make other products. Fluid milk products average about 2 percent fat, so almost half the fat received by those plants will be sent to another plant, such as an ice cream operation. Since butter-powder plants make distinct products with either zero fat or very high fat content, they can accept whatever component other plants have in excess.

Product shares and component shares by product have evolved over time in California and in other markets. In particular, fluid milk products used more than 30 percent of milk fat in the early 1980s. That share fell steadily as total milk production rose, and a small share of all milk went to fluid products. At the same time, however, California consumers used less fluid milk per capita. U.S. average

Table 6.6. California Dairy Processing Costs, 2016

	Butter	Nonfat Dry Milk	Cheese
	Dollars per Pound		
Processing Labor	0.0754	0.0538	0.0626
Processing Non-Labor	0.0724	0.1129	0.0882
Packaging	0.0138	0.0152	0.0244
Other Ingredients	0.0038	N/A	0.0286
General and Administrative	0.0193	0.0140	0.0355
Return on Investment	0.0101	0.0123	0.0061
Total Cost	0.1938	0.2082	0.2454

Source: CDFA Manufacturing Costs Exhibit; the background data for 2016 are available from the author.
Note: Costs are the weighted average cost for all plants in California.

consumption of fluid milk fell from 26 gallons per capita in 1987 to 17 gallons in 2018. Over the same 30-year period, the share of whole milk fell from half to about one-third.

MILK PROCESSING COSTS AND CONCERNS

California's milk processing industry supplies California, the rest of the United States, and the rest of the world. As discussed, milk and milk components comprise the main input into making dairy products, but other inputs are also important in the manufacturing process. For fluid milk products used by consumers in California, the payments for farm milk comprise about half the retail price. For cheddar cheese, the farm share of U.S. consumer expenditure is about 28 percent, reflecting in part that more cheese is consumed away from home.

Milk processing uses labor and other material, which is a part of the cost of moving milk from the farm to customers, whether they be retailers, food service establishments, or further processors. Table 6.6 provides the most recent data on input costs for making butter, nonfat dry milk, and cheese in California. The total non-milk costs range from about $0.194 per pound for butter to $0.245 for cheese. The biggest cost aggregate is the direct processing costs other than labor, which includes utilities and equipment costs. The cost of energy for drying milk is significant, especially for nonfat dry milk. Processing labor is about one-quarter of total costs for nonfat dry milk and cheese. California has high construction, energy, and labor costs relative to

other major dairy states, which tends to raise processing costs. Because California processors compete in national and global markets for these products, the consequence of higher processing costs in California is lower farm milk prices.

DEMAND FOR CALIFORNIA DAIRY PRODUCTS

We have discussed several demand issues in the previous sections. The most important factor is that most California milk is destined for national and global markets or competes with shipments of products into the state for customers in California. Of course, demand from California customers is important for California-produced fluid milk products, but these products now use only about 12 percent of the milk produced in California.

Demand for milk components has trended gradually over time with income, and food and nutrition information. The decline in demand for milk fat caused in part by concerns about obesity in children and adults, has moderated as nutritional information has shifted to raise more concern about carbohydrate consumption and place less emphasis on fat consumption. While the shift to plant-based foods has continued to place pressure on dairy consumption, current nutritional information has reduced the stigma of milk fat in fluid milk products, yogurt, and butter.

Per capita fluid milk consumption has fallen by one-third since 1990, while per capita butter consumption has risen by one-third, and per capita cheese consumption has risen

by 42 percent. Yogurt consumption rose by a remarkable 244 percent over this period. Since 1990, U.S. consumption of per capita milk fat has risen by 14 percent. Overall, domestic commercial use of milk fat has risen by 42 percent since 1995 while domestic commercial use of nonfat solids has risen by 22 percent. Exports of the nonfat solid milk component have grown much more rapidly over this period.

PRICE TRENDS AND ISSUES

Against these steady trends in domestic milk demand, milk price variations are driven by variations in milk supply and cost of production and export demand for U.S. and California milk. Demand for exports depend mainly on global dairy product demand trends and variation in conditions among competing milk suppliers.

Figure 6.9 shows the annual average U.S. and California farm milk prices (nominal) over the period from 2000 through 2018. Notice first that the California price is consistently slightly below the U.S. price, but follows the same trend and has the same annual ups and downs. In recent

Figure 6.9. California and U.S. Farm Price of Milk, 2000–2018

Source: USDA, NASS, QuickStats; https://quickstats.nass.usda.gov/results/240496B2-AB0F-31D7-A1k8E-FFDFC8B5D1D6

Table 6.7. Organic Milk Sales in California		
	Gallons (per Capita)	Share of Fluid Milk Sales (Percent)
2009	31.3	4.16
2010	35.7	4.83
2011	42	5.80
2012	46	6.40
2013	54	7.65
2014	54	7.98
2015	49	7.54
2016	47	7.61
2017	51	8.45
2018	41	8.52

Source: CDFA, Retail milk sales.

The organic segment of the California milk industry is distinct in several ways, including the situation and outlook for demand. California organic sales tend to be dominated by fluid milk, where the organic share has been growing. Table 6.7 shows that the organic share of California fluid milk quantity has risen from about 4 percent in 2009 to about 8.5 percent in 2018. However, the decline of overall fluid milk sales meant that the peak quantity per capita was 2013 and 2014. The organic share of fluid milk revenue is much higher than the share of volume because the retail price of organic fluid milk is about double the retail price of conventionally produced fluid milk. About 12 percent of California milk quantity sells as fluid products, which implies that about 1.3 percent of California milk sells as organic fluid milk. Based on cow numbers and productivity, about 2 percent of California-produced farm milk is organic, which leaves about 0.7 percent of California milk or about one-third of organic milk to sell as organic yogurt and other products.

years, the correlation between the two series on a monthly basis has been about 0.98. Notice the extreme price swings such as the $6/cwt increase from 2006 to 2007, followed by a $5/cwt decline from 2008 to 2009, and then a gain of more than $6/cwt over the two-year period from 2009 to 2011. The high milk prices in 2014 were followed by a period of low prices since 2015. Recent monthly data show that milk prices rose gradually through the beginning of 2020, before the collapse in the spring of 2020, by about $7 per cwt to a price level not seen since 2009.

As shown above, feed costs are more than half of the cost of milk production. USDA economists created an index of prices of common milk cow feeds, which include corn, soybeans, and alfalfa hay that they use to compute the cost of a common dairy cow feed ration. The often-cited ratio of milk price to dairy ration cost ranged between 2.5 and 3.5 in the 1990s, before spiking to about 3.6 in 1999. The ratio remained above 2.5 until a feed price spike in 2008 drove the ratio to 2.01. This precipitated a collapse in milk prices in 2009, leaving the ratio at 1.78, which was the lowest in at least 30 years. With feed prices again high in 2012, the ratio of milk price to dairy ration cost was even lower at 1.52. Even with peak milk prices in 2014, the milk price to feed cost ratio was only 2.54, less than what the industry considered a moderate ratio two decades before. Given these relatively low milk prices, technical and managerial productivity allowed the U.S. and California dairy industries to remain in business.

EXPORTS

Dairy products were California's third-largest farm export category in 2018 measured by export value, following almonds, and about equal to pistachios and wine. Based on port data, product mix, and industry sources, UC Agricultural Issues Center estimates that about $1.7 billion in dairy exports were shipped outside the United States in 2018, up marginally from 2017, even though milk prices were down. As a share of farm production, the UC Agricultural Issues Center estimates that about 35 percent of California-produced milk is exported, which is more than 40 percent of the dairy products other than fluid milk. California exports about a third of all U.S. dairy exports, about twice its share of national production.

California exports a portfolio of products; however, like the U.S. as a whole, nonfat solids comprise a larger share of exports than they do in domestic consumption. Nonfat dry milk, whey and other milk powders, and lactose are major export items. California also produces and exports substantial quantities of cheese, and the whey and lactose by-products of cheese production are prominent among exports.

Figure 6.10 documents the broad portfolio of California dairy export product destinations, by value share. Even

Figure 6.10. California Dairy Product Destinations, Share of 2018 Exports

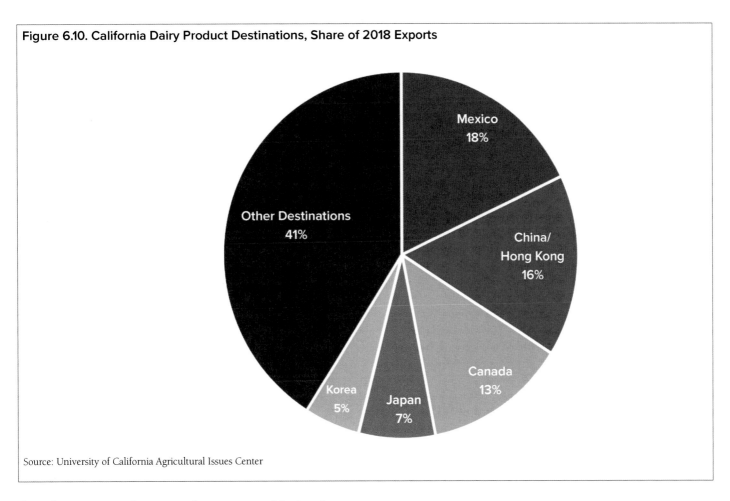

Source: University of California Agricultural Issues Center

though 2018 was a down year for exports to Mexico, it remained the top destination for dairy product exports. Exports increased to China and Hong Kong (considered together) and to Canada. Exports to Japan and Korea depends in part on the market opening accomplished by multilateral and bilateral trade agreements (Lee, Sumner, and Ahn, 2006). Exports to these markets have been relatively steady, and they have remained among the top five export destinations. Partly because of locational advantages and reflecting competitive conditions, the major destinations for dairy exports are North America or Northeast Asia (Matthews et al., 2016).

DAIRY POLICY

The dairy industry is subsidized and regulated through a series of state and federal commodity policies that date back to the Great Depression of the 1930s. Government dairy programs have been influencing dairy farm prices, revenues, and costs for almost 90 years. This section first considers the current set of federal government support policies, some of which disadvantage California dairy farms. I then turn to the Federal Milk Marketing Order (FMMO) for California that replaced the state-government marketing order in November 2018. Finally, recent data and analysis on the California milk pool "quota" program describes impacts of what remains of the California marketing order.

FEDERAL SUPPORT FOR DAIRY FARMS

For many decades, until about 20 years ago, the United States maintained high internal milk prices using a government-set price of manufactured dairy products at which USDA would purchase standardized butter, cheese, and nonfat dry milk. The resultant milk prices were periodically well above market-clearing prices, and the government acquired substantial stocks of dairy products, which it subsequently attempted to dispose of through foreign and domestic food assistance. To maintain high internal prices, the government established detailed and elaborate tariffs and import quotas. As recently as the negotiations of the Free Trade Agreement with Australia in the early 2000s, the United States resisted relaxing import barriers for dairy products (Alston et al., 2006).

As U.S. dairy productivity improved, federal milk policy gradually shifted. Congress allowed government-set prices to decline relative to market prices, domestic food assistance programs bought dairy products, and export subsidies faded away. For most of a decade, the support price program was ineffectual in that the minimum price was so low it provided little income support. For much of the recent period, high feed prices and a low margin of milk price over feed cost were the main concerns of the dairy industry. At the same time, there was little interest in raising the purchase price for milk products. Neither Congress nor industry groups wanted the federal government to

again acquire substantial stock of milk products (Balagtas and Sumner, 2012). The farm bill of 2014 eliminated the federal program supporting milk prices with purchases of manufactured dairy products, and was the authority for export subsidies (Sumner, 2018b).

The U.S. federal dairy policy in the 2018 Farm Bill has at its centerpiece the Dairy Margin Coverage (DMC) program, which is a revision of the Margin Protection Program that had been operating with relatively little farm participation (Sumner, 2018; Lee and Sumner, 2019). Like the program it replaced, the new DMC offers payments to make up the differences in milk price-feed cost margins. The coverage starts at $4.00 margins, which is free, but rare and so low as to be disastrous for most dairy farms. The program makes available highly subsidized coverage up to $9.50 per cwt for the first 5 million pounds of milk produced on a farm (the annual milk production from a bit more than 200 cows). For more than 5 million pounds of milk, the maximum coverage is $8.00 per cwt, and premium rates have much less subsidy. Margins of less than $9.50 per cwt are quite common, and thus, the "insurance" is likely to payout regularly (see Table 6.8 for 2019 margins).

Since premiums are highly subsidized for the first 5 million pounds of milk, the program is essentially a production subsidy that provides smaller dairy farms an incentive to expand. This means that for smaller farms, that predominate in the East and Midwest, the program is likely to generate substantial positive returns relative to revenue. It is likely to stimulate additions to the herd and more milk production on these farms. The result is more milk production from smaller farms and a lower national milk price than would otherwise prevail. A simple example, based on that in Lee and Sumner (2019), will help explain the operation of the program and illustrate the concern for conventional dairy farms in California. This example is similar in some ways to the impact of the Northeast Dairy Compact that was operating temporarily about 20 years ago (Balagtas and Sumner, 2003)

Consider two farms that enrolled in the DMC. The San Joaquin Valley farm has 1,600 cows and produces 40 million pounds of milk per year, which is somewhat above the

California average herd size shown in Table 6.3. The New York farm, in our example, has 160 cows and produces 4 million pounds of milk per year, which is somewhat larger than average shown in Table 6.3. The California farm has milk revenue of about $6 million, but negative net revenue based on a California price of $15 per cwt. The New York farm has revenue of $680,000, but negative net revenue based on the New York prices of $17 per cwt. As an example, assume both farms enroll 3.8 million pounds of milk at the $9 coverage level and pay the low premium of $0.11 per cwt or $4,180 for each farm.

The DMC bases the margin used for payment on national average milk prices and feed costs. Assume for simplicity that the actual margin is $8.00. Both farms get a payment of $38,000 for the investment of $4,180. For the California farm, this is a small addition to revenue and is intramarginal and thus does not add to the incentive to maintain or expand the herd. For the New York farm, the higher revenue is about $0.89 per cwt or about 5 percent and applies to all the milk production. This 5 percent increase in expected revenue is more than a 10 percent increase in the margin. If we assume the average response is a 10 percent increase in milk production on these smaller farms, which produce about 20 percent of U.S. milk, we get a 2 percent total U.S. milk output, even if moderate-sized and larger farms have no change in milk output. If the demand elasticity is -0.5, the price of milk falls by about 4 percent. In our example, this is $0.60 per cwt or $240,000 in lost milk revenue on the California dairy farm.

Table 6.8 shows that the milk price-feed cost margin in the DMC program was in the range to make payments in each of the first seven months of 2019 of between $1.29 / cwt in January and $0.23 / cwt in July. The margin coverage at $8.00, available for milk above 5 million pounds per farm, was unattractive given that premium rates were high and payout unlikely. The rest of 2019 had margins above the $9.50 maximum margin. The 2020 year started with margins above the $9.50 maximum, but that was set to change for months after April, and a farm that paid the very small premium for the DMC coverage for 5 million pounds again received a significant subsidy.

The point of this illustration is to indicate that a "subsidy" program such as the DMC that is structured to benefit selected farms in a way to stimulate production can be a net loss for the unfavored farms. Federal dairy programs

Table 6.8. Dairy Margin Coverage, Milk Price, Feed Cost, and Margins for 2019

Month	All Milk Price	Feed Costs for DMC	Margin for DMC
	Dollars per Hundredweight ($/cwt)		
January	16.60	8.89	7.71
February	16.80	8.89	7.91
March	17.50	8.84	8.66
April	17.70	8.88	8.82
May	18.00	9.00	9.00
June	18.10	9.47	8.63
July	18.70	9.43	9.27
August	18.90	9.05	9.85
September	19.30	8.89	10.41
October	19.90	9.02	10.88
November	21.00	8.79	12.21
December	20.70	8.75	11.95

Source: USDA Farm Service Agency. https://www.fsa.usda.gov/programs-and-services/dairy-margin-coverage-program/index

Note: Payments were possible at margins below $9.50/cwt, depending on the level of coverage chosen.

routinely favor small, mostly eastern, dairy farms in this way. Further, the recently enacted COVID-19 farm subsidies seem likely to have a similar impact because total payment limits per farm will leave most California milk production outside the benefit range.

CALIFORNIA FEDERAL MILK MARKETING ORDER

In November 2018, the federal milk marketing order (FMMO) system began to regulate milk markets in California after a three-year formal rule-making process. The details of the new order differ from the California state government policy that had regulated prices paid by milk processors and prices received by farmers in California since the 1930s. However, the basic purpose and form of the regulations have not changed. Under the goal of "orderly marketing," government regulators set minimum prices paid by processors within the order for milk components that differ by the end use of the milk components purchased. To be eligible for the program, milk must be classified as Grade A, meaning it meets sanitary requirements for fluid uses. In the early days, that was a significant restriction, but is no longer a binding constraint, in

Table 6.9. FMMO Milk Classes Used in Pricing by "End Use"	
FMMO Pricing Class	**"End Use" Products Within Class**
Class I	Fluid milk products
Class II	Soft and frozen products such as cottage cheese, yogurt, cheese and ice cream
Classes III	Cheese, including cream cheese
Class IV	Butter, nonfat dry milk, and other dry milk products,

Source: https://www.cafmmo.com/download-file/?s=true&folderMap=order.language&fileName=Code+of+Federal+Regulations%2c+Title+7%2c+parts+1051.pdf&ia=inline, Adapted and simplified from Section 1051.40

part because of the incentives created by the marketing orders (Balagtas, Smith, and Sumner, 2007). The marketing order provides for pooling the revenue generated by these minimum prices before the order distributes revenue to dairy farms in proportion to each farm's delivery of milk components.

Specific rules and regulations have changed a bit over the decades, but the principle of end-use prices paid by processors and pooled prices received by dairy farms has long been central to the marketing order system. In the current system, the minimum prices paid by processors apply to milk components—fat, protein, and other solids—with these prices linked to selected market prices received for specified dairy products. In particular, national market prices of butter, nonfat dry milk, cheese, and whey powder determine component values used in minimum price formulas. These price formulas set minimum prices that change each month based on movements in product market prices and differ by end-use class (Table 6.9).

The FMMO can generate added revenue for dairy farms because the minimum prices of milk components used for fluid products (designated Class I) in California are higher than they would otherwise be by a fixed price differential of an average of about $2.00 per cwt. The size of the Class I differential is limited by political limits on how much additional revenue can be extracted from local fluid milk users (Ahn and Sumner, 2009). Thus, there is little scope to raise

the payoff to the marketing order by raising the Class I differential.

The change in program rules and program administration from the California Milk Marketing Order followed several years, during which California milk producers became especially concerned about low prices in the state relative to prices in many other regions of the country. As was shown above in Figure 6.9, California milk prices are lower than those in many other regions of the United States and have been lower for many decades. But, the lower California prices are due to the fact that California is a net exporter of milk products to the rest of the United States and the world, and not because of identified deficiencies in government regulations. The new federal regulations do not change the supply and demand fundamentals for milk produced and processed in California. Therefore, the rules leave little scope for the federal order to cause major increases in milk prices compared to the California program that it replaced.

An important change from the California regulations is that under FMMO rules, Class III and Class IV processors, which previously had been required to remain in the marketing order, may opt out of the regulations if they find doing so to be financially advantageous. Fluid milk processors are required to remain in the pool, so there will always be a small Class I differential in the pool. "Depooling" has become common in California because the $2.00 differential is small and only about 12 percent of milk solids receive the differential. That means the Class I differential only adds about $0.24 per cwt (about 1.5 percent) to the pool price, and the difference between the additional payments required for processors of different products can easily exceed that difference.

A processor of cheese will tend to remain in the order when the Class III minimum price is near to or below the Class IV minimum price. Similarly, a processor of butter and dry milk powder will tend to remain in the order when the Class IV minimum price is near to or below the Class III minimum price. The reasoning is straightforward. When the market price of butter and milk powder has been low so that Class IV minimum price is sufficiently low, the price that a Class III processor must pay into the pool will be above what the farms that deliver to that Class III processor will receive as a pool price. That means the

Class III processor will be able to pay more for milk and have higher profits if they are outside the FMMO and pay farmers directly. A further complication is that once out of the order, a processor is allowed to re-enter only gradually. That means processors base decisions to exit or re-enter on long-term projections.

In fact, in November 2018, when the FMMO pricing began in California, the Class III minimum price was well below the Class IV minimum, and the Class IV processors stayed out of the order. Then, as the Class III price rose relative to the Class IV price, the roles reversed and much of the milk volume of Class III processors left the FMMO and has remained out of the order through May of 2020, the last month available as this chapter was finalized.

The complications of processors entering and leaving the order, make interpreting price minimums and pool prices complicated, which makes understanding the impacts of the FMMO more difficult to interpret. Nonetheless, the simple economic relationships and incentives are clear. The scope to raise the average market price of milk for farmers through a Class I differential is severely limited in a market such as California, where less than 15 percent of milk is used for Class I products and the Class I differential is only about 15 percent of typical average market price (Sumner, 2018a).

The FMMO system has small effects on milk price in California, but it can have larger impacts in other regions, raising further complications. By encouraging additional milk production and reducing the amount of milk used for local Class I products, the FMMO system encourages more production of butter, milk powder and cheese that are distributed nationally and internationally. The Class I differential reduces the prices of tradable dairy products to the disadvantage of producers in regions that specialize in these products, such as California and some international competitors (Sumner, 1999; Sumner, 2018a).

Two additional factors make the FMMO system more flexible and more complicated. First, the minimum pricing rules do not apply to the payments from cooperatives to their members. As owners of their cooperatives, payments to members are internal transactions, and farmers share broadly in gains and losses of the cooperative roughly in proportion to the milk they deliver. Therefore, to regulate the price of milk paid to a cooperative member would

not regulate the return for milk that a member would receive. Of course, in order to maintain its membership, the expected returns to a cooperative member must be competitive with what that farm could expect to receive by selling directly to proprietary processors or to being a member of a different cooperative. These same competitive pressures affect milk contracts offered by proprietary processors and cooperative alike, but the FMMO more directly regulates prices of the proprietary firm.

Second, the enforcement of government-set minimums does not preclude processors from paying more. These additional payments, called over-order premiums, are common. They are based in part of the quality characteristics of milk delivered and in part on competitive conditions prevailing in the market. Naturally, milk purchase and delivery contracts are complex. They have many features specifying bonuses for delivered quality and quantity as well as prices generally set as some amount over the minimum required under the FMMO in order to attract producer milk. Overall, market supply and demand conditions drive the processed product prices that determine FMMO minimum prices for each component in each end-use. Therefore, expected competition among processors, including cooperatives, determines over-order premiums that are written into contracts.

MILK POOL QUOTA IN CALIFORNIA

A unique feature of the California milk marketing order was a system, going back to 1969, under which some producers drew funds out of the pool based on their ownership of "pool quota." During the California milk marketing order, quota operations were incorporated as an implicit revenue transfer from all California producers to those who owned quota.

The FMMO has no provisions for the quota program. Therefore, in order to maintain the quota, producers voted in favor of keeping the quota program essentially unchanged after the shift to the California FMMO. The administration of the quota assessments and payments would remain with the California Department of Food and Agriculture. For the past 18 months, under the FMMO, state regulations specify an assessment of about $0.35 per cwt that is deducted before milk revenue is distributed to

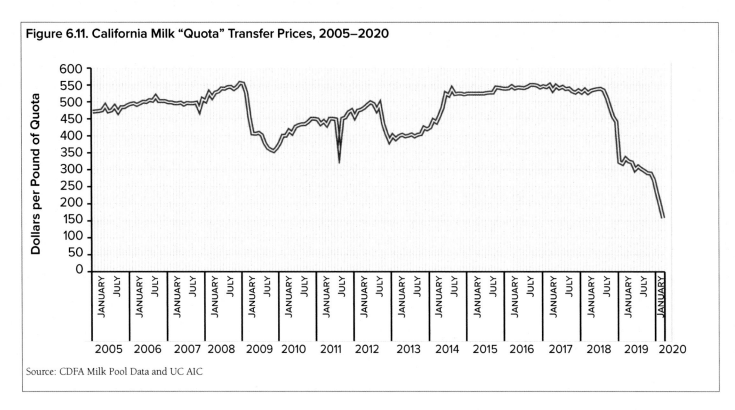

Figure 6.11. California Milk "Quota" Transfer Prices, 2005–2020

Source: CDFA Milk Pool Data and UC AIC

producers. The assessment collected is then paid to quota owners in proportion to their quota ownership.

When California established the program about five decades ago, farms received quota roughly according to how much of their milk had been delivered for fluid uses. In the early days, the value of quota moved up and down with the demand for fluid milk products in California (Sumner and Wolf, 1998). However, the program also allocated additional quota for a few years to new producers (Sumner and Wilson, 2000). For most of the past five decades, the quota has been bought and sold, in a market where California milk producers could own quota up to the quantity of their milk production.

To be very clear, the ownership of quota places no restrictions on milk production or marketing. It simply conveys to the quota owner the right to receive a specified amount of revenue each month. Annual revenue per unit of quota is $71.25 payable monthly. Since the amount of revenue per unit of quota is fixed, the value of quota is simply the capitalized value of this revenue flow over the expected horizon of the payments (Wilson and Sumner, 2004; Sumner and Wilson, 2005).

Variation in the capitalized value of the quota depends on how long the payments are expected to last and any chance

that they may be reduced or increased. Moreover, since only dairy farms can participate in the market, the price of quota depends on the discount rate relevant to California dairy farms (Wilson and Sumner, 2004; Sumner and Yu, 2014). In times of financial stress, more dairies will sell quota to raise liquidity, and fewer will have the ready cash or credit to buy quota; therefore, the price of quota will fall.

Figure 6.11 shows the capital value of quota over the 15-year period from January 2005 through March of 2020. Since quota ownership generated income on $71.25 per year, a price of $500 implies an annual return of about 14 percent, if no capital gains or losses are expected. A quota owner that purchased quota at that price in 1995 would have experienced that remarkably high rate of return year after year for 25 years. Generally, high returns are associated with high risk, and in this case, the applicable risk is that the program will not last or that the owner will sell the quota at a time of lower quota prices. Given the amount of quota, at $500 per unit, the total capital value of all quota was about $1 billion.

Quota price dropped to about $350 per unit in 2009 when milk prices were low, and dairy feed costs were high and dropped again in 2012, before rising in 2014 as economic conditions improved. There were no obvious changes in the likelihood of program termination during these periods. However, the precipitous drop in the price of quota from more than $500 in the summer of 2018 to less than $350 in early 2019 was clearly associated with a subtle change in the program.

For the first time in November 2018, the assessment that paid for quota benefits was listed explicitly on the milk checks of all California dairy farms. Each producer could then see precisely how much the quota program reduced milk revenue. For example, a dairy farm with 2,000 cows and average productivity and prices would pay about $16,000 per month or close to $200,000 per year into the quota program. While this amounted to a small share of total revenue for the farm, as a transfer to other dairies with no obvious benefit to the farm making the payment, the heightened awareness of the quota assessment caused agitation for change. Dairy operators filed a petition to end the program, while quota beneficiaries have moved to build support to keep the program. This activity has reduced the perceived expectation that the program will continue for many more years, and the price fell to about $150 in June 2020, with very few transactions so far this year.

PROSPECTS FOR THE FUTURE

After remarkable growth for a half century, during which it supplied milk products for California's expanding population and began to ship products around the world, the California dairy industry abruptly stopped growing about a dozen years ago. Given expected economic pressures and environmental constraints, the prospects for renewed rapid expansion seem limited, at least under probable scenarios. The more likely outcome is for California dairy to continue as a mature industry that competes effectively by adopting innovative technologies and management strategies to deal with challenges. To maintain production, the California dairy industry, and the forage crop industry upon which it depends, must compete locally for land, water, and labor with other industries in the San Joaquin Valley. On the demand side, the California dairy industry must compete with milk production and processing industries for dairy product markets nationally and globally.

The California dairy industry has faced many economic pressures related to state, national, and global markets for milk, national and global markets for grain and oilseeds, and local costs of forage and labor, among other challenges. The costs of dairy farming and dairy product manufacturing have risen in California during the same period over which global economic competition has become stronger. These California cost challenges relate to costs of land, water, electricity, and labor (among others) that are due, in part, to California regulatory choices.

The industry was an early adopter of large-scale milk production and processing that lowered costs and attracted top managers. With rapid consolidation and strong economic incentives, only the best managers have remained in the business. These economic incentives and pressures continue, and consolidation continues. Table 6.10 summarizes the projection of continued farm consolidation. It suggests that the number of milk cows on dairy farms with less than 500 cows will decline by more than 64 percent over the next two decades. The rate of decline might be even faster, except that small organic farms remain to serve that specialty local market. The number of cows on dairies with between 500 and 2,000 cows is projected to decline by about 26 percent and the number of cows on the farms with more than 2,000 is projected to rise by 26 percent. The model calibrated these growth rates with current cow numbers such that the overall size of the industry remains roughly constant, in terms of milk production.

A significant cost pressure on milk production is related to the success of the tree nut industry in the San Joaquin Valley, which has increased the demand for land and irrigation water and caused a shift away from field crops. Reduced availability and higher costs of irrigation water have reduced regional acreage of hay and silage. Local silage production has declined, and more high-quality hay has shipped in from regions such as Northern California and Idaho, which causes the price of feed for California dairies to be higher than that of competitors.

One benefit to the California industry has been the increased availability of by-product forage feeds, led by almond hulls, but including grape pomace and many other by-products from fruit and vegetable production and food processing. Nonetheless, the California dairy industry will likely continue to have more expensive feed than its low-cost competitors.

As emphasized above, only a small share of California milk is used to make locally-consumed fluid milk products that sell in markets insulated from other dairy milk competition. However, the California and national trends toward less beverage milk consumption have been continuing for decades, with no indication of any reversal. Recently, plant-based alternatives to cow's milk have further diverted some demand. This shift has been significant and long-lasting enough that it seems likely to endure.

Therefore, most California milk will continue to be used to make processed products that compete in national and international markets. With relatively open borders, the prices in these markets are determined globally. As dairy production has become more efficient in other competitive regions, national and international prices are lower. Some of the efficiency gains in other parts of the United States

Table 6.10. A Projection of the Distribution of Cows across Dairies by Herd Size

Size Category	Annual Rate of Change	Implied Accumulated Percentage Change Over Each Horizon		
	Percent	5 years	10 years	20 years
Number of Cows		Percent		
Less than 500	-5.0	-22.6	-40.1	-64.2
500–2,000	-1.5	-7.3	-14.0	-26.1
More than 2,000	NA	7.8	14.7	26.3
Organic	0	0	0	0

Source: Author's projections.

Note: Based on annual rates of change consistent with historical changes over the past two or three decades. We expect the negative changes for smaller herd sizes to be mainly in farm exits, for midsize herd size some farms are moving to the larger size category. Increase in average herd sizes is likely to represent most of the growth in cow numbers for the larger groups. Assumes organic production associated with smaller herds remains. The percentage shifts in each size category are consistent with almost no change in numbers of cows.

have been due to their adoption of scale and management for which California was long known. In other places, pasture-based, seasonal milk production is the lower-cost alternative. Growing efficiency among competitors means that the inflation-adjusted prices of dairy products are likely to continue to decline even as demand grows, especially with income growth in developing countries.

Because California remains a large net exporter of dairy products and the costs of dairy product manufacturing have risen in California, the price of raw milk is relatively low compared to places where California dairy products are shipped. This straightforward price relationship has been a source of frustration for milk producers, who point to higher farm prices elsewhere. The other reason for lower farm milk prices in California is the cost pressure on milk processors here. These processors have innovated, but much of that effort has been in response to increasing demands for regulatory compliance. Given that they sell as price takers in national and international markets, where non-milk costs rise for processors, their demand for raw milk shifts down, and they offer lower prices to farms. These cost pressures on processors seem likely to continue.

None of the underlying cost pressures seem likely to change materially in the next few decades; hence, a return to rapid growth of California milk production seems unlikely. However, the inherent strengths of the California dairy industry remain. Therefore, it also seems unlikely that significant aggregate declines in California milk production are on the horizon. California milk output

has been roughly constant, with many moderate ups and downs, for about 13 years. That aggregate pattern seems likely to continue. Of course, unforeseeable events may be on the horizon. As this is written, in May 2020, expecting the unexpected seems more appropriate than ever. Any projections, therefore, must be handled with caution.

CONCLUSION

This chapter describes the economic relationships driving the largest of California farm industries as measured by farm sales. However, we have also examined many challenges. The uncertain conditions in the spring of 2020 makes the concept of resilience even more salient for the California dairy industry.

At the end of 2019 and beginning of 2020, milk prices were rising and forecasts projected a return to profitability for much of the dairy industry. Demand for dairy products was rising and feed costs were moderate. The situation changed dramatically in February and March as the economic lock-downs accompanying the pandemic began to disrupt markets. Processing and packaging were misaligned to service consumers who were no longer consuming away from home. Some milk was dumped at farms because of a lack of processing and storage capacity. A looming global recession and disrupted export markets caused milk prices to collapse by one-third from $17/cwt to $11/cwt for milk used to process cheese or butter and milk powder. An expected recovery for the dairy industry turned into an economic disaster.

In response to these economic pressures, farm subsidies ramped up. The Dairy Margin Coverage program, developed to deal with unexpected declines in the milk price-feed cost margins, did not replace enough revenue to maintain dairy incomes. The federal government responded with supplemental direct payments to milk producers. The fund of about $3 billion, about 7 percent of annual industry revenue, was designated for the national dairy industry. This political response, however, focused support on the most politically powerful parts of the dairy industry, which tend to be the small and numerous farms in the east. Limits on payments per farm mean that for a typical eastern dairy, payments will cover most losses. In contrast, for a typical California dairy, payments may be limited to about $0.25 per cwt, even though the two farms faced the same decline in milk prices.

As the pandemic continued, demand for cheese expanded, partly from government programs, and the price of cheese rose to record heights. Dairy farm incomes improved such that, when government subsidies are included, dairy farm revenues for 2020 are likely to be above that in recent years.

Despite the pandemic and policy responses that curtailed much economic activity, food consumption continues, and dairy product demand remains substantial. Global demand growth has slowed, and it will be a few years before we catch up to where milk demand would have been. Nonetheless, those dairy farms and processors that weather the storm will face growing markets and the same challenges they faced before the 2020 disaster. The California dairy industry is positioned to remain a major part of California agriculture for decades to come.

REFERENCES

Ahn, B. and D.A. Sumner. 2009. "Political Market Power Reflected in Milk Pricing Regulations." *American Journal of Agricultural Economics* 91(3): 723-37.

Alston, J.M., J.V. Balagtas, D.A. Sumner, and H. Brunke. 2006. "Supply and Demand for Commodity Components: Implications of Free Trade versus AUSTFA for the U.S. Dairy Industry." *Australian Journal of Agricultural and Resource Economics* 50(2): 131-152.

Balagtas, J.V. and D.A. Sumner. 2012. "Evaluation of US Policies and the Supply Management Proposals for Managing Milk Margin Variability." *American Journal Agricultural Economics* 94(1): 403-423.

Balagtas, J.V., D.A. Sumner, and A. Smith. 2007. "Effects of Milk Marketing Order Regulation on the Share of Fluid Grade Milk in the United States." *American Journal of Agricultural Economics* 89(4): 839-51.

Balagtas, J.V. and D.A. Sumner. 2003. "The Effect of the Northeast Dairy Compact on Producers and Consumers, with Implications of Compact Contagion." *Review of Agricultural Economics* 25(1): 123-144.

Balagtas, J.V., F.M. Hutchinson, J. M. Krochta, and D.A. Sumner. 2003. "Ex Ante Analysis of R&D: Anticipating Market Effects of New Uses for Whey and Evaluating Returns to R&D." *Journal of Dairy Science* 86(4): 1662-1672.

Blaney, D.P. 2002. "The Changing Landscape of U.S. Milk Production." Washington DC: U.S. Department of Agriculture. Economic Research Service, Statistical Bulletin No. 978. Available at: https://www.ers.usda.gov/webdocs/publications/47162/17864_sb978_1_.pdf?v=41056

Kaffka, S., T. Barzee, H. El-Mashad, R. Williams, S. Zicari, and R. Zhang. 2016. "Evaluation of Dairy Manure Management Practices for Greenhouse Gas Emissions Mitigation in California." Final Technical *Report to the State of California Air Resources Board.*

Key, N. and S. Sneeringer. 2014. "Potential Effects of Climate Change on the Productivity of U.S. Dairies." *American Journal of Agricultural Economics* 96(4): 1136-1156.

Lee, H. and D.A. Sumner. 2019. "California Farm Commodities and the 2018 Farm Bill." *ARE Update* 22(3): 2–5. University of California Giannini Foundation of Agricultural Economics. Available at: https://s.giannini.ucop.edu/uploads/giannini_public/85/89/8589b847-56cd-4115-9176-2022deba741d/v22n3_2.pdf.

Lee H. and D.A. Sumner. 2018. "Dependence on Policy Revenue Poses Risks for Investments in Dairy Digesters." *California Agriculture* 72(4): 226-235. Available at: https://doi.org/10.3733/ca.2018a0037.

Lee, H., D.A. Sumner, and B. Ahn. 2006. "Consequences of Further Opening of the Korean Dairy Market." *Food Policy* 31(3): 238-248.

MacDonald, J. M., J. Cessna, and R. Mosheim. 2016. "Changing Structure, Financial Risks, and Government Policy for the U.S. Dairy Industry." Washington DC: U.S. Department of Agriculture. Economic Research Service, Economic Research Report No. 105. Available at: https://www.ers.usda.gov/webdocs/publications/45519/56833_err205_errata.pdf?v=0.

Matthews, W.A. and D.A. Sumner. 2019. "Contributions of the California Dairy Industry to the California Economy in 2018." A Report for the California Milk Advisory Board. University of California Agricultural Issues Center. Available at: https://aic.ucdavis.edu/wp-content/uploads/2019/07/CMAB-Economic-Impact-Report_final.pdf.

Matthews, W. A., G.T. Gabrielyan, D.A. Putnam, and D.A. Sumner. 2016. "The Role of California and Western U.S. Dairy and Forage Crop Industries in Asian Dairy Markets." *International Food and Agribusiness Management Review* 19(B): 147-162.

National Agricultural Statistics Service, USDA Quick Stats. Available at: https://www.nass.usda.gov/ .

National Agricultural Statistics Service, USDA Agricultural Census, (2017). Available at: https://www.nass.usda.gov/AgCensus/.

Romain, R.F. and D.A. Sumner. 2001. "Dairy Economics and Policy Issues between Canada and the United States." *Canadian Journal of Agricultural Economics* 49(4): 479-492.

Sumner, D.A. 1999. "Domestic Price Regulations and Trade Policy: Milk Marketing Orders in the United States." *Canadian Journal of Agricultural Economics* 47(5): 5-16.

Sumner, D.A. 2018a. "New California Milk Marketing Regulations Will Not Change Economic Fundamentals" *Choices* 33(4). Agricultural & Applied Economics Association. Available at: https://ageconsearch.umn.edu/record/279868/files/cmsarticle_660.pdf.

Sumner, D.A. 2018b. "Dairy Policy Progress: Completing the Move to Markets." *American Enterprise Institute.* Available at: https://www.aei.org/wp-content/uploads/2018/01/Dairy-Policy-Progress.pdf.

Sumner, D.A. 2014. "American Farms Keep Growing: Size, Productivity, and Policy." *Journal of Economic Perspectives* 28(1): 147-66.

Sumner, D.A. and J.D. Leiby. 1987. "An Econometric Analysis of the Effects of Human Capital on Size and Growth Among Dairy Farms." *American Journal of Agricultural Economics* 69(2): 465-470.

Sumner, D.A. and Q. Pan. 2019. "Water into Wine and Cheese: Implications of Substitution and Trade for California's Perennial Water Woes." In: S. Msangi and D. MacEwan (eds), *Applied Methods for Agricultural and Natural Resource Management and Policy*, Springer, Cham Switzerland: 173-188.

Sumner, D.A. and N.L.W. Wilson. 2005. "Capitalization of Farm Policy Benefits and the Rate of Return to Policy-Created Assets: Evidence from California Dairy Quota." *Review of Agricultural Economics* 27(2): 245-258.

Sumner, D.A. and N.L. Wilson. 2000. "Creation and Distribution of Economic Rents by Regulation: Development and Evolution of Milk Marketing Orders in California." *Agricultural History* 74(2): 198-210.

Sumner, D.A. and C. Wolf. 1996. "Quotas without Supply Control: Effects of Dairy Quota Policy in California." *American Journal of Agricultural Economics* 78(2): 354-366.

Sumner, D.A. and C. Wolf. 2002. "Diversification, Vertical Integration and the Regional Pattern of Dairy Farm Size." *Review of Agricultural Economics* 24(2): 442-457.

Sumner, D.A. and J.Y. 2014, "The Agricultural Act of 2014 and Prospects for the California Milk Pool Quota Market." *Journal of Agribusiness* Vol 32(2): 193-206.

Wilson, N.L.W. and D.A. Sumner. 2004. "Explaining Variations in the Price of Dairy Quota: Flow Returns, Liquidity, Quota Characteristics, and Policy Risk." *Journal of Agricultural and Resource Economics* 29(1): 1-16.

Wolf, C. and D.A. Sumner. 2001. "Are Farm Size Distributions Bimodal? Evidence from Kernel Density Estimates of Dairy Farm Size Distributions." *American Journal of Agricultural Economics* 83(1): 77-88.

Zhang, W. 2018. "Costs of a Practice-based Air Quality Regulation: Dairy Farms in the San Joaquin Valley." *American Journal of Agricultural Economics* 100(3) 762-785.

CHAPTER 7. CALIFORNIA'S FRUITS AND TREE NUTS

RACHAEL E. GOODHUE, PHILIP L. MARTIN, AND LEO K. SIMON

ABSTRACT

California produces three-fourths of U.S. fruits and nuts. The state's fruits and nuts were worth $22 billion in 2017, 44 percent of the state's $50 billion in farm sales. Nuts were worth over $8 billion, including almonds, $5.6 billion; walnuts, $1.6 billion; and pistachios, $1 billion. Grapes were worth $6.5 billion, including over 60 percent from wine grapes and almost 20 percent each from table grapes and raisins. Berries were worth $3.7 billion, including $3.1 billion from strawberries, $450 million from raspberries, and $138 million from blueberries. The most valuable tree fruits are oranges, worth $1.9 billion in 2017; lemons, $820 million; avocados, $383 million; and peaches, $540 million. Plums were worth $345 million and cherries $330 million. The acreage of tree nuts is rising, while the acreage of citrus, peaches, pears, and plums is declining.

ABOUT THE AUTHORS

Rachael E. Goodhue is a professor and chair of the Department of Agricultural and Resource Economics at UC Davis. She can be contacted by email at regoodhue@ucdavis.edu. Philip L. Martin is an emeritus professor in the Department of Agricultural and Resource Economics at UC Davis. He can be contacted by email at plmartin@ucdavis.edu. Leo Simon is an adjunct professor in the Department of Agricultural and Resource Economics at UC Berkeley. He can be contacted at leosimon@berkeley.edu. All are members of the Giannini Foundation of Agricultural Economics.

California leads among U.S. states in the production of 28 fruits and nuts. Nut crops are three of California's top five agricultural exports. In 2017, almonds were California's largest agricultural export commodity by value at $4.5 billion.

Photo Credit: Brittney Goodrich, UC Davis

CHAPTER 7. TABLE OF CONTENTS

INTRODUCTION

California leads among U.S. states in the production of 28 fruits and nuts, and was the sole commercial producer of 11 fruits and nuts (CDFA, 2018). U.S.-produced fruits and nuts were worth $29 billion in 2018, and California's $22 billion was three-fourths of U.S. fruit and nut cash receipts. This chapter covers six major fruits: oranges, lemons, peaches, avocados, prunes and plums, and cherries, and three major tree nuts: almonds, walnuts, and pistachios.

Figure 7.1 shows that California accounted for three fourths of US fruit and nut cash receipts in 2018. Nut acreage has been increasing and fruit acreage decreasing, with the exception of berries and cherries. Almonds stand out for having rapidly rising acreage and value of production.

Figure 7.1. California Accounted for Three-Fourths of U.S. Fruit and Nuts Cash Receipts in 2018

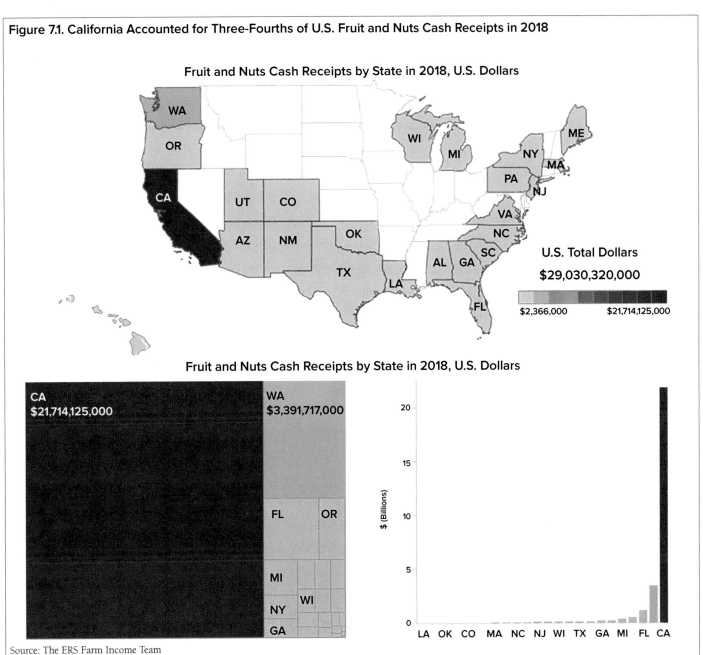

Source: The ERS Farm Income Team

Data Source: https://www.ers.usda.gov/data-products/farm-income-and-wealth-statistics.aspx released November 27, 2019

Note: States without shading have no production for this commodity or are included in miscellaneous crops or all other animals and animal products.

FRUIT

The U.S. produced fresh fruit worth almost $20 billion in 2018, including $16.4 billion worth of noncitrus fruit and $3.3 billion worth of citrus (ERS Fruit and Tree Nut Yearbook, Table A-3). The leading U.S. fruits by value were grapes for all uses, $6.6 billion in 2018; apples, $3.0 billion; strawberries, $2.7 billion; and oranges, $1.8 billion; these four fruits accounted for 70 percent of U.S. fresh fruit production in 2018.

Over half of U.S. fresh fruit is imported, up from a quarter in 1975. One reason is year-round availability that led to increased per capita consumption of mangoes, limes, avocados, grapes, asparagus, artichokes, and squash. Mexico provides about half of U.S. fresh fruit imports, followed by Chile with 15 percent and Guatemala with 10 percent. Projections suggest that three-fourths of U.S. fresh fruits and half of U.S. fresh vegetables may be imported by 2030, up from one-half and 30 percent today.

U.S. fresh fruit consumption declined 127 pounds per capita during 1994–98 to 119 pounds in 2007–08, reflecting less orange juice consumed and fewer oranges and stone fruits such as peaches and nectarines eaten (Linn and Morrison, 2016). Between 2009 and 2014, the number of "consumption events," instances of people consuming fruit, decreased from an average 315 to 296 a year, driven by the decline in fruit juice consumption, according to the Produce for Better Health Foundation in 2015.

The number of consumption events increased for store-bought fresh fruit and declined for all other fruit. Among fruit consumed "as is" and in other dishes, berries accounted for 24 consumption events a year, oranges for 14 events, melons for 13, grapes for 12, and peaches for six. Overall, 83 percent of fruit consumption events involved fruit eaten without additional preparation.

California's top agricultural exports in 2017 included several fruits: table grapes (No. 6, $795 million worth of exports); oranges (No. 7, $677 million); strawberries (No. 10, $415 million); raisins (No. 16, $307 million); and lemons (No. 17, $219 million). The state's agricultural exports were $19 billion, so these five fruits accounted for 12 percent of all agricultural exports (CDFA, 2016).

California produces a wide variety of fresh fruits, led by grapes and strawberries. San Joaquin Valley is the U.S. fruit and nut bowl, where most of California's fruits and nuts are produced. California had 23,000 farms producing noncitrus fruits in 2017 from 1.2 million acres of orchards; 6,581 farms producing citrus fruits from 312,162 acres; and 13,676 farms producing tree nuts from 2 million acres (COA, Table 37).

For each type of fruit and nut, most producers are small, with fewer than 100 acres, but these smaller producers account for less than half of the total acreage with the exception of avocados. Table 7.1 shows that half of the farms producing noncitrus fruits produced grapes, and one-seventh of grape farms that had 100 or more acres of vineyard accounted for 82 percent of all grape vineyards. Grapes are the noncitrus fruit most concentrated on farms with 100 acres or more, and avocados are the least concentrated; only a quarter of avocado acreage is on farms with 100 or more acres of avocados. In the other fruits, less than 10 percent of farms had 100 acres or more, and they accounted for over half of total acreage.

Citrus crops are similar in having most acreage on relatively few farms with 100 or more acres. Less than 10 percent of lemon and orange farms are 100 or more acres, but these farms accounted for 60 percent or more of total acreage. A higher share of nut farms, 20 to 30 percent, have 100 or more acres, but these larger farms accounted for 80 to 90 percent of the acreage of almonds, pistachios, and walnuts.

Table 7.1. California Fruit and Nut Farms in 2017

	Farms	Acres	Farms	Acres
			Percent Share > 100 acres	
All Noncitrus Fruit	22,977	1,300,428		
Avocados	4,826	57,192		
>100 acres	107	15,390	2	27
Cherries	1,254	36,853		
>100 acres	83	21,302	7	58
Grapes	11,812	935,272		
>100 acres	1,610	769,175	14	82
Olives	2,124	42,421		
>100 acres	72	22,287	3	53
Peaches	1,688	44,987		
>100 acres	121	29,231	7	65
Plums	1,642	64,702		
>100 acres	158	41,783	10	65
Citrus				
Lemons	2,254	58,190		
>100 acres	115	33,789	5	58
Oranges	4,145	170,241		
>100 acres	381	116,860	9	69
Mandarins (tangerines)	1,747	66,965		
>100 acres	100	47,910	6	72
Nuts				
Almonds	7,611	1,265,815		
>100 acres	2,364	1,103,519	31	87
Pistachios	1,515	334,949		
>100 acres	479	305,668	32	91
Walnuts	5,676	416,201		
>100 acres	1,004	326,000	18	78

Source: Table 37, COA 2017

Note: Walnuts >100 acres acreage is estimated.

Table 7.2. Oranges, 1985–2015

	1985	1995	2005	2015
Harvested Acreage (acres)	173,899	202,804	193,005	167,077
Yield (tons/acre)*	9.06	11.46	12.60	14.80
Value of Production ($1,000)	1,398,273	1,392,333	1,306,184	1,425,949
Revenue ($/acre)	8,041	6,865	6,768	8,535

Source: CDFA, 2015
Note: *Yield data for navel oranges.

Table 7.3. Lemons, 1985–2015

	1985	1995	2005	2015
Harvested Acreage (acres)	46,376	48,893	45,054	46,743
Yield (tons/acre)	13.04	15.61	15.59	16.14
Value of Production ($1,000)	501,737	520,189	408,779	772,265
Revenue ($/acre)	10,819	10,639	9,073	16,522

Source: CDFA, 2015

CITRUS: ORANGES AND LEMONS

Most of California's citrus is from Tulare and Kern counties. Navel and Valencia oranges consumed fresh are the most valuable citrus, worth three times more than lemons, and most are from the San Joaquin Valley.

Orange groves typically yield commercial harvests three or four years after planting, and yields stabilize ten years after planting. A 2015 UC Cooperative Extension costs and returns study for the Southern San Joaquin Valley found that accumulated net cash costs to establish an orange grove were $9,000 an acre at the end of the fifth year. Annual operating costs at full production are $6,000 an acre, with harvest costs accounting for over half of operating costs while pest and disease management costs are 10 percent (O'Connell, Kallsen, Klonsky, and Tumber, 2015).

Table 7.2 shows that orange yields increased by a third between 1985 and 2015, contributing to the increase in the value of orange production despite a reduction in acreage. Orange acreage increased 17 percent between 1985 and 1995, declined 5 percent between 1995 and 2005, and declined a further 13 percent between 2005 and 2015. In 2015, revenues per acre and the total value of production were slightly higher than in 1985, although 1995 and 2005 values were substantially lower.

California has about half as many lemon farms as orange farms, and lemons account for one-third as much acreage as oranges. Lemons are the one citrus fruit that is not concentrated in the San Joaquin Valley, since Ventura and Riverside counties have about half of the state's acreage.

Lemon groves typically yield commercial harvests in the third or fourth year; yields increase until year 8 and then plateau. A 2015 UC Cooperative Extension costs and returns study for the Southern San Joaquin Valley assumed a 40-year orchard life and found at the end of the fifth year, net accumulated cash costs (operating and cash overhead) were $4,300 per acre. In full production, total operating costs are slightly under $8,800, including two-thirds for harvest costs and 10 percent for pest and disease management and pruning (O'Connell et al., 2015).

Lemon acreage remained stable between 1985 and 2015, while yields increased by 20 percent. Revenues per acre, which are determined by yield and price, increased by one-third. The total value of production increased by 50 percent.

California produced almost all U.S. tangerines (mandarins); 96 percent of U.S. cash receipts of $576 million in 2018 from 59,000 acres. California also produces some grapefruit.

Table 7.4. Peaches, 1985–2015

	1985	1995	2005	2015
Harvested Acreage (acres)	58,623	69,566	78,778	55,532
Yield (tons/acre)*	18.00	15.44	15.66	17.58
Value of Production ($1,000)	518,165	497,383	570,006	665,054
Revenue ($/acre)	8,839	7,064	7,236	11,976

Source: CDFA, 2015
Note: *Yield data for clingstone peaches.

Table 7.5. Plums and Prunes, 1985–2015

	1985	1995	2005	2015
Harvested Acreage (acres)	106,232	129,318	105,165	71,144
Yield (tons/acre)	NA	NA	NA	NA
Value of Production ($1,000)	579,683	614,632	432,058	467,536
Revenue ($/acre)	5,457	4,753	4,108	6,572

Source: CDFA, 2015

TREE FRUITS: PEACHES AND PLUMS

California peaches were worth $372 million in 2018 and plums and prunes $345 million. California had almost 1,700 peach farms with 45,000 acres in 2017, and the 120 that had 100 or more acres accounted for two-thirds of total acreage. There are two major types of peaches, clingstone and freestone, with similar acreage and value. Clingstone peaches have pits to which the fruit clings, and most are used for canning and freezing. Freestone peach fruit is more easily separated from the pit, most are sold as fresh fruit. Clingstone peach production is concentrated in the Northern San Joaquin and Sacramento Valleys, while freestone peach production is concentrated in Fresno and Tulare counties.

A 2017 UC Cooperative Extension costs and returns study for processing peaches assumed commercial yields in the third year and an orchard life of 18 years. Four years after planting a new orchard, net accumulated cash costs are $6,600 an acre. Total operating costs are $5,600 per acre, of which harvest costs are a third. Pest and disease management costs are 14 percent, and fruit thinning is 20 percent (Hasey, Duncan, Sumner, and Murdock, 2017).

Peach acreage decreased between 1985 and 2015, although in 2005 acreage was a third higher than in 1985. Yields fluctuated between 16 and 18 tons an acre, and revenues per acre and the value of production increased by a third to $12,000 an acre.

Some 1,600 farms reported 65,000 acres of plums and prunes in 2017, including 158 with 100 or more acres and 65 percent of total plum acreage. The difference in the size distribution of farms producing plums reflects the different cultivars used in plum production for the fresh market and plum production of the prune (dried plum) market. Farms that grow plums for the fresh market tend to be smaller and concentrated in Fresno and Tulare counties, while farms that grow prunes or dried plums tend to harvest later and are located mostly in the Sacramento Valley.

A 2016 UC Cooperative Extension costs and returns study in the Southern San Joaquin Valley reported that fresh plums generate a commercial crop in year 3 and reach yield maturity in years 5 to 7, and then continue yielding for 18 years. Establishment costs are $7,000 an acre, the total accumulated net cash cost at the end of year 3. Once in production, annual operating costs are $11,366 per acre, with three-fourths reflecting harvest costs. Irrigation costs are 8 percent of total operating costs, thinning is 4 percent, and pest and disease management costs are about 3 percent (Day, Klonsky, Sumner, and Stewart, 2016).

The most recent cost study for prune production was conducted in 2012. Prunes achieve economic production in the fourth year after planting and reach full production beginning in year 7, with orchard life estimated to be 30 years. The establishment cost at the end of year 4 is

169

Table 7.6. Avocados, 1985–2015

	1985	1995	2005	2015
Harvested Acreage (acres)	73,533	61,614	67,825	55,081
Yield (tons/acre)	3.14	2.78	2.81	2.68
Value of Production ($1,000)	377,814	434,156	477,961	400,386
Revenue ($/acre)	5,138	7,046	7,047	7,269

Source: CDFA, 2015

Table 7.7. Cherries, 1985–2015

	1985	1995	2005	2015
Harvested Acreage (acres)	10,243	16,045	27,143	39,712
Yield (tons/acre)	2.69	1.28	1.80	2.28
Value of Production ($1,000)	95,659	123,598	218,737	351,907
Revenue ($/acre)	9,338	7,703	8,059	8,861

Source: CDFA, 2015

$7,635 per acre, and accumulated net cash costs increase through year 7. Once in full production, annual operating costs are $3,200 per acre, with harvest costs 60 percent and pest management costs 10 percent of total operating costs (Buchner et al., 2012). Plum and prune acreage declined by a third between 1985 and 2015, and revenue per acre and the total value of production declined by a fifth.

AVOCADOS AND CHERRIES

California produced 113,000 tons of avocados in 2018 from 51,000 acres, accounting for 98 percent of U.S. production. The state's avocado production peaks during the summer. California had 4,800 avocado farms with 57,000 acres in 2017 (including non-bearing acres), and the 107 avocado farms that each had 100 or more acres accounted for 27 percent of the state's avocado acreage. Avocados are grown primarily in San Diego and Ventura counties.

Avocados are a climacteric fruit that matures on the tree but ripens off the tree. Avocados are picked when they are hard and green, and ripen at room temperature in two weeks, or faster if exposed to ethylene gas. Avocados can remain on trees without damage for weeks.

Avocado harvests begin in year 3 and trees reach full production in year 5. A 2011 UC Cooperative Extension study estimated accumulated cash costs in year 4 of $21,800 an acre in Ventura and Santa Barbara counties, and

annual operating costs of $4,600 an acre, with harvest costs accounting for 40 percent of operating costs. Irrigation accounts for 20 percent of costs, and pest and disease management costs are 7 percent (Takele, Faber, and Vue, 2011).

Avocado acreage and yield declined between 1985 and 2015. Revenues per acre increased by 40 percent due to higher prices that reflected higher consumption. Per capita use of avocados was over seven pounds per person in 2015/16, double the per capita consumption in 2005/06.

California had 1,254 farms producing sweet fresh cherries in 2017. The 83 cherry farms that each had 100 or more acres accounted for almost 60 percent of the state's almost 39,000 acres. San Joaquin County accounted for slightly over half of California cherry acreage in 2015.

Cherries reach economic yields in year 4 and full yields in year 9, and are viable for 25 years. A 2017 UC Cooperative Extension costs and returns study estimated net cash costs at the end of year 4 at $8,688 per acre and operating costs per acre at $15,000, with harvest costs accounting for 80 percent of operating costs. Pruning was 6 percent of costs and pest and disease management 5 percent (Grant, Caprile, Sumner, and Murdock, 2017). Cherry acreage almost quadrupled between 1985 and 2015. Yields declined by 15 percent, and revenue per acre declined by around 5 percent, but the total value of production increased sharply.

PACKERS AND SHIPPERS

There are a relatively small number of buyers of most fruits. For example, the California Avocado Society reported that 12 packer/shippers handled 93 percent of the state's avocados, while the California Avocado Commission lists 16. Calavo, formed as a grower cooperative in 1924 and now a publicly traded company, shipped 35 percent of the avocados consumed in the U.S. in 2005. The California Cherry Board lists 23 shippers, while the California Dried Plum Board lists 23 packers, and the California Canning Peach Association lists six processors.

Many fruits have marketing orders that collect grower-paid fees to engage in activities such as advertising the commodity and research to deal with pest management and other issues. If the majority of growers representing the majority of production acreage approve, all growers can be compelled to support these activities, with first handlers collecting a fee for each box or bin handled. Boards, commissions, and other groups may be created by state or federal law. The California Avocado Commission, California Cherry Board, Citrus Research Board and California Citrus Nursery Program, California Cling Peach Advisory Board, and California Dried Plum Board are state organizations.

Cooperatives and voluntary associations are also important. Sunkist, a grower cooperative, markets a significant share of California citrus production, while the California Canning Peach Association is a bargaining cooperative for peach growers. The California Fresh Fruit Association is a voluntary trade association that focuses on public policy issues for its members, who produce 95 percent of deciduous tree fruit shipped from California and 85 percent of table grapes. California Citrus Mutual is a voluntary trade association that focuses on public policy issues and advocates for citrus producers.

TRENDS

Figure 7.2 shows that cantaloupes and Valencia oranges each declined by more than 100,000 acres over the past two decades. Valencia oranges are typically used to make orange juice. Their acreage began to decline in the early 2000s and has continued to fall as orange juice consumption drops. Raisin grapes, avocados, and dried plums had the next largest declines in acreage. Fruits with the largest decreases in acreage were also those with the largest decreases in the value of production.

Valencia oranges, cantaloupes, and raisin grapes had large declines in value and declines in acreage, followed by plums and prunes and grapefruit. Declining consumption of dried fruit and increased competition from lower-cost imports means that nuts are replacing some raisin grape vineyards and dried plum orchards.

On a percentage basis, raspberries displayed the largest percentage increase in acreage, but from a very low base. Cherries displayed the second-largest percentage increase in acreage. The three remaining fruits in the top five percentage increases in acreage were strawberries, wine grapes, and freestone peaches. Figure 7.3 shows the three

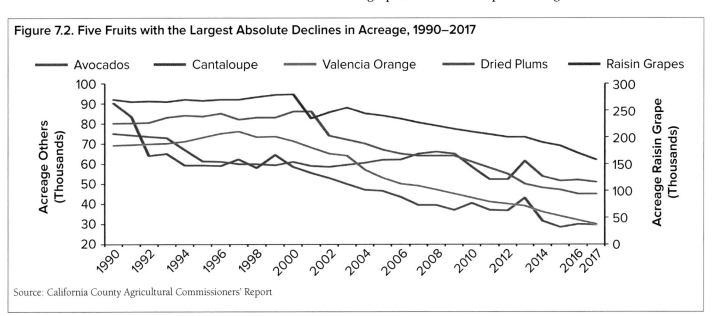

Figure 7.2. Five Fruits with the Largest Absolute Declines in Acreage, 1990–2017

Source: California County Agricultural Commissioners' Report

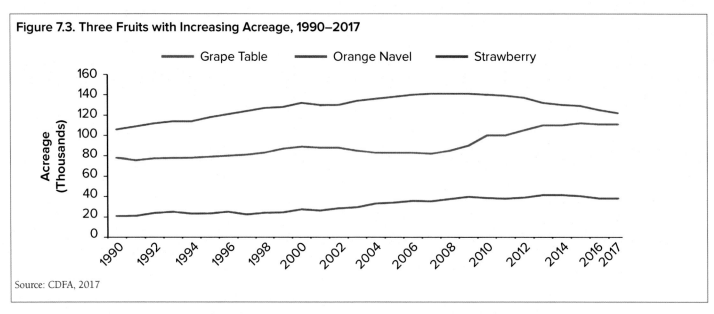

Figure 7.3. Three Fruits with Increasing Acreage, 1990–2017

Source: CDFA, 2017

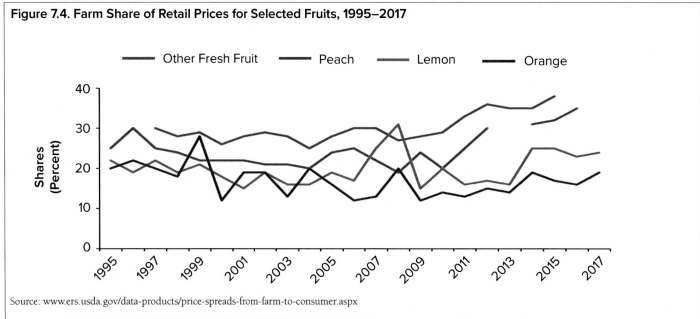

Figure 7.4. Farm Share of Retail Prices for Selected Fruits, 1995–2017

Source: www.ers.usda.gov/data-products/price-spreads-from-farm-to-consumer.aspx

fruits with the largest increases in acreage, led by strawberries, and then table grapes and navel oranges.

Figure 7.4 plots the farm share of the retail price for selected fresh fruit. Since the mid-1990s, the farm share of the retail price has increased for all fresh fruit except oranges, lemons, and peaches.

TREE NUTS

Almonds, pistachios, and walnuts are California's major tree nuts. Almonds were California's most valuable crop in 2017, walnuts were ranked seventh, and pistachios were ranked ninth (CDFA, 2018). U.S. per capita tree nut consumption increased by 62 percent between 1994 to 1998; between 2007 and 2008, it increased again from 1.7 to 2.6 pounds (ERS, 2016). The substantial increase in nut consumption over the past two decades has been associated with their health benefits (Ros, 2010).

Most California tree nuts are exported. California is the world's largest almond producer, accounting for 80 percent of world production. Approximately two-thirds of the California crop was exported in 2015 (CDFA, 2016). California is the world's third-largest producer of walnuts, after China and Iran.

Nut crops are three of California's top five agricultural exports. In 2017, almonds were California's largest agricultural export commodity by value, $4.5 billion; followed by dairy products, $1.6 billion; pistachios, $1.5 billion; and wine and walnuts, $1.4 billion each. The three nut crops accounted for over one-third of all agricultural exports. Table 7.8 ranks nut crops by their 2017 value of production.

California had 7,600 almond farms in 2017, including 2,364 with 100 or more acres; 31 percent of almond farms had 100 or more acres, and they accounted for 87 percent of the state's almond acreage. Most almond acreage is in the San Joaquin Valley, with half in four counties: Kern, Fresno, Stanislaus, and Madera. There are roughly 100 almond processors and handlers (Agricultural Issues Center and Romero, 2015).

Almond acreage increased by 170 percent between 1985 and 2015, and revenues per acre increased by 267 percent in inflation-adjusted dollars. The total value of almond production increased ninefold.

A 2016 UC Cooperative Extension costs and returns study for almond production in the Southern San Joaquin Valley estimated an establishment cost of $8,072 per acre, with annual operating costs of $4,027 per acre, including 10 percent or $421 per acre for harvesting and $400 an acre in pollination costs. Pest and disease management costs are 15 percent of total operating costs, and winter sanitation is an additional 6 percent (Yaghmour et al., 2016).

A 2016 UC Cooperative Extension study for almond production in the Sacramento Valley estimated an establishment cost of $4,591 per acre and annual operating costs of $2,267 per acre, including harvest costs of 17 percent and pollination costs of 20 percent (Pope et al., 2016). In 2016, the cost of irrigation water was the major difference between the Sacramento and San Joaquin Valleys: $392 per acre in the Sacramento Valley and $2,490 per acre in the San Joaquin Valley.

California's Sustainable Groundwater Management Act (SGMA) may limit growth in almond acreage in the San Joaquin Valley, where yields are 30 percent higher than in the Sacramento Valley, which has more access to water. Critically overdrafted groundwater basins are required to have plans to limit overpumping by 2020, which may slow the expansion of almond acreage in the San Joaquin Valley. Almond consumption in China and India, countries with over a third of the world's people, is less than a tenth of the U.S. average of 2.6 pounds per person per year. There

Table 7.8. California Tree Nuts by Value, 2017

Rank	Crop	2017 Value of Production ($1,000)
1	Almond	5,603,950
2	Walnut	1,593,900
3	Pistachio	1,014,507
4	Pecan	11,500

Source: CDFA, 2017

Table 7.9. Almonds, 1985–2015

	1985	1995	2005	2015
Harvested Acreage (acres)	409,670	429,113	611,723	1,109,526
Yield (tons/acre)	0.62	0.45	0.83	0.94
Value of Production ($1,000)	716,331	1,464,126	3,444,807	7,130,359
Revenue ($/acre)	1,749	3,412	5,631	6,426

Source: CDFA, 2015

Table 7.10. Walnuts, 1985–2015

	1985	1995	2005	2015
Harvested Acreage (acres)	179,005	200,404	238,087	363,705
Yield (tons/acre)	1.35	1.23	1.75	1.97
Value of Production ($1,000)	383,746	510,531	732,886	1,549,118
Revenue ($/acre)	2,144	2,548	3,078	4,259

Source: CDFA, 2015

Table 7.11. Pistachios, 1985–2015

	1985	1995	2005	2015
Harvested Acreage (acres)	31,909	58,375	115,349	291,339
Yield (tons/acre)	0.47	1.29	1.46	0.50
Value of Production ($1,000)	102,702	240,186	860,811	895,894
Revenue ($/acre)	3,219	4,115	7,463	3,075

Source: CDFA, 2015

is little competition from other countries that produce almonds; so if almond consumption keeps increasing in China and India, and almonds are used to make commodities from milk to butter, U.S. production and prices could continue to increase.

California had almost 5,700 walnut farms in 2017, including 1,000 with 100 or more acres that accounted for almost 80 percent of walnut acreage. Walnut production occurs throughout the Central Valley, from Shasta County in the north to Kern County in the south. There are about 100 walnut processors (Boriss, Brunke, and Krieth, 2015).

A 2015 UC Cooperative Extension costs and returns study estimated an establishment cost of $7,212 per acre for orchards expected to produce for 30 years. Annual operating costs are $2,241 per acre and harvest costs are half of total operating costs, while pest and disease management costs are one-quarter of costs.

Walnut acreage more than doubled between 1985 and 2015, and yields increased by a third. Revenues per acre, reflecting changes in both yield and prices, effectively doubled and the total value of production quadrupled (Hasey et al, 2015).

There were 1,500 pistachio farms in 2017, including 480 with 100 or more acres and 3 percent that accounted for over 90 percent of the total acreage. Almost all pistachio acreage is in the San Joaquin Valley, including a third in Kern County. Pistachios must be processed within 24 hours of being harvested.

A 2015 UC Cooperative Extension costs and returns study estimated an establishment cost of $11,207 per acre for a pistachio orchard in the Southern San Joaquin Valley and annual operating costs of $2,641 per acre. Harvest costs are 15 percent of operating costs, pest and disease management 18 percent, and winter sanitation 5 percent (Brar et al., 2015). Pistachio acreage increased eightfold between 1985 and 2015, and the value of the crop increased almost eightfold as well.

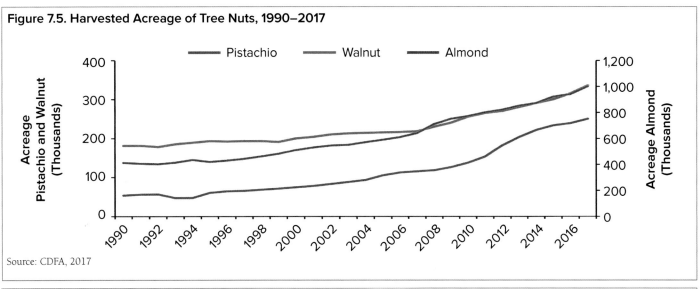

Figure 7.5. Harvested Acreage of Tree Nuts, 1990–2017

Source: CDFA, 2017

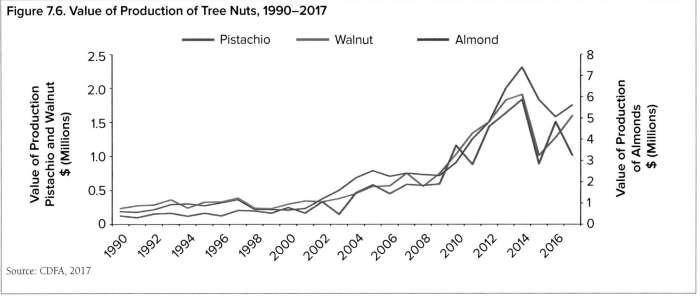

Figure 7.6. Value of Production of Tree Nuts, 1990–2017

Source: CDFA, 2017

TRENDS

Figure 7.5 plots harvested acreage for California tree nuts from 1985 to 2015. Acreage of the three major nuts—almonds, walnuts, and pistachios—increased. Almond acreage is substantially higher than that of the other two nuts, and is plotted against the right-hand axis.

As shown in Figure 7.6, the value of production followed a similar path until 2015, when the price of almonds fell from $4.00 per pound in 2014 to $2.84 per pound (CDFA, 2016). Walnuts also experienced a significant price decrease, from $3,340 a ton to $1,620 a ton, while pistachio prices and yields fell substantially: from $3.57 to $2.48 per pound and from 2,330 to 1,160 pounds per acre.

LABOR CHALLENGES

Half of the 80 top policy issues mentioned by the Board of Directors of the California Fresh Fruit Association between 2010 and 2017 involved labor, including potential enforcement to prevent the hiring of unauthorized workers, immigration reform to provide a legal workforce, and federal and state laws dealing with unionization, health and safety, and minimum wages and overtime (www.cafreshfruit.org/top-10-issues).

The state's largest peach grower, Gerawan Farms, was embroiled in a dispute with the United Farm Workers (UFW) between 2012 and 2018, including an unsuccessful challenge to the state's 2002 Mandatory Mediation and Conciliation (MMC) law. In November 2017, the California

175

Supreme Court held that a union remains certified to represent farm workers until that union is decertified lawfully by current workers. However, the votes cast in a November 2013 decertification election were counted in 2018, revealing that workers voted 197 to retain the UFW and 1,098 to decertify the UFW as bargaining agent; with another 660 votes disputed.

The Agricultural Labor Relations Act (ALRA) was enacted in 1975 "to ensure peace in the agricultural fields by guaranteeing justice for all agricultural workers and stability in labor relations." Contemporary observers expected the ALRA to usher in an era when most of the state's farm workers would work on farms with collective bargaining agreements. In fall 1975, there were almost 100 elections a month, and unions won over 95 percent of those whose results were certified.

Election activity slowed in the 1980s and 1990s after internal UFW changes, Republican appointments to the Agricultural Labor Relations Board (ALRB), and rising unauthorized migration. Despite a unique make-whole remedy for bad-faith bargaining that requires employers who fail to bargain in good faith to make their employees whole for any wage and benefit losses while the employer failed to bargain as required, the UFW charged that employers were delaying bargaining, and discouraging workers from voting for union representation.

The UFW in 2002 persuaded the California Legislature to enact the MMC law to reduce employer-caused delays after unions were certified to represent workers by ensuring a collective bargaining agreement within a year of a union being certified. After bargaining for six months, MMC allows unions or employers to request a mediator to help reach an agreement. If mediation fails, the mediator becomes an arbitrator and develops a contract that the ALRB can order the parties to implement.

The expectation was that MMC would unleash a wave of organizing, elections, and collective bargaining agreements at farms that never had elections or contracts. Instead, MMC was invoked at so-called "old certifications," cases where a union was certified to represent workers before 2002, the employer committed an unfair labor practice, and a collective bargaining agreement was never signed.

Gerawan was an old certification. The ALRB certified the UFW as the bargaining representative for Gerawan workers in July 1992, but no contract was negotiated during a February 1995 bargaining session, and there were no further negotiations.

The UFW in 2012 requested bargaining and, after several bargaining sessions, the UFW requested mediation. Many of Gerawan's workers objected to UFW representation, pointing out that only a few workers who voted for the UFW in 1990 were still at Gerawan in 2012. In November 2013, the workers asked the ALRB to supervise an election to decertify the UFW. However, the ALRB found that Gerawan unlawfully interfered with the decertification election, and the votes were not counted.

Meanwhile, a mediator developed a Gerawan-UFW contract that the ALRB ordered Gerawan to implement. Gerawan refused and challenged the constitutionality of MMC, arguing that MMC allowed the state to impose different rules on different farms. The 5th District Court of Appeal in May 2015 agreed that MMC was unconstitutional, and also agreed that Gerawan should have been able to challenge the UFW's continued right to represent Gerawan employees after almost two decades of no contact between the UFW and Gerawan.

The California Supreme Court reversed the 5th District Court and upheld the constitutionality of the MMC law and upheld the ALRB's finding that a union remains certified to represent farm workers until it is decertified. The Supreme Court found that a mediator can take into account the unique circumstances of each farm and variance in wages and benefits by commodity and area, so mediator-imposed contracts do not violate equal protection guarantees.

After the ruling, the UFW said that Gerawan owed workers $10 million based on the difference between the mediator's contract and the wages and benefits that were paid by Gerawan since 2013. Gerawan disputed this assertion, saying it would not have agreed to a contract with higher wages and benefits even with good-faith bargaining. After the ALRB upheld the certification of the UFW, the make-whole issue became moot. Gerawan Farming and Wawona Packing agreed to merge in September 2019 to create the largest U.S. stone fruit producer, accounting for a third of the state's peaches and nectarines.

MECHANIZATION

Labor costs are rising for all farmers who hire workers, but especially for growers of fresh fruit. Machines grasp the trunks of trees and shake tree nuts to the ground, where they are swept into rows, picked up by machine, and cleaned and sorted before being processed. Fresh fruit trees are often picked multiple times, and the fruit is sometimes obscured by leaves and limbs, posing a difficult challenge for harvesting machines.

There are experiments underway to make fruit trees more amenable to machine harvesting, including planting dwarf trees so that the fruit falls a shorter distance, and improving machine-vision systems to detect ripe fruit and robotic arms to pick it. Another approach is to develop new varieties of apples and peaches that produce fruit that ripens more uniformly. If 80 to 90 percent of the fruit could be harvested in one pass through the field, shake-and-catch machines with catching skirts that surround the tree so that the fruit does not touch the ground, could spread quickly.

Most analysts expect a wave of mechanization in fresh fruit orchards by 2030 in reaction to higher labor costs. Until then, many farmers are experimenting with mechanical aids, including hydraulic lifts that eliminate the use of ladders to harvest tree fruit, which make these jobs more appealing to older workers and women. The most recent comprehensive survey of the status of mechanization in fresh fruit harvesting concluded that mechanization required "new varieties, new cultural practices, and pre- or post-harvest treatments to improve ripeness uniformity and decrease both the susceptibility to and consequences of produce damage." (Sarig, 2000)

DECLINING FRUIT CONSUMPTION

Fruit consumption, whether measured in pounds or consumption events, has declined. For example, the per capita consumption of peaches declined from almost 11 pounds per person in the mid-1980s, including 6 pounds consumed as fresh peaches, to less than 5 pounds of fresh peaches. There are more at-home consumption events for fresh fruit purchased from stores, 130 in 2004 and 150 in 2014, but this increase in events does not compensate for declining consumption of frozen, canned, dried, juice, and homegrown fruit.

One barrier to increasing fruit consumption is meals away from home. Restaurants account for 10 percent of all meals but only 2 percent of fruit consumption events. Seniors consume the most fruit, but their consumption per capita has declined the most among all demographic groups. Declining domestic consumption, all else equal, reduces prices and increases the importance of exports.

Of California's top 15 fruits, only berries have realized significant gains in consumption events. Bananas (46 events), a non-California crop, and apples (32), a smaller California fruit crop, account for a substantially larger share of consumption events than the next three most commonly consumed fruits: berries (24), oranges (14), and grapes (12) (Produce for Better Health Foundation, 2015). Seasonality means that California's market share is not constant throughout the year, and consumption events do not represent only California fruits.

There are many fruits, and the organizations representing one commodity, such as apples or pears, tend to focus on enhancing demand for their commodity rather than for all fruit. Since 1991, the "Five a Day" public-private program has promoted fruit and vegetable consumption with several organizations cooperating to promote increased consumption. The Produce for Better Health Foundation was formed in 1991 by commodity groups, and supports the "Fruits and Veggies: More Matters" initiative.

INVASIVE SPECIES

An invasive species is a non-native plant, animal, microbe or pathogen that causes economic or environmental damage in one or more agricultural or natural systems. In addition to reducing marketable yields and negatively impacting plant health and future yields through direct damage and the transmission of disease, invasive species can negatively affect exports due to phytosanitary regulations in importing countries. Pimente, Zuniga, and Morrison (2005) estimated that for the U.S. as a whole, losses due to invasive species are $120 billion a year.

The California Department of Food and Agriculture's (CDFA) Plant Health and Pest Prevention Services Division is responsible for state efforts to detect, eradicate, and manage invasive species. CDFA had detection and emergency projects for 18 insect pests and three diseases regarded as significant sources or potential sources of economic and environmental damage in 2017 (CDFA, 2017b). Sumner, Brunke, and Krieth (2006) estimated that each state dollar spent on this program has a benefit-cost ratio ranging from 2.8 to 5.1 in terms of economic damages averted.

Not all non-native species become invasive species. A species must first be introduced, become established, and spread. Means of addressing invasive species include: prevention (trapping), inspection or restriction of movement between borders (quarantines), eradication, and ongoing management. According to the Center for Invasive Species Research (CISR) at the University of California, Riverside, 10 percent of species that enter a new ecosystem will survive, and 10 percent of the survivors will become invasive (CISR, 2017).

Three invasive species of current concern in California fruit crops include the polyphagous shot hole borer, the Mediterranean fruit fly, and the Asian citrus psyllid. The Polyphagous Shot Hole Borer (PSHB) is an economic pest in avocados that carries the fungal pathogen, *Fusarium euwallaceae*, and causes Fusarium dieback disease, which disrupts the tree's ability to transport water and nutrients (Eskalen, Dimson, and Kabashima, 2015). The pest and the disease it carries have many other host species, but the largest potential economic impact is associated with avocados (Eskalen, 2017).

The Mediterranean fruit fly (medfly) has appeared repeatedly in California, leading to significant damage and disruption. The fly lays eggs under the skin of fruit, making it unmarketable. The medfly was detected in San Mateo County in December 2017, leading CDFA to place a quarantine on parts of the county. California seeks to eradicate the medfly when it is detected by releasing sterile males and using targeted applications of the organic pesticide spinosad (CDFA, 2017a).

The California citrus industry is currently facing a serious invasive species problem: Asian citrus psyllid, which can transmit huanglongbing disease (HLB) (also known as citrus greening disease). In the nymphal stage, the Asian citrus psyllid survives on the new flush tips of citrus leaves and injects a substance that is toxic to the tree, causing the leaves to stop growing properly. More importantly, infected psyllids can spread a bacterium that causes huanglongbing

disease. Diseased trees produce commercially undesirable fruit that is small, unattractively colored, and distorted in shape with bitter juice; it can also kill the tree in as little as 5 years.

The spread of huanglongbing disease in Florida was associated with a substantial decline in citrus acreage. In California, the disease was detected in backyard citrus a decade ago, prompting efforts to remove infected plants. If the disease were to appear in commercial citrus production regions, the cost of eradicating diseased trees would be significant (Grafton-Cardwell, 2017).

CONCLUSION

Tree fruits and nuts account for 40 percent of the state's farm sales, and tree nuts such as almonds are important agricultural exports. California's tree nut acreage and production are increasing, while the acreage and production of tree fruits such as peaches and oranges is decreasing.

Tree fruits face more challenges than nuts, which have enjoyed rising production and prices but may face market saturation and water issues. Harvesting tree fruit is a labor-intensive process that is now done largely by unauthorized workers. The costs of labor are rising with the state's minimum wage, prompting efforts to mechanize pruning and harvesting. Meanwhile, the fruit industry must grapple with declining consumption and threats from invasive species.

REFERENCES

Agricultural Issues Center, updated by C. Romero. 2015. "Almonds." Agricultural Marketing Center and University of California Agricultural Issues Center. Available at: https://www.agmrc.org/commodities-products/nuts/almonds/.

Boriss, H., updated by C. Romero. 2015. "Pistachios." Agricultural Marketing Center and University of California Agricultural Issues Center. Available at: https://www.agmrc.org/commodities-products/nuts/pistachios.

Boriss, H., H. Brunke, and M. Krieth, updated by Christina Romero. 2015. "English Walnuts." Agricultural Marketing Center and University of California Agricultural Issues Center. Available at: https://www.agmrc.org/commodities-products/nuts/english-walnuts/.

Brar, G.S., D. Doll, L. Ferguson, E. Fichtner, C.E. Kallsen, R.H. Beede, K. Klonsky, K.P. Tumber, N. Anderson, and D. Stewart. 2015. "Sample Costs to Establish and Produce Pistachios, San Joaquin Valley - South: Low-Volume Irrigation." Available at: https://coststudies.ucdavis.edu/en/.

Buchner, R.P., J.H. Connell, F.J. Niederholzer, C.J. DeBuse, K. Klonsky, and R.L. De Moura. 2012. "Sample Costs to Establish a Prune Orchard and Produce Prunes (Dried Plums), Sacramento Valley: French Variety & Low-Volume Irrigation." Available at: https://coststudies.ucdavis.edu/en/.

California Department of Food and Agriculture. 2016. *California Agricultural Statistics Review, 2015-2016.* Available at: https://www.cdfa.ca.gov/statistics/PDFs/2016Report.pdf.

California Department of Food and Agriculture. 2015. *California County Agricultural Commissioners' Report* Available at: https://www.nass.usda.gov/Statistics_by_State/California/.

California Department of Food and Agriculture. 2017a. "Press Release: Medfly Quarantine in Portion of San Mateo County." Release #17-082. December 19. Available at: https://www.cdfa.ca.gov/egov/Press_Releases/Press_Release.asp?PRnum=17-082.

California Department of Food and Agriculture. 2017b. "Target Diseases and Pests." Available at: http://www.cdfa.ca.gov/plant/PDEP/target_pests.html.

Center for Invasive Species Research, University of California, Riverside. 2017. "Frequently Asked Questions about Invasive Species." Available at: http://cisr.ucr.edu/invasive_species_faqs.html#what percent20are percent20invasive percent20species.

Day, K.R., K. Klonsky, D.A. Sumner, and D. Stewart. 2016. "Sample Costs to Establish and Produce Plums, San Joaquin Valley-South: Fresh Market-Double Line Drip Irrigation." Available at: https://coststudies.ucdavis.edu/en/.

Economic Research Service, United States Department of Agriculture. 2016. "Table 1. Annual U.S. per Capita Loss-adjusted Food Availability: Total, Children, and Adults." Available at: https://www.ers.usda.gov/data-products/commodity-consumption-by-population-characteristics/.

Economic Research Service, United States Department of Food and Agriculture. 2017. "Tree Nuts : Bearing Acreage, Yield Per Acre, Gross Returns per Acre, Production and Value, Price, and Supply and Utilization." Available at: https://www.ers.usda.gov/data-products/fruit-and-tree-nut-data/fruit-and-tree-nut-yearbook-tables/#Tree Nuts.

Eskalen, A. 2017. "Polyphagous Shot Hole Borer (*Euwallacea sp.*) and Fusarium Dieback (*Fusarium sp.*)." Center for Invasive Species Research, University of California, Riverside. Available at: http://cisr.ucr.edu/polyphagous_shot_hole_borer.html.

Eskalen, A., M. Dimson and J. Kabashima. 2015. "Polyphagous Shot Hole Borer and Fusarium Dieback: A Pest Disease Complex on Avocado in CA." University of California Division of Agriculture and Natural Resources. Available at: http://ucanr.edu/sites/pshb/files/238251.pdf.

Federal Reserve Bank of Saint Louis. 2017. "Consumer Price Index for All Urban Consumers: All Items" Available at: https://fred.stlouisfed.org/series/CPIAUCSL.

Grafton-Cardwell, E. 2017. "Asian Citrus Psyllid." Center for Invasive Species Research, University of California, Riverside. Available at: http://cisr.ucr.edu/asian_citrus_psyllid.html.

Grant, J.A., J.L. Caprile, D.A. Sumner, and J. Murdock. 2017. "Sample Costs for Sweet Cherries to Establish an Orchard and Produce Sweet Cherries, San Joaquin Valley-North: Micro-Sprinkler Irrigation." Available at: https://coststudies.ucdavis.edu/en/.

Hasey, J.K., R.P. Bucher, K. Klonsky, D.A. Sumner, N. Anderson, and D. Stewart. 2015. "Sample Costs to Establish and Produce English Walnuts in the Sacramento Valley: Micro Sprinkler Irrigated." Available at: https://coststudies.ucdavis.edu/en/.

Hasey, J.K., R. Duncan, D.A. Sumner, and J.Murdock. 2017. "Sample Costs to Establish and Produce Processing Peaches Cling and Freestone Late Harvested Varieties, Sacramento and San Joaquin Valley." Available at: https://coststudies.ucdavis.edu/en/.

Lin, B.-H. and R. Mentzer Morrison. 2016. "A Close Look at Declining Fruit and Vegetable Consumption Using Linked Data Sources." *Amber Waves*. July 5. Available at: https://www.ers.usda.gov/amber-waves/2016/july/a-closer-look-at-declining-fruit-and-vegetable-consumption-using-linked-data-sources/.

O'Connell, N., C.E. Kallsen, K. Klonsky, and K.P. Tumber. 2015. "Sample Costs to Establish an Orange Orchard and Produce Oranges." Available at: https://coststudies.ucdavis.edu/en/.

Pimentel, D., R. Zuniga, and D. Morrison. 2005. "Update on the Environmental and Economic Costs Associated with Alien-invasive Species in the United States." *Ecological Economics*, 52(3), pp.273-288.

Pope, K.S., D.M. Lightle, R.P. Buchner, F. Niederholzer, K. Klonsky, D.A. Sumner, D. Stewart, and C.A. Gutierrez. 2016. "Sample Costs to Establish and Orchard and Produce Almonds, Sacramento Valley: Micro-Sprinkler Irrigation." Available at: https://coststudies.ucdavis.edu/en/.

Produce for Better Health Foundation. 2017. "Our Donors." Available at: https://fruitsandveggies.org/wp-content/uploads/2019/03/PBH_Annual_Report_2017.pdf.

Produce for Better Health Foundation. 2016. "Scorecard." Available at: https://pbhfoundation.org/pdfs/about/org_plan/PBHScorecardInfographic2016.pdf.

Produce for Better Health Foundation. 2015. State of the Plate, 2015 Study on America's Consumption of Fruit and Vegetables. Available at: https://fruitsandveggies.org/.

Ros, E. 2010. Health Benefits on Nut Consumption. *Nutrients* 2:652-682. Available at: https://www.ncbi.nlm.nih.gov/pmc/articles/PMC3257681/pdf/nutrients-02-00652.pdf.

Sarig, Y., J.F. Thompson, and G.K. Brown. 2000. "Alternatives to Immigrant Labor?" Center for Immigration Studies. Available at: https://cis.org/Alternatives-Immigrant-Labor.

Sumner, D.A., H. Brunke, and M. Kreith. 2006. "Aggregate Costs and Benefits of Government Invasive Species Control Activities in California." University of California Agricultural Issues Center. Available at: https://coststudies.ucdavis.edu/en/.

Takele, E., B. Faber, and M. Vue. 2011. "Avocado Sample Establishment and Production Costs And Profitability Analysis For Ventura, Santa Barbara, And San Luis Obispo Counties, Conventional Production Practices." Available at: https://coststudies.ucdavis.edu/en/.

United States Department Of Agriculture. 2017. *Fruit and Tree Nuts Yearbook*. Available at: http://usda.mannlib.cornell.edu/usda/ers/89022/2017/FruitandTreeNutYearbook2017.pdf.

United States Department of Agriculture. 2017. Quick Stats. Available at: https://quickstats.nass.usda.gov/.

Yaghmour, M., D.R. Haviland, E.J. Fichtner, B.L. Sanden, M. Viveros, D.A. Sumner, D.E. Stewart, and C.A., Gutierrez. 2016. "Sample Costs to Establish an Orchard and Produce Almonds, San Joaquin Valley South: Double Line Drip Irrigation." Available at: https://coststudies.ucdavis.edu/en/.

CHAPTER 8. GRAPE AND WINE PRODUCTION IN CALIFORNIA

JULIAN M. ALSTON, JAMES T. LAPSLEY, AND OLENA SAMBUCCI

ABSTRACT

Grapes were California's most valuable crop in 2017. They are grown throughout the state for wine production and, in the San Joaquin Valley, for raisins, fresh table grapes, grape-juice concentrate, and distillate. This chapter outlines the broader grape-growing industry as a whole to provide context for a more detailed discussion of wine grapes and wine. We discuss the regional variation in wine grape yields and prices within California, and the evolving varietal mix; the economic structure of the grape-growing and wine-producing industry; and shifting patterns of production, consumption, and trade in wine. We interpret these patterns in the context of recent changes in the global wine market and the longer economic and policy history of grape and wine production in California.

ABOUT THE AUTHORS

Julian Alston is a Distinguished Professor in the Department of Agricultural and Resource Economics and the director of the Robert Mondavi Institute Center for Wine Economics at the University of California, Davis, and a member of the Giannini Foundation of Agricultural Economics. He can be contacted by email at jmalston@ucdavis.edu. Jim Lapsley is an academic researcher at the UC Agricultural Issues Center; an adjunct associate professor in the Department of Viticulture and Enology, University of California, Davis; and emeritus chair of the Department of Science, Agriculture, and Natural Resources for UC Davis Extension. He can be reached by email at jtlapsley@gmail.com. Olena Sambucci is an assistant project scientist in the Department of Agricultural and Resource Economics at the University of California, Davis. She can be contacted by email at osambucci@ucdavis.edu.

ACKNOWLEDGEMENTS

The work for this project was partly supported by the National Institute of Food and Agriculture, U.S. Department of Agriculture, under award number 2011-51181-30635 (the *Vitis*Gen project), and award number 2015-51181-24393 (the Efficient Vineyard project). The authors are grateful for this support. Views expressed are the authors' alone.

In 2017, California had 935,000 acres of grapes planted, which produced about 6.5 million tons of grapes, worth some $5.7 billion at the farm. Of this total, about $3.6 billion was for wine grapes, $1.6 billion for table grapes, and $0.5 billion for raisin grapes.

Photo Credit: UC Davis

CHAPTER 8. TABLE OF CONTENTS

INTRODUCTION

Grapes have been cultivated in the United States for more than 400 years and in California for more than 200 years. However, California's grape and wine industry did not really take off as such until the end of the 19th century. As discussed and documented in detail by Pinney (1989, 2005) and summarized by Alston et al. (2018), the longer history of grape and wine production in America reflects several significant influences. These include ongoing struggles against the biological barriers to development of an industry, eventually overcome about 150 years ago when the industry was first established in California; the subsequent destruction of the wine industry by government fiat in 1920, with consequences that lasted well beyond Repeal after 14 years of Prohibition; the recovery and reconstruction of the industry and a return to specialized wine grapes through the middle of the 20th century, which was both hindered and hastened by government policies; and seismic shifts in patterns of consumption and production in the modern era, with increased attention to quality and product differentiation.

In the late 18th century, Franciscan missionaries introduced European (*Vitis vinifera*) "Mission" grapes to California for making wine; the first vintage was probably 1782 (Pinney, 1989). This was the main form of grape cultivation in California until the 1850s when, on the heels of the 1849 gold rush, the new state of California emerged as a major supplier of wine. California rose to a position of national preeminence in wine and wine grape production by 1880, a status it has held since. Much changed over the subsequent decades, and it was not all plain sailing, but the ultimate outcome was the creation of a thriving, vibrant, fascinating industry. The United States today is recognized globally as a significant wine producer, and the lion's share of the total U.S. value and volume of wine production is sourced in California.

In parallel with the growth in production of grapes for winemaking came the development of industry segments dedicated to growing grapes for other end-uses, including drying for raisins, packing as table grapes for fresh consumption, and crushing for grape juice concentrate and distillation. In the early days, multipurpose grape varieties—such as Thompson Seedless—could be grown for any and all of these end-uses, and flexibly allocated among them from one season to the next. Nowadays, varieties, trellises, and other aspects of the production system are much more specialized for particular end-uses, and the different parts of the grape industry are much less integrated with one another. In many ways, they are now altogether separate industries, each of which is complicated and interesting in its own ways. Taken together, table, raisin, and wine grapes have been ranked as California's most valuable crop in many years and grapes continue to vie for that status with almonds (Sambucci and Alston 2017). In 2017, California had a total of 829 thousand bearing acres of grapes, which produced about 6.5 million tons of grapes, worth some $5.7 billion (2017 dollar values) at the farm. Of this total, about $3.6 billion was for wine grapes, $1.6 billion for table grapes, and $0.5 billion for raisin grapes.

This chapter provides an economic overview of the grape and wine industries in California, paying attention to the major developments in the history of those industries and the main influential forces, many of which continue to play a role, including the evolving global and domestic market context. The chapter begins with a broad overview of the grape-producing industry as a whole, and then provides more detail on each of the main grape industries, defined according to the end-use of the grapes. Most of the chapter is devoted to wine grapes and wine, and less to the other end-uses of grapes, partly because it is a more complicated and diverse sector, as will be explained, and partly because we deal with the wine industry as well as the industry producing its primary input: wine grapes.

CURRENT GRAPE PRODUCTION PATTERNS — AN OVERVIEW

The production of grapes and wine in California dates back at least to the beginnings of European settlement, in the 17th century. Native American pests and diseases (such as phylloxera, Pierce's disease, powdery mildew, and downy mildew, among others), combined with unfavorable climatic conditions, frustrated earlier attempts to establish an industry in the eastern states based on European *Vitis vinifera* grape varieties (Pinney, 1989). The consequences of the Gold Rush of the 1850s, combined with technological advantages, California's more favorable climate, and practices for managing the main pest and disease problems, made *Vitis vinifera* cultivation sustainable and enabled the wine industry to take off in the late 1800s, only to be shut down by government fiat a few decades later. While California's wineries were closed by Prohibition (1920–33), grape growing flourished, producing varieties suitable for shipping east for home wine-making, as well as for raisins and fresh consumption.

Repeal in 1933 left an enduring legacy in terms of the varietal mix and industry structure and Byzantine state-specific regulations over wine production and marketing. Following World War II, which imposed different policy strictures and introduced new incentives for reorganizing production, grape and wine production in California entered an era of growth and change, as discussed by Alston et al. (2018). Especially in the past 20–30 years, the industry has evolved considerably in terms of the product mix and quality emphasis, with implications for varieties planted and cultivation practices in vineyards. In this section, we review the current status of the California grape-growing industry in the context of developments over the past half-century, emphasizing the more recent trends.

AREA, VOLUME, AND VALUE OF PRODUCTION

Grapes have multiple end-uses, with some varieties being suitable for more than one end-use, and complete information is not available on the actual utilization of these multipurpose varieties. Even when we know the utilization, it is not always straightforward to compare quantities and values of grapes across end-uses. When they leave the farm, raisins and especially table grapes are close to their final product forms, whereas wine grapes must undergo considerable further processing, with much value-adding, before they become retail wine. Thus, comparing farm-gate values is different from comparing either values at harvest or final values among end-uses of grapes.[1]

Further complications arise when we discuss production patterns among regions within California, because the available information is based on reports by County Agricultural Commissioners, which are not necessarily comparable among counties. The aggregation of the county-level data yields totals that are not entirely consistent with the totals reported by the United States Department of Agriculture (USDA), National Agricultural Statistics Service (NASS) for the state as a whole. We seek to provide consistent and meaningful measures, properly explained.

Figure 8.1 shows the trends in 50 years of annual observations of the total bearing area, volume, and value of production at the farm level for each of the three main categories of grapes—wine, table, and raisin—based on the classification of varieties of grapes among these three main end-uses, though they might not all have been used as such.[2] Figure 8.1 shows that the total bearing area of wine grapes has grown considerably both in absolute terms and relative to table grapes and raisin grapes, with notable surges in the 1970s and the 1990s. Raisins have lost ground, especially in the past two decades, while table grapes have crept up fairly steadily. The trends of bearing area are reflected in the trends in volume of production. However, the production patterns exhibit more variability, reflecting the boom and bust cycles of production and investment as well as weather effects on yields.

---

1   In the case of raisin production, we sometimes observe quantities and prices of the dried fruit, and have to use conversion factors to infer the quantity of fresh fruit used to produce them; sometimes the converse.

2   In particular, we know that considerable quantities have been used for the production of grape juice concentrate and distillate. Nowadays, this production is predominantly based on "wine grapes" (say, 20–30 percent of the total annual "crush"), particularly from the Southern San Joaquin Valley. Fifty years ago a much greater share of production for this and all end-uses would have been from Thompson Seedless grapes, a truly multipurpose variety.

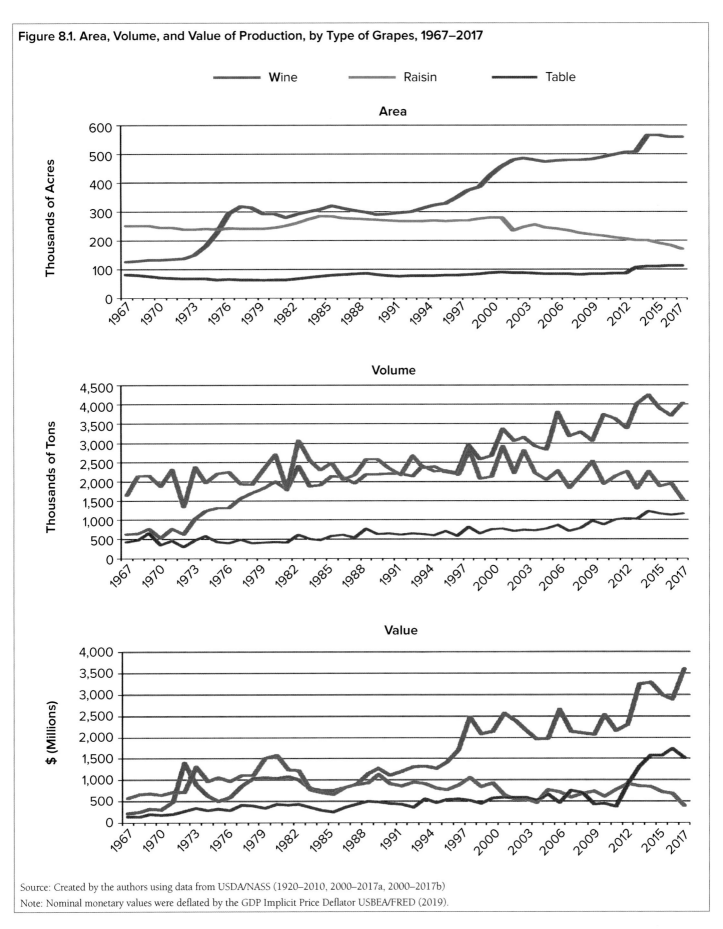

Figure 8.1. Area, Volume, and Value of Production, by Type of Grapes, 1967–2017

Source: Created by the authors using data from USDA/NASS (1920–2010, 2000–2017a, 2000–2017b)
Note: Nominal monetary values were deflated by the GDP Implicit Price Deflator USBEA/FRED (2019).

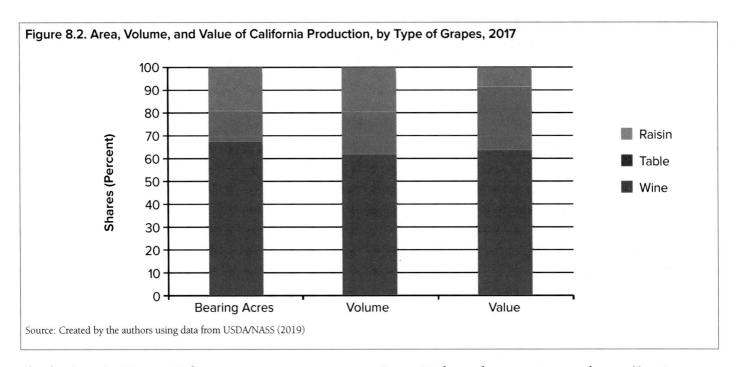

Figure 8.2. Area, Volume, and Value of California Production, by Type of Grapes, 2017

Source: Created by the authors using data from USDA/NASS (2019)

The third panel of Figure 8.1 shows an even more pronounced divergence in the trends in real (2017 dollars) value of production among the different end-uses. This pattern reflects a "premiumization" of wine production in terms of both the varietal mix and regional location of production within California, as documented by Alston, Anderson, and Sambucci (2015), and, more recently, a rapid rise in the average unit value of California table grapes.

Figure 8.3. Grape-Producing Areas of California

■ North Coast

■ Central Coast

■ N. San Joaquin Valley

■ S. San Joaquin Valley

■ Other California

Source: Created by the authors

Figure 8.2 shows the contemporary shares of bearing area, volume, and value of production among the three main types of grapes grown. Wine grapes dominate the picture in every dimension. Table grapes have large shares of volume and especially value compared with their share of bearing area—comparatively high yields per acre and especially high average values per ton; raisins have, conversely, a small share of value compared with their shares of area and volume of production.

Wine grapes are grown in significant quantities in many parts of the state, whereas production of table grapes and raisin grapes is concentrated in the Southern San Joaquin Valley. Table 8.1 includes details on the bearing area, volume, and value of production of each of the three main categories of grapes in each of five main regions of the state (Figure 8.3), based on county-specific data from the County Crop Reports published by the Agricultural Commissioner's office for each respective county (see References for a complete list of reports), and the sum of those elements, representing the state as a whole. For comparison, the table also includes the corresponding state totals obtained from USDA/NASS (2019), which are generally similar but with some notable discrepancies, such as the average unit values and consequently the total value of raisins and table grapes.

Table 8.1. Area, Volume, and Value of Production, by Types of Grapes and Region, 2017

Region	Grape Types			Total
	Wine Grapes	Raisin Grapes	Table Grapes	
Total Area, Thousand Bearing Acres				
North Coast	129			129
Central Coast	119			119
N. San Joaquin Valley	176			176
S. San Joaquin Valley	142	132	133	407
Other California	17	2	7	26
Total California	582	134	140	856
NASS Total California	560	158	111	829
Total Production, Thousand Tons				
North Coast	452			452
Central Coast	460			460
N. San Joaquin Valley	1,295			1,295
S. San Joaquin Valley	1,684	1,351	1,529	4,564
Other California	68	22	49	139
Total California	3,959	1,372	1,578	6,910
NASS Total California	4,014	1,268	1,200	6,482
Average Unit Value, $ Per Ton				
North Coast	3,311			3,311
Central Coast	1,574			1,574
N. San Joaquin Valley	590			590
S. San Joaquin Valley	332	438	1,813	860
Other California	1,281	455	2,389	1,546
California Average	917	438	1,831	1,031
NASS Total California	927	380	1,330	894
Total Value, $ Millions				
North Coast	1,496			1,496
Central Coast	724			724
N. San Joaquin Valley	764			764
S. San Joaquin Valley	559	559	2,772	3,923
Other California	87	10	118	215
Total California	3,630	601	2,890	7,122
NASS Total California	3,721	482	1,596	5,799

Sources: Created by the authors using data from CDFA (2018); County Crop Reports for Glenn, Stanislaus, and Tehama counties were obtained from the Agricultural Commissioner's Office for each county (see references); NASS state totals are from USDA/NASS (2019)

Note: Volume of production and price per ton for raisin grapes are reported using fresh equivalent basis.

Table 8.2. Total Grape Area and Number of Grape-Producing Farms, 2017

Region	Total Grape Area		
	Farms	Acres	Acres/Farm
North Coast (NC)	4,156	150,481	36.2
Central Coast (CC)	1,694	131,697	77.7
N. San Joaquin Valley NSJV)	1,336	188,244	140.9
S. San Joaquin Valley (SSJV)	2,610	434,808	166.6
Other (OC)	2,016	30,042	14.9
Total California	11,812	935,272	79.2

Source: Created by the authors using data from USDA/NASS (2017b)

Most of the total value and volume of grape production comes from the Southern San Joaquin Valley, which produces all of California's raisin and table grapes and also a significant share of the state's total volume, but a much smaller share of the total value of production of wine grapes. The wine grapes produced in this region have a comparatively low average unit value, offset to some extent by high yields, and they are used to produce very low-cost wine, grape juice concentrate, and distillate. The other four regions produce only wine grapes in significant quantities, and they vary in their market outlets and structure of production in interesting ways that are discussed in detail in subsequent sections.

STRUCTURE OF THE GRAPE-GROWING INDUSTRY

In 2017, the most recent year for which census data are available, California had 11,812 farms that grew grapes. The total area (including non-bearing vines) was 935 thousand acres planted to grapes, an average of 79 acres per farm (USDA/NASS, 2017b). These statewide average figures mask some variation among regions, some of which stems from different types of grape production. In the San Joaquin Valley, with an average of more than 140 acres of grapes per producer, grape production generally is conducted at a larger scale compared with the coastal regions, especially the North Coast, with an average of 36 acres of grapes per producer (Table 8.2).

Not surprisingly, wine grape growers in California's Central Valley have mechanized, adopting mechanical pruning and harvesting at a higher rate than coastal growers, who generally continue to rely on hand labor for many operations. Over 80 percent of California's wine grapes are harvested by machine. Machine pruning is less widely adopted (Dokoozlian, 2013). In contrast, table grape production, in particular, is highly labor intensive, as table grapes are picked by hand and packed in the field, leaving the vineyard ready for direct delivery to the supermarket. Nevertheless, table grape operations tend to be relatively large scale, employing large crews of hired labor during the harvest.

Table 8.3 contains more information on the size distribution of grape producers in terms of area planted to grapes— again, including all end-uses of grapes. As is typical of farm-size distributions, this distribution is heavily skewed to the right. The vast majority of grape producers have relatively small vineyards and, while the average area is 79 acres of vines, the median is closer to 15 acres. Reflecting this skewness, the roughly 55 percent of growers who had less than 15 acres of vines collectively accounted for less than 3 percent of the total vineyard area, while the 92 growers (less than 1 percent of the total) who had 1,500 acres or more were responsible for almost 32 percent of the total area. More than half the total vineyard area is on farms with 500 or more acres of vineyard. Of course, and as noted above, these distributional figures for the statewide industry as a whole will not be equally representative of all segments. In particular, very large vineyards are much more likely to be found in the San Joaquin Valley than in the premium coastal valleys where land values are very much higher.

Table 8.3. California: Size Distribution of Grape Producers, 2017				
Size Range	**Total Bearing and Non-Bearing Grapes**		**Cumulative Total**	
	Farms	Acres	Acres	Percent
0.1 to 0.9 acres	1,359	528	528	0.06
1.0 to 4.9 acres	3,118	6,997	7,525	0.80
5.0 to 14.9 acres	2,238	19,322	26,847	2.87
15.0 to 24.9 acres	1,181	22,068	48,915	5.23
25.0 to 49.9 acres	1,269	44,443	93,358	9.98
50.0 to 99.9 acres	1,037	72,738	166,096	17.76
100.0 to 249.9 acres	885	133,980	300,076	32.08
250.0 to 499.9 acres	382	132,348	432,424	46.24
500.0 to 749.9 acres	128	78,341	510,765	54.61
750.0 to 999.9 acres	58	49,413	560,178	58.89
1,000.0 to 1,499.9 acres	65	78,730	638,908	68.31
1,500.0 acres or more	92	296,363	935,271	100.00
All Farms	11,812	935,271		

Source: Created by the authors using data from USDA/NASS (2017a)

UTILIZATION OF GRAPES GROWN IN CALIFORNIA

Several features of grape production make an economic analysis of this industry particularly complicated. First, like other perennial crops, grapes are capital intensive, with a large share of the total costs of production tied up in the biological capital—the vines themselves—and the associated physical capital in trellising and irrigation infrastructure. This biological capital takes years to create on the farm—with a gestation period of several years before vines become fully productive, followed by a productive life of 20 years or more. Eventually, this capital stock depreciates economically, either because of changes in demand for the particular variety, or because of physical deterioration,

owing to the burden of chronic diseases (often "trunk diseases") or pest infestations reducing the productivity of the vineyard.[3]

In the short run, grape production is largely pre-determined (supply is highly inelastic with respect to current

---

3 In perennial crops, pests and diseases can cause a loss of the current year's output but also a reduction in the capacity to produce future output. When Pierce's disease kills grapevines, it destroys valuable capital that takes years to replace. This leads to a loss in output for several years, in addition to the cost of replanting the vineyard.

Table 8.4. Utilization of California's Grape Crush, 2000–2017

Crush Year	Crush Volume				Shares of Total Volume		
	Total	Concentrate	Distilled	Wine	Concentrate	Distilled	Wine
	Thousand Tons				Percent		
2000	3,951	745	749	2,458	18.9	18.9	62.2
2001	3,368	537	651	2,180	15.9	19.3	64.7
2002	3,787	752	808	2,227	19.9	21.3	58.8
2003	3,370	507	654	2,209	15.0	19.4	65.5
2004	3,615	658	623	2,334	18.2	17.2	64.6
2005	4,329	550	565	3,214	12.7	13.0	74.2
2006	3,489	463	541	2,485	13.3	15.5	71.2
2007	3,674	516	509	2,649	14.1	13.9	72.1
2008	3,673	748	507	2,418	20.4	13.8	65.8
2009	4,095	499	532	3,064	12.2	13.0	74.8
2010	3,986	536	578	2,872	13.4	14.5	72.1
2011	3,874	598	581	2,695	15.4	15.0	69.6
2012	4,387	529	569	3,290	12.1	13.0	75.0
2013	4,699	655	729	3,315	13.9	15.5	70.5
2014	4,143	470	699	2,975	11.3	16.9	71.8
2015	3,868	435	661	2,772	11.2	17.1	71.7
2016	4,227	393	504	3,330	9.3	11.9	78.8
2017	4,242	404	448	3,390	9.5	10.6	79.9
Average	3,932	555	606	2,771	14.3	15.5	70.2

Source: Created by the authors using data from USDA/NASS (2000–2017a)

Note: Tons crushed for distillate computed assuming 170 gallons per ton applied to total distillate from U.S. Treasury/TTB (2017a).

prices), and prices must adjust to absorb shifts in demand or changes in total production that reflect prior investments or yield shocks from weather or pests (or, as in 2017, wildfires). These features of the production system can give rise to pronounced boom-and-bust cycles and leave grape producers vulnerable to sharp changes in markets (including shifts in demand as different varieties of table grapes or wine grapes become more or less fashionable). The wine grape industry, in particular, has seen some dramatic demand shifts.

Second, unlike most other perennial crops, production of grapes is highly differentiated both in terms of the varieties of grapes grown—classified according to their primary end-use—and, especially within the wine grape sector, in terms of the market "quality" segment and corresponding methods of production. Both within and especially among regions of California, the normal yields and prices of wine grapes vary enormously, more so than for any other farm commodity. This diversity complicates the analysis of the economics of production at the farm level as well as in the retail markets for wine where prices range from a few dollars to hundreds of dollars per 750 ml bottle.

TABLE GRAPES

Over the past 30 years, as shown in Figure 8.1, annual production of table grapes grew steadily—from 540 thousand tons on 84 thousand bearing acres in 1987 to 1,200 thousand tons on 111 thousand bearing acres in 2017. Over the same period, the real value of that production grew even faster—from $444 million to $1,596 million (2017 dollars)—reflecting a considerable increase in average price per ton, especially during the current decade.

At least some of that increase in unit value is due to new varieties of table grapes with enhanced quality traits, for which consumers are happy to pay more—such as large seedless berries, with the desired color, sensory attributes, and seasonal availability. In table grapes, varietal innovation is proceeding rapidly, including proprietary private varieties developed and owned by individual producers as well as public varieties developed by grape breeders supported by a mixture of government and industry funding.

In 2017, the California Grape Acreage Report (USDA/NASS 2018a) listed details of area planted for more than 70 table grape varieties, of which 15 had at least 1,000 acres

planted and together accounted for the lion's share (83 percent) of the total. As one indicator of the rapid rate of varietal change, all of the bearing acreage for several of the current varieties was planted at least 10 years ago, while for several others, all of the current acreage was planted within the past five years. Varieties that had the largest share of bearing acreage in 2017 (Flame Seedless, 18.1 percent; Crimson Seedless, 10.2 percent; Red Globe, 8.6 percent) had much smaller shares of non-bearing acreage (a combined total of 6.7 percent) compared with some up-and-coming varieties (Allison, 10.9 percent; Scarlet Royal, 10.5 percent; Autumn King, 8.13 percent).

Table grapes are typically picked and packed in a single operation, such that they leave the field in retail packs ready for cold storage and shipment to retailers around the world. Quality control is paramount, and growers incur significant labor and other costs both before and during the harvest. University of California Cost and Return Studies indicate that in 2017, table grape growers incurred annual operating costs on the order of $14,000–$18,000 per acre for newer, popular varieties (about 45 percent of these costs was for labor), to generate income of about $30,000 per acre (Fidelibus et al., 2018a, 2018b). Significant issues for growers in this industry include continued access to a sufficient supply of skilled labor, improved varieties, and pesticides and other compounds used in grape production and management as well as pests and diseases. New concerns about labor supply have promoted enhanced interest in mechanization and the use of information technologies to allow more effective and efficient use of labor, water, and other resources. Promising possibilities are being developed.

Table grapes are available to U.S. consumers year-round. California itself has an extended growing season, because it combines diverse regions and varieties with different harvest times. The winter months are covered by imports from Mexico and the Southern Hemisphere—especially Chile and, more recently, Peru. California exports table grapes to other countries, especially Canada and China, as well as countries throughout the Southern Hemisphere.

RAISINS

Production of raisin grapes peaked in the early 1980s, after which, as shown in Figure 8.1, the trend in annual area and production was flat for many years, while the real (2017 dollar) value trended down. Since 2000, both area and production have trended down along with value: from 280 thousand bearing acres yielding 2,921 thousand tons fresh equivalent valued at $670 million (compared with 2,112 thousand tons valued at $964 million in the previous year, 1999), down to 170 thousand bearing acres yielding 1,536 thousand tons valued at $482 million in 2017. The patterns of fluctuating (and fading) fortunes for California raisin producers reflect a pronounced pattern of fluctuating production and thus prices—with years of high yields (and low prices) followed next year by low yields (and high prices)—in the context of a static or declining demand. The upshot is a shrinking of the industry and responses by government and industry attempting to mitigate the consequences.

Although raisins are traded internationally, patterns of prices and production indicate that the California industry faces a significantly downward sloping demand. The Raisin Administrative Committee (RAC, a federal marketing order established in 1949) sought to exploit that relationship by using its reserve (supply management) program to divert raisins away from the normal market and thereby to increase the price (and hence, the value) of the crop. In June 2015, the Supreme Court outlawed the RAC's reserve program on the grounds that it represented an unconstitutional taking of property (see, e.g., Crespi, Saitone, and Sexton, 2016). The marketing cooperative, Sun-Maid, almost 100-years old, and the California Raisin Marketing Board (CRMB, a state marketing order created in 1998), continue to provide other industry "collective" goods, but neither of these organizations can manage supply.

Of course, some producers will continue to succeed and even flourish. Varietal innovation has been slow in this industry, compared with table grapes. In 2016, 86 percent of the total area of raisin grapes was still Thompson Seedless, most of which were planted at least 10 years ago, with Fiesta (8 percent), and Selma Pete (4 percent) accounting for most of the rest. However, innovative producers have been adopting new trellises and production systems—such as dried on the vine—that will allow them to operate with less labor and on a larger scale, and thus at lower cost and on an economically more sustainable basis, as indicated by recent University of California Cost and Return Studies (Fidelibus et al., 2016a, 2016b).

JUICE CONCENTRATE AND DISTILLATE

Some so-called "raisin grapes" are diverted to other uses, especially when prices for raisins are low. In 2017, 94 thousand tons of raisin grapes were crushed, potentially for use as wine or other uses including grape juice concentrate or distillate; and, in the same year, a further 132 thousand tons of "table grapes" were crushed. These amounts are significant, but small relative to the quantities of raisin grapes and table grapes and the total crush: more than 4 million tons. Nevertheless, juice concentrate and distillate is a significant end-use of California grape production, accounting for a surprisingly large share of the total grape crush.

Our estimates indicate that, since the year 2000, at least 20 percent (and, in one year more than 40 percent) of the total annual grape crush has gone for uses other than wine, including juice concentrate (primarily for use in the food manufacturing industry as a "natural," "healthy" substitute for sugar and other sweeteners), and to make distillate for use to produce brandy or fortified wine (Table 8.4).

The total quantity going to these non-wine uses varies with the fortunes of the various industry segments. On average, during the period 2000–2017, 14.3 percent of the crush has been used to make grape juice concentrate and 15.5 percent for distillate, leaving 70 percent for wine. On average during this period, out of 3.9 million tons of grapes crushed per year, 2.7 million tons were used to make wine, and 1.2 million tons were used for other purposes (i.e., to make grape juice concentrate and distillate). The grapes used for these other purposes are likely to have been sold for comparatively low prices—perhaps in the range of $200–300 per ton—and would almost all have come out of the Southern San Joaquin Valley. This would leave less than half of the total grape crush from that region (1.6 million tons in 2017) for wine making.

WINE GRAPES AND WINE

In 2017, the United States crushed 4.4 million tons of grapes—representing about 9.4 percent of the world's wine volume (OIV, 2019). Four states accounted for the lion's share (97 percent) of that total: California (CA), Washington (WA), Oregon (OR), and New York (NY). California dominates that group, accounting for about 90 percent of the four-state total. California differs from the other major producing states, and itself contains several distinct wine production regions that differ in terms of terrain, climate, soil types, mixture of varieties grown, and quality of grapes and wines produced. Data on production and prices of wine grapes in California are available in some cases by county (of which there are 58, not all of which grow wine grapes) and in others by crush district (of which there are 17). Some crush districts contain several counties or parts of counties. In Table 8.5, these data are organized into five contiguous regions, defined such that each crush district fits entirely into one of the five regions (see Figure 8.3).[4] Treating each of the other significant

wine-producing states (i.e., WA, OR, and NY) as a region, we have eight primary U.S. wine-producing regions comprising these three plus the five in California.

Table 8.5 includes some detail on the salient features of the eight main U.S. wine-producing regions in 2017 (see Appendix Table 8.5A for more detail). Several distinct patterns are apparent in this table, as illustrated in Figure 8.4. First, California dominates the nation's total area, volume, and value of wine production. Second, the regional shares differ significantly among measures of area, volume, and value of production. In particular, the Southern San Joaquin Valley has a much larger share of volume compared with area or especially value of production, while the North Coast region has a much smaller share of volume compared with area and value of production. These patterns reflect the relatively high yield per acre (and correspondingly low price per ton) of grapes from the Southern San Joaquin Valley and the conversely low yield and high price per ton in the North Coast. In 2017, in Napa County, the average yield was 3.3 tons/acre and the average crush price was $5,225/ton, almost 10 times the average crush price in the Southern San Joaquin Valley where the average yield was 17.3 tons/acre (Appendix Table 8.5A). The other regions were distributed between these extremes with higher yields generally associated with lower prices per ton.

---

4   These regions are North Coast or NC (comprising crush districts 1, 2, 3, and 4); Central Coast or CC (crush districts 6, 7, and 8); Northern San Joaquin Valley or NSJV (crush districts 5, 11, 12, and 17); Southern San Joaquin Valley or SSJV (crush districts 13 and 14); and Other California or OC (crush districts 9, 10, 15, and 16).

Table 8.5. Characteristics of U.S. Wine Grape-Growing Regions, 2017

Region	Total Acreage	Volume	Crush price	Value
	Acres	Tons	$/Ton	$ Millions
North Coast (NC)	126,096	467,119	3,268	1,527
Central Coast (CC)	100,308	543,766	1,535	835
N. San Joaquin Valley (NSJV)	123,983	1,273,899	579	737
S. San Joaquin Valley (SSJV)	93,764	1,624,184	309	503
Other California (OC)	16,286	104,715	893	93
Total California (CA)	460,437	4,031,684	921	3,695
Washington (WA)	53,000	229,000	1,210	277
Oregon (OR)	23,000	77,000	2,234	172
New York (NY)	10,058	57,000	649	37
Total United States (U.S.)	546,495	4,376,684	955	4,181

Sources: USDA/NASS (2017a,b; 2019).

Note: Appendix Table 8.5A provides more detail.

Within the United States, in 2014 five varieties (Chardonnay, Cabernet Sauvignon, Merlot, Pinot Noir, and Zinfandel) accounted for 52.3 percent of the total volume and 63.2 percent of the total value of production from the four states included in Table 8.5. As discussed in detail by Alston, Anderson, and Sambucci (2015), these five varieties predominate in several of the main production regions—in particular in the premium price regions within California, as well as in Washington and Oregon—but the emphasis varies among the premium price regions and some regions are quite different. In particular, the hot Southern San Joaquin Valley (dominated by French Colombard and Rubired used to produce grape juice concentrate as well as bulk wine) and New York (dominated by non-vinifera American varieties, Concord, and Niagara) are quite unlike the other regions climatically and in terms of their grape varietal mix.

Chardonnay is the most important variety in terms of total bearing area nationally and is highly ranked throughout the premium regions. However, the North Coast region is especially known for its Cabernet Sauvignon, which historically and increasingly is its most important variety. The same can be said for Washington. The cooler coastal regions—in particular, Oregon and the Central Coast region of California—are relatively specialized in Chardonnay and Pinot Noir and other cool-climate varieties. Zinfandel is more significant in the Northern San Joaquin Valley and other mid-price regions, and these patterns reflect this variety's dual roles in serving as both a premium red varietal wine and as lower-priced "blush" (white zinfandel) wine.

Prices vary systematically among regions—in general, the North Coast region has higher prices than other regions for all varieties, and the Southern San Joaquin Valley has lower prices. In addition, prices vary systematically among varieties—generally among the premium varieties grown in significant quantity, Cabernet Sauvignon ranks higher than Chardonnay, and Zinfandel generally ranks lower. But the sizes of the premia, and even the rankings of varieties, vary among regions. For example, Pinot Noir ranks above Cabernet Sauvignon almost everywhere, but not in Oregon where Pinot is by far the dominant variety, nor in the Napa-Sonoma region. Chardonnay ranks above Cabernet Sauvignon in the Central Coast region.

Box 8.1. Evolving Demand for California Wine and the Media

As discussed and documented by Alston, Lapsley, and Sambucci (2018), the 1970s boom in California wine production and consumption was driven by demand from the "baby boom" cohort reaching adulthood, combined with a trend of improving quality—a trend reflecting increased emphasis on table wine rather than fortified wine, greater use of premium varieties of specialized winegrapes, and improved winemaking methods.

The improved quality of California wines was confirmed on 24 May 1976 when, at the so-called "Judgment of Paris," French judges in blind tastings of top-quality red and white wines from France and California rated California wines best in each category (Stag's Leap Wine Cellars 1973 Napa Valley S.L.V. Cabernet Sauvignon, and Chateau Montelena 1973 Napa Valley/Calistoga Chardonnay). This event made it undeniable that California was producing world-class wines (Taber, 2005).

The 1990s saw a second surge in bearing area of wine grapes in California—from 120,000 hectares in 1992 to 190,000 hectares in 2001—a 60 percent increase. Red wine consumption tripled. A contributing factor to the shift to red wine was a public perception of health advantages, which some ascribe to a report by Morely Safer on "The French Paradox" aired on the news magazine show 60 Minutes on 17 November 1991. This report noted the low incidence of cardiovascular disease among the French and suggested this might be linked to their high per capita consumption of red wine. Americans were open to such a convenient theory: sales of red wine in the United States increased by 39 percent in 1992 (Frank and Taylor, 2016).

That wine demand might be susceptible to sudden swings is also illustrated by the so-called "Sideways Effect." In the Academy Award-winning movie, Sideways, released in October 2004, one of the leading characters—Miles Raymond, a neurotic wine snob played by Paul Giamatti—venerated Pinot Noir and denigrated Merlot. This had surprising consequences in the wine market. While the size of the effect is hard to measure precisely, and it may have worn off by now, Cuellar, Karnowsky, and Acostac (2009) estimated a reduction in sales of Merlot by 2 percent over the interval 2005–2008, while sales of Pinot Noir increased considerably.

Figure 8.4. U.S. Wine Regions: Area, Volume, and Value of Production, 2017

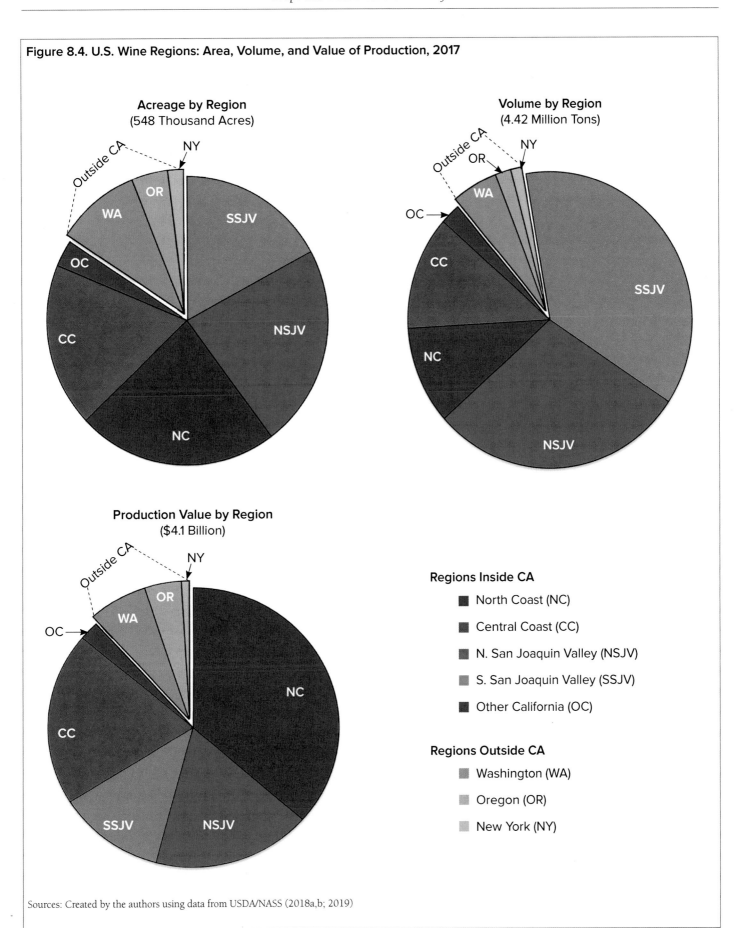

Acreage by Region
(548 Thousand Acres)

Volume by Region
(4.42 Million Tons)

Production Value by Region
($4.1 Billion)

Regions Inside CA

- North Coast (NC)
- Central Coast (CC)
- N. San Joaquin Valley (NSJV)
- S. San Joaquin Valley (SSJV)
- Other California (OC)

Regions Outside CA

- Washington (WA)
- Oregon (OR)
- New York (NY)

Sources: Created by the authors using data from USDA/NASS (2018a,b; 2019)

Table 8.6. Characteristics of California Wine Grapes Crushed, 2017

Region	Total Tons Crushed	Purchased Tons Crushed	Custom Crush	Own Tons Crushed*	Own Share of Total Tons Crushed
	Tons				Percent
North Coast (NC)	467,119	295,726	21,026	150,376	32
Central Coast (CC)	543,766	363,852	11,307	168,608	31
N. San Joaquin Valley (NSJV)	1,273,899	1,068,832	3,560	201,507	14
S. San Joaquin Valley (SSJV)	1,624,184	1,553,882	694	69,608	4
Other California (OC)	104,715	53,654	1,456	49,608	47
Total California (CA)	4,013,684	3,335,943	38,044	639,697	16

Source: Created by the authors using data from USDA/NASS (2018b)

Notes: * Indicates the winery owns the vineyard that grew the grapes; Appendix Table 8.6A provides more detail.

Because grape-growing location has become recognized as an important element of perceived wine quality, the vineyard location is often identified on the wine label. Prior to 1978, wineries could use only geopolitical locations, such as counties or towns, on labels. In 1983, the federal government responded to desire from the industry to include more precise vineyard locations on wine labels by creating a new type of location, the so-called "American Viticultural Areas" (AVAs—see U.S. Treasury / TTB, 2013). AVAs are defined geographic areas that may be quite large and cross state or county lines, or may be quite small and lie within a county or, in some cases, another AVA. The Napa Valley AVA is, for instance, a large AVA located within Napa County. The Oakville AVA is a much smaller AVA that is located within the Napa Valley AVA. In contrast, the Carneros AVA is a defined AVA in the southern portion of Napa and Sonoma Counties. Today, wineries may identify the grapes used in a wine as coming from an AVA if 85 percent of the grapes were grown in the AVA.

WINERIES

California includes a diverse mixture of wine production models. A vineyard may be vertically integrated with a winery, in a single enterprise, or the two enterprises may be entirely separate. In some cases, a winery may crush and bottle only estate-grown fruit while, next door, a vineyard sells all its production to a winery somewhere else. Because grape growing and wine production are often separate businesses in California, most wineries contract with grape growers for at least some of their volume. Goodhue et al. (2003) reported that 90 percent of California

growers sold grapes under contract and that 10 percent of contracts were pre-planting contracts in which the winery contracted to purchase grapes from a not-yet-established vineyard. Production models vary from region to region within California, and Table 8.6 provides details of the balance between purchased, custom crush, and own tons crushed by wineries (Appendix Table 8.6A provides more detail). For the state as a whole, only 16 percent of tons crushed were own-grown; the vast majority were purchased. This pattern was even more pronounced in the Southern San Joaquin Valley where about 4 percent of the crush was own-grown. In the premium coastal regions, the share of own-grown fruit in the total crush was closer to 30 percent.

Some wineries may have a cellar door from which they sell at retail whereas others may leave the retailing to others. Reflecting this diversity, California has an active market for wine grapes—whether under contract or for spot sales—as well as markets for bulk wine and bottled wine. Particular sizes of vineyards—depending on the location and market segment to be served—are more or less appropriate for these different business models. Some wine businesses in California are engaged in every aspect: growing grapes, making wine, offering custom crush and winemaking services, importing and exporting bulk or premium wine, and providing cellar door experiences at boutique winery estates.

Among countries, the United States is the world's fourth-largest producer of wine, and the largest consumer and importer (OIV, 2019; ITC, 2018). The quantity of wine consumed in the United States grew by 60 percent over the

Table 8.7. Gallons of Bottled Wine Removed, Tax-Paid* into the U.S. Market, 2005 and 2017

Wine Type	2005	2017	Percentage Change
	Millions of Gallons		Percent
Still Wine	457.2	615.1	34.5
Cider	4.9	45.8	834.7
Effervescent	19.4	29.7	53.1
Flavored Wines	15.8	23.7	50.0
Wine Coolers	30.3	22.2	−26.7
Total Taxable Removals	527.6	736.5	39.6

Sources: Created by the authors based on data from U.S. Treasury/TTB (2005, 2017a)

Note: *We use "removed tax paid" as a measure of domestically produced wine that enters the U.S. market.

past 20 years, from 581 million gallons in 1997 to just over 861 million gallons in 2017 (OIV, 2019). This expansion is a result of both population growth and an increasing rate of adult per-capita consumption. Both trends are expected to continue. U.S. growth trends stand in marked contrast to declines in volume of wine consumed in France, Italy, and Spain (OIV, 2020).

DOMESTIC PRODUCTION AND CONSUMPTION

Still wine accounts for the vast majority of domestically produced and bulk imported wine that is bottled and consumed in the United States, although smaller volumes of other types of wine are produced, and about 10–11 percent of production is used for distillation. According to data from U.S. Treasury/TTB (2017a), over 6,015 million gallons of still wine were bottled and "removed" after payment of tax for domestic consumption; this represented 86 percent of the approximately 718 million gallons of domestically bottled wine.[5] Since 2005, the volume of tax-paid, domestically bottled wine (including cider) entering the U.S. market has increased by almost one-third. Cider consumption increased almost tenfold, from 4.9 million gallons to 45.8 million gallons, while still wine grew by 34.5 percent, and wine cooler volume declined (Table 8.7).

---

5   Here, "wine" includes cider. The term "removed" here refers to removal of the product from a bonded warehouse, as it enters commerce and, if it is destined for domestic sale, incurs excise tax.

California produces the vast majority of wine produced in the United States. In 2017, the TTB reports approximately 888.6 million gallons of still wine produced in the United States, with California responsible for 716.3 million gallons, or 84.3 percent. Washington State, with 44.8 million gallons, and New York State, with 28.1 million gallons, were second and third in production (U.S. Treasury/TTB, 2017a). All of California's, Oregon's, and Washington State's wine production is from *Vitis vinifera* grape varieties, while New York State's production includes fruit wines and wines produced from native grape species and hybrids. The increase in U.S. demand for wine is reflected in an increase in the number of wineries, which has more than doubled in the past decade. In 2004, there were 4,325 federally licensed wineries or wine blenders in the United States, with 2,059 located in California; by 2017, the number of U.S. wineries had increased to 11,996, with 4,661 located in California. Other major states with wineries are Washington, 1,005; Oregon, 679; and New York, 551. However, every state has a few wineries and produces some wine (U. S. Treasury/ TTB, 2017a).

Although almost 12,000 wineries or wine blenders are operating in the United States, a handful of large wineries dominate production and distribution of wine. Over the past 20 years, the largest U.S. wine producers have become marketers of wine as well as producers, importing bulk wine to be bottled under their own brands, and importing and distributing bottled wines from foreign producers. Industry analysts estimated that in 2016, the three largest U.S. wine producers, E & J Gallo, The Wine Group, and Constellation Brands, together produced or imported

Table 8.8. Shares of all California Licensed Wineries (2017) and Tons of Wine Grapes Crushed (2017) by Region

Region	Grapes Crushed in 2017	Licenses Issued in 2017	Share of Total Tons Crushed	Share of Total Licenses
	Thousand Tons	Count	Percent	Percent
North Coast (NC)	467	2,195	11.6	47.1
Central Coast (CC)	544	1,369	13.5	29.4
Northern San Joaquin Valley (NSJV)	1,274	239	31.7	5.1
Southern San Joaquin Valley (SSJV)	1,624	77	40.5	1.7
Other California (OC)	105	781	2.6	16.8
Total California	4,014	4,661	100.0	100.0

Sources: Created by the authors based on data from USDA/NASS (2018b); U.S. Treasury/TTB (2017b)
Note: Appendix Table 8.8A provides more detail.

approximately 46 percent of all wine sold in the United States. The top 10 producers account for over 61 percent of U.S. sales, and the top 30 are estimated to be responsible for approximately 631 million gallons of the 949 million gallons of wine consumed in 2016, or 66 percent of sales (*Wine Business Monthly*, 2016, 2017). The remaining smaller firms or importers supply the other 318 million gallons.

Since the TTB does not release production data at the firm level, it is not possible to report precise figures of the volume produced by wineries. However, given that there were more than 11,000 wine producers in 2016 and having estimated that the remaining U.S. total wine consumption, after subtracting sales by the top 30 wine firms, was approximately 318 million gallons (including imported bottled wine not sold by the largest firms), it follows that the typical U.S. winery is very small, perhaps producing 20,000 gallons of wine after allowing for imported wines. An examination of wine production by region within California reinforces this conclusion. Using TTB data of California wine producer and blender permit holders at the end of 2017, we sorted wineries by production region. Then, for each region, we computed its share of California's wine grape tonnage and its share of the total number of California wineries. Table 8.8 shows the results of our calculations (see also Appendix Table 8.8A).

As noted above, California's Northern and Southern San Joaquin Valley vineyards (crush districts 5, 11, 12, 13, 14, and 17) produce approximately 72 percent of California's wine grapes. However, this productive grape growing region has only 6.8 percent of California's wineries. Central Valley wineries are quite large and efficient, processing almost 3 million tons of grapes in 2017 and producing inexpensive wine. Almost 77 percent of California's wineries are located in coastal areas (crush districts 1–8) yet, collectively, these areas produced less than 26 percent of all California wine grapes. For the most part, these coastal wineries, along with wineries in California's Sierra Nevada foothills, are quite small, each producing small quantities of more expensive wines.

Wines sold in the United States may bear a varietal designation on the label if 75 percent or more of the wine was produced from the named grape variety. Nielsen data for table wine sales for the 52 weeks ending in October 2015, show that approximately 85 percent of wine by value carried a varietal label. Chardonnay, at 19 percent, and Cabernet Sauvignon, at 16 percent, were the two most popular varieties, followed by Pinot Grigio, Pinot Noir, Merlot, and Sauvignon Blanc, which collectively accounted for 28 percent of the value of table wine sold in the United States. In 2015, red wine represented just over 50 percent of Nielsen-tracked wine sales by value, followed by white wines at 43 percent of value and rose or blush wines at 6 percent (*Wine Business Monthly*, 2016).

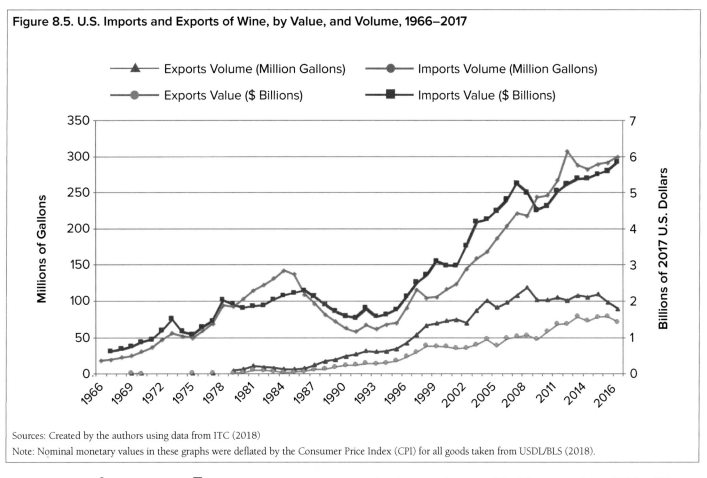

Figure 8.5. U.S. Imports and Exports of Wine, by Value, and Volume, 1966–2017

Sources: Created by the authors using data from ITC (2018)

Note: Nominal monetary values in these graphs were deflated by the Consumer Price Index (CPI) for all goods taken from USDL/BLS (2018).

IMPORTS AND EXPORTS

The United States consumes more wine than it produces, but even though a net importer, the country exports significant quantities of wine: for the past decade approximately 100 million gallons each year, just over 10 percent of its total production in 2017, if distilling material is included. The United States is also a major importer of wine and, for the past decade, approximately one-third of all wine consumed in the United States has been imported. Figure 8.5 shows the total volume and value of U.S. exports and imports of wine by year.

The share of imported wine in total consumption has increased slightly since 2005, but much of the increase in import volume has been in inexpensive bulk wine rather than in bottled wine. In 2005, U.S. wineries imported 10.3 million gallons of wine in containers larger than four liters (here referred to as "bulk wine"), a volume that represented approximately 6 percent of all imported wine. Twelve years later, in 2017, bulk wine imports had grown to 87.7 million gallons, accounting for 28 percent of all imported wine volume. During the same period, bottled

wine imports increased by 29 percent from 176.0 million gallons to 227.6 million gallons in 2017 (ITC, 2018).

The growth in volume of imported bulk wine has become an issue for wine grape growers in California's Southern San Joaquin Valley. Their concern centers on a trade policy referred to as "drawback," which allows an importer to recapture up to 99 percent of taxes paid on imported goods when goods defined as "interchangeable" are exported.

In 2003, the U.S. Bureau of Customs and Border Protection allowed drawback on imported wine for the first time and defined interchangeable wine as wine under 14 percent alcohol by volume (ABV), of the same color, and within 50 percent of value per unit. Such tax refunds could be as high as $1.60 per gallon for wines imported in large containers from countries without free trade agreements. Since prices of bulk wine imported into the United States have ranged around $3.80 per gallon for the past decade, the incentive is strong, and the potential drawback is significant. Some Central Valley grape growers fear that drawback encourages California wineries to import increased quantities of bulk wine, rather than to purchase California grapes.

However, Sumner, Lapsley, and Rosen-Molina (2012) concluded that when imports exceed exports, the drawback policy encourages exports, which should increase demand for California grapes. Bulk import volumes have exceeded bulk export volumes since 2011.

The United States exports both bottled and bulk wine. Over the past decade, the volume of exports decreased by 17 percent, from 107.8 million gallons in 2007 to 89.5 million gallons in 2017. During the same period, the value of exported wine increased by over 130 percent, from $1 billion in 2007 to $1.4 billion in 2017. The U.K. is the largest importer by volume of U.S. wine and took 32 percent of all U.S. exports by volume. However, most of the exports to the U.K. are shipped in bulk and at an average price of only about $7.20 per gallon. By value, Canada is the most important importer of U.S. wine, buying bottled wine at an average price of over $23 per gallon and receiving 19.4 percent of U.S. wine exports by volume in 2017. Over the past decade, China (Hong Kong and mainland China) has emerged as a major market for U.S. wine, growing from just over 2 million gallons in 2007 to 3.4 million gallons in 2017. Most of this is bottled wine with an average price of about $21 per gallon. Although volume and value of wine exported have increased in the past 11 years, it seems that most U.S. producers are focused more on the expanding domestic market than on export opportunities.

CONCLUSION

The production of grapes and wine in the United States is concentrated in the western United States, dominated by California. California produces four-fifths of the total wine and nine-tenths of the total grapes produced in the United States, including almost all of the table grapes and raisin grapes, as well as wine grapes. While the other segments remain significant, wine grapes have increased in absolute as well as relative importance in the California and U.S. grape industry over the past 20–30 years. At about $6 billion in farm value, grapes have been a valuable crop grown in California, and significant value is added to the crop in producing high-value consumer products—especially in the case of wine. California shipped a record of 279 million cases of wine in 2017, of which 241 million cases went to U.S. consumers for an estimated retail value of $40.5 billion (Wine Institute, 2020).

Wine grapes are best understood as a high-value specialty crop, whose high prices are driven by an increasing demand for wine on the part of American consumers. This increased demand has been met by an expansion of vineyard acreage across the United States, by an increase in importation of bulk and bottled wine, and by a doubling of the number of U.S. wineries over the past decade. Among nations, the United States is now the world's largest consumer of wine, even though it remains a nation of primarily beer drinkers, spirit drinkers, and teetotalers. Although the experiment with Prohibition has left as its legacy a patchwork of laws throughout the nation, making wine distribution cumbersome and costly, increased consumer demand for wines of all types is forcing changes in distribution. These changes, coupled with increased rates of per-capita consumption and population growth, should ensure that the United States remains the world's major wine-consuming country for the first half of the 21st century.

Box 8.2. U.S. Per Capita Consumption of Wine in Context

Compared with most other countries, the United States is a nation of beer drinkers, spirit drinkers, and teetotalers, with comparatively low rates of per capita consumption of wine, reflecting the fact that a majority of Americans do not drink any! It is only because of its sheer size, in terms of total population, that the nation ranks first in total wine consumption. The table below shows per capita consumption of wine, beer, and spirits in the United States and selected other countries in 2010–14. The United States consumes a similar total quantity of alcohol per capita, compared with other high-income countries, but a much smaller share is in the form of wine and a much larger share is in the form of spirits.

Country	Total Alcohol Consumption, 2010–2014	Volume Shares of Wine, Beer, and Spirits		
		Wine	Beer	Spirits
	LAL/capita/year	Percent		
France	9.2	**59**	19	23
United Kingdom	8.0	**41**	37	22
Australia	7.3	40	**46**	14
Germany	9.6	28	**53**	19
United States	7.0	18	**49**	34
China	3.3	4	44	**52**
World	2.7	15	**43**	42

Source: Based on a more-detailed table in Holmes and Anderson (2017), Table 3

Notes: Data are volume-based in liters of alcohol (LAL) per capita per year, measured as 5-year averages.

The bold number in each row highlights the largest share for that country; measured as shares of total LAL consumed in each form.

REFERENCES

Alston, J.M., K. Anderson, and O. Sambucci. 2015. "Drifting Towards Bordeaux? The Evolving Varietal Emphasis of U.S. Wine Regions." *Journal of Wine Economics* 10(3): 349-378.

Alston, J.M., J.T. Lapsley, O. Sambucci, and D.A. Sumner. 2018. "United States." In Kym Anderson and Vicente Pinilla, eds, *Wine's Evolving Globalization: Comparative Histories of the Old and New World.* Cambridge: Cambridge University Press.

California Department of Food and Agriculture (CDFA). 2018. *California County Agricultural Commissioners' Reports Crop Year 2016–2017.* Sacramento, CA, December. Available at: https://www.cdfa.ca.gov/statistics/pdfs/2017cropyearcactb00.pdf.

County of Glenn Department of Agriculture/Weights and Measures. 2018. *Glenn County 2017 Annual Crop & Livestock Report.* Willows, CA, September. Available at: https://www.countyofglenn.net/sites/default/files/Agriculture/Crop_Reports/Glenn%20County%20Crop%20Report%202017.pdf.

County of Stanislaus Agricultural Commissioner's Office. 2018. *Stanislaus County Agricultural Crop Report 2017.* Modesto, CA. Available at: http://www.stanag.org/pdf/cropreport/cropreport2017.pdf.

County of Tehama Department of Agriculture. 2018. *2017 Annual Crop Report.* Red Bluff, CA. Available at: https://www.co.tehama.ca.us/images/stories/agriculture/2017_crop_report_final_a.pdf.

Crespi, J., T. Saitone, and R.J. Sexton. 2016. "The Supreme Court's Decision in the 'Raisin Case': What Does it Mean for Mandatory Marketing Programs?" *ARE Update* 18(6): 1-4. University of California Giannini Foundation of Agricultural Economics. Available at: https://s.giannini.ucop.edu/uploads/giannini_public/b3/39/b3397c5c-8162-4a3a-9c4b-bdca6e38538e/v18n6_1.pdf.

Cuellar, S.S., D. Karnowsky, and F. Acostac. 2009. "The Sideways Effect: A Test for Changes in the Demand for Merlot and Pinot Noir Wines." *Journal of Wine Economics* 4(2): 1-14.

Dokoozlian, N. 2013. "The Evolution of Mechanized Vineyard Production Systems in California." *Acta Horticultura* 978: 265-278.

Fidelibus, M., A. Ferry, L. Jordan, G. Zhuang, D.A. Sumner, and D.Stewart. 2016a. "Sample Costs to Establish a Vineyard and Produce Dry-on-Vine Raisins, Open Gable Trellis System, Early Maturing Varieties, San Joaquin Valley-2016." Davis, CA. Available at: https://coststudies.ucdavis.edu.

Fidelibus, M., A. Ferry, L. Jordan, G. Zhuang, D.A. Sumner, and D.Stewart. 2016b. "Sample Costs to Establish a Vineyard and Produce Dry-on-Vine Raisins, Overhead Trellis System, Early Maturing Varieties. San Joaquin Valley-2016." Davis, CA. Available at: https://coststudies.ucdavis.edu.

Fidelibus, M., A.El-kereamy, G. Zhuang, D. Haviland, K.Hembree, D. Stewart, and D.A. Sumner. 2018a. "2018 Sample Costs to Establish and Produce Table Grapes, Joaquin Valley South, Scarlet Royal Mid-Season Maturing." Available at: https://coststudies.ucdavis.edu.

Fidelibus, M., A.El-kereamy, D. Haviland, K.Hembree, G. Zhuang, D. Stewart, and D.A. Sumner. 2018b. "2018 Sample Costs to Establish and Produce Table Grapes, San Joaquin Valley South, Autumn King, Late Maturing." Available at: https://coststudies.ucdavis.edu.

Frank, M. and R. Taylor. 2016. "Journalist Morley Safer, Who Highlighted Red Wine's Potential Health Benefits, Dies at 84," *Wine Spectator*, May 19. Available at: http://www.winespectator.com/webfeature/show/id/Morley-Safer-Dies-at-84.

Goodhue, R.E., D.M. Heien, H. Lee, and D.A. Sumner. 2003. "Contracts and Quality in the California Winegrape Industry." *Review of Industrial Organization* 23(3): 267-282.

Holmes, A.J. and K. Anderson. 2017. "Convergence in National Alcohol Consumption Patterns: New Global Indicators." *Journal of Wine Economics* 12(2): 117-148.

International Organization of Vine and Wine (OIV). 2019. *2019 Statistical Report on World Vitiviniculture.* Paris, FR. Available at: http://oiv.int/public/medias/6782/oiv-2019-statistical-report-on-world-vitiviniculture.pdf.

International Organization of Vine and Wine (OIV). 2020. Statistical Database. Available at: http://www.oiv.int/en/statistiques/recherche.

Lapsley, J.T. 2010. "Looking Forward: Imagining the Market for California Wine in 2030." *ARE Update* 13(6): 12–15. University of California Giannini Foundation of Agricultural Economics. Available at: https://s.giannini.ucop.edu/uploads/giannini_public/8d/b2/8db2aab0-d270-4086-8c29-b2f8c8417eb4/v13n6_5.pdf.

Pinney, T. 1989. *A History of Wine in America: From Beginning to Prohibition: Volume 1*. Berkeley, CA: University of California Press.

Pinney, T. 2005. *A History of Wine in America: From Prohibition to the Present: Volume 2*. Berkeley, CA: University of California Press.

Sambucci, O., and J.M. Alston. 2017. "Estimating the Value of California Winegrapes." *Journal of Wine Economics* 12(2): 149-160.

Sumner, D.A., J.T. Lapsley, and J.T. Rosen-Molina. 2012. "Economics of Wine Import Duty and Excise Tax Drawbacks." *ARE Update* 15(4): 1-4. University of California Giannini Foundation of Agricultural Economics. Available at: https://s.giannini.ucop.edu/uploads/giannini_public/3c/02/3c02299a-90e3-4ee7-ade6-4e6619801610/v15n4_1_1.pdf.

Taber, G.M. 2005. *Judgment of Paris*, New York NY: Scribner.

U.S. Bureau of Economic Analysis, Federal Reserve Bank of St. Louis (USBEA/FRED). 2019. "Gross Domestic Product: Implicit Price Deflator" [A191RI1A225NBEA]. Available at: https://fred.stlouisfed.org/series/A191RI1Q225SBEA.

U.S. Department of Agriculture, National Agricultural Statistics Service (USDA/NASS). 1920–2010. *California Grapes, 1920–2010*. Revised, February 2014.

———. 2017a. United States Department of Agriculture Census of Agriculture. Volume 1, Chapter 1. Available at: https://www.nass.usda.gov/Publications/AgCensus/2017/Full_Report/Volume_1,_Chapter_1_State_Level/California/st06_1_0037_0037.pdf.

———. 2000–2017a. California Grape Crush Reports, 2000–2017. Retrieved From: https://www.nass.usda.gov/Statistics_by_State/California/Publications/Specialty_and_Other_Releases/Grapes/Crush/Reports/index.php.

———. 2017b. United States Department of Agriculture Census of Agriculture. Volume 1, Chapter 2. Available at: https://www.nass.usda.gov/Publications/AgCensus/2017/Full_Report/Volume_1,_Chapter_2_County_Level/California/st06_2_0031_0031.pdf.

———. 2011–2017b. California Grape Acreage Reports, 2000–2017. Retrieved from: https://www.nass.usda.gov/Statistics_by_State/California/Publications/Specialty_and_Other_Releases/Grapes/Acreage/Reports/index.php.

———. 2018a. California Grape Acreage Report, 2017. Available at: https://www.nass.usda.gov/Statistics_by_State/California/Publications/Specialty_and_Other_Releases/Grapes/Acreage/2019/201904gabtb00.pdf.

———. 2018b. Grape Crush Report, Final, 2017. Available at: https://www.nass.usda.gov/Statistics_by_State/California/Publications/Specialty_and_Other_Releases/Grapes/Crush/Final/2017/201703gcbtb00.pdf.

———. 2019. Noncitrus Fruits and Nuts 2018 Summary. Washington DC. Available at: https://www.nass.usda.gov/Publications/Todays_Reports/reports/ncit0619.pdf.

U.S. Department of Labor/Bureau of Labor Statistics (USDL/BLS). 2018. Consumer Price Index (CPI) Databases–All Urban Consumers (Current Series). Available at: https://www.bls.gov/cpi/data.htm.

U.S. Department of The Treasury, Alcohol and Tobacco Tax and Trade Bureau (U.S. Treasury/TTB). 2005. *Monthly Statistical Report—Wine, January 2005–December 2005*.

———. 2013."American Viticultural Area (AVA)." Available at: https://www.ttb.gov/wine/american-viticultural-area-ava.

———. 2017a. Statistical Report–Wine, January–December 2017. Available at: Available at: https://www.ttb.gov/wine/wine-statistics.

———. 2017b. "List of Permittees." Available at: http://www.ttb.gov/foia/frl.shtml.

U.S. International Trade Commission (ITC). 2018. Trade Database. Available at: https://dataweb.usitc.gov/.

Wine Business Monthly. 2016. "Retail Sales Analysis." January.

———. 2017. "WBM 20 List." February.

Wine Institute. 2020. *California Wine Shipments*. Available at: https://wineinstitute.org/our-industry/statistics/california-wine-shipments/.

Appendix Table 8.5A. Characteristics of U.S. Wine Grape-Growing Regions, 2017

Region	Crush District	Total Acreage	Volume	Crush Price	Value
	Number	Acres	Tons	$/Ton	$ Millions
North Coast	1	16,443	70,752	1,698	120
(NC)	2	8,771	47,857	1,756	84
	3	57,603	206,097	2,806	578
	4	43,279	142,413	5,225	744
	Total	126,096	467,119	3,268	1,527
Central Coast	6	6,699	28,448	1,177	33
(CC)	7	46,977	282,090	1,405	396
	8	46,632	233,228	1,737	405
	Total	100,308	543,766	1,535	835
N. San Joaquin Valley	5	3,469	17,986	1,041	19
(NSJV)	11	70,699	743,360	610	454
	12	29,283	354,231	459	163
	17	20,532	158,372	646	102
	Total	123,983	1,273,899	579	737
S. San Joaquin Valley	13	73,137	1,311,813	309	405
(SSJV)	14	20,627	312,371	311	97
	Total	93,764	1,624,184	309	503
Other California	9	6,965	74,781	647	48
(OC)	10	6,982	22,118	1,470	33
	15	683	967	696	1
	16	1,656	6,849	1,742	12
	Total	16,286	104,715	837	93
California (CA)		**460,437**	**4,013,684**	**921**	**3,695**
Washington (WA)		**53,000**	**229,000**	**1,210**	**277**
Oregon (OR)		**23,000**	**77,000**	**2,234**	**172**
New York (NY)		**10,058**	**57,000**	**649**	**37**
Total United States		546,495	4,376,684	955	4,181

Sources: USDA/NASS (2018a,b; 2019)

Notes: This appendix includes tables that provide data at the level of crush districts as well as for the regional aggregates (obtained by summing across crush districts) provided in their counterpart text tables, and they are named accordingly – i.e., Table 8.5A corresponds to Table 8.5, and so on.

Acreage of wine grapes in NY was calculated by applying the share of volume of wine grapes to the total grape acreage reported in USDA/NASS (2019), as data on wine grape acreage were not available. The U.S. totals encompass only the four states (CA, WA, OR, and NY). The Wine Institute (2018a) reports a national total of 4.67 million tons compared with the 4.38 million tons reported here for the four-state (U.S.) total.

Appendix Table 8.6A. Characteristics of California Wine Grapes Crushed, 2017

Region	Crush District	Total Tons Crushed	Purchased Tons Crushed	Custom Crush	Own Tons Crushed*	Own Share of Total Tons Crushed
	Number	Tons				Percent
North Coast	1	70,752	46,490	9,901	14,361	20
(NC)	2	47,857	32,393	4,894	10,569	22
	3	206,097	132,710	3,033	70,354	34
	4	142,413	84,133	3,198	55,083	39
	Total	467,119	295,726	21,026	150,367	32
Central Coast	6	28,448	18,973	608	8,868	31
(CC)	7	282,090	179,926	730	101,434	36
	8	233,228	164,952	9,970	53,306	25
	Total	543,766	363,852	11,307	168,608	31
N. San Joaquin Valley	5	17,936	15,812	134	1,991	11
(NSJV)	11	743,360	675,144	2,398	65,818	9
	12	354,231	241,132	396	112,702	32
	17	158,372	136,744	633	20,996	13
	Total	1,273,899	1,068,832	3,560	201,507	16
S. San Joaquin Valley	13	1,311,813	1,251,784	563	59,467	5
(SSJV)	14	312,371	302,098	132	10,142	3
	Total	1,624,184	1,553,882	694	69,608	4
Other California	9	74,781	36,009	688	38,084	51
(OC)	10	22,118	13,980	377	7,761	35
	15	967	631	197	139	14
	16	6,849	2,145	194	3,624	53
	Total	104,715	53,652	1,456	49,608	47
Total California		4,013,684	3,373,988	38,044	639,697	16

Sources: Created by the authors using data from USDA/NASS (2018b)

Note: * Indicates the winery owns the vineyard that grew the grapes.

Appendix Table 8.8A. Shares of all California Licensed Wineries and Tons of Wine Grapes Crushed by Region, 2017

Region	Crush District	Grapes Crushed in 2016	Licenses Issued in 2017	Share of Total Tons Crushed	Share of Total Licenses
		Tons	Count	Percent	Percent
North Coast	1	70,752	121	1.8	2.6
(NC)	2	47,857	53	1.2	1.1
	3	206,097	909	5.1	19.5
	4	142,413	1,112	3.5	23.9
	Total	467,119	2,195	11.6	47.1
Central Coast	6	28,448	397	0.7	8.5
(CC)	7	282,090	124	7.0	2.7
	8	233,228	848	5.8	18.2
	Total	543,766	1,369	13.5	29.4
N. San Joaquin Valley	5	17,936	29	0.4	0.6
(NSJV)	11	743,360	174	18.5	3.7
	12	354,231	17	8.8	0.4
	17	158,372	19	3.9	0.4
	Total	1,273,899	239	31.7	5.1
S. San Joaquin Valley	13	1,311,813	69	32.7	1.5
(SSJV)	14	312,371	8	7.8	0.2
	Total	1,624,184	77	40.5	1.7
Other California	9	74,781	135	1.9	2.9
(OC)	10	22,118	307	0.6	6.6
	15	967	60	0.0	1.2
	16	6,849	279	0.2	6.0
	Total	104,715	781	2.6	16.8
Total California		4,013,684	4,661	100.0	100.0

Sources: Created by the authors based on data from USDA/NASS (2018b), U.S. Treasury/TTB (2017b)

CHAPTER 9. LIVESTOCK AND RANGELAND IN CALIFORNIA

TINA L. SAITONE

ABSTRACT

U.S. farm sales in 2017 totaled $365 billion, including $190 billion from crops and $175 billion from livestock and animal products. Unlike other states, where animal products generate more farm sales than crops, in California crops account for roughly three-fourths of farm sales. California's $12 billion in livestock-related sales are about 6 percent of total U.S. livestock sales. California is home to 2 percent of the nation's 31 million beef cows and 10 percent of the 5.5 million sheep in the U.S.

The beef cattle industry has distinct subsectors. Cow-calf operations raise calves until they are about 7 months old and weigh 600 pounds. This is the most common type of operation in California. Calves are sold from cow-calf to stocker operations that feed them on pasture until they are about 1-year. Yearling cattle are sold to feed lots and fattened with grain before slaughter at 1,300 pounds. Almost three-fourths of "cattle on feed" in the U.S. were in the Midwest; meaning that yearling cattle leave California on trucks and return as beef.

I emphasize several distinct attributes of California's cattle industry: reliance on public lands for forage for cattle, inter-annual shipment of cattle to access different forage resources, limited in-state meat processing facilities, and regulations on antibiotics and transportation that will increase the costs for California ranchers. Many of these issues are relevant to California sheep producers as well.

Cattle and sheep ranchers need low-cost forage, which is disappearing with increased regulation of grazing on federal lands. Ranchers believe that the big four meatpackers who process over 85 percent of cattle are able to depress prices. The use of antibiotics to prevent disease is being restricted in order to slow antibiotic resistance, and new rest requirements for truck drivers may make it more expensive to ship cattle to Midwest feedlots.

ABOUT THE AUTHOR

Tina L. Saitone is a Cooperative Extension specialist in the Department of Agricultural and Resource Economics at the University of California, Davis, and a member of the Giannini Foundation of Agricultural Economics. She can be contacted at tlsaitone@ucdavis.edu.

More than 45 percent of California's acreage is federally owned and managed, which makes many livestock producers in California reliant upon on the availability of federal grazing permits.

Photo Credit: Tina L. Saitone, UC Davis

Chapter 9. Table of Contents

BEEF CATTLE

The United States is the largest producer of beef in the world, facilitated, in large part, by the nation's ample grasslands and substantial feed-grain production. Cattle production in the U.S. accounted for $78.2 billion in cash receipts in 2015, 21 percent of the total receipts for agricultural commodities. In 2015, California cash receipts associated with livestock and livestock products were $12 billion, 25 percent of the state's total $47 billion (CDFA, 2016), including dairy products ($6.3 billion),[1] cattle and calves ($3.4 billion), poultry and eggs ($1.7 billion), hogs and pigs ($29 million), and miscellaneous livestock ($554 million).[2] Ranching is a part-time business for many operators. According to the 2012 Census of Agriculture (USDA, 2012), 87 percent of beef cattle operators made less than half of their income from farming.

The U.S. beef supply chain is generally characterized by four relatively distinct segments of the supply chain: 1) cow-calf operations, 2) stocker operations, 3) feeding operations, and 4) slaughter and packing.

COW-CALF AND STOCKER OPERATIONS

A typical cow-calf operation manages a commercial herd of beef cows that are bred to produce calves. Calves are raised at their mother's side on rangelands until they are weaned at roughly 6–8 months of age, weighing between 500 and 650 lb. Given the reliance of cow-calf operations on pasture-based forage resources, these operations characterizing this initial stage in the supply chain are geographically diffuse and are present in nearly all states throughout the United States. Figure 9.1 is a dot density plot of calf inventories in the U.S. on January 1, 2017, where each dot represents 1,500 head. In 2012, 727,906 farms in the U.S. had beef cows, with an average herd size of 40

cows per operation (USDA, 2012). Cow-calf operations are especially important in the western and southeastern United States (Blank, Saitone, and Sexton, 2016).

The size of the beef cow herd in the U.S. has been declining since its peak in 1975. Despite reductions in reproductive capacity, beef production has increased as the industry has become more efficient. Figure 9.2 overlays U.S. beef cow inventories and annual commercial beef production from 1940 to 2017. In 1975, the U.S. produced 23.7 billion pounds of beef with a beef cow herd of 45.7 million head. By 2017, a beef-cow herd of less than 30.2 million produced 25.2 billion pounds of beef. The size of the dairy-cow herd affects total commercial beef production, as dairy-bred steers and culled cows enter the beef supply chain.

As of January 1, 2017, California was home to 2.1 percent of the nation's 31.2 million beef cows. California's beef cow herd has been declining monotonically since its peak in 1982 (nearly 1.2 million head) until 2015 (590,000 head). In very recent years, the state's herd has begun rebuilding following substantial herd reductions due to severe drought conditions that persisted from 2013–2015.

Small operations (less than 100 head of beef cows) manage one-quarter of the state's beef-cow herd, while medium-sized operations (100–499 head) manage 35 percent, and large operations (500 head) account for the remaining 40 percent (USDA, 2012). These operations are distributed across the state, with Kern, San Luis Obispo, and Siskiyou counties having the largest county-level herds. Figure 9.3 is a dot density plot that shows how beef-cow inventories are distributed across counties in California with each dot representing 500 head.[3]

After weaning, calves are typically sold to stocker operations through local sales yards or satellite video

---

1 Although dairy cattle are considered part of the state's livestock industry, the prominence and regulatory specifics associated with the industry warrant more detailed consideration than can be provided here. For more information on the California dairy industry, please consult Chapter 6.

2 Miscellaneous livestock includes sheep and lambs and goats used for milking and meat production.

3 Dots are not location specific and are simply used to show within-county density. County-level beef cow inventories are not available for Alameda, Alpine, Amador, Imperial, Los Angeles, Mariposa, Mendocino, Modoc, Mono, Monterey, Napa, Placer, Plumas, San Benito, Santa Barbara, Sierra, and Yolo counties. In total, these counties accounted for 161,700 (25 percent) beef cows in 2017.

Figure 9.1. Dot Density Plot of Calf Inventories, January 1, 2017

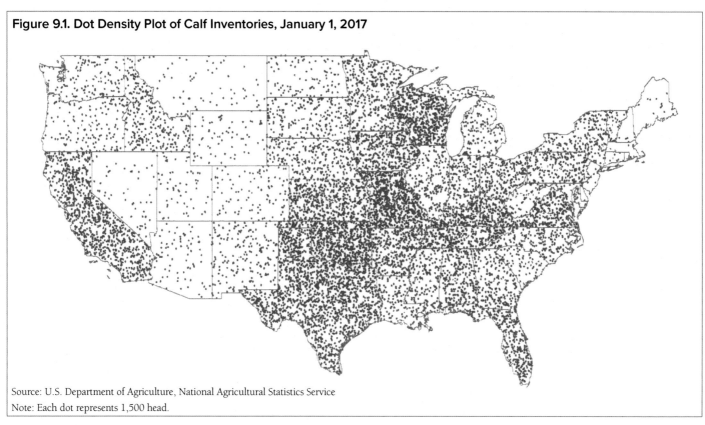

Source: U.S. Department of Agriculture, National Agricultural Statistics Service

Note: Each dot represents 1,500 head.

Figure 9.2. U.S. Beef Cow Inventories and Commercial Beef Production, 1940–2017

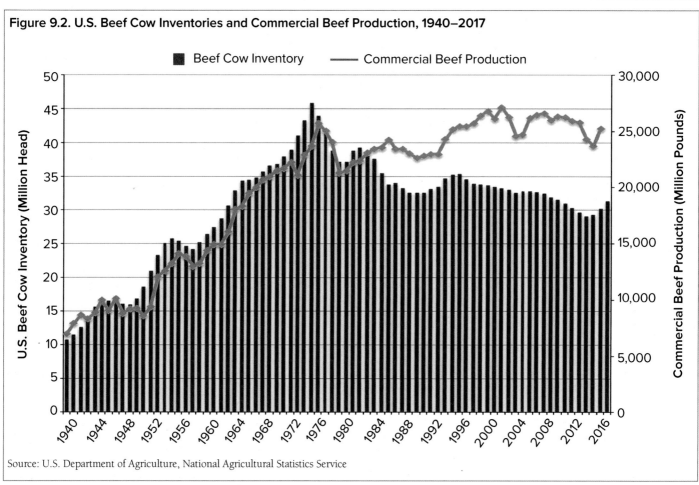

Source: U.S. Department of Agriculture, National Agricultural Statistics Service

Figure 9.3. Dot Density Plot of California Beef Cow Inventories by County, January 1, 2017

Source: California Department of Food and Agriculture
Note: Each dot represents 500 head.

auctions, although some cow-calf operations retain calves through the stocker phase. The standard stocker operation feeds animals on pasture for roughly six months, until the animals weigh between 800 and 950 lb. These "yearling" cattle are then typically sold to feeding operations to add weight before slaughter.

Available statistics specific to the stocker phase of the supply chain in California are limited. However, much like cow-calf operations, stocker operations typically market cattle via sales yards or satellite video auctions to feeding operations, most of which are in the Midwest. The lack of feeding and processing capacity in California and the western U.S. is an important consideration, and causes cattle born in California to be sold at discounted prices, relative to comparable stock raised in close proximity to feedlots, to compensate for the costs of transportation. For example, Blank, Saitone, and Sexton (2016) found that from

2009–2013, calves were discounted $0.82/cwt. for every 100 miles they were from the concentration of feeding and processing capacity in Nebraska. This was a $14.63/cwt. discount for calves raised roughly 1,600 miles from Nebraska (e.g., in Northern California).

RANGELAND AND PASTURE-BASED FORAGE

Livestock grazing is California's most extensive land use. California's total land area consists of nearly 101 million acres, of which 25.4 million acres are farmland. Approximately 63 million acres (62 percent) of the state's land area is considered to be rangeland. Ninety percent of the state's grazed forage is supplied by approximately 41 million acres (CDFF, 1988). Annual grasslands in the state, roughly 10 million of the 41 million grazed acres, produce the majority (70 percent) of the forage consumed by livestock.[4] Cattle and other livestock typically are grazed on marginal lands that are not suitable for other agricultural or productive uses. Mottet et al. (2017) estimate that on a global scale, 57 percent of the land used for livestock forage is not suitable for food production.

A unique feature of California and the western United States is the presence of publicly owned land that is managed by state and federal agencies. More than 45 percent of California's acreage is federally owned and managed, which makes many livestock producers in California reliant upon on the availability of federal grazing permits.

Livestock grazing on public lands began during the last half of the 19th century and increased to unsustainable levels around World War I. In response to the damage caused by unregulated grazing pressure, grazing allotments were established and allocated to individual producers beginning in the mid-1920s and culminating in the mid-1950s. During the 1990s, a regulatory paradigm shift changed the management of federal lands to include grazing utilization standards and integrated riparian management conservation policies, which reduced livestock grazing on federal lands by 15 percent across

---

4   Annual grasslands are characterized as open grasslands or woodlands dominated by an understory of annual plants and are primarily in the state's valleys and low-elevation mountains and foothills.

Figure 9.4. Dot Density Plot of Commercial Slaughter Total, 2016

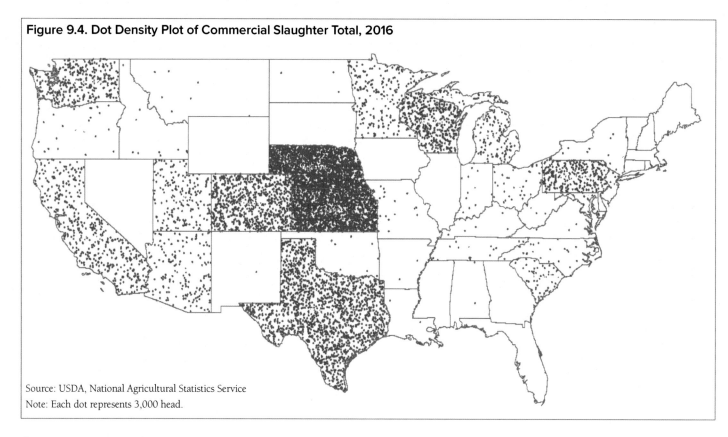

Source: USDA, National Agricultural Statistics Service
Note: Each dot represents 3,000 head.

the 11 western states from 2000 to 2015, and by 36 percent in California (Oles et al., 2017). Despite these reductions, ranchers in the western U.S. continue to get roughly 17 percent of their annual forage needs from public lands (Rimbey, Tanaka, and Torell, 2015).

CATTLE FEEDING AND PROCESSING

The majority of cattle in the U.S. are fed the last 4–6 months before slaughter on concentrated, grain-based rations (i.e., "grain-fed").[5] The U.S. Department of Agriculture's National Agriculture Statistics Service defines "cattle on feed" as cattle receiving a ration of grain, silage, hay, and/or protein supplements for the slaughter market, and expected to produce a carcass that will grade as select or better. At this stage in the beef supply chain, most yearlings have been shipped out of California to the Great Plains to feedlots located in close proximity to processing facilities.

5   Alternatively, some feeding operations choose not to use grain-based rations and instead use pasture and hay to add weight prior to slaughter. Finishing cattle on grass takes longer, and these operations are highly dependent on sufficient grass supplies. Thus, grass-fed cattle are typically older at time of slaughter (22–26 months) and somewhat lighter (1,000–1,200 lb), relative to their grain-fed counterparts.

Seventy-one percent of the cattle on feed in 2017 were being fed in just five states (Nebraska, Texas, Kansas, Iowa, and Colorado). Only 3 percent (430,000 head) of cattle received feed in California in 2017.

Cattle-processing operations are specialized to handle either steers and heifers or culled cows (including dairy) and bulls. Cow and bull plants are scattered across the country, reflecting the location of dairy operations. In 2016, dairy cows accounted for 9.6 percent of cattle slaughtered. Steer and heifer plants provide most of the high-valued muscle cuts of beef, such as steaks and roasts. The Midwest has the greatest concentration of processing operations for steers and heifers, with Nebraska, Texas, Kansas, and Colorado accounting for 70 percent of all commercial slaughtering in 2016. Nearly 55 percent of cattle slaughtered in 2016 were steers, and roughly 26 percent were heifers. California accounted for only 4 percent (1,218,800 head) of total commercial slaughter, with an estimated 50 percent comprised of culled dairy cows and bulls. Figure 9.4 is a dot density plot of commercial slaughter totals for 2016, with each dot representing 3,000 head slaughtered, and highlights the concentration of plants in the Midwestern states and major dairy states including California, Wisconsin, and Pennsylvania.

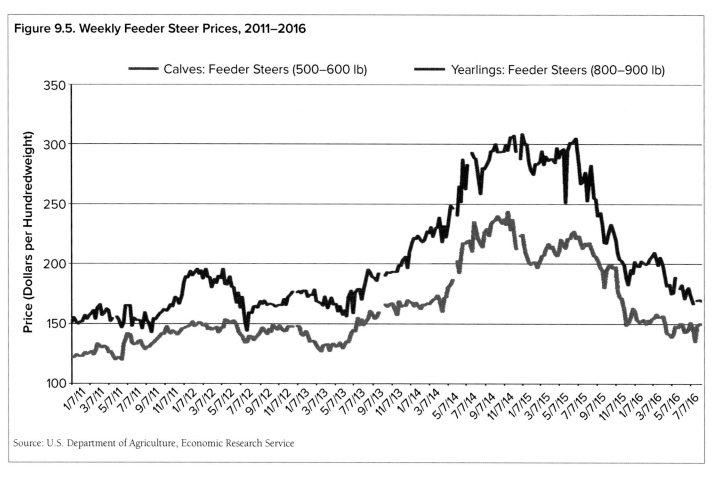

Figure 9.5. Weekly Feeder Steer Prices, 2011–2016

Source: U.S. Department of Agriculture, Economic Research Service

Four firms dominate meatpacking (JBS, Cargill, Tyson, and National Beef), slaughtering 85 percent of the steers and heifers in the United States. At time of slaughter, cattle are between 14–22 months of age and weigh between 1,200–1,400 lb. Geographic concentration continues to intensify when moving downstream from the feeding to the processing stage. A number of factors account for this geographic concentration. They include minimization of labor costs, avoidance of unionized labor, and improved technology in fabrication (i.e., boxed beef). (See Wohlgnant, 2013 for a comprehensive summary.)

MARKETING

Cow-calf and stocker operations typically use either local sales yards or satellite video auctions to market their calves and yearlings. Research suggests that satellite video auctions attract higher-quality cattle and offer producers access to a larger pool of potential buyers. In addition, satellite video auctions allow producers to differentiate their product, which is increasingly important as consumer tastes and preferences evolve. With food purchases

accounting for less than 10 percent of the budget for a typical American household, consumers can afford to pay premium prices for quality characteristics that they want, including how the foods they eat were produced. For livestock products, many consumers want to know, for example, if the animal received antibiotics or hormones, and whether it was raised in a humane manner.

Ranchers are using different management practices (e.g., non-hormone treated, natural, Global Animal Partnership certified) to increase the value of their cattle. Studies have shown that these value-added management practices often command price premiums at video auctions (Blank, Saitone, and Sexton 2016; Zimmerman et al., 2012). For example, calves raised as "natural" (i.e., without the use of antibiotics, ionophores, synthetic hormones, or given supplements containing animal by-products) sold for $1.20/cwt. more than cattle not participating in this program (Blank, Saitone, and Sexton, 2016). Further, non-trivial premiums for respiratory vaccines and weaning are confirmed by many studies, as these practices have been shown to improve performance at the feeding stage. Of

Figure 9.6. Total U.S. Cattle Inventories Across 11-Year Cattle Cycles, 1994–2017

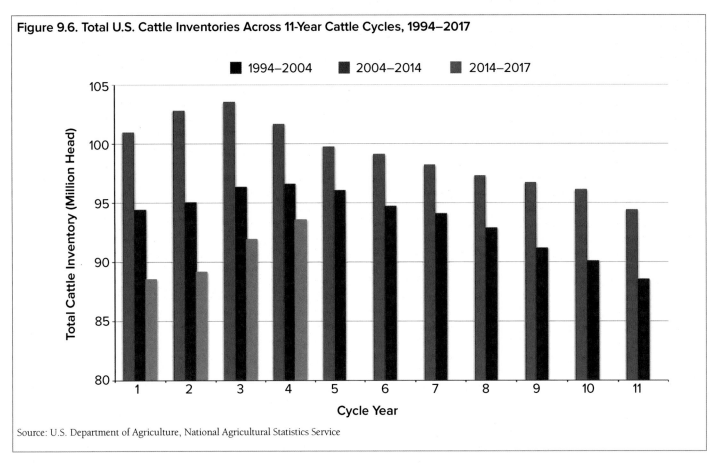

Source: U.S. Department of Agriculture, National Agricultural Statistics Service

course, ranchers earn premiums at the expense of higher costs of production, so they must weigh carefully what quality characteristics they seek to provide in their cattle.

Even when ignoring these opportunities for differentiation, the market for live cattle is inherently volatile, characterized by large fluctuations in price. Figure 9.5 shows weekly average prices for calves (feeder steers 500–600 lb) and yearlings (feeder steers 800–900 lb) from January 2011 to August 2016. During this roughly five-year period, prices ranged from $1.43/lb to a maximum of $3.09/lb for feeder steers in the 500–600 lb range. Similar volatility is present in the market for yearlings, although these larger cattle sell at a lower price per pound.

Some of the underlying price volatility is due to a periodic "cattle cycle," wherein cattle inventories vary in a somewhat predictable cyclical fashion. Figure 9.6 depicts total U.S. cattle inventories and shows how the cattle cycle ebbs and flows over 11-year periods, with each cattle cycle characterized by progressively lower total U.S. cattle numbers. Prices, not surprisingly, are lower during periods of higher inventories, which translate into increased supplies of cattle to the market.

Many ranchers seek to offset the risks of cattle ranching by diversifying their operations and also raising crops or other types of livestock or, alternatively, engaging in off-farm work. Ranchers can also attempt to hedge against adverse price movements in live cattle markets by buying and selling on organized futures markets.

Ultimately, the price that ranchers receive for their cattle is derived from the prices that consumers pay in grocery stores and restaurants for beef products. The farm-to-retail price spread measures the difference, on a per-pound basis, between the value of the animal at the farm and its value at the grocery store, after adjusting for the fact that a pound of beef on the hoof produces less than a pound at retail due to inedible parts of the live animal.

The price spread includes two components: farm to wholesale and wholesale to retail. Figure 9.7 shows that the farm-to-wholesale price spread has been relatively stable; fluctuating a maximum of 66.2 cents over a more than 11-year period. At the same time, the wholesale-to-retail price spread has been trending upward from a minimum of $1.54 per pound in June 2006 to a maximum of $2.99 in September 2016, a difference of more than $1.44 per pound.

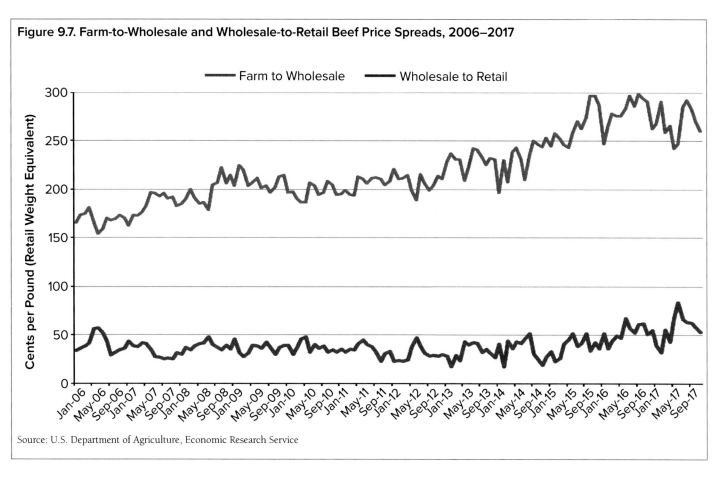

Figure 9.7. Farm-to-Wholesale and Wholesale-to-Retail Beef Price Spreads, 2006–2017

Source: U.S. Department of Agriculture, Economic Research Service

CATTLE AND BEEF TRADE

The United States is a net importer of live cattle, importing from Canada or Mexico. In 2017, the U.S. imported more than 1.7 million head of cattle—55 percent coming from Canada and 44 percent from Mexico. Over the most recent three years for which data are available (2014–2016), on average, the U.S. imported 40 percent of cattle for feeding (i.e., between 400–700 lb) and another 30 percent for slaughter. In 2016, the U.S. exported nearly 70,000 head of cattle, mostly to Canada and Mexico.

The majority of the beef exported from the U.S. is high-value, grain-finished muscle cuts. At the same time, the U.S. imports predominantly lower-valued, grass-fed beef to combine with fat to produce ground beef. While still a net importer of beef and veal, the U.S. earned the distinction of being the world's largest beef exporter measured by value in 2016—$6.343 billion (U.S. Meat Export Federation, 2016). In total, the U.S. exported more than 2.55 billion pounds of beef in 2016 to Japan (655.4 million lb), South Korea (459.2 million lb), and Mexico (395.0 million lb), among others, while importing more than 3.0 billion pounds of beef from Australia (767.2 million lb), Canada (717.8 million lb), and New Zealand (612.5 million lb), among others.

U.S. beef exports are expected to continue to increase over time despite sanitary, phytosanitary, and traceability requirements (Pendell et al., 2013). For example, in 2017, China lifted its 13-year ban on fresh beef imports from the United States. O'Donoghue and Hansen (2017) predict that imports of beef to China will increase by 42 percent over the next decade. Yet, the U.S. may be slow to respond to this opportunity, as there are limited volumes of cattle in the U.S. to meet the export requirements (e.g., only 0.27 percent of the cattle slaughtered by Tyson each week currently meet the specifications [*Bloomberg News*, 2017]). As demand in specific export markets rises, processors have begun to search for cattle that meet the characteristics required or desired in these markets (e.g., age- and source-verified, and hormone-free).

SHEEP

Although the U.S. at one time was home to more than 56.2 million sheep, inventories have been declining since their peak in 1942. Figure 9.8 shows sheep and lamb inventories in the United States and California from 1940 through 2017. Following precipitous declines in the 1940s and 1960s, the U.S. flock has stabilized at roughly 5.5 million head. The decrease is due to declining domestic per capita consumption of lamb; increased foreign competition in the markets for lamb, mutton, and wool; available synthetic textile substitutes for wool; predator pressures resulting in substantial death losses; and price volatility with persistent periods where prices were below costs for many producers.

According to the most recent Census of Agriculture, more than 88,000 farms in the U.S. had sheep and lamb inventories in 2012. Many of these farms are relatively small, with 92 percent of farms having less than 100 head on their operations. Larger operations with 1,000 head or more account for less than 1 percent of farms but have nearly 44 percent of total inventories. The sheep and lamb

inventories in California have followed the same general trend as the United States, stabilizing at roughly 600,000 head. The top five sheep- and lamb-producing states in the U.S., in order of total inventories in 2017, were Texas, California, Colorado, Wyoming, and Utah.

The majority of sheep in the U.S. are raised for both meat and wool production. Total wool production in the United States has been declining due to sheep inventory reductions, as well as reduced demand for wool for use in textiles. Although Texas has larger sheep and lamb inventories, California has more sheep shorn and the largest wool production numbers of any state in the nation. In 2016, 410,000 sheep were shorn in California, producing 2.7 million pounds of wool.

In 2017 California produced 20 percent (250,000 head) of the market lambs and 13 percent (10,000 head) of the market sheep in the United States. During 2016, there were 16 federally inspected processing plants in the state for

Figure 9.8. United States and California Sheep and Lamb Inventories, 1940–2017

Source: U.S. Department of Agriculture, National Agricultural Statistics Service

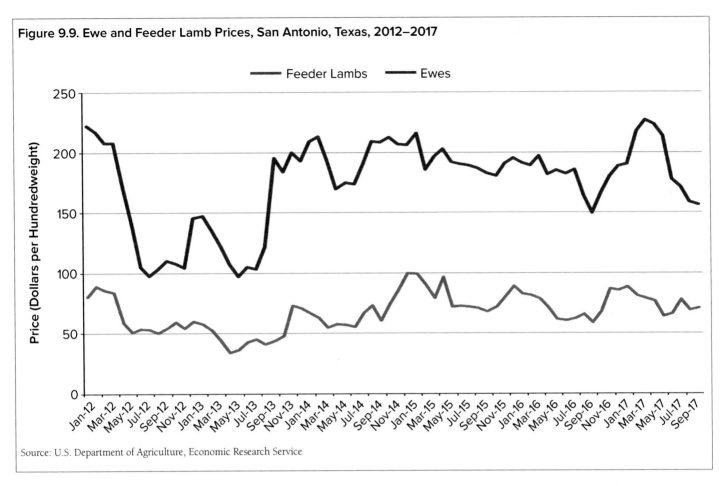

Figure 9.9. Ewe and Feeder Lamb Prices, San Antonio, Texas, 2012–2017

Source: U.S. Department of Agriculture, Economic Research Service

sheep and lamb processing.[6] In the same year, California had the second largest commercial sheep and lamb slaughter total (314,600 head), 14 percent of the national total.

MARKETING AND TRADE

In general, the lamb supply chain today is much like the beef supply chain. Lambs destined for slaughter are fed in feedlots and then marketed to processors. Over time, processors have substantially reduced the amount of purchases that they make via "formula," from roughly 70 percent of purchases in 2007 to approximately 40 percent in 2016. At the same time, the portion of lambs owned and fed by processors has increased from less than 20 percent in 2007 to nearly 40 percent in 2016. Much like cattle, the market for ewes and feeder lambs is quite volatile. Figure 9.9 shows average monthly ewe and feeder-lamb prices for the past six years.

The United States is a net exporter of live sheep. Exports of live sheep in 2016, totaling 51,638 head, were destined for more than 20 countries around the world. The vast majority of sheep exported went to the United Arab Emirates (60 percent) and Mexico (26 percent).[7] In the same year, all live sheep imports, totaling 14,272 head, originated from Canada.

The U.S. is a net importer of lamb and mutton, which primarily comes from Australia or New Zealand. Over 50 percent of U.S. lamb exports were destined for Mexico. Mexico is the primary export market for the U.S. (38 percent of the mutton exports in 2016), with the remaining volume shipping to more than 50 export destinations. In 2016, all live sheep imports, totalling 14,272 head, originated from Canada.

7 The United Arab Emirates was a new export destination for U.S. sheep beginning in 2016. In prior years, the majority of sheep exported went to Canada and Mexico.

6 In 2016, 94 percent of commercial slaughter in California was at federally inspected plants. State-inspected facilities processed the remaining animals.

ISSUES, CHALLENGES, AND OPPORTUNITIES

As livestock producers continue to struggle to manage their operations profitably, they are confronted with new and unprecedented challenges. While the gamut of challenges facing the livestock industry is too vast to cover fully in this chapter, the subsequent sections discuss a few key issues especially relevant to California.

FORAGE RESOURCES

A persistent and ongoing challenge for cow-calf and stocker operations, the segments of the supply chain most prevalent in California, is sufficient forage. One of the strongest predictors of profitability on an operational scale is non-pasture feed costs, with producers who are able to minimize the need and amount of supplement feed remaining the most solvent. Given this dependence on rangeland and pasture-based forage supplies, climate, environmental, and regulatory changes that restrict access, availability, and efficient use of these resources are of paramount concern to California livestock producers.

Climate change is expected to result in more variable weather patterns, with longer and more severe droughts being one likely outcome. California's ranching community, which is reliant on rain-fed (i.e., climate-sensitive), pasture-based forage systems, is likely one of the most vulnerable to climate variability and drought (Roche, 2016). Simultaneously, there is growing societal pressure for sustainable food production and expanding expectations for land conservation, making the management of both private and public rangelands increasingly complex (Roche et al., 2015). These challenges have often resulted in conservation strategies that reduce livestock stocking rates or remove livestock altogether on public lands, despite evidence that grazing pressure is currently at a level that balances livestock production and conservation goals (Oles et al., 2017).

Beyond supporting agricultural production, California's rangelands simultaneously provide a wide array of benefits, often referred to as ecosystem services, that include recreation, wildlife habitat, open space, nutrient cycling, carbon sequestration, water, and timber. Yet, the quality and quantity of these ecosystem services are at risk. In the 14 years between 1990 and 2004, urbanization contributed to the loss of 100,000 acres of grazing land. Forecasts are that by 2040, an additional 750,000 acres will be urbanized (CDFF, 2010; Kroeger et al., 2009). Beyond reductions in land available for grazing, urbanization, as well as exurban parcelization, creates ecosystem fragmentation. This fragmentation is a major threat to ecosystem services and biodiversity that is dependent upon large, contiguous areas of land (Hobbs et al., 2008). Attempts to curb these trends include conservation strategies to reduce property taxes for agricultural lands (i.e., the Williamson Act), conserve grasslands through voluntary, publicly funded restoration incentives, and create mitigation banks (e.g., habitat or water) (Cameron and Holland, 2014).

CONCENTRATION, VERTICAL INTEGRATION, AND VERTICAL COORDINATION

The concentration of processors in the beef industry has been a focal point for researchers, policymakers, and those involved in the supply chain dating back to the early 1900s. Yet, despite investigations by the U.S. Federal Trade Commission and the U.S. Department of Justice (DOJ), private antitrust lawsuits, and regulatory attempts through the development and enforcement of the Packers and Stockyards Act, the concentration in processing has continued to increase apace from the mid-1970s to present. From 1976 to 1998, the four-firm concentration ratio in steer and heifer slaughter increased from 25 percent to 80 percent (Ward, 2002), and by 2015, was 85 percent (USDA, 2016).[8] Although the preponderance of empirical evidence in the academic literature fails to find processors exercising their buying power (monopsony power) in order to depress cattle prices, concerns among industry participants

---

8 The four-firm concentration ratio (CR4) is one measure used to quantify concentration. It is calculated by summing the market shares of the largest four firms in the industry.

persist to this day.[9] One recent example is a cattle-producer group's (R-CALF USA) petitioning the U.S. Senate Judiciary Committee to investigate the U.S. beef processor industry's role in the precipitous decline in cattle prices in and around 2015.

National concentration metrics likely understate concentration in the local or regional areas where individual livestock producers operate. Ranchers, particularly those operating feedlots, say they have only one, or at most a few, prospective buyers. This was a recurring theme at the joint USDA-DOJ listening sessions conducted across the country in 2010. The following comment from a cattle producer is representative:

"While potentially there are four market participants, what we see typically region by region is that there are really one to two meaningful participants, rarely three, and four meaningful participants is very much an oddity." (U.S. Dept. of Justice 2010a, p. 211).

Inextricably related to processor concentration is the use of vertical integration and contracting to procure cattle. Large cattle processors are dependent upon a steady supply of cattle to process in order to operate their facilities at efficient capacity and remain profitable. As a consequence, packers have increasingly relied upon vertical integration into cattle feeding and/or vertical coordination through contracts in order to assure their supply.

In the 1970s, the share of cattle marketed under vertical coordination mechanisms was similar to the shares observed in other agricultural product industries (around 10 percent by 1980), but this share for cattle roughly doubled in the subsequent 20 years. By 2007, the share of fed cattle purchased using spot-type mechanisms (e.g., auctions, private sales, etc.) was 60 percent, but by 2016, it had declined to just 30 percent (USDA, 2016). The rate of increase in vertical coordination through contracts in the United States has been most pronounced in the livestock sector—representing about 60 percent of all contracts in U.S. agriculture (Crespi, Saitone, and Sexton, 2012).

While the cattle feeding and processing segments of the supply chain remain the most concentrated and coordinated, these trends, coupled with the potential for increased efficiency, have caused speculation surrounding whether or not the upstream portions of the beef supply chain will follow hog and broiler production.

It is imperative that the beef supply chain evolves in order to satisfy consumer preferences, while simultaneously complying with sanitary, phytosanitary, and traceability requirements imposed by trading partners in order to increase demand. Concurrently, processors must employ procurement strategies that facilitate the sourcing of animals with very specific suites of characteristics. This is a monumental task considering the geographically diverse and often small-scale and autonomous set of producers that characterize the cow-calf and stocker segments of the supply chain.

Upstream livestock producers may use this situation to create opportunities to reduce uncertainty and increase profitability by either increasing the specificity (i.e., production of specific quality characteristics) of their marketed animals to attract or target particular buyers, or coordinating with buyers via contracts to guarantee a market for their animals, thereby reducing risk and price volatility.

REGULATIONS AND RESTRICTIONS

Like other businesses operating in California, ranchers face a number of state-specific regulations and geographically based challenges. While state-specific regulations often penalize in-state production relative to production in other locales (Sumner, 2017), some of the challenges are simply an artifact of the geographic location of California's livestock operations. A key example of a California-specific regulation is that beginning in 2018, livestock producers face more restrictions in the use of antibiotics on their operations. New commercial transportation laws that will likely increase costs associated with livestock hauling are a key case of a national regulation that may affect California ranchers disproportionately. Further, an increasing number of Northern California producers must deal with increased predator pressure from wolves.

---

9   The literature on the exercise of market power (e.g., Azzam and Schroeter 1995; Morrison-Paul, 2001) has found modest departures from competition but overall, has concluded that the efficiency advantages of consolidation outweighed any negative potential impacts from the exercise of market power.

VETERINARY FEED DIRECTIVE AND CALIFORNIA SB 27

Antibiotic resistance is one of the most pressing public health challenges. While concerns about resistance are paramount in both the human- and animal-health arenas, the food-producing animal segment (e.g., beef cattle, dairy cattle, poultry) of the supply chain has been widely criticized for using antibiotics for growth promotion and enhanced feed efficiency (i.e., subtherapeutic uses), as when antibiotics are administered for an extended period of time. According to the Center for Disease Control, this type of long-term, low-level exposure contributes to the survival and growth of resistant bacteria. In response to these concerns, regulations have been put into place to limit the use of antibiotics in food-producing animals for growth promotion and to increase feed efficiency.

The Department of Heath and Human's Service's Food and Drug Administration (FDA) amended the Animal Drug Availability Act of 1996 to create a new avenue to distribute antibiotics used in or on animal feed or administered through water. This change was implemented on January 1, 2017, and barred the use of "medically important" antibiotics for subtherapeutic treatments i.e., an antibiotic used in both humans and animals. Moreover, this class of drugs can only be used to treat, prevent, or control disease in animals under the supervision of a licensed veterinarian. A veterinary feed directive (VFD), which closely resembles a prescription for feed- or water-based antibiotic treatment, provides this supervision.

At roughly the same time as that VFD rule went into effect, California Governor Jerry Brown signed Senate Bill 27 ("Livestock: Use of Antimicrobial Drugs"). This bill, which became effective on January 1, 2018, implements regulations in California that are similar to, and more stringent than, the federal rules. Beyond expanding the regulatory oversight and use restrictions in the state, SB 27 also mandates that the California Department of Food and Agriculture develop and distribute stewardship guidelines for judicious use of antibiotics, put in place requirements for data collection on the use of antibiotics, conduct surveillance for antimicrobial resistance, and survey management practices and associated health outcomes.

Restricting the use of antibiotics through regulations is likely to have economic ramifications, with farm-level production costs expected to increase as a result. The costs associated with veterinary consults to facilitate the use of feed- or water-based antibiotic treatments will be borne by producers, with small operations likely experiencing higher costs on a per-unit basis. Further, the cost of feed-based antibiotic treatment is likely to rise as feed mills and feed distributors are required to mix and sell medicated feeds in compliance with regulations while engaging in more stringent record-keeping obligations. Finally, as producers substitute away from medically important antibiotics to unregulated alternatives, prices for these alternative treatments may increase. And, given that the California regulations are more stringent, these anticipated cost increases and production challenges are likely to be more severe here relative to other parts of the country.

ELECTRONIC LOGGING DEVICE REGULATIONS

The lack of cattle feeding and processing capacity in California and the western U.S. causes ranchers to receive lower prices for cattle, compared to their counterparts in the Midwest, in order to compensate buyers for the costs associated with transportation (Blank, Saitone, and Sexton, 2016; Saitone et al., 2016). This price differential is anticipated to become larger due to new transportation regulations governing commercial cattle haulers. In December 2017, the Federal Motor Carrier Safety Administration (FMCSA) implemented Electronic Logging Device (ELD) regulations that will monitor and limit both driving and on-duty time for commercial transportation services.[10] While regulations limiting drive and on-duty time are needed for safety, there are potentially significant cost and animal-welfare implications associated with the implementation of these regulations for live-animal commercial haulers.

Cattle hauled from California to the center of feeding and processing capacity in the Midwest travel between

---

10 At the time that this chapter went to press, commercial haulers of agricultural products, including cattle, have been given a 90-day extension to ELD implementation.

1,500 and 1,700 miles. Under EDL regulations, this will require a mandated 8-hour rest period for a single driver or require the use of a second driver. Further, the auctions through which cattle are purchased and shipped can create inefficiencies and delays that require haulers to spend limited on-duty time in trucks waiting for lots to be aggregated and loaded. The stress of shipment on cattle will only be exacerbated if haulers are required to unload and re-load cattle in order to comply with these regulations, especially given the few locations where this would be possible.

Western ranchers, particularly those in California, are at substantial locational disadvantage and, as a consequence, are estimated to have received $0.82/cwt. less for every mile that they are from Omaha, NE, controlling for quality and value-added characteristics (Blank, Saitone, and Sexton, 2016). The EDL rule and associated cost increases will put Western ranchers at further disadvantage due to their location.

PREDATOR PRESSURES

While livestock producers in other states (e.g., Montana, Idaho, and Oregon) have been forced to deal with predation pressure from wolves for some time, California ranchers have not faced this challenge until relatively recently. Wolves were removed from the California landscape at the beginning of the 20th century.

The first gray wolf confirmed to have re-entered California (named OR-7) did so in late 2011. OR-7 originated in Oregon, frequently crossed the Oregon-California border from 2011–2013, and, while he eventually remained in Oregon, his presence marked the beginning of concern and anticipation of the return of wolves to California's landscape. Since this time, trail cameras in remote areas of Northern California have confirmed the presence of other wolves and wolf pups in the state. By July 2017, there were a minimum of two wolf packs in the state—the Shasta Pack and the Lassen Pack—and the state's first confirmed wolf kill of livestock occurred in October 13, 2017, in Lassen County.

Gray wolves are listed under both the state and federal endangered species acts. Due to the protections afforded by the act, it is prohibited by law to "harass, harm, pursue, hunt, shoot, wound, trap, capture, or collect, or to attempt to engage in any such conduct." Given these protections, ranchers with herds in areas with wolves are constrained to using non-lethal depredation strategies to attempt to protect their animals from harm. These strategies—including carcass removal, guardian animals, and range riders—have limited effectiveness in deterring wolf predation while increasing production costs. Potential losses due to predation could have substantial negative consequences for cattle and sheep operations in the state. Yet, the indirect production impacts associated with predator pressures (e.g., lower conception rates, reduced weight gain, increased stress, etc.) have been shown to have more substantial economic consequences for producers than direct (i.e., death) losses (Ramler et al., 2014).

A number of government- and nonprofit-funded initiatives have attempted to provide compensation for direct losses incurred by livestock producers due to wolves, while other proposals have created cost-share funding for producers who wish to adopt non-lethal predator protection techniques. Historically, these programs have not been successful, as the losses sustained by producers have often outpaced government-based funding and/or donations. Consequently, livestock producers, particularly those in Northern California, will have to reassess their operational procedures (e.g., timing and location of calving, location and timing of pasture, etc.) in order to maximize profits under a new risk paradigm and subject to a dynamic set of constraints from predator pressures.

CONCLUSION

California's livestock sector accounts for nearly one-quarter ($12 billion in 2015) of the state's total cash receipts. Cattle and sheep in California transform forage into protein and fiber using predominantly marginal lands that would otherwise not facilitate agricultural production. California's livestock producers face persistent disadvantages associated with their geographic location that cause them to receive lower prices for their animals. Further, additional factors are looming on the horizon that may exacerbate the challenges associated with engaging in livestock production in California. Yet, California ranchers are resilient and resourceful. Opportunities exist for producers to earn premiums in a modern food market environment and access to California's niche markets may be an untapped prospect. Finally, policymakers need to recognize the importance of this key agricultural industry and the challenges it faces as they contemplate rules and regulations that impact this sector of our economy.

REFERENCES

Azzam, A. and J.R. Schroeter. 1995. "The Tradeoff between Oligopsony Power and Cost Efficiency in Horizontal Consolidation: An Example from Beef Packing." *American Journal of Agricultural Economics* 77(4): 825-836.

Blank, S.C., T.L. Saitone, and R.J. Sexton. 2016. "Calf and Yearling Prices in the Western United States: Spatial, Quality, and Temporal Factors in Satellite Video Auctions." *Journal of Agricultural and Resource Economics* 41(3): 458-480.

Bloomberg News. 2017. "U.S. Beef is Back on China's Shelves -- But China Doesn't Care." Available at: https://www.bloomberg.com/news/articles/2017-08-03/trump-s-vaunted-return-of-u-s-beef-to-china-risks-turning-a-dud.

California Department of Food and Agriculture (CDFA). 2016. *California Agricultural Statistics Review, 2015.* Sacramento CA. Available at: https://www.cdfa.ca.gov/Statistics/PDFs/2016Report.pdf.

California Department of Forestry and Fire (CDFF). 1988. *California's Forests and Rangelands: Growing Conflict Over Changing Uses.* Sacramento CA: Forest and Rangeland Resources Assessment.

California Department of Forestry and Fire (CDFF). 2010. *California's Forests and Rangelands: 2010 Assessment.* Sacramento CA: Fire and Resource Assessment Program.

Cameron, D.R. and M.J. Holland. 2014. "Whither the Rangeland? Protection and Conversion in California's Rangeland Ecosystems." *PLoS ONE* 9(8): e103468.

Crespi, J.M., T.L. Saitone, and R.J. Sexton. 2012. "Competition in U.S. Farm Product Markets: Do Long-Run Incentives Trump Short Run Market Power?" *Applied Economic Perspectives and Policy* 34(4): 669-695.

Food and Agricultural Organization of the United Nations. 2006. *World Agriculture Towards 2030/2050 Interim Report: Prospects for Food, Nutrition, Agriculture and Major Commodity Groups.* Rome IT: Global Perspective Studies Unit.

Hobbs, N.T., K.A. Galvin, C.J. Stokes, J.M. Lackett, A.J. Ash, R.B. Boone, R.S. Reid, and P.K. Thronton. 2008. "Fragmentation of Rangelands: Implications for Humans, Animals, and Landscapes." *Global Environmental Change* 18(4): 776-785.

Kroeger, T., F. Casey, P. Alvarez, M. Cheatum and L. Tavassoli. 2009. "An Economic Analysis of the Benefits of Habitat Conservation on California Rangelands." Conservation Economics White Paper, Conservation Economics Program. Washington DC: Defenders of Wildlife.

Morrison-Paul, C.J. 2001. "Cost Economies and Market Power: The Case of the U.S. Meat Packing Industry." *Review of Economics and Statistics* 83: 531-540.

O'Donoghue, E. and J. Hansen, and D. Stallings. 2018. "USDA Agricultural Projections to 2027." *Agricultural Projections No. OCE-2018-1.* Washington DC: U.S. Department of Agriculture. Available at: https://www.ers.usda.gov/publications/pub-details/?pubid=87458.

Oles, K.M., D.A. Weixelman, D.F. Lile, K.W. Tate, L.K. Snell, and L.M. Roche. 2017. "Riparian Meadow Response to Modern Conservation Grazing Management." *Environmental Management* 60: 383-395.

Pendell, D.L., G.T. Tonsor, K.C. Dhuyvetter, G.W. Brester, and T.C. Schroeder. 2013. "Evolving Beef Export Market Access Requirements for Age and Source Verification." *Food Policy* 43: 332-240.

Ramler, J.P., M. Hebblewhite, D. Kellenberg, and C. Sime. 2014. "Crying Wolf? A Spatial Analysis of Wolf Locations and Depredations on Calf Weight." *American Journal of Agricultural Economics* 96(30): 631-656.

Rimbey, N. R., J. A. Tanaka, and L. A. Torell. 2015. "Economic Considerations of Livestock Grazing on Public Lands in the United States of America." *Animal Frontiers* 5: 32-35.

Roche, L.M. 2016. "Adaptive Rangeland Decision-Making and Coping with Drought." *Sustainability* 8(12): 13 p.

Roche, L.M., T.K. Schohr, J.D. Derner, M.N. Lubell, B.B. Cutts, E. Kachergis, V.T. Eviner, and K.W. Tate. 2015. "Sustaining Working Rangelands: Insights from Rancher Decision Making." *Rangeland and Ecology Management* 68(5): 383-389.

Saitone, T.L., L.C. Forero, G.A. Nader, and L.E. Forero. 2016. "Calf and Yearling Prices in California and the Western United States." *California Agriculture* 70(4): 179-186.

U.S. Department of Agriculture (USDA). 2016. *Packers and Stockyards Program: 2016 Annual Report.* Washington DC: Grain Inspection, Packers, and Stockyards Administration. Available at: https://www.gipsa.usda.gov/psp/publication/ar/2016_PSP_Annual_Report.pdf.

U.S. Meat Export Federation. 2016. "Global Beef Exports Held Steady in 2016." Available at: https://www.usmef.org/global-beef-exports-held-steady-in-2016/.

Ward, C.E. 2002. "A Review of Causes for and Consequences of Economic Concentration in the U.S. Meatpacking Industry." *Current Agriculture, Food & Resource Issues* 3: 1-28.

Wohlgenant, M.K. 2013. "Competition in the U.S. Meat-packing Industry." *Annual Review of Resource Economics* 5: 1-12.

Zimmerman, L.C., T.C. Schroeder, K.C. Dhuyvetter, K.C. Olson, G.L. Stokka, J.T. Seeger, and D.M. Grotelue-schen. 2012. "The Effect of Value-Added Management on Calf Prices at Superior Livestock Auction Video Markets." *Journal of Agricultural and Resource Economics* 37(1): 128-143.

CHAPTER 10. CALIFORNIA VEGETABLES

RACHAEL E. GOODHUE AND PHILIP L. MARTIN

ABSTRACT

High-value, year-round production and marketing, and sensitivity to labor costs distinguish fresh vegetables from California's other crops. Fresh vegetables are relatively small-acreage crops with big values: some 250,000 acres of lettuce produced $2.4 billion worth of output in 2017, making California lettuce three times more valuable than four million acres of U.S. barley. Grower-shippers who market vegetables year-round are the key actors, producing in several areas, and importing to ensure a steady supply of vegetables for grocery chains and food-service firms. Labor costs are often one-third of variable costs to produce fresh vegetables; rising labor costs have set up a race between rising imports, labor-saving machines, and guest workers for how and where fresh vegetables are produced.

ABOUT THE AUTHORS

Rachael E. Goodhue is a professor and chair of the Department of Agricultural and Resource Economics at UC Davis. She can be contacted by email at regoodhue@ucdavis.edu. Philip L. Martin is an emeritus professor in the Department of Agricultural and Resource Economics at UC Davis, who can be contacted at plmartin@ucdavis.edu. Both authors are members of the Giannini Foundation of Agricultural Economics.

With a value of $6.1 billion, California accounted for over half of U.S. fresh vegetable production in 2018.

Photo Credit: Shermain Hardesty, UC Davis

CHAPTER **10**. TABLE OF CONTENTS

VEGETABLES

Americans have about 150 pounds of fresh vegetables available to them each year, including U.S. production and imports. The U.S. produced $14.2 billion worth of fresh vegetables in 2019, imported $8 billion and exported $2.3 billion, for a fresh vegetable trade deficit of $5.7 billion (Parr, Bond, and Minor, 2020, ERS Vegetables and Pulses Yearbook Tables 7, 8). Over half of U.S. fresh vegetable production is in California ($6.1 billion), followed by 10 percent ($1.2 billion) in Arizona.

Excluding fresh potatoes, U.S. residents consumed (or had available to consume) an average 144 pounds of fresh vegetables in 2016, including 27 pounds of lettuce, 21 pounds of tomatoes, 19 pounds of onions, and 11 pounds of bell peppers. These four fresh vegetables accounted for over half of the fresh vegetables available to U.S. residents (Minor and Bond, 2017, Table 5).

Table 10.1. California: Six Major Fresh Vegetables, 2017

	Acres	Tons	Value	CA Share
		1,000	$ (Millions)	Percent
Broccoli	119,000	952	850	92
Carrots	58,500	1,082	615	89
Celery	23,500	734	302	96
Lettuce, All	199,700	3,044	2,415	66
Peppers, Bell	15,900	334	282	57
Tomatoes, Fresh	NA	331	206	63
Subtotal	NA	6,478	4,671	

Source: CDFA, *California Agricultural Statistics Review*

Note: CA share is for all peppers and all tomatoes; CA share is based on value of commodity.

Table 10.2. Broccoli

All Broccoli	1985	1995	2005	2015
Harvested Acreage (acres)	94,902	122,178	122,702	120,035
Yield (tons/acre)				
Value of Production ($1,000)	228,173	329,697	292,647	356,372
Revenue ($/acre)	2,404	2,698	2,385	2,969

Source: CDFA, 2015

Fresh Broccoli	1985	1995	2005	2015
Harvested Acreage (acres)	48,320	96,023	77,868	60,100
Yield (tons/acre)	6.15	6.32	6.98	7.15
Value of Production ($1,000)	126,910	236,200	181,000	193,200
Revenue ($/acre)	2,626	2,460	2,324	3,214

Source: CDFA, 2015

Figure 10.1. Acreage of Six Vegetables, 1990–2017

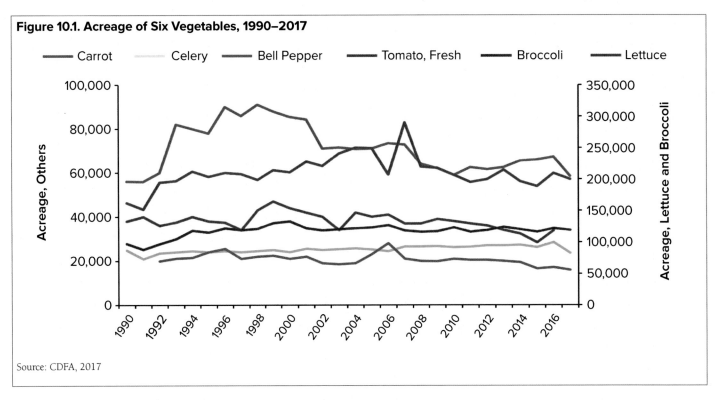

Source: CDFA, 2017

Table 10.3. Carrots

	1985	1995	2005	2015
Harvested Acreage (acres)	33,087	58,018	58,970	51,076
Yield (tons/acre)*	17.03	25.82	23.99	23.12
Value of Production ($1,000)	271,908	237,749	240,034	193,842
Revenue ($/acre)	8,218	4,098	4,070	3,795

Source: CDFA, 2015
Note: *Yield data for fresh market carrot.

Six Vegetables

California's six most valuable fresh vegetables in 2015 were lettuce, worth $2.3 billion; broccoli, $866 million; carrots, $639 million; bell peppers and celery worth about $430–440 million each; and fresh tomatoes, $330 million (Table 10.1). These six commodities were farmed on less than 500,000 acres and generated almost $5 billion worth of commodities in 2015. By contrast, Kansas harvested over 8 million acres of wheat that generated $1.5 billion in sales in 2016.

Figure 10.1 plots acreage over time for these vegetables between 1985 and 2015. Lettuce and broccoli account for two-thirds of the acreage of the six major vegetables. Figure 10.1 data are from County Agricultural Commissioners' Reports and may provide duplicate counts.

Lettuce acreage increased until the mid-2000s, and has fallen since then, while broccoli acreage increased significantly between 1985 and 1995 and has been fairly stable since. Carrot acreage fluctuated, while fresh tomato and bell pepper acreage declined. Celery has registered a fairly steady increase in acreage. These data include acreage harvested, and multiple crops of lettuce and celery grown on the same land in one year.

The value of California broccoli has increased from stable acreage since 1995, reflecting higher yields and prices (Table 10.2). Fresh broccoli acreage increased, while broccoli for processing and other uses decreased. These data are from County Agricultural Commissioners' Reports and do not match the state's annual summary data precisely.

Table 10.4. Celery

	1985	1995	2005	2015
Harvested Acreage (acres)	21,761	23,805	26,883	31,160
Yield (tons/acre)*		34.39	38.28	32.70
Value of Production ($1,000)	251,115	275,132	179,265	237,482
Revenue ($/acre)	11,539	11,558	6,668	7,621

Source: CDFA, 2015
Note: *Yield data for fresh market celery.

Table 10.5. Lettuce

	1985	1995	2005	2015
Harvested Acreage (acres)	195,536	205,828	205,023	191,212
Yield (tons/acre)*	14.04	10.60	16.46	13.96
Value of Production ($1,000)	1,251,212	1,291,369	1,021,351	991,103
Revenue ($/acre)	6,399	6,274	4,982	5,183

Source: CDFA, 2015
Note: *Yield data for lettuce leaf.

Table 10.6. Bell Peppers

	1985	1995	2005	2015
Harvested Acreage (acres)	10,324	23,851	20,048	16,196
Yield (tons/acre)	12.97	14.65	18.93	25.90
Value of Production ($1,000)	87,983	152,894	157,551	118,202
Revenue ($/acre)	8,522	6,410	7,859	7,298

Source: CDFA, 2015

The yield and the value of carrots have fluctuated, along with acreage (Table 10.3). Revenues per acre have recovered to the 1985 level of over $8,000 an acre. The value of celery production has increased with acreage and prices, but yields fluctuate.

Lettuce acreage and yields do not display consistent trends (Table 10.5). Revenues per acre and the value of production have increased, and the shift from head lettuce to leaf lettuce and romaine have increased revenues per acre.

Bell pepper yields and revenues per acre have increased, which increased the value of production. (Table 10.6). However, harvested acreage declined between 2005 and 2015.

The value of fresh tomatoes declined between 2005 and 2015, reflecting a sharp drop in acreage but higher yields (Table 10.7).

STRUCTURE OF PRODUCTION: FEWER AND LARGER GROWER-SHIPPERS

Consumers expect a year-round supply of fresh vegetables, and the consolidating grocery and food-service industries want to deal with grower-shippers who can provide a year-round supply. As a result, production of the major fresh vegetables is concentrated among a relative handful of large firms.

While the trend is well-recognized by industry members and observers, limited government data are available on the concentration of fresh vegetable production. These data show that the largest 50 farms account for 50 to 90 percent of total acreage and production of most fresh vegetables.

Table 10.7. Fresh Tomatoes

	1985	1995	2005	2015
Harvested Acreage (acres)	28,142	37,917	35,782	22,544
Yield (tons/acre)	14.83	14.02	13.74	17.80
Value of Production ($1,000)	282,596	217,005	183,388	128,237
Revenue ($/acre)	10,042	5,723	5,125	5,688

Source: CDFA, 2015

Table 10.8. Largest Vegetable Growers: West, 2014

	Acreage	Crops	Other Crops
Grimmway	57,787	Carrots	Other Vegetables
D'Arrigo	36,847	Lettuce	Broccoli
Tanimura & Antle	25,527	Lettuce	Broccoli & Other Vegetables
Ocean Mist	24,890	Lettuce	Artichokes & Other Vegetables
Nunes	19,223	Lettuce	Broccoli & Other Vegetables
Subtotal	164,274		

Source: *Growing Produce*, http://www.growingproduce.com/vegetables/2014-top-25-vegetable-growers-west/

Note: Not all of these large vegetable growers are classified as vegetable farms. Grimmway Farms, which reports processing 80 percent of U.S.-grown carrots (http://www.grimmway.com/carrots/), is included in miscellaneous crop farming (NAICS 111998) rather than vegetable farming (http://www.labormarketinfo.edd. ca.gov/aspdotnet/databrowsing/empDetails.aspx?menuchoice=emp&geogArea=0604000029&empId=641807581). The *Growing Produce* list excludes Dole Fresh Vegetables, which produces and markets a range of fresh vegetables but is considered a fruit and vegetable merchant wholesaler (NAICS 424480) rather than a farmer, as are Bud of California, Mann Packing, and Taylor Farms (www.labormarketinfo.edd.ca.gov/majorer/countymajorer.asp?CountyCode=000053).

Table 29 of the Census of Agriculture reported almost 4,900 vegetable farming operations in California that harvested 1.2 million acres in 2017, down from 6,100 operations but the same 1.2 million acres harvested in 2012 (https://www.nass.usda.gov/Quick_Stats/CDQT/chapter/2/table/29/state/CA). Over 90 percent of California vegetable farming operations, and three-fourths of the vegetable acres harvested, are produced for the fresh market.

There were 812 broccoli farming operations that harvested 109,423 acres in 2017, almost all for the fresh market; broccoli had a farm gate value of $850 million in 2017. The 36 broccoli farming operations that harvested 1,000 or more acres accounted for almost 60 percent of all broccoli acreage. There were 785 carrot farming operations that harvested 62,700 acres in 2017, almost all for the fresh market; carrots were worth $615 million in 2017. The 25 carrot farming operations that harvested 500 or more acres accounted for two-thirds of the harvested carrot acreage. There were 323 celery farming operations that harvested almost 30,000 acres in 2017, 98 percent for the fresh market; celery was worth $302 million in 2017.

Lettuce is the most valuable vegetable grown in California, worth $2.4 billion in 2017. There were 1,114 lettuce farming operations that harvested almost 250,000 acres in 2017, all for the fresh market. The 67 lettuce farming operations that harvested 1,000 or more acres accounted for 80 percent of the harvested lettuce acreage, which included 102,000 acres of head lettuce, 90,000 acres of romaine lettuce, and 58,000 acres of leaf lettuce.

Some 780 bell pepper farming operations harvested 15,800 acres in 2017, including 80 percent for the fresh market; bell peppers were worth $282 million in 2017. The 49 bell pepper farming operations that harvested 100 or more acres accounted for 85 percent of the bell pepper acreage. There were 1,900 fresh tomato farming operations that harvested 24,300 acres in 2017; fresh tomatoes were worth $206 million in 2017. The 58 fresh tomato farming operations that harvested 100 or more acres accounted for 83 percent of the harvested fresh tomato acreage.

As shown in Figure 10.2 for California's six major fresh vegetables, the largest farms were less than 10 percent of all farms producing each commodity, but they accounted for 60 to 85 percent of the harvested acreage of each vegetable.

The value of California broccoli, carrots, celery, lettuce, bell peppers, and fresh tomatoes was $4.7 billion or 56 percent of the value of the state's vegetables. The acreage of broccoli harvested for the fresh market rose by 14 percent between 2012 and 2017; the acreage of carrots for the fresh market increased by 5 percent, and the acreage of lettuce rose by 8 percent. The acreage of bell peppers harvested for the fresh market fell by 20 percent between 2012 and 2017, and the acreage of tomatoes for the fresh market fell almost 40 percent. Other vegetable commodities include processing tomatoes worth $848 million in 2017; garlic, $390 million; cauliflower, $304 million; and mushrooms, $275 million.

The value of U.S. vegetables, potatoes, and melons was $20 billion in 2017; California's vegetable, potato, and melon sales were $8.4 billion or 43 percent of the U.S. total. The Census of Agriculture (COA) reports data in several ways, including by the North American Industry Classification System (NAICS) code in Table 75, and vegetables are NAICS 1112. There were 45,165 U.S. vegetable farms

in 2017, with sales of $19.7 billion, including $17.2 billion worth of vegetables. However, the 9,900 U.S. vegetable farms that had sales of $50,000 or more accounted for 98 percent of U.S. vegetable sales.

Cook (2011) reported that the four largest iceberg lettuce producers controlled 60 percent of the market, and the eight largest had 80 percent, with new entrants deterred by the scarcity of high-quality land for year-round production and the need for contracts with produce buyers. The top two bagged salad firms, Fresh Express and Dole, accounted for almost 60 percent of sales in 2010, and the top four had 70 percent. Seven large produce firms studied for how they dealt with food safety had average sales of almost $200 million a year for lettuce and other leafy greens (Calvin, Jensen, Klonsky, and Cook, 2017). Most of these firms had lettuce as their major commodity (Table 10.8).

Growing Produce lists large vegetable growers by acreage. Its most recent list in 2014 reported that the five largest California-based growers had 164,000 acres, a third of the state's total fresh vegetable acreage, led by Grimmway and D'Arrigo, who together accounted for about 20 percent of the state's total vegetable acreage (Table 10.8).

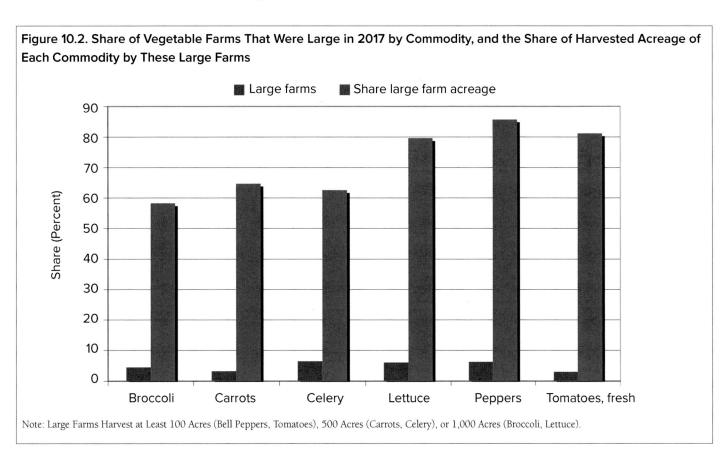

Figure 10.2. Share of Vegetable Farms That Were Large in 2017 by Commodity, and the Share of Harvested Acreage of Each Commodity by These Large Farms

Note: Large Farms Harvest at Least 100 Acres (Bell Peppers, Tomatoes), 500 Acres (Carrots, Celery), or 1,000 Acres (Broccoli, Lettuce).

Due to the organization of production, some government statistics do not provide information that helps determine the importance of major firms. In spite of their acreage and crop mixes, D'Arrigo, Tanimura & Antle (T&A), Ocean Mist, and Nunes are not listed among the major employers in Monterey County, reflecting the practice of many growers to use farm labor contractors to obtain workers rather than employing workers directly. Five farm labor contractors and harvesters listed as major Monterey County employers include: Al Pak Labor, Azcona Harvesting, Quality Farm Labor, and RC Packing; most are in the NAICS 115115 farm labor contractor category (www.labormarketinfo.edd.ca.gov/majorer/countymajorer.asp?CountyCode=000053). These contractors may or may not work with the large Monterey County grower-shippers on the *Growing Produce* list.

Large grower-shippers provide fresh vegetables to grocery chains and food-service firms year-round by producing in several areas. The best example may be lettuce, most of which is produced from April through November in the Salinas area and then directly east in the San Joaquin Valley for a month. Between December and March, lettuce and other leafy greens are produced mostly in the Yuma, Arizona area. The same grower-shippers are involved in all these areas and they harvest a variety of lettuces, including head, leaf, and romaine. Some deliver lettuce to bagged salad firms that have contracts to deliver particular quantities each week to grocery chains and food-service firms, prompting some growers to plant lettuce in Mexico as insurance against problems with cold weather in Yuma.[1]

Food Safety

Many factors favor fewer and larger grower-shippers of fresh vegetables, including economies of scale in production that mirror the consolidation of supermarkets and food-service firms. Another factor is food safety, especially for fresh vegetables that are often consumed without cooking. The number of produce-linked illnesses doubled between 1980–87 and 1987–95, prompting government and industry efforts to implement Good Agricultural Practices

(GAPs) to prevent the contamination of fresh produce (Martin, 2016).

Bagged spinach on September 14, 2006, linked to an E. coli O157:H7 outbreak, killed three people and hospitalized over 100. The contaminated spinach, eventually traced to a 51-acre field leased by a spinach grower from a cattle rancher, was less than 1,000 pounds of the 680 million pounds of spinach consumed by Americans, but led to the recall of all bagged spinach and a slow recovery in fresh spinach sales and prices. Mixing contaminated spinach with other spinach meant that, instead of sickening only a few, thousands became ill (Calvin, 2007).

Spinach's so-called "9/14 moment", the day contaminated spinach was discovered, convinced industry leaders of the need for food-safety standards to restore consumer confidence in leafy green vegetables, which the voluntary California Leafy Green Marketing Agreement (LGMA) of 2007 embodied. The 71 handlers who accounted for 99 percent of the leafy greens produced in California agreed to buy produce only from growers with best practices to ensure that their produce was safe. Growers were required to have trace-back systems to link retail produce with the field and crew where it was grown and packed. The food-safety compliance system helped to overcome the externality that one producer's unsafe produce can adversely affect all producers by requiring everyone to adhere to food safety standards (Cook, 2011).

Calvin et al. (2017) examined the costs of seven fresh produce firms that implemented the LGMA and found that labor costs, including the cost of food safety staff and field supervisor[2] time to monitor protocols, accounted for two-thirds of these firms' compliance costs. The cost of audits was one-sixth of produce firms' costs, and lost product due to safety concerns was 10 percent. In other words, most of the cost of compliance with the LGMA was labor costs to implement and monitor safety protocols, not the cost of being unable to sell suspect produce.

---

1 In 2010, costs of lettuce production were similar in Central Mexico and Yuma, AZ, as lower Mexican wages were offset by lower Mexican yields (Calvin and Martin, 2010).

2 The average salary of the harvest foremen who monitor their workers, toilet and hand-washing facilities, and to ensure that harvest knives are sanitized several times a day, was reported to be $47,000 a year (Calvin et al., 2017). Foremen also look for animal intrusions that could contaminate the vegetables.

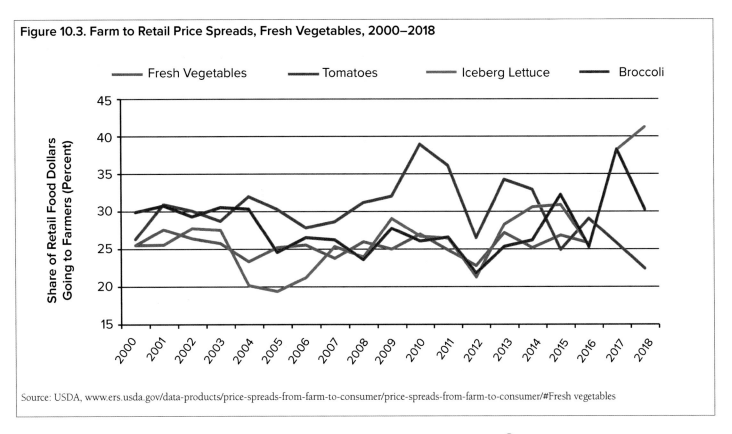

Figure 10.3. Farm to Retail Price Spreads, Fresh Vegetables, 2000–2018

Source: USDA, www.ers.usda.gov/data-products/price-spreads-from-farm-to-consumer/price-spreads-from-farm-to-consumer/#Fresh vegetables

The Food Safety Modernization Act of 2011 (FSMA, PL 111-353) gave the U.S. Food and Drug Administration (FDA) authority to regulate on-farm food safety practices, including requiring farms to document their efforts to prevent contamination. FDA issued a Produce Safety Rule in November 2015, that incorporated many of the best practices developed by the LGMA to govern how U.S. fruits and vegetables are grown, harvested, cooled, and transported. The rule included worker training on health and hygiene, and monitoring irrigation water, fertilizers, animals near fields, and sanitizing equipment (Collart, 2016).

Compliance with the Produce Safety Rule was required beginning in January 2018 for farms with annual gross revenues of $500,000 or more. The definition and enforcement of the provisions regarding agricultural water have been delayed, and industry concerns remain regarding the functionality of water-testing requirements. Self-regulation will be supplemented by government enforcement in the event of a food safety problem.

CHALLENGES

California vegetable growers pioneered the separation of production and consumption of fresh vegetables by working with University of California and private scientists to develop plants that produce crops that could travel thousands of miles and be preferred to local produce. Both farm and nonfarm developments, including interstate highways and trucking deregulation, aided the growth of vegetable production in California.

Figure 10.3 shows that farmers receive an average 25 percent of the retail price of fresh vegetables. The farm share of average retail prices has been stable over the past two decades, fluctuating more for field-grown fresh tomatoes than for broccoli and lettuce. Retail vegetable prices do not reflect grower prices, which can change daily, and instead, reflect stable "everyday low prices" or feature sales that advertise one produce item on sale. Some food-service firms make contracts with grower-shippers that include prices or link prices to daily or weekly averages, reducing grower profit when prices are high and grower losses when prices are low.

Large grower-shippers have developed labels and packaging to differentiate their fresh vegetables. Most California vegetable producers provide both organic and conventional produce, and many sell produce under their own label as well as under private store labels. New types of packaging and value-added, fresh vegetable-based products also contribute to differentiation.

The fresh vegetable industry wants to make produce more accessible to consumers. Consumers typically get less than the 2 pounds they would get from a head of lettuce in a bagged salad, but are willing to pay for the convenience of ready-to-eat salads. Bagged salad firms have moved from offering only lettuce or spinach to complete salad meals and snacks with condiments, so that consumers can buy ready-to-eat salads. Higher-income households spend more on fresh vegetables, and are most likely to pay extra for convenience.

Is there a threat to California vegetable growers from vertical farms that produce near consumers? Farms in converted warehouses near major U.S. cities such as New York aim to compete with produce grown in open fields in California. New York City-based BrightFarms builds 1-acre or 43,560-square-foot rooftop farms for about $2 million that generate vegetable sales of $1 million to $1.5 million a year. In 2016, BrightFarms raised $30 million in venture capital funds by touting its use of less water and land to produce local produce.[3] Columbia University professor Dickson Despommier estimated that a 30-story, one-square-block farm could yield as much food as 2,400 outdoor acres.

Over the next decade, there is little prospect that indoor and local vegetable production will present serious threats to California vegetable growers, who have achieved economies of scale and developed an infrastructure to produce safe fresh vegetables efficiently. Grower prices of fresh vegetables fluctuate, and are often below total production costs, although growers continue to harvest if the prices they receive cover their harvesting costs and some of their fixed costs. Finding the labor to hand-harvest fresh vegetables is one of the major challenges facing California growers.

LABOR

Harvest labor costs for major fresh vegetables range from 15 to 50 percent of production costs, with the higher percentages often including the cost of the container into which produce is packed for sale and marketing costs. Labor costs are often a third of variable production costs in fresh vegetables, and harvesting costs can be 70 to 90 percent of labor costs.

A 2010 University of California Cooperative Extension (UCCE) study of iceberg or head lettuce put total costs per 24-head, 42-pound carton at $12 for yields of 800 cartons an acre, with harvesting costs of $5.85 per carton accounting for almost half of production costs (Tourte and Smith, 2010).[4] These harvest labor costs include selling costs, but not the $1 a carton charge to cool harvested lettuce.

A similar 2017 study of broccoli in the Central Coast estimated non-land production costs at $8,000 an acre (Tourte, Smith, Murdock, and Sumner, 2017), including $4,200 to harvest and pack 700 14-bunch and 21-pound cartons per acre at a cost of $6 per carton, making harvesting costs over half of production costs (excluding land costs but including the cost of the carton into which broccoli is packed). A celery cost study for 2012–13 estimated harvesting costs of $5 per 55-pound carton (Takele, Daugovish, and Vue, 2017).

Most carrots are machine harvested and cut into "baby carrots," minimizing harvest labor costs. The most recent bell pepper study is for 2000 in Imperial County. It estimated harvesting costs at $4.40 per carton, or half of total costs of $8.75 per carton for yields of 1,000 30-pound cartons per acre, including land rent (Mayberry, 2000).

A 2007 study of mature-green fresh tomatoes in the San Joaquin Valley put harvesting costs at $62 a ton, including wages to pickers, payroll taxes, and contractor overhead and profit (Stoddard, LeStrange, Aegerter, Klonsky, and De Moura, 2007). Farm workers harvest tomatoes into 5-gallon buckets that hold 25 to 30 pounds, and pickers normally fill a bucket every two minutes before walking full buckets to a truck to dump the tomatoes and receive credit for what they have picked. Picking costs of $1,116 were 20 percent of total costs of $5,548 per acre, including land costs. Once

---

3 "BrightFarms (www.brightfarms.com) raises $30.1 million to set up futuristic greenhouses across the U.S.," September 21, 2016. TC News. https://techcrunch.com/2016/09/21/brightfarms-raises-30-1-million-to-set-up-futuristic-greenhouses-across-the-u-s/.

---

4 Land rent and taxes were assumed to be $1,200 per acre or $1.50 per carton, and were included in production costs.

taken to packing sheds, harvested tomatoes are sorted and packed into 25-pound cartons. Stoddard et al. assumed a yield of 18 tons per acre and a pack-out rate of 72 percent, so that an acre of fresh tomatoes yields 1,040 cartons, each weighing 25 pounds. Harvesting costs were $1.07 per packed carton, hauling costs $0.21 a carton, and packing and marketing costs were $2.50 per carton.

Lettuce and fresh tomatoes are commodities in which some of the major producers have union contracts. The United Farm Workers (UFW) represents workers employed by lettuce and other vegetable growers D'Arrigo and George Amaral Ranches, and Teamsters Local 890 has long represented Dole vegetable workers. The UFW in May 2016 reported contracts with tomato grower Pacific Triple E covering 450 workers; Gargiulo Tomatoes, 350 workers; and San Joaquin Tomatoes, 350 workers.[5]

For most of the 1990s and early 2000s, the piece rate for mature-green picking tomatoes was $0.475 a bucket or about 1.6 cents a pound. However, piece rates increased after several of the firms lost cases in which the UFW charged they failed to bargain in good faith. In the Pacific Triple E contract, piece rates increased to $0.625 per bucket or 2.1 cents a pound between 2015 and 2018.[6] The UFW said that tomato harvesters average $18 to $20 an hour picking mature-green tomatoes.[7] The workers employed on fresh-vegetable farms are similar to those employed throughout California agriculture—namely, mostly Mexican-born men who are not authorized to work in the United States (Martin, 2017).

MECHANIZATION

The slowdown in Mexico-U.S. migration since the 2008–09 recession and, more recently, the increase in California's minimum wage to $11 an hour in 2018 and scheduled to be

$15 an hour in 2022, puts upward pressure on labor costs. Other state labor-law changes, including requiring overtime pay for farm workers after eight hours of work a day or 40 hours a week by 2022, and a requirement that piece-rate workers receive their average hourly earnings while on paid rest breaks, add to rising labor costs.[8]

Fresh vegetable growers have responded to rising labor costs in several ways, including hastening efforts to develop machines to replace workers and requesting more H-2A guest workers. Lettuce and broccoli are usually field packed, meaning that workers cut and trim these crops and place them on a slow-moving platform traveling ahead of harvesters that carries workers who wrap and pack produce into cartons. Field conveyor belts reduce the need for workers to carry harvested produce, making them more productive.

Baby leaf and romaine lettuce can be harvested by machines that use water jets to cut the lettuce just above the ground. Water-jet machines are in development to harvest cabbage and celery. Ramsey Highlander developed a water-jet machine that it says can harvest 12,000 pounds of romaine lettuce an hour into tote containers, and harvest faster by putting the heads of lettuce in bulk containers[9].

The major issue slowing mechanization in head lettuce, broccoli, and other fresh vegetables is non-uniform ripening. The once-over harvesters common throughout U.S. agriculture make one pass through the field, but using a once-over harvester for head lettuce would mean losing up to one-quarter of the crop. Plant genetics and transplants can increase uniform ripening, facilitating the use of once-over harvesters.

Transplanting lettuce reduces labor needs by ensuring a uniform crop without thinning, and allows growers to harvest two or more crops a year on the same land. Machines can thin seeded lettuce, so the plants that survive produce

---

5   See: https://migration.ucdavis.edu/rmn/more.php?id=1978.

6   Pacific Triple E signed a three-year agreement with the UFW on May 22, 2012, even though the UFW was certified to represent Triple E workers in 1989. The 2012–15 contract guaranteed tomato pickers at least $8.50 an hour and $0.56 to $0.575 per bucket. The contract prohibited Triple E from requiring "cupped" or overfull buckets and discouraged workers from "fluffing" their buckets to make them appear fuller than they are. https://migration.ucdavis.edu/rmn/more.php?id=1717.

7   See: https://migration.ucdavis.edu/rmn/more.php?id=1924.

8   AB 1066 requires 1.5 times normal wages after eight hours of work in a day and 40 hours a week by 2022; employers with 25 or fewer employees have extra time to comply. AB 1513 requires California farmers to pay piece-rate workers at their average hourly earnings for mandatory rest periods and other nonproductive time. https://migration.ucdavis.edu/rmn/more.php?id=2016.

9   See: http://www.ramsayhighlander.com/products/romaine/green-leaf-lettuce-harvester.htm.

marketable heads.[10] Plant breeders, who in the past focused on maximum yields and disease resistance, are now developing plants more amenable to machine planting and harvesting. As labor costs rise, more farmers may decide that once-over harvesting machines are more profitable even if they can sell only 80 percent of the marketable heads. Machine harvesting and sorting costs for 80 percent of the crop generate more profits than the hand-labor costs of marketing closer to 100 percent of the crop.

An alternative to uniformly ripening crops and once-over harvesters is selective harvesters, machines that select ripe heads of lettuce and do not damage immature heads. Selective harvesters are more difficult to develop because they must be able to distinguish between ripe and unripe crops, a much greater engineering challenge than simply harvesting everything in the field and later sorting the harvested produce.

H-2A Guest Workers

Fresh vegetable growers are also hiring more H-2A guest workers. The H-2A guest worker program requires farmers anticipating labor shortages to satisfy three major requirements—namely, try and fail to recruit U.S. workers, provide free housing for guest workers and out-of-area U.S. workers, and pay an Adverse Effect Wage rate of $14.77 an hour in California in 2020. Farm employers must prepare job orders spelling out wages and work requirements and promise work or wages for three-fourths of the contract period.[11]

There were 3,000 jobs in California certified to be filled by H-2A workers in FY12, and 23,000 in FY19, a sevenfold increase in seven years. Most of the statewide increase in H-2A workers is in the Salinas area, where vegetable and berry farms employ guest workers.

Housing costs in the area discourage prospective workers, making the H-2A program more attractive for growers. The Monterey County "salad bowl" has relatively high-cost housing, making it difficult for low earners to find affordable housing. The 40th percentile Fair Market Rent (FMR) for Monterey County in 2018 was $1,433 for a two-bedroom apartment, meaning that 40 percent of the two-bedroom rental units in the county rented for $1,433 or less, and 60 percent for $1,433 and more.[12] A worker earning $12 an hour and employed 160 hours a month would earn $1,920, so a one-earner household paying the FMR would devote 75 percent of gross earnings to rent, far more than the usual rule of devoting less than 30 percent. East Salinas includes areas with very high population density, reflecting several families sharing one home with converted garages and backyard sheds rented out to farm workers.

High housing costs also mean that the most difficult requirement for employers in the Salinas area is housing. Many of the H-2A workers currently in the Salinas area live in motels that do not satisfy standards for major chains. However, several growers have or are building new farm worker housing, often over the objections of local residents. T & A opened a $17 million, 800-bed facility ($21,000 a bed) in Spreckels meant for H-2A workers in 2016, but found that many of its current solo male workers were willing to pay $125 a month for beds in 900 square-foot, two-bedroom, two-bath units. The Nunes Company plans a $20 million, 600-bed complex ($33,000 a bed) in North Salinas.

Fresh vegetable production is consolidating on large and specialized farms that rely on hired workers whose cost is rising, prompting efforts to make workers more productive with mechanical aids and to reduce the need for hand labor with labor-saving machines. Many fresh vegetable firms have operations around the U.S. and abroad, making trade the third major factor affecting the future of California's fresh vegetable industry.

---

10 Tanimura & Antle uses Plant Tape to transplant lettuce seedlings, while other lettuce producers continue to seed lettuce and use the See and Spray machine developed by Blue River Technology to thin lettuce plants after they emerge from the ground. Geoffrey Mohan, "As California's labor shortage grows, farmers race to replace workers with robots," *Los Angeles Times*, July 21, 2017. http://www.latimes.com/projects/la-fi-farm-mechanization/.

11 These job offers are available in a public job registry at: https://icert. doleta.gov/.

---

12 See: www.huduser.org/datasets/fmr.html.

TRADE

Almost a third of the fresh vegetables available to Americans are imported, up from less than 10 percent in the early 1990s. Mexico, the most important source of fresh vegetable imports, exported fresh vegetables worth $7.5 billion to the U.S. in 2016 (including potatoes and mushrooms). Mexico accounted for 74 percent of the value of U.S. fresh vegetable imports, followed by Canada with 13 percent and Peru with 4 percent (Minor and Bond, 2017).

Some labor-intensive fresh vegetables that were once widely grown in California are now mostly imported, including asparagus, whose acreage fell from 37,000 in 2000 to 8,000 in 2016. Asparagus is a perennial plant whose spears must be harvested several times a week during a 60- to 90-day harvest season. A machine harvester is in development, but may arrive too late to offset asparagus imports from Peru, the major source of U.S. fresh asparagus.

Climate is Mexico's major competitive advantage in producing fresh vegetables for U.S. consumers. Mexico can produce some vegetables when there is little or no U.S. production, except in Florida, just as Chile can produce and export a variety of fresh fruits during the winter months when there is little U.S. production.

What began as off-season production in other countries has become more direct competition for U.S. producers, as foreigners extend the period in which they produce and export fresh vegetables. Mexico is a leader in protected culture farming, using structures that protect plants from pests and disease. Mexico had 21,000 hectares of greenhouses, plastic-covered frames, and other protected culture structures in 2014, which produced 3.5 million tons of mostly vegetables worth $1.5 billion. Sinaloa, (22 percent), Jalisco (15 percent), and Baja California (12 percent) had half of the protected culture area in Mexico.

Protected culture has implications for California farmers, as sheltering plants reduces pest and disease issues, increases yields, and extends the shipping season for produce. Americans have shown a preference for vine-ripened over mature-green tomatoes, which is one reason Mexico now supplies over half of the fresh tomatoes consumed in the United States. Protected culture also changes labor relations, extending periods of farm work and encouraging previously migrant workers to settle near the farms where they can work for longer periods.

CONCLUSION

California has a vibrant fresh vegetable industry that accounts for almost 20 percent of the state's farm sales from 5 percent of the state's irrigated crop land. High-value fresh vegetables are capital-intensive and risky, making grower-shippers in vegetables the key players in these commodities. Vegetable grower-shippers agree to supply broccoli or lettuce year-round, and do this by planting in areas with climates that allow production at various times of the year.

Americans are consuming more fresh vegetables. The number of buyers is shrinking as supermarkets and the food-service industry consolidates, which reinforces trends toward fewer and larger grower-shippers and marketers. Larger growers and marketers have the capital and expertise to operate in many areas and to manage production abroad and imports. There is more concentration in the fresh vegetable than in the tree fruit industry, which includes more diverse and smaller growers with perennial crops who often market their crops via co-ops. New challenges, from food safety to recruiting guest workers, reinforce incentives to get larger or get out of the vegetable industry.

Most fresh vegetables are labor-intensive, with harvest labor costs 15 to 40 percent of variable production costs. Efforts to develop once-over harvesters appear more promising than efforts to develop selective harvesters that can make multiple passes through a field, harvesting only mature produce. Commodities that do not ripen uniformly and are fragile are most difficult to mechanize, often requiring changes in farming practices such as elevated rows with hard edges to guide machines.

Trade poses challenges and opportunities for California's fresh vegetables. Rising incomes abroad increase the demand for California produce, while free-trade agreements and improved technologies facilitate imports from countries with lower wages. The major source of imported fresh fruit and vegetables is Mexico, whose expanding export sector has developed with the help of California producers and marketers. Mexican imports, which once complemented California production while competing with Florida production, are arriving earlier and

continuing longer, so they overlap with California production of the same commodity. Direct competition between California and Mexico may increase as Mexico expands production under protected culture structures that reduce risks and increase yields.

California's fresh vegetable industry has overcome many challenges, from growing to marketing, to emerge as the most vibrant in the United States. The major current challenge may be labor costs, which are rising rapidly due to fewer unauthorized immigrants and high housing costs in the coastal areas of California, where fresh vegetable production is concentrated. As labor costs continue rising, there is likely to be more labor-saving mechanization, more reliance on guest workers, and more imports of fresh vegetables. Trade and migration policies, combined with the pace of new developments in plants and machines, will shape California's vegetable industry.

REFERENCES

Calvin, L., H. Jensen, K. Klonsky, and R. Cook. 2017. *Food Safety Practices and Costs Under the California Leafy Greens Marketing Agreement*. Washington DC: U.S. Department of Agriculture, Economic Research Service, Economic Information Bulletin No. 173, June. Available at: www.ers.usda.gov/webdocs/publications/83771/eib-173.pdf?v=42893.

Calvin, L. and P. Martin. 2010. "The U.S. Produce Industry and Labor: Facing the Future in a Global Economy." Washington DC: U.S. Department of Agriculture. Economic Research Service, *Economic Research Report* No. 106. Available at: https://www.ers.usda.gov/publications/pub-details/?pubid=44766.

Calvin, L. 2007. "Outbreak Linked to Spinach Forces Reassessment of Food Safety Practices." *Amber Waves*, June. Available at: https://www.ers.usda.gov/amber-waves/2007/june/outbreak-linked-to-spinach-forces-reassessment-of-food-safety-practices/.

Collart, A.J. 2016. "The Food Safety Modernization Act and the Marketing of Fresh Produce." *Choices* 31(1). Available at: http://www.choicesmagazine.org/UserFiles/file/cmsarticle_489.pdf.

Cook, R. 2011. "Fundamental Forces Affecting the U.S. Fresh Berry and Lettuce/Leafy Green Subsectors." *Choices* 26(4). Available at: http://ageconsearch.umn.edu/record/120009.

Cook, R. and L. Calvin. 2005. "Greenhouse Tomatoes Change the Dynamics of the North American Fresh Tomato Industry." Washington DC: U.S. Department of Agriculture, Economic Research Service, *Economic Research Report* No. 2, April. Available at: ucce.ucdavis.edu/files/datastore/234-447.pdf.

MacDonald, J., R. Hoppe, and D. Newton. 2018. "Three Decades of Consolidation in U.S. Agriculture." Washington DC: U.S. Department of Agriculture, Economic Research Service, *Economic Information Bulletin* No. 189, March. Available at: https://www.ers.usda.gov/publications/pub-details/?pubid=88056.

Martin, P. 2017. "Immigration and Farm Labor: Challenges and Issues." Special Report, University of California, Giannini Foundation of Agricultural Economics, June. Available at: http://bit.ly/2tvaUSw.

———. 2016. "Labor Compliance in Fresh Produce: Lessons from Food Safety." *Choices* 31(3). Available at: http://www.choicesmagazine.org/choices-magazine/submitted-articles/labor-compliance-in-fresh-produce--lessons-from-food-safety.

Mayberry, K.S. 2000. "Sample Cost to Establish and Produce Bell Peppers. Imperial County – 2000." Available at: https://coststudies.ucdavis.edu/en/.

Minor, T. and J. Bond. 2017. "Vegetables and Pulses Outlook." Washington DC: U.S. Department of Agriculture, *Economic Research Service, Situation and Outlook*, VGS-358, April. Available at: http://usda.mannlib.cornell.edu/usda/ers/VGS//2010s/2017/VGS-04-28-2017.pdf.

Parr, B., J. Bond, and T. Minor. 2019. "Vegetables and Pulses Outlook." Washington DC: U.S. Department of Agriculture, *Economic Research Service, Situation and Outlook*, VGS-363, October. Available at: https://usda.library.cornell.edu/

Stoddard, C.S., M. LeStrange, B. Aegerter, K. Klonsky, and R. De Moura. 2007. "Sample Costs to Produce Fresh Market Tomatoes. San Joaquin Valley. Furrow Irrigated." Available at: https://coststudies.ucdavis.edu/en/.

Takele, E., O. Daugovish, and M. Vue. 2012-2013. "Costs and Profitability Analysis for Celery Production, Ventura County." Available at: https://coststudies.ucdavis.edu/en/.

Tourte, L., R. Smith, J. Murdock, and D.A. Sumner. 2017. "Sample Costs to Produce and Harvest Broccoli. Central Coast Region. Monterey, Santa Cruz, and San Benito Counties." Available at: https://coststudies.ucdavis.edu/en/.

Tourte, L. and R. Smith. 2010. "Sample Production Costs for Wrapped Iceberg Lettuce. Sprinkler Irrigated – 40-inch Beds. Central Coast. Monterey, Santa Cruz, and San Benito Counties 2010." Available at: https://coststudies.ucdavis.edu/en/.

APPENDIX

Appendix Figure 10.1A. Vegetables and Melons Cash Receipts by State in 2018, U.S. Dollars

California Accounted for 43 Percent of $18.5 Billion in U.S. Vegetable and Melon Sales in 2018

Total U.S. Dollars

$18,547,443,000

$1,970,000 $7,878,047,000

Vegetables and Melons Cash Receipts by State in 2018, U.S. Dollars

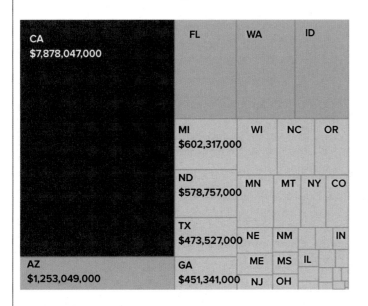

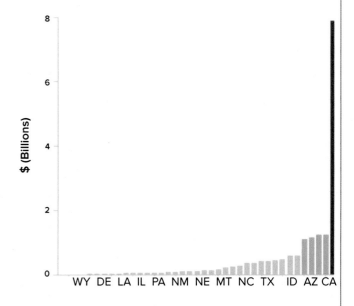

Source: The ERS Farm Income Team

Data Source: https://www.ers.usda.gov/data-products/farm-income-and-wealth-statistics.aspx released November 27, 2019

Note: States without shading have no production for this commodity or are included in miscellaneous crops or all other animals and animal products.

Appendix Figure 10.2A. Lettuce Cash Receipts by State in 2018, U.S. Dollars

Lettuce is the Most Valuable Vegetable; California Accounted for 67 Percent of U.S. Lettuce Sales in 2018

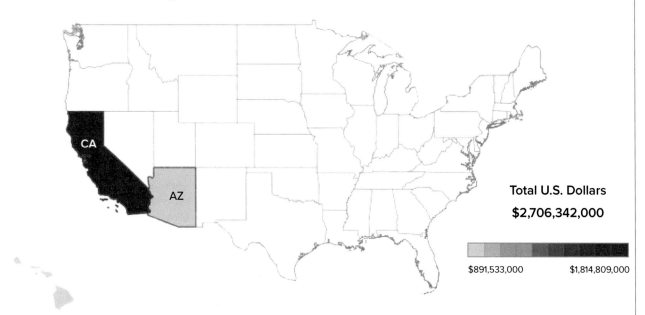

Total U.S. Dollars

$2,706,342,000

$891,533,000 $1,814,809,000

Lettuce Cash Receipts by State in 2018, U.S. Dollars

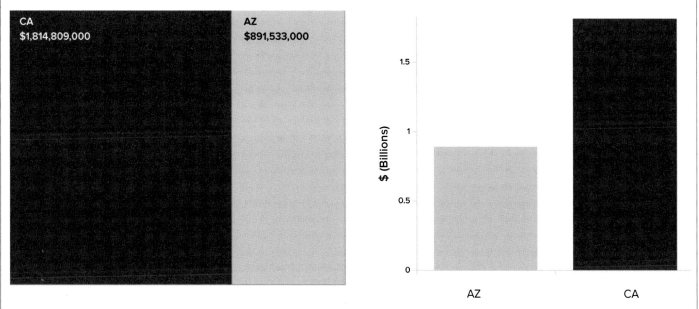

CA
$1,814,809,000

AZ
$891,533,000

Source: The ERS Farm Income Team

Data Source: https://www.ers.usda.gov/data-products/farm-income-and-wealth-statistics.aspx released November 27, 2019

Note: States without shading have no production for this commodity or are included in miscellaneous crops or all other animals and animal products.

Appendix Figure 10.3A. Tomatoes, Fresh Cash Receipts by State in 2018, U.S. Dollars

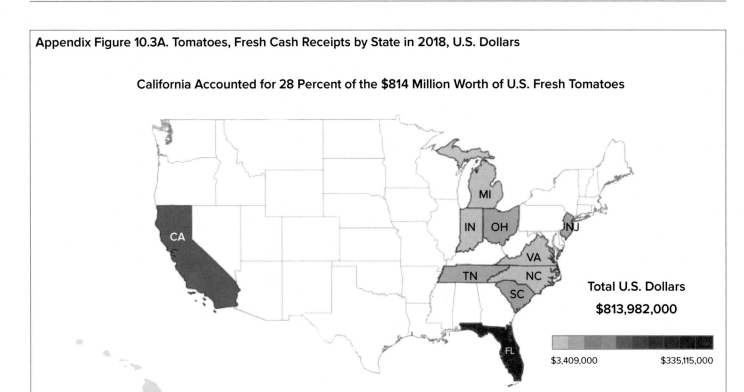

California Accounted for 28 Percent of the $814 Million Worth of U.S. Fresh Tomatoes

Total U.S. Dollars

$813,982,000

$3,409,000 $335,115,000

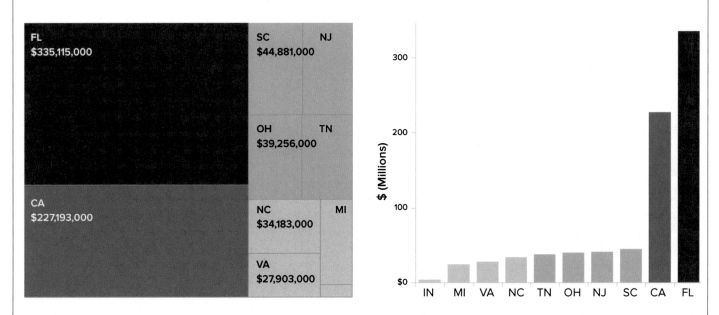

Fresh Tomatoes Cash Receipts by State in 2018, U.S. Dollars

FL
$335,115,000

SC
$44,881,000

NJ

OH
$39,256,000

TN

CA
$227,193,000

NC
$34,183,000

MI

VA
$27,903,000

Source: The ERS Farm Income Team

Data Source: https://www.ers.usda.gov/data-products/farm-income-and-wealth-statistics.aspx released November 27, 2019

Note: States without shading have no production for this commodity or are included in miscellaneous crops or all other animals and animal products.

Appendix Figure 10.4A. Artichokes Cash Receipts by State in 2018, U.S. Dollars

California Accounted for All of the $64 Million Worth of U.S. Artichokes

Total U.S. Dollars

$63,032,000

$63,032,000

Artichokes Cash Receipts by State in 2018, U.S. Dollars

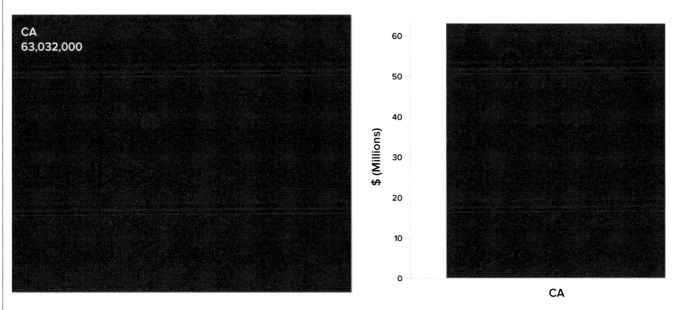

Source: The ERS Farm Income Team

Data Source: https://www.ers.usda.gov/data-products/farm-income-and-wealth-statistics.aspx released November 27, 2019.

Note: States without shading have no production for this commodity or are included in miscellaneous crops or all other animals and animal products.

CHAPTER 11. CALIFORNIA BERRIES

RACHAEL E. GOODHUE AND PHILIP L. MARTIN

ABSTRACT

California's berry industry generates 7 percent of California's farm sales from less than 1 percent of the state's farmland. The berry industry includes two major subsectors: strawberries that are usually planted each year and cane or bush berries, such as blueberries, raspberries, and blackberries. Cane berries can produce berries for a decade or more, although most growers replant them after several years. California produces over 80 percent of U.S. strawberries and raspberries, and has a rapidly expanding blueberry sector. Berries are high-value and high-risk crops, generating revenues of over $50,000 an acre, but exposing growers to disease, labor, and market risks. Land, disease, and labor constraints may slow the berry industry's expansion after two decades of rapid growth.

ABOUT THE AUTHORS

Rachael E. Goodhue is a professor and chair of the Department of Agricultural and Resource Economics at UC Davis. She can be contacted by email at regoodhue@ucdavis.edu. Philip L. Martin is an emeritus professor in the Department of Agricultural and Resource Economics at UC Davis. He can be contacted by email at plmartin@ucdavis.edu. Both are members of the Giannini Foundation of Agricultural Economics.

California's fresh berries were worth $3.7 billion in 2017, including 84 percent from strawberries and 12 percent from raspberries.

Photo Credit: Jon Bovay, UC Davis, 2013.

CHAPTER 11. TABLE OF CONTENTS

CALIFORNIA BERRIES

Demand for fresh berries has been rising with their perceived health benefits as well as year-round availability and convenient packaging, making berries the highest-value fresh produce item sold in U.S. supermarkets. In 2017, strawberries represented 47 percent of the $6.4 billion in U.S. retail fresh berry sales, followed by blueberries at 26 percent, raspberries at 14 percent, and blackberries at 9 percent (Cook, 2017).[1]

U.S. strawberry consumption per person doubled from 4 to 8.3 pounds between 2001 and 2017, while blueberry consumption quadrupled from 0.5 pounds to 2 pounds. Raspberry and blackberry consumption are each less than a pound per person per year, but their rate of increase is much faster, up eightfold since 2001 (Cook, 2017).

California's fresh berries were worth $3.7 billion in 2017, including 84 percent from strawberries and 12 percent from raspberries (Table 11.1). While all berries have grown in value, bush berries increased on a percentage basis. Monterey County accounted for 22 percent of the value of strawberry sales in 2016, followed by Ventura County with 19 percent. The value of raspberries exceeded the value of all peaches and was four times the value of pears.

Total wages paid to berry workers were almost $1.1 billion in 2018, including 73 percent paid to strawberry workers.

The strawberry share of total wages has been falling as the other berry sectors have grown. The average weekly wages of other berry workers were higher than their weekly earnings in strawberries until 2015. However by 2018, strawberry workers earned an average $604 a week, while workers employed in other berries earned an average $559.

California and Mexico can produce the four major berries almost year-round. Most of the strawberries available to U.S. consumers are produced in California, while most blackberries, blueberries, and raspberries are imported. The share of imports in U.S. strawberry consumption is 14 percent, compared to 53 percent for blueberries[2] and 55 percent for raspberries (there are no data on blackberries, but almost all U.S. blackberry imports are from Mexico). Mexico's strawberry exports peak between December and March,[3] and Mexican raspberry exports peak between October and May.[4] Most blackberry imports are from Mexico, except during the summer months when California and Oregon are producing.

---

1 Cook (2017) reported that fresh berries worth $6.4 billion in 2017 were 20 percent of the $31 billion in U.S. retail fresh fruit sales. Total retail fruit sales are not fully counted, but are at least $31 billion. Berries are high-value commodities; they were only eight percent of the quantity of fresh fruit sold in U.S. supermarkets.

2 Chile is the leading supplier of imported blueberries, followed by Canada, Mexico, Peru, and Argentina. Chile exported 103,000 metric tons of blueberries in 2016/17, two-thirds to the U.S., while Peru exported 40,000 metric tons, 55 percent to the United States. Peru's blueberry exports are rising fast, often due to investments by Chilean firms and shipments by sea to the United States. The La Liberdad region of northwestern Peru is ideal for growing blueberries, but housing for workers is scarce.

3 Mexico exports one-third of the strawberries that it produces, almost all to the United States.

4 The U.S. produced about 80,000 metric tons of raspberries in 2016, and imported 60,000 metric tons, almost all from Mexico.

Table 11.1. California Berries, 2017

	Acres	Tons	Value	CA Share of U.S.	CA Share of Total Berries
			$ Million	Percent	
Blueberries	6,600	31,500	138	7	4
Raspberries	9,000	75,200	452	88	12
Strawberries, All	38,200	1,462,200	3,100	89	84
Subtotal	53,800	1,568,900	3,690	100	100

Source: CDFA, California Agricultural Statistics Review, 2017–18
Note: CA share is based on value of commodity.

CANE OR BUSH BERRIES

There were 15,000 U.S. farms with 113,200 acres of blueberries in the 2017 Census of Agriculture (COA), including 246 farms that each had 100 or more acres and accounted for over half of the total blueberry acreage. There were 7,800 U.S. farms with 23,250 acres of raspberries, and 9,000 farms with 16,700 acres of blackberries, dew berries, and marionberries, but no size distribution data.

California had 6,400 acres of blueberries in 2016 that produced 605,000 hundredweight (cwt) of blueberries worth $109 million. Between 2007 and 2016, acreage almost tripled (from 2,300 in 2007), production rose almost fourfold (from 165,000 hundredweight in 2007), and the value of blueberries rose almost fourfold (from $30 million in 2007).

California accounts for a much higher share of U.S. raspberry and strawberry production than of blueberries. Blueberry production is concentrated in eight states, led by Michigan and Georgia with almost half of the cultivated blueberry acreage in the United States. California blueberry acreage is increasing rapidly, as growers take advantage of rising consumer demand and the development of blueberry varieties suitable for California production areas (Figure 11.1). California is second to Oregon in the value of blueberries produced.

California has the highest yields of blueberries–10,000 pounds per acre–worth an average $2.60 per pound in 2018 for the fresh market. This explains why the value of California blueberries was much higher than the value of Georgia blueberries, where yields of 4,100 pounds per acre were worth $2 a pound for the fresh market.

A 2009 UC Cooperative Extension (UCCE) cost and return study estimated 1,000 hours of labor were needed to pick 10,000 marketable pounds of blueberries per acre, suggesting that pickers average 10 pounds an hour working for piece-rate wages of about $0.85 a pound or $8.50 an hour when the state's minimum wage was $8. Blueberries, especially those used for processing, are more amenable to machine harvesting than other berries. However, machines damage more fruit and prices for processing blueberries are significantly lower than fresh market prices. Improvements in mechanical harvesters and a decrease in the gap between fresh and processing blueberry prices would speed the adoption of mechanical blueberry harvesters (Gallardo and Zilberman, 2016).

Most berry workers are not organized into unions. However, Klein Management (Gourmet Trading Company) blueberry workers in McFarland, California, voted 347 to 68 in

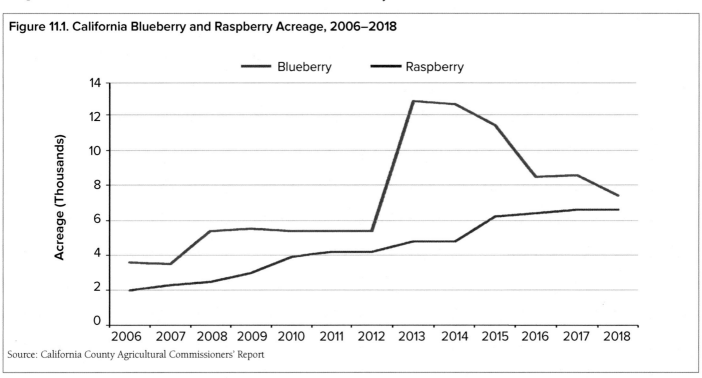

Figure 11.1. California Blueberry and Raspberry Acreage, 2006–2018

Source: California County Agricultural Commissioners' Report

favor of representation by the United Farm Workers (UFW) in May 2016 after a brief strike over wages; the Agricultural Labor Relations Board (ALRB) said that 627 workers were eligible to vote. The workers, who were mostly from Oaxaca, Mexico, complained that Klein Management reduced the piece rate from $0.95 a pound at the beginning of the season to $0.70 a pound as production increased. The UFW reported a contract with Klein Management covering blueberry workers.[5]

California had 9,700 acres of red raspberries in 2016 that produced 2.1 million hundredweight of raspberries worth $358 million. California leads the U.S. in the production of fresh red raspberries, while Washington leads in the production of red raspberries for processing.

Raspberries are a perennial crop that can produce for a decade or more, but are commonly replanted on a two- or three-year cycle. Coastal raspberry growers switched in the 1980s from floricane spring-bearing varieties to proprietary primocane fall-bearing varieties that thrive, even with inadequate chill, to achieve two harvests a year (Tourte et al., 2016). Most of the raspberries in coastal California are grown under protected structures, typically plastic-covered, high-hoop tunnels. The impacts of this switch are apparent in Table 11.2, which shows that harvested acreage increased by a factor of six between 1985 and 1995, and continued to increase after 1995.

Raspberries are handpicked into 6-ounce plastic clam shells; 12 filled clamshells make a 4.5-pound flat. Piece rates vary, but average $6.50 per flat or tray, with pickers averaging two to four flats an hour. Yields average 4,750 trays an acre and, at an average grower price of $15 a tray, revenues are over $71,000 an acre. Total costs of production for second-year raspberries are $48,000 an acre, including 80 percent for harvest costs (Tourte, Bolda, and Klonsky, 2016). Net returns can be $25,000 per acre or more.

Raspberry production expanded into land that was previously pasture and thus had few pathogens and little pest pressure, which facilitated organic production; the limits of such expansion may have been reached. Pre-plant soil fumigation is used within conventional production systems, making organic production more dependent on new acreage.

In 2016, the ALRB found that Premier Raspberries (Dutra Farms) unlawfully required its 800 employees to agree to arbitration of labor disputes, a provision of employee contracts that the ALRB found violated state labor laws giving workers the right to organize and bargain collectively with their employers or refrain from union activities.[6] After a brief strike, Premiere Raspberries workers voted 269 to 236 in favor of UFW representing them in an August 9, 2017 election, and the ALRB certified the UFW October 11, 2017.

6 The ALRB found that a similar arbitration policy at strawberry grower T.T. Miyasaka was unlawful.

5 See: https://ufw.org/overwhelming-vote-ufw-blueberry-workers-mcfarland-ranch-627-workers/.

Table 11.2. California Raspberries, 1985–2015

	1985	1995	2005	2015
Harvested Acreage (acres)	266	1,627	4,145	10,345
Yield (tons/acre)	4.24	7.02	12.02	10.57
Value of Production ($1,000)	9,377	63,452	233,756	471,190
Revenue ($/acre)	35,252	39,000	56,395	45,548

Table 11.3. California Blackberries, 1985–2015

	1985	1995	2005	2015
Harvested Acreage (acres)	n/a	3	41	2,088
Yield (tons/acre)	n/a	n/a	2.78	4.72
Value of Production ($1,000)	n/a	17	538	60,768
Revenue ($/acre)	n/a	5,667	13,125	29,103

Source for Tables 11.2 and 11.3: California County Agricultural Commissioners' Report

Premiere Raspberries challenged the certification of the UFW as the bargaining representative of its workers by engaging in a technical refusal to bargain in order to have courts review the ALRB's certification of the UFW as the representative of its workers. However, the ALRB ordered mandatory mediation and conciliation to generate a UFW-Premiere Raspberries collective bargaining agreement. Premiere Raspberries refused to implement the agreement, prompting the UFW to call a strike in September 2018 that involved picketing Well-Pict, which distributes Premiere Raspberries.

California's blackberry acreage has increased rapidly, but most U.S. blackberries are imported from Mexico. A 2013 UC Cooperative Extension cost study includes time for establishment and five production-harvest cycles. Most varieties are floricane bearing and produce fruit for six to eight weeks in summer. Growers normally plant several varieties to harvest from mid-June through September.

Harvest labor costs are a significant portion of cash operating costs. The 2013 cost study assumed that pickers receive a seasonal average piece rate of $4.25 per five-pound tray, with growers adjusting piece rates upward at the beginning and end of the season when yields are lower. Total costs of production for second-year blackberries are estimated to be $43,000 an acre, including 70 percent for harvest costs (Tourte et al., 2016). Net returns can be $12,000 per acre or more.

Strawberries

California dominates the production of U.S. fresh strawberries, accounting for almost 85 percent of the $2.7 billion in strawberry cash receipts in 2018 from two-thirds of U.S. strawberry acreage. California's long growing season, high yields, and high quality allow most of the state's strawberries to be sold fresh, increasing the value of California's strawberries.

Table 38 of the 2017 COA reported 8,964 U.S. farms with 60,162 acres of strawberries, including 130 farms that each had 100 or more acres and accounted for two-thirds of total strawberry acreage. The midpoint acreage of strawberry farms was 180 in 2012, meaning that half of strawberry acres were on farms with 180 acres or more and half were on farms with less than 180 acres (MacDonald, Hoppe, and Newton, 2018).

As shown in Figure 11.2, California's strawberry acreage has been declining but, as Table 11.4 shows, production continues to increase because of higher-yielding varieties. California had 34,000 acres of strawberries in 2018, including 4,000 acres of organic strawberries, but production is expected to set new records. Due to the end of methyl bromide fumigation before planting, farmers are planting new varieties that yield more despite pressure from soil-borne diseases.[7]

Plant breeders are developing disease-resistant strawberries, and growers are seeking ways to produce strawberries

---

7 Over 80 percent of strawberry acreage is planted in the fall for winter, spring, and summer strawberry harvesting.

Table 11.4. California Strawberries, 1985–2015

	1985	1995	2005	2015
Harvested Acreage (acre)	15,085	18,995	33,928	40,022
Yield (ton/acre)*	22.14	19.90	28.89	32.34
Value of Production ($1,000)	725,005	890,744	1,405,433	2,442,681
Revenue ($/acre)	48,061	46,894	41,424	61,033

Source: California County Agricultural Commissioners' Report
Note: *Yield data for fresh market strawberries.

Figure 11.2. California Strawberry Acreage, 2006–2018

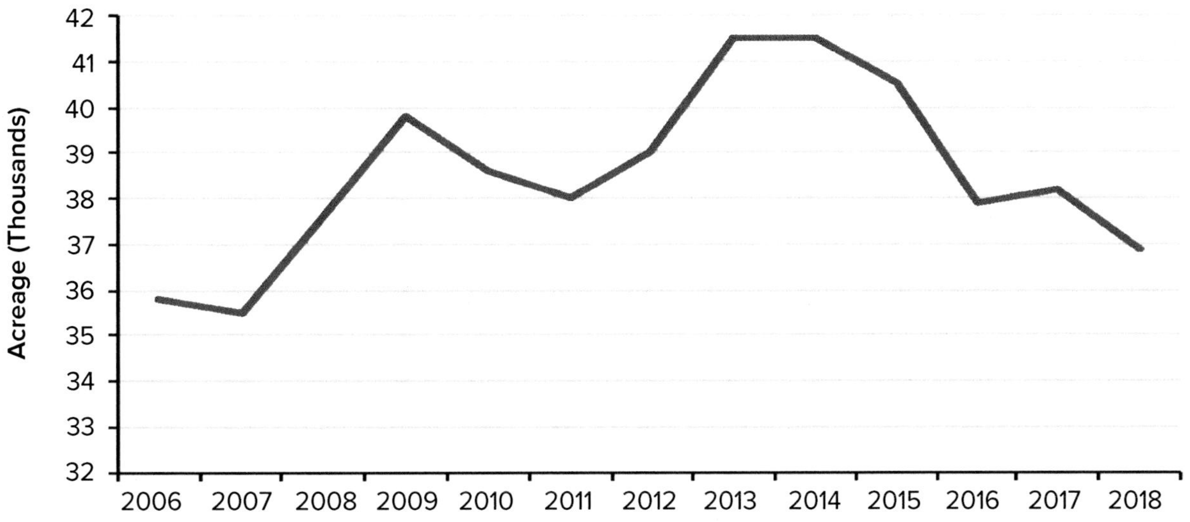

Source: California County Agricultural Commissioners' Report

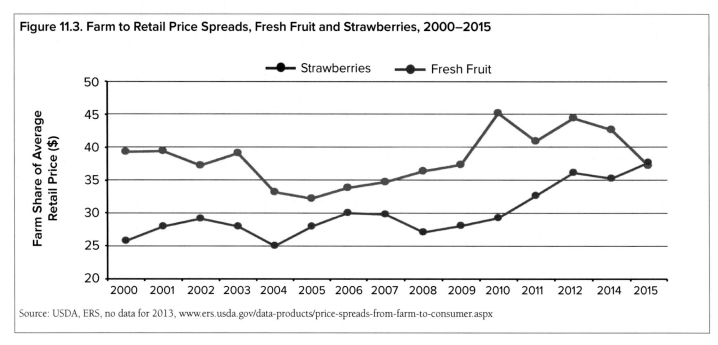

Figure 11.3. Farm to Retail Price Spreads, Fresh Fruit and Strawberries, 2000–2015

Source: USDA, ERS, no data for 2013, www.ers.usda.gov/data-products/price-spreads-from-farm-to-consumer.aspx

with less hand labor (Holmes, Mansouripour, and Hewavitharana, 2020).

Four firms, led by Driscoll's, market most fresh strawberries.[8] Driscoll's is also the dominant marketer of raspberries, accounting for 90 percent of U.S. raspberry sales from farms in California and Mexico.[9] Naturripe Farms is the leading U.S. marketer of blueberries, and also markets other berries. Both Driscoll's and Naturripe market blackberries from Central Mexico.

Figure 11.3 shows that farmers receive an average of 38 percent of the retail price of strawberries, more than the average 30 percent farm share of the retail price of fresh fruit. Apple and grape growers receive about 25 percent of the average retail price of these commodities, and fresh orange growers receive an average of 16 percent of the retail price. Note that the farm share of retail fresh fruit prices rose in recent years, while the farm share of strawberry prices fell to 37–38 percent in 2015.

VARIETIES AND FUMIGATION

The University of California's Public Strawberry Breeding Program developed many of the major strawberry varieties planted in California fields. The diffusion of the program's 30 patented varieties, including Albion, the most widely planted strawberry, helped to raise average yields from 6 tons an acre in the 1950s to over 30 tons an acre today. UC-developed varieties are planted on about 60 percent of the state's acreage, and proprietary varieties on 40 percent. UC licenses its strawberry patents to nurseries and received about $7 million in revenue from its strawberry patents in 2015.

Between the 1960s and 2016, strawberries were often planted on land that was covered first with plastic and injected with 300 to 400 pounds of methyl bromide per acre to fumigate the soil. This practice killed plant pathogens, nematodes, weeds, and soil-borne pests, which raised strawberry yields (Tourte et al., 2016).[10] By fumigating the soil before planting, strawberries could be grown on the same land year-after-year, allowing yields to rise to 30 tons an acre by 2010; yields of organic strawberries are much lower—15 to 17 tons an acre.

Methyl bromide depletes the ozone layer that protects the earth. And the Montreal Protocol called for an end

---

8   Driscoll's markets about a third of U.S. fresh berries, and two-thirds of organic fresh berries.

9   Goodyear (2017) reported that Driscoll's controlled a third of U.S. strawberry sales. The Reiter family reportedly owns 70 percent of Driscoll's, and Reiter Farming provides a third of the Driscoll's berries.

10 Chloropicrin, first applied in the 1950s, was often mixed with methyl bromide to fumigate the soil.

to methyl bromide use by 2005. Because technically and economically viable alternatives were not easily found, the strawberry industry was able to receive critical-use exemptions that allowed continued use of methyl bromid until 2016. Methyl bromide has been replaced by chloropicrin and/or 1,3-dichloropropene to fumigate soil used for conventional strawberries, but these chemicals are not as effective as methyl bromide. Some diseases have re-emerged, prompting experiments with non-fumigant alternatives such as steam, anaerobic soil disinfestation (ASD), and crop rotations.

Soil fumigation is regulated by federal, state, and local (county) governments. Many strawberries are grown in densely populated areas, prompting increasingly stringent buffer zones for preplant soil fumigation (Goodhue, Schweisguth, and Klonsky, 2016). Soil fumigations cannot be conducted within one-eighth of a mile of a school, and applicators are required to notify nearby property owners and post warnings on the fumigated acreage. Growers can sometimes reduce buffer zones by dividing a field into multiple application blocks.

LABOR AND WAGES

Strawberries are likely the most labor-intensive crop in California, involving about 1.5 workers per acre and 50,000 to 60,000 workers statewide, mostly to harvest strawberry fields twice a week. The strawberry harvest begins in the southern part of the state and moves north. From January through March, Florida also supplies strawberries. Most strawberry growers are specialized, but some Salinas vegetable growers have added strawberries. This contributes to the $725 million value of strawberries in Monterey County in 2016, which is second only to lettuce ($1.3 billion) in value.

Strawberries are soft fruits that are susceptible to damage in handling, and a strawberry field may be picked 40 to 50 times a season. Labor represents 60 percent of strawberry production costs (Tourte et al., 2016), prompting efforts to make hand harvesters more productive. Many growers place slow-moving conveyor belts in front of workers so that they can place full flats of berries on the belt. This practice eliminates the need for workers to walk full flats to the end of the row to receive credit for their work, thus giving them more time to pick. To harvest strawberries,

workers push a light wheelbarrow containing the plastic clamshells in which strawberries are sold while they pick from two adjacent elevated rows.

Two major wage systems are used to pay berry workers: hourly wages and piece rates. Most farm jobs pay hourly wages, but most berries are picked for piece rate or incentive wages. Piece-rate earnings are the product of the rate per unit of work accomplished times the number of units completed, such as $2 for picking a flat of strawberries times six trays an hour or 48 trays a day, yielding $12 an hour or $96 a day. Piece-rate wages keep grower costs constant regardless of variation in worker productivity, unless growers elect to keep low-productivity workers and make up their earnings to the minimum wage. Most workers are paid piece-rate wages, such as $1.75 a tray or flat, with a guarantee of at least the minimum wage ($12 an hour in 2019). Some growers offer workers an hourly wage of $5 an hour and a piece rate of $1.10 a flat that has 12 twelve-ounce pints or 8 one-pound clamshells. Workers typically pick five to seven flats an hour, earning more than the minimum wage. Piece rates are lower in fields with conveyor belts that serve up to 60 pickers because workers can pick faster.

The combination of the government-set minimum wages and employer-set piece rates creates minimum productivity standards, or the number of trays workers must pick per hour or day to earn the minimum wage. Employers must "make up" the earnings of slow pickers so that they receive at least the minimum wage or terminate slow pickers. In 2014, when the state's minimum wage was $9 an hour and the Adverse Effect Wage Rate for H-2A guest workers was $11 an hour, surveys found two major wage systems: $5 an hour plus $1.10 a tray, and $1.70 a tray. Figure 11.4 shows that workers who were paid only a per-tray piece rate had to pick more trays per hour than those who were paid a combination per hour and per tray piece rate.

Many of the workers who harvest strawberries are limited-Spanish speakers from southern Mexican states such as Oaxaca and Chiapas. There are often several members of a family and their relatives in a crew, so that strawberry crews are more diverse than the solo male work crews that dominate the harvest of tree fruits, meaning there is more variance in productivity among strawberry harvesters.

Table 11.5. California Strawberry and Other Berries, 2006–2018

	Average Employment		Total Wages ($1,000)		Average Weekly Pay ($)	
	Strawberries	Other Berries	Strawberries	Other Berries	Strawberries	Other Berries
2006	21,622	3,059	411,165	69,508	366	437
2007	23,652	3,488	483,831	77,893	393	429
2008	26,165	4,060	531,696	92,377	391	438
2009	27,211	4,441	553,971	95,777	392	415
2010	26,934	5,275	568,954	122,525	406	447
2011	27,088	6,103	595,540	142,953	423	450
2012	27,073	6,981	650,248	176,023	462	485
2013	26,727	8,876	666,975	234,274	480	508
2014	25,939	9,719	698,466	265,284	518	525
2015	25,975	10,618	716,825	289,569	531	524
2016	25,501	10,942	780,319	285,017	588	501
2017	25,376	10,241	780,506	275,926	591	518
2018	24,897	10,018	782,029	291,150	604	559
Percent Change Over Time						
2006–18	15	227	90	319	65	28
2006–12	25	128	58	153	26	11
2011–18	−8	44	20	65	31	15

Source: U.S. Department of Labor, Bureau of Labor Statistics, QCEW (www.bls.gov/cew): Strawberries, 111333; Other berries, 111334

Most strawberry harvesters are hired directly by farmers rather than brought to farms by contractors, and many farmers keep older and slower workers on their payrolls in order to retain their younger and faster relatives.

The strawberry labor market is "fluid," with workers often changing employers. Some workers monitor yields to determine where they are most likely to maximize their piece-rate earnings, and seek jobs at the best fields. In the past, some growers refused to rehire workers who quit during the season and went elsewhere, but since the slowdown in unauthorized Mexico-U.S. migration after the 2008–2009 recession, few growers maintain no-rehire-during-the-season policies.

Strawberry harvesting crews typically include 60 workers, and the key figure is the crew supervisor who is responsible for ensuring that the crews include 50 to 60 workers. Crew supervisors are responsible for recruiting additional workers to replace those who move to other farms.

The arrival of fewer unauthorized newcomers from Mexico has prompted many growers to use the H-2A program to employ legal Mexican guest workers. Many of these H-2A workers are provided by Fresh Harvest, a labor contractor based in the Imperial Valley that is the state's largest employer of guest workers.[11] Perhaps half of the Salinas-Watsonville strawberries were picked by H-2A workers in 2017. Berries were the most common type of job filled by H-2A workers in FY19, accounting for 10 percent of the 258,000 farm jobs certified to be filled with guest workers.

The combination of fewer unauthorized newcomers and more H-2A guest workers, who must be paid an Adverse Effect Wage Rate that is higher than the state's minimum wage ($13.92 in 2019 when the state's minimum wage was $12 an hour), has put upward pressure on earnings. Average employment in California's strawberry industry (NAICS 111333) rose from 21,600 to 25,000 between 2006 and 2018—up 15 percent. However, as Table 11.5 shows,

---

11 See: http://freshharvestusa.com/

Figure 11.4. Minimum Productivity Standards to Pick Strawberries, 2014

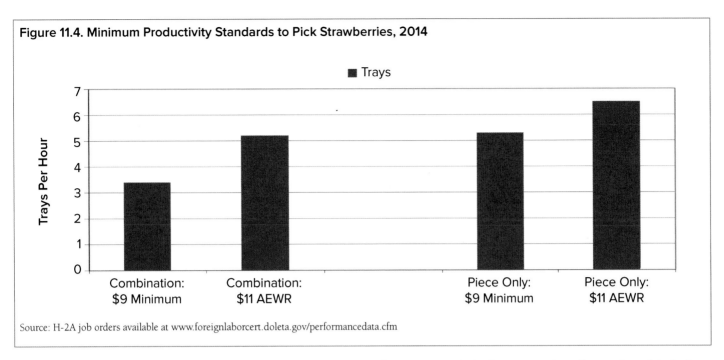

Source: H-2A job orders available at www.foreignlaborcert.doleta.gov/performancedata.cfm

average strawberry employment rose 25 percent between 2006 and 2012, and has since fallen. Other berry employment (blackberries, blueberries, and raspberries) rose much faster, up 227 percent over the decade and, as with strawberries, rose faster between 2006 and 2012 than between 2012 and 2018. There were seven full-time equivalent strawberry jobs for each other berry job in 2006, but only 2.5 in 2018, demonstrating the rapid growth in other berry employment.

Total wages paid to berry workers were almost $1.1 billion in 2018, including 73 percent paid to strawberry workers. The strawberry share of total wages has been falling. These employment and earnings data are from 12 monthly snapshots, as employers report employment and earnings for the pay period that includes the 12th of each month. Most berry workers are not employed the entire year, so their annual earnings are less than what a full-year worker would earn. Unpublished data from the Employment Development Department for 2015 found 38,800 workers who were primarily employed in strawberry farming, meaning their highest earnings were from strawberry establishments (Martin, Hooker, and Stockton, 2017). They earned a total of $690 million in 2015 or an average of $17,850. However, for workers who had only a job in strawberries in 2017, average earnings were $23,800, reflecting year-round workers, managers, and supervisors.

There were 16,150 who were primarily employed in "other berries" in 2015. They earned a total of $270 million or an average of $16,700. However, workers employed only in "other berries" earned an average $9,150, suggesting that there were many workers employed only short periods in "other berries." It should be noted that there are no data on the commodity of workers brought to farms by labor contractors. There were 294,000 workers who had their highest earnings with labor contractors in 2015, and they earned an average $9,900, the lowest of any category.

Several efforts are underway to mechanize strawberry harvesting, which is difficult because the fruit is soft and fields must be re-picked repeatedly during the season. The $100,000 Spanish Agrobot has 16 mechanical arms to pick strawberries and place them on a conveyor belt as it moves down rows with hardened sides that guide the machine and pick the berries growing over the hard sides. Another version of the Agrobot will have 60 arms to harvest strawberries grown on raised, hydroponic beds instead of low, dirt fields. The British-based Autonomous Strawberry Harvesting and Management Robot (AUTOPIC) project aims to develop a robotic picker to harvest soft fruit on a 24/7 basis.[12]

---

12 See: http://ict-agri.eu/node/36238

SHARECROPPING

Strawberries may be the only major California commodity in which the majority of growers are Hispanic, in part a legacy of sharecropping.[13] Some strawberry marketers made contracts with farmers who planted strawberries on leased land, received technical help while plants grew, and harvested and delivered the crop to the marketer, who deducted any loans advanced to the farmer and marketing costs. If yields and prices were high, the sharecropper farmer made a profit; if not, sharecroppers could lose money because marketers were repaid for their loans and costs before forwarding the balance to growers.

A federal suit filed in 1975, Real v. Driscoll's Strawberry Associates (DSA), alleged that 15 sharecropper farmers were employees of Driscoll's. The farmers sought payment of the minimum wage from DSA, which prepared the land, provided the plants and irrigation equipment, and monitored the development of the berries. Sharecropper farmers harvested the berries, delivered them to Driscoll's, and received the "net proceeds" after deductions for preharvest loans and marketing costs. A federal district court dismissed the farmers' claim but, after the U.S. Court of Appeals for the 9th Circuit overruled that decision and allowed the minimum-wage case to proceed, DSA settled with the 15 farmers in 1981.[14]

Cucumber sharecroppers near Gilroy made similar arguments, asserting that they were employees entitled to workers compensation despite contracts identifying them as independent contractors. This S.G. Borello case went to the California Supreme Court, which in 1989 declared that the "sharefarmers" were employees.[15] The Supreme Court laid out a six-factor test to distinguish employees from independent contractors:

1) who controls the work,
2) what is the farmer's opportunity for profit or loss,
3) what investment does the farmer make in equipment,
4) what skills are required of the farmer,
5) how permanent is the relationship between farmer and marketer, and
6) is the farmer's service integral to the marketer's business?

The Real and Borello cases reduced strawberry sharecropping. One legacy is the hundreds of relatively small growers, often ex-harvesters, who sign contracts with berry marketers to raise patented plants, harvest the berries, and deliver them to the marketer. Marketers no longer advance funds, but other entities may make loans that are repaid when the berries are sold. The practical problem for a small grower with 5 or 10 acres is that when yields are low and berries are sold at low prices, checks from marketers may not provide sufficient funds to pay the 10 to 20 workers needed to harvest the berries. Despite these challenges, many harvesters want to become small growers, and some have become successful large berry growers.

UNIONIZATION AND CERTIFICATION

Workers at VCNM Farms, which marketed its berries through Well-Pict, voted to be represented by the UFW in August 1995. Before a contract was negotiated, VCNM destroyed its remaining crop and went out of business, an action deemed unlawful by the ALRB. VCNM paid $113,000 to the displaced workers in March 1996.[16]

Since much of the land used to grow strawberries is leased, and many strawberry farms are partnerships that may be reconstituted from year-to-year, the UFW concluded that it would have to organize the entire strawberry industry rather than individual farms. The UFW in April 1996 announced a "Five Cents for Fairness" campaign to raise then-prevailing strawberry piece rates of $1.20 per flat or

---

13 There are no official data, but industry observers say that 55 percent of strawberry growers (not acreage) are Hispanic, 25 percent are of Japanese ancestry, and 20 percent are non-Hispanic white. Before World War II, Japanese farmers grew more than 90 percent of California's strawberries, but plant and soil diseases and the internment of Japanese during WWII took many out of the industry.

14 See: https://openjurist.org/603/f2d/748/ca-79-3000-real-v-driscoll-strawberry-associates-inc-d-j

15 See: https://law.justia.com/cases/california/supreme-court/3d/48/341.html

16 Stuart Silverstein, "The Strawberry Jam: Dispute Between Growers and Farm Workers Heats Up," *Los Angeles Times*, December 27, 1996. http://articles.latimes.com/1996-12-27/business/fi-12876_1_strawberry-growers

$5 an hour and $0.10 per 12-pint, 12-ounce flat.[17] The UFW noted that a worker picking 10 flats an hour earned $6 per hour when the state's minimum wage was $4.75.

Increasing the piece rate by five cents a pint would have raised the piece rate from $1.20 to $1.80, a 33 percent wage increase. If workers maintained a 10-flat an hour picking rate, average worker earnings would have raised to $10.80 an hour, more than twice the minimum wage in 1995.

The UFW deployed 40 full-time organizers in summer 1996 to organize 15,000 workers employed on 270 strawberry farms in the Salinas-Watsonville area. The UFW called strawberries "La Fruta del Diablo" (the fruit of the devil) because of the stooping required to pick them. The UFW's effort in strawberries drew support from the AFL-CIO and national media attention, and opposition from the Strawberry Workers & Farmers Alliance.

The UFW's organizing campaign failed to achieve election victories and union contracts despite union-friendly investors purchasing the largest strawberry grower, Coastal Berry, which did not oppose efforts to unionize its 1,000 workers.[18] Coastal Berry workers in summer 1997 complained of "harassment" by UFW organizers, and an August 1998 election saw the UFW lose to the local Coastal Berry Farm Workers Committee, 410 to 523. There were several more elections, and the UFW lost the June 3-4, 1999 election to the Committee on a 598 to 688 vote.[19]

Coastal Berry had operations in Northern and Southern California, and the UFW won 311 to 266 in Oxnard, while losing 268 to 416 in Watsonville. The ALRB allowed Coastal Berry's Northern and Southern California farms to be considered separate bargaining units, and recognized the UFW as the bargaining agent for Coastal Berry's southern workers and the Committee for Coastal Berry's northern workers. The UFW eventually won the right to represent all Coastal Berry workers and Coastal Berry was sold to Dole in 2004; Dole stopped berry farming in 2017. The UFW had one strawberry contract in 2018, with Swanton Berry.

Instead of union contracts, some berry farms have been certified as in compliance with farm labor protocols aimed at protecting farm workers. The Equitable Food Initiative (EFI),[20] launched in 2012 by Oxfam America and the United Farm Workers (UFW) union with the support of Costco, has standards covering labor protections, food safety, and environmental sustainability. EFI's labor standards call for full compliance with federal, state, and local labor laws, and go beyond labor laws to require farm workers to be "trained in their rights and responsibilities, educated about the standards and constructive methods of communicating with their employers, and afforded opportunities for professional development."

The EFI facilitates worker involvement through "an authorized worker liaison team or through traditional labor union representation." Workers are paid while they are being trained, both men and women are on liaison teams, and collective bargaining agreements take precedence over EFI standards if their provisions exceed EFI standards (Martin, 2016). Trained supervisors and workers, the multistakeholder teams at the heart of EFI, extend their knowledge to the farm's entire workforce to ensure compliance. Costco rewards certified growers with preferential access to its buyers.

The EFI aims to reassure consumers that their food is safe and was picked by workers who were treated well; EFI notes that hundreds of workers trained to identify food-safety issues are better than government inspectors or third-party auditors who visit farms periodically. Several Andrew & Williamson's strawberry farms in California have been certified, as well as berry and vegetable operations in Mexico.

EFI aims to be a one-stop shop for growers seeking certification of their compliance with labor, food safety, and sustainability protocols, but being certified by EFI does not exempt farms from inspections by government agencies that enforce labor, food safety, and environmental laws. EFI staff are supported by foundation grants to publicize the program, train leadership teams on farms, and work with growers and buyers.

---

17 Many strawberries are picked into flats or trays that contain 12 dry pints each weighing 12 ounces, or a total 144 ounces or 9 pounds of strawberries; full trays weigh 10.5 to 11 pounds, including the weight of the tray. Some strawberries are picked into one-pound clamshells.

18 See: https://migration.ucdavis.edu/rmn/more.php?id=210

19 See: https://migration.ucdavis.edu/rmn/more.php?id=383

---

20 www.equitablefood.org

The effects of EFI on farm worker earnings, productivity, and turnover have not been evaluated. Some anecdotal evidence suggests that certified growers believe that worker turnover has decreased in response to higher pay, worker feelings of belonging to an organization that cares about them, and end-of-season bonuses (Martin, 2016).

TRADE

In 2017, the U.S. supply of fresh strawberries was 3 billion pounds, including 367 million pounds or 12 percent imports.[21] U.S. consumption was 2.7 billion pounds or 8.3 pounds per person, and 290 million pounds of U.S. strawberries were exported, almost all to Canada. The U.S. is a net importer of fresh strawberries, most of which are from Mexico.

Mexico had 28,000 acres of strawberries in 2018, double the acreage of a decade earlier, with strawberry production concentrated in Michoacán (60 percent of Mexican production), Guanajuato, and Baja California; Irapuato, calls itself "Mexico's strawberry capital." There are 150,000 workers employed in Mexico's berry sector, which also includes blackberries,[22] blueberries, and raspberries, most of which are exported to the United States.

Over 85 percent of Mexico's fresh berries are exported, and Mexico's export-oriented berry industry continues to expand with the help of U.S. and Chilean partners, producing berries worth almost $1.3 billion in 2017.[23] Florida strawberry growers, who compete most directly with Mexican producers, experience variable weather that can lead to fluctuations in supply and grower prices. Some Florida growers blame imports from Mexico for variable prices, but Mexican exporters counter that Florida produces mostly conventional rather than organic strawberries, and sells most of its berries east of the Mississippi River, limiting competition with Mexican berries sold in the western states.

Mexico is the source of about half of U.S. fruit imports and three-fourths of its vegetable imports; fruits and vegetables were 54 percent of the $23 billion in agricultural imports from Mexico in 2016. The U.S. exported farm commodities to Mexico worth $18 billion, meaning that the U.S. had an agricultural trade deficit with Mexico.

Mexico produced about 850,000 metric tons of berries in 2016, including 55 percent strawberries, 29 percent blackberries, and 13 percent raspberries (Cook, 2017). One-third of Mexican strawberries and almost all of its raspberries and blackberries are exported to the United States. Chile, Canada, and Peru are the leading sources of imported blueberries, but Mexican blueberry exports are expanding rapidly, especially during the early spring period.

The import share of berries varies, but Mexico supplies almost all imports of strawberries (100 percent of imports), raspberries (98 percent), and blackberries (95 percent). The growth in strawberry imports from Mexico has led to a stabilization of strawberry production in Florida. By contrast, the availability of Mexican raspberries appears to have enlarged the U.S. market, much as the availability of Mexican avocados expanded U.S. avocado consumption.

---

21 An additional 494 million pounds of strawberries were frozen in 2016 and, with 384 million pounds of frozen strawberry imports plus 236 million pounds of beginning stocks, the supply of frozen strawberries was a billion pounds. (ERA FTS 364. Table 11).

22 Mexico's 10,000 hectares of blackberries produced about 30 percent of the world's crop in 2016. http://www.freshplaza.com/article/156566/Mexico-Blackberries-will-continue-to-grow-throughout-the-world.

23 Robbie Whelan, "Mexico's Berry Bounty Fuels U.S. Trade Dispute," *Wall Street Journal*, October 7, 2017. The WSJ reported a total 88,000 acres of berries in Mexico, and quoted a Georgia blackberry grower who complained that Mexico was selling 12 six-ounce clamshells for $10 when his cost of production was $12 for a flat, citing his labor costs of $200 a day as the reason for higher U.S. costs. Few U.S. harvest workers average $200 a day; $100 a day is far more typical.

CONCLUSION

California has a vibrant fresh berry industry that accounts for 7 percent of the state's farm sales from less than 1 percent of the state's irrigated crop land. High-value fresh berries are capital-intensive and risky. Berry marketers are the key players, developing proprietary varieties that are leased to growers, providing advice to growers, and marketing the berries. Most marketers source berries from around the U.S. and abroad so that they can supply fresh berries year-round to the shrinking number of supermarket chains and food-service buyers.

Fresh berries are among the most labor-intensive and risky commodities produced in California. Currently, harvest costs account for 50 to 70 percent of total production costs. By 2022, the minimum wage will raise to $15 an hour. This effect is amplified in agriculture due to overtime laws that require growers to pay 1.5 times the usual wages after eight hours or 40 hours a week. Growers who face a minimum wage of $15 an hour in 2022 are looking for ways to make workers more productive, as with conveyor belts in fields that reduce walking. Further ahead, some growers hope to harvest strawberries by machine, while others hope that blueberry harvesting machines will improve to allow harvesting fruit for the fresh market.

Berry growers today face the challenge of finding sufficient harvesters at a time of reduced Mexico to U.S. migration. Picking berries seasonally is often a first U.S. job for Mexican-born workers from rural areas with little education, and fewer are arriving as the Mexico-U.S. border becomes more difficult to cross illegally. Some strawberry growers are turning to the H-2A guest worker program, which allows them to employ legal guest workers from Mexico. They face the challenge of finding housing for guest workers in coastal areas with high housing costs and restrictive regulations that reduce the ability to build more.

Trade poses challenges and opportunities for California's berry industry. Rising incomes abroad increase the demand for California berries, while free-trade agreements and improved varieties and technologies that are transferred abroad facilitate imports from countries with lower wages. Mexico's export-oriented berry industry is expanding rapidly, and berries that once complemented California production are increasingly competing with the state's berries. Direct competition between California and Mexico is likely to increase as Mexico expands production under protected culture structures that reduce risks and increase yields, and will likely first affect Southern California berry operations.

California's fresh berry industry has expanded rapidly, and overcome the challenge of losing access to the most common soil fumigant after a half century. Labor and pests are the top challenges facing the industry. New varieties continue to be developed in response to disease, labor, and other challenges. The berry industry's past successes in overcoming barriers to producing high-quality fresh fruit suggest that berry growers will be able to overcome today's disease, labor, and water challenges.

REFERENCES

Bolda, M., L. Tourte, and R. DeMoura. 2005. "Sample Costs to Produce Fresh Market Raspberries. Central Coast Region. Santa Cruz and Monterey Counties." Davis, CA. Available at: https://coststudies.ucdavis.edu/en/.

Brat,I. 2015. "Robots Step Into New Planting, Harvesting Roles," *Wall Street Journal*, April 23. Available at: https://www.wsj.com/articles/robots-step-into-new-planting-harvesting-roles-1429781404.

Cook, R. 2011. "Fundamental Forces Affecting the U.S. Fresh Berry and Lettuce/Leafy Green Subsectors." *Choices* 26(4). Available at: http://ageconsearch.umn.edu/record/120009.

Cook, R. 2017. "Global Fresh Berry Trends: Focus on the European Market." Paper presented at Amsterdam Product Show, Amsterdam NE, 15–17 November.

Gallado, K. and D. Zilberman. 2016. "The Economic Feasibility of Adopting Mechanical Harvesters by the Highbush Blueberry Industry." *HortTechnology* 26(3):299-308. Available at: http://horttech.ashspublications.org/content/26/3/299.full.pdf+html.

Goldberg,C. 1996. "The Battle of the Strawberry Fields," *New York Times*, July 3. Available at: http://www.nytimes.com/1996/07/03/us/the-battle-of-the-strawberry-fields.html.

Goodhue, R., M. Schweisguth, and K. Klonsky. 2016. "Revised Chloropicrin Use Requirements Impact Strawberry Growers Unequally." *California Agriculture* 70(3):116-123. Available at: http://calag.ucanr.edu/Archive/?article=ca.2016a0002.

Goodyear, D. 2017. "How Driscoll's Reinvented the Strawberry." *New Yorker*, August. Available at: https://www.newyorker.com/magazine/2017/08/21/how-driscolls-reinvented-the-strawberry.

Guthman, J. 2017. "Paradoxes of the Border: Labor Shortages and Farmworker Minor Agency in Reworking California's Strawberry Fields." *Economic Geography* 93(1):24-43. Available at: http://www.tandfonline.com/doi/abs/10.1080/00130095.2016.1180241.

Holmes, G., S. M. Mansouripour, and S. Hewavitharana. 2020. "Strawberries at the Crossroads: Management of Soilborne Diseases in California Without Methyl Bromide." *Phytopathology*. Vol 110. No 5. Available at https://apsjournals.apsnet.org/doi/10.1094/PHYTO-11-19-0406-IA.

Jimenez, M., K. Klonsky, and R. DeMoura. 2009. "Sample Costs to Establish and Produce Fresh Market Blueberries. San Joaquin Valley South. Tulare County." Davis, CA. Available at: https://coststudies.ucdavis.edu/en/.

MacDonald, J., R. Hoppe, and D. Newton. 2018. "Three Decades of Consolidation in US Agriculture." Washington DC: U.S. Department of Agriculture. Economic Research Service, *Economic Information Bulletin* No. 189 Available at: https://www.ers.usda.gov/webdocs/publications/88057/eib-189.pdf?v=43172.

Martin, P. 2017. "Immigration and Farm Labor: Challenges and Issues." Special Report, University of California, Giannini Foundation of Agricultural Economics, June. Available at: http://bit.ly/2tvaUSw.

Martin, P. 2016. "Labor Compliance in Fresh Produce: Lessons from Food Safety." *Choices*. Quarter 3. Available at: http://www.choicesmagazine.org/choices-magazine/submitted-articles/labor-compliance-in-fresh-produce-lessons-from-food-safety.

Martin, P., B. Hooker, and M. Stockton. 2017. "Employment and Earnings of California Farm Workers in 2015." *California Agriculture*, published online:1-7. Available at: http://calag.ucanr.edu/archive/?type=pdf&article=ca.2017a0043.

Silverstein, S. 1996. "The Strawberry Jam: Dispute Between Growers and Farm Workers Heats Up," Los Angeles Times, December 27. Available at: http://articles.latimes.com/1996-12-27/business/fi-12876_1_strawberry-growers.

Tourte, L., M. Bolda, and K. Klonsky. 2016. "The Evolving Fresh Market Berry Industry in Santa Cruz and Monterey Counties." *California Agriculture* 70(3):107-115. Available at: https://doi.org/10.3733/ca.2016a0001.

CHAPTER 12. CALIFORNIA'S NURSERY AND FLORAL INDUSTRY

HOY F. CARMAN

ABSTRACT

Nursery and floral production is an important component of California's agricultural output, accounting for 7.5 percent of the state's farm sales. Annual sales of $3.5 billion mean that California accounts for 20 percent of U.S. sales of nursery and floral products. Nursery and flower production occurs throughout California, but is mostly concentrated in Central Coast and South Coast counties near the largest population centers; a third of sales are in San Diego County.

ABOUT THE AUTHOR

Hoy F. Carman is an emeritus professor in the Department of Agricultural and Resource Economics at the University of California, Davis, and a member of the Giannini Foundation of Agricultural Economics. Hoy can be contacted by email at carman@primal.ucdavis.edu.

Nursery and floral production is an important component of California's overall agricultural output and annual farm income. California's nursery and flower crops returned average cash revenues of over $3.73 billion annually for the five crop years 2013 through 2017.

Photo Credit: UC Davis

CHAPTER 12. TABLE OF CONTENTS

NURSERY AND FLORAL PRODUCTION

Nursery and floral production is an important component of California's overall agricultural output and annual farm income. California's nursery and flower crops returned average cash revenues of over $3.73 billion annually for the five crop years 2013 through 2017. Only three California crops exceeded this annual average for the 5-year period: dairy and milk, $7.18 billion; almonds, $6.08 billion; and, all grapes, $5.51 billion. Overall, the annual nursery and floral share of total agricultural sales ranged between 6.2 to 7.5 percent from 2013 to 2017, with a 5-year average of 6.9 percent. Nursery and flower production is located throughout California, with at least one farm operation reported in 56 of 58 counties. The industry has a definite urban orientation, with the majority of production taking place in the most populated counties.

NURSERY AND FLORAL INDUSTRY SALES

California nursery and floriculture production and sales enjoyed a 15-year expansion, with sales rising from $1.96 billion in 1993 to a record high of $3.98 billion in 2007. Nursery and floral sales were increasing relative to the rest of California, production through 2002, when they accounted for 12.5 percent of total California agricultural sales (Figure 12.1).

While nursery and floral sales continued to grow through 2007, growth of total agricultural sales resulted in the nursery sales percentage of total sales remaining rather constant in a range of 11.5 to 12.5 percent before dropping to 10.9 percent in 2007 (Figure 12.1). While California's total agricultural sales increased from $36.4 billion in 2007 to almost $59.4 billion in 2014, nursery and floral sales relative to total agricultural sales dropped to a low of 6.2 percent in 2014. Between 2014 and 2016, the increase in nursery and floral relative to total agricultural sales was the result of total agricultural sales decreasing to $50.95 billion, while nursery and floral sales increased to $3.8 billion in 2016. All sales increased in 2017, but total agricultural sales increased faster than did nursery and floral sales.

Figure 12.2 shows annual floral and nursery sales. The largest components of the floral crop category include cut flowers and greens and potted flowering plants. Floral sales ranged from a low of $932 million in 2000 to a high of $1.112 billion in 2012, before dropping to $770 million in 2016 and 2017. The largest components of annual nursery sales are ornamental plants and nursery stock. Total nursery sales ranged from a low of $2.087 billion in 2001 to a high of $2.962 billion in 2007, then decreased to

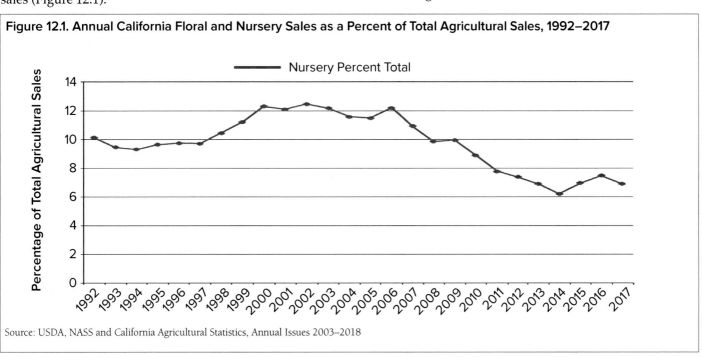

Figure 12.1. Annual California Floral and Nursery Sales as a Percent of Total Agricultural Sales, 1992–2017

Source: USDA, NASS and California Agricultural Statistics, Annual Issues 2003–2018

Figure 12.2. Annual Value of California Floral and Nursery Production, 2000–2017

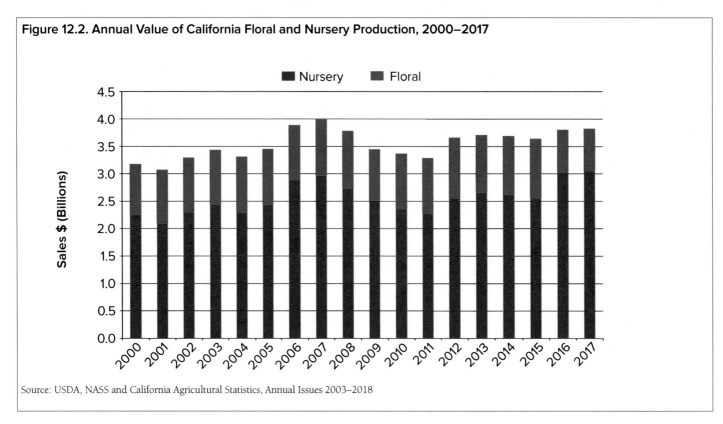

Source: USDA, NASS and California Agricultural Statistics, Annual Issues 2003–2018

$2.275 billion in 2011 before recovering to $3.05 billion in 2017. Note that average annual sales of floral products were $953 million from 2013 through 2017, while average annual sales of nursery products were $2.781 billion for the same period. The split for total floral and nursery sales are typically 25 to 30 percent floral and 70 to 75 percent nursery.

California's nursery and floral industry plays a leading role nationally. The USDA 2014 Census of Horticultural Specialties, which gathered data for all horticultural operations with sales greater than $10,000, reported that 1,710 California operations had 2014 total sales of $2.878 billion, accounting for almost 20.9 percent of total U.S. sales of $13.79 billion. California was followed by Florida, (13%); Oregon, (6.8%); Michigan, (4.7%); Texas, (4.3%); and North Carolina, (4.1%). Thus, the top six states accounted for 53.8 percent of total U.S. sales of horticultural specialty crops.

USDA, NASS annually surveys commercial floricultural operations with sales of more than $100,000. They reported that 685 California producers with floricultural sales of $1.08 billion accounted for 25 percent of the U.S. wholesale value in 2015. California accounted for 14 percent of bedding and garden plants, 34 percent of potted flowering plants, and 78 percent of the total cut flower wholesale value (*California Agricultural Statistics Review*, 2015–2016).

STRUCTURE OF CALIFORNIA'S NURSERY AND FLORAL INDUSTRY

The Census of Agriculture reported that total California sales of nursery and floriculture crops increased from just over $1.413 billion in 1987 to almost $3.65 billion in 2007, and then dropped to $2.51 billion in 2012 before recovering to $2.934 billion in 2017 (Table 12.1).

Data in each row of Table 12.1 describe changes occurring over time in the California nursery and floral industry. The number of farms producing nursery and floriculture products increased steadily from 2,993 in 1987 to 4,388 in 2002 and then dropped back to 2,758 in 2017. With total sales of nursery products growing relative to the number of nursery farms, average sales per farm also grew through 2002 then jumped significantly in 2007 when total sales increased, and farm numbers decreased. However, a significant decrease in total sales with a small decrease in the number of farms in 2012 resulted in average sales returning to 2002 levels. Finally, with a loss of 632 farms between 2012 and 2017 and rebounding total sales, average sales reached an all-time high of $1.06 million per farm in 2017. A similar pattern of growth is shown for the average value of land and buildings and the average value of machinery and equipment, although average values in 2017 remained below 2012 levels.

The average age of the principal operator of California nursery and floriculture farms increased from 51.5 years in 1987 to 58.9 years in 2012 and ended at 56.8 years in 2017. This pattern is similar to the average for all California farms, where average age increased from 53.6 years in 1987 to 60.1 years in 2012, and then decreased to 59.2 years in 2017.

The legal structure of California nursery operations has also changed over time. The distribution of nursery farms by legal organization in 1982 was sole proprietors, 61 percent; partnerships, 14 percent; corporations, 24 percent; and other, 1 percent[1]. In 1997, this had changed to sole proprietors, 69 percent; partnerships, 11 percent; corporations, 18 percent; and other, 2 percent. In the 2007 census, the legal structure was sole proprietors, 67 percent; partnerships, 9 percent; corporations, 22 percent; and

---

1 "Other" category includes cooperatives, estates and trusts, institutions, etc.

Table 12.1. Selected Characteristics of California Nursery and Floriculture Farms, 1987–2017

Selected Characteristics	Census Year						
	1987	1992	1997	2002	2007	2012	2017
Number of Farms	2,993	3,319	4,285	4,388	3,549	3,390	2,758
Total Sales ($ Billions)	1.413	1.662	2.211	3.287	3.647	2.514	2.934
Average Sales ($/farm)	470,816	495,688	513,761	756,416	1,025,524	741,489	1,063,928
Average Acres per Farm	45	54	45	50	52	90	50
Average Value of Land & Buildings ($/farm)	612,352	742,937	624,267	866,017	1,995,792	1,133,108	1,760,990
Average Value of Machinery & Equipment ($/farm)	70,580	86,284	82,328	101,289	153,103	114,973	133,323
Average Age of Operator	51.5	52.3	54.0	54.8	56.3	58.9	56.8

Source: USDA, Census of Agriculture for each census year

other, 2 percent. The most recent census (2017) reported sole proprietors, 62 percent; partnerships, 9 percent; corporations, 26 percent; and other, 3 percent. The share of corporations that were family-owned remained relatively constant at 81 percent in 1982 and 84 percent in 2017. Note that the corporate share of farms is larger for nursery farms (26 percent) than for any other sector in California agriculture, with corporations accounting for 10.3 percent of all California farms. Nursery and floriculture farms accounted for just 3.9 percent of all California farms in 2017, while at the same time accounting for 9.8 percent of all California farm corporations.

The California floral and nursery sector's ties to the real estate industry and the unique nature of its crops contributed to uninterrupted sales growth between 1993 and 2007. This growth continued in spite of major challenges presented by shipping restrictions related to pests and diseases, increased competition from imported flowers, the impact of increased energy costs on production and transportation, limited and expensive water supplies, and less than ideal weather conditions. The effects of the 2007 "burst" of the "housing bubble" and the economic recession impacted much of California agriculture and particularly nursery and floral products. Then, just as sales began to recover in 2012, the effects of California's drought hit. The continuing effects of recession and the drought are evident throughout the industry, ranging from the sales of plants and material to structural aspects of wholesale and retail product distribution.

LOCATION OF PRODUCTION

Nursery and flower production occurs throughout California, but is mostly concentrated in Central Coast and

Table 12.2. California Gross Value of Production of Nursery, Flowers, and Foliage in 2014 through 2017, Top 15 Counties in 2017 with 2017 Share of State Total

| | Value of Production | | | | Share of State Total |
| | 2014 | 2015 | 2016 | 2017 | 2017 |
Top 15 Counties	Thousands of Dollars				Percent
San Diego	1,182,614	1,146,814	1,233,942	1,232,557	32.19
Stanislaus	286,577	313,689	276,423	271,049	7.08
Monterey	228,114	244,339	254,882	256,102	6.69
Ventura	138,884	169,887	204,797	247,873	6.47
Santa Barbara	196,271	195,881	160,268	190,985	4.99
Riverside	172,910	158,648	150,426	153,749	4.01
Siskiyou	155,666	149,580	140,085	138,968	3.63
San Joaquin	62,725	46,773	116,186	117,294	3.06
Kern	96,396	104,820	107,387	113,705	2.97
San Mateo	93,776	83,274	102,318	102,770	2.68
Los Angeles	119,238	94,954	97,922	90,840	2.37
Santa Cruz	119,690	119,120	93,612	84,375	2.20
Santa Clara	133,576	92,399	92,399	82,951	2.17
San Luis Obispo	84,394	100,138	86,933	82,802	2.16
Tulare	78,396	67,635	83,292	72,141	1.88
Top 15 County Total	3,149,227	3,087,951	3,200,872	3,238,161	84.56
Rest of State	516,351	524,099	605,402	591,238	15.44

Source: California County Agricultural Commissioners' Reports, 2012–2017

South Coast counties.[2] Among the 15 California counties with the largest nursery, flower, and foliage production in 2017, there were 10 counties with over $100 million of production. As shown in Table 12.2, San Diego County dominated with 32.2 percent of total state production in 2017. The next five counties—Stanislaus, Monterey, Ventura, Santa Barbara, and Riverside—combined for 29.2 percent of total California production. The remaining nine of the top 15 counties accounted for 23.1 percent of production. Eight of the 15 largest-producing counties border the Pacific Ocean, and Santa Clara County has a coastal climate. Among the four Central Valley counties (Stanislaus, San Joaquin, Kern, Tulare), three had an annual production of over $100,000 during at least one of the four years. The ten counties with production over $100 million in 2017 accounted for $2.83 billion (73.8 percent) of California's 2017 nursery, flower, and foliage production. There were five counties with nursery, flower, and foliage production in the range of $72 to $100 million. They accounted for 10.8 percent of total 2017 production. Overall, 15 counties produced 84.6 percent of California's total 2017 nursery, flower, and foliage crops. Among all crops grown in these top 15 counties, nursery and floral crops ranked No. 1 in value of production in San Diego, Los Angeles, San Mateo, and Santa Clara counties.

Nursery and flower producers continue to located in the most urbanized areas of the state. The climatic conditions favorable for nurseries are also very attractive to people, and population and housing growth have been high in areas where nurseries have traditionally located. There were nine California counties with a population exceeding 1 million persons in 2017. Five of these counties (Los Angeles, Orange, San Diego, Santa Clara, and Riverside) were among the largest nursery and flower producers (Appendix Table 12.1A), and have a combined population of 21.07 million. The 15 largest nursery- and flower-producing counties have a population of 23.14 million and accounted for almost 58.6 percent of California's 2017 population. The proximity of nursery and floral production to urban population centers has advantages and disadvantages. Short distribution channels tend to have comparatively low transportation costs while providing a fresh and quality product. Many nurseries distribute their product directly to retailers, and some also integrate into retailing. However, other costs, such as water and land, are comparatively high. An important consideration for urban locations, given the recent economic issues facing the industry, is that the land resource can easily and quickly shift to other uses. Thus, it may be very difficult to re-establish an urban nursery, once closed.

2 The gross value of nursery, flower, and foliage production by county is in Appendix Table 12.1A. Note that the County Agricultural Commissioners' Reports do not include nursery and flower sales for four counties that do have producers listed in the CDFA Directory, Nurserymen and Others Licensed to Sell Nursery Stock in California available July 2013 (http://plant.cdfa.ca.gov/nurserylicense/nlmenu.asp). These counties and the number of producers include (1) Colusa, (2) Kings, (3) Mono, and (4) Plumas.

CROPS PRODUCED

The wholesale value of California nursery, flower, and foliage production during 2017 totaled almost $3.83 billion (Table 12.3). Of the total value, floral products contributed $423.3 million, while nursery production during the same period was just over $3.4 billion. Nursery, flower and foliage producers market a wide variety of plant materials ranging from cut flowers, potted flowering plants, flower seeds, bedding and garden plants, bulbs, and ornamentals to fruit and nut trees and strawberry plants. Buyers include consumers, landscape contractors, institutions, and agricultural producers. The most recent data available indicate that the largest wholesale value of plant materials produced by the California nursery, flower, and foliage industry totaled $3.98 billion in 2008 (Table 12.3). Table 12.3 shows values for the various categories of nursery products for the fiscal years ending in 2001, 2008, and 2017. Comparable data for the entire period of 2001 through 2017 are available in Appendix Table 12.2A.

The product categories used by the CDFA Nursery Program and shown in Table 12.3 differ from those reported in annual *California Agricultural Statistics Reports* and *California County Agricultural Commissioners' Reports*. Briefly, the latter two reports include a category for flowers and foliage that includes more products than does the Floral Products Total in Table 12.3. A comparison for 2017 has the floral products total in Table 12.3 equal to $423,345,000, while the Flowers and Foliage category in *California Agricultural Statistics* reports a value of $774,407,000. The annual total of nursery products and floral and flower products for the two data series are similar in magnitude, but they tend to differ slightly from year to year.

There is a considerable range of wholesale values for the 12 categories of floral and nursery products included in Table 12.3. There are other important differences, including the pattern of changing values over time, variation in customers and target markets, and factors affecting values for each category. Using column 2017 values, the largest five categories account for a value of almost $3.68 billion or 96 percent of the 2017 total.

These categories and their percentage of total 2017 wholesale value are: cut flowers and cut greens, 10.8 percent; potted plants, 16.3 percent; bedding plants, 10.9 percent; ornamentals, 24.7 percent; and nursery stock 33.3 percent. The other seven categories of floral and nursery products individually range from $4.7 to $53.5 million and have a combined total of just $150.36 million (4 percent). The wholesale value of California-produced floral products reached a maximum of $521.46 million in 2007 while the maximum wholesale value of nursery products ($3.46 billion) and the high of combined floral and nursery wholesale value of $3.98 billion occurred in 2008. While seven of the product categories had higher wholesale values in 2008 than in 2001, only four (cut flowers and cut greens, potted plants and flowering foliage, ornamentals, and nursery stock) had higher values in 2017 than in 2001. Overall, the total wholesale value of California nursery and floral products increased 23.6 percent from 2001 to 2017.

TOTAL SALES TRENDS

The California floral and nursery industry reports total wholesale value and total sales data, but separate observations for price and quantity for the various product categories are not available. Total wholesale value and total sales data are reported for California floral and nursery products but separate observations for price and quantity for the various product categories are not available. Because of this data shortfall, there are no quantitative estimates of supply and demand parameters available. There are no estimates for price elasticity of demand and underlying determinants for observed changes in total sales revenues are unknown.

Given that there are a variety of market segments for the 12 product categories in Table 12.3, one would expect the sales impact of different factors to vary by product. For example, one would expect a significant portion of sales for cut flowers and cut greens are to consumers in retail outlets, while sales of a product such as turf and sod are mainly to landscapers and other installers. While incomes or expected incomes are likely a factor in sales of all floral and nursery products, other factors such as housing

Table 12.3. Wholesale Value of California Floral and Nursery Products by Major Categories, 2001, 2008, and 2017

Floral Products	2001 Value	2008 Value	2017 Value
	Thousands of Dollars		
Cut Flowers and Cut Greens	383,102	505,036	413,709
Flower Seeds	5,831	7,932	4,682
Christmas Trees	10,686	6,547	4,954
Floral Products Total	399,618	519,515	423,345
Nursery Products			
Potted Plants and Flowering Foliage	615,772	677,820	624,911
Bulbs, Corm, Roots and Tubers	10,295	10,456	6,737
Flowering Propagative Materials	75,590	61,0112	53,517
Bedding Plants	465,045	438,602	418,810
Rose Plants	45,936	45,704	18,903
Woody, Deciduous and Evergreen Ornamentals	772,006	1,239,919	947,101
Herbaceous Perennials	30,069	46,135	25,270
Turf and Sod	42,750	124,708	36,298
Nursery Stock other than Ornamentals	639,509	817,324	1,273,956
Nursery Products Total	2,696,974	3,461,678	3,405,503
Grand Total	3,096,592	3,981,193	3,828,848

Source: California Department of Food and Agriculture. Value of Nursery Products, Fiscal Year; CDFA Nursery Program, Nursery Advisory No.01-2002, Nursery Advisory No. 01-2009, January 16, 2009, and Nursery Advisory No. 01-2019, April 30, 2019

Figure 12.3. Index of Total Wholesale Value by Crop, 2001–2017

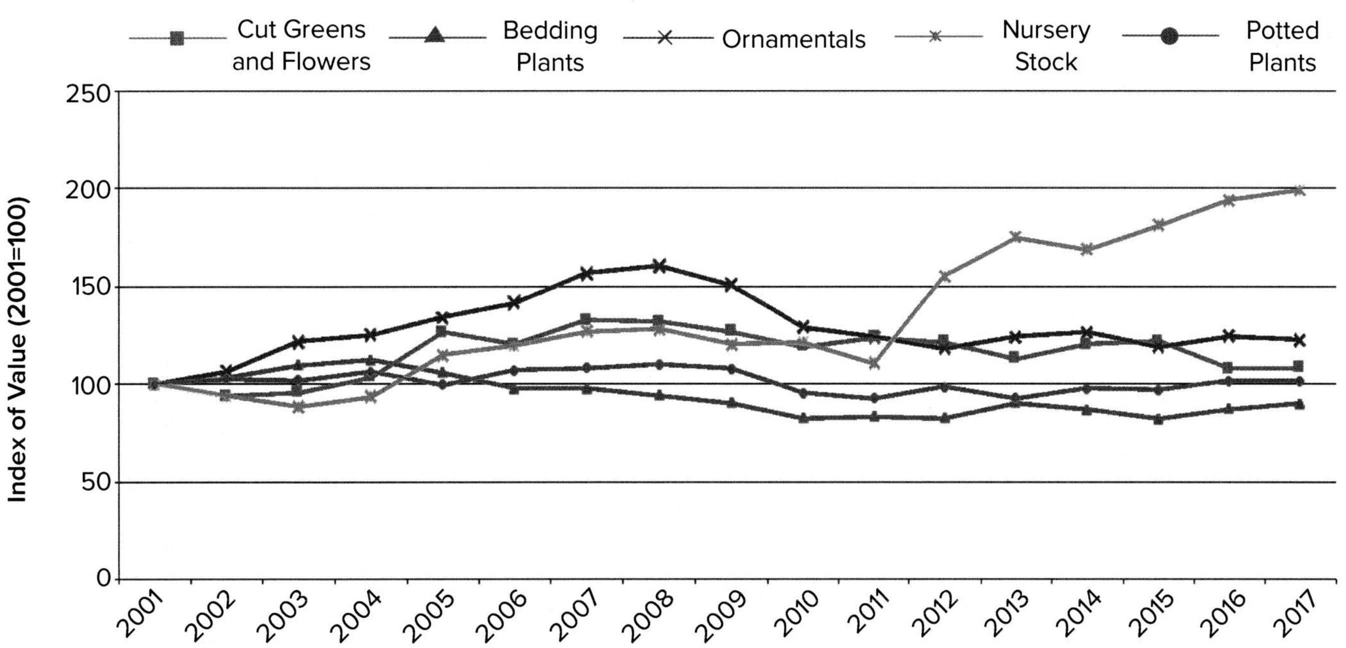

Source: California Department of Food and Agriculture. Value of Nursery Products, Fiscal Year. CDFA Nursery Program, Nursery Advisory. Annual Issues

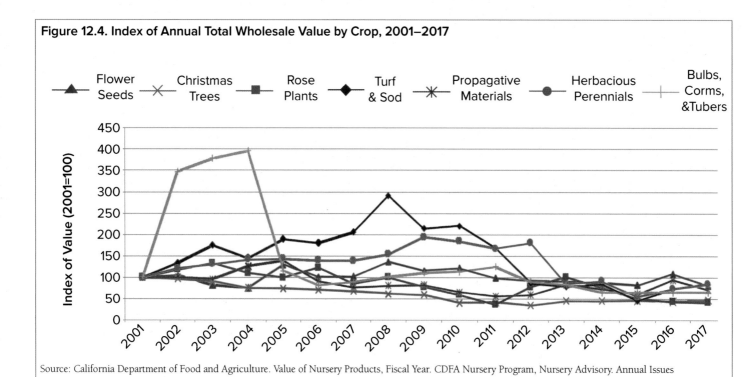

Figure 12.4. Index of Annual Total Wholesale Value by Crop, 2001–2017

Source: California Department of Food and Agriculture. Value of Nursery Products, Fiscal Year. CDFA Nursery Program, Nursery Advisory. Annual Issues

Note: This figure includes seven floral and nursery crop categories with the smallest annual sales.

starts, expected prices for fruit and tree nut crops, rainfall, drought, plant disease, energy prices, and other major input costs may also be important. A brief examination of sales trends for each of the product categories indicates that the factors listed above have differential impacts.

In Table 12.3, for the years 2001 through 2017, we calculate an index of annual sales for each floral and nursery crop using 2001 as the base year (2001=1.0). Figure 12.3 shows the values of the index for the five crop categories with largest wholesale values (sales). The sales trends differ for each of the five products, with nursery stock exhibiting the largest divergence. Most of the nursery stock sells to producers for replacement or new plantings of fruit and tree nut acreage, and most of the production is under contract between the nursery and buyer. 2017 nursery stock sales are 1.99 times greater than in 2001, which is due to recent acreage expansions for tree nuts (almonds, walnuts, and pistachios).

Figure 12.4 illustrates sales indexes for the seven floral and nursery crop categories with the smallest annual sales. While the 16-year pattern of sales differs for each product, all of the products ended the 16-year period with fewer sales than in 2001. Christmas tree sales had a strong downward trend from 2001, having only 34.5 percent of beginning sales in 2012 before recovering slightly to 46.4

percent of 2001 sales in 2017. Turf and sod sales increased almost three-fold to 2008 and then decreased steadily to only 42.5 percent of beginning sales in 2015 before recovering to 84.9 percent of 2001 sales in 2017. California's housing collapse, the recession, several cities' programs that paid homeowners to remove grass lawns, and increased water charges are probably related to decreased sales of turf and sod products. Sales for most of the products decreased after the recession officially began in 2008, although herbaceous perennials' sales increased and remained high from 2009 through 2012 before collapsing from 2013 to 2017. Flower seeds sales decreased from their 2008 high of 1.36 times their 2001 level to 80.3 percent of their 2001 level in 2017. Each of the other minor crops ended 2017 with lower sales relative to 2001 sales.

RETAIL SALES

The channels of distribution for California floral and nursery production tend to be short and direct, with many nurseries having outlets on-premise to serve retail customers. Direct sales to landscape contractors and gardeners purchasing products ranging from specimen trees to bedding plants, and agricultural producers purchasing trees and strawberry plants, are also important. California is the largest market for lawn and garden products in the U.S., accounting for about 10 percent of annual retail sales. The majority of California floral and nursery production sells in California, with the distribution of sales varying by product. A survey of California flower growers conducted in 2000 found that 59 percent of California-produced flowers were sold in California, 40 percent were shipped to other states, and 1 percent were exported to other countries (Prince and Prince, 2000). The spatial distribution of California nursery product sales, based on industry estimates, is approximately 79 percent in California, 20 percent shipped to other states, and 1 percent exported to other countries.

Partial data on retail floral and nursery product sales in California are available from government statistics. The California State Board of Equalization publishes sales data by type of retail outlet but not by product line. There are annual retail sales data for florists and farm and garden supply stores, two types of stores that tend to specialize in floral and nursery products. The Board of Equalization revised their "type of business" classification in 2009 from the Standard Industrial Classification (SIC) to the North American Industry Classification System's (NAICS) classifications. Farm and garden supply stores became "lawn and garden equipment and supplies stores" while florists continued as "florists." There are also aggregate sales data for large multi-product retailers such as food stores, hardware stores, and general merchandise. Still, it

Year	Florists	Farm and Garden	Total	Change from Prior Year
		Thousands of Dollars		Percent Change
2000	983,396	2,060,713	3,042,436	5.52
2001	988,022	2,059,040	3,047,062	0.15
2002	998,781	2,135,472	3,134,253	2.86
2003	1,005,452	2,266,142	3,271,594	4.38
2004	1,077,694	2,386,377	3,464,071	5.88
2005	1,133,896	2,662,956	3,796,852	9.61
2006	1,172,658	2,930,230	4,102,888	8.06
2007	1,203,148	2,965,697	4,168,845	1.61
2008	793,882	2,751,233	3,545,115	-14.96
2009	461,349	2,216,767	2,678,116	-24.46
2010	449,893	2,269,297	2,719,190	1.53
2011	464,761	2,392,542	2,857,303	5.08
2012	484,517	2,492,977	2,977,494	4.21
2013	493,526	2,732,246	3,225,772	8.34
2014	537,808	2,857,008	3,394,816	5.24
2015	557,740	3,174,133	3,731,873	9.93
2016	568,050	3,367,663	3,935,713	5.46
2017	594,779	3,492,113	4,086,892	3.84
2018	578,379	3,420,648	3,999,027	-2.15

Table 12.4. Statewide Taxable Sales by California Retail Florists and Farm and Garden Supply Stores, 2000–2018

Source: California State Board of Equalization, Annual Reports

is not possible to determine the share of floral and nursery product sales for each of these retail store categories. Table 12.4. shows taxable retail sales reported by California florists and farm and garden supply stores for the 19-year period 2000 through 2018. Note that combined sales for the two types of stores increased from $3.04 billion in 2000 to almost $4.17 billion in 2007. The steady sales increase was interrupted in 2008 when total sales for the two types of outlets dropped almost 15 percent to $3.55 billion. Then, 2009 total sales for florists and farm and garden stores were down another 24.5 percent to $2.68 billion, a total that was below the 2000 level. Retail sales then increased slightly in 2010, with the sales increase for farm and garden stores offsetting the loss for florists. Total sales for both types of retailers then increased annually through 2017 before decreasing 2.15 percent in 2018.

Changes in store numbers and average annual sales for California florists between 2000 and 2011 are dramatic (Table 12.5). The number of California florists increased from 5,161 in 2000 to a peak of 6,427 in 2008 (24.5 percent), with store numbers increasing in 2008 even as sales began to plunge. Annual florists' sales decreased over 34 percent from 2007 to 2008, 41.9 percent from 2008 to 2009, and another 2.5 percent from 2009 to 2010. Total sales by California florists in 2010 were only 37.4 percent of their level just three years earlier in 2007. Large numbers of florists began closing in 2008, decreasing 25.3 percent by 2011 (from 6,427 in 2008 to 4,798 in 2011). Average sales per florist were highest in 2006, a year before total sales peaked in 2007; average sales then began to increase as the number of florists continued to decrease, and total sales increased. Sales per florist took a dive in 2015 with a surprising 44 percent increase in store numbers overwhelming the 3.7 percent increase in total sales (Table 12.5). The number of florists continued to increase, reaching a high of 7,153 in 2018, with the lowest average sales since 2000.

Sales for California lawn and garden stores increased from just over $2.06 billion in 2000 to a high of over $2.96 billion in 2007. They then decreased over 25.2 percent the next two years before increasing slightly in 2010 (Table 12.5). However, the number of stores increased each year from 2000–2011. Average sales per farm and garden store reached a high in 2006 and then decreased to a low in 2010 before increasing slightly in 2011. Total sales for lawn and garden stores increased steadily from 2010 through 2017,

reaching a high of $3.49 billion in 2017, before decreasing slightly to $3.42 billion in 2018. Sales per store increased through 2014 but then dropped sharply when the number of stores increased from 4,977 in 2014 to 6,564 in 2015—a 31.9 percent, one-year increase in store numbers. Increased total sales with stabilization of store numbers from 2016–2018 resulted in average sales per store in a range of $517,465 to $529,993.

FIRMS LICENSED TO SELL NURSERY PRODUCTS

Firms must be licensed by the California Department of Food and Agriculture to sell nursery products in California and the annual Directory of Nurserymen and Others Licensed to Sell Nursery Stock in California lists licensed firms. There was a significant reduction in the number of retailers between 2003 and 2011, with a slight recovery in 2013 and again in 2018. There were also less dramatic decreases in the total numbers of middlemen (wholesalers, jobbers, and brokers), as well as landscapers and producers from 2011 to 2013 and continuing to 2018.

The USDA's *2014 Census of Horticultural Specialties* included all operations that reported producing and selling $10,000 or more of horticultural specialty products. The census counted a total of 23,221 operations in the U.S., and 1,710 (7.36 percent) of these were in California. U.S. sales were $13.79 billion, with California operations accounting for 20.87 percent of the total. The average California horticultural specialty crop producer had 2014 sales of $1,683,030 as compared to the U.S. average of $593,818. The census reported wholesale and retail sales by California firms. Among the total 1,710 firms, 1,306 reported wholesale sales of $2.625 billion for average wholesale sales of $2,010,487 per operation. There were 835 operations with $252 million in retail sales for an average retail sales of $302,139 per firm. From total sales of $2.878 billion, 91.2 percent were at wholesale, and the remaining 8.8 percent were retail.

Comparison of the 2009 and 2014 *Census of Horticultural Specialties* indicates that the number of U.S. producers with annual sales over $10,000 increased from 21,585 in 2009 to 23,221 in 2014 (7.6 percent), while total sales increased from $11.687 billion to $13.789 billion (18 percent). The same comparison for California indicates that the total number of producers increased from 1,611 in 2009 to 1,710 in 2014 (6.1 percent), while total sales increased from $2.283 billion to $2.878 billion (26.1 percent).

Table 12.5. Number of Retailers and Average Sales Per Retailer, California Florists and Farm and Garden Retailers, 2000–2018

Year	Florists			Farm and Garden Stores		
	Number*	Sales ($1,000)	Sales per Florist ($)	Number*	Sales ($1,000)	Sales per Store ($)
2000	5,161	983,396	190,544	3,601	2,060,713	572,261
2001	5,338	988,022	185,092	3,711	2,059,040	554,848
2002	5,474	998,781	182,459	3,834	2,135,472	556,983
2003	5,572	1,005,452	180,447	3,943	2,266,142	574,725
2004	5,703	1,077,694	188,970	4,061	2,386,377	587,633
2005	5,708	1,133,896	198,650	4,188	2,662,956	635,854
2006	5,825	1,172,658	201,315	4,188	2,930,230	699,673
2007	6,160	1,203,148	195,316	4,285	2,965,697	692,111
2008	6,427	793,882	123,523	4,715	2,751,233	583,506
2009	5,070	461,349	90,996	5,133	2,216,767	431,866
2010	4,950	449,893	90,887	5,427	2,269,297	418,149
2011	4,798	464,761	96,866	5,600	2,392,542	427,240
2012	4,779	484,517	101,385	5,557	2,492,977	448,619
2013	4,606	493,526	107,149	5,204	2,732,246	525,028
2014	4,504	537,808	119,407	4,977	2,857,008	574,042
2015	6,487	557,740	85,978	6,564	3,174,133	483,567
2016	6,670	568,050	85,165	6,508	3,367,663	517,465
2017	6,741	594,779	88,233	6,589	3,492,122	529,993
2018	7,153	578,379	80,858	6,563	3,420,648	521,202

Source: California State Board of Equalization. Taxable Sales in California, 2000–2018

Note: * Number of licenses, July 1 of each year.

Table 12.6. Number of California Firms Licensed to Sell Nursery Stock by Category and Total, 2003, 2011, 2013, and 2018

Year	Cut Flowers & Greens Wholesalers	Jobbers & Brokers	Landscapers	Producers*	Incidental Retailers**	Retailers***	Total
2003	853	476	454	2,999	2,715	3,756	9,821
2011	880	460	463	2,959	736	2,158	5,848
2013	854	447	421	2,833	842	2,180	5,834
2018	798	409	426	2,790	848	2,270	5,674

Source: CDFA, Directory of Nurserymen and Others Licensed to Sell Nursery Stock in CA. To source directory: http://plant.cdfa.ca.gov/nurserylicense/nlmenu.asp

Notes: * A producer is a commercial producer who grows and sells a total of $1,000 or more of nursery stock in one year.

    ** An incidental retailer is an operator of a retail sales outlet for nursery stock that is handled incidental to other merchandise. Retailers such as Home Depot, Wal-Mart, Lowes and supermarkets are in this category.

    *** A retailer is an operator of a sales outlet that has no growing grounds except small areas devoted to the production of plants for local distribution and those producing less than $1,000.

STRUCTURAL CHANGES

Since 1992, there are changes in the number of California nursery and floricultural producers, changes in sales per firm and industry sales, and changes in the share of total California agricultural sales. The number of California farms producing nursery and floricultural products grew to a high of 4,388 in 2002 (Table 12.1). Nursery and floral sales reached 10.5 percent of total California agricultural sales in 1998, increased to a high of 12.5 percent in 2002 and remained above 10 percent through 2007. The highest combined nursery and floral sales occurred in 2007, when sales totaled $4 billion, accounting for 10.9 percent of total California agricultural sales. Nursery and floricultural sales as a share of total agricultural sales decreased to 6.2 percent in 2014 before recovering slightly in 2015.

Retail sales for California florists and lawn and garden stores also peaked during 2007, with total retail sales of almost $4.17 billion (Table 12.4). Then, with the onset of the economic recession in 2008, retail sales for florists and lawn and garden stores plunged over 14.9 percent in 2008 and another 24.5 percent in 2009, reaching a low of almost $2.68 billion. While total retail sales began to increase slowly in 2010, a total of nearly $4 billion in 2017 was still well below the 2007 peak.

The impacts of the economic recession on the number of firms producing and marketing California nursery and floral products point to some rather basic structural changes, with implications for both producers and consumers. First, is the sharp reduction in the number of California florists and their total sales associated with the recession. The number of florists in 2011 dropped 1,629 (25.3 percent) from the peak of 6,427 in 2008, while sales decreased $753.26 million (62.6 percent) from 2007 to 2010. The change in farm sales of floral products was much less dramatic. California farm-level floral product sales reached a high of $1.036 billion in 2007. Sales then dropped to $1.015 billion in 2008 and further to $937 million in 2009, before recovering to $1.015 billion in 2010. The large decrease in sales by florists with only a small change in farm-level sales is presumed to be due to a significant change in retail market shares for floral products. Specifically, other outlets, such as supermarkets,

gained market share for floral products at the expense of individual florists.

The situation for lawn and garden equipment and supplies stores is different. While total sales decreased after the peak occurring in 2007, the number of retail licenses continued to increase throughout the recession, reaching 5,600 in 2011 (Table 12.5). This is not the case for other retailers handling nursery products, as reported by CDFA. As shown in Table 12.6, there were fewer licensed producers (including some with direct sales to consumers) as well as incidental and specialized nursery retailers in 2011 as compared to 2003. The number of retailers licensed to sell nursery stock decreased from a total of 6,471 in 2003 to 2,894 in 2011 (55.3 percent) before increasing to 3,022 in 2013 and 3,118 in 2018. Given much smaller reductions in wholesale as compared to retail sales, the surviving retailers are larger on average and probably have smaller operating margins than was typical for either specialized florists or lawn and garden retailers.

Surges in the number of retail florists and farm and garden stores in 2015 as reported by the California State Board of Equalization show the number of retail florists increased from 4,504 in 2014 to 6,487 in 2015 (44 percent) while the number of farm and garden stores grew from 4,977 to 6,564 (31.9 percent). As reported by CDFA, the number of licensed retailers increased only by 96 (3.2 percent) between 2013 and 2018. The difference in the number of sales tax licenses and the number of CDFA licenses is significant. The best explanation is that most of the new sales tax licenses are to retailers who sell only cut flowers and greens and plants used indoor and are not required to be licensed by CDFA. There could also be some new entrants that are not familiar with CDFA licensing requirements and have not applied for the required licenses.

This very significant reduction in licensed California retailers handling nursery and floral products has implications for both producers and consumers. Some producers undoubtedly lost their major retail customers, while many lost important retail outlets. The impact of the loss of outlets was not uniform, but it was widespread. Products are not as widely available at the consumer level as before the recession, which tends to reduce consumer choice and negatively impact impulse buying. This consolidation of outlets may offer some economies in distribution but the impact on floral and nursery product sales has been negative. A change from specialized to multi-product retailers tends to reduce customer service and may reduce product assortments. And, the changes noted may be associated with more market power in the hands of surviving retailers. Recent increases in the number of retail outlets should have a positive effect on production and sales, especially for cut flowers and greens.

REFERENCES

California Department of Finance. 2017. *E-1 Population Estimates for Cities, Counties and the State – January 1, 2016 and 2017*. Sacramento, CA, May. Available at: http://www.dof.ca.gov/Forecasting/Demographics/Estimates/E-1.

California Department of Food and Agriculture. Various Years. *Value of Nursery Products, Fiscal Year*. Sacramento, CA: CDFA Nursery Program, Nursery Advisory.

California Department of Food and Agriculture. No Date. "Directory of Licensed Nurseries." Available at: https://plant.cdfa.ca.gov/nurserylicense/nlmenu.asp.

California Department of Food and Agriculture, National Agricultural Statistics Service (NASS). 2000–2017. *California County Agricultural Commissioners' Reports*. Available at: https://www.nass.usda.gov/Statistics_by_State/California/Publications/AgComm/index.php.

California State Board of Equalization. 2000–2018. *Taxable Sales in California Annual Report*. Sacramento, CA. 2000-2015 available at: https://www.boe.ca.gov/annual/table5.htm. and 2016-2017 available at https://www.boe.ca.go/annual/annualrpts.htm.

Carman, H. and A. M. Rodriguez. 2004. "Economic Contributions of the California Nursery Industry." *Giannini Foundation Information Series* No. 04-1, July. Berkeley: University of California Agricultural Experiment Station. Available at: https://s.giannini.ucop.edu/uploads/giannini_public/94/31/9431f0f7-cc14-473a-8f85-7fc284672ea1/041-nursery.pdf.

Carman, H. 2011. "Economic Aspects of the California Nursery and Floral Industry, 2001–2009." *Giannini Foundation Information Series* No. 11-1, December. Berkeley: University of California Agricultural Experiment Station. Available at: https://s.giannini.ucop.edu/uploads/giannini_public/a6/a5/a6a5c4f8-4267-4d2f-b84a-66901359ba37/111-nursery.pdf.

Carman, H. 2013."Some Impacts of Recession on California's Nursery and Floral Industry." *ARE Update* 16(5):9-11. University of California Giannini Foundation of Agricultural Economics. Available at: https://s.giannini.ucop.edu/uploads/giannini_public/08/25/0825e2f3-91f8-4fb3-a7e1-af11c9657dfe/v16n5_3.pdf.

Morey, J. 2004. "Market Share Report, 2004." *Nursery Retailer*, January/February, pp. 81-85.

Prince & Prince, Inc. 2000. *California Cut-Flower Production and Industry Trends 2000: A State-Wide Survey of Cut-Flower Growers*. Marketing Research Report, June. Columbus, Ohio.

U.S. Department of Agriculture, NASS, California Field Office. 2003-2016. *California Agricultural Statistics, Annual Issues*. Sacramento, California. Available at: https://www.nass.usda.gov/Statistics_by_State/California/Publications/index.php.

U.S. Department of Agriculture, NASS. 2007. *Census of Agriculture 2007, California State and County Data, Vol. 1, Geographic Area Series, Part 5*. Washington DC, February. Available at: https://www.nass.usda.gov/Publications/AgCensus/2007/Full_Report/Volume_1,_Chapter_2_County_Level/California/cav1.pdf.

U.S. Department of Agriculture, NASS. 2012. *Census of Agriculture 2012, California State and County Data, Volume 1, Chapter 2: County Level Data, Table 44*. Washington DC. Available at: https://www.agcensus.usda.gov/Publications/2012/Full_Report/Volume_1,_Chapter_2_County_Level/California/st06_2_044_044.pdf.

U.S. Department of Agriculture, NASS. 2017. *Census of Agriculture 2017, California State and County Data, Vol. 1, Chapter 2:County Level Data, Table 44*. Available at: https://www.nass.usda.gov/Publications/AgCensus/2017/Full_Report/Volume_1,_Chapter_2_County_Level/California/st06_2_0044_0044.pdf.

U.S. Department of Agriculture, NASS. 2014. *Census of Horticultural Specialties*. Washington DC. Available at: https://www.nass.usda.gov/Surveys/Guide_to_NASS_Surveys/Census_of_Horticultural_Specialties/index.php.

APPENDIX

Appendix Table 12.1A. Population (2017), Value of Nursery and Floral Production (2017), and Number of Greenhouse, Nursery, and Floriculture Producers (2017) by California County

County	Population Jan. 1, 2017	Value of Nursery Product ($1,000)	Number of Farms 2017	County	Population Jan. 1, 2017	Value of Nursery Product ($1,000)	Number of Farms 2017
Alameda	1,645,359	7,256	17	Orange	3,194,024	61,670	53
Alpine	1,151	0	0	Placer	382,837	8,643	54
Amador	38,382	218	9	Plumas	19,819	13	6
Butte	226,404	14,399	29	Riverside	2,384,783	153,749	178
Calaveras	45,168	259	14	Sacramento	1,514,770	32,182	25
Colusa	22,043	0	3	San Benito	56,854	7,686	14
Contra Costa	1,139,513	8,717	17	San Bernardino	2,160,256	51,441	68
Del Norte	27,124	10,237	8	San Diego	3,316,192	1,232,557	604
El Dorado	185,062	5,284	104	San Francisco	874,228	0	3
Fresno	995,975	38,247	79	San Joaquin	746,868	117,294	33
Glenn	28,731	7,017	2	S.Luis Obispo	280,101	82,802	73
Humboldt	136,953	55,945	68	San Mateo	770,203	102,770	51
Imperial	188,334	7,682	8	Santa Barbara	450,663	190,985	106
Inyo	18,619	1,185	0	Santa Clara	1,938,180	82,951	68
Kern	895,112	113,705	25	Santa Cruz	276,603	84,375	108
Kings	149,537	0	5	Shasta	178,605	12,181	16
Lake	64,945	925	15	Sierra	3,207	4	1
Lassen	30,918	36	3	Siskiyou	44,688	138,968	26
Los Angeles	10,241,278	90,840	210	Solano	436,023	44,627	16
Madera	156,492	29,382	4	Sonoma	505,120	35,411	145
Marin	263,604	243	19	Stanislaus	548,057	271,049	21
Mariposa	18,148	69	3	Sutter	96,956	47,350	20
Mendocino	89,134	1,577	44	Tehama	63,995	23,293	6
Merced	274,665	57,648	13	Trinity	13,628	4	15
Modoc	9,580	0	6	Tulare	471,842	72,141	38
Mono	13,713	20	1	Tuolumne	54,707	138	25
Monterey	442,365	256,102	60	Ventura	857,386	247,873	130
Napa	142,408	652	5	Yolo	218,896	19,068	19
Nevada	98,828	531	58	Yuba	74,577	0	7
				STATE	39,523,613	3,829,399	2,758

Source: Population data are from State of California, Department of Finance, Report E-1,Population Estimates for Cities, Counties and the State, January 1, 2016 and 2017.Sacramento, CA, May, 2017; Nursery and floral production from California Department of Food and Agriculture, California County Agricultural Commissioners' Reports, Crop Year 2016-2017, December 28, 2018; Number of greenhouse, nursery and floriculture producers from USDA, NASS, Census of Agriculture 2017, California State and County Data, Vol. 1, Chapter 2: County Level Data, Table 44

Appendix Table 12.2A. Annual Value of California Nursery Products by Category, 2001–2017

YEAR	Cut Flowers & Cut Greens	Flower Seeds	Xmas Trees	Total Floral Products
	Annual Value $ (Thousands)*			
2001	383,102	5,831	10,686	399,618
2002	359,811	6,074	10,305	376,190
2003	365,945	4,776	9,637	380,358
2004	396,748	4,380	7,975	409,103
2005	484,151	7,556	7,918	499,625
2006	460,419	5,862	7,507	473,788
2007	508,274	5,955	7,234	521,463
2008	505,036	7,932	6,547	519,515
2009	485,608	6,704	6,256	498,568
2010	456,493	7,086	4,3112	467,891
2011	473,513	5,737	4,442	483,691
2012	464,287	5,335	3,6823	473,305
2013	431,942	5,303	4,728	441,973
2014	459,813	5,084	4,742	469,638
2015	465,6901	4,779	4,829	475,299
2016	412,324	6,316	4,662	423,303
2017	413,709	4,682	4,954	423,345

YEAR	Potted Plants & Flowering Foliage	Bulbs,Corms, Roots, and Tubers	Flowering Propagative Materials	Bedding Plants	Rose Plants	Woody, Deciduous, and Evergreen Ornamentals
	Annual Value $ (Thousands)*					
2001	615,772	10,295	75,590	465,045	45,936	772,006
2002	631,386	35,712	75,701	480,438	54,062	823,256
2003	628,213	38,962	71,9767	509,310	61,047	940,436
2004	654,605	40,750	94,934	522,660	50,558	966,152
2005	612,803	11,830	105,047	492,449	45,353	1,035,598
2006	658,588	8,330	68,870	453,665	56,251	1,092,487
2007	665,904	9,090	57,931	454,220	38,982	1,208,605
2008	677,820	10,4556	61,012	438,602	45,704	1,239,919
2009	663,093	11,415	62,0856	419,378	35,6278	1,164,761
2010	585,716	11,711	49,170	383,405	27,201	996,500
2011	569,480	12,842	42,206	387,885	16,600	956,878
2012	604,840	9,127	44,509	384,256	35,621	912,435
2013	569,282	8,508	63,055	420,648	46,367	958,078
2014	601,310	6,701	55,561	403,653	35,444	975,360
2015	595,588	6,701	46,188	381,955	22,970,	918,654
2016	626,110	6,737	70,655	404,916	19,885	960,000
2017	624,911	6,737	53,517	418,810	18,903	947,101

Appendix Table 12.2A. Continued

YEAR	Herbaceous Perennials	Turf & Sod	Nursery Stock Other than Ornamentals	Total Nursery Products	Total Floriculture and Nursery
			Annual Value $ (Thousands)*		
2001	30,069	42,750	639,509	2,696,974	3,096,592
2002	36,176	56,725	598,607	2,792,062	3,168,252
2003	39,135	74,853	564,753	2,928,685	3,309,043
2004	42,37	61,827	597,499	3,031,353	3,440,456
2005	42,905	80,877	732,811	3,159,671	3,659,297
2006	41,752	76,966	763,397	3,220,305	3,694,093
2007	41,577	87,845	810,579	3,374,731	3,896,194
2008	46,135	124,708	817,324	3,461,678	3,981,193
2009	58,255	91,397	769,332	3,275,344	3,773,912
2010	55,273	94,197	776,989	2,980,161	3,448,052
2011	50,178	72,001	705,552	2,813,621	3,297,313
2012	54,175	37,091	990,779	3,072,833	3,546,138
2013	25,564	33,460	1,117,666	3,242,627	3,684,601
2014	27,277	35,925	1,079,007	3,220,237	3,689,876
2015	16,443	19,303	1,157,518	3,165,319	3,640,617
2016	21,907	31,428	1,240,808	3,382,445	3,805,748
2017	25,270	36,298	1,273,956	3,405,503	3,828,848

Source: California Department of Food and Agriculture. Value of Nursery Products, Fiscal Year. CDFA Nursery Program, Nursery Advisory. Annual Issues
Note: * Dollar Values Rounded to Nearest Thousand.

Chapter 13. Cannabis in California

Daniel A. Sumner, Robin Goldstein, William A. Matthews, and Olena Sambucci

Abstract

In November 2016, two decades after legalizing medicinal cannabis, California voted to legalize, tax, and regulate "adult-use" (recreational) cannabis. Subsequent legislation unified adult-use and medicinal cannabis taxation and regulation under a single structure. Implementation of the new licensed cannabis system was introduced in stages from January 1, 2018, to early 2019. However, as of 2020, lack of publicly available data still make it difficult to understand the emerging licensed market. Media reports suggest that these are difficult times for licensed cannabis businesses. At the same time, a vibrant unlicensed market continues to exist. We discuss the reasons why unlicensed cannabis markets can continue to thrive even after licensed systems have been implemented. We assess the situation for the industry in 2020, from cultivation through retail. We estimate that less than one-third of in-state retail sales are currently in the legal, regulated, and taxed segment. Finally, we assess briefly the impact of COVID-19 (Coronavirus) on the cannabis industry.

About the Authors and Acknowledgements

Daniel A. Sumner is the Frank H. Buck, Jr. Distinguished Professor in the Department of Agricultural and Resource Economics, University of California, Davis; Director of the University of California Agricultural Issues Center (AIC); and a member of the Giannini Foundation of Agricultural Economics. He can be contacted by email at dasumner@ucdavis.edu. Goldstein, Matthews, and Sambucci are project scientists at UC Davis. This chapter represents the views of the authors, not those of any institution with which they are affiliated nor that of any funding agency or any source which they reference. They thank Raffaele Saposhnik and other members of the large UC Davis team that has worked on the projects related to cannabis, staff at the California Bureau of Cannabis control, teams at ERA Economics and Humboldt State University, and others who have provided information, assistance, and interpretations related to data, regulations, and markets.

With the passage of Proposition 64 in 2018, which legalized recreational cannabis, California set up a system of state licensing, regulation, and taxation. However, cannabis sale, purchase, and possession remain prohibited under federal law.

Photo Credit: UC Davis

CHAPTER 13. TABLE OF CONTENTS

INTRODUCTION

Cannabis production, processing, sale, purchase, and possession by California residents with a doctor's recommendation was first allowed under the Compassionate Use Act of 1996, a voter initiative that allowed California residents with doctor's recommendations to purchase and possess cannabis without being subject to criminal penalties. Two decades later, in November 2016, Proposition 64 (another voter initiative) decriminalized cannabis purchase and possession by all adults 21 and over, without medical recommendations or California residency requirements. Proposition 64 also set up a system of state licensing, regulation, and taxation to be governed by several state agencies starting in 2018. Cannabis sale, purchase, and possession remain prohibited under federal law, with potentially severe penalties. This status of cannabis under federal law continues to mean that cannabis is not a normal farm product in the context of interstate trade, finance, and banking.

This chapter deals with two broad questions. First, what is the economic situation of the cannabis industry in California from farm cultivation through processing, marketing, and retailing? Second, what is the likely evolution of the industry in the future?

For our examination of the wholesale and retail markets, we draw on our research developed at the University of California Agricultural Issues Center (AIC) (Sumner et al., 2018, 2019, 2020; Goldstein, Saposhnik, and Sumner, 2020; Goldstein and Sumner, 2019; Goldstein, Sumner, and Fafard, 2019; Valdes-Donoso et al., 2019, 2020). For the discussion of cultivation and manufacturing, we draw on reports prepared to inform the California regulatory process (MacEwan et al., 2017; Eschker et al., 2018).

In broad terms, the dimensions of cannabis in California are as follows. Production is about 16 million pounds of raw dried flower. We do not think this number has changed substantially since before adult-use legalization and the implementation of state cannabis taxes, regulations, and licensing at the beginning of 2018. We estimate 2019 consumption in California, by weight, at about 2.8 million pounds, about 2.3 million pounds of which were illegal (unlicensed) and about 540,000 pounds of which were legal (licensed). This represents a modest shift from the legal retail market to the illegal

retail market since 2017, when we estimated total consumption at 2.8 million pounds, with the illegal (unlicensed) cannabis market at 2.1 million pounds and the legal (licensed) cannabis market at 700,000 pounds. We estimate that in 2019, as in 2017, about 80 percent of total cannabis production by weight was illegally exported to destinations outside the state. We stress that the estimates of total production and illegal shipments out of California are based on very limited and indirect data sources.

A variety of factors have contributed to the small size of the licensed market relative to the unlicensed market. First of all, for several reasons, unlicensed prices are relatively low. Licensed cannabis is more expensive to produce on the farm in part because licensed producers must pay taxes and satisfy a long list of regulations and standards. These include payroll and income taxes, and environmental, labor, transport and other rules.

The second factor keeping the licensed cannabis market relatively small is that licensed cannabis businesses throughout the supply and retail chain must also comply with a set of cannabis-specific regulations and taxes. Cannabis manufacturing, distributing, and retail regulations, introduced in 2018, added compliance costs and capital barriers to licensed cannabis but not to unlicensed cannabis. Compliance costs include license fees, locally and state-compliant renovations, the installation and maintenance of special security apparatus, taxes at two or three levels, compliance with track-and-trace software systems, labeling and child-proof packaging requirements, waste disposal rules, and legal and business consultants necessary to comply with these and other new regulations.

The third major barrier for would-be licensed cannabis businesses has been the difficulty of getting local approval for their plans. As of early 2020, more than 70 percent of local jurisdictions in California have prohibited all or most cannabis businesses. These local prohibitions were enabled under the so-called "local control" provisions of Proposition 64, which made state licensing contingent on local licensing. Many investors and industry observers were surprised by how many local jurisdictions chose to forgo local cannabis taxes and enact prohibitions. Because of local control, in

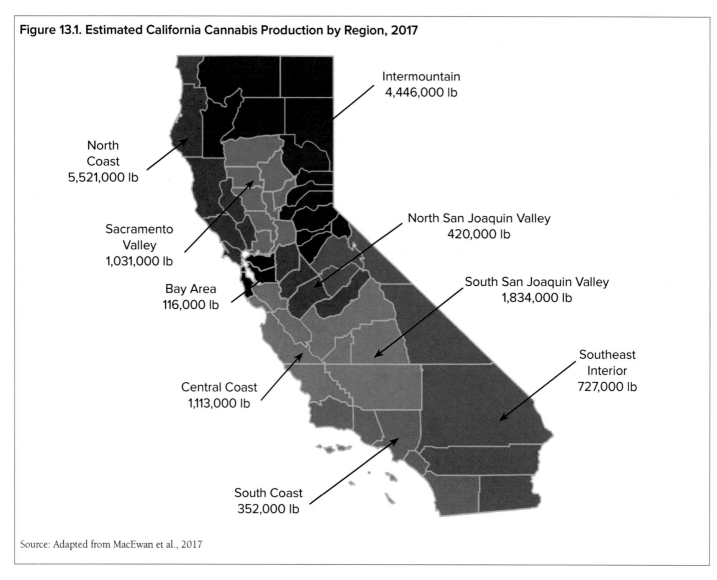

Figure 13.1. Estimated California Cannabis Production by Region, 2017

North Coast
5,521,000 lb

Intermountain
4,446,000 lb

Sacramento Valley
1,031,000 lb

North San Joaquin Valley
420,000 lb

Bay Area
116,000 lb

South San Joaquin Valley
1,834,000 lb

Central Coast
1,113,000 lb

Southeast Interior
727,000 lb

South Coast
352,000 lb

Source: Adapted from MacEwan et al., 2017

many parts of the state, pre-existing businesses that were legally operating in the medicinal segment in 2017 never had any path to becoming legal under the new state system. Delivery from licensed cannabis retailers is allowed throughout the state, but this has not compensated for lack of storefront licenses across many regions in California.

Barriers to entry, including the costs of running any legal business in California, cannabis-specific start-up compliance costs, and local control, have all restricted the supply of licensed businesses and subjected licensed businesses to higher costs (of becoming and staying licensed, complying with regulations, and paying taxes). These effects may help account for the fact that only a minority of farm cultivators appear to have become compliant as of late 2019 (by some accounts, less than 10 percent of the growers in Humboldt County have entered the licensed system).

The remainder of this chapter discusses in greater detail the structure and economics of the current California cannabis industry, using the latest data available as of early 2020, including the full-year 2019 cannabis tax collections announced by the California Department of Tax and Fee Administration (CDTFA) on March 6, 2020. We divide the remainder of the chapter into brief reviews of California cannabis cultivation, manufacturing, and retail followed by a more general discussion about the economics of California cannabis.

CANNABIS CULTIVATION IN CALIFORNIA

We estimate that between one-quarter and one-third of domestic cannabis consumed, by weight, is currently being sold through licensed channels in California. As discussed, the wholesale and farm prices (defined below) of cannabis differ by growing method, potency, other product characteristics, and regulation status. As of March 2020, according to Cannabis Benchmarks (2020), which surveys a selected and not necessarily unbiased set of wholesale transactions each week, the wholesale price of medicinal cannabis averaged about $1,200 per pound, with lower prices for cannabis grown outdoors (about $850 per pound), and higher prices for cannabis grown indoors (about $1,800 per pound). Prices for cannabis grown in greenhouses was similar to the volume-weighted market average of $1,200 per pound.

Because most cannabis grown in California is illegal, estimates of the quantity of cannabis production in California must be assembled from a variety of sources. MacEwan et al. (2018) used information from satellite imagery, law enforcement reports, local interviews, and many other sources to estimate 2017 production by region. Figure 13.1 displays their estimates. The data are displayed in what we term "dried cannabis flower equivalent" units, which includes estimates of a small contribution from leaves and trimmings (sold at much lower prices—as low as one-tenth of dried flowers or less).

Of the 15.6 million pounds of production in 2017, MacEwan et al. (2018) estimated that about 11 million pounds came from Northern California, where cannabis has long been grown in mountains and valleys, often in remote areas. Another 3 million pounds came from the San Joaquin Valley and the mountain and desert interior counties. That left about 1.5 million pounds in the coastal regions from San Diego up to San Francisco, where the bulk of the California population resides and where most California cannabis consumption occurs.

Table 13.1 shows the estimated distribution of production in each region by the share of production method—outdoor, indoor, and greenhouse. The final column in Table 13.1 shows the share of California production in each region based on the production quantities reported in Figure 13.1. More than 70 percent of California production comes from Northern California. These regions, like most others, have the majority of production outdoors, but the 51 percent grown outdoors in the North Coast region is below the statewide average of 58 percent grown outdoors. The share grown in greenhouses ranges from 54 percent in the South San Joaquin Valley and 43 percent in the North Coast region, to only 8 percent in the Southeast Interior and 9 percent in the North San Joaquin Valley. Finally, only 9 percent of California cannabis is grown indoors with the highest shares in the more urban regions of the Bay Area and the South Coast.

Table 13.1. Share of Production Measured in Pounds by Method by Region, 2016–17

	Outdoor	Indoor	Mixed Light	Total Share
	Percent			
Intermountain	63	9	27	29
North Coast	51	6	43	35
Sacramento Valley	77	8	15	6.6
Bay Area	26	61	13	0.7
North San Joaquin	74	17	9	2.7
Central Coast	74	6	20	7.2
South San Joaquin	43	3	54	12
Southeast Interior	83	8	8	4.7
South Coast	48	30	22	2.4
Statewide	58	9	33	100

Source: Adapted from MacEwan et al., 2017

Notes: Figures may not add exactly due to rounding; Mixed Light includes greenhouse.

These production estimates from 2017 include the roughly 80 percent of cannabis that is shipped outside California, similar to many other California commodities. There are two major differences for cannabis. First, evidence suggests that relatively little cannabis is exported from the U.S. (with Canada as the potential exception). Second, unlike other farm products, cannabis is illegal to ship to other U.S. states.

The other difference is that much of the production remaining in California is also being sold outside the regulated and taxed legal market. Although cannabis is legal to buy and possess (buying cannabis from unlicensed sellers is not a crime), selling cannabis outside the licensed, taxed, and regulated system is subject to criminal penalties.

Compared with other agricultural products, cannabis canopy area per farm is small (a fraction of an acre on average for all methods). Canopy is the designated area that will contain mature plants, and is measured in square feet. Cannabis output per square foot varies significantly by cultivation method: outdoor, indoor, and greenhouse (mixed light). Given wholesale prices, however, cannabis farms are not small as measured by total revenue.

Outdoor production typically has one harvest per year and, for the surveyed farms, yields an average of only 0.019 pounds, or 0.3 ounces, of dried flowers per square foot of canopy area. Indoor operations average only about 60 percent of the area of outdoor operations, but produce several harvests per year and, in this sample, yield almost 10 times as much cannabis per square foot as outdoor production. Greenhouse production is much closer to indoor in terms of square feet per operation, and averages about 0.105 pounds of cannabis per square foot. Indoor cultivation is much more intense and has very high annual yields of dried flowers per square foot compared to the outdoor operations in this sample. The canopy area per operation is about 60 percent of the outdoor canopy, thus the indoor cultivators averaged about six times as much cannabis as the average outdoor cultivator. The average greenhouse cultivator produced about 3.6 times as much as the outdoor cultivator in this sample.

The prices in 2016–17 were much higher per pound for indoor and greenhouse cannabis. Before legal adult-use cannabis retail sales began in California in 2018, revenue per farm averaged about $411,000 for outdoor cultivators, compared to $3,687,000 for indoor and $1,646,000 for greenhouse cultivators. Reported direct expenses are only about half of revenue indicating very high returns to management and risk.

In April 2018, farm prices were reported to be between $800–$900 per pound for outdoor-grown cannabis and between $1,500–$1,600 per pound for indoor-grown cannabis, with greenhouse-grown again in the middle (Cannabis Benchmarks, 2018). Two years later, in March 2020, these farm prices had remained remarkably stable, averaging about $850 for outdoor cannabis, $1,800 for indoor cannabis, and about $1,200 for greenhouse-grown cannabis. These are reported as prices that apply to sales within the legal and licensed market channel.

Note that we distinguish "farm prices" as discussed above (i.e., the price for the raw material of one pound of dried cannabis flower) from what we call "wholesale prices" above (which, imputed from CDTFA, based on about $1.3 million in 2019 wholesale sales and 540,000 pounds, would suggest an average wholesale price about $2,400 per pound).

The wholesaling stage in the supply chain (which is sometimes integrated by firms that are licensed to conduct cultivation, manufacturing, or retail operations) adds value by being responsible for labeling, packaging, and distribution to retailers. Wholesalers are also responsible for arranging for and paying for mandatory testing that must be conducted by an independent entity. For operations that are vertically integrated (except for testing), prices at each stage cannot be cleanly separated.

Taxes and regulations that were implemented in 2018 and revised in 2020 affect the cannabis cultivation industry both directly and through market relationships. In January 2020, state cultivation taxes were raised to $154 per pound of dried flower. The state requires a track-and-trace system starting at the farm, as well as surveillance to implement the system and provide security. The California Department of Food and Agriculture (CDFA) is responsible for licensing cannabis growers and issuing several license types based on cultivation method, farm size, and whether the cannabis is to enter the medicinal or adult-use segment. The cannabis itself may be identical in these license categories.

License fees per square foot rise with the area of canopy and are higher for greenhouse and indoor methods to reflect higher production and prices per square foot of canopy. Producers may obtain several licenses.

We estimate that state regulations add about $50 per pound to cultivation costs, not including cultivation taxes. Local governments, mainly counties and cities, also implement taxes and regulations on cultivators. These vary by medicinal versus adult-use cannabis and by cultivation method—outdoor, indoor, or greenhouse. Although local taxes and regulations are still in flux and much harder to gauge, local taxes were estimated to add approximately $130 per pound to the costs of supplying cannabis from the farm (MacEwan et al., 2018). One complication is that growers tend to avoid high-tax, high-regulation areas. Some taxes are on a per-square-foot basis and thus favor growing systems with high-yields of cannabis per square foot. The overall tax rate per pound thus depends in part on how production methods evolve and where production concentrates across jurisdictions.

The evolution of a licensed, taxed, and regulated cultivation industry will favor those firms adept at attracting relatively sophisticated management and adequate capital to meet the new regulatory setting. This new setting includes not only cannabis-specific taxes and regulations, but an array of labor, health and safety, environmental, and other regulations and taxes about which many incumbent cannabis growers have not been knowledgeable or compliant. We expect many growers who were well suited to the long-standing unlicensed and unregulated system to be less suited to the new system than many new entrants. Many of these incumbents may therefore choose to remain unlicensed. Since the size of illegal market is likely to remain large relative to the regulated market, these producers can remain in the cannabis business without attempting to navigate a system in which they may have little comparative advantage.

In general, the prospect of becoming licensed is less appealing to outdoor cannabis producers than to greenhouse or indoor cannabis producers. The first disadvantage to outdoor producers is that pesticide restrictions on cannabis have been at a more restrictive level than the restrictions on any other agricultural product in California (Valdes-Donoso, Goldstein, and Sumner, 2018). It is more difficult for outdoor growers than it is for indoor growers to comply with zero-tolerance standards in areas where there are already residual nonzero amounts of pesticides in the air from neighboring farms.

The second disadvantage is that there is a fixed cost per square foot associated with building state-compliant premises, and cannabis grown indoors or in greenhouses can yield four or five times more cannabis per square foot by inducing multiple harvests per year.

Third, there is a tax disadvantage for outdoor producers. Many local jurisdictions also tax cannabis per square foot, and the state cultivation tax is a tax by weight (rather than by value). Thus lower-yield cannabis cultivation per square foot and cheaper cannabis, both of which are associated with outdoor-grown cannabis, face high taxes per dollar of revenue versus indoor-grown or greenhouse-grown cannabis. California government officials have publicly discussed changing the structure of taxation in ways that may shift this balance to some extent (Schroyer, 2020).

In spite of these challenges, outdoor-grown cannabis has kept the plurality of the California market by volume, perhaps because of its foothold on the low-priced end of the retail market. The relative shares of outdoor-grown, indoor-grown, and greenhouse-grown cannabis fluctuate throughout the year, with outdoor-grown cannabis taking a larger share in the months following the fall harvest. But even four or six months after the last outdoor harvest, in March 2020, about 40 percent of wholesale transactions observed by Cannabis Benchmarks were for outdoor-grown cannabis. Indoor-grown cannabis was about 30 percent of wholesale transactions, and greenhouse-grown cannabis was about 30 percent of wholesale transactions. (It is not clear how representative Cannabis Benchmarks' measures are, but they are the only widely cited source for this information.)

Why does outdoor-grown cannabis still maintain a plurality of the licensed market? Probably the resilience of outdoor-grown is because of its foothold in the low-price segment of the market, where dried cannabis flower can sell at or below $5 per gram (less than half the statewide average retail price). Electricity is relatively expensive in California, and outdoor-grown cannabis, which uses natural light, saves on this major input into greenhouse-grown and indoor-grown cannabis production. Some large outdoor farms have opened in sunny and sparsely populated areas of the state with advantageous climates and local laws and tax structures that impose fewer costs on growers, such as Kings County and Coachella Valley. Outdoor growers also tend to sell in the largest batch sizes per transaction, thus reducing testing costs per unit.

CANNABIS MANUFACTURING AND RETAIL IN CALIFORNIA

Most retail cannabis is sold as dried flowers for smoking, but a significant minority of the retail market is manufactured cannabis products derived from cannabis flowers, leaves, and trim. Manufactured products are made using cannabis materials that are extracted using a variety of methods, including pressurized solvent-based extraction, distillation, pressing, tumbling, and dry sifting. The retail products using these concentrated extractions are roughly divided into three product categories:

(1) Concentrates, e.g., Butane Hash Oil (BHO) and CO_2 oil, typically sold at retail as vape pens, cartridges, or rosin. Oil typically has 60–75 percent THC content by volume.

(2) Edibles, e.g., cannabis-infused foods and beverages generally manufactured using cannabis concentrates.

(3) Topicals, e.g., creams, lotions, oils, or balms manufactured using cannabis concentrates as ingredients.

Eschker et al. (2018) estimated that manufactured products, including concentrates, edibles, and topicals, comprised about 30 percent of California's legal medicinal cannabis segment (by revenue) in 2017, and had a similar share of the licensed and regulated market that includes adult-use cannabis. Using the AIC estimate of a legal retail market of about $2.5 billion in 2019 (the same as the $2.5 billion medicinal market in 2017), this would translate to a retail value of about $750 million for the manufactured products segment in 2019.

Eschker et al. (2018) estimated an average ratio of wholesale to retail prices for manufactured products of 0.4 during 2017 (lower than the 0.5 ratio we impute from CDTFA tax data). That ratio implies that retail sales value of $750 million means a wholesale revenue of about $300 million for manufactured products in the medicinal cannabis market.

Sales volumes within manufactured cannabis products in the medicinal segment is about 75 percent concentrates, 22 percent edibles, and 3 percent topicals. Manufactured products in the unlicensed segment are almost all concentrates (in the form of vape pens and cartridges).

In 2018, the California Department of Public Health (CDPH) began regulating manufactured cannabis products. Separate license types are required for extracts using nonvolatile solvents and extracts using volatile solvents. CDPH also enforces rules covering food safety, the security of licensed manufacturing premises, compliance with the track-and-trace system, packaging and labeling, and other areas of regulatory oversight. Eschker et al. (2018) estimate costs of the licenses plus state regulations. In general, the licensed share of manufactured products seems to be higher than the licensed share of dried flower products, but reliable data on quantities by product type are not available.

The price of retail cannabis varies widely by region and location, regulation status, and product characteristics. One distinct difference between retailers is whether or not they are licensed. Most retailers that advertise public listings—72 percent, in data we collected for July 2019 (Goldstein, Saposhnik, and Sumner, 2019)—were unlicensed. The highest proportions of unlicensed retailers were in Southern California (83 percent of all retailers) and the Los Angeles area (78 percent). The lowest proportions of unlicensed retailers were in eastern California, including Sacramento (43 percent), and the greater Bay Area, including Napa and Sonoma (44 percent). Note these data do not include sales from retailers that do not advertise publicly, which may apply to a significant share of the market among some segment of buyers and some locations.

As of mid-2019, in a sample of more than 200,000 retail prices for cannabis flower in California, we observed that licensed storefront retailers listed prices that were 25 percent higher than prices of unlicensed retailers for dried flower, and licensed delivery-only retailers listed prices that were 7 percent higher than those of unlicensed delivery-only retailers.

We observed average retail prices, before sales tax, of about $11.50 per gram ($5,200 per pound) at licensed storefront retailers, $9.20 per gram ($4,200 per pound) at unlicensed storefronts, $11.80 per gram ($5,400 per pound) at licensed delivery-only retailers, and $11.00 per gram ($5,000 per pound) at unlicensed delivery-only retailers (Goldstein, Saposhnik, and Sumner, 2019). Both of these retail averages are higher than the 2017 price of cannabis in the medicinal retail market, which was about $8 per gram. For most retailers, these prices include the state and local excise taxes. But, based on a limited survey, there remains some variation across retailers in whether or not these excise taxes are included in the listed prices.

CANNABIS TAXES AND MARKET SIZE IN CALIFORNIA

Since MAUCSRA was implemented in January 2018, the California Department of Tax and Fee Administration (CDTFA) has published quarterly information about cannabis tax collections. In Table 13.2, we show all tax collections reported by CDTFA in the first two years of California's regulated cannabis system.

These data show a rapid jump in tax collections as more farms and firms became licensed in 2018. Total state tax collections, as shown in Table 13.2, increased from $347 million to $620 million in 2019. Growth in tax collections continued in 2019, but at a much slower pace.

In Table 13.2, California's revenue from its taxes on cannabis is separated into the three levels of state taxation. The left most column shows the cultivation taxes collected from farms based on weight produced, which in 2018 and 2019 were fixed at $9.25 per ounce, or $148 per pound. The second column, moving right, shows the excise taxes collected from distributors, which in 2019 were 24 percent of the wholesale price. The third column shows the state

sales taxes collected from retailers, which we estimate at an average of 8.3 percent (including a 7.25 percent base sales and a 1.05 percent average county tax that may or may not be incorporated into CDTFA's reported sales tax figures). Note that Table 13.2 does not report any cannabis-specific tax collections from local governments.

In the remainder of this section, we estimate some basic market characteristics for cannabis in California based on CFTDA's reported tax numbers shown in Table 13.2. The retail market size, as measured by total (aggregate) retail revenue, can be estimated directly from CDTFA's sales tax collections, or indirectly through CDTFA's excise tax collections. Excise tax collections also give a window onto the wholesale market size, as measured by total (aggregate) wholesale revenue.

Cultivation taxes are on a per-pound basis. CDTFA reports its total cultivation tax collections each quarter. These reports can be used, along with some simple arithmetic, to approximate the size of the licensed market in California in

Table 13.2. California Cannabis Taxes Collected from Licensed Activities, 2018–2019

2018	Cultivation Tax Collections	Excise Tax Collections	Sales Tax Collections	Total Tax Collections	Annual Growth
	$ (Thousands)				
Qtr 1	1,600	32,000	27,300	60,900	
Qtr 2	4,500	43,500	26,200	74,200	
Qtr 3	12,600	53,300	34,900	100,800	
Qtr 4	17,200	55,600	39,100	111,900	
Total	35,900	184,400	127,500	347,800	
2019					
	$ (Thousands)				Percent
Qtr 1	17,100	3,100	40,600	120,800	98
Qtr 2	22,900	75,800	58,200	156,900	111
Qtr 3	22,700	84,400	63,000	170,100	69
Qtr 4	23,600	84,400	64,700	172,700	54
Total	86,300	307,700	226,500	620,500	78

Source: Based on quarterly tax reports by CDTFA (2018–2020), including later revisions

Note: Does not include local municipal cannabis taxes.

Table 13.3. Size of California's Licensed Cannabis Market Estimated from Tax Collections, 2018–2019

Year	Total Weight (lb), Estimated Based on Cultivation Taxes	Total Wholesale Revenues, Estimated Based on Excise Taxes	Total Retail Revenues, Estimated Based on Excise Taxes[1]	Total Retail Revenues, Estimated Based on Sales Taxes[2]
2018	Pounds	Millions of U.S. Dollars		
Qtr 1	10,811	133	293	329
Qtr 2	30,405	181	399	316
Qtr 3	85,135	222	489	420
Qtr 4	116,216	232	510	471
Total	242,568	768	1,690	1,536
2019	Pounds	Millions of U.S. Dollars		
Qtr 1	115,541	263	578	489
Qtr 2	154,730	316	695	701
Qtr 3	153,378	352	774	759
Qtr 4	159,459	352	774	780
Total	583,108	1,282	2,820	2,729

Source: Based on quarterly tax reports by CDTFA (2018–2020), including later revisions

Notes: Does not include local municipal cannabis taxes.

[1] Assumes an actual retail markup of 120 percent. This is meant to apply to the 2018–2019 markets only. Note that in our simulation model, we assume a lower markup (85 percent) so that our results can be more generally relevant to future markets, where we think the average markup will fall over time from the effects of technology, efficiency, and competition.

[2] Assumes that CDTFA reported tax collections include both state and county taxes, thus an average sales tax rate of 8.3 percent.

each quarter since California's regulated cannabis market began. In our simple model, the implied quantities are just CDTFA's reported tax revenue ($86.3 million for all of 2019) divided by the tax rate ($148 per pound at the farm in 2019), which generates an estimate of $86,300,000/$148 = 583,000 pounds cultivated in 2019.

As shown in Table 13.3, from 2018 to 2019, the total weight of licensed cannabis cultivated in California more than doubled, from about 243,000 pounds to about 583,000 pounds. Note that these and other calculations discussed above and shown in Table 13.3 do not incorporate complications from accounting for leaves and trim, which have a low tax rate and farm price and, as discussed above, are used in manufactured products.

Next, we use CDTFA's excise and sales tax collections to estimate total wholesale and retail revenues in California. Excise taxes provide a direct window onto licensed wholesale revenues and an indirect window onto licensed retail revenues. In 2018 and 2019, California's cannabis excise tax rate was 24 percent of wholesale revenue. We

estimate total wholesale revenues by dividing total CDTFA excise tax collections ($307.7 million for all of 2019) by 0.24 (24 percent) to get our estimate of $1.3 billion total wholesale revenues in California in 2019. This estimate is shown and broken down by quarter in the second ("total wholesale revenues") column of Table 13.3.

Officially, the state arrived at 24 percent by assessing a 15 percent tax on the product of the wholesale price times an assumed "markup" multiple of 1.6. But this is simply equivalent to a 24 percent tax on wholesale price. In 2020, although the published excise tax rate of 15 percent remained constant, the effective excise tax increased to 27 percent because the assumed markup multiple increased to 1.8. (This excise tax increase is discussed below and modeled as Simulation Scenario 1.)

Retail revenue can also be estimated, indirectly, from CDTFA's excise tax collections by assuming an average wholesale-to-retail markup and multiplying total wholesale revenues by the average markup. (Here, we mean the *actual* average markup in the California marketplace, not to be confused with CTDFA's assumed markup multiple that is used in calculating excise taxes.) We assume a wholesale-to-retail markup of 120 percent, based on our own price data and our previous findings on the overall cannabis market in California (Goldstein et al., 2019; Sumner et al., 2018). By multiplying our estimate of total wholesale revenues, as above ($307.7 million / 24% = $1.3 billion) by 2.2 (100% + 120% markup = 220%), we get our estimate of $2.8 billion in total retail revenues. Total retail revenue estimates based on excise taxes are broken down by quarter for 2018 and 2019 in the third column of Table 13.3.

California assesses a fixed state sales tax on all retailers, including cannabis retailers, plus an additional local sales tax that varies by county. In 2019, state sales tax was set at 7.25 percent and county sales tax averaged 1.05 percent, for a statewide average sales tax rate of about 8.3 percent (Sumner et al., 2018). Dividing total sales tax collections from cannabis purchases ($226.5 million in 2019) by 8.3 percent (our assumed sales tax rate) generates a California cannabis retail market size estimate of about $2.7 billion of total retail revenues in 2019—similar to the $2.8 billion estimate we arrived at via excise tax collections, assuming a 120 percent markup. Total retail revenue estimates based on sales taxes are broken down by quarter for 2018 and 2019 in the fourth column of Table 13.3.

Retail revenue increased by almost 80 percent year-over-year from 2018 to 2019. However, retail revenue did not grow substantially between quarters 3 and 4 of 2019. Despite the track-and-trace system, some cannabis that did not pay the cultivation tax may leak into the licensed retail market. If that is the case, then our estimate of quantity sold at the licensed retailers is an underestimate.

The fact that 583,000 pounds of cannabis were legally produced on California farms in 2019 does not mean that 583,000 pounds of cannabis were legally sold by California retailers in 2019. Cannabis, like many other agricultural products, must be processed, tested, packaged, labeled, distributed, received, priced, and listed before being sold at retail There is a time lag between production and retail sale and the quantity produced in a year does not directly line up with the quantity sold in the same year. Cannabis comes in many forms whose shelf life and consumer popularity vary considerably.

California's cannabis industry is new and expanding rapidly making a given year's quantity grown or manufactured a relatively poor estimate of the same year's quantity sold at retail. Data are not yet available (e.g., from California's track-and-trace system) about the length of the average retail cycle in the cannabis industry from "seed-to-sale." We handle the above uncertainties by making

About 700,000 pounds of cannabis were sold legally in California through medicinal cannabis retailers in 2017, and about 600,000 pounds of cannabis were sold legally in California through licensed cannabis retailers in 2019. However, about 2.1 million pounds were sold through the illegal market in 2017, and about 2.4 million pounds were sold through the unlicensed market in 2019.

Photo Credit: joshuaraineyphotography

Table 13.4. Estimates of the California Cannabis Market Size, Prices, and Quantities

Assumption	Assuming Retail Sale in Same Month of Production[1]	Assuming Retail Sale 3 Months after Production[2]	Assuming Retail Sale 6 Months after Production[3]
2019 Market Size Estimates Based on CDTFA Reported Sales Tax Collections			
7.25% Average Sales Tax[4]	583,000 lbs x $5,400/lb = $3.1B Retail Revenue	540,000 lbs x $5,800/lb = $3.1B Retail Revenue	472,000 lbs x $6,600/lb = $3.1B Retail Revenue
8.3% Average Sales Tax[5]	583,000 lbs x $4,700/lb = $2.7B Retail Revenue	540,000 lbs x $5,100/lb = $2.7B Retail Revenue	472,000 lbs x $5,800/lb = $2.7B Retail Revenue
2019 Market Size Estimates Based on CDTFA Reported Excise Tax Collections			
80% Actual Wholesale-to-Retail Markup	583,000 lbs x $4,000/lb = $2.3B Retail Revenue	540,000 lbs x $4,300/lb = $2.3B Retail Revenue	472,000 lbs x $4,900/lb = $2.3B Retail Revenue
120% Actual Wholesale-to-Retail Markup	583,000 lbs x $4,800/lb = $2.8B Retail Revenue	540,000 lbs x $5,200/lb = $2.8B Retail Revenue	472,000 lbs x $6,000/lb = $2.8B Retail Revenue
Averages of 200,000 California Online Retail Flower Prices We Collected in July 2019			
Statewide Averages	Average Storefront Price: $5,200/lb Average Delivery Price: $5,400/lb		
Our Estimated Range for 2019 Licensed Market	520,000–560,000 lbs x $5,000–$5,400/lb = $2.6B–$3B Retail Revenue		

Source: Estimated based on CDTFA reported sales tax, excise tax, and cultivation tax collection

Notes: Our estimates of cannabis quantity from CDTFA reported cultivation tax collections assume that all cannabis is dried flower taxed at $9.25/ounce in 2019. We do not account for lower-potency trim that is taxed at a lower level.

[1] 583,000 lb = estimated pounds of cannabis on which cultivation taxes were collected by CDTFA in 2019 Q1–Q4.

[2] 540,000 lb = estimated pounds of cannabis on which cultivation taxes were collected by CDTFA in 2018 Q4 + 2019 Q1–Q3.

[3] 472,000 lb = estimated pounds of cannabis on which cultivation taxes were collected by CDTFA in 2018 Q3–4 + 2019 Q1–Q2.

[4] 7.25 percent is the base state sales tax rate that is kept by the state. CDTFA is not clear in its reported sales tax revenue from cannabis whether or not the revenue includes additional county sales taxes that are collected by the state in addition to the 7.25 percent sales tax and then remitted back to local jurisdictions. Therefore we vary the sales tax rate assumption (including versus not including additional county tax) in the first two rows of this Table 13

[5] 8.3 percent is our estimate of the average sales tax rate including county taxes averaging 1.05 percent statewide in addition to the 7.25 percent base state sales tax.

market estimates, shown in Table 13.4, using three different assumptions about the average time from farm to retail sale: less than one month, three months, and six months.

In Table 13.4, the left most column of numbers, an unlikely boundary case, assumes that cannabis is sold at retail in the same month that it is produced and taxed at the farm. In this scenario, the 2019 estimate of 583,000 licensed pounds produced would correspond to 583,000 licensed pounds sold. However, the assumption of less than a one-month lag time between farm and retail sale is likely to overestimate the number of pounds actually sold at retail in 2019 (or in any given span of quarters within the data set of eight CDTFA reports since Q1 2018).

In the second column of Table 13.4, we assume—more reasonably, we think—that the average time from farm taxation to retail sale is three months (one quarter). Thus we assume that the volume of cannabis sold in 2019 quarters 1 through 4 would be best approximated by the volume of cannabis produced from 2018 quarter 4 through 2019 quarter 3. Using this assumption of retail sale averaging three months after production, there are 540,000 licensed pounds (43,000 fewer than in the initial no-lag scenario). Column 3 uses an even more conservative assumption about quantity by volume: a six-month average time from farm taxation to retail sale, where only 472,000 licensed pounds are sold at retail in 2019.

THE ECONOMIC PAST AND PRESENT OF CALIFORNIA CANNABIS

From 1996 to 2017, the medicinal cannabis segment operated for 21 years with no significant state regulation and a small and highly variable degree of regulation under local jurisdictions. In many municipalities, no cannabis retail storefronts were allowed, but delivery services made cannabis available to customers with medicinal recommendations.

Until 2017, medicinal cannabis buyers, in order to enter a retail store or order from a delivery service, were required to obtain, and renew annually, a medical document (not a prescription) signed by a California physician indicating that cannabis was recommended. In practice, such recommendations could be obtained via a very quick in-person visit. A patient would self-report medical symptoms indicating cannabis, and show that he or she (or his or her parent or legal caretaker) was a California resident aged 18 or over. The typical fee for an in-person appointment was about $50.

Starting around 2015, some doctors began offering these recommendations via websites with video-chat functionality. No video chat was required—only completion of an online form, proof that the patient was a California resident of legal age, and access to payment by credit card. Fees for online appointments were somewhat lower and permission was available within minutes. It is instructive to note that despite the ease of meeting the medicinal requirements, most cannabis remained outside this California-legal retail segment.

Proposition 64 legalized cannabis consumption. In June 2017, the California State Legislature enacted the Medicinal and Adult Use Cannabis Regulation and Safety Act (MAUCRSA), which specified the framework for taxing and regulating cannabis in California. The first set of regulations went into effect on January 1, 2018. Some MAUCRSA rules, however, were not enforced until later. Mandatory pesticide-testing rules went into effect between July 1, 2018 and January 1, 2019.

There are several specific challenges that complicate economists' contributions to helping policymakers, the public, and market participants understand the economics of the rapidly evolving legal and regulatory environment for cannabis in California. First, there are no official price or quantity data from the State of California or other government sources. Moreover, as documented above, most California

production and use has been and remains outside the legal channels for medical production, processing, sale, and use. Thus, a large industry developed in California that avoided compliance with auxiliary government regulations such as those administered by environmental, labor, public health, or tax authorities.

An important area of current regulation covers implementation of the track-and-trace system, which starts with seeds used in cultivation and continues through retail sales. Security measures require cameras, video archival, record keeping, security guards, secure destruction and disposal, and secure childproof packaging. Even more costly is the requirement that each batch of cannabis (with maximum batch size of 50 pounds) must be tested for a long list of microbial and chemical contaminants as well as for THC levels, moisture, and for some manufactured products, uniformity. The wholesalers are required to hold the cannabis products during testing and are responsible for submitting state excise and cultivation taxes.

Sumner et al. (2018) find that tests themselves are likely to cost more than $50 per pound. However, the largest cost derives from loss of product that fails the required tests, given zero tolerance for contaminants such as pesticides and microbials and the difficulty for growers to meet the very tight standard. Valdes-Donoso et al. (2019, 2020) estimate costs when a significant percent of product fails a test and must be destroyed as a result. The costs of testing and of lost inventory from failed batches depends on two main inputs: the average batch size and the failure rate. For instance, assuming a 5-pound average batch size and a 7 percent failure rate, the average testing compliance cost would be about $200 per pound. Given the same failure rate of 7 percent, if the batch size increased to 50 pounds (the legal maximum), then the cost per pound would be cut in half, to about $100.

Failure rates and batch sizes are rapidly changing. Recent data from the Bureau of Cannabis Control suggests that the failure rate has recently fallen below 5 percent (Valdes-Donoso et al., 2020). Cannabis Benchmarks (2020) reports the current average batch size at only about 4 pounds, but this may represent a biased sample of sellers. Considering the best available evidence, we estimate that in 2020, average testing costs may fall slightly below $100 per pound.

Table 13.5. Summary of Regulatory and Tax Costs Per Pound for California Cannabis Market, 2020

Estimated Regulatory Costs per lb of Cannabis	2019 Licensed Costs	2020 Licensed Costs	2019 and 2020 Unlicensed Costs
	U.S. Dollars per Pound		
Cultivators' Costs of Regulatory Compliance	50	50	0
Manufacturers' Costs of Regulatory Compliance	100	100	0
Testing Costs, Including Cost of Rejected Product	100	100	0
Distribution, Packaging, and Retail Regulatory Compliance	200	200	0
Total Estimated Regulatory Costs in $ per lb	450	450	
Estimated Tax Costs per lb			
State Cultivation Taxes	148	154	0
Local Cultivation, Testing, and Manufacturing Taxes	180	180	0
Local Cannabis Retail Taxes	5% of Retail Price[1] ~ $230	5% of Retail Price[2] ~ $240	0
State Excise Taxes[1]	24% of Wholesale Price[1] ~ $570	27% of Wholesale Price[1] ~ $640	0
State Sales Taxes	8.3% of Retail Price[1] ~ $450	8.3% of Retail Price[2] ~ $470	0
Total Estimated Tax Costs $ per lb	1,580	1,680	0
Total Estimated Taxes and Regulatory Costs $ per lb	**$2,030 per lb**	**$2,130 per lb**	**$0 per lb**

Notes: Tax calculations assume $5,000 per pound licensed retail price; U.S. dollars per pound of dried flower equivalent cultivated. Estimates rounded to nearest $5.

[1] Wholesale price assumed to be ~$2,375 (based on CDTFA excise tax, and retail price assumed to be ~$5,200 including state excise taxes (~120 percent retail markup). Excise tax calculated as (15% x 1.6 x wholesale price) for 2019, and (15% x 1.8 x wholesale price) for 2020. Local cannabis retail taxes applied to retail price not including state excise taxes or state sales taxes. State sales taxes imposed on retail price including state excise taxes and local cannabis retail taxes.

[2] Retail price for 2020 is adjusted upward to incorporate: (1) an additional $6 in cultivation tax that (assuming farm price of $1,200 and constant markup percentage) translates to $6 x (5200/1200) = $26 per pound; (2) an additional $70 in excise tax that (assuming wholesale price of $2,375 and constant markup percentage) translates to $70 x (5200/2375) = $153 per pound; so the total retail price is $26 + $153 = $179, which we round to $180 and add it to the 2019 retail price of $5,200 to get a 2020 retail price of $5,380.

Table 13.5 provides a summary of taxes, fees, and regulatory costs including those at the cultivation, manufacturing, wholesale and retail stages in 2019 and 2020. The retail taxes for cannabis are added in several steps from both state and local jurisdictions. As discussed above, the cultivation tax is $148 per pound in 2019 and $154 per pound in 2020. The state excise tax is 24 percent in 2019 and 27 percent in 2020; and the sales tax remains constant in 2019–2020 at about 8.3 percent.

The sales tax does not apply to medicinal cannabis sales if the buyer has a county-issued medical card in addition to the required medical recommendation. However, by all accounts, this exemption is rarely used by consumers.

Local cannabis retail taxes vary widely across the state. A survey of local taxes and fees that were implemented, scheduled, or likely in early 2018 indicated an average of 8.2 percent for adult-use cannabis and 7.8 percent for medicinal cannabis (Sumner et al., 2018). We assume that local cannabis retail taxes are applied to retail price not including excise or state sales tax, whereas state sales taxes are applied to retail price including state excise and local cannabis retail taxes. We recognize that retailers tend to avoid high-tax

Table 13.6. Estimated California Retail Cannabis Quantities, Prices, and Revenues, Legal vs. Illegal, 2017 vs. 2019

Market Segment	2017	2019
Legal Market	Medicinal in 2017	Licensed in 2019
Total Weight Sold at Retail (lb)	700,000	540,000
Average Retail Price Without Any Taxes ($/lb)	3,600	4,300
Average Retail List Price (Incl Cultivation & Excise Taxes but Not Sales & Local Cannabis Retail Taxes) ($/lb)	3,600	5,200
Average Retail Price After All Taxes ($/lb)	3,600	5,900
Total Retail Revenue (Incl Cultivation & Excise Taxes but Not Sales and Local Cannabis Retail Taxes) ($ Billion)	2.5	3.2
Legal's Share of Total Market by lb (%)	25	20
Legal's Share of Total Market by Revenue, Incl Cultivation & Excise Taxes but Not Sales & Local Cannabis Retail Taxes (%)	33	36
Illegal Market	Non-medicinal in 2017	Unlicensed in 2019
Total Weight (lb)	2,100,000	2,220,000
Average Retail Price ($/lb)	2,400	2,500
Total Retail Revenue ($ Billion)	5	5.6
Illegal's Share of Total Market by lb (%)	75	80
Illegal's Share of Total Market by Revenue (%)	67	64
Aggregate Market (Legal + Illegal)		
Total Weight (lb)	2,800,000	2,760,000
Average Retail Price ($/lb)	2,700	3,200
Total Retail Revenue	$7.5 billion	$8.7 billion

places for retail operations; especially given that regulations do not limit delivery operations from delivering across regulatory jurisdictions. We expect that many customers are willing to travel (or order from delivery services) across jurisdictions for a lower price. We thus use 5 percent as a statewide average local cannabis retail tax.

Table 13.6 shows our estimates of the prices and quantities in the legal and illegal (or unlicensed) California retail cannabis market in 2017, before MAUCRSA regulations were implemented; and in 2019, the second complete year under MAUCRSA. We estimate that about 700,000 pounds of cannabis were sold legally in California through medicinal cannabis retailers in 2017, and that about 600,000 pounds of cannabis were sold legally in California through licensed cannabis retailers in 2019. We estimate that 2.1 million pounds were sold through the illegal market in 2017, and that about 2.4 million pounds were sold through the unlicensed market in 2019.

SIMULATION OF LIKELY EFFECTS OF CHANGES IN TAX RATES AND REGULATIONS

What are the impacts of taxes and regulations on cannabis purchases in the legal (licensed) and illegal (unlicensed) segments? We designed a simulation model to assess how changes in taxes on licensed cannabis producers and distributors affect the two market segments for cannabis in California. Cannabis is assumed to be available in two types: licensed and unlicensed. For simplicity, we assume that the retailer is also the distributor and that there is no intermediate wholesaler or manufacturer in the supply chain.

Licensed cannabis gets taxed at two stages. First, cultivation tax is applied to cannabis produced by licensed cultivators (growers). Cultivation tax is additive and is applied in dollars per pound of dried flower equivalent. We convert this specific tax to an ad valorem equivalent in order to simplify log-transformation of this model. The wedge between wholesale and retail prices includes wholesale-to-retail markup, excise taxes, sales taxes, and local taxes. First, excise tax is applied to wholesale price plus a multiple that the state calls a "markup" (but is distinct from the actual markup as we discuss it elsewhere). Local municipal tax is applied to a cannabis price exclusive of the excise tax. State sales taxes—which include California state tax and county sales tax—are applied to a cannabis price that already includes cultivation, excise, and local municipal taxes.

Our model allows us to calculate changes in quantities and prices for licensed and unlicensed cannabis as a function of exogenous demand shifters and taxes. We parameterize our model using values of initial prices and quantities, markups and taxes, and elasticities. Reliable data and parameter values to calibrate the model and specify the demand and supply equations are difficult to develop for cannabis. Little or no useful econometric estimations for cannabis have been published. Moreover, even basic data on quantities (and, to a lesser degree, prices) is not available from normal sources.

We use our best estimates of key supply and demand parameters for licensed and unlicensed cannabis, and

substitutability between cannabis from the two market channels taken from interviews with industry sources and by analogy with other farm products that share similar characteristics with some aspects of cannabis. That is, we use information from other products and our own experience with the industry to specify the models.

We assume some consumer willingness to pay extra for legal cannabis because of testing, product security, and perhaps convenience or customer service advantages. The notion that safety testing and government assurances of testing and safety can increase willingness to pay is widely incorporated in analysis of demand for other agricultural products (Pouliot and Sumner, 2008; Saitone, Sexton, and Sumner, 2016; and Gray et al., 2005).

The farm supply elasticity of cannabis in each segment is 5.0, which reflects the fact that cannabis requires few specialized resources and will be a very small share of the space available in greenhouses, warehouses, or outdoor plots (Matthews and Sumner, 2017). The demand elasticity for cannabis overall is taken to be quite inelastic. We use -0.2 from Jacobi and Sovinsky (2016), but this parameter is of little importance in the main results. We assume own-price demand elasticities to be –2 for both licensed and unlicensed cannabis, and calculate cross-price elasticities between licensed and unlicensed cannabis. Cross-price elasticity between licensed and unlicensed cannabis is calculated to be 7.57, and between unlicensed and licensed cannabis: 0.40.

Other parameters included in the model are volumes and prices for licensed and unlicensed cannabis, as well as taxes for licensed cannabis, which are discussed at length earlier in this chapter.

Table 13.7. Simulated Impacts of Small Changes in Tax Rates and Regulations

	Simulation Scenarios	
	1 **Small Tax Rate Increase** **(Changes Implemented January 1, 2020)**	**2** **Allowing More Retail Hours** **of Operation per Day**
Variables	Percent Change	
Total Quantity of Cannabis	−0.1	0.4
Quantity of Licensed Cannabis	−2.3	8.4
Quantity of Unlicensed Cannabis	0.4	−1.5
Retail Price of Licensed Cannabis	1.5	1.7
Retail Price of Unlicensed Cannabis	0.1	−0.3
Price Received by Licensed Suppliers	−0.5	1.7
Price Received by Unlicensed Suppliers	0.1	−0.3

SCENARIO 1. HIGHER TAXES

On January 1, 2020, the State of California raised its two main cannabis taxes: the cannabis cultivation tax (from $148 to $154 per pound of cannabis flower cultivated) and the cannabis excise tax. The markup used to calculate the excise tax rate also increased from 0.6 to 0.8, resulting in an effective excise tax increase from 24 percent of wholesale price to 27 percent of wholesale price (a 12.5 percent increase in the excise tax rate). This is the first simulation scenario we consider. Results are reported in Table 13.7.

In Simulation Scenario 1, the quantity of licensed cannabis is projected to decline by about 2.3 percent, or about 12,000 pounds, while quantity of unlicensed cannabis is projected to increase by about 0.4 percent, or about 9,000 pounds. As a result, total quantity of cannabis will decline slightly by 0.1 percent, or about 3,000 pounds. Therefore, the new tax policy accomplishes a slight reduction in the total amount of cannabis consumed in California, but with a shift of 9,000 pounds from the licensed to the unlicensed market segment.

SCENARIO 2.
MORE HOURS OF OPERATION

The state may want to consider implementing regulations that increase the share of licensed cannabis relative to unlicensed cannabis, while causing few changes in costs to the state. Currently, licensed cannabis retailers have restricted hours of operation from 9 a.m. to 10 p.m.. This regulation makes licensed cannabis less available to consumers who want to shop outside of those hours.

In 2017, we estimated that about 13 percent of the opening hours of medicinal cannabis retailers that existed in the unregulated pre-MAUCRSA market fell outside of legally allowable hours of operation for licensed cannabis retailers under MAUCRSA (Sumner et al., 2018). Between 10 p.m. to 2 a.m., which are busy hours for cannabis delivery in some areas, unlicensed retailers are the only option available to consumers. Some consumers will adjust to the 10 p.m. curfew and buy in advance from licensed retailers, whereas others will not.

In California, we assume that eliminating this restriction on operating hours would increase consumer demand for licensed cannabis by 7 percent, defined as an outward (right) shift in demand. This is the second simulation scenario we consider. Results are reported in Table 13.7.

Under Scenario 2, demand for licensed cannabis is estimated to increase by 8.4 percent, or about 45,000 pounds; the demand for unlicensed cannabis—to decrease by 1.5 percent, or about 33,000 pounds, and total demand for cannabis to increase by about 0.4 percent, or 12,000 pounds.

COVID-19

In spring 2020, the spread of COVID-19 (Coronavirus) resulted in the declaration of state and Federal emergencies and several temporary regulations governing retail markets and buying behavior. These included statewide and local "shelter-at-home" orders. Initially, many cannabis retailers reported a bump in revenues as consumers rushed to buy cannabis. Although many licensed storefronts remained open after cannabis was deemed by the state to be an "essential" good, we expect that COVID-19 will result in an overall shift away from storefront retailers and toward delivery-only retailers.

Preliminary data in late March 2020 indicate an increase of 230 percent in cannabis revenues reported by Weedmaps in the first week after Governor Newsom issued his "shelter-in-place" order (*Wall Street Journal*, 2020). We assume that this increase in revenues came from a combination of licensed and unlicensed retailers, although no statements were made by Weedmaps or the journalists covering the story about the license status of retailers that had experienced increases in business during COVID-19 lockdown.

Our research suggests that a larger share of delivery-only retailers are unlicensed, whereas licensed retailers have a higher proportion of storefronts. The shift to delivery generated by COVID-19 restrictions is thus likely to cause a temporary increase in the share of unlicensed cannabis, and a decrease in the share of licensed cannabis, in the California market for in-state consumption.

Effects of COVID-19 on overall consumption are unclear, but with consumers spending more time at home, recreational consumption may increase as other forms of recreation are limited by COVID-19 restrictions. This is consistent with the early Weedmaps data (*Wall Street Journal*, 2020).

CONCLUSION

After the first two years of the introduction of California state cannabis regulations and taxes, it is clear that the licensed cannabis market will continue to account for only a minority of retail sales for as long as unlicensed and untaxed sellers continue to maintain a substantial price advantage, as they do now. Licensed producers and sellers could eventually gain more market share if their prices fall as scale increases, the industry consolidates, and a few large, highly efficient producers and distributors dominate the market. This happened historically in other highly regulated industries, where significant compliance costs are introduced by the government, such as tobacco, alcohol, and pharmaceuticals. A policy option would be to lower costs of taxes and regulations enough that prices in the licensed market could decline substantially. So far, this option has not been pursued in California. On the contrary, state cannabis tax rates were raised in 2020, which we expect will have the effect of expanding the unlicensed market and shrinking the licensed market.

REFERENCES

Bureau of Cannabis Control (BCC). 2019. Cannabis Regulations. Available at: www.bcc.ca.gov.

CDTFA. 2020. California Department of Tax and Fee Administration Reports Cannabis Tax Revenues for the Fourth Quarter of 2019. News Release, March 6, 2020. Available at: https://www.cdtfa.ca.gov/news/20-03.htm.

Cannabis Benchmarks, 2018–2020. Premium Reports, Wholesale Price Data Archive. New Leaf Data Services. Available at: www.cannabisbenchmarks.com.

Eschker, E., J. Kaplan, J. Zender, F. Krissman, J. Meisel, and A. Silvaggio, 2018. "Standardized Regulatory Impact Assessment (SRIA). Proposed Regulations for Manufacturers of Adult-Use and Medicinal Cannabis." Humboldt Institute for Interdisciplinary Marijuana Research. Available at: http://www.dof.ca.gov/Forecasting/Economics/Major_Regulations/Major_Regulations_Table/documents/SRIA_Manufacturers_Cannabis_CDPH_4-11-18.pdf.

Goldstein, R. 2019. "Half-blind Tasting: A Deception-Free Method for Sizing Placebo and Nocebo Responses to Price and Packaging Attributes." *Journal of Wine Economics* 14(3): 321-331.

Goldstein, R., and D.A. Sumner 2019. "California Cannabis Regulation: An Overview." *California Agriculture* 73 (3–4): 101-102.

Goldstein, R., R. Saposhnik, and D.A. Sumner. 2020. "Prices of Cannabis in California from Licensed and Unlicensed Retailers." *ARE Update* 23(3): 1–4. University of California Giannini Foundation of Agricultural Economics. Available at: https://s.giannini.ucop.edu/uploads/giannini_public/70/d1/70d16c7a-3e45-4769-8e6c-f78e2c6f3135/v23n3_1.pdf.

Goldstein, R., D.A. Sumner, and A. Fafard. 2019. "Retail Cannabis Prices in California Through Legalization, Regulation and Taxation." *California Agriculture* 73 (3–4):136-145.

Gray, R.S., D.A. Sumner, J.M. Alston, H. Brunke, and A.K.A. Acquaye. 2005. "Economic Consequences of Mandated Grading and Food Safety Assurance: Ex Ante Analysis of the Federal Marketing Order for California Pistachios." Monograph 46. University of California Giannini Foundation of Agricultural Economics, March 2005. Available at: http://giannini.ucop.edu/publications/historic/monographs/.

Jacobi, L. and M. Sovinsky. 2016. "Marijuana on Main Street? Estimating Demand in Markets with Limited Access." *American Economic Review* 106-8: 2009-45.

MacEwan, D., D. Newman, R.E. Howitt, J. Noel, and M. Driver. 2017. "Economic Impact Analysis of CalCannabis Cultivation Licensing Program Regulations. Standardized Regulatory Impact Assessment (SRIA)." ERA Economics LLC. Available at: http://www.dof.ca.gov/Forecasting/Economics/Major_Regulations/Major_Regulations_Table/documents/Cultivation_SRIA_CDFA_1-5-2018.pdf.

Matthews, W.A., D.A. Sumner, J. Medellín-Azuara, and T. Hanon. 2017. "Economics of the California Cut Flower Industry and Potential Impacts of Legal Cannabis." University of California Agricultural Issues Center. Available at: http://www.cafgs.org/assets/docs/final_calflower_report-web.pdf.

Pouliot, S., and D.A. Sumner. 2008. "Traceability, Liability and Incentives for Food Safety and Quality." *American Journal of Agricultural Economics* 90(1): 15-27.

Saitone, T.L., R.J. Sexton, and D.A. Sumner. 2015. "What Happens When Food Marketers Require Restrictive Farming Practices?" *American Journal of Agricultural Economics* 97(4): 1021-1043.

Schroyer, J. 2020. "Proposed Regulatory and Tax Reforms in California Could Make Life Simpler for Marijuana Businesses." *Marijuana Business Daily*, January 16, 2020. Available at: https://mjbizdaily.com/proposed-regulatory-and-tax-reforms-in-california-could-make-life-simpler-for-marijuana-businesses/.

Substance Abuse and Mental Health Services Administration. 2014. Results from the 2013 National Survey on Drug Use and Health: Summary of National Findings. NSDUH Series H-48, HHS Publication No. (SMA) 14- 4863. Substance Abuse and Mental Health Services Administration.

Sumner, D.A., R.S. Goldstein, H. Lee, W.A. Matthews, Q. Pan, J. Medellin-Azuara, T. Hanon, P. Valdes-Donoso, and J. Lapsley. 2018. "Economic Costs and Benefits of Proposed Regulations for the Implementation of the Medicinal and Adult Use Cannabis Regulation and Safety Act (MAUCRSA)." Standardized Regulatory Impact Analysis, including Appendix.

Valdes-Donoso, P., D.A. Sumner, and R.S. Goldstein. 2019. "Costs of Mandatory Cannabis Testing in California." *California Agriculture* 73(3–4): 154-160.

Valdes-Donoso, P., D.A. Sumner, and R.S. Goldstein. 2020 "Costs of Cannabis Testing Compliance: Assessing Mandatory Testing in the California Cannabis Market." PLOS One, forthcoming.

Wall Street Journal. 2020. Staff Editorial. "California Deems Pot an Essential Coronavirus Business." 24 March 2020. Available at: https://www.wsj.com/articles/california-deems-pot-an-essential-coronavirus-business-11585005903.

Weedmaps. Available at: http://weedmaps.com

CHAPTER 14. MARKETING CALIFORNIA'S AGRICULTURAL PRODUCTION

HOY F. CARMAN

ABSTRACT

Efficient marketing of California's agricultural output is critical for the long-run survival of the industry. Marketing costs typically account for more than 75 percent of the retail price of food products due to processing, packing, transportation, retail sales, and other marketing functions. California producers are relatively distant from many important markets and they have high input costs, especially for labor, land, and water. They have been able to overcome these issues and effectively compete in national and international markets through constant technical and economic innovations. California producers have embraced mandated marketing programs as a tool to fund production, marketing, and nutritional research, to develop and fund product grades and standards, to coordinate product shipments, to fund demand-enhancing advertising and promotion programs, and to provide current information on crop production, prices, and shipments. California now has 61 government-mandated commodity programs, including 38 marketing orders and 20 commissions that recently collected and spent over $317 million on programs to improve their returns.

ABOUT THE AUTHOR

Hoy F. Carman is an emeritus professor in the Department of Agricultural and Resource Economics at the University of California, Davis, and a member of the Giannini Foundation of Agricultural Economics. Hoy can be contacted by email at carman@primal.ucdavis.edu.

The widespread use of government-mandated marketing programs is a distinguishing feature of marketing California agricultural products. The California walnut industry has had a federal marketing order since 1948 that supports domestic promotion and research programs. Above is an example of point-of-sale materials created for the California Walnut Board's American Heart Month campaign.

Photo Credit: California Walnut Board

CHAPTER **14.** TABLE OF CONTENTS

INTRODUCTION

Marketing California's agricultural output presents unique opportunities and challenges. California's climate permits production of the most diversified mix of crops in the United States, including a large variety of specialty products that are not grown extensively in the other 49 states. Because of the large variety and sheer volume of products, seasonality of production, customer preferences, product features, and distance to major markets, marketing this annual output is complex, costly, and critically important to the long-term maintenance of a profitable and dynamic agricultural economy.

The California Department of Food and Agriculture estimates that the state produces over 400 crop and livestock commodities and is the leading U.S. producer of 74 (*California Agricultural Statistics Review*, 2015–2016). Among these commodities, California is the sole producer (99 percent or more) of 14 crops, with nut crops (almonds, walnuts, and pistachios) being the most important in terms of cash income. California's cash income from agricultural commodities marketed during 2015 totaled $47.07 billion. The horticultural sector accounted for approximately 65 percent of total cash income, with fruit and nut crops contributing $17.98 billion (38 percent), vegetables and melons contributing $8.85 billion (19 percent), and nursery products and floriculture adding $3.92 billion (8 percent). Livestock and poultry (25 percent), field crops (5 percent), and all other crops (5 percent) accounted for the remaining 35 percent of commodity cash income.

California's leading position in U.S. fruit, vegetable, and tree nut production is explained by climatic, technological, and infrastructure advantages, as well as the market- and consumer-driven orientation of its agribusiness managers. Given the importance of horticultural crops to California agriculture and to the nation, the discussion of marketing institutions, programs, and strategies draws heavily on examples from this sector.

California producers and supply chain intermediaries face many challenges in providing high-quality, safe, nutritious, and readily available specialty crop products to national and international consumer markets. Many of California's fruits and vegetables are highly perishable and

bulky, the majority of markets are distant, and production is seasonal. In addition, the major markets are mature, meaning that population growth rates and the income elasticity of demand for food are low, so that aggregate food consumption expands very slowly, if at all.

U.S. consumers are generally well fed, the share of per-capita income allocated to food has decreased over time, and firms are essentially competing for "share of stomach." This competition has intensified given the high rate of new product introductions and the expanded, year-round availability of formerly seasonal items, often through imports. These factors have led to a greater array of substitute products, increased services as part of the product bundle, and increased competition for shelf space as retailers attempt to optimize product assortments.

A growing segment of U.S. consumers is focusing on the nutritional and health benefits of food products when making their purchasing decisions. Producers, commodity firms, and marketing organizations are well aware of this market segment and continue to respond with changes in the supply chain that emphasize choice of crops, production practices, distribution, and communication with their target consumers. Government diet recommendations emphasize increased consumption of fruits and vegetables, grower organizations are funding research on the nutritional attributes of their products and the health benefits from their consumption, and firms at all levels of the marketing channel are promoting nutrition, health, and fitness.

Dissemination of favorable research results, through public relations and promotion, about the contributions to health and disease prevention of almonds, walnuts, pistachios, blueberries, avocados, strawberries, and grapes are associated with increases in demand for these commodities. A research-backed health claim can be a powerful marketing tool, but the FDA's standards for approval of such a claim are high. The demand for certified organic products increased, and organic production has shifted from small to larger growers as retailers have expanded their offerings (Klonsky and Richter, 2011). The U.S. Department of Agriculture's (USDA) National Agricultural Statistics Service (NASS) 2014 Organic Survey found that

California led the nation in organic sales, accounting for $2.2 billion (40 percent) of the total $5.5 billion United States organic sales[1] (*USDA Census of Agriculture, Organic Survey*).

California's agricultural bounty presents marketing opportunities. Through the diversity of its agricultural production, firms marketing California produce have the opportunity to provide food retailers with complete lines of fruits, vegetables, and nuts. Because California produces a large share of the U.S. supply of key commodities—almonds, lemons, olives, lettuce, navel oranges, prunes, raisins, strawberries, table grapes, pistachios, processing tomatoes, and walnuts—California producers and marketers traditionally had unique opportunities to exercise control over the markets for those commodities. However, the expanding world supply of many commodities has reduced California's share, increasing competition and presenting new marketing challenges.

---

1   Washington ranked 2nd (515 million) and Oregon was 4th (237 million) for U.S. organic sales in 2014.

THE IMPORTANCE OF MARKETING

This chapter documents the importance of marketing for both U.S. and California agricultural products and highlights the institutions that have emerged and the strategies that have been pursued by California's food marketing sector to compete effectively in constantly evolving national and international markets.

Marketing functions account for the largest share of each U.S. dollar spent for food, and the percentage of total food costs attributed to marketing has been increasing over time. Food marketing costs thus will continue to have an important impact on the welfare of both farmers and consumers. The U.S. Department of Agriculture (USDA) maintains two general measures of relative food costs. The market basket consists of the average quantities of food that are purchased for consumption at home and mainly originate on U.S. farms. USDA tracks retail food prices and the associated producer revenues for nine major commodity groups including meats, poultry, eggs, dairy products, fats and oils, fresh fruits, fresh vegetables, processed fruits and vegetables, and bakery and cereal products.

Carman, Cook and Sexton (2003) used the original Economic Research Service (ERS), USDA marketing bill series to trace the farm share of the market basket for all food from 1950 through 2000. They noted that the farm share of the market basket declined from 41 percent in 1950 to 31 percent in 1980, 24 percent in 1990, and 15.8 percent in 2000. Using data through 2001, they pointed out that meat, dairy and poultry products, which traditionally had farm values of more than 50 percent of the retail value, all returned less than half of the retail value to farmers. Because of measurement problems and discontinuation of several data series used for the share calculations, ERS replaced the marketing bill series with a new series named the food dollar series.

Table 14.1. Distribution of U.S. Food Marketing Costs for Each Dollar Spent on: All Food, Food at Home, and Food Eaten Away From Home, Each with Farm Share, $U.S., 2015

	All Food	Food at Home	Food Away from Home
Marketing Cost Categories		Cents per Food Dollar	
Agribusiness	2.2	3.5	0.7
Farm Production	8.6	13.5	3.0
Food Processing	15.6	24.8	5.0
Packaging	2.5	3.0	2.1
Transportation	3.5	5.1	1.6
Wholesale Trade	9.3	14.4	3.4
Retail Trade	12.7	23.3	0.5
Foodservices	34.4	1.0	72.1
Energy	4.0	4.5	3.6
Finance and Insurance	3.4	3.6	3.2
Advertising	2.6	2.3	3.3
Legal and Accounting	1.3	1.1	1.6
Total	100.0	100.0	100.0
Farm Share	15.6	24.1	5.3

Source: Economic Research Service (ERS), U.S. Department of Agriculture (USDA) Food Dollar Series, https://www.ers.usda.gov/data-products/food-dollar-series/

The new food dollar series is composed of three primary data series (Canning). They include: (1) the marketing bill series; (2) the industry group series; and (3) the primary factor series. The marketing bill series divides the food dollar between farm and marketing shares. The industry group series identifies the distribution of the food dollar among 10 distinct food supply chain industry groups. Finally, the primary factor series identifies the distribution of the food dollar in terms of U.S. worker salaries and benefits, rents to food industry property owners, taxes and imports. Each of the three primary series is disaggregated into two commodity groupings (food and food & beverage) and three expenditure categories (total food, food at home, and food away from home).

For example, a trend affecting U.S. food marketing is the changing ratio of food expenditures at home and away from home, with an increasing portion of total food expenditures occurring away from home. This is important because marketing costs are higher per dollar of food expenditures made away from home. While the overall farm share of all food expenditures was 15.6 percent in 2015, the farm share for food expenditures made away from home was only 5.3 percent versus a farm share of 24.1 percent for food expenditures at home.

The present supply chain and institutional framework used by California producers to market diverse products have evolved over time and continues to change. They are a function of market development, the changing structure of competition, forward-thinking, and informed leadership.

CALIFORNIA AGRICULTURAL MARKETING COOPERATIVES

Cooperatives are firms owned by the producers who utilize the firm's services, although many cooperatives also do business with nonmembers (cooperative law specifies that at least 50 percent of business volume must be conducted with members). Commodity producers who are members of a marketing cooperative can be viewed as having vertically integrated downstream into the packing or processing and marketing of their production. A number of incentives can account for producer cooperative integration, including avoidance of processor market power and the reduction of both margins and risks (Sexton and Iskow, 1988).

Marketing cooperatives have had an important role in the growth and development of California's specialty crop sector. In fact, marketing cooperatives are closely linked with the development of many important California crops even as their roles have changed over time. Many consumers continue to identify the commodity with a cooperative brand, such as Blue Diamond (almonds), Calavo (avocados), Diamond (walnuts), Sunsweet (prunes), Sunkist (citrus), and Sunmaid (raisins). The market share of California marketing cooperatives has tended to decrease over time as production practices, competition, and markets have evolved. Large and once-dominant firms that no longer operate as cooperatives include Calavo and Diamond (both converted to public firms listed on the stock exchange); Tri-Valley Growers, a fruit and vegetable processor; the Rice Growers Association, a rice miller; and Blue Anchor, a diversified fresh fruit sales organization. The latter three declared bankruptcy in 2000.

The other four marketing cooperatives listed above rank among the 100 largest U.S. cooperatives in 2016 and 2015, as measured by gross revenue (USDA). In 2016, Blue Diamond Growers had revenues of $1.674 billion (#10); Sunkist Growers, Inc. had revenues of $1.208 billion (#18); Sunmaid Growers of California had revenues of $383 million (#78). In 2015, Sunsweet Growers, Inc. had revenues of $315 million (#98). Other California cooperatives in 2016's top 100 include California Dairies, Inc. with revenues of $3.002 billion (#6) and Pacific Coast Producers with revenues of $634 million (#47).

While cooperatives continue to be important in marketing California commodities, the loss of those mentioned above raised concerns among many observers about the future of cooperatives in the 21st century. All firms must adjust to a changing competitive environment; the question is whether or not marketing cooperatives can make the needed adjustments. Changes in food distribution, particularly at the retail level, pose challenges. Large retailers prefer to deal with suppliers who can provide products across an entire category during the whole year while satisfying product specifications such as the use of particular inputs, methods of production, and product traceability.

Traditionally, cooperatives are organized around a single or limited number of commodities and production is likely to be seasonal. Cooperatives can attempt to surmount these difficulties by undertaking marketing joint ventures and sourcing product from nonmembers, including internationally. Dealing with nonmembers, however, can create legal and equity issues for cooperatives that investor-owned competitors do not face. It is interesting to note that among the first actions taken by both Diamond and Calavo after converting to investor-owned firms were broadening of product lines and year-round and international sourcing of perishable product.

Cooperatives may also face challenges in procuring the consistent, high-quality production that the market place now demands. Cooperatives usually employ some form of pooling mechanism to determine payments to members. In essence, revenues from product sales and costs of processing and marketing flow into one or more "pools." The producer's share of the product marketed through each pool then determines his/her payment. The problem with some pooling is that high-quality and low-quality products are commingled, and producers receive a payment based upon the average quality of the pool. Such an arrangement represents a classic adverse selection problem, and tends to drive producers of high-quality products out of the cooperative to the cooperative's ultimate detriment. Cooperatives can solve this pooling problem by operating multiple pools and/or designing a system of premiums and discounts based upon quality, but the key point is that investor-owned competitors face similar hurdles in paying for the qualities of products they desire. Despite these limitations, large, well-managed marketing cooperatives can, at least, partially offset the market power of large food retailers.

THE ROLE OF MANDATED MARKETING PROGRAMS

The widespread use of government-mandated marketing programs is a distinguishing feature of marketing California agricultural products. California producers were at the forefront in adopting both federal and state marketing order and agreement programs authorized by the federal Agricultural Marketing Agreement Act of 1937 (AMAA) and the California Marketing Act of 1937, with amendments. The mandatory nature of the programs overcame the free-rider problems that had earlier led to a breakdown of cooperative-organized quality and supply control marketing efforts. The 1937 AMAA authorizing

marketing orders and agreements has been supplemented by federal legislation for individual commodities authorized by Congress and signed by the President as well as by the Commodity Promotion, Research and Information Act of 1996 that gives the USDA broad-based authority to establish national generic promotion and research programs for nearly all commodities either at its own initiative or upon the request of an industry group.[2] Commodity commissions and councils, each established by a specific law passed by the State Legislature and signed by the governor, supplement California's Marketing Act.

The procedures and requirements for establishing a government-mandated marketing program are spelled out in the enabling legislation and available on government websites. Basically, a group of producers and/or handlers of a particular commodity requests these programs, the Secretary of Agriculture or the state equivalent approves it, an industry vote gives further approval, and an assessment on all producers finances the program for the covered commodity. A critical requirement for obtaining a government-sponsored marketing program is the existence of strong and effective industry leadership. The leadership for several of California's early mandated marketing programs came from marketing cooperatives but, as cooperative influence waned, individuals and other groups provided the leadership. This leadership must work with commodity producers and handlers to define the nature of the commodities' economic problems and the suitability of available provisions for solving these problems.

The proposed legislation must be approved or enacted by government, typically after a series of public hearings, and then submitted to producers and handlers for a vote. The program submitted for an industry vote will include details on the provisions included, geographic coverage, assessment rates, operating procedures, governing structure, and requirements for approval and termination. Requirements for periodic evaluation of program performance and/or continuation are often included. The Secretary of Agriculture can terminate or suspend any federal marketing order that does not effectuate declared

---

2 Prior to 1996, all federal check-off programs to fund generic advertising and research were authorized by specific legislation for each individual commodity.

policy or whenever the Secretary determines that a majority of producers favor termination.

Marketing orders authorize three broad categories of activities: (a) quantity controls, (b) quality control, and (c) market support, such as advertising and research. Quantity or supply control provisions may take the form of producer allotments, allocation of product between markets based on location or product form (e.g., foreign and domestic or fresh and processed), reserve pools, and market flow regulations. Orders may also have quality control provisions that permit the establishment of minimum grades, sizes, and maturity standards. Advertising and promotion account for the majority of market support expenditures, with research in a distant second place; other market support activities include container regulations, price posting, and prohibition of unfair trade practices.

California producers utilize Federal and state marketing orders and agreements, commodity commissions and councils for solutions to their marketing problems and as a competitive tool to improve crop returns through research and demand expansion programs. Being able to select different programs operating under different legislative frameworks provides a flexible approach to tailoring a solution to the problem situation. The Agricultural Marketing Agreement Act of 1937, as amended, provides the framework for Federal marketing orders and agreements for fruits, vegetables, nuts and specialty crops.

A Federal marketing order can cover production in one or several states and may contain provisions for one or more of the following: generic advertising and sales promotion; production, processing and marketing research; quality regulations with inspection; supply management or volume control; the standardization of containers or packs; and the prohibition of unfair trade practices. California marketing orders and agreements, authorized by the California Agricultural Marketing Act of 1937, are available for a wider range of commodities and allow for more activities than federal orders but only cover California production. California legislation permits programs for advertising and promotion, research, the prohibition of unfair trade practices, product inspection, stabilization pools and the regulation of grades and standards.

California commodity commissions and councils are each established by a specific law passed by the state legislature and signed by the governor. While the provisions available to each commission are numerous, most concentrate on advertising, promotion and research. Councils tend to concentrate on education programs, promotion and research. The establishment of a commission typically requires an industry referendum, and the voting requirements are usually the same as for a marketing order. Councils have been established without an industry vote. California commodity commissions and councils have more program and budget autonomy than do marketing orders. They develop their own operating plans and budgets, with CDFA concurrence, and can hire executives and elect commission members without the CDFA's prior approval. Because of their flexibility, several existing commissions are replacements for marketing orders.

Each marketing order or commission program specifies a maximum assessment rate, usually in terms of dollars per unit of weight or as a percentage of total revenue. The Secretary of Agriculture (or California counterpart) approves assessment rates based on the budget recommendation of the marketing program administrative committee. To facilitate payment, the first handler level in the supply chain (channel of distribution) usually collects the marketing program assessments. Thus, for fruits, nuts, and vegetables, the assessments are paid by packinghouses and processors on behalf of the producers who deliver the product. Handlers and processors, in turn, deduct the assessments from payments to their producers.

Examples of recent levels of assessment for California programs include an assessment rate of $.04 per kernel weight pound for walnuts; California almonds also have an assessment rate of $.04 per pound effective August 1, 2016, through July 31, 2019, when the rate returned to $.03 per pound; the California Table Grape Commission had an assessment rate of $0.006087 per pound for the year ended April 30, 2016, and the California Avocado Commission had an assessment rate of $0.023 per dollar of sales on all varieties of avocados produced in California, effective from November 1, 2016, through October 31, 2017. Note that California avocado producers also paid an assessment of $0.025 cents per pound to the Hass Avocado Board for all Hass avocados sold.

Table 14.2. Number of Mandated Marketing Programs by Type, California, 1985–2016

Mandated Marketing Programs in California	Year			
	1985	1995	2005	2016
Federal Marketing Order	17	13	11	9
CA Marketing Order/Agreement	21	28	29	29
CA Commodity Commission	7	16	20	20
CA Commodity Council	2	4	3	3
Total	47	61	63	61

Sources: Data for 1985 and 1995 are from Lee et al., 1997; 2005 data are from Carman, 2007a

SCOPE OF PROGRAMS COVERING CALIFORNIA COMMODITIES

Government-mandated marketing programs cover commodities accounting for about two-thirds of the total value of California's agricultural output. In 2004, for example, the value of production of California commodities covered by 63 active marketing programs was almost $21.2 billion out of a total output of $31.8 billion. California producers paid marketing assessments of over $226 million in 2004–2005 and budgeted $154 million for advertising and promotion, $25 million for research, and almost $8.8 million for inspection programs. The number of active programs has changed over time in response to changing marketing issues. Overall, the trend in California has been an increase in the total number of programs, with the number of federal marketing orders decreasing and the number of California commodity commissions increasing (Table 14.2). More than half of the current programs have been established since 1980. Note that the number of programs has stabilized over the past decade. Current program coverage for California crops includes nine federal marketing orders, 29 California marketing orders and agreements, 20 commodity commissions, and three commodity councils for a total of 61 programs.

California commodity producers have been able to choose from several mandated marketing programs, with the selection depending on the problems faced and the goals of the particular commodity group. As noted, the programs chosen have tended to change over time as the nature of marketing problems changed. For example, increasing imports free-riding on U.S. commodity promotion and research programs were a catalyst for the Commodity Promotion, Research, and Information Act of 1996 that

facilitates assessments on imports to support domestic commodity promotion and research programs. The increasing number of California commodity commissions, each established by a specific law passed by the State Legislature and signed by the governor, can be explained by their increased flexibility in program provisions and group activities when compared to either federal or state marketing orders.

Commodity groups have changed programs over time, and some participate in more than one mandated marketing program. For example, California avocado growers conducted their promotion and research under a state marketing order program from 1961 until 1980 when they switched to a commodity commission. Then, faced with growing imports that were free-riding on their programs, California avocado growers, working through their commission, were instrumental in gaining passage of the Hass Avocado Promotion and Research Order (HAPO) in 2002. Now all Hass avocados sold in the U.S. (including imports) pay an assessment to support promotion and research programs.[3]

The California walnut industry has had a federal marketing order since 1948 that has supported domestic promotion and research programs. They added the California Walnut Commission in 1986 to take advantage of cost sharing

---

3 Note that the Hass variety accounts for over 95 percent of annual U.S. fresh avocado sales. Other varieties, often referred to as "green skins," are not widely available and typically sell at a significant discount relative to the Hass variety. Florida, which has its own federal avocado marketing order, is the main source of the other varieties available in the U.S. market. Green skin varieties typically account for less than 1.0 percent of California production and imports.

Table 14.3. Federal Marketing Orders for California Commodities: Budgeted Expenditures by Category, 2016–2017

| Federal Marketing Orders | Expense Category* | | | | Total Budgeted Expenditures |
	Administration	Promotion	Inspection	Research	
	U.S. Dollars				
Almonds	14,380,292	47,802,089		14,678,121	76,860,502
Dates	52,500				52,500
Grapes – CA Desert	80,000			28,500	108,500
Kiwifruit	108,450	2,500		10,000	120,950
Olives	513,000	823,500	98,000	390,830	1,825,330
Pistachios	547,900			125,000	672,900
Prunes – Dried	1,037,705	5,283,205		580,150	6,901,060
Raisins	1,625,750	3,577,178		35,000	5,237,928
Walnuts	1,769,170	19,447,830	825,000	2,098,000	24,140,000
Total	20,114,767	76,936,302	923,000	17,945,601	115,919,670

Source: Budget data for individual federal marketing orders are from two sources: the orders' administrative committees and USDA, AMS information provided in response to FOAI request 2018-AMS-01243-F

Note: * The data in the expenditure categories provide a broad overview of each program's activities but should not be regarded as an exact accounting for several reasons. Expenditures vary by program and often do not fit consistently into the four categories listed, some programs allocate what are essentially overhead expenses to research and promotion activities while others treat the same expenses as administration, and different programs may classify a particular activity, such as marketing research, in administration, research, or promotion.

U.S. government export promotion programs, with both programs administered by the same staff. Prunes also have two programs with the federal marketing order for dried prunes that emphasizes domestic promotion, and the state marketing order for dried plums that does export marketing activities.[4] Pistachios have both federal and state marketing orders with research accounting for most program spending. Pistachios also had a commodity commission that focused on promotion, but it was terminated in 2007 because growers supporting continuation represented only 41 percent of the voted volume (Cline, 2007). Raisins also have two programs—a federal marketing order and a state marketing order.

National Research and Promotion Programs

California producers also participate in National Research and Promotion Programs, commonly referred to as National Check-Off Programs. As noted on the USDA, Agricultural Marketing Service website, there are currently 22 of these programs, which establish a framework to pool resources to develop new markets, strengthen existing markets, and conduct important research and promotion activities.[5] Two of the national programs, the Paper & Packaging Board and the Softwood Lumber Board, serve large manufacturing companies. California agricultural producers participate in 15 of the remaining 20 national boards, councils, and programs including those for eggs, lamb, beef, Christmas trees, cotton, fluid milk, Hass avocados, Highbush blueberries, mushrooms, dairy products, honey, pork, processed raspberries, watermelon, and potatoes. The most recent annual budgets and assessment revenues for the 22 programs totaled over $639 million. Imports are subject to assessments to fund research and promotion for 17 of the 22 programs.

Federal and State Marketing Orders

The AMAA, as amended, provides the framework for federal marketing orders and agreements for fruits,

---

4 Dried prunes and dried plums are the same product. Prunes is the traditional descriptor but some prefer to use dried plums after motivational research found negative connotations associated with prunes.

5 For details on the individual programs, see: https://www.ams.usda.gov/rules-regulations/research-promotion.

Table 14.4. California Marketing Order and Agreement Programs: Budgeted Expenditures by Category, 2016–2017

	Expense Category*				Total Budgeted Expenditures
	Administration	Promotion	Inspection	Research	
California Marketing Orders		U.S. Dollars			
Alfalfa Seed Research	34,170			28,134	62,304
Artichoke	82,340	3,700		114,000	200,040
Dry Bean	135,160	53,060		81,000	269,220
Cantaloupe	105,700	113,000	155,000		373,700
Fresh Carrot	107,600	144,900		399,697	652,197
Celery Research	71,950			199,597	271,547
Cherry Mktg & Research	242,200	1,103,437		380,000	1,725,637
Citrus Nursery	62,164	26,425		303,161	391,750
Citrus Research	1,488,796			8,686,340	10,175,136
Dried Fig	528,550	820,884		4,200	1,353,634
Garlic & Onion Dehydrator	148,960		257,767	0	406,727
Garlic & Onion Research	78,800			137,730	216,530
Leafy Greens Research	348,650	0		1,204,097	1,552,747
Melon Research	106,050	0		102,160	208,210
Milk Processor	643,450	16,775,397			17,418,847
Market Milk	2,100,000	36,688,888		1,950,000	40,738,888
Cling Peach Grower	134,300	1,183,522		276,654	1,594,476
Pear	415,500	979,590		170,000	1,565,090
Pistachio Research	260,200			5,370,000	5,630,200
Dried Plum	1,367,000	6,778,096		930,000	9,075,096
Potato	75,660			70,566	146,226
Raisin Marketing	487,900	37,500		40,000	565,400
Rice Research	318,025			3,845,243	4,163,268
Wild Rice	40,200	68,862		41,000	150,062
Processing Strawberry	563,639		672,230	50,000	1,285,869
Processing Tomato	558,000		4,901,967	223,500	5,683,467
California Marketing Agreements					
California Grown	95,000	1,489,188			1,584,188
Leafy Green Handler	471,294	698,484	1,382,716		2,552,494
Wine Grape Inspection	99,235		1,861,600	75,000	2,035,835
Total	11,170,493	66,964,933	9,231,280	24,682,079	112,048,785

Source: Current California marketing program budget information provided by California Department of Food and Agriculture Marketing Branch, Sacramento, CA

Note: * The data in the expenditure categories provide a broad overview of each program's activities but should not be regarded as an exact accounting for several reasons. Expenditures vary by program and often do not fit consistently into the four categories listed; some programs allocate what are essentially overhead expenses to research and promotion activities while others treat the same expenses as administration, and different programs may classify a particular activity, such as marketing research, in administration, research, or promotion.

Table 14.5. California Commodity Commission and Council Programs: Budgeted Expenditures by Category, 2016–2017

	Expense Category*				Total Budgeted Expenditures
	Administration	Promotion	Inspection	Research	
CA Commodity Commissions			U.S. Dollars		
Apple	363,050	212,250		50,000	625,300
Asparagus	149,800	46,555		1,000	197,355
Avocado	3,375,000	8,710,000		647,000	12,732,000
Blueberry	159,800	209,800		40,000	409,600
Cut Flower	516,908	581,940		37,500	1,136,348
Date	91,300	219,900		497,400	808,600
Grape Rootstock	84,217			650,000	734,217
Olive Oil	155,500	60,000	95,000	191,000	501,500
Pepper	75,440			93,708	169,148
Rice	1,727,750	4,995,332	0	20,000	6,743,082
Sea Urchin	71,700	22,150		15,000	108,850
Sheep	75,333	137,084		6,364	218,781
Strawberry	2,477,491	6,317,358		4,394,640	13,189,489
Table Grape	790,537	15,195,204		1,599,312	17,585,053
Walnut	1,340,500	14,906,337		3,155,000	19,401,837
Wheat	334,000	263,681		330,000	927,681
Wine Grapes					
Lake County	163,189	252,776		187,380	603,345
Lodi	824,671	1,619,000		151,500	2,595,171
Sonoma	586,075	1,719,516		444,245	2,749,836
Councils					
Beef Council	812,250	1,088,455			1,900,705
Dairy Council	832,304	5,581,862		29,677	6,443,843
Salmon Council	38,122	0		0	38,122
Total	15,044,937	62,139,200	95,000	12,540,726	89,819,863

Source: Current California marketing program budget information provided by California Department of Food and Agriculture Marketing Branch, Sacramento, CA

Note: * The data in the expenditure categories provide a broad overview of each program's activities but should not be regarded as an exact accounting for several reasons. Expenditures vary by program and often do not fit consistently into the four categories listed, some programs allocate what are essentially overhead expenses to research and promotion activities while others treat the same expenses as administration and different programs may classify a particular activity, such as marketing research, in administration, research or promotion.

vegetables, nuts, and specialty crops. A federal marketing order can cover production in one or several states and may contain provisions for one or more of the following programs: generic advertising and sales promotion; production, processing, and marketing research; quality regulations with inspection; supply management or volume control; standardization of containers or packs; and the prohibition of unfair trade practices. California marketing orders and agreements are available for a wider range of commodities and allow for more activities than do federal orders but are only applicable to California production. California legislation permits programs for advertising and promotion, research, prohibition of unfair trade practices, product inspection, stabilization pools, and regulation of grades and standards.

The number of federal marketing orders applicable to California commodities decreased over the last three decades as producer and processor interest moved away from supply control programs. There are currently nine federal marketing orders applicable to California-produced commodities, down from the 17 that were effective in 1985 (Table 14.2). As shown in Table 14.3, the nine commodity programs' most recent annual budgets totaled over $115.9 million with the majority of the funds spent on advertising and promotion. The distribution of 2016–2017 program expenditures was 66.4 percent for promotion and 15.5 percent for research as compared to 2004–2005 program expenditures of 59.6 percent for promotion and 8.6 percent for research (Carman, 2007a). Total budgeted expenditures increased from $41,634,024 in 2004–2005 to $115,919,670 in 2016–2017, an increase of 278 percent. Comparison of budgets for the two periods reveals that almonds and walnuts, each of which experienced significant growth in acreage, production, and total crop income over time, accounted for a large portion of the increase.

There has been little variation in the number of California marketing orders since 1995 (Table 14.2), while total budgets have increased. Prior to the year 2000, overall budget increases tended to fund advertising and promotion programs. Spending during the most recent decade has moved away from promotion and toward research in both absolute and percentage terms. California state marketing order and agreement budgets totaled $101.4 million during 2004–2005, with $71.4 million allocated to advertising and promotion and $13.1 million to research programs (Carman, 2007a, p. 180). The total of the most recent budgets is just over $112.0 million, with the advertising and promotion budgets decreasing to $64.8 million and the research budgets increasing to $24.6 million (Table 14.4).

Different commodities emphasize different program activities. Among the largest programs, dairy (milk processor and market milk) dominates in the advertising and promotion expense allocation while the marketing orders for citrus, pistachios, and rice dominate commodity research spending.

Table 14.5 lists the most recent budgeted expenditures for California's commodity commissions and councils. The overall number of commissions decreased from 20 to 19 between 2005 and 2017 while councils remained steady at three. In terms of specific commodities, the Forest Products, Kiwifruit, Pistachio, and Tomato Commissions ceased operations while producers initiated new commissions for blueberries, olive oil, and Sonoma wine grapes. Overall,

California commodity commission budgets increased from $83.9 million in 2004–2005 (Carman, 2007a) to $89.8 million in 2017. The distribution of budgeted expenditures changed from 68.9 percent promotion and 10.0 percent research in 2004–2005 to 69.2 percent promotion and 14.0 percent research in 2017. Government-mandated marketing programs that focus on California commodities spent over $226.7 million in 2004–2005 with 67.9 percent of the total expenditures on promotion and 11.0 percent on research (Carman, 2007a). The total amount budgeted for federal marketing orders and California state marketing programs increased to almost $317.8 million in 2017, with 64.8 percent of expenditures on promotion and 17.3 percent on research (Tables 14.3, 14.4, and 14.5).

THE ECONOMIC EFFECTS OF MANDATED PROGRAMS

An objective of mandated marketing programs, as stated in the enabling legislation, is to improve producer returns through orderly marketing. Determination of the degree to which each program has met its objectives can sometimes be difficult to determine. Further, it almost always leads to serious discussions among producers concerning returns from advertising and promotion, the effectiveness of minimum quality and maturity standards, the benefits of industry supply controls, and the returns from industry-funded research. Possible impacts on other groups, including consumers and trading partners as well as overall effects on economic welfare, add to the controversy.

Disagreement over the impacts and effectiveness of mandated marketing program provisions have resulted in numerous public hearings and frequent litigation as critics have sought to modify or terminate specific programs. Legal challenges have included actions against provisions in the marketing orders for peaches and nectarines, kiwifruit, plums, apples, grape rootstocks, cut flowers, almonds, milk, cling peaches, California/Arizona citrus (lemons, Navel oranges & Valencia oranges), and table grapes. In recent years, four court cases, three concerning advertising and promotion and one on volume controls, were decided by the U.S. Supreme Court as discussed below.

VOLUME CONTROLS

Marketing order provisions that control the amount of product marketed can be a powerful economic tool when the commodity group controls most of the production and marketing of the commodity, demand is inelastic, and/ or there are different (separate) markets with different price elasticities of demand. Under these conditions, the commodity group can gain a measure of monopoly power and enhance returns by restricting the supply marketed, or by practicing price discrimination between markets. However, since marketing orders allow producers to control the amount of product marketed but not entry or the amount of product produced, any short-run price enhancement leads to longer-run supply response. It is not surprising that volume controls have been controversial— monopoly-pricing practices reduce the economic welfare of some consumers as well as distorting resource allocation decisions, while producers face all of the problems of maintaining a cartel. Marketing orders allow California commodity groups to control the quantity of product marketed by one or more methods: (a) market allocation, (b) reserve pools, and (c) market controls.

Market allocation programs control the amount of product going to a primary market with the remainder going to uncontrolled markets. In practice, controls were usually on the more inelastic fresh market, with uncontrolled product being processed or exported. In the case of the state marketing order for cling peaches (used only for canning), supply was controlled using a "green drop," tree removal, and cannery diversion (disposal of fruit that had been picked). Almonds, dates, raisins, and walnuts have implemented market allocation.

Reserve pools may require diverting a portion of a crop to a secondary (or noncompeting) market, or setting aside a portion of the crop for return to the market when prices are more favorable. The impact of a reserve pool depends on disposition of the product. If the product is diverted to a secondary market, the pool's impact is the same as a market allocation program; if the pool product is returned to the primary market, the impact is similar to a market flow program. The almond, walnut, raisin, and prune industries have utilized reserve pools. Market flow controls regulate the amount of product reaching a specified market during a given time period. Citrus prorates that controlled

weekly shipments of California/Arizona lemons or oranges to the domestic fresh market has been the principal use of this provision. The continuous use of weekly prorates essentially converts these flow controls to an allocation program where the crop is allocated between the domestic fresh market (with the most inelastic demand) and other outlets consisting of processing or exports.

While quantity control provisions were very popular during the early years of marketing orders, their use has decreased over time as a result of problems associated with monopoly pricing and lack of supply control. Six of California's nine marketing orders contain provisions for supply controls, but none are presently in use and there is little prospect for their use in the future. A brief review of supply controls for citrus, raisins, and almonds provides some insights concerning problems limiting their future use.

The Secretary of Agriculture terminated the federal marketing orders for citrus at the end of the 1993–1994 crop year, after more than 50 years of almost continuous use, because of a large number of lawsuits for violations of the prorate rules. The citrus prorates set the amount of lemons and oranges for shipping to the domestic fresh market on a weekly basis. Fruit in excess of a handler's fresh market prorated quantity could be exported or processed without limits. The fresh market demand facing lemon and orange packers is very inelastic relative to the demands in the export and processing markets. Thus, price discrimination in the domestic fresh market was both possible and profitable by restricting weekly fresh market sales.

Increased producer prices without any controls on entry (new plantings) led to increased new plantings for both lemons and Navel oranges. As these plantings reached bearing age and production increased, the administrative committees were forced to direct increasing proportions of the annual crop to exports and processing to maintain domestic fresh market prices. Average producer returns from all markets decreased over time as total production increased, until new plantings were no longer profitable. When compared to competitive market equilibrium, prorate resulted in increased acreage and production of citrus, as well as increased exports and processed products (Thor and Jesse, 1981; Shepard, 1986).

The economic impacts of marketing order prorate on the California/Arizona lemon industry were the focus of research studies by Smith (1961); French and Bressler (1962); Lenard and Mazur (1985); Kinney, Carman, Green, and O'Connell (1987); Carman and Pick (1988, 1990); and Richards, Kagan, Mischen, and Adu-Asamoah (1996). These studies found that weekly quantity controls could be used to enhance short-run prices and increase producers' revenues; that, over time, higher prices resulted in a supply response with increased cyclical acreage, production, and prices; in equilibrium, total lemon acreage tended to be greater with prorate; supply response to short-run price enhancement required increased diversions over time to processing and export markets to maintain total crop revenues; restrictive quantity controls increased consumer prices and reduced consumer surplus; that, because of supply response, long-term producer benefits from lemon prorate were likely quite limited; and the way prorate is used might determine the size of lemon marketing margins.

Some opponents of the citrus volume regulations, who had been sued in 1983 by the United States for violations of prorate, discovered evidence of over-shipments by a large number of competing orange and lemon packing houses. A series of lawsuits, investigations, and proposals for penalties under AMAA forfeiture rules threatened to keep the industry in court for many years and create economic hardships for industry participants, prompting the Secretary of Agriculture to terminate the California/Arizona citrus marketing orders on July 31, 1994, "to end the divisiveness in the citrus industry caused by over 10 years of acrimonious litigation."

California raisins provide another example of the long-term use of marketing order volume controls. Under the federal raisin marketing order, first effective in 1949, annual production was divided between free tonnage and a reserve pool controlled by the Raisin Administrative Committee (RAC). Only free tonnage could be sold on the domestic market, but the RAC could allow packers to buy additional tonnage for free use from the reserve when the RAC determined that supply and demand conditions justified such actions. The RAC disposed of the reserve raisins in "noncompeting" market outlets including exports, government programs (school lunch and charitable food distribution), sales to wineries for distilling into alcohol, donations to charity, and cattle feed.

Until 1977, prices for the majority of exported raisins in the reserve pool were much lower than prices received for free tonnage sold on the domestic market. Thus, the RAC sought to restrict sales in the domestic market where demand is inelastic and to sell the excess in export markets where demand is much more elastic. Conditions and markets changed, however, and beginning in 1977, exports were considered free tonnage shipments, and the initial free tonnage was increased to serve favorable export markets. Since 1977, the RAC has often exported reserve pool raisins at prices competitive with world prices but below prices on the domestic market.

The federal raisin marketing order has not implemented a reserve program since 2009 and is unlikely to do so in the future as a result of the U.S. Supreme Court's decision in the "Raisin Case." This case, decided in 2015, stemmed from the RAC's decision to set aside 47 percent of the 2002–2003 raisin crop. Marvin and Lena Horne were raisin growers and packers located in Kerman, California, and they objected to the program as an illegal taking of their property. After they refused to comply with the reserve provisions, they faced penalties of $695,000 for their noncompliance since 2002.

The Hornes' case eventually made its way to the U.S. Supreme Court, which ruled in an 8–1 decision that the raisin marketing orders' supply-management system violates the Takings Clause in the U.S. Constitution's Fifth Amendment. The Supreme Court also found that there is no difference between real and personal property and set aside the Hornes' fines and civil penalties. The Supreme Court's decision fueled numerous articles in the popular press concerning the need for and future of marketing order programs. As noted by Crespi, Saitone, and Sexton (2015), the raisin marketing order had unique features relative to other authorized volume-control provisions. They concluded, "Most importantly, the court's opinion does not challenge in any way the existence of mandatory marketing programs and the function they most often perform, such as funding research and promotions, and implementing grades and standards."

Finally, the experience of the California almond industry illustrates how changing market conditions can alter the effectiveness of volume controls. The federal marketing order for California almonds includes provisions for market allocation and a reserve pool. At the beginning of each marketing season, the Almond Board of California recommends to the Secretary of Agriculture a maximum annual quantity for sale in domestic and export markets (the market allocation) and the quantity that are not for sale (the reserve pool). The reserve may be designated unallocated or allocated reserve. The unallocated reserve is essentially forced storage; nuts can be released from the unallocated reserve as the season progresses or carried over to the following season. The allocated reserve must be utilized in noncompetitive outlets such as almond butter, almond oil, airline samples, or cattle feed.

The reserve provision of the almond marketing order was used to encourage export sales through 1972, while maintaining higher prices in the domestic market than in the export market. This price discrimination ended when export markets became an important outlet for California almonds (over two-thirds of the crop is now exported annually), with price elasticities tending to equalize between domestic and export markets. Recent work indicates that the price elasticity of demand for almonds is now more elastic in the domestic market than in major export markets, leading to the result that short-run revenue maximization through price discrimination could involve restricting sales to export markets (Alston et al., 1995). Recent models of acreage response to changing returns indicate that U.S. and Spanish producers each increase production when returns appear favorable (Murua, Carman, and Alston, 1993). Thus, if the Almond Board were to use the reserve to practice price discrimination and raise world almond prices, increased prices would stimulate production in Spain as well as the United States. As a consequence of these various considerations, the almond industry has not implemented volume controls for many years.

QUALITY CONTROLS

All existing federal marketing orders for California fruits, vegetables, and nuts include provisions for grades and minimum quality standards. However, only 10 California marketing programs include quality standards and inspection provisions and just seven actively use the provisions. The purpose of minimum quality standards is to maintain or enhance demand for a commodity by keeping inferior products off the market, thus avoiding the "lemons" problem, which occurs when a product has unobservable

characteristics for which the seller has much better information than the buyer. Fresh fruit prices normally decline over the season, giving growers strong incentives to ship fruit as early as possible, despite possible lack of maturity. Most consumers are unable to judge the maturity of fruit from appearance and may find that fruit that "looks good" does not "taste good." While the individual producer obtains a high price for this fruit, consumer dissatisfaction can adversely affect prices and subsequent sales of high-quality product by other producers later in the season. Indeed, representatives of many commodity groups believe that shipments of immature fruit have a negative impact on total sales and overall average prices because consumers delay repeat purchases. Maturity standards based on sugar content, firmness, and color are used by several marketing orders to determine when fruit is mature enough to be shipped.

The economic impact of minimum quality standards may be to: (1) increase the retail demand for a product, resulting in higher prices and/or increased sales; (2) reduce marketing margins—by reducing waste, with benefits accruing to —with benefits accruing to both producers and consumers; and (3) reduce supply, which can increase total revenue to producers if demand is inelastic. Any effective minimum quality standard will restrict the total quantity of commodity marketed, but supply control tends to be a by-product rather than the focus of such standards. Federal marketing order regulations on grade, size, quality, or maturity also apply to imports of the same commodities from other countries during the period the regulations are effective for the domestic product.

The use of some minimum quality standards has been controversial. Concerns include charges that quality standards are a hidden form of supply control, wasting edible fruit with the primary impact being on the poorest consumers, and that quality standards are sometimes not equitable because of seasonal and regional variations in production conditions. While empirical analyses of the economic impact of minimum standards of grade, size, and maturity for California commodities are limited, those available indicate that it is probably relatively small (U.S. GAO, 1985).

Assuring food safety is the newest use of minimum quality standards and inspection by mandated marketing programs. The purpose of these standards is to enhance product demand by reducing the chances of a food-safety incident, thereby increasing consumer confidence and preventing the costs of product recall or rejection. There are three California marketing programs currently stressing food safety: the Leafy Greens Products Handler Marketing Agreement (LGMA), the federal marketing order for pistachios, and the federal marketing order for almonds. The LGMA is a unique and rigorous science-based food safety system that protects public health by reducing potential sources of contamination and establishes a culture of food safety on the farm.[6] The LGMA emphasizes research-based standards and industry-wide training programs with mandatory government audits.

The main provisions of the federal marketing order for pistachios set standards and require testing for quality and aflatoxin, a cancer-causing mold that can contaminate many nuts and grains. Producers' concerns about the possible negative effects of an aflatoxin poisoning event were the major factor leading to the creation and adoption of the marketing order for pistachios, with support by more than 90 percent of the growers in a 2004 vote. Analysis of the pistachio marketing order program by Gray et al. (2005) projected significant positive returns from the growers' assessments, with benefit-cost ratios ranging from 3:1 to greater than 6:1, with 60 percent of the overall benefits going to domestic consumers.

Similarly, the Almond Board of California initiated a pasteurization program in 2006 in response to two food safety events. In 2001, a Salmonella outbreak in Canada was traced back to raw almonds from three orchards in California. Then in spring 2004, foodborne illnesses in Oregon from Salmonella were traced to raw almonds purchased from a retailer who obtained all supplies from one California handler. The handler initiated a voluntary recall that involved approximately 15 million pounds of almonds. All raw, natural almonds entering the domestic food distribution system are now pasteurized, and it is used in other markets, as requested, based on their local food safety preferences. In addition, California almonds transitioned from a Voluntary Aflatoxin Sampling Plan program to a Pre-Export Checks (PEC) program in August 2015. PEC was developed by the California almond industry to provide an aflatoxin-sampling plan for the

analysis of ready-to-eat products equivalent to that used by the European Union (EU) for official testing of incoming consignments. The program ensures the industry is not vulnerable to inconsistent or arbitrary controls (ABC, 2016).

ADVERTISING AND PROMOTION

Generic advertising and promotion account for the majority of funds collected by mandated marketing programs in the United States. The purpose of these expenditures is to increase demand for the advertised commodity so that the same amount of commodity sells for a higher price and/or more sells for the same price. The distribution of program benefits and the "free-rider problem" provide the basis for the rationale for mandatory support by all producers.[7] Research has documented significant increases in product demand and prices as a result of commodity advertising and promotion programs, with the net monetary benefits to producers being much greater than costs (Kaiser et al., 2005). For example, promotions led to statistically significant increases in demand and price in case studies for eight California crops (table grapes, eggs, prunes, avocados, almonds, walnuts, raisins, and strawberries) and benefit-cost estimates for four national checkoff programs (dairy, beef, pork, and cotton). Kaiser et al. (2005) wrote that "the overwhelming conclusion . . . is that mandated commodity marketing programs have been very profitable for California's agricultural producers. In every case, the evidence suggests that one can be reasonably confident that the benefits have well exceeded the costs and that it would have been profitable for producers to have increased expenditures on the programs."

Producer support for promotion programs is strong, but not unanimous, and litigation over mandatory assessments for advertising and promotion has occupied a number of programs since the 1980s. Several large growers have sued to avoid making payments for reasons that range from philosophical opposition to government interference

---

6 Interested readers can access information on the LGMA on the website: http://www.caleafygreens.ca.gov/

7 It is usually not economical for small, individual commodity producers to advertise, even with extremely high returns, as can be shown by a simple example. Suppose that returns from a generic advertising program are $200 for each dollar spent and that there are 1,000 equally small producers of the commodity. If an individual producer were to spend $100, the benefits to the industry would be $20,000 but since the benefits are distributed equally based on sales, the individual will obtain a return of only $20 for this $100 expenditure.

in marketing their products, a belief that they could obtain a better return promoting their own brand, and basic disagreements with the promotion message or operation of the program. Three cases concerning the constitutionality of generic promotion programs have been heard by the U.S. Supreme Court (Kaiser et al., 2005). In the 1997 case of Glickman v. Wileman Bros. & Elliott, Inc., et al., the Supreme Court ruled that federally mandated generic advertising for California peaches, plums, and nectarines did not violate the First Amendment of the U.S. Constitution. In the 5–4 ruling, the Court noted that the business entities that are compelled to fund generic advertising do so as part of a broader collective enterprise in which the regulatory scheme already constricts the freedom to act independently.

However, in 2001, the Supreme Court ruled in U.S. v. United Foods, that the national Mushroom Promotion Act of 1990 violated the First Amendment, setting off a flood of litigation against other promotion programs, with lower courts striking down several. Then in 2005, the Supreme Court agreed to hear a third promotion program case on an Eighth Circuit Court ruling that the national beef checkoff program was unconstitutional. In Livestock Marketing Association v. USDA, the Supreme Court ruled (May 23, 2005) that the national beef check-off program is constitutional. The ruling, which overturned lower court decisions, stated that the beef promotion messages were government speech that is not subject to certain First Amendment challenges. This ruling helped to settle pending litigation for several generic promotion programs and seemed to increase producer interest in promotional programs.

In addition to producer-funded promotion by marketing orders and commissions, the U.S. government also provides funds to many of the same organizations to expand agricultural commodity exports. The USDA's Foreign Agricultural Service's Market Access Program (MAP) provided $173.5 million in fiscal year 2017 funding to 70 nonprofit organizations and cooperatives. Included was over $30 million to California groups, with the majority of the funds directed to important export commodities (almonds, walnuts, pistachios, table grapes, raisins, citrus, prunes, and wine). California producers also benefitted from grants to national organizations supporting exports of dry beans, poultry and eggs, wheat and grains, rice,

cotton, and potatoes. The Foreign Agricultural Service also allocated Foreign Market Development Program (FMD) funds totaling $26.6 million in fiscal year 2017 to 26 trade organizations that represent U.S. agricultural producers. The FMD focuses on generic promotion of U.S. commodities, rather than consumer-oriented promotion of branded products, and organizations that represent an entire industry or are nationwide in membership and scope receive preference.

A recent study of the MAP and FMD programs indicates that they contributed $309 billion to farm export revenue between 1977 and 2014, an average of $8.2 billion per year (Williams et al., 2016). This study also found that from 2002 through 2014, the programs boosted average annual farm cash income by $2.1 billion, annual U.S. economic output by $39.3 billion, annual gross domestic product (GDP) by $16.9 billion, and annual labor income by $9.8 billion. In addition, the programs generated economic activity that directly created 239,000 new jobs, including 90,000 farm sector jobs.

RESEARCH

There were 28 California mandated marketing programs with research expenditures totaling almost $8.5 million in 1992 (Lee et al., 1996); this increased to 45 programs with expenditures of over $21.2 million in 2003–2004 (Kaiser et al., 2005), and further to 48 programs with expenditures over $25 million in 2004–2005 (Carman, 2007a). The research portion of California state programs increased to $37.22 million for 44 active programs in 2016–2017 (Tables 14.4 and 14.5). The share of total program expenditures dedicated to research increased from about 7.5 percent in 1992 to about 11 percent in 2004–2005, and further to 18.4 percent in 2016–2017. Historically, research funded by California marketing programs focused on production problems and issues. A sampling of research topics includes new variety development, insect and pest management, irrigation and water management, disease control, pollination, harvest methods/machinery, crop management, and postharvest quality control. More recently, California marketing programs have maintained production-oriented research while increasing funds devoted to nutrition and health research.

There are numerous examples of the benefits to producers from research expenditures by mandated marketing programs. Research has produced cost savings from the reduced use of inputs (water, pesticides, and fertilizer) and changes in the input mix, yield increases, reductions in postharvest losses, improved crop characteristics, and new management techniques. Several California commodity groups have funded research at UC that has helped them become the most efficient producers in the United States and the world. Included are almonds, walnuts, pistachios, strawberries, lettuce, and grapes (Alston and Zilberman, 1998). California producers have gained a short- to intermediate-term competitive edge from these research-enabling improvements and, over time, benefits have flowed to consumers in the form of increased supply and availability, improved quality, and lower prices.

The California Walnut Commission became the first California-mandated marketing program to specifically fund health and nutrition research. In 1990, the commission contracted with Loma Linda University for research on the protective effects of walnut consumption on the risk of coronary heart disease. The motivation for walnut nutrition research was to counter the popular perception, at that time, that walnut consumption was unhealthy because of their high oil content. Likewise, the Almond Board of California initiated a Nutrition Research Program and established a Nutrition Subcommittee in 1995. In 1997, the California Avocado Commission began to communicate the nutritional benefits of avocados through national public relations and outreach efforts. In 2003, the California Strawberry Commission funded its first nutrition research projects. These early changes in research emphasis soon yielded results that have helped to improve the impact of advertising and promotion programs, increase consumer knowledge of the nutritional composition of major specialty crops, and increase demand for these same crops.[8]

The California walnut industry submitted its research results for a heart health claim to the U.S. Food and Drug Administration (FDA), and the almond industry submitted its as part of a petition filed by the International Tree Nut Council Nutrition Research and Education Foundation to the FDA for a heart health claim for nuts. (Walnuts were also included in the International Tree Nut Council petition.) The FDA approved a qualified health claim for

walnuts, and another for almonds and other selected nuts, on July 15, 2003, which states: "Scientific evidence suggests but does not prove that eating 1.5 ounces per day of (specify nut) as part of a diet low in saturated fat and cholesterol may reduce the risk of heart disease."

Commodity health and nutrition research has tended to focus on analyses detailing each commodity's chemical and nutritional composition, including the amount and type of fat, calories, vitamins, phytochemicals, antioxidants, and minerals. The presence of particular components, already associated with favorable health outcomes has helped focus research on important health topics. Many commodity groups are seeking evidence that consuming their product may reduce the risk of heart disease or that product components may help to lower the risk of certain cancers. In addition, it is important to document whether or not commodities contain antioxidants known to slow the aging process and protect against heart disease and various forms of cancer. Several commodities have examined the role they might play in diets to control weight gain and if they can be part of a healthy diet for managing and controlling diabetes. California commodities devoting substantial funds supporting research related to health and nutrition include walnuts, almonds, pistachios, avocados, strawberries, table grapes, and blueberries.

INFORMATION PROGRAMS

Pricing efficiency in agricultural commodity markets requires current information on supply and demand factors affecting prices, with more information preferred to less. Typically, this information is not easy to obtain and, when available, it is often expensive. Access to current data can be a source of market power and can provide a competitive advantage. Public market information for agricultural commodities has decreased over time in response to changing channels of distribution and reduced government funding. Terminal market price and arrival data have decreased because these markets have become less important as large buyers deal directly with larger grower-shippers; market reports have also been reduced and suspended in response to government budget reductions. In the continuing search for market information, developments in information technology and the spread of personal communication devices offer potential breakthroughs for marketing firms. California producers are

---

8 Carman (2007b) includes a discussion of the health and nutrition research programs for these four organizations.

developing information programs through their commodity organizations.

In addition to having an organized commodity group, an important and often overlooked benefit of mandated marketing programs is the value of the information gathered, organized, and disseminated in administering each program. These data on production, prices, bearing and nonbearing acreage, reported by region, are useful for determining trends, estimating annual demand functions, forecasting production, and measuring aggregate economic contributions, but contribute little to day-to-day pricing negotiations and decisions. Efforts to collect and disseminate information on daily prices by grade and shipments are in progress. A current example is the information program conducted by the California Blueberry Commission (CBC).

The CBC is a relatively new program. California blueberry producers voted to establish the CBC in 2009, and founded the commission on March 1, 2010. An important activity of the commission was to fund the Blueberry Marketing Resource Information Center (BMRIC), which collects and provides important real-time marketing data to the industry. BMRIC also publishes summaries of weekly shipments, pack-out volume, and daily f.o.b. prices by size of package (container) in their annual reports.[9] While these data do not cover all California production, they are representative of commercial production and are readily available to registered users. Note that the California Avocado Commission operates a similar program with a similar name, the Avocado Marketing Resource Information Center (AMRIC).

The Hass Avocado Board, which collects a $0.025 cents per pound assessment on all Hass avocados sold in the United States to fund promotion and research, also conducts a web-based program to exchange crop and marketing information among 100 packers and over 20,000 producers who serve the U.S. market. This program collects, tracks, analyzes, and disseminates information relevant to marketing Hass avocados in the United States. It provides all market participants with 24-hour access to market data that drive decisions about growing, shipping, distribution,

and marketing Hass avocados. In an evaluation of the information program, Carman, Li, and Sexton (2010) found evidence that improved market information had contributed to reduced price variability that benefited both avocado producers and consumers.

Information-sharing cooperatives, relatively unique to California, can reduce marketing costs and improve pricing efficiency. These cooperatives provide a means of communication regarding production plans and pricing strategies that would ordinarily be illegal under U.S. antitrust laws, but lawful under the Capper-Volstead Act. Information-sharing cooperatives are helpful for highly perishable commodities whose production is concentrated in the hands of relatively few grower-shippers, including iceberg lettuce, melons, table grapes, fresh stone fruits, mushrooms, and fresh tomatoes. Successful coordination of production and marketing in these industries can be a major advantage in terms of avoiding the periods of over supply and low prices. Sexton and Sexton (1994) includes a discussion of experience with an information-sharing cooperative in the California iceberg lettuce industry.

Information websites that provide promotional materials to consumers as well as retailers, foodservice, and media are maintained by most of California's mandated marketing programs.[10] Review of websites reveals a wide range of content including such things as press releases, nutrition and health information, recipes, advertising and promotional copy, program descriptions, data on prices and shipments (ranging from aggregate to detailed), links to blogs, information on production, product availability, care of the product, point-of-sale displays and other retail materials, fact sheets, image libraries, links to research results, promotional and training videos, plus other product-related information. These websites are both interesting and informative.

---

10 Note that 45 of California's 51 mandated programs maintain active websites. The California Department of Food and Agriculture provides a directory of commodity program websites with links at: https://www.cdfa.ca.gov/mkt/mkt/BoardCommissionSites.html.

---

9 The California Blueberry Commission only represents growers that produce 5 acres or more of blueberries. An example of some of the summary data published is available in Carman (2017).

CONCLUSION

Marketing California's agricultural output is complex and expensive. The costs of performing the physical functions of moving products from the farm to the final consumer have grown absolutely and as a proportion of total consumer expenditures, reflecting consumer demand for new product attributes and services. Another reason is that the share of meals consumed away from home has increased, and marketing costs are higher for food away from home.[11] The institutional framework for marketing California food products continues to evolve as new retail formats compete with traditional supermarkets and large-scale general merchandise retailers increase their share of food sales. Menu and ingredient choices by large-scale fast-food restaurants, limited dining, and take-out establishments can have major impacts on agricultural producers and the food supply chain. Decisions made to gain a competitive edge, such as deciding to offer breakfast items or to extend the hours in which they are offered, can significantly increase demand for basic ingredients (eggs, bacon, sausage, etc.), or banning use of certain inputs such as antibiotics fed to livestock can add significant costs to meet the new requirements.[12] California commodity producers continue to support mandated marketing programs, but their focus has changed from federal marketing orders with supply control provisions to California commodity commissions with an emphasis on research and promotion.

Growing interest in the diet, health, and possible disease preventative properties of food products provide examples of attributes desired by segments of consumers. There are also growing demands for organically and locally grown products that may be a proxy for a desire to support small farms amidst concerns about the environmental impacts

of production and consumption of particular products.[13] Mandated marketing programs provide a framework for discovering and verifying product dimensions that can be directed toward market segments using effective promotion and public relations programs. Health and nutritional research programs conducted on behalf of commissions representing walnuts, almonds, avocados, and strawberries have demonstrated the positive impacts that producer-funded marketing programs can have on product demand (Carman, 2007b). Other commodities that have health and nutrition programs to provide input to their promotion programs include table grapes, blueberries, dried plums, and dates.

Developing information technology and artificial intelligence may offer significant improvements in pricing and productive efficiency from decisions on commodity production, distribution, and marketing. Collecting and sharing harvest, inventory, packing, shipment, and pricing data can achieve an "orderly marketing" objective for mandated marketing programs. Producer-funded information programs, such as for avocados and blueberries, can contribute to a reversal of trends that have reduced the availability and timeliness of government market and price information. The widespread availability of marketing information and data is a theoretical requirement for competitive markets. Industry marketing programs operating with government sanction have an exemption from antitrust laws so that producers and shippers may share market information and stabilize shipments and prices. Producers and consumers can benefit from decreased price variability when price transmission is asymmetric, as is the case for many perishable commodities (Carman, Li, and Sexton).[14] Information programs that smooth the flow of product from producers to final consumers can reduce price variability, leading to smaller marketing margins that benefit producers with higher average f.o.b. prices and consumers with lower average retail prices.

---

11 Even though marketing costs are higher for food consumed away from home, savings for the household due to the opportunity costs of meal preparation may increase net household income.

12 Saitone, Sexton, and Sumner examine the economic effects of limitations on the use of antibiotics in U.S. pork production. They found that, in the absence of demand growth, less pork is sold due to higher costs in the restricted segment, and both pork consumers (on average) and producers are harmed.

---

13 See Philpott and Lurie for some of the issues related to almonds' use of water during drought years, and Darnton and Rickenbrode for issues related to deforestation in Mexico and increased greenhouse emissions from increased avocado imports.

14 With asymmetric price transmission, one finds that retail prices respond quicker and more fully to shipping-point price increases than to shipping-point price decreases. As a result, retail price margins tend to increase with larger and more frequent price changes or decrease with smaller and less frequent price changes

REFERENCES

Alston, J.M., H.F. Carman, J.E. Christian, J. Dorfman, J.R. Murua, and R.J. Sexton. 1995. *Optimal Reserve and Export Policies for the California Almond Industry: Theory, Econometrics and Simulations.* Giannini Foundation Monograph No. 42. Davis CA: Department of Agricultural and Resource Economics, University of California. Available at: https://s.giannini.ucop.edu/uploads/giannini_public/ff/39/ff39c94d-2a97-41bb-8db6-806514e289a6/42_almonds.pdf.

Alston, J.M. and D. Zilberman. 1998. "Science and Technology in California Agriculture." *Issues Brief* No. 4, February. University of California Agricultural Issues Center. Available at: http://aic.ucdavis.edu/pub/briefs/brief4.html.

California Department of Food and Agriculture. 2016. *California Agricultural Statistics Review* 2015-2016. Sacramento CA. Available at: https://www.cdfa.ca.gov/statistics/PDFs/2016Report.pdf.

Canning, P. 2011. *A Revised and Expanded Food Dollar Series: A Better Understanding of Our Food Costs.* Economic Research Report Number 114. Washington DC: U.S. Department of Agriculture, Economic Research Service, February. Available at: https://www.ers.usda.gov/webdocs/publications/44825/7759_err114.pdf?v=42132.

Carman, H.F. 2007a. "California Farmers Adapt Mandated Marketing Programs to the 21st Century." *California Agriculture* 61(4): 177-183, October-December. Available at: http://calag.ucanr.edu/archive/?article=ca.v061n04p177.

———.2007b. "Discovering and Promoting Commodity Health Attributes: Programs and Issues." *International Food and Agribusiness Management Review* 10(2): 99-116.

———. 2017. "The Organic Premium for California Blueberries." *ARE Update* 20(6): 9-11. University of California Giannini Foundation of Agricultural Economics. Available at: https://s.giannini.ucop.edu/uploads/giannini_public/9c/17/9c17359a-a7d1-4ebe-b3f2-1ba83565c4e4/v20n6_3.pdf.

Carman, H.F., R. Cook, and R.J. Sexton. 2003. "Marketing California's Agricultural Production." In J. Siebert, ed. *California Agriculture: Dimensions and Issues.* Berkeley CA: University of California, Giannini Foundation of Agricultural Economics, pp. 89-119. Available at: https://s.giannini.ucop.edu/uploads/giannini_public/4e/a8/4ea8b9cc-df88-4146-b1ae-e5467736e104/escholarship_uc_item_9145n8m1.pdf.

Carman, H.F., L. Li, and R.J. Sexton. 2010. "Can Improved Market Information Benefit Both Producers and Consumers? Evidence from the Hass Avocado Board's Internet Information Program." *ARE Update* 13(4): 5-8. University of California Giannini Foundation of Agricultural Economics. Available at: https://s.giannini.ucop.edu/uploads/giannini_public/14/17/14171977-731c-4211-87b0-d7edb84d2612/v13n4_2.pdf.

Carman, H.F. and D.H. Pick. 1988. "Marketing California-Arizona Lemons Without Marketing Order Shipment Controls." *Agribusiness* 4(3): 245-259.

———.1990. "Orderly Marketing for Lemons: Who Benefits?" *American Journal of Agricultural Economics* 72(2): 346-357.

Carman, H.F., L. Li, and R.J. Sexton. 2010. "Can Improved Market Information Benefit Both Producers and Consumers? Evidence from the Hass Avocado Board's Internet Information Program." *ARE Update* 13(4): 5-8. University of California Giannini Foundation of Agricultural Economics. Available at: https://s.giannini.ucop.edu/uploads/giannini_public/14/17/14171977-731c-4211-87b0-d7edb84d2612/v13n4_2.pdf.

Carman, H.F. and R.J. Sexton. 2011. "Effective Marketing of Hass Avocados: The Impacts of Changing Trade Policy and Promotion/Information Programs." *International Food and Agribusiness Management Review* 14(4): 37-50.

Cline, H. 2007. "Paramount Farming Kills California Pistachio Commission." *Western Farm Press*, March. Available at: http://www.westernfarmpress.com/paramount-farming-kills-california-pistachio-commission.

Crespi, J., T. Saitone, and R.J. Sexton. 2015. "The Supreme Court's Decision in the 'Raisin Case': What Does it Mean for Mandatory Marketing Programs?" *ARE Update* 18(6): 1-4. University of California Giannini Foundation of Agricultural Economics. Available at: https://s.giannini.ucop.edu/uploads/giannini_public/6d/1e/6d1ed400-5715-4afc-9a9e-0afdab20869d/v18n6.pdf.

Darnton, J. and V. Rickenbrode. 2017. "Avocado Consumption: Environmental and Social Considerations." *Michigan State University Extension Newsletter*, August 24. Available at: http://msue.anr.msu.edu/news/avocado_consumption_environmental_and_social_considerations.

French, B.C. and R.G. Bressler. 1962. "The Lemon Cycle." *Journal of Farm Economics* 44(4): 1021-1036.

Gray, R.S., D.A. Sumner, J.M. Alston, H. Brunke, and A.K.A. Acquaye. 2005. *Economic Consequences of Mandated Grading and Food Safety Assurance: Ex Ante – Analysis of the Federal Marketing Order for California Pistachios.* Giannini Foundation Monograph 46. Davis CA: Giannini Foundation of Agricultural Economics, University of California. Available at: https://s.giannini.ucop.edu/uploads/giannini_public/5f/65/5f651bff-93e6-47a4-b0b2-38757c3a3294/46_pistachios.pdf.

Kaiser, H.M., J.M. Alston, J.M. Crespi, and R.J. Sexton. 2005. *The Economics of Commodity Promotion Programs: Lessons from California.* New York NY: Peter Lang Publishing.

Kinney, W., H.F. Carman, R.D. Green, and J. O'Connell. 1987. *An Analysis of Economic Adjustments in the California-Arizona Lemon Industry.* Gianinni Foundation Research Report No. 337, April. Berkeley CA: University of California Agricultural Experiment Station. Available at: https://s.giannini.ucop.edu/uploads/giannini_public/88/a8/88a84399-23c9-4473-b28e-cd3d2b690c83/337-lemons.pdf.

Klonsky, K. and K. Richter. 2011. *Statistical Review of California's Organic Agriculture 2005-2009.* Davis CA: Agricultural Issues Center, University of California. Available at: http://aic.ucdavis.edu/publications/Statistical_Review_05-09.pdf.

Lee, H., J.M. Alston, H.F. Carman, and W. Sutton. 1996. *Mandated Marketing Programs for California Commodities.* Giannini Foundation Information Series No. 96- 1, August. Berkeley CA: University of California Division of Agriculture and Natural Resources. Available at: https://s.giannini.ucop.edu/uploads/giannini_public/a4/d3/a4d30a2d-58c5-49eb-8f54-1fa56cb10273/961-marketing.pdf.

Lenard, T.M. and M.P. Mazur. 1985. "Harvest of Waste: The Marketing Order Program." *Regulation*, pp. 19-26.

Philpott, T. and J. Lurie. 2015. "Here's the Real Problem With Almonds." *New Republic*, December 31. Available at: https://newrepublic.com/article/125450/heres-real-problem-almonds.

Polopolus, L.C., H.F. Carman, E.V. Jesse, and J.D. Shaffer. 1986. *Criteria for Evaluating Federal Marketing Orders: Fruits, Vegetables, Nuts and Specialty Commodities.* Washington DC: U. S. Department of Agriculture, Economic Research Service.

Richards, T., A. Kagan, P. Mischen, and R. Adu-Asamoah. 1996. "Marketing Order Suspensions and Fresh Lemon Retail-FOB Margins." *Journal of Agricultural and Applied Economics* 28(2): 263-277.

Saitone, T.L., R.J. Sexton, and D.A. Sumner. 2015. "What Happens When Food Marketers Require Restrictive Farming Practices?" *American Journal of Agricultural Economics* 97(4): 1021-1043.

Sexton, R.J. and T.A. Sexton. 1994. "Information-Sharing Cooperatives; Market Coordination or Cartel Behavior." In R.W. Cotterill, ed. *Competitive Strategy Analysis for Agricultural Cooperatives.* Boulder CO: Westview Press.

Shepard, L. 1986. "Cartelization of the California-Arizona Orange Industry." *The Journal of Law and Economics* 29(1): 83-123.

Smith, R.J. 1961. "The Lemon Prorate in the Long Run." *Journal of Political Economy* 69(6): 573-586.

Thor, P.K. and E.V. Jesse. 1981. "Economic Effects of Terminating Federal Marketing Orders to California-Arizona Oranges." Washington DC: U.S. Department of Agriculture, Economic Research Service, Technical Bulletin No. 1664.

U.S. Department of Agriculture. 2016. "Top 100 Agricultural Cooperatives, 2016 and 2015, by Total Gross Business Revenue ($billion)." Available at: https://www.rd.usda.gov/files/USDA2016NewTop100AgCoop.pdf.

U.S. Department of Agriculture, Economic Research Service. 2017. "Food Dollar Series." Available at: https://www.ers.usda.gov/data-products/food-dollar-series.

U.S. Department of Agriculture, Foreign Agricultural Service. 2017. "MAP Funding Allocations – FY 2017." Available at: https://www.fas.usda.gov/programs/market-access-program-map/map-funding-allocations-fy-2017.

U.S. Department of Agriculture, National Agriculture Statistics Services. 2014. *Census of Agriculture, 2014 Organic Survey (2014), Vol. 3, Special Studies, Part 4.* Available at: https://www.agcensus.usda.gov/Publications//Organic_Survey/.

U.S. General Accounting Office. 1985. "The Role of Marketing Orders in Establishing and Maintaining Orderly Marketing." Gaithersburg MD: GAO/RCED-85-57, July 31.

Williams, G.W., J.J. Reimer, R.M. Dudensing, B.A. McCarl, H. Kaiser, and J. Somers. 2016. *Economic Impact of USDA Export Market Development Programs.* Washington DC: Informa Economics IEG. Available at: https://www.fas.usda.gov/sites/default/files/2016-10/2016econimpactsstudy.pdf.

CHAPTER 15. INTERNATIONAL TRADE AND CALIFORNIA AGRICULTURE

COLIN A. CARTER

ABSTRACT

A large share of California's agricultural supply chain is devoted to international trade. On average, more than 44 percent of California's agricultural output is sold into over 60 foreign markets, making California agriculture more orientated towards export markets, compared to other major agricultural producing states in the United States. This means that California agriculture has a big stake in more liberalized agricultural trade, unlike some other regions in U.S. agriculture. The dynamics of the world market have encouraged California agriculture to be highly competitive and innovative. It has achieved these characteristics by exporting fruits, vegetables, tree nuts, and dairy products.

ABOUT THE AUTHOR

Colin A. Carter is a Distinguished Professor in the Department of Agricultural and Resource Economics at University of California, Davis, and a member of the Giannini Foundation of Agricultural Economics. He can be reached by email at cacarter@ucdavis.edu.

California agriculture has had an increased dependence on international trade. International exports as a share of California agricultural output rose from 25.2 percent in 2000 to 43 percent in 2015. As of 2017, leading export destinations for California agricultural commodities included the European Union ($3.415 billion), Canada ($3.287 billion), China and Hong Kong ($2.27 billion), Japan ($1.452 billion), Mexico ($1.057 billion), South Korea ($1.011 billion), and Taiwan ($305 million).

Photo Credit: Heidi Schweizer, UC Davis, 2017

Chapter 15. Table of Contents

INTRODUCTION

This chapter summarizes the importance of international trade for California's agricultural sector. It outlines the trade dimensions, trade environment, challenges, and prospects for the continued role of international trade as a driver of California agriculture. We briefly discuss what it means for California agriculture to be "competitive" in an increasingly globalized marketplace. We review the importance of the state's key agricultural trading partners, including the role of China as both a market and a competitor. Foreign markets are growing in importance for California agriculture, and increased trade liberalization will be beneficial to most California producers since they competitively supply high-valued specialty products, despite facing some important and, in some cases, growing barriers to trade in important foreign markets.[1] The main section of this chapter describes California's agricultural trade up until 2017, before the beginning of the U.S.-China trade war.[2] Because China's retaliatory import tariffs were somewhat targeted at agricultural trade, there is a section towards the end of the chapter that addresses the implications of the trade war for California's agriculture.

Historically, the major crops in California (i.e., fruits, vegetables, and tree nuts) have not benefitted from federal farm subsidy programs and other forms of protectionism provided by U.S. Congress to the main program commodities (such as grains, oilseeds, cotton, sugar, and milk). Therefore, we argue that California agriculture would benefit from reduced subsidies to midwestern U.S. agriculture and concomitant increased access to markets abroad. Thus, to the extent that the political fallout from the protectionist 2014 and 2018 U.S. Farm Bill results in a less ambitious World Trade Organization (WTO) agreement, this is costly for the California agricultural sector. The 2017 U.S. withdrawal from the Trans-Pacific

Partnership (TPP)—with 11 trading nations in the Pacific Region—has also hurt California agriculture, especially regarding more access to the Japanese market. It goes without saying that the U.S.-China trade war was detrimental to California agriculture. The North American Free Trade Agreement (NAFTA)—now called the Canada–U.S.–Mexico Agreement (CUSMA)—was renewed in 2020, which is a good thing for California agriculture because a withdrawal from that agreement would have been costly like the withdrawal from TPP was.

Globalization describes the phenomenon of greater integration of international markets, including more cross-border movement of goods, services, and factors of production (such as capital, technology, and labor). Classical economic theory predicts benefits to economies as a whole from the integration of markets. The benefits arise because factors of production like land, labor, and capital will be allocated more efficiently across international borders, and consumers will have access to a wider variety of products at a lower price. Put another way, trade allows a region to shift its pattern of production so that it can produce more with the same endowment of resources—just like technological change, which allows a country to do more with less. Historical examples bear out economists' predictions; production for international markets rather than the domestic market alone has led to rising average incomes and higher profitability for firms.

Some fear that California's agricultural future is bleak because of globalization. They even go so far as to claim that without protection, California agriculture will go out of business, because it cannot compete with developing countries. This view emphasizes that agriculture is becoming less important in the state's economy, and the lower wage rates and weak domestic regulations in developing countries means California growers' costs will be too high to compete successfully internationally.

However, neither low wage rates nor weak domestic regulations in developing countries mean an end to California agriculture. The fact that California agriculture continues to thrive despite trade barriers in foreign markets underscores the fact that California agriculture

---

1 Beckman et al. report that sanitary and phytosanitary trade barriers and other non-tariff barriers to trade in agricultural products are growing, with increasing international disagreement over the scientific basis for rejecting imports.

2 2018 trade statistics can be found at: www.cdfa.ca.gov/statistics/pdfs/AgExports2018-2019.pdf. However, 2018 exports were affected by the trade war.

remains efficient and competitive.[3] Productivity growth in California agriculture has been relatively high, holding costs down. California farmers reduce the unit costs of production by substituting capital and technology for land and labor. A recent analysis suggests that California agriculture productivity grew at about 1.7 percent per year from 1980–2004,[4] faster than most of U.S. manufacturing.

Several other trends also work in favor of California agriculture. There is a continuing shift in global food demand towards high-value, differentiated products like those produced in California. For instance, the U.S. Department of Agriculture (USDA) annually projects U.S. agricultural exports; and the latest projections (2020) support the view that world demand for California agricultural products will continue to expand. The USDA projects that U.S. dairy and horticultural exports will grow by 42 and 27 percent, respectively, from 2018 to 2029. This is a significant growth rate compared to a number of other agricultural products.

Economies of scale and technological "spillovers" in California agriculture, which are not as common in other regions of the world that produce specialty crops, help to keep California's production costs low. The state has a dependable climate, cutting-edge technology, advanced human capital, productive labor, and world-class marketing networks, institutions, and infrastructure. As a result, agricultural producers using these inputs are likely to compete successfully in an increasingly globalized marketplace. For example, the U.S. (led by California) is the largest exporter of horticultural products in the world,[5] despite their generally labor-intensive nature. Tree nut exports to Asia have been especially strong. For instance, California almond exports were valued at $4.5 billion in 2017, compared to only $0.65 billion in 2000—an exceptional growth in production and export sales. In California, bearing almond orchards now cover more than 1 million acres, up from 510,000 acres in 2000.

Despite these trends, not all crop and livestock producers in California will benefit from increasing globalization. The cost of production for specific agricultural products may indeed be higher in California than in foreign countries. However, for more than one reason, this information alone gives little guidance as to the competitiveness of California's agricultural sector. First, comparing the cost of garlic production in California to the cost of garlic production in China, for example, obscures the point that today's garlic growers need not grow garlic tomorrow. A structural transformation within the sector, towards products that capitalize on the state's strengths, will allow California agriculture to most effectively meet the challenges and opportunities of globalization.

Second, marketing costs, including transportation, are often a high share of total delivered costs. This makes foreign suppliers much less competitive during California's production season for many fresh commodities. Indeed, even for many crops with a high import share, most of the imports enter off-season; the advantage of other countries is not cost, but latitude and climate. California firms can and do exploit the state's climatic advantages by shifting fruit and vegetable production towards fresher rather than processed products. The state has also moved out of field crops towards more and more tree nuts. More generally, increased trade exposes producers to more competition; the most efficient and productive growers and firms will do the best.

---

3   See McCalla and Johnston for an excellent discussion of the booms and busts that California agriculture has experienced.

4   See: https://www.ers.usda.gov/data-products/agricultural-productivity-in-the-us/.

CALIFORNIA'S AGRICULTURAL TRADE

California's agricultural trade is characterized by: (1) a large and growing share of exports relative to production, (2) a diversity in exports that matches changing global food demand, (3) significant sales to rich-country markets and high-income consumers, despite trade barriers in these markets, and (4) new competition for access to these markets from Mexico, China, and other temperate-zone emerging food exporters.

Compared to agricultural commodity producers in other states, and with some notable exceptions, California agriculture competes largely on its own merits in a complex and dynamic global environment; but managing foreign competition and accessing protectionist markets remain a challenge. California agricultural producers rely on foreign markets for a significant portion of their revenues. Table 15.1 reports that the value of California agricultural exports total about $22 billion, or about 44 percent of the value of agricultural commodities produced in California (almost $50 billion)—based on a five-year 2012–2016 average.[6] The second largest agricultural state

Table 15.1. Summary Statistics: Top Five Agricultural States, 2012–2016 Average

State	Agricultural Production	Agricultural Exports	Export Share
	$ (Billions)		Percent
CA	49.985	22.077	44.2
IA	29.513	10.682	36.2
NE	23.287	6.637	28.5
MN	19.105	7.256	38.0
TX	22.741	6.173	27.1

Sources: Compiled from https://www.ers.usda.gov/data-products/farm-income-and-wealth-statistics/
and https://www.ers.usda.gov/data-products/state-export-data/

in the United States, Iowa, produces about $29 billion in agricultural products per year and exports about 36 percent of that production to international markets. While California generates 13 percent of national farm cash receipts, it accounts for an estimated 16 percent of total U.S. agricultural export revenue.[7] Keep in mind for some products, such as tree nuts, the share of state output that is exported ranges up to 70 percent.

California exports a wide variety of high-value, specialty food products. As shown in Figure 15.1, according to the California Department of Food and Agriculture (CDFA), the top six food product exports from California in 2017 (and for most recent years) were almonds, dairy products, walnuts, wine, pistachios, and table grapes. Tree nuts (almonds, walnuts, and pistachios) are the No. 1 agricultural product group exported by California, but the diversity of California's exports is also an important industry characteristic. The top 10 products account for less than 70 percent of California's agricultural exports by value. Even when exports are aggregated into commodity groups, the range of products exported by California is notable (Figure 15.2). According to available estimates of state-level trade statistics, fruit exports (including wine) comprise 17 percent of the state's agricultural exports, followed by tree nuts (33 percent), vegetables (13 percent), animal products (7 percent), wine (7 percent) and field crops (6 percent).

---

6 Data analyses in this chapter are constrained by the fact that detailed state-level trade data are very limited. For example, there are no reliable data on California's agricultural imports. Almost all trade data are collected at the national level rather than the state level. However, the California Department of Food and Agriculture (CDFA) and the U.S. Department of Agriculture (USDA) do estimate state-level export values. The USDA method uses state exports based on U.S. farm-cash-receipts data, under the assumption that California's share of U.S. exports for a particular commodity is equal to California's share of national production for that commodity. The CDFA uses a slightly different method and provides a more disaggregate breakdown of the commodities compared to the USDA data. The USDA estimates can be found at: https://www.ers.usda.gov/data-products/state-export-data/. The CDFA estimates (in conjunction with the UC Agricultural Issues Center) can be found at https://www.cdfa.ca.gov/statistics/PDFs/AgExports2015-2016.pdf. The resulting estimates of aggregate exports are quite similar from the two sources. For instance, for 2015, the CDFA estimated California's agricultural exports to be $20.69 billion, and the USDA estimate was $21.4 billion. Both sources estimate that the agricultural industry in California exports about 44 percent of its production, based on value. However, for some specific commodities, the export estimates are substantially different. The CDFA estimated dairy (and products) exports to be $1.632 billion in 2015, whereas the USDA estimated California dairy product exports to be $922.7 million in that same year. This discrepancy is not surprising because California is only one of several dairy states and it is difficult to apportion the percent of state production exported overseas. Alternatively, almost all of the U.S. almonds, pistachios, and walnuts are produced in California, so for these products, the estimated California exports are most likely very accurate. Hereafter, when we refer to CDFA export estimates, please note these estimates are published in conjunction with the University of California Agricultural Issues Center (https://aic.ucdavis.edu/).

---

7 https://www.ers.usda.gov/data-products/farm-income-and-wealth-statistics/.

Figure 15.1. California's Main Agricultural Exports, 2017

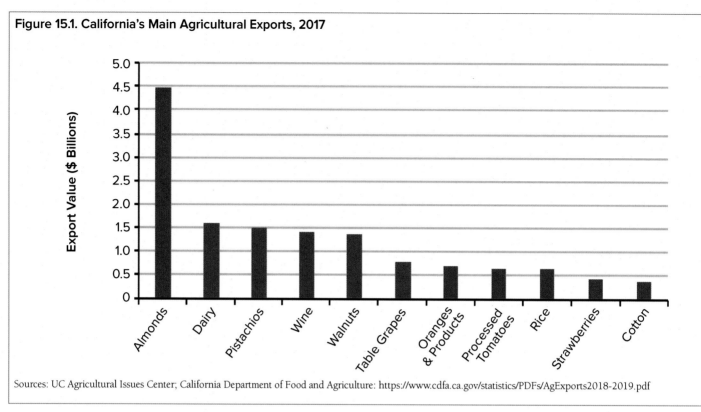

Sources: UC Agricultural Issues Center; California Department of Food and Agriculture: https://www.cdfa.ca.gov/statistics/PDFs/AgExports2018-2019.pdf

Figure 15.2. California Agricultural Export Shares, 2018

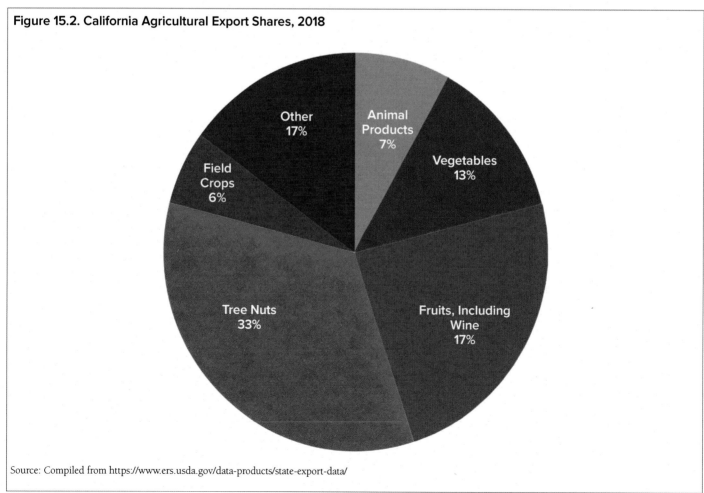

Source: Compiled from https://www.ers.usda.gov/data-products/state-export-data/

Figure 15.3. California's Main Agricultural Exports, 2016

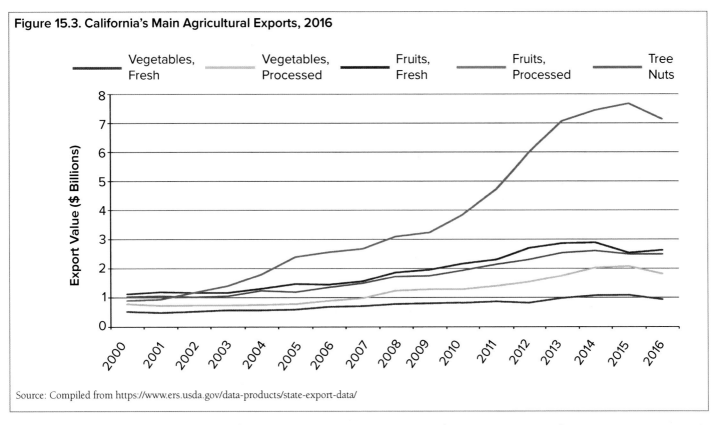

Source: Compiled from https://www.ers.usda.gov/data-products/state-export-data/

There have been significant changes in the make-up of California's agricultural exports in the past 20 years. For instance, cotton was the second most important export commodity in 2002, and now it barely ranks in the top 10. Table grapes moved down from the top four to the top seven. At the same time, exports of dairy (and products), walnuts, and pistachios have moved up the rank of top export commodities. Over the past 15 years, the relative importance of tree nuts as a share of the state's agricultural exports has increased from 15 to 33 percent. In fact, tree nuts are also the nation's third-largest agricultural export, with soybeans and corn No. 1 and No. 2, respectively. The share of (fresh and processed) vegetables in California exports rose from 9 to 13 percent. At the same time, the share of exports of fruits and products (excluding wine) fell from 25 to 17 percent. There was a dramatic change in the role of field crops, falling from 17 percent of exports in 2002 to only 6 percent in 2017.

Figure 15.3 further illustrates, these trends in the make-up of the state's agricultural exports. In the early 2000s, the value of tree nut exports began to break away from the value of fruit and vegetable exports, and tree nut export sales rose much more rapidly, from $2.4 billion in 2005 to $7.1 billion by 2016. Figure 15.3 shows that export growth in fresh fruits has outperformed export growth in fresh

vegetables. The differential growth rate between processed fruits and processed vegetables is less, but the percentage growth in processed fruit exports has exceeded the growth in processed vegetable exports.

This assortment of agricultural exports from California differentiates the state from other important agricultural states in the U.S., which tend to specialize in only a few commodities. The agricultural sector in Iowa and Illinois is concentrated on just three commodities: corn, soybeans, and hogs, which account for 75 to 85 percent or more of each of those states' farm cash receipts. Nebraska's production of corn and cattle generates over 75 percent of that state's farm receipts. Texas depends on the cattle sector, which produces over 40 percent of its farm cash receipts, with cotton generating another 10 percent.[8]

A notable development for California agriculture has been the dramatically increased dependence on international trade. As shown in Table 15.2, international exports as a share of California agricultural output rose from 25.2 percent in 2000 to 43 percent in 2015. On the one hand, this is positive because it reveals that California

8 The figures are compiled from https://www.ers.usda.gov/data-products/farm-income-and-wealth-statistics/.

Table 15.2. California's Growing Dependence on International Trade, 2000–2017

	Value of CA Ag Production	Value of CA Exports	Export Share
	$ (Billions)		Percent
2000	27.19	6.85	25.2
2005	34.56	9.67	28.0
2010	40.68	15.37	37.8
2015	52.17	22.84	44.0
2017	52.55	22.66	43.0

Sources: Agricultural production from USDA/ERS Farm finance indicators, state ranking: https://data.ers.usda.gov/reports.aspx?ID=17839; Value of exports from: https://www.ers.usda.gov/data-products/state-export-data/

agriculture is dynamic and responsive to changing market conditions. The shift away from field crops into tree nuts is no doubt partially driven by export opportunities. On the other hand, the increased trade dependence exposes California agriculture to the vagaries of the world market, which is more unpredictable than the domestic market. Exchange rates, trade agreements, trade wars, third market competition, and protectionism in foreign markets all come into play in the international market. Perhaps this is no more evident than in the case of the downturn in the global dairy market that began in 2013.

The USDA estimated the value of California dairy exports fell from $1.27 billion in 2013 to $825 million in 2016, a 35 percent drop.[9] This was partly due to the EU removing its dairy production quotas in 2015, a relatively strong U.S. dollar relative to competitor currencies (Australia, New Zealand, and the EU), a drop in China's import demand, and a Russian import embargo.

As of 2017, leading export destinations for California agricultural commodities included the European Union ($3.415 billion), Canada ($3.287 billion), China and Hong Kong ($2.270 billion), Japan ($1.452 billion), Mexico ($1.057 billion), South Korea ($1.011 billion), and Taiwan ($305 million). This is not surprising because the top five markets for U.S. agricultural exports are Canada, Mexico, the EU, China, and Japan. Major agricultural products sent to these key markets are summarized in Table 15.3. This table again shows the diversity of California's exports, but also suggests that products are targeted to different markets; each market is dominated by a different set of products, with little overlap between them.

In 2017, almond exports from California were primarily destined for the EU (35 percent), India (15 percent), China/Hong Kong (11 percent), Canada (6 percent), and Japan (5 percent). Most of the walnuts in 2017 were sold into the EU, Turkey, China and Hong Kong, Japan, South Korea, Vietnam, and Canada. The EU serves as the major market for California wine, followed by Canada, China/Hong

---

9 https://www.ers.usda.gov/data-products/state-export-data/.

Table 15.3. California's Major Export Markets, $ (Millions), 2017

EU	Canada	China/ Hong Kong	Japan	Mexico	S. Korea
Almonds (1,568)	Wine (376)	Pistachios (663)	Almonds (226)	Dairy (447)	Oranges (229)
Wine (521)	Strawberries (284)	Almonds (501)	Rice (190)	Table Grapes (96)	Almonds (174)
Walnuts (491)	Lettuce (279)	Wine (185)	Walnuts (131)	Proc. Tomatoes (80)	Beef (95)
Pistachios (462)	Proc. Tomatoes (270)	Dairy (175)	Beef (127)	Almonds (75)	Walnuts (93)
Raisins (70)	Almonds (256)	Oranges (124)	Hay (117)	Nursery (41)	Rice (85)
Total* (3,415)	Total* (3,287)	Total* (2,270)	Total* (1,452)	Total* (1,057)	Total* (996)

Source: UC Agricultural Issues Center, California Department of Food and Agriculture, https://www.cdfa.ca.gov/statistics/PDFs/AgExports2018-2019.pdf

Note: * Total dollar value is for all commodities exported to each region, not just those listed in the table.

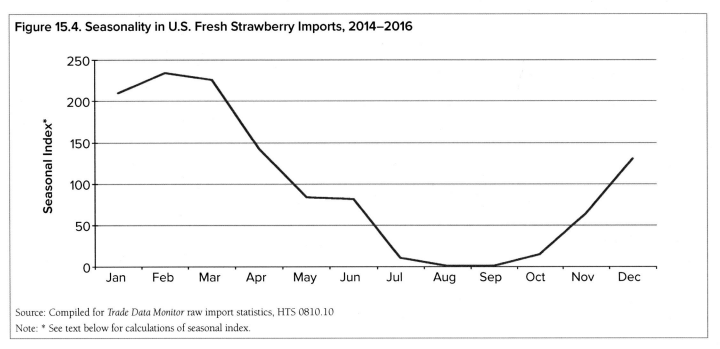

Figure 15.4. Seasonality in U.S. Fresh Strawberry Imports, 2014–2016

Source: Compiled for *Trade Data Monitor* raw import statistics, HTS 0810.10

Note: * See text below for calculations of seasonal index.

Kong, and Japan. Canada and Mexico imported 41 percent of California's table grapes in 2017, with Canada buying 29 percent alone. The EU, China/Hong Kong, and Canada are the largest importers for California pistachios (accounting for about 80 percent of export sales). Processed tomato exports were shipped primarily to Canada (42 percent), Mexico (12 percent), and the EU (8 percent). A large share of the rice exports from California (30 percent) were sold to Japan, with S. Korea and Jordan purchasing 13 and 14 percent of rice exports, respectively, in 2017.

California's integration into world agricultural markets is not unidirectional. Residents of the state also consume significant amounts of agricultural imports. For commodities not grown in the U.S., such as cocoa, coffee, and bananas, California relies entirely on imports. While data on import value by state is not readily available, we can estimate the sense of the magnitude of import consumption by relying on the proportion of the U.S. population residing in California (12 percent in 2016). In 2016, the U.S. as a whole imported beef and veal worth $4.8 billion, $5.1 billion worth of cocoa and related products, $6.0 billion worth of coffee and related products, $2.3 billion worth of bananas and plantains, and $1.8 billion worth of cane sugar. If 12 percent of these products were destined for California, then consumers in this state spent about $2.4 billion on imports of these commodities alone.

As mentioned above, there is strong seasonality associated with U.S. exports and imports of agricultural products

produced in California. For instance, in the winter months, California's production of some fresh products, such as strawberries, declines due to the relatively cold weather. Figure 15.4 illustrates the seasonal pattern of U.S. strawberry imports for 2014–2016. We calculate the seasonal index by expressing the average volume of imports for each month as a percentage of the overall monthly average import volume (for all months combined) over the entire time period. For the time period covered in Figure 15.4, in January the three-year average import volume was 27.421 thousand metric tons. At the same time, the overall monthly average import volume for all months was 13.038 thousand metric tons. Therefore, the January index is (27.421/13.028) * 100 = 210.3. In other words, the January import volume was 210 percent above the typical monthly import volume over the time period (2014–2016). We see from Figure 15.4 that U.S. strawberry imports are typically high in December, January, February, and March, when the California harvest is virtually dormant. Imports then drop off to almost zero in the summer months when the California harvest of fresh strawberries is in full swing.

GLOBAL AGRICULTURAL TRADING ENVIRONMENT RELEVANT TO CALIFORNIA

From 2006–2016, the nominal value of total U.S. agricultural exports grew by about 90 percent, while California's agricultural exports increased by about 106 percent. The fortunes of California's commodities have

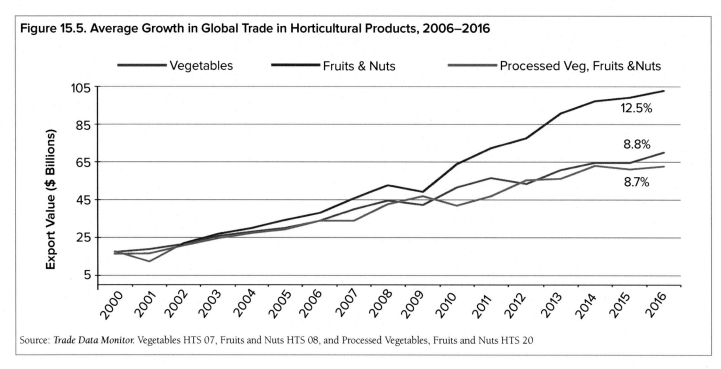

Figure 15.5. Average Growth in Global Trade in Horticultural Products, 2006–2016

Source: *Trade Data Monitor.* Vegetables HTS 07, Fruits and Nuts HTS 08, and Processed Vegetables, Fruits and Nuts HTS 20

been mixed; exports of some commodities important to California grew more rapidly, while others rose less rapidly than the national average. Over this time period, the nominal value of California dairy exports increased by 135 percent and fresh vegetable exports increased by only 39 percent. On the other hand, tree nut exports expanded by about 180 percent in value.[10]

Figure 15.5 displays the annual growth in the dollar value in international trade in horticultural products. From 2000 to 2016, trade in vegetables grew from $17.4 to over $70 billion per year. At the same time, trade in fruits and nuts increased from $17.7 to $102.8 billion, and processed fruits, nuts, and vegetables grew from $16.3 to $62.7 billion. The trade growth rate in fruits and nuts was most impressive, increasing by 12.5 percent per year, on average. The other two categories shown in Figure 15.5 experienced trade growth close to 9 percent per year, which is very high compared to most non-agricultural products.

California agriculture is suited to supply agricultural products to countries whose markets are experiencing strong demand growth due to international trends in income, urbanization, heightened food safety, and healthy lifestyles. The summary statistics in Table 15.4 document that the U.S. is the world's largest export supplier of the combination of fruits, vegetables, and tree nuts, and most of these crops originate in California and Florida. However, Florida does not export tree nuts. Although the

state-level export data are imprecise, the USDA estimates that California exports about 38 percent of the nation's vegetables (fresh and processed) and accounts for 58 percent of the nation's fruit exports (processed and fresh). Florida accounts for 6 percent of the vegetable exports and 8.5 percent of the fruit exports.[11]

As shown in Table 15.4, the U.S. is very dominant in the global fruit and nut market, with annual exports totaling $14.46 billion, on average, from 2014–2016. Spain ranks second with exports of $9.12 billion. Alternatively, China is dominant in the exports of vegetables, supplying $9.27 billion in annual exports. In vegetables, the U.S. ranks fifth on the list, behind Mexico. When it comes to processed vegetables, fruits, and nuts, the U.S. ranks No. 2 as a world exporter behind China. If we aggregate all three categories in Table 15.4 (see rightmost column), the U.S. nudges out China as the largest exporter with annual sales of $27.22 billion. Spain, the Netherlands, and Mexico rank behind China. These data indicate that California's strongest export competitors in the world horticultural sector are China, European suppliers, and Mexico. However, some of this competition is outside of the California harvest season.

California agriculture faces a complex international trading environment, characterized by import tariffs and tariff-rate

11 Compiled from https://www.ers.usda.gov/data-products/state-export-data/.

334

Table 15.4. Major Exporters of Fruits, Vegetables, and Tree Nuts, 2014–2016 Average				
	Vegetables	**Fruits & Nuts**	**Processed Vegetables, Fruits & Nuts**	**Total**
Exporter	$ (Billions)			
USA	4.52	14.46	8.23	27.22
China	9.27	4.99	9.81	24.06
Spain	6.28	9.12	5.18	20.58
Netherlands	7.30	5.35	5.05	17.69
Mexico	5.94	4.75	2.40	13.09

Source: Compiled from UN Comtrade, Vegetables HTS 07, Fruits and Nuts HTS 08, and Processed Vegetables, Fruits and Nuts HTS 20, https://comtrade.un.org/data/

quotas (TRQs), non-tariff trade barriers (such as certain phytosanitary requirements), geographical indicators, fluctuating exchange rates, and low-cost competitors. Increasing foreign export competition and import barriers in foreign markets have raised the importance of further trade liberalization. For instance, the California Farm Bureau Federation supported the TPP[12] because it would have likely increased state agricultural exports and farm cash receipts.[13] Liberalizing imports in Japan, Vietnam, Malaysia, and other TPP markets would increase gains from trade. Japan would have likely eliminated its high imports tariffs on oranges, cheese, grapes, avocados, strawberries, raspberries, blueberries, kiwifruit, and watermelon, and TPP would have harmonized wine import tariffs that now favor Australia and others over California. Within the Asian region, trading partners now have regional trade agreements that give non-U.S. exporters advantages in certain markets. Important for California agriculture, the TPP would have leveled this playing field.

The U.S. International Trade Commission (USITC, 2016) has documented certain areas where California agriculture would have benefited from TPP membership. These include

- Increased dairy exports to Canada and Japan.

- Increased market access to Japan and Vietnam for U.S. exports of fresh fruits, vegetables, and nuts.

- Increased wine exports to Japan resulting from reduced import tariffs.

- Reduction in the impact of sanitary and phytosanitary (SPS) measures on trade as TPP will require that SPS measures are science- and risk-based and not being used as a protectionist non-tariff import barrier.

- Reduction in high tariffs on processed foods exported to Japan, Malaysia, and Vietnam.

In the last 25 years, the most significant agricultural import growth in world markets has been in high-valued and processed food products like those exported from California. From 1995–2014, the share of fruits/nuts and vegetables in world agricultural trade declined slightly, while the share of high-value, processed agricultural products increased (Beckman et al., 2017). The fact that fruit and vegetable trade did not increase any faster than total agricultural trade is very surprising given the growing per-capita demand in developed and transition countries for fresh fruits and vegetables. The stagnant share of fruit and vegetable trade no doubt reflects the high level of protectionism around the world for these food categories. For instance, two-tiered tariffs known as tariff-rate quotas (TRQs) are commonly used to restrict imports of fruits and vegetables. Worldwide, there are more than 350 TRQs placed on fruits and vegetables, and more than 25 percent of all agricultural TRQs are concentrated in the fruit and vegetable trade (Skully, 2001), which critically affects California agriculture.

---

12 The Trans-Pacific Partnership (TPP) originally had 12 member countries before the U.S. dropped out. The trade agreement created a platform for economic integration across the Asia-Pacific region, and encompassed existing free trade agreements (FTAs), such as NAFTA. The U.S. does not have FTAs with all TPP nations, and this was a significant reason why the TPP was a good idea for the United States. The U.S. has no FTA with Brunei, Japan, Malaysia, New Zealand, and Vietnam (all TPP members). After the U.S. dropped out of TPP, the agreement's name was changed to the Comprehensive and Progressive Agreement for Trans-Pacific Partnership (CPTPP).

13 http://www.cfbf.com/top-issues/?tab=Trade+%26+Transportation.

Table 15.5. U.S. International Trade in Fruits, Vegetables, and Tree Nuts

Commodity	2000	2005	2010	2015
Exports	$ (Billions)			
Vegetables	1.89	2.42	3.78	4.36
Fruits & Nuts	3.98	6.39	10.14	14.46
Processed Vegetables, Fruits & Nuts	2.22	2.41	3.78	5.43
Imports				
Vegetables	2.65	4.32	6.49	8.66
Fruits & Nuts	3.37	4.88	7.58	12.68
Processed Vegetables, Fruits & Nuts	2.68	3.90	5.48	7.22
Net Trade (Exports – Imports)				
Vegetables	- 0.76	- 1.90	- 2.70	- 4.30
Fruits & Nuts	0.61	1.51	2.56	1.78
Processed Vegetables, Fruits & Nuts	- 0.46	- 1.49	- 1.70	- 1.79

Source: *Trade Data Monitor*, Vegetables HTS 07, Fruits and Nuts HTS 08, and Processed Vegetables, Fruits and Nuts HTS 20

As an exporter of high-value food commodities, California must contend with the fact that import tariffs in important markets, such as the EU, are generally higher on processed agricultural products than on the primary commodities. This tariff wedge between a processed commodity (e.g., processed fruit) and its corresponding primary commodity (e.g., fresh fruit) is referred to as tariff escalation, and this poses a significant obstacle to California exports. Tariff escalation produces a trade bias against processed agricultural and value-added products. There is general evidence of tariff escalation in OECD countries (such as Australia, Canada, the EU, and New Zealand), especially for fruits, vegetables, and nuts, which are major California exports. For many countries, bound tariffs w[14] tend to be higher for processed agricultural products than for unprocessed products, and many importers also practice discriminatory trade behavior, favoring domestic products over imported products. For example, in 2017, the United States launched a trade enforcement action against Canada at the WTO, challenging regulations that discriminate against the sale of U.S. wine in grocery stores. In 2018, Australia initiated a similar WTO case against Canada over trade discrimination in the wine market.

On the import side, the vast majority of U.S. agricultural imports are classified as high-value products, as opposed to bulk commodities. The top horticultural imports by value are legumes, fresh and processed vegetables, processed fruits, nuts, grapes, apples, and citrus. Table 15.5 shows that the U.S. international trade deficit in vegetables grew (in nominal dollars) from $760 million in 2000 to $4.3 billion in 2015. The trade deficit in processed vegetables, fruits, and nuts also grew (from $460 million to $1.79 billion), but if we adjust for inflation, the increase is minimal. Turning to fruits and nuts in Table 15.5, the U.S. trade surplus increased from $610 million to $1.78 billion. One way to interpret the trade statistics in Table 15.5 is to conclude that California's horticultural exports (especially fruits and nuts) have helped to lower the U.S. trade deficit in fruits and vegetables. Although the U.S. share of total world agricultural exports has fallen (Beckman et al., 2017), from 23 percent of global value in 1995 to 12.5 percent in 2013, the agricultural industry in California has lessened the drop.

---

14 A bound tariff is the maximum import duty allowed by the WTO for imports from any member state.

NAFTA

The North American Free Trade Agreement (NAFTA) has impacted California agriculture in a positive way by reducing agricultural trade barriers on the continent. It has improved competition and facilitated foreign investment by California agribusiness in farm production and food processing in Mexico. The trade agreement was signed by the United States, Canada, and Mexico on January 1, 1994, and this trade pact has benefitted producers and consumers in all three member countries. As a result of NAFTA, the agricultural sectors in North America have become more integrated, leading to more trade in a wide range of agricultural products, substantial levels of cross-border investment, and regional changes in production that have lowered costs (Zahniser et al., 2015).

U.S. farm exports to Canada and Mexico rose from $8.9 billion in 1993, before NAFTA implementation, to $38 billion in 2016. In 2016, the U.S. exported $17.6 billion in agricultural products to Mexico and $20.4 billion to Canada. Canada is the No. 2 market for California agricultural exports and Mexico ranks fifth. Canada and Mexico account for about 20 percent of California's agricultural exports. On the import side, Mexico and Canada are both large suppliers to the U.S.; in 2016, the U.S. imported $22.5 and $21.4 billion in agricultural products from these two countries, respectively.[15]

At the outset of NAFTA, there was significant opposition to the agreement from U.S. agriculture. Opposition came from producers of wheat, sugar, peanuts, citrus, and winter fruits and vegetables (Orden, 1996). Some agricultural interests in California opposed NAFTA because of fear of competition from low-wage Mexican agriculture in the production of labor-intensive crops. Proponents argued that NAFTA would enhance the competitiveness of California's agriculture.

Factor price equalization lay at the root of the debate over the effects of liberalized trade on the competitiveness of California agriculture precisely because a large percentage of California's agricultural production is labor-intensive, using a relatively high proportion of labor relative to other inputs such as land and capital. This includes the production of fruits and vegetables, nuts, and various horticultural crops, where labor costs are a relatively high percentage of total production costs.

Despite protectionism on both sides of the border, NAFTA led to freer trade and more cross-border investment between the U.S. and Mexico.[16] For instance, in 1996 the U.S. opened its market to Mexican avocados for the first time in 82 years. Prior to this ruling, phytosanitary rules banned unprocessed Mexican avocados imports and provided considerable protection to California growers. The U.S. decision to import avocados extended beyond that single market and helped to persuade Mexico to reduce import trade barriers on certain fruits.

While the California dairy industry has experienced strong exports sales to Mexico under NAFTA, some of the fruit and vegetable industry (e.g., asparagus) have faced increased competition from rising imports. This suggests that increasing trade flows will entail both risks and benefits for California agricultural producers.

Starting in 2020, the new NAFTA will be known as the USMCA and the changes will only have incremental impacts on California agriculture. This is a good thing because Canada and Mexico are two of the largest trading partners with California agriculture and the freeing up of trade through NAFTA will be preserved with USMCA.

OTHER FOREIGN MARKETS

Despite the fact that Japanese agriculture receives high levels of government support, Japan is also one of the world's largest net importers of agricultural products. The United States supplies roughly 15 percent of Japan's agricultural imports, and in 2016, Japan's agricultural imports from the U.S. were valued at $11 billion.[17] About 15 percent of these U.S. exports to Japan originated in California. Japan is California's fourth largest export market for agricultural products, with rice, almonds, and alfalfa hay ranking as the top commodities (Table 15.3). The U.S. withdrawal from the Trans-Pacific Partnership (TPP) will mean that U.S. agricultural exporters to Japan will be

16 https://www.cfr.org/backgrounder/naftas-economic-impact.

17 https://www.ers.usda.gov/data-products/foreign-agricultural-trade-of-the-united-states-fatus/calendar-year/.

15 USDA, ERS, *Outlook for U.S. Agricultural Trade*, AES-102, Nov. 30, 2017.

at a competitive disadvantage vis-à-vis Japan's TPP trading partners who will face lower import duties under the TPP.

Japan continues to restrict imports of horticultural products, livestock products, and processed foods, all of which are important exports for California. Under the appearance of phytosanitary concerns, Japan restricts imports of U.S. fresh fruit, vegetables, and other horticultural crops, keeping Japanese domestic prices of horticultural products artificially high. Government subsidies encourage farmers to divert land out of rice production and into vegetables. Japan also has country-of-origin labeling requirements for agricultural products, which principally affects fruits, vegetables, and animal products and acts as a non-tariff barrier to trade. Japan maintains high tariffs on beef, citrus, and processed foods. In addition, imported, high-quality California rice is strictly controlled and rarely reaches the consumer food table in Japan. The over-quota rice tariff in Japan exceeds 400 percent.

In the case of fresh oranges and lemons, the U.S. (primarily California and Arizona) is the largest supplier to Japan, accounting for over 80 percent of Japan's imports. Other exporters of oranges and lemons of lesser importance in Japan are Australia, Chile, and South Africa. The Japanese government continues to impose a high import tariff on fresh oranges. The tariff rate is 32 percent for imports during the December–May period, (during the marketing season for domestically produced citrus) and 16 percent during June–November.[18] Japan's import tariffs on table grapes are also relatively high—17 percent from March to October. Import tariffs on wine can range up to 57.7 percent. California is a large supplier of processed fruit to Japan (such as raisins, prunes, and frozen strawberries) and California competes directly with China and other Asian exporters in the Japanese market.

An ongoing trade dispute between the U.S. and the EU concerns the use of geographical indicators (GIs), especially for wine and dairy products. For instance, the EU has over 2,800 wine GI registrations (R. Johnson, 2017). While some GIs are allowed under WTO rules, the EU wants to extend the list of protected products and prohibit foreign producers of food and beverage products

from labeling products with European regional names on hundreds of cheeses, meats, and spirits (e.g., French Champagne and Chablis wine, Italian Parma ham, or French Roquefort cheese). The list of products that will receive this protection is an ongoing subject of negotiations at the WTO.

For California, there is a trade-off associated with GI protection. On the one hand, California would have to stop exporting products using certain names if the EU is successful (e.g., Basmati rice or Feta cheese as these names refer to regions of other countries). This means that U.S. Feta cheese (for example) could not be exported to the EU because any Feta cheese sold in the EU must originate from regions with GI certification. On the other hand, California agriculture could use GI protection to develop niche markets for its food and beverage products, potentially capturing a price premium. In fact, the Napa Valley wine growers support the EU attempt to expand the use of GIs in the U.S. market (R. Johnson, 2017). The TPP will address the regulation of GIs in the Pacific region. Regional free trade agreements that include GI protections but exclude the U.S. can and will affect U.S. trade with that region.

California's agricultural industry is carefully watching developments in China's agricultural trade. China's land area sown to fruits, nuts, and vegetables has grown rapidly in the past decade and trade is expected to take on a greater importance for China in coming years. China's horticultural exports account for a large share of its agricultural exports. Given China's rich agricultural resources, abundant labor supply, and large population, it has great potential to play a much more prominent role in agricultural trade in the coming years, as both an exporter and an importer.

China uses both tariff and non-tariff barriers to restrict agricultural imports. China has in place import tariffs on certain agricultural commodities currently exported by California, such as citrus, table grapes, wine, beef, and dairy products. China has import tariffs on citrus and table grapes of approximately 10 percent and maintains a restrictive tariff rate quota (TRQ) on cotton.

Domestic developments in China, not directly related to trade policy but related to rising incomes, present opportunities for California agricultural exports. For example, the growing importance of Western-style super-

---

18 USDA, FAS GAIN Report, JA7150, Dec. 2017.

markets in Chinese cities may present a new opportunity for California producers to supply pre-packaged or processed products and products that require refrigeration. Another example of the effect of increasing incomes on potential demand for California products is the increasing popularity of wine among China's urban middle class.

China has become a serious export competitor with the U.S. in third markets for horticultural products. This is partly a result of the relative size of the two countries; the harvested area of fruits and vegetables in China is about 22 million hectares, or seven times the U.S. area for these products. As China's agricultural sector moves away from its historical focus on land-intensive grains and concentrates more on labor-intensive cash crops, markets in other parts of Asia will be subject to increased competition from China. The U.S. response to China's production and exports of these products will affect how competition from China impacts California producers.

A skirmish over the garlic market was an example of the policy response to the emergence of China as a competitor. California accounts for over 80 percent of U.S. garlic production but experienced competition from China in the mid-1990s. U.S. imports of Chinese garlic increased from about 3 million pounds a year in 1992 to 64 million pounds by 1994. This raised concerns among California producers. California garlic growers lobbied and won import relief from Chinese imports in 1994, when the U.S. government issued an antidumping order and imposed a 376 percent tariff on garlic imports from China.

Garlic production in California is highly concentrated, with less than 10 producers accounting for about 80 percent of the annual harvest. These growers joined together to seek protection from foreign competition, and they were quite successful at first. China eventually regained its market share after the antidumping case. In 1994, when the case was initiated, the value of U.S. imports of garlic from China decreased from $11.9 million to $4.1 million, a drop of 65.5 percent. However, while China's exports to the United States fell to $250,000 in 1995, Mexico's exports nearly doubled to $20 million, and Argentina's exports increased by an additional 19 percent to $3.9 million. Today, China is once again the No. 1 foreign supplier of garlic to the U.S., and imports from China totaled $145 million in 2016. Other large suppliers to the U.S. include Spain, Mexico, and Argentina.

After joining the World Trade Organization (WTO) in 2001, China increased its trade dependence on agriculture. As of 2019, it was the fourth largest exporter and second largest importer of agricultural products in the world, according to WTO trade statistics.[19] China's import growth has been driven by a shift in its domestic production mix, and changing consumer diets with rising incomes and urbanization. China's substantial increase in fruit and vegetable production is a major factor behind its agricultural export growth. With imports growing faster than exports during the post-WTO accession years, China reversed its long-time status as a net agricultural exporter to that of a net importing country since 2004. Very strong growth in exports of horticultural products (e.g., garlic, apples, pears, and citrus), semi-processed food products (e.g., animal products and pet food), and aquaculture (e.g., fish fillets) have dominated the changing structure of China's agricultural exports.

China is an emerging competitor for U.S. farmers in some specialty crops and China has a positive trade balance with the U.S. on horticultural crops, although the total dollar value is a relatively small share of total agricultural trade. China's growing demand for almonds, pistachios, and walnuts is a positive development for U.S. agriculture. And per-capita consumption of these specialty crops is still very low in China, as Chinese per-capita consumption of almonds is only 5 percent of U.S. levels.

Impediments to foreign market access are an issue for Chinese agribusiness firms. For instance, China's agricultural exports of horticultural products have been adversely affected by antidumping (AD) investigations against them launched by firms in both developing and developed countries. Globally, there have been about 23 AD cases against China's agriculture since that market opened up in the early 1980s, and many of the AD actions in agriculture targeted horticultural products—resulting in very high tariff rates against Chinese firms. Most antidumping cases are nothing more than hidden protectionism. Under U.S. AD law, China is treated as a "non-market economy" and as a result, its exporters have been assessed tariffs higher than typical AD rates applied

---

19 https://www.wto.org/english/res_e/statis_e/wts2020_e/wts2020_e.pdf.

Table 15.6. California Market Access Program Allocations

Trade Organization	FY 2018 Award ($ Millions)
Blue Diamond Growers/Almond Board of California	5.007
California Agricultural Export Council	1.012
California Cherry Marketing and Research Board	0.566
California Cling Peach Growers Advisory Board	0.470
California Fresh Fruit Association	0.405
California Prune Board	2.910
California Strawberry Commission	0.148
California Table Grape Commission	3.285
California Walnut Commission	3.910
Raisin Administrative Committee	2.814
Wine Institute	5.526
Cotton Council International	14.589
Sunkist Growers, Inc	1.720
USA Rice Federation/ U.S. Rice Producers Association	2.488
U.S. Dairy Export Council	4.626
Total	49.47

Source: https://www.fas.usda.gov/programs/market-access-program-map/map-funding-allocations-fy-2018

Notes: Payments to cotton, rice, and dairy producers are not limited to California. Sunkist products are grown in Arizona and California.

to so-called market economies.[20] U.S. AD cases against China's exports have targeted imports of fresh garlic, preserved mushrooms, apple juice concentrate, shrimp, and crawfish tail meat. With the exceptions of honey and shrimp, these cases have had mixed success at keeping out Chinese exports for more than a few years. But in each and every case, the U.S. consumer has paid higher prices as a result of the dumping orders.

The trade war between the U.S. and China that started in 2018 impacted the U.S. and California in a significant way. Average foreign tariffs on agricultural and food products increased from 8.3 percent to 28.6 percent, targeting 1,118 products and affecting more than $28.9 billion US (37.1 percent) of agricultural and food exports of the United States (Carter and Steinbach, 2020a; Balistreti et al., 2020) found that California incurred the largest 'net' welfare loss among all states due to the trade war. Below, we discuss the impacts of the trade war in more detail.

20 U.S. Government Accountability Office (GAO) "U.S.-China Trade: Eliminating Nonmarket Economy Methodology Would Lower Antidumping Duties for Some Chinese Companies" (10-JAN-06, GAO-06-231).

FEDERAL GOVERNMENT SUPPORT FOR CALIFORNIA AGRICULTURE

As previously noted, California agriculture receives relatively few subsidies from the federal government compared to other states. Agricultural producers in California received $425 million in federal assistance in 2016; of this, about $290 million came as crop insurance subsidies. Disaster programs provided $66.6 million and commodity programs paid $62.7 million directly to California farmers. The remainder of government payments to farmers came in the form of conservation programs.[21]

California agriculture receives less than 1 percent of federal commodity payments even though the state produces about 13 percent of national farm output (as of 2016). Federal subsidies to California have also been on the decline as the total was around $800 million in 2001. Farms in California receiving these government payments are growing cotton, rice, and wheat. California has dropped in the national subsidy ranking as cotton production in California has waned.

California also benefits from several smaller government programs designed to either explicitly subsidize exports or promote demand for California specialty products in foreign markets. Government programs that help farmers include marketing and promotion programs, crop insurance and disaster assistance, and trade assistance. In addition to the trade-orientated programs, the USDA purchases fruits, vegetables, and tree nuts for domestic distribution under various subsidized meal programs such as the school lunch program and child nutrition programs. Johnson (2014) reported government purchases of fruits and vegetables totaled $660 million in 2013.

Among the promotion programs, the most important to California producers is the Market Access Program (MAP),

and the Foreign Market Development Program (FMD), both of which subsidize market development activities overseen by trade organizations. In addition, the Technical Assistance for Specialty Crops Program (TASC) funds projects that address technical barriers to the export of specialty crops, such as sanitary and phytosanitary trade barriers.

MAP[22] spends over $49 million per year promoting California crops such as almonds, citrus, kiwifruit, peaches, pears, pistachios, prunes, strawberries, table grapes, tomatoes, tree fruits, and walnuts (see Table 15.6). The California dairy industry benefits from the FMD program, which spends funds to expand foreign imports of U.S. dairy products.

Economic theory predicts that programs like the MAP or FMD are not cost-effective uses of public budgets; it is difficult to find economic evidence in favor of the MAP. If the private benefits of marketing efforts exceed their cost, firms should find it profitable to undertake these efforts without government assistance. Government assistance uses taxpayers' money to underwrite marketing efforts with high costs relative to benefits. Well-known arguments are made for government support for investments that have "externalities"; that is, benefits that accrue to many groups whether they pay the cost of the investment or not. However, the marketing of name-brand agricultural products is not likely to be such an investment.

---

22 https://www.fas.usda.gov/programs/market-access-program-map.

---

21 https://farm.ewg.org/region.php?fips=06000&progcode=total&yr=2016. Twenty-six states received higher total federal government payments to agriculture than California in 2016. Since these states are smaller than California in both area and population, even this ranking understates the extent to which California receives relatively little federal government subsidy to agriculture.

U.S.–CHINA TRADE WAR[25]

In 2018, the U.S. started a trade war with China and other trading partners by introducing import "safeguard" tariffs and quotas on washing machines and solar panels. This was followed up by tariffs on steel and aluminum, apparently imposed for national security reasons, and then followed by additional tariffs on hundreds of Chinese products. One of President Trump's stated goals was to use import trade barriers as leverage to force China to change its policies regarding intellectual property rights and government subsidies. In response, China imposed retaliatory import tariffs, specifically targeting U.S. agricultural exports. These retaliatory tariffs reduced U.S. agricultural exports to China by close to $14.4 billion per year, eliminating China as the No. 1 export market for U.S. agriculture. Some of the agricultural products targeted by China's retaliatory tariffs are important California exports, including almonds, walnuts, pistachios, wine, oranges, and table grapes.

In addition to China, other countries also imposed retaliatory tariffs on U.S. agricultural and food exports in response to the U.S. tariffs on their exports. In 2018, tariffs were imposed by Canada on prepared meats, fruits,

and vegetables, coffee, and whiskey; by Mexico on pork, prepared fruits and vegetables, cheese, and vegetables; by the EU on prepared vegetables and legumes, grains, fruit juice, peanut butter, and whiskey; and by Turkey on tree nuts, rice, some prepared foods, whiskey, and tobacco.

The impact of retaliatory tariffs was particularly significant for agricultural and food trade with China. U.S. exports of these products to China decreased by 63 percent between 2017 and 2018. The trade effects are concentrated in Washington, Louisiana, Texas, California, and Oregon, which together accounted for nearly 80 percent of the overall U.S. exports to China (Carter and Steinbach, 2020b). All states but Oregon saw double-digit percent declines in the value of agricultural exports to China. Several of the retaliatory tariffs were lifted as a result of ongoing negotiations. In May 2019, Canada and Mexico lifted their retaliatory tariffs to clear the way for the ratification of the USMCA, as the United States also lifted its tariffs on steel and aluminum from Mexico and Canada. Moreover, the United States and China reached a trade deal in early January 2020, with China agreeing to resume purchasing U.S. agricultural exports. However the COVID-19 virus further disrupted trade in 2020 and delayed the implementation of this agreement between the U.S. and China.

---

25 This section draws heavily on Carter, 2018 and Carter and Steinbach, 2020b.

Table 15.7. China Import Tariffs in Response to U.S. Tariffs: Selected California Export Products

HS Code	Commodity	Former Tariffs	2018 Tariffs	2019 Tariffs
			Percent	
80211	Almonds, In Shell	10	25	60
80212	Almonds, Shelled	10	25	60
80231	Walnuts, In Shell	25	40	75
80232	Walnuts, Shelled	20	35	70
80251	Pistachios, In Shell	5	20	55
80252	Pistachios, Shelled	5	20	55
80510	Oranges, Fresh	11	26	61
80610	Grapes, Fresh	13	28	63
220410	Sparkling Wine	14	29	54
220421	Wine	14	29	54

Source: USDA FAS GAIN Report Number: CH2019-0194, 1/05/20

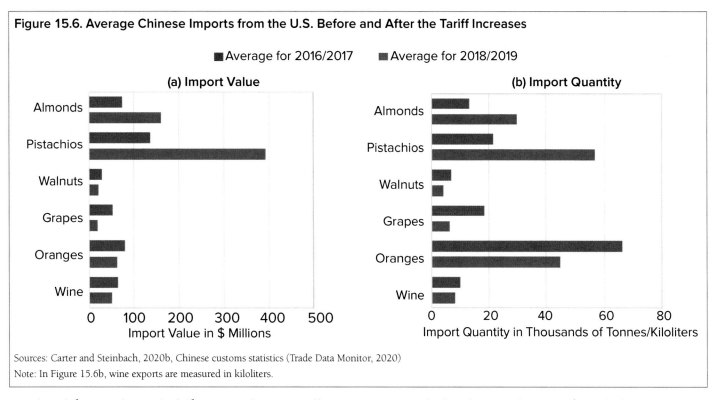

Figure 15.6. Average Chinese Imports from the U.S. Before and After the Tariff Increases

■ Average for 2016/2017   ■ Average for 2018/2019

(a) Import Value

Almonds, Pistachios, Walnuts, Grapes, Oranges, Wine

Import Value in $ Millions (0, 100, 200, 300, 400, 500)

(b) Import Quantity

Almonds, Pistachios, Walnuts, Grapes, Oranges, Wine

Import Quantity in Thousands of Tonnes/Kiloliters (0, 20, 40, 60, 80)

Sources: Carter and Steinbach, 2020b, Chinese customs statistics (Trade Data Monitor, 2020)
Note: In Figure 15.6b, wine exports are measured in kiloliters.

I analyzed the initial round of China's retaliatory tariffs in 2018 (Carter, 2018) and concluded that for wine, walnuts, and table grapes, there would be little export price impact but a loss of market share for California exporters in the Chinese market. For almonds and pistachios, it looked as though the volume of U.S. exports would not be unduly impacted, and this turned out largely to be the case. With the retaliatory tariffs in place, Chinese consumers ended up paying higher prices for almonds and pistachios; nevertheless, imports of these tree nuts from the U.S. remained steady because of the U.S. position as the dominant global supplier. In the case of almonds and pistachios, the U.S. has 86 percent and 71 percent of world exports, respectively. The U.S. share of walnut exports is lower (54 percent), and China is actually a net exporter of walnuts. As a result, U.S. walnut exports to China declined somewhat due to the trade war.

Following the initiation of the trade war between China and the United States, the federal administration decided to spend $28 billion US in 2018 and 2019 on 'trade war compensation' programs for farmers to repay them for the adverse effects of the trade war (mainly with China) (Carter and Steinbach, 2020b). Most of this money was given to farmers in the form of direct payments for eligible commodities. The 2018 and 2019 'trade aid' programs provided special subsidies for three commodity groups—

grains and oilseeds, specialty crops (mainly fruits and nuts), and animal products (hogs and dairy). These subsidy payments were made on a per-unit or per-acre base. Some research has found that the federal administration overpaid farmers for certain commodities because the government did not account for lost exports that may have been diverted to other third countries (Glauber, 2019).

Table 15.7 shows the escalation of China's retaliatory tariffs in 2018 and 2019. California farmers are the primary U.S. supplier of the seven targeted products listed in Table 15.7. Before the trade war, China's import tariffs on the commodities listed in Table 15.7 ranged from 5 percent on pistachios to 25 percent on walnuts. China's initial World Trade Organization tariffs on walnuts were relatively high (20 to 25 percent) to protect its large domestic industry. The annual production of walnuts in China is close to 1 million metric tons, compared to less than 600,000 metric tons in the United States. China is self-sufficient in walnuts but remains reliant on world markets for pistachio and almond supplies. For instance, China is the world's largest pistachio importer. It is the third-largest importer of almonds and the third-largest importer of fresh oranges.

In the first wave of retaliation, China raised its tariffs to the 20–40 percent range. Then, in the second wave, some of China's retaliatory tariffs more than doubled from 2018 to

Table 15.8. Average U.S. Market Share in China for 2016/17 and 2018/19 and Potential Trade Losses

Commodity	Column A Average U.S. Market Share for 2016/2017	Column B Average U.S. Market Share for 2018/2019	Column C 2019 Imports from the U.S.	Column D 2019 Imports from the U.S. Assuming Average 2016/2017 Market Share	Column (C - D) / C
	Percent		$ (Millions)		Percent Change
Almonds	97.4	44.0	197.1	511.9	-159.7
Pistachios	90.8	67.8	483.4	734.5	-52.0
Walnuts	87.8	66.2	14.3	24.1	-68.9
Grapes	8.7	3.1	6.0	56.2	-829.8
Oranges	25.9	14.7	38.2	103.3	-170.8
Sparkling Wine	0.4	0.3	0.1	0.4	-472.1
Wine	2.7	2.2	32.9	59.1	-79.4

Sources: Carter and Steinbach, 2020b; Chinese customs statistics (Trade Data Monitor, 2020)

2019. By 2020, U.S. walnut exports faced the highest tariff (75 percent), while the tariff on pistachios was 55 percent, up from 5 percent before the trade war (see Table 15.7).

The market impact of the Chinese retaliatory tariffs is evaluated by using international trade data from 2016 and 2017 as a benchmark. Data from 2016/2017 is the "before" the retaliatory tariffs period and 2018/2019 is the "after" period. Figure 15.6a illustrates the before and after value of imports into China from the United States and Figure 15.6b reports import quantities.

The annual value of Chinese imports of the seven targeted U.S. products (in Table 15.7) increased from $439 to $706 million from 2016/2017 to 2018/2019, according to Chinese customs statistics. We see from Figure 15.6 that the annual average value of Chinese almond imports from the United States increased from $75 to $160 million and pistachios from $137 to $394 million in 2018/2019 over 2016/2017. In contrast, the annual value of China's imports from the United States declined by 20 percent and 29 percent for wine and walnuts, respectively. Therefore, it appears there was some trade destruction for the targeted products, but this was countered by the substantial growth in China's pistachio imports from the United States.[26]

Although the U.S. remains a major supplier of these seven products to China, it lost significant market shares to foreign competitors partially due to the trade war. Table 15.8 summarizes changes in U.S. market shares in China and shows the maximum potential trade losses due to the tariffs as the percent difference between columns C and D. As shown in columns A and B in Table 15.8, all products experienced a significant drop in market share, with the U.S. market share for almonds dropping by more than 53 percent, from 97.4 percent to 44 percent. Therefore, lost trading opportunities amplified the effects of the trade destruction.

Assuming average 2016/17 market shares for 2019, Chinese imports from the U.S. could have been double their 2019 level ($1,489 million instead of $772 million). Although there is sufficient supply in the market, in a "but for" world, the U.S. may have chosen not to meet all of the increased import demand in China.

There was some degree of trade diversion, and export sales losses for walnuts, almonds, and table grapes largely account for this diversion. The data indicate that Australia (almonds, grapes, oranges, walnuts), Peru (grapes), Chile (walnuts, grapes), Egypt (oranges), and Iran (pistachios) gained from the Chinese tariffs against the United States. For instance, California was the most important exporter of walnuts to China but with the retaliatory tariffs in place, China has shifted to Chile and Australia for imported walnuts—that is what we call trade diversion.

---

26 Trade destruction means U.S. exporters lose sales to China.

CONCLUSION

California's agricultural trading environment holds both new challenges and new opportunities. Established markets in developed countries continue to erect non-tariff barriers against imports of California's specialty crops. The rapidly changing Chinese market holds uncertain benefits, but also the promise of new competition. Further trade liberalization in agriculture is a promising avenue for the expansion of California's agricultural trade. As such, California producers should guard against the temptation to support the expansion of domestic U.S. policies and non-tariff barriers that make far-reaching trade liberalization less likely. Farms in other parts of the U.S. can afford to be protectionist because they are not so dependent on foreign markets; California growers have no such luxury.

Coordinated liberalization does expose California growers to new competition from Mexico and China, especially. Market integration may also lead to new food safety concerns, as with BSE (i.e., mad cow disease). But higher incomes and urbanization abroad should also translate into increased demand for high-value fresh produce and wine. Product differentiation is an important competitive strategy for California, which has a reputation as a high-quality producer and increasingly, as a producer of value-added agricultural and food products. As the trend toward adding value continues to unfold, agricultural goods will less and less be homogenous. There are new opportunities for business in emerging markets as well as competitive challenges.

Not all California agricultural producers win from increased trade liberalization. Ending government support for agriculture and lowering tariff barriers will inevitably benefit some more than others. Coordinated liberalization that affords California increased access to these markets, even if at the expense of increased competition from China and Mexico, could be an important opportunity. This is all the more true because most of California's agricultural producers have few subsidies to give up. Even the loss of the export-promotion programs would not be very costly; these programs provide little benefit to the industries they support.

Finally, the 2018 trade war started by the U.S. administration has been costly for California agriculture in the short-run and could have serious consequences for the long-run as key California agricultural export products lost market share in the growing China market. There could be long-lasting consequences for California associated with China looking elsewhere for export suppliers, diversifying international supply chains.

REFERENCES

Arthur, T., C.A. Carter, and A.P. Zwane. 2003. "International Trade and the Road Ahead for California agriculture." In Jerry Siebert, ed. *California Agriculture Dimensions and Issues*." Berkeley CA: Giannini Foundation of Agricultural Economics, pp. 120–156. Available at: https://s.giannini.ucop.edu/uploads/giannini_public/4e/a8/4ea8b9cc-df88-4146-b1ae-e5467736e104/escholarship_uc_item_9145n8m1.pdf.

Balistreri, E.J., W. Zhang, and J. Beghin. 2020. "The State-level Burden of the Trade War: Interactions between the Market Facilitation Program and Tariffs." *Agricultural Policy Review*, 2020(1):1. Iowa State University. Available at: https://www.card.iastate.edu/ag_policy_review/article/?a=103.

Beckman, J., J. Dyck, and K.E.R. Heerman. 2017. "The Global Landscape of Agricultural Trade, 1995–2014." Washington DC: U.S. Department of Agriculture, Economic Information Bulletin 181 for Economic Research Service, November.

Carter, C.A. 2018. "China's Retaliatory Tariffs and California Agriculture" *ARE Update* 21(4):1-4. University of California Giannini Foundation of Agricultural Economics. Available at: https://giannini.ucop.edu/publications/are-update/issues/2018/21/4/chinas-retaliatory-tariffs-and-california-agricult/.

Carter, C.A. and Steinbach, S. 2020a. "The Impact of Retaliatory Tariffs on Agricultural and Food Trade." Paper presented at NBER Agricultural Markets and Trade Policy Conference, April 30–May 1.

Carter, C.A. and Steinbach, S. 2020b. "Impact of the U.S.-China Trade War on California Agriculture." *ARE Update* 23(3):9-11. University of California Giannini Foundation of Agricultural Economics. Available at: https://giannini.ucop.edu/publications/are-update/issues/2020/23/3/impact-of-the-us-china-trade-war-on-california-agr/.

Glauber, J. W. 2019. "Agricultural Trade Aid: Implications and Consequences for U.S. Global Trade Relationships in the Context of the World Trade Organization." American Enterprise Institute: Washington D.C.

Johnson, R. 2014. "Fruits, Vegetables, and Other Specialty Crops: Selected Farm Bill and Federal Programs." Washington DC: Congressional Research Service Report R42771 prepared for Members and Committees of Congress, July.

Johnson, R. 2016. "The U.S. Trade Situation for Fruit and Vegetable Products." Washington DC: Congressional Research Service Report RL34468 prepared for Members and Committees of Congress, December.

Johnson, R. 2017. "Geographical Indicators (GIs) in U.S. Food and Agricultural Trade." Washington DC: Congressional Research Service Report R44556 prepared for Members and Committees of Congress, March.

McCalla, A.F. and W.E. Johnston. 2004. "Whither California Agriculture?" Special Report, University of California, Giannini Foundation of Agricultural Economics, August. Available at: https://s.giannini.ucop.edu/uploads/giannini_public/43/84/4384fd4a-266c-434a-b85c-83a1ec11e385/escholarship_uc_item_4232w2sr.pdf.

Orden, D. 1996. "Agricultural Interest Groups and the North American Free Trade Agreement." In Anne O. Krueger, ed. *The Political Economy of American Trade Policy*, Chicago IL: University of Chicago Press, pp. 335-382.

Skully, D.W. 2001. "Economics of Tariff-Rate Quota Administration." Washington DC: Market and Trade Economics Division, Economics Research Service, U.S. Department of Agriculture, Technical Bulletin No. 1893, April.

U.S. Department of Agriculture. 2017. "USDA Agricultural Projections to 2026." Washington DC: Interagency Agricultural Projections Committee, Office of the Chief Economist, World Agricultural Outlook Board, Long-Term Projections Report OCE-2017–1, February.

U.S. International Trade Commission. 2016. "Trans-Pacific Partnership Agreement: Likely Impact on the U.S. Economy and on Specific Industry Sectors." Washington DC: Publication 4607, Investigation No. TPA-105-001, May.

Zahniser, S., S. Angadjivand, T., Hertz, L. Kuberka, and A. Santos. 2015. "NAFTA at 20: North America's Free-Trade Area and its Impact on Agriculture." Washington DC: U.S. Department of Agriculture, Economic Research Service, Outlook Report No. WRS-15-01, February.

Chapter 16. Climate Change and California Agriculture

Katrina Jessoe, Pierre Mérel, and Ariel Ortiz-Bobea

Abstract

Recent climate projections indicate an unambiguous warming across California and all seasons over the 21st century. Projections regarding the amount of precipitation are less clear, but it is likely that rising temperatures will reduce mountain snowpack, which provides critical natural water storage for irrigated agriculture. Changes in the timing, and potentially the quantity, of runoff will likely disrupt surface water distribution, placing agricultural operations at risk. Climate variability is also predicted to increase with more frequent occurrence of droughts.

Climate change is expected to reduce yields of major field crops, including cotton and wheat. Impacts on fruit and nut crops appear unclear, and highly dependent on the crop considered and the modeling approach used. One prominent study predicts stagnating yields for almonds and table grapes and declining yields for strawberries and cherries by mid-century. The suitability of California regions for premium wine grape production could also be negatively affected by climate change.

Animals will also be affected by rising temperatures, with milk yields likely declining due to heat stress. Workers tend to be less productive at low (under 55°F) and high (over 100°F) temperatures. Agriculture could adapt, moving dairy cows to cooler regions, but perhaps raising the cost of feed procurement. Farm workers could work at night, necessitating lighting systems and perhaps premium wages.

To combat climate change, the state has enacted a series of important legislation, starting with the 2006 Global Warming Solutions Act. While it is unclear whether California will succeed in changing the path of global climate, it is likely that constraints on greenhouse gas emissions in California will come at a cost. California farms may be affected by the state's climate policies through higher energy prices and lower processing capacity, as food-processing plants are covered by the state's cap-and-trade program and may lose competitiveness relative to unregulated regions. The dairy and livestock sector, the main contributor to agricultural greenhouse gas emissions in California, is also expected to reduce its methane emissions greatly in the near future.

About the Authors

Katrina Jessoe is an associate professor in the Department of Agricultural and Resource Economics at the University of California, Davis. She can be contacted by email at kkjessoe@ucdavis.edu. Pierre Mérel is a professor in the Department of Agricultural and Resource Economics at the University of California, Davis. He can be contacted by email at merel@primal.ucdavis.edu. Both are members of the Giannini Foundation of Agricultural Economics. Ariel Ortiz-Bobea is an assistant professor at the Charles H. Dyson School of Applied Economics and Management at Cornell University. He can be contacted by email at ao332@cornell.edu.

Changing temperature and precipitation patterns may create serious challenges for irrigation water management across the state. As a result, farms will likely face an overall reduction in available surface water. During the recent drought, many almond orchards were abandoned in the Central Valley due to lack of available water.

Photo Credit: Pierre Mérel

CHAPTER 16. TABLE OF CONTENTS

INTRODUCTION

Nowhere has the field of agricultural economics transformed more over the last 15 years than in the area of climate change. In the previous edition of this book, little more than five paragraphs were devoted to the topic. Since then, California has introduced pioneering legislation to reduce greenhouse gas emissions and weathered a historic drought; the topic of climate change and agriculture regularly appears in headlines and on the news; and researchers across a number of disciplines have dedicated themselves to understanding the links between weather, climate, and agriculture. In short, the intersection of climate change and agriculture has taken center stage in discussions among farmers, policymakers, and researchers alike.

This chapter seeks to take a stock of the state of knowledge on climate change and agriculture in California, and provide an overview of climate change and how it relates to California agriculture. We begin by describing the historic and variable climate that characterizes the state, and then lean on climate change models to make projections about changes in temperature and precipitation under various warming scenarios. Next, we summarize the implications of these projected changes in temperature and precipitation for irrigated water supplies. We then ask: "what does climate change mean for agricultural outcomes?" where we focus on impact assessment for farm profitability, crop yields, animal productivity, and labor productivity. After highlighting a number of primary channels through which climate change could affect agriculture in California, we evaluate the role adaptation can play in reducing the negative effects of climate change on agriculture. Our discussion of adaptation looks at the potential of crop switching to reoptimize outcomes under a new climate regime. Given California's aggressive and trailblazing efforts to reduce greenhouse gas emissions, we also survey the efforts taken by the state to mitigate agricultural greenhouse gas emissions.

A review of the literature cited in this paper reveals a young, exciting, growing, and collaborative field, and this chapter seeks to provide a primer on the essentials of this literature for the setting of California. While this survey of the literature is broad, it is not exhaustive. For this reason, we view this chapter as a starting point on the potential impacts of climate change on California agriculture. Fortunately, to get a broader understanding for the fields of climate change economics, climate change and agriculture, or the methodologies underpinning this work one can seek counsel from an array of comprehensive papers on these topics (Auffhammer et al., 2013; Auffhammer and Schlenker, 2014; Blanc and Reilly, 2017; Carleton and Hsiang, 2016a; Dell et al., 2014; Tol, 2018).

While the state of knowledge has advanced substantially over the past decade, substantial uncertainty still surrounds the relationship between agriculture and climate change in California. To see this, simply look at projections about changes in the amount of precipitation across climate change models. Some project increases in precipitation; others foresee no change; and others anticipate decreases in precipitation. What emerges from these models is little consensus on the projected changes in California precipitation. These gaps in our understanding about climate change and agriculture stem in part from the complex nature of the question in the context of California. The natural and built landscape vary substantially across the state, implying that climate change may manifest itself very differently depending on the weather, topography, infrastructure, and built resilience of a region. As we discuss in the chapter, this variation makes the question of the climate change impacts on agriculture complicated, and ripe for future research.

PAST CLIMATE TRENDS
AND PREDICTED CLIMATE CHANGES IN CALIFORNIA

To set the stage for an assessment of the effect of a changing climate on California agriculture, we first look at recent trends in climatology across California regions. Then, we present future prospects of climate derived from climate models and warming scenarios for the mid-century period. The advantage of looking at past climate trends, in addition to projections of future climate, is that although historical trends may not continue into the future, their derivation largely relies on actual observations and is therefore subject to less uncertainty than climate model output. While recent trends can stem from natural weather variability, they remain important to put future projections in context.

Historical trends in weather are calculated using daily gridded weather data at a 4 km resolution over the

years 1981–2016 from the PRISM database.[1] The PRISM Climate Group uses climate observations from a range of monitoring networks to develop spatially explicit climate databases that reveal short- and long-run climate patterns.

Figure 16.1 shows the resulting trends in precipitation, computed as the percentage change in 18-year averages between the periods 1981–1998 and 1999–2016 for annual precipitation (panel (a)), and as absolute changes in

---

1   There are several tradeoffs associated with reporting weather trends, including regarding geographical resolution and time coverage. The PRISM data is a high-resolution dataset that is particularly well suited to analyzing California's heterogenous landscape. We chose to utilize the more recent PRISM data, which covers the years 1981 to present, because the longer time series stops in 2005. PRISM Climate Group, Oregon State University, http://prism.oregonstate.edu, created 29 Jul 2016.

Figure 16.1. Recent Trends in Precipitation

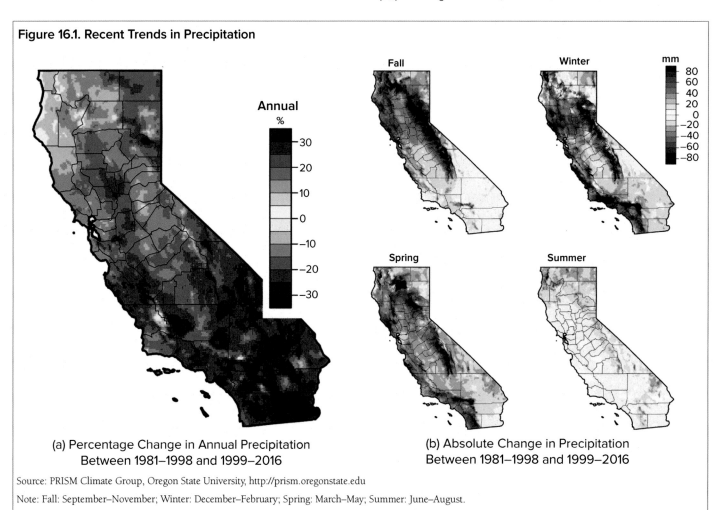

(a) Percentage Change in Annual Precipitation
Between 1981–1998 and 1999–2016

(b) Absolute Change in Precipitation
Between 1981–1998 and 1999–2016

Source: PRISM Climate Group, Oregon State University, http://prism.oregonstate.edu

Note: Fall: September–November; Winter: December–February; Spring: March–May; Summer: June–August.

millimeters (mm) for each season (panel (b)). The figure shows decreases in precipitation of about 20 percent in the recent period, with more pronounced declines in the southern part of the state. The largest absolute reductions in rainfall have occurred in places with higher rainfall, which generally correspond to higher-altitude areas— mainly the northern part of the state (Klamath mountains), the Sierra Nevada, the Northern and Southern Coast Ranges, and the Transversal and Peninsular Ranges in the south. Because these trends are computed using 18-year averages, rather than 30-year averages as would normally be required to obtain climate normals, one should be

cautious in interpreting them. In particular, the recent multi-year drought partially drives these trends, and its impact might be attenuated when using longer time series.

Figure 16.2 describes changes in temperature over the period 1981–2016, also using 18-year averages. Panel (a) shows changes in February minimum temperature, a weather indicator that has been shown to impact almond yields (see Impacts on Key Crops, p. 360), changes in chilling hours (hours with temperature between 0 and 7°C) and changes in chilling-degree hours (a related measure that gives more weight to temperatures closer to the

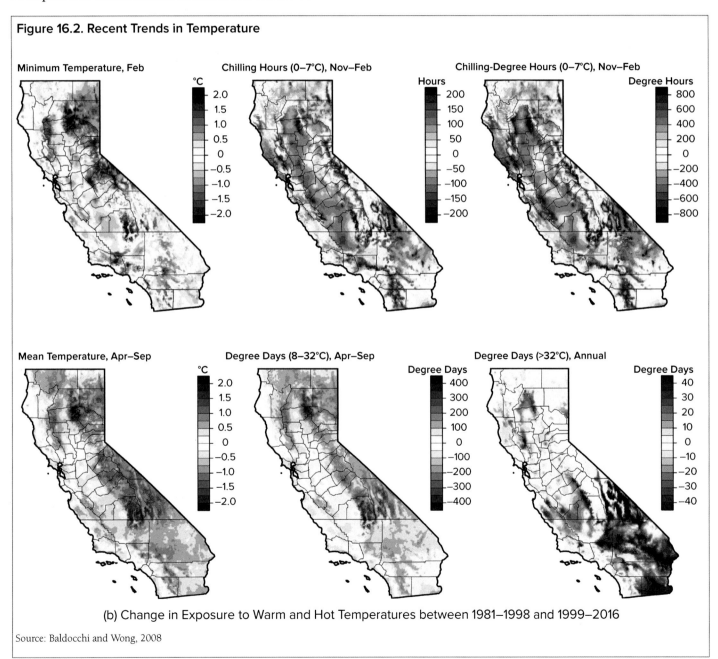

Figure 16.2. Recent Trends in Temperature

Minimum Temperature, Feb

Chilling Hours (0–7°C), Nov–Feb

Chilling-Degree Hours (0–7°C), Nov–Feb

Mean Temperature, Apr–Sep

Degree Days (8–32°C), Apr–Sep

Degree Days (>32°C), Annual

(b) Change in Exposure to Warm and Hot Temperatures between 1981–1998 and 1999–2016

Source: Baldocchi and Wong, 2008

bottom threshold of 0°C).[2] Chilling hours are a relevant climatic indicator for California agriculture because an extended period of cool temperatures is needed for many fruit trees to become and remain dormant and subsequently set fruit.[3] Panel (a) reveals geographically heterogeneous trends. Regions of higher altitude have experienced warming trends with higher February minimum temperature, and higher chilling hours from November to February due to a reduction of exposure to freezing temperatures. Low-altitude regions, notably the Central Valley, have experienced a cooling trend in February but an overall warming in other months. Notably, the regions of the state with fruit and nut crops have seen a decline in chilling hours which, if exacerbated by climate change, may jeopardize some key California crops (Baldocchi and Wong, 2008).

Panel (b) of Figure 16.2 describes historical trends in exposure to warm temperatures during the spring-summer growing season. The first graph shows that, except for a narrow coastal band and the Sacramento-San Joaquin River Delta, California has seen an increase in average April–September temperature of about +0.5°C across the Central Valley, with more pronounced warming in the Sierra Nevada and both the northern and southern parts of the state. When looking at degree days accumulation between 8 and 32°C, a measure of time exposure to beneficial temperatures agronomically relevant for many crops, this warming pattern persists.[4] One exception is the Central Valley, where some regions have experienced slightly more

degree days and others slightly less. The desert region to the southeast of the state, including the Imperial Valley, appears to have experienced an increase in degree days accumulation, as well as a large increase in exposure to heat, as captured by harmful degree days (i.e., °C exposure beyond a threshold of 32°C).

Figures 16.3 and 16.4 describe projected changes in precipitation and temperature by mid-century (2036–2065) relative to the reference period 1971–2000, based on an average of models from the ensemble of General Circulation Models (GCMs) in the Coupled Model Intercomparison Project Phase 5 (CMIP5), the latest set of climate projections of the Intergovernmental Panel on Climate Change (IPCC, 2013).[5] We consider projections under four Representative Concentration Pathways (RCPs). RCPs refer to greenhouse gas concentration trajectories and range from rapid emissions reductions (RCP 2.6) to continued emissions increases (RCP 8.5). We focus on the mid-century period because end-of-century projections are arguably subject to greater uncertainty. The native climate change projections in CMIP5 typically have low spatial resolution (about 100 km), so we rely on downscaled projections (1/8 deg or about 14 km) from the Downscaled CMIP3 and CMIP5 Climate and Hydrology Projections archive. These projections are corrected for biases introduced in the statistical downscaling procedure.

The climate model ensemble projects modest increases in annual precipitation in the northern and central parts of California, in the order of 5 percent, but reductions in the southern part of the state. Most precipitation in California occurs during the winter period, and this model ensemble indicates the largest increases in absolute precipitation during winter months, particularly in higher altitude areas (up to about 30 mm). The highest increases in winter precipitation seem to happen under the most rapid warming scenario RCP 8.5. These precipitation changes remain

2 Specifically, chilling degree hours are calculated as a weighted summation over winter months of the number of hours of exposure to temperatures between 0 and 7°C, with higher weights given to cooler temperatures within this range. For instance, one hour of exposure to a temperature of 6°C would result in one chilling degree hour, whereas one hour of exposure to 4°C would result in three chilling degree hours. Temperatures below 0°C or above 7°C do not contribute chilling hours or chilling degree hours.

3 For instance, almonds need between 400 and 700 chilling hours. (Baldocchi and Wong, 2008).

4 Degree days between 8 and 32°C represent the total time spent at a temperature between 8 and 32°C, with warmer temperatures being counted more heavily than cooler ones—up to the 32°C threshold. For instance, one day of exposure to 9°C counts as one degree day, while one day of exposure at 10°C counts two degree days, and one day of exposure at 32°C or above counts 24 degree days. Exposure below 8°C does not contribute to degree days.

5 In Appendix Table 16.1A. we indicate, for each climatic variable and RCP scenario, the set of GCMs that were used to compute the average projection. We acknowledge the World Climate Research Programme's Working Group on Coupled Modelling, which is responsible for CMIP, and we thank the climate modeling groups (listed in Table 16.1A of this chapter) for producing and making available their model output. For CMIP the U.S. Department of Energy's Program for Climate Model Diagnosis and Intercomparison provides coordinating support and led development of software infrastructure in partnership with the Global Organization for Earth System Science Portals. https://gdo-dcp.ucllnl.org/downscaled_cmip_projections/ (Reclamation 2013)

Figure 16.3. Projected Changes in Precipitation by Mid-Century

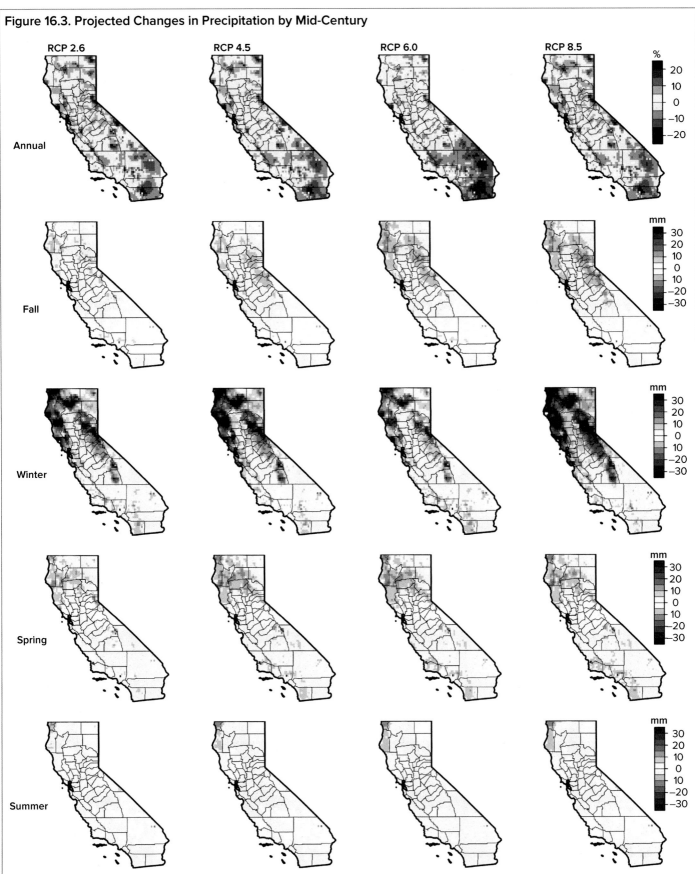

Note: Each panel represents an average of projected changes by 2036–2065 relative to the reference period 1971–2000 across several climate models (see Table 16.1A), for a given RCP scenario. Fall: September–November; Winter: December–February; Spring: March–May; Summer: June–August.

modest, highly dependent on geography, and sometimes contradict earlier predictions, e.g., Cayan et al., 2008. They should thus be interpreted with caution. Moreover, higher temperature may affect the snowpack at high altitudes, so winter precipitation has a higher chance of resulting in rainfall rather than snowfall.

Unlike precipitation patterns, temperature effects seem to be consistent across the year and geographically, and in line with earlier studies at least in term of direction (Hayhoe

et al., 2004; VanRheenen et al., 2004; Cayan et al., 2008). Our model ensemble projects unequivocal warming in virtually every part of the state and across seasons. Winter minimum temperatures are projected to rise by 1–2°C, and more under scenario RCP 8.5. Both mean and maximum temperatures are projected to increase during the months of April to September, by 2–3°C, and more under scenario RCP 8.5. Maximum temperature during those months is predicted to increase more than mean temperature.

Figure 16.4. Projected Changes in Temperature by Mid-Century

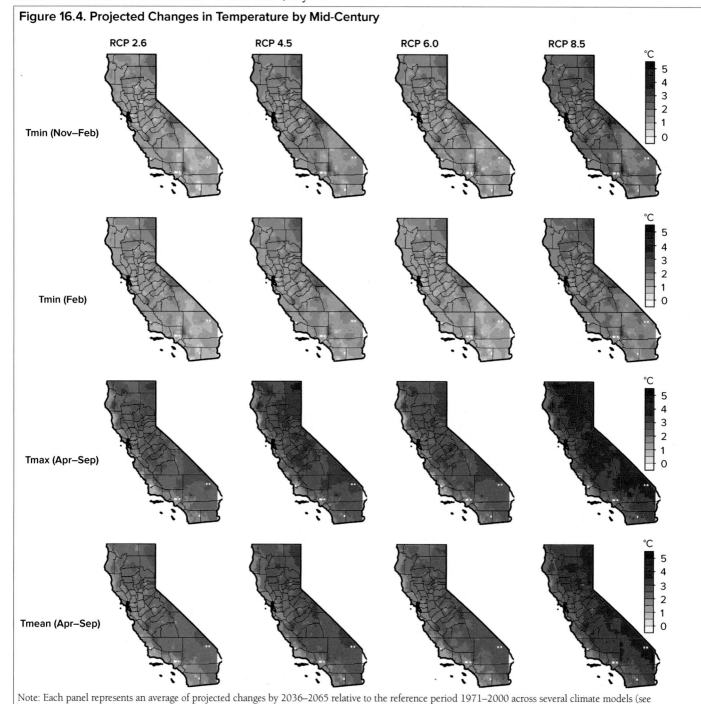

Note: Each panel represents an average of projected changes by 2036–2065 relative to the reference period 1971–2000 across several climate models (see Table16.1A), for a given RCP scenario.

CLIMATE CHANGE IMPACTS ON IRRIGATION WATER AVAILABILITY

Climate change may substantially alter irrigation supplies in California, though there is limited consensus on exact trends in precipitation patterns across climate models. Given the irrigated nature of California agriculture, and the potential of irrigation to mitigate some of the effects of increasing temperature on plants and animals alike, it is expected that changes in surface water supplies and groundwater availability will strongly influence the costs of climate change. This section provides a brief overview of the natural, built, and legal architecture that defines the state's water supply, and discusses how irrigated water availability may evolve with climate change.

Contrary to common belief, California is a relatively water abundant state with more than 200 million acre-feet of precipitation occurring in an average year. Local surface water, imported surface water, and groundwater serve as the primary water supplies. Snow and rain occurring mostly between November and April and mainly in the mountainous north supply sufficient moisture for plants during these months. Reservoirs, aquifers, and snowpack are critical for shifting water, allowing winter precipitation to be accessed during the dry months of May to October, when demand for water is greatest. Groundwater provides a stored source of water that becomes increasingly important and relied upon during periods of drought.

California's extensive water conveyance and storage systems have helped to align supply and demand geographically. To meet growing agricultural and urban demands, large city, state, and federal water projects were built in the early and mid-1900s. Led by the city of Los Angeles' diversions from Owens Valley in 1906, and San Francisco's damming of the Hetch Hetchy in Yosemite National Park in 1928, regional, federal, and state governments soon followed with larger water projects that connected major water users with streams throughout California's Central Valley, the Trinity River, and the Colorado River. Each of these projects has a colorful history. The complex network of dams, reservoirs, and canals, funded and supported by numerous agencies, helps explain how agriculture and cities can thrive in water-scarce regions of the state (e.g., Los Angeles).

An important foundation for determining the distribution and consumption of water is the legal framework that guides the assignment of water rights. California has a peculiar mix of old English and western "first-in-time, first-in-right" priority water rights. An extensive system of water contracts that govern the distribution and operation of water from water projects supplements this water rights system. During drought, lower-priority rights holders face curtailments or are denied water, regardless of the value they attach to water. Many respond by pumping additional groundwater, which has led to long-term over-pumping of less regulated groundwater in some areas.

Climate change models project changes to the variability, timing, and form of precipitation in the state. This arises from changes in precipitation patterns and warming temperatures. The warming temperatures projected under almost all climate change scenarios imply that less precipitation will fall as snow, the snowpack will melt earlier, and increased evaporation will reduce soil moisture and surface water availability. This will impact the state's ability to store irrigated water, and to manage when irrigation occurs.

Projected temperature increases will shift precipitation from snow to rain and will reduce the state's capacity to store water in the Sierra Nevada and southern Cascades snowpack. In a given year, California's snowpack stores over 15 million acre-feet and supplies approximately one-third of the water used by agriculture and cities. With climate change, the snowpack may be reduced by between 29 to 89 percent by the end of the century (Maurer, 2007; VanRheenen et al., 2004; Vicuna et al., 2007).

Warming temperatures will impact when the existing snowpack melts, and as a result when irrigated water can be accessed. In California, a mismatch exists between the timing of precipitation and demand for irrigation: precipitation occurs mainly between November and April while demand peaks between May to October. The melting of the snowpack into river basins that supply water to the State Water Project and Central Valley Project provides a natural process to align supply with demand. Warming temperatures are associated with declines in fractional spring stream flow and an increase in the amount of total annual runoff occurring in the winter (as opposed to the spring and summer) (Vicuna and Dracup, 2007; Maurer, 2007). A change in the timing of when surface water supplies are available may have implications for the storage and delivery of irrigated water (Vicuna et al., 2007).

It may appear that the average annual precipitation in California may not change. At a state level, there is little consensus on changes in annual average state rainfall, with some predicting increases, others predicting decreases, and still others projecting minimal changes (Cayan et al., 2008; VanRheenen et al., 2004; Maurer and Duffy, 2005; Vicuna et al., 2007). These discrepancies in annual projections about the quantity of annual rainfall mask some consistent and important findings that emerge from the literature. Variability in interdecadal precipitation is expected to increase, with both droughts and floods becoming more frequent and more severe. So while average annual rainfall may change little, the variability from year to year is likely to increase (Hayhoe et al., 2004).

Climate change models project that the length, frequency, and severity of extreme droughts will increase, with the proportion of years categorized as dry or critical increasing from 32 percent to 50–64 percent by the end of the century (Hayhoe et al., 2004), and the co-occurrence of dry and extremely warm weather conditions increasing as well (Diffenbaugh et al., 2015). In addition to an increase in dry periods, winter flooding may also increase. The increased risk of winter flooding is attributable to earlier melting of the snowpack. An increase in both droughts and floods sets up a new water dilemma in the state: water managers must decide whether to increase reserve capacity in reservoirs to protect against winter flooding or increase the quantity of water stored in reservoirs to insure against droughts and/or reduced springtime runoff.

If agriculture responds to reductions in surface water supplies through increased reliance on groundwater resources, groundwater overdraft may be an indirect effect of climate change. While one cannot directly point the arrow from climate change to groundwater overdraft, droughts in California are strongly correlated with increased groundwater extraction. Recent work highlights that groundwater depletion in the Central Valley increases during droughts (Scanlon et al., 2012; Famiglietti et al.,

2011). The relationship between droughts and groundwater extraction was on display during the recent drought in California. Surface water deliveries to agriculture from the Central Valley Project and State Water Project decreased by a third, and farmers offset approximately 70 percent this reduction through an increase in groundwater use (Howitt et al., 2015). While groundwater serves as a critical source of water, particularly during droughts, management has not been optimal and there are concerns that this resource may not be available to cope with future droughts. In the last year of this drought (2014), the state passed the Sustainable Groundwater Management Act, which requires local groundwater plans to achieve sustainability. More active groundwater storage management could substantially reduce the costs of future drought to agriculture.

Changing temperature and precipitation patterns will create serious challenges for irrigation water management across the state. With less rainfall stored as snowpack and a limited capacity to hold water in existing storage systems, total water storage is likely to decrease. As a result, farms will likely face an overall reduction in available surface water, potentially exacerbated by increasing demands from urban and environmental sectors. While groundwater pumping may, as in recent times of drought, partially compensate for reductions in water deliveries, this response is not a sustainable solution to long-run surface water reductions. Increasing groundwater recharge during the wet period through controlled flooding may represent one of the most promising adaptation avenues.

CLIMATE CHANGE IMPACTS ON AGRICULTURE

California is the leading U.S. state in terms of agricultural cash receipts, largely due to its ability to grow high-value specialty crops thanks to fertile soils, favorable climate, and large investments in both public and private irrigation infrastructure. Climate change may affect California agriculture through two main channels: the direct effect of weather on crops and animals, (e.g., through increased exposure to extreme heat), and the ability of California's natural and man-made water reserves to deliver water to crops at the time when they need it. While the impacts of a warming climate in terms of heat exposure are well documented in other parts of the U.S., evaluating the impact of climate change on California agriculture presents unique challenges due to the diversity and specificity of its main crops and its reliance on irrigation as the main source of water supply, as opposed to rainfall. In this section, we aim to take a careful look at the available evidence on the impact of climate on farm profitability, crop yields, and animal productivity.

METHODOLOGICAL APPROACHES

Much of the uncertainty surrounding the impacts of foreseeable climate change on California agriculture largely stems from its very specificity in the U.S. agricultural landscape, which has constrained the set of methods that can be leveraged to assess climate impacts. There are three main ways to assess the possible impacts of climate change on agriculture: (i) direct experimental evidence, (ii) biophysical models, and (iii) statistical methods that directly rely on historical agricultural outcomes data.

Method (i) would consist of experimentally changing one or more aspects of weather, e.g., temperature in a controlled environment, to track how plants or animals would fare under a different climate. This method can be costly to implement, and because it is impossible to submit comprehensive natural and human systems such as a farm to experimentally designed environmental signals, it will generally fall short of delivering the net impact of climate change on agricultural outcomes.

Method (ii) is a partial answer to these challenges. Biophysical models are stylized representations of the relationships between soils, weather, biophysical processes, and, where relevant, human actions that are calibrated using observational or experimental data. They can be used to predict outcomes (e.g., yields or crop quality) under conditions outside of those used for calibration, negating the need for additional experimental data collection. For important food crops such as wheat, agronomic models are still the method of choice to predict climate change impacts (e.g., Asseng et al., (2015). However, because these models usually require extensive experimental or observational data as a basis for calibration, and because they are more easily developed for annual than perennial crops, a large set of California specialty crops has so far escaped the attention of crop modelers. Another drawback of process-based crop models is that they usually cannot account for pests and diseases, which is particularly problematic for fruit and nut crops (Lobell et al., 2007).

As a result, method (iii), estimation of statistical relationships, has so far been the method of choice in the literature to decipher climate change impacts for many California crops. This stands in sharp contrast to the large body of experimental and model-based evidence for major field crops such as wheat or corn. One of the traditional challenges associated with the statistical approach is the selection of relevant weather covariates to explain observed outcomes such as yield. Nowhere is this issue more salient than for California perennial cropping systems, which may respond to a large suite of weather signals spanning more than a calendar year.

PROFITABILITY OF FARM OPERATIONS

Within statistical methods, two main approaches have been introduced to infer climate impacts on agriculture. The cross-sectional or Ricardian (a.k.a. "hedonic") approach, introduced by Mendelsohn et al. (1994) in their study of U.S. agriculture, compares agricultural outcomes such as farmland values across places with differing climates, controlling for an array of potentially confounding factors such as soils, proximity to urban centers, or population.

Other things being held constant, comparing land values in a "warm" vs. "cool" location will reflect the impact of warming, net of any of the adjustments made by humans to adapt to climatic conditions. The appeal for this method lies in the fact that the recovered impact implicitly includes adjustments made in response to warmer climate, such as changes in input intensity, planting dates, crop varieties, cropping patterns, etc. The main drawbacks are that these adjustments remain implicit (i.e., one does not learn how agents have adapted to climate) and that the Ricardian estimates are vulnerable to omitted variables bias; that is, the possibility that differences in outcomes across differing climates may be due to factors other than climate but correlated with it, such as unobserved soil quality attributes.

The second approach, known as the panel approach, addresses this last criticism by using panel (as opposed to cross-sectional) data and non-parametrically controlling for time-invariant confounding factors through the inclusion of locational fixed effects. The linear panel approach uses year-to-year fluctuations in weather, rather than cross-sectional climate differences, to identify the effect of climate on agricultural outcomes such as profits, revenues, or yields. As a result, panel estimates have been criticized for failing to include long-run adaptations to climate (Mendelsohn and Massetti, 2017). As indicated by Hsiang (2016), these issues reveal a tradeoff between the causality of the statistical estimate of the climate-outcome relationship and its relevance as an indicator of net climate change impacts. Thankfully, both Ricardian and panel approaches have been implemented for California, so that one may compare results from the two approaches.

Schlenker et al. (2007) is a reference study that implements the Ricardian approach on a sample of farms spanning agricultural regions of California. The authors regress geo-referenced farmland values obtained from the June Agricultural Survey of the U.S. Department of Agriculture on a set of climatic and soil variables, as well as a measure of average surface water deliveries per acre at the level of the water district. Access to groundwater is proxied using depth to groundwater, itself interpolated from well-level data. One of the innovations in the study by Schlenker et al. (2007) relative to prior work is that the effect of temperature on farmland values is modeled

through growing degree days rather than average monthly temperature over selected months of the growing season. Growing degree days are a measure of the time exposure (over the growing season) to temperatures deemed to be beneficial for plant growth; that is, neither too cool nor to hot. Depending on the initial distribution of temperature exposure, warming may result in more or less growing degree days. Heat degree days, in contrast, represent time exposure to detrimental hot temperatures. For instance, assuming that heat degree days are measured starting at a temperature threshold of 34°C, one day at 35°C would translate into one heat degree day, while one day at 36°C would translate into two heat degree days. Uniform warming would unambiguously result in more heat degree days as more time is spent at temperatures above the threshold.

The analysis by Schlenker et al. (2007) reveals that farmland values respond nonlinearly to growing degree days (calculated over the six-month period between April and September between the thresholds of 8°C and 32°C, see footnote 4), in the sense that there is a degree day "optimum," at about 2,500 degree days. This means that

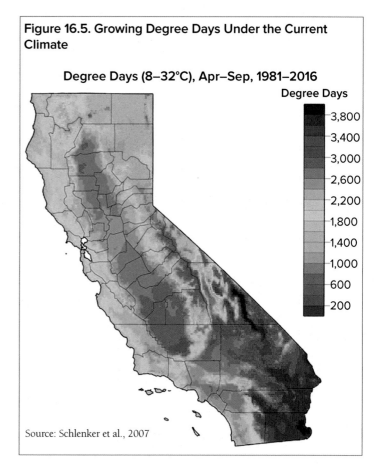

Figure 16.5. Growing Degree Days Under the Current Climate

Degree Days (8–32°C), Apr–Sep, 1981–2016

Degree Days

3,800
3,400
3,000
2,600
2,200
1,800
1,400
1,000
600
200

Source: Schlenker et al., 2007

farmland values decrease if growing degree days are either too small (not enough useful heat accumulation) or too large (perhaps a proxy for extreme heat, which negatively affects crop growth and thus farmland values). Figure 16.5 shows growing degree days across California, computed as an average across the years 1981–2016 using the PRISM dataset referenced previously.

The map shows that most of California's Central Valley is already at or near the optimum growing degree days, and the southern part of the San Joaquin Valley is above it. In contrast, the Imperial Valley is far beyond the optimum. Further warming would thus hurt agriculture in these regions, particularly in the southern part of the state. Schlenker et al. (2007) also show that water deliveries strongly capitalize into farmland values, as expected given the irrigated nature of California agriculture. Specifically, depending on the controls included in the hedonic regression, the capitalized value of 1 acre-foot of surface water delivery, net of any charges levied by water districts, ranges from $ 568/acre to $ 852/acre, for an average farmland value of $4,177 in the sample. Reductions in water deliveries caused by climate change thus have the potential to affect farmland values significantly and therefore the profitability of agriculture in California.[6]

Deschenes and Kolstad (2011) implement a panel approach by combining county-level profit outcomes from the Census of Agriculture for the years 1987, 1992, 1997, and 2002 with detailed daily weather station data. They regress farm profits on three main weather indicators: annual growing degree days, annual precipitation, and annual heat degree days. One drawback when implementing the panel approach on farm profits, as indicated by Fisher et al. (2012) and acknowledged by the authors of the California study, is that yearly profits may only partially reflect the impact of yearly weather on agricultural productivity, since farmers may store products across years to smooth income. In the limit, if the smoothing were perfect, yearly profits would be completely disconnected from yearly weather realizations.

Perhaps surprisingly, the estimates in Deschenes and Kolstad (2011) suggest that farm profits are decreasing in growing degree days, increasing in heat degree days, and decreasing in precipitation. Only the precipitation effect is statistically significant, and implies that an additional 100 mm of rainfall decreases yearly profits by about $28 per acre. The authors then use their coefficient estimates to infer the impact of changing temperature and precipitation, as predicted by the CCSM model (version 3) from the National Center for Atmospheric Research under two warming scenarios, on farm profits. They look at two warming scenarios, a "business as usual scenario" (IPCC scenario A2) and a more moderate warming scenario (IPCC scenario B1), and two prediction horizons, 2010–2039 and 2070–2099. Their results indicate that California farm profits would increase in the medium term (+4.2 percent under scenario A2 and +6.1 percent under scenario B1) while the effect is ambiguous in the long term (0.6 percent and –2.8 percent). These effects are imprecisely estimated, however.[7]

To provide some context to the above damage estimates, it might be useful to compare them to estimates of the economic impact of recent droughts on California agriculture. Howitt et al. (2015) estimate the total economic impact of the 2015 drought to be $2.7 billion, of which $1.8 billion represent direct costs to agricultural farms. Assuming that climate change affects agriculture principally through reduced water availability, say by 2 acre-feet per acre as extrapolated by Schlenker et al. (2007), the Ricardian model implies an impact on farmland values ranging from $1,136 to $1,704 per irrigated acre. Using an estimate of 10 million acres of irrigated farmland, this impact translates into an economic loss of $11.4–17.0 billion. Assuming a discount rate of 5 percent, the drought impact estimated by Howitt et al. (2015) would translate into a net present value of $36 billion. Although it is

---

6   One caveat to this last point is in order. To the extent that the opportunity costs of agricultural water deliveries are not fully reflected in the retail costs paid by farmers (i.e., subsidized water), then the capitalized value of water above would overstate the actual social value of water, and the ensuing social damages from reduced water availability due to climate change.

7   The authors also estimate a model wherein the five-year moving averages of past weather variables are included as separate regressors. The regression implies much larger and negative effects of predicted climate change on farm profits, –42.7 percent and –28.1 percent under scenarios A2 and B1, respectively. While this specification is more flexible, it is not clear to us how to interpret the coefficients on the moving average, conditional on the realized yearly weather. It is the (negative) coefficient on the moving average of annual degree days that drives the large negative impacts found by the authors.

difficult to compare the two studies as their geographical scope and the set of included farming activities differ, one could speculate that the lower damage estimate implied by the Ricardian estimate reflects adaptation channels not captured in the impact study of Howitt et al. (2015). Note, however, that none of these impact estimates account for the fact that long-term climate change may reduce the amount of groundwater available to compensate for reduced surface water availability. As such, the net impact of climate change may be much larger than suggested by these estimates.

IMPACTS ON KEY CROPS

Although perhaps less prominently considered in the literature, field crops play an important part in California agriculture. For example, alfalfa (used for hay) occupied 21 percent of crop acreage in 2006, while cotton and corn (grain and silage) each occupied 8 percent (Lee et al., 2011). The large California dairy industry uses several of these field crops as a production input. Milk and cream are the top agricultural commodity in terms of value (CDFA, 2016).

Lee et al. (2011) use a biogeochemical crop model calibrated to California conditions (the DAYCENT model, Del Grosso et al., 2008; De Gryze et al., 2010) to study the impacts of climate change on key California field crops under current management practices, with irrigation water assumed to be non-limiting. While their yield predictions differ significantly across the climate models and downscaling methods used to predict future climatic variables, they find that the yields of most field crops will decline under climate change. Specifically, their model predicts null to moderate yield declines by 2050 compared to 2009, followed by substantial declines by 2094 under warming scenario A2 (medium-high emissions): –25 percent for cotton, –24 percent for sunflower, –14 percent for wheat, –10 percent for rice, and –9 percent for tomato and maize. The only field crop found to be unaffected by climate change is alfalfa. These yield declines are mostly attributed to increases in temperature, and do not account for the potentially mitigating effects of CO_2 fertilization on yields and water demand.

Because most crop growth models are not calibrated for specialty crops, particularly perennial crops for which biophysical relationships are difficult to establish due to slow growth, most of the available evidence on the effects of climate change on California crops comes from statistical studies. The panel study by Deschenes and Kolstad (2011) discussed above includes estimates of the effect of weather variables on key California crops such as tree nuts, vegetables, grapes, cotton, and citrus, based on county-level data for the period 1980–2005. The authors include annual growing degree days and annual precipitation as regressors, and investigate impacts on both crop revenues (holding acreage constant) and physical yields. Most coefficients are imprecisely estimated and not significantly different from zero. Exceptions for the crop revenue relationships include table grapes and wine grapes, which respond positively and negatively to degree days, respectively. Pistachios and walnuts also respond negatively to degree days. (The regression does not control for heat degree days, which may correlate positively with growing degree days.) Perhaps surprisingly, lettuce and strawberry revenues respond negatively to annual precipitation. To a large extent, these effects carry out to physical yields. The study also provides estimates of climate change impacts based on predictions from the CCSM model under IPCC scenario A2 (business as usual), for the period 2070–2099.

Most predicted crop revenue impacts are not precisely estimated, except for avocados (–69 percent), cotton (+50 percent), table grapes (+205 percent), and strawberries (–51 percent). Yield effects are not always consistent with these revenue impacts. The authors conclude that the impacts of climate change on California crops will be heterogenous.

Lobell et al. (2007) use yield data aggregated at the state level over the period 1980–2003 for 12 major California crops to determine the weather characteristics that have the most explanatory power for yield anomalies. They construct yield anomalies by netting out linear trends (to capture the effect of smooth technological change) as well as past yield realizations (to capture the effect of alternate bearing for perennials). In contrast to the study by Deschenes and Kolstad (2011), the authors allow for the effects of weather to vary by month of the year. They also consider minimum (nighttime) and maximum (daytime) temperature as opposed to degree days, and allow weather over a 24-month period covering the calendar harvest year and the year prior to harvest to affect crop yields.[8]

Their results for the three highest-revenue crops over the period are as follows. Wine grape yields increase in April nighttime temperature (due to lower risk of frost during the post-budbreak period) and in June precipitation (which may be detrimental to grape quality, however). Lettuce yields increase in April daytime temperature (up to about 23°C) and in the daytime temperature of the month of October of the prior year. The authors speculate that temperatures during these particular months are affecting lettuce crop yields in different parts of the state. Finally, almond yields decrease markedly in February nighttime temperature (likely due to a shortened dormancy period) and January rainfall (perhaps due to lower pollination and increased disease risk).

Lobell et al. (2006) use the regression models estimated on historical data by Lobell et al. (2007) to predict the impact of climate change on the yields of six major perennial crops, accounting for uncertainty in climate predictions and in the statistical estimation of the climate-yield relationship. They assess uncertainty in climate predictions by utilizing six climate models and three emissions scenarios. The authors address uncertainty related to the fact that the projected climate may exceed the extremes of the historical climate ("projection" uncertainty) by allowing a variant of their predictions to constrain projected yields within the bounds observed in the historical record. This method implicitly assumes that the new climate will not result in yield realizations that lie outside of past extreme realizations.

Under this conservative assumption, the authors find that wine grape yields will not be affected much by climate change over the 21st century, but that the yields of other perennials, namely almonds, table grapes, oranges, walnuts, and avocados, will likely decline, particularly for avocados (about –40 percent by the end of the century).

---

8 To avoid model overfitting due to the large number of potentially relevant covariates, they select up to three weather indicators, each allowed to affect yield in a quadratic fashion, based on measures of in-sample fit (R-squared). For example, a weather indicator may be average maximum temperature during the month of May of the harvest year.

For these five crops, when accounting for climate model and estimation uncertainty, these negative effects remain statistically significant. Allowing projected yields to exceed historical realizations has two main effects on predictions. First, uncertainty surrounding estimates increases markedly, and more so for predictions for later years. Second, except for oranges, yield predictions appear more negative. For instance, yield effects for table grapes reach about –35 percent by the end of the century, versus –20 percent with constrained yields.

Lobell and Field (2011) extend the previous study by considering 20 California perennials in California counties over the period 1980–2005 and greatly refining the model specification and the model selection method used in Lobell et al. (2007). As such, they offer the most reliable study to date on the likely impacts of climate change on California perennials. In order to determine whether the historical record is conducive to reliable statistical inference, the authors use different statistical models and compare results across models, keeping only crops for which model results are consistent and pass a simple out-of-sample validation test. In particular, they exploit the panel structure of their data to evaluate the robustness of their predictions to the inclusion of county fixed effects, which control for time-invariant factors that may be correlated with local climate, such as soils. Out of 20 perennials crops, only four crops exhibit statistical climate-yield relationships that appear robust enough as a basis for climate change predictions: almonds, strawberries, table grapes, and cherries.

To assess the overall response of these crops to warming, the authors first investigate the impacts of uniform increases in temperature by +2°C, holding precipitation constant. Almond yields appear to be hurt by higher nighttime temperatures in February and April, but benefit from higher nighttime temperatures in May and July. This is in contrast to the results of Lobell et al. (2006) that only consider the effects of warmer nighttime temperature in February. Strawberry yields are declining in nighttime temperatures during the months of March through May, and increasing in nighttime temperatures during the months of June through August (but they are hurt by higher daytime temperatures during these summer months). In contrast, cherries appear to suffer from higher temperatures throughout the months of November to

February, particularly at night, consistent with the view that reduced chilling is driving the yield impacts of warming. Finally, table grapes appear relatively insensitive to warming except for a sensitivity to higher daytime temperatures during the month of June.

The authors then use the predictions of six climate models and two warming scenarios (A2 and B1), downscaled to California counties' agricultural areas, to predict the yields of these four crops by 2050. Predicted almond yields exhibit a slightly positive trend with a projected increase of less than 5 percent by 2050 relative to the 1995–2005 climate. Predictions for table grape yields indicate no large effect of climate change on yield, with relatively high precision. In contrast, the yields of strawberries and cherries are predicted to decline significantly by 2050 (particularly for cherries, about –15 percent by 2050), although the uncertainty surrounding the actual declines remains large.

Gatto et al. (2009) also implement a statistical panel approach for premium wine grapes. Their study covers four counties in Northern California (Napa, Sonoma, Lake, and Mendocino) and focuses on temperature and precipitation effects on yield and price (a proxy for quality). Unlike Lobell and Field (2011), they only consider three weather indicators: April minimum temperature, July–August maximum temperature, and dormant season precipitation, selected exogenously. They estimate quadratic relationships in each weather indicator, separately for cool and warm weather varieties. They then use the climate projections in Cayan et al. (2008) to infer impacts on revenue per acre by 2034. Their study suggests increases in crop revenue in Sonoma, Lake, and Mendocino but decreases for Napa driven by price reductions.

White et al. (2006) analyze how climate change by the end of the 21st century may affect the suitability of U.S. land for premium wine grape production. An area is deemed suitable in their study if its climate meets a certain growing degree day requirement (1,111–2,499 GDD between April and October), an average growing season temperature requirement (13–20°C), as well as a series of requirements related to exposure to both very hot and very cold temperatures during key stages of the production cycle. Although the study does not discriminate areas according to factors such as soils or altitude, it indicates a reduction

in the suitability of current California regions, likely due to increased average growing season temperature and increased exposure to extreme heat (>35°C).

Hayhoe et al. (2004) use an even more parsimonious model based on the average monthly temperature at the time of ripening to infer the suitability of future climate for wine production in current California wine regions. They find that grape ripening will happen two months earlier and at higher temperatures, leading to a degradation in wine quality by the end of the century (2070–2099) in all wine regions except the cool coastal region.

IMPACTS ON ANIMAL AGRICULTURE

Animal agriculture is an essential part of California agriculture. Dairy is the top commodity in the state in terms of value before almonds and grapes (CDFA 2016). It generated more than $6 billion in revenue in 2015. Cattle and calves rank fourth. Broiler and egg production are also important, ranking in the top 20 commodities by value.

Unfortunately, while the literature on the effects of climate change on California crops has grown significantly in the recent past, there are still relatively few studies looking at the impact of climate on animal agriculture. A quick search, in fact, reveals that the most commonly debated aspects of climate change and animal production in California are proposed measures by the state to reduce greenhouse gas emissions due to livestock, the major contributor to greenhouse gas emissions from California agriculture (e.g., Alexander, 2016).[9] As such, the California animal sector may face more challenges from climate regulation than from climate change itself.

That is not to say that animal production is insensitive to climate change. Indeed, in July 2006, and again in June 2017, thousands of cows died from heat waves in the San Joaquin Valley. The heat also affected the poultry sector (CNBC, 2017). More generally, heat stress has been documented to have a negative impact on dairy

---

9 Agriculture contributed about 8 percent of California greenhouse gas emissions in 2015. Out of these, enteric fermentation and manure management from livestock were the main contributors, with about two thirds of emissions. Dairies themselves accounted for 60 percent of total agricultural emissions (California Air Resource Board, 2017b).

productivity. A Cooperative Extension report from the University of California, Davis indicates that temperatures exceeding 38°C can cause significant stress on cattle and other livestock, exacerbated by high humidity. In cattle, heat stress may result in decreased milk production, poor reproductive performance, an increase in the frequency and severity of infections, and death (Moeller, 2016). Lower dietary intake under heat stress partially drives the decrease in milk yield. Heat stress also affects the quality of milk through lower fat, solids-not-fat, and protein content. (Aggarwal and Upadhyay, 2013). Hayhoe et al. (2004) compute statewide losses for the dairy sector by the end of the century (2070–2099) ranging from zero to 22 percent depending on the emissions scenario considered, the climate model used, and the assumed sensitivity of milk production to heat.

IMPACTS ON FARM LABOR PRODUCTIVITY

Like animals, humans are generally less productive under environmental stress, notably high temperatures. California's specialty crop agriculture can be labor-intensive, particularly for crops requiring manual harvests such as lettuce, berries, premium wine grapes, or peppers. These industries are particularly sensitive to labor market conditions such as seasonal labor shortages. A climate-change-induced reduction in labor productivity could have serious consequences for them.

Several studies document the effects of heat exposure on labor supply and labor productivity, including Graff Zivin and Neidell (2014) and Carleton and Hsiang (2016b). Studies specific to agriculture and to California are much more rare. Stevens (2017) uses worker-level information in the California blueberry industry to estimate the relationship between ambient temperature and labor productivity, as measured by the weight of berries picked by unit of time, controlling for an array of potentially confounding factors. He finds that worker productivity is negatively affected by both very low (between 50–55°F) and very high (above 100°F) temperatures, but that farms have partially adapted to heat by scheduling picking prior to the hottest part of the day.

ADAPTATION

Human societies have two main avenues to respond to the potential threat of climate change: adaptation and mitigation. Adaptation consists of a suite of behavioral changes that allow achievement of a new economic optimum under the new climate and thus improve on outcomes obtained under the old behavior (Antle and Capalbo, 2010). Mitigation consists of taking measures to reduce greenhouse gas emissions and concentrations to curb changes in climate.

The issue of adaptation has become prominent in the climate change literature (Moore and Lobell, 2014; Burke and Emerick, 2016). Because many studies project detrimental impacts on economic biophysical or economic outcomes, the extent to which such impacts already account for adaptation, and the extent to which further adaptation measures could lessen these impacts, have become central questions for climate policy. Climate research can provide answers to both questions. As indicated above, Ricardian damage estimates are usually interpreted as net of any adaptations taken in the past. While they cannot account for new adaptation that may occur as a result of new technologies, they are generally considered to be a better predictor of net impacts than estimates based on year-to-year weather fluctuations or output from biophysical process models. Identifying the behavioral changes that could lessen climate change-induced damages has also been the focus of many climate studies related to agriculture (Rosenzweig and Parry, 1994; Ortiz-Bobea and Just, 2013).

In the context of California agriculture, a few studies have attempted to delineate possible adaptation measures. Scientific research on adaptation is particularly relevant and important for perennial plants. These plants are distinct because they are commonly grown for several decades (e.g., 25 years for grapes, or more for premium wine grapes (Diffenbaugh et al., 2011), leaving little opportunity for individual farmers to experiment in the face of a changing climate. It also means that publicly funded or incentivized adaptation measures may be justified from a social perspective to speed up and facilitate coordinated adaptation (Gatto et al., 2009).

Lobell et al. (2006) provide county maps of projected perennial crop yields under either +2°C or +4°C warming as a percentage of current statewide average yields in order to provide insights into possible adaptation through crop reallocation across regions. Under +2°C warming, walnut yields would be lower than the current state average in every single county, meaning that adaptation through geographical relocation could likely not buffer against yield effects. For almonds, table grapes, and avocados, current yields could be maintained only at the cost of relocating to areas mostly disjoint from current production regions. Predictions are even bleaker under the +4°C scenarios, except perhaps for wine grapes, although maintaining current yields would still require significant relocation for this crop.

In a less normative exercise, Lee and Sumner (2015) investigate the link between historical acreage allocation and climatic indicators such as precipitation, growing degree days, and chilling hours in Yolo County, California, controlling for price expectations. They project that warmer winters, particularly from 2035 to 2050, will cause lower wheat acreage and more alfalfa and processing tomato acreage. Only marginal changes in acreage are projected for tree and vine crops, in part because chilling hours would remain above critical values. Their study also indicates that price expectations have played a much larger role in the historical acreage allocation among their set of crops than climatic factors.

Lobell and Field (2011) investigate whether specific almond varieties are less sensitive to higher minimum temperatures in the critical month of February (see Impacts on Key Crops, p. 13) using statewide almond production data by almond variety. Unfortunately, they fail to find significant differences in the sensitivity of output to weather, indicating that selecting among currently available varieties offers little promise to cancel climate change impacts on yield.

Regarding the California dairy industry, which might be susceptible to more frequent and/or severe heat waves, a possible adaptation measure, beyond shade provision and the use of sprinklers, would be the relocation of production to cooler areas. The location of dairies is partially linked to the production of animal feed such as silage corn and alfalfa. This means an increase in the procurement cost of feed if these activities cannot be moved simultaneously due to soil or climatic limitations or competing land uses.[10]

Diffenbaugh et al. (2011) investigate the impacts of warming on the suitability of current wine regions for premium wine production in the Western U.S., including the North and Central Coast regions of California. Their suitability requirements combine a growing degree day window (850–2,700 GDD between April and October) with average growing season temperature (<20°C) and exposure to extreme heat (less than 15 days with maximum temperature exceeding 35°C). While the GDD window itself does not appear to affect much the suitability of the North and Central Coast regions under climate warming by 2030–2039, suitability (as measured in loss of suitable area) is substantially affected once the extreme heat and average growing season temperature are considered, as exemplified by Napa County (about –50 percent in suitable area) and Santa Barbara County (–30 percent in suitable area).

Relaxing the extreme heat requirement from less than 15 to less than 30 days would greatly diminish these predicted losses, suggesting that one pathway of adaptation would be to increase plant's ability to withstand extreme heat. The study also suggests a decline in the quality of wine produced in these regions driven by the increase in growing degree days. The authors suggest that available adaptation measures include shifts in vineyard location, shifts in varietals, changes in vineyard management (e.g., adapting trellising systems), and changes in winery processing (e.g., acidification or alcohol removal). Nicholas and Durham (2012) further mention the increased use of irrigation (which may be a limited option under decreased water supplies), application of a kaolin clay that acts as a sunscreen, or installation of an evaporative cooling system.

---

10 For example, in 2015 the top five counties for milk and cream were Tulare, Merced, Kings, Stanislaus, and Kern. The top five counties for silage production were Tulare, Merced, Stanislaus, San Joaquin, and Kings.

CLIMATE MITIGATION EFFORTS BY THE STATE

California's Global Warming Solutions Act of 2006, also known as Assembly Bill 32 (AB 32), established a greenhouse gas (GHG) emissions target for statewide emissions by 2020 equal to 1990 emission levels. In 2016, Senate Bill 32 (SB 32) codified a reduction target of 40 percent below 1990 emission levels by 2030. One of the many instruments to achieve these emissions reductions is California's GHG cap-and-trade program, overseen by the California Air Resources Board (ARB). Firms that are under the cap must cover their emissions with an emission permit (allowance).

Allowances are allocated to firms or auctioned off and can be subsequently exchanged in the allowance market. By controlling the aggregate quantity of allowances, ARB can reduce aggregate emissions in covered sectors over time. Emitters in uncovered sectors do not need permits to cover their emissions. However, they may be able to participate in emission reductions by generating offsets, that is, voluntary emission reductions that are then purchased by emitters to cover emissions in lieu of an allowance. The incentive for the offsetting firm to engage in costly emission reductions is that the unit price of the offset may be higher than the cost of reducing emissions for that firm.

Agriculture has so far been kept out of the sectors covered by California's cap-and-trade program, perhaps because agricultural emissions represent a modest, though non-negligible share of statewide emissions (8 percent), but also because of the difficulty of accurately and reliably measuring greenhouse gas emissions from animals and working lands (Garnache et al., 2017). Despite these difficulties, there is some evidence that the agricultural sector may be able to supply GHG emission reductions at a competitive price, suggesting that it could play a larger role in future GHG reduction targets, if not as part of the capped sector, at least through the possibility of generating offsets (Pautsch et al., 2001; De Gryze et al., 2009, 2011; Garnache et al., 2017). In its 2017 Scoping Plan, which lays down a strategy to achieve California's 2030 greenhouse gas target, ARB indicates that "the agricultural sector can reduce emissions from production, sequester carbon, and build soil carbon stocks [...]" suggesting an increased

contribution of agriculture to GHG reduction efforts in the future.

METHANE EMISSIONS FROM THE DAIRY AND LIVESTOCK SECTORS

As the No. 1 source of agricultural GHG in the state (60 percent), methane emissions from the dairy and livestock sectors are likely to become one of the primary levers to reduce the carbon footprint of California agriculture. In 2016, Senate Bill 1383 (SB 1383) set a target for statewide reductions of methane emissions to 40 percent below 2013 levels by 2030. Manure management and enteric fermentation in the dairy and livestock sectors represent a large share of the state's methane emissions, 65 percent in 2013 according to ARB (CARB, 2017d, Appendix C). Livestock and dairy manure management is singled out (along with organic waste management) in SB 1383 and the ensuing Short-Lived Climate Pollutant Reduction Strategy developed by ARB (CARB, 2017d) as an essential lever to reach the statewide methane reduction target.

One of the main avenues to reduce emissions of methane from manure is the installation of anaerobic digesters that capture methane and either use it on site to generate electricity or funnel it into a methane pipeline. Barriers to the widespread adoption of digesters are the very high infrastructure and maintenance costs involved (Ashton, 2016),[11] the need for procurement contracts for the surplus energy generated on-farm, and the disposal of by-products. As a result of these hurdles, voluntary adoption of digesters in the dairy and livestock sector has been slow, despite existing incentives from various state agencies.

Besides direct subsidies to the installation of infrastructure on the farm, which have been channeled through CDFA's Dairy Digester Research and Development Program, existing incentives include the possibility to claim the greenhouse gas reductions attributed to the capture of

---

11 The California Department of Food and Agriculture reports that 18 dairy digester projects were funded in 2017 across California. The average total project cost was in excess of $6 million per project (CDFA, 2017).

methane in a digester either as an offset under the state's cap-and-trade program or, when using captured methane as a transportation fuel, as a credit pursuant to the state's low-carbon fuel standard (CARB, 2017c). Beyond current incentive programs, SB 1383 directs ARB to begin regulating methane emissions from dairy and livestock manure management operations no sooner than 2024, and provided the proposed regulations are technically and economically feasible, with a goal to achieve a 40 percent reduction below the sector's 2013 levels by 2030.

In 2015, ARB adopted an offset protocol for rice cultivation in order to incentivize practices that reduce methane emissions from flooded rice fields (CARB, 2015). As of December 2017, no offsets had been claimed pursuant to this protocol, either in or outside of the state (CARB, 2017a).

CARBON SEQUESTRATION

Sequestration of carbon in agricultural soils has the potential to contribute to net reductions in agricultural GHG emissions. Cultivation practices that have been shown to promote carbon sequestration in soils in California include reduced tillage, manure application, and winter cover cropping (De Gryze et al., 2011). The California Department of Food and Agriculture (CDFA) currently encourages adoption of such practices through its Healthy Soils Program. In 2017, the program awarded $3.75 million for projects ranging from the establishment of hedgerows to the use of cover crops or compost application in fields.[12]

---

12 CDFA also incentivizes GHG emission reductions through its State Water Efficiency and Enhancement Program, which aims to promote the adoption of water- and energy-saving irrigation systems throughout the state.

EFFECTS OF CALIFORNIA'S CLIMATE POLICY ON ENERGY PRICES AND THE LOCAL FOOD PROCESSING INDUSTRY

California's new ambitious target to achieve GHG emissions 40 percent below 1990 levels by 2030 likely means that California businesses, including farms, will see a rise in energy prices relative to a world without constraints on emissions. Energy costs represent a non-negligible share of operating costs for many farming activities (use of mechanical power for field work, groundwater pumping, indoor climate control and lighting, powering of processing equipment).

Downstream processors like tomato or milk processing plants are also affected by rising energy prices, which may reduce their demand for farm output as the profitability of their operations declines. Food processors in California directly emit GHG through the burning of natural gas, and as such are covered by the cap under the cap-and-trade program. A gradual tightening of the emissions cap over time means that these processors will face higher total costs of energy procurement, which may dramatically affect their competitiveness and lead to a reallocation of food-processing plants towards unregulated regions outside California (Hamilton et al., 2016).

Since many farm products cannot be economically transported over long distances for processing, relocation of plants outside California implies that supplying farms will either need to shut down or convert to production of other, less-affected commodities. For instance, Hamilton et al. (2016) predict that a carbon price of $20 per metric ton, without allowances handed in to California processors, would lead to a more than 7 percent decline in the California supply of processing tomatoes. The authors find more modest effects in the cheese, wet corn, and sugar sectors. While it is difficult to predict the extent to which these effects will impact the agricultural sector as a whole, absent compensating mechanisms, farmers should anticipate reduced profitability from policies that directly raise energy prices for farms and the food-processing sector.

CONCLUSION

In this chapter, we review the scientific, agronomic, and economic literature to provide a broad survey on the topic of climate change and agriculture in California. This area of study is distinct in its topical and methodological breadth. Economists, hydrologists, climate scientists, engineers, and agronomists have brought their disciplines to bear on questions about the effects of climate change on temperature and precipitation patterns, irrigated water supplies, and agricultural outcomes, and the role adaptation can play in mitigating the costs of climate change. Despite the remarkable development of climate-related research, many key questions remain unanswered.

The available scientific evidence, even when gathered across a relatively large array of disciplines, does not paint a clear picture of the impact of climate change on California agriculture over the next century. We expect that in the next iteration of this book series, a new generation of research on this still nascent topic will provide further clarity on the complex relationship between agriculture and climate change in California.

REFERENCES

Aggarwal, A. and R. Upadhyay. 2013. "Heat Stress and Milk Production." *Heat Stress and Animal Productivity*. Springer, pp. 53-77.

Alexander, K. 2016. Climate Fight Targeting Cows May Reshape California Dairies." *San Francisco Chronicle*, 29 September 2016. Available at: http://www.sfchronicle.com/bayarea/article/Climate-fight-targeting-cows-may-reshape-9401293.php.

Antle, J.M. and S.M. Capalbo. 2010. "Adaptation of Agricultural and Food Systems to Climate Change: An Economic and Policy Perspective." *Applied Economic Perspectives and Policy*, 32(3): 386-416.

Ashton, A. 2016. California's dairy industry knows how to cut its greenhouse gas emissions, but can it afford to? *Sacramento Bee*, 17 September 2016. Available at: http://www.sacbee.com/news/local/environment/article101657322.html.

Asseng, S. 2014. "Rising Temperatures Reduce Global Wheat Production." *Nature Climate Change*, 5:143-147. Available at: https://www.nature.com/articles/nclimate2470.

Auffhammer, M., S. Hsiang, W. Schlenker and A. Sobel. 2013. "Using Weather Data and Climate Model Output in Economic Analyses of Climate Change." *Review of Environmental Economics and Policy* 7(2): 181–198.

Auffhammer, M. and W. Schlenker. 2014. "Empirical Studies on Agricultural Impacts and Adaptation." *Energy Economics*, 46: 555-561.

Baldocchi, D. and S. Wong. 2008. "Accumulated Winter Chill is Decreasing in the Fruit Growing Regions of California." *Climatic Change*, 87(1): 153-166.

Blanc, E. and J. Reilly. 2017. "Approaches to Assessing Climate Change Impacts on Agriculture: An Overview of the Debate." *Review of Environmental Economics and Policy*, 11(2): 247-257.

Brekke, L., B.L. Thrasher, E.P. Maurer and T. Pruitt. 2013. "Downscaled CMIP3 and CMIP5 Climate and Hydrology Projections: Release of Downscaled CMIP5 Climate Projections, Comparison with preceding Information, and Summary of User Needs." *U.S. Department of the Interior, Bureau of Reclamation, Technical Services Center*. Denver, Colorado. 47 pp.

Burke, M. and K. Emerick. 2016. "Adaptation to Climate Change: Evidence from U.S. Agriculture." *American Economic Journal: Economic Policy*, 8(3): 106-140.

California Air Resource Board. 2015. *Compliance Offset Protocol Rice Cultivation Projects*. June 2015. Sacramento, CA.

———. 2017a. *ARB Offset Credits Issued*. December 2017. Sacramento, CA.

———. 2017b. *California GHG Emission Inventory* 2017 Edition. Sacramento, CA.

———.2017c). *Draft Guidance on the Impact of Adopting Regulations Pursuant to SB 1383 on the Ability to Continue to Generate Credits Under the LowCarbon Fuel Standard and Cap-and-Trade Programfor the Reduction of Methane Emissions from Manure Management Operations*. December 2017. Sacramento, CA.

———.(2017d). *Short-Lived Climate Pollutant Reduction Strategy*. March 2017. Sacramento, CA.

California Department of Food and Agriculture. 2016. *California Agricultural Statistics Review*, 2015-216. Sacramento, CA.

———. 2017. 2017 *Dairy Digester Research and Development Program, Projects Selected for Award of Funds*. December 2017. Sacramento, CA.

Carleton, T.A. and S. M. Hsiang. 2016a. "Social and Economic Impacts of Climate." *Science*, 353(6304):aad9837.

———.(2016b). "Social and Economic Impacts of Climate." *Science*, 353(6304):aad9837.

Cayan, D.R., E.P. Maurer, M.D. Dettinger, M. Tyree, and K. Hayhoe. 2008. "Climate Change Scenarios for the California Region." *Climatic Change*, 87: 21-42.

Daniels, J. 2017. "California's Triple-digit Heat Slows Milk Production, Threatens Crops and Livestock." CNBC. Available at: https://www.cnbc.com/2017/06/27/californias-triple-digit-heat-slows-milk-production-threatens-crops.html.

De Gryze, S., M.V. Albarracin, R. Catalá-Luque, R.E. Howitt and J. Six. 2008. "Modeling Shows that Alternative Soil Management Can Decrease Greenhouse Gases." *California Agriculture*, 63(2): 84-90.

De Gryze, S., J. Lee, S. Ogle, K. Paustian and J. Six. 2011. "Assessing the Potential for Greenhouse Gas Mitigation in Intensively Managed Annual Cropping Systems at the Regional Scale." *Agriculture, Ecosystems & Environment* 144(1): 150-158.

De Gryze, S., A. Wolf, S.R. Kaffka, J. Mitchell, D.E. Rolston, S.R. Temple, J. Lee, and J. Six. 2010. "Simulating Greenhouse Gas Budgets of Four California Cropping Systems Under Conventional and Alternative Management." *Ecological Applications* 20(7): 1805-1819.

Del Grosso, S., A. Halvorson, and W. Parton. 2008. "Testing DAYCENT Model Simulations of Corn Yields and Nitrous Oxide Emissions in Irrigated Tillage Systems in Colorado." *Journal of Environmental Quality* 37(4): 1383-1389.

Dell, M., B. F. Jones, and B. A. Olken. 2014. "What Do We Learn from the Weather? The New Climate-Economy Literature." *Journal of Economic Literature* 52(3): 740-98.

Deschenes, O. and C. Kolstad. 2011. "Economic Impacts of Climate Change on California Agriculture." *Climatic Change*, 109(1): 365-386.

Diffenbaugh, N.S., D.L. Swain and D. Touma. 2015. "Anthropogenic Warming Has Increased Drought Risk in California." *Proceedings of the National Academy of Sciences*, 112(13): 3931-3936.

Diffenbaugh, N.S., M.A. White, G.V. Jones, and M. Ashfaq. 2011. "Climate Adaptation Wedges: A Case Study of Premium Wine in the Western United States." *Environmental Research Letters* 6(2):024024.

Famiglietti, J. S., M. Lo, S.L. Ho, J. Bethune, K.J. Anderson, T.H. Syed, S.C. Swenson, C.R. de Linage and M. Rodell. 2011. "Satellites Measure Recent Rates of Groundwater Depletion in California's Central Valley." *Geophysical Research Letters* 38(3).

Fisher, A.C., W.M. Hanemann, M.J. Roberts and W. Schlenker. 2012. "The Economic Impacts of Climate Change: Evidence from Agricultural Output and Random Fluctuations in Weather: Comment." *The American Economic Review*, 102(7): 3749-3760.

Garnache, C., P.R. Mérel, J. Lee and J. Six. 2017. "The Social Costs of Second-best Policies: Evidence from Agricultural GHG Mitigation." *Journal of Environmental Economics and Management*, 82: 39-73.

Gatto, J., B. Kim, P. Mahdavi, H. Namekawa and H. Tran. 2009. "The Future Impact of Climate Change on the California Wine Industry and Actions the State of California Should Take to Address It." *Report*. International Policy Studies Program, Stanford University.

Graff Zivin, J. and M. Neidell. 2014. "Temperature and the Allocation of Time: Implications for Climate Change." *Journal of Labor Economics* 32(1): 1-26.

Hamilton, S.F., E. Ligon, A. Shafran and S. Villas-Boas. 2016. "Production and Emissions Leakage from California's Cap-and-Trade Program in Food Processing Industries: Case Study of Tomato, Sugar, Wet Corn and Cheese Markets." *California's Air Resources Board*. Sacramento, CA.

Hayhoe, K., D. Cayan, C.B. Field, P.C. Frumhoff, E.P. Maurer, N.L. Miller, S.C. Moser, S.H. Schneider, K.N. Cahill, E.E. Cleland, et al. 2004. "Emissions Pathways, Climate Change, and Impacts on California." *Proceedings of the National Academy of Sciences of the United States of America* 101(34): 12422-12427.

Howitt, R., J. Medellín-Azuara, D. MacEwan, J. Lund, and D. Sumner. 2015. "Economic Analysis of the 2015 Drought for California Agriculture." Davis, CA. *Center for Watershed Sciences, University of California – Davis*.

Hsiang, S. 2016. "Climate Econometrics." *Annual Review of Resource Economics* 8:43–75.

Intergovernmental Panel on Climate Change. 2013. "Climate Change 2013: The Physical Science Basis." Geneva, Switzerland. 1535 pp.

Lee, H. and D.A. Sumner. 2015. "Economics of Downscaled Climate-Induced Changes in Cropland, with Projections to 2050: Evidence from Yolo County, California." *Climatic Change* 132(4): 723-737.

Lee, J., S. De Gryze and J. Six. 2011. "Effect of Climate Change on Field Crop Production in California's Central Valley." *Climatic Change* 109(1): 335-353.

Lobell, D.B., K.N. Cahill, and C.B. Field. 2007. "Historical Effects of Temperature and Precipitation on California Crop Yields." *Climatic Change* 81(2):187–203

Lobell, D.B. and C.B. Field. 2011. "California Perennial Crops in a Changing Climate." *Climatic Change* 109(1): 317-333.

Lobell, D.B., C.B. Field, K.N. Cahill and C. Bonfils. 2006. "Impacts of Future Climate Change on California Perennial Crop Yields: Model Projections with Climate and Crop Uncertainties." *Agricultural and Forest Meteorology* 141(2): 208-218.

Maurer, E.P. 2007. "Uncertainty in Hydrologic Impacts of Climate Change in the Sierra Nevada, California, Under Two Emissions Scenarios." *Climatic Change* 82: 309-327.

Maurer, E.P. and P.B. Duffy. 2005. "Uncertainty in Projections of Streamflow Changes Due to Climate Change in California." *Geophysical Research Letters* 32(3).

Mendelsohn, R., W.D. Nordhaus, and D. Shaw. 1994. "The Impact of Global Warming on Agriculture: A Ricardian Analysis." *The American Economic Review* 84(4): 753-771.

Mendelsohn, R.O. and E. Massetti. 2017. "The Use of Cross-Sectional Analysis to Measure Climate Impacts on Agriculture: Theory and Evidence." *Review of Environmental Economics and Policy* 11(2): 280-298.

Moeller, R.B. 2016. "Heat Stress in Cattle." *Extension report, University of California, Davis.* Davis, CA. Available at: http://cahfs.ucdavis.edu/local_resources/pdfs/fact%20sheets/Heat_stress_fact_sheet_2016.pdf.

Moore, F.C. and D.B. Lobell. 2014. "Adaptation Potential of European Agriculture in Response to Climate Change." Nature *Climate Change* 4(7): 610-614.

Nicholas, K.A. and W.H. Durham. 2012. "Farm-scale Adaptation and Vulnerability to Environmental Stresses: Insights from Winegrowing in Northern California." *Global Environmental Change* 22(2): 483-494

Ortiz-Bobea, A. and R.E. Just. 2013. "Modeling the Structure of Adaptation in Climate Change Impact Assessment." *American Journal of Agricultural Economics* 95(2): 244- 251.

Pautsch, G.R., L.A. Kurkalova, B.A. Babcock, and C.L. Kling. 2001. "The Efficiency of Sequestering Carbon in Agricultural Soils." *Contemporary Economic Policy* 19(2): 123-134.

Rosenzweig, C. and Parry, M. L. (1994). "Potential Impact of Climate Change on World Food Supply." *Nature*, 367(6459): 133-138.

Scanlon, B.R., C.C. Faunt, L. Longuevergne, R.C. Reedy, W.M. Alley, V.L. McGuire and P.B. McMahon. 2012. "Groundwater Depletion and Sustainability of Irrigation in the U.S. High Plains and Central Valley." *Proceedings of the National Academy of Sciences* 109(24): 9320-9325.

Schlenker, W., W.M. Hanemann, and A.C. Fisher. 2007. "Water Availability, Degree Days, and the Potential Impact of Climate Change on Irrigated Agriculture in California." *Climatic Change* 81(1): 19-38.

Stevens, A. W. 2017. "Temperature, Wages, and Agricutural Labor Productivity." *Working paper*, University of California, Berkeley.

Tol, R. S. 2018. "The Economic Impacts of Climate Change." *Review of Environmental Economics and Policy*, 12(1): 4-25.

VanRheenen, N.T., A.W. Wood, R.N. Palmer and D.P. Lettenmaier. 2004. "Potential Implications of PCM Climate Change Scenarios for Sacramento–San Joaquin River Basin Hydrology and Water Resources." *Climatic Change* 62(13): 257-281.

Vicuna, S. and J. Dracup. 2007. "The Evolution of Climate Change Impact Studies on Hydrology and Water Resources in California." *Climatic Change* 82: 327-350.

Vicuna, S., E.P. Maurer, B. Joyce, J.A. Dracup and D. Purkey. 2007. "The Sensitivity of California Water Resources to Climate Change Scenarios." JAWRA *Journal of the American Water Resources Association* 43(2): 482-498.

White, M. A., N. Diffenbaugh, G.V. Jones, J. Pal and F. Giorgi. 2006. "Extreme Heat Reduces and Shifts United States Premium Wine Production in the 21St Century." *Proceedings of the National Academy of Sciences* 103(30): 11217-11222.

APPENDIX

Appendix Table 16.1A. Set of GCMs Used to Derive Average Projections by 2036–2065, for Each Climatic Variable and RCP

GCM	Precipitation				Temp. mean				Temp. max				Temp. min			
	RCP 2.6	RCP 4.5	RCP 6.0	RCP 8.5	RCP 2.6	RCP 4.5	RCP 6.0	RCP 8.5	RCP 2.6	RCP 4.5	RCP 6.0	RCP 8.5	RCP 2.6	RCP 4.5	RCP 6.0	RCP 8.5
access1-0		×		×		×		×		×		×		×		×
access1-3		×		×		×		×								
bcc-csm1-1		×	×	×		×	×	×		×	×	×		×	×	×
bcc-csm1-1m		×		×		×		×		×		×		×		×
canesm2	×	×		×	×	×		×	×	×		×	×	×		×
ccsm4	×	×	×	×	×	×	×	×	×	×	×	×	×	×	×	×
cesm1-bgc		×		×		×		×		×		×		×		×
cesm1-cam5	×	×	×	×	×	×	×	×	×	×	×	×	×	×	×	×
cmcc-cm		×		×		×		×								
cnrm-cm5		×		×		×		×		×		×		×		×
csiro-mk3-6-0	×	×	×	×	×	×	×	×	×	×	×	×	×	×	×	×
ec-earth	×	×		×	×	×		×	×	×		×	×	×		×
fgoals-g2	×	×			×	×			×	×			×	×		
fgoals-s2	×	×		×	×	×		×	×	×		×	×	×		×
fio-esm	×	×	×	×	×	×	×	×								
gfdl-cm3	×	×	×	×	×	×	×	×	×	×	×	×	×	×	×	×
gfdl-esm2g	×	×	×	×	×	×	×	×	×	×	×	×	×	×	×	×
gfdl-esm2m	×	×	×	×	×	×	×	×	×	×	×	×	×	×	×	×
giss-e2-h-cc		×	×			×	×			×	×			×	×	
giss-e2-r	×	×	×	×	×	×	×	×	×	×	×	×	×	×	×	×
giss-e2-r-cc		×				×				×				×		
hadgem2-ao	×	×		×	×	×		×	×	×		×	×	×		×
hadgem2-cc		×		×		×		×		×		×		×		×
hadgem2-es	×	×		×	×	×		×	×	×		×	×	×		×
inmcm4		×		×		×		×		×		×		×		×
ipsl-cm5a-lr	×	×	×	×	×	×	×	×	×	×	×	×	×	×	×	×
ipsl-cm5a-mr	×	×	×	×	×	×	×	×	×	×	×	×	×	×	×	×
ipsl-cm5b-lr		×		×		×		×		×		×		×		×
miroc-esm	×	×	×	×	×	×	×	×	×	×	×	×	×	×	×	×
miroc-esm-chem	×	×	×	×	×	×	×	×	×	×	×	×	×	×	×	×
miroc5	×	×	×	×	×	×	×	×	×	×	×	×	×	×	×	×
mpi-esm-lr	×	×		×	×	×		×	×	×		×	×	×		×
mpi-esm-mr	×	×		×	×	×		×	×	×		×	×	×		×
mri-cgcm3	×	×	×	×	×	×	×	×	×	×	×	×	×	×	×	×
noresm1-m	×	×	×	×	×	×	×	×	×	×	×	×	×	×	×	×
noresm1-me	×	×	×	×	×	×	×	×	×	×	×	×	×	×	×	×
Total	24	36	18	33	24	36	18	33	23	33	17	30	23	33	17	30

CHAPTER 17. RESEARCH, INNOVATION, SUPPLY CHAINS, AND PRECISION AGRICULTURE IN CALIFORNIA

BEN GORDON, OLENA SAMBUCCI, ITAI TRILNICK, AND DAVID ZILBERMAN

ABSTRACT

California agriculture has benefited from modern sciences through the educational-industrial complex where public research and extension introduce new innovations that are implemented by the private sector. Key features of modern agriculture are continuous innovation and increased precision. Innovations result in new products and expansion of value-added provided by agrifood sector, and its implementation requires creative design of supply chains. Precision agriculture increases input use efficiency and reduces side effects. The efficiency of California agriculture is an outcome of public policy supporting research, regulating pollution, and providing education to California's agrifood sector. We highlight two cases of innovation: a process innovation, the management of powdery mildew in wine grapes, and a product innovation, precise irrigation systems, to show the transformation of research to product and adoption. We also show how new cross-sector technologies, such as remote sensing and information technology, as well as shifting consumer preferences, demand and accelerate innovation and development, especially in response to 21st century challenges.

ABOUT THE AUTHORS

Ben Gordon is a research assistant in the Department of Agricultural and Resource Economics at UC Berkeley, Olena Sambucci is an assistant project scientist in the Department of Agricultural and Resource Economics at UC Davis, Itai Trilnick is a Ph.D. student in the Department of Agricultural and Resource Economics at UC Berkeley. David Zilberman is a professor and holds the Robinson Chair at the Department of Agricultural and Resource Economics at UC Berkeley and is a member of the Giannini Foundation of Agricultural Economics. He can be contacted at zilber11@berkeley.edu.

Precision agriculture is heavily integrated into vertical farming systems (farming indoors with multiple layers of production), which can be quite profitable in the production of high-value crops, such as microgreens and lettuce.

Photo Credit: Don Goodwin, GoldenSun Marketing

373

CHAPTER 17. TABLE OF CONTENTS

INTRODUCTION

California is known for its advanced agricultural sector, which, for more than a century, has utilized frontier knowledge to produce high-value products under adverse conditions. This chapter provides an overview of the linkages between research, innovation, technology adoption, and productivity in California agriculture. New scientific knowledge and technological capabilities have contributed to the emergence of new agricultural technologies. For example, the internal combustion engine eventually led to the introduction of mechanized innovations, breakthroughs in chemistry led to fertilizers and pesticides, and recent innovations in information, nano, and biological technologies increase productivity through increased precision.

The first part of the chapter highlights the importance of technology in California agriculture. An overview of the innovation process and the transformation of knowledge into applied technology in California agriculture will follow We will then assess the processes of technology adoption in California and their implications. We then assess the economics of precision agriculture. Finally, we overview the supply chain that transforms innovations to products. We finish with a conclusion.

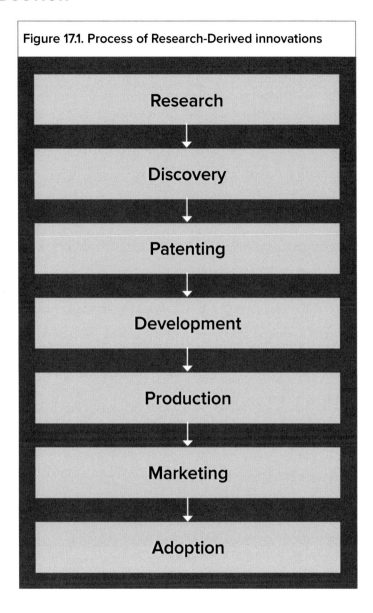

Figure 17.1. Process of Research-Derived innovations

Research

Discovery

Patenting

Development

Production

Marketing

Adoption

INNOVATION SUPPLY CHAIN AND THE EDUCATIONAL-INDUSTRIAL COMPLEX

Innovations, which are ideas about new products, institutions, and location and processes of production, are often induced by economic conditions (Hayami and Ruttan, 1971). For instance, labor scarcity may lead to automation, and water scarcity may lead to advanced irrigation technologies. The large economic literature on innovation (Sunding and Zilberman, 2001) views innovation that leads to new technologies as a multi-stage process depicted in Figure 17.1. New technologies frequently start from an idea obtained through research or practice by practitioners, who have been supplanted in the past century by the educational-industrial complex. Innovations originate with university research and are often developed and commercialized by industry—a process that plays a major role in transforming California's economy and agriculture and provides a model for the world.

As Figure 17.1 suggests, research-derived innovations are frequently concepts proven on a small scale. These discoveries are often the source of intellectual property, which can be embodied in different arrangements for further development. Once a viable product is identified, a production system and commercialization strategy are needed to produce, market, and adopt the innovation. Of course, this is a schematic description, and the reality is more complex with an iterative process and often overlapping steps.

California's educational-industrial complex begins with research at universities and research institutes, funded by both the public and private sectors under public-private partnerships (Rausser, Amaden, and Stevens, 2016). For example, UC Berkeley had major agreements with British Petroleum to develop second-generation biofuels, and Mars has supported multiple research projects at UC Davis. Wright et al. (2014) show that this private research enhances valuable innovation.

The UC system uses several mechanisms to transfer technology to potential users. First, of course, is educating students whom, upon graduation, are employed by the industry. Graduates of the UC system embody knowledge and skills acquired at universities. University faculty

provide consulting services and conduct contract-based work for the government, private sector, and non-governmental organizations (NGOs). Universities also register patents and transfer the rights to use them, as well as trade secrets, to the private sector and government.

Most research universities manage much of their intellectual property through an Office of Technology Transfer (OTT). For instance, the UC system has a portfolio of over 12,000 active inventions and has accumulated close to 5,000 active patents for various innovations including plant varieties.[1] Universities may receive compensation for the rights to use its patents, and a key objective of these offices is to ensure that university knowledge is impactful in the world (Graff, Heiman, and Zilberman, 2002).

In some cases, the innovations are transferred to major companies, while in other cases university researchers establish their own firm. These start-ups may then become major companies, or be acquired by established firms. In the life sciences, major California companies, like Genentech and Amgen, are manifestations of this educational-industrial complex. In agriculture, the University of California spawned companies like Calgene, which was then acquired by Monsanto, and Mendel, which holds major patents in agricultural biotechnology. One measure is the rate of return, while another is the location of biotechnology companies (94 percent are within 35 miles of a UC campus {King, 2007}). We see the emergence of clusters of companies around major research universities, such as Berkeley, Davis, San Diego, Riverside, Los Angeles, and San Francisco. Table 1 provides a partial list of agricultural biotechnology companies originating at UC campuses.

UC Cooperative Extension (UCCE) is a unique and important mechanism of technology transfer in California. UCCE includes specialists based on UC campuses as well as farm advisors in counties and research stations throughout the state. Extension professionals conduct applied research in collaboration with UC faculty, and provide information and technical assistance to major constituents that include government, NGOs, agribusiness, and farmers. Knowledge and information are key inputs for a successful agricultural sector.

Just et al. (2002) investigate the most important sources of information used by a sample of economic agents in California, Iowa, and Washington agriculture. They distinguish between end-users (e.g., farmers, processors, input suppliers) and information intermediaries (e.g., private consultants, extension, media). They also distinguish between primary data and knowledge (e.g., weather data, academic studies) and targeted information, as well as between formal information and informal information (word of mouth). They find that intermediaries rely more on formal information than farmers, and that 52 percent of information used by farmers is informal (mostly about production practices, reliability of suppliers, business opportunities, etc.). They also find that growers of specialty crops (e.g., tomatoes) with less developed formal information networks rely more heavily on informal information than farmers of major commodities (e.g., wheat).

Different intermediaries have different relative advantages. For example, the public sector is a major source of economic information (supply and demand, international forecasts) as well as of technological information. Commodity associations are especially valuable for regulatory information, while commercial vendors provide pricing information. Wolf et al. (2001) find that among intermediaries, extension provides the most informational value, as measured by the conversion rate of primary data to targeted information. Furthermore, while end-users perceive that only 30 percent of their information comes from public sector services, in reality it is 70 percent because private consultants and media rely on and transmit information from the public sector. Information provision is a crucial element of the last stage of the innovation process in the adoption of new technology or product by final users—be it farmers, agribusiness, or consumers.

Table 17.1. Companies Associated with University of California Campus Research

UC Campus	Company	Technology/Product
Berkeley	A/F Protein	Antifreeze proteins for control of cold-induced damage
Berkeley	Acacia Biosciences, Inc.	Biopharmaceuticals and agricultural chemicals
Berkeley	Berkeley Lights Inc.	Single cell annotation and genomics
Berkeley	Caribou Biosciences Inc.	CRISPR applications
Berkeley	Enable Biosciences, Inc.	Ultra-sensitive antibody detection
Berkeley	Molecular Dynamics	DNA sequence and analysis systems
Berkeley	Magnetic Insight	Clinical and translational research imaging
Berkeley	Ventria Bioscience	GM crop-based protein production system
Berkeley	20n Labs, Inc.	Engineered microbes
Berkeley	Juvenon	Supplements for energy and cellular health
Berkeley	Mendel Biological Solutions	Biological crop solutions to enhance yield
Berkeley	The Two Blades Foundation	Disease resistance in crops
Berkeley	GO2 Water Inc.	Reclaim water, energy, and nutrients from wastewater
Davis	Arcadia Biosciences	GM food crops to reduce environmental impact
Davis	AstRoNA	Pathogen ID with molecular biology and nanotech
Davis	AcenXion Biosystems	Polymerase chain reaction (PCR) systems
Davis	AimRNA	Improved RNA therapeutics
Davis	Circularis	Gene expression for crop and livestock traits
Davis	Glycohub	Production of complex glycans with enzymes
Davis	InnovaNutra	Stabilizer for food, supplements, and cosmetics
Davis	Inserogen	Repurpose tobacco plant for vaccines and therapeutics
Davis	Luminance Biosciences	Companion diagnostics and therapeutics
Davis	RF Biocidics	Elimination of food-related pathogens, pests, and fungi
Davis	Tule Technologies	Sub-field irrigation IT and monitoring
Davis	XTB Laboratories	Detection and response to agricultural disease infestations
Los Angeles	AvidBiotics	Proteins developed for therapeutics and livestock
Los Angeles	Aragon Pharmaceuticals	Treatment of hormonally-driven cancers
Los Angeles	ImaginAb	Antibody technology for in vivo imaging
Los Angeles	Lyxia	Microalgaue biofuel production
Los Angeles	Water Planet Engineering	Desalination and water resuse solutions
Irvine	Antigen Discovery Inc	Proteomic biomarker discovery and immune profiling
Irvine	Velox Biosystems,LLC	Food safety testing
Riverside	Biagro Western Sales, Inc.	Nutrient solutions for crops (Phosphite)
Santa Barbara	Apeel Sciences	Plant-based crop and harvest protection
Santa Barbara	Diagnostic Biochips, Inc	Biosensors for diagnostics
Santa Barbara	SerImmune	Diagnostics and therapeutics for autoimmune diseases
Santa Barbara	Spectradyne LLC	Nanoparticle analysis
Santa Cruz	Five 3 Genomics	Rapid sequence analysis algorithms
Santa Cruz	Two Pore Guys	Nanopore technologies for genome sequencing and diagnostics
Santa Cruz	Dovetail Genomics	In vitro method for long-range sequencing libraries

Source: OTT at each UC campus

TECHNOLOGY ADOPTION

The literature on technology distinguishes between adoption (the uptake of a technology by an individual) and diffusion (measured by the percentage of users or land that use a technology). Early studies found that successful diffusion is an S-shape function of time (Figure 17.2), with a low adoption rate initially followed by a period of rapid uptake, and then plateauing during later stages of diffusion. There is another stage of dis-adoption of technologies and replacement by new ones. Initially, in the 1950s, adoption was modeled as a process of imitation, with few early adopters setting the way for a larger group of followers (Rogers, 2010). But the threshold model of adoption is a more complete framework (Zilberman, Zhao, and Heiman, 2012).

The threshold framework has three components. First, is individual behavior by farmers or consumers. In particular, it assumes that farmers pursue profit subject to risk and financial considerations, and consumers pursue benefits from consumption of goods and services, also taking into account risk and other constraints. The second element is heterogeneity among potential adopters. Some individuals are better positioned to adopt a technology

than others. The third element is dynamic processes that include learning-by-doing by manufacturers that reduces the price of a technology, learning-by-using by adopters that increases the benefit and reduces the cost and risks of the technology, as well as network externalities where the benefit from adoption increases with the number of adopters (e.g., the internet).

Biophysical phenomena are another set of dynamic processes that may lead to adoption of technologies. They include pesticide resistance build-up leading to adoption of alternative pest control strategies, and depletion of groundwater leading to adoption of improved water management strategies. A good marketer is aware of these processes and will target a technology to the lowest hanging fruit. For example, a technology will be introduced first to regions where it will be most profitable and then move to other regions.

There are many applications that illustrate the threshold framework in California. In the case of mechanized innovation (e.g., laser levelers, combines, harvesters) the early adopters in California were large farmers, and firms that provided custom services allowing smaller farmers

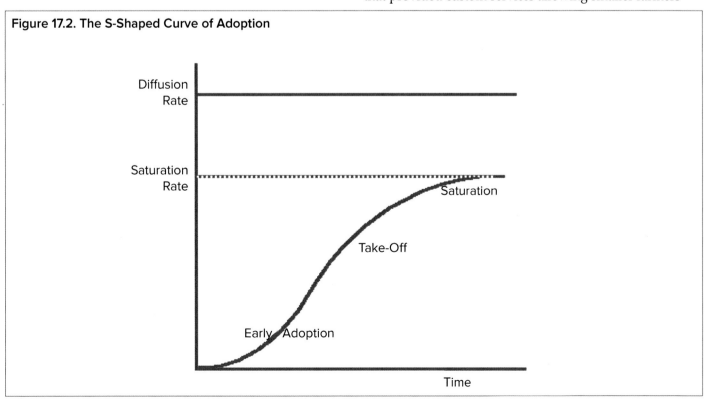

Figure 17.2. The S-Shaped Curve of Adoption

to adopt the technology on a partial basis. Over time, consolidation of farms and the reduction of technology costs and risks led to increased technology adoption.

In the case of drip irrigation, major sources of heterogeneity were biophysical conditions such as water-holding capacity as well as the price of water and final product. Therefore, avocado growers in San Diego who were early adopters of drip, produced high-value crops on steep hills using expensive water. As drip irrigation became less expensive and more reliable, adoption moved to other crops and regions. While in 1985, 5 percent of California agricultural land adopted drip or micro irrigation, in 2014 they were used on 40 percent of land, including relatively low-revenue crops like processing tomatoes. The adoption of drip irrigation accelerated during periods of drought where the price of water was increasing and availability was declining, as well as during periods of high commodity prices (Taylor and Zilberman, 2016).

In the case of computers in agriculture, early adopters were larger farmers and packing houses that had access to a labor force with higher levels of education. Over time, use of computers became commonplace, and the intensity of adoption of computer software and applications in farming systems increased. Again, while some larger farmers adopt computerized management systems outright (e.g., irrigation scheduling), others rely on intermediary consultants that set-up and oversee these management systems.

In general, early adopters of pest control are located in regions with high levels of pest infestation. While diffusion of Bt cotton was intensive in the Mississippi Delta and areas of Texas with high rates of bollworm infestation, it was low in California where bollworm infestation is low. Alternative pest control strategies were introduced both due to regulations and build-up of resistance to chemical pesticides that increase the cost of their application and reduce their effectiveness. Weddle, Welter, and Thomson (2009) argue that resistance build-up and environmental constraints led to the gradual diffusion of biological controls and integrated pest management (IPM) in pear production in California over 50 years starting in 1960. Regulation of pesticide residue, the build-up of resistance, and the high cost of chemicals led to the adoption of IPM

in other crops. University research and extension efforts that increase the effectiveness of alternative pest control strategies, diffuse information through media, and educate pest control consultants all contributed to the adoption of IPM strategies.

The availability of new technologies and improved production opportunities may lead to an expansion of the area where a crop is suitable and profitable. New technologies or other innovative arrangements may provide regions with newfound relative advantages in agricultural. Some of California's desert and water-scarce counties became world-leading agricultural regions because of large-scale water projects and modern irrigation technologies. Because of the favorable conditions of California, it has become a hub of organic farming. Meemken and Qaim (2018) find that organic farming tends to reduce productivity and increase costs. However, in some locations, the yield losses are relatively small, and the organic label can be a source for enhancing value-added from agriculture. In some moderately dry regions in California, the relatively low level of pest infestations and high level of human capital led to the adoption of organic practices, when the price premiums for production compensate for the extra costs and lower crop yields.

According to the United States Department of Agriculture's (USDA) 2016 survey on certified organic production, California had a million acres of certified organic farms, 20 percent of the U.S. acreage. A state focusing on high-value crops, California's income from organic production is about $2.9 billion, 38 percent of the U.S. total, and almost double its share in acreage. The organic sector has seen very rapid growth in recent years. According to previous surveys by the University of California, the 2016 figures represent an 80 percent increase in acreage and a 92 percent increase in sales value from 2012. California's relative agricultural strengths seem to be reflected in its organic production as well. In dollar value of sales, the state produces 95 percent of the total organic citrus, 87 percent of grapes, 84 percent of tree nuts, and 64 percent of vegetables.

PRECISION AGRICULTURE

Precision agriculture is a set of technologies that are capable of adjusting input application to spatial or temporal variability at the micro level, which may be a specific field or farm operation (NRC, 1997). Both demand and supply factors contribute to the development of these technologies, and their introduction and availability became feasible as a result of improvements in remote sensing and communication technologies, improved computing power, and the emergence of big data and nano technologies. The demand for these technologies stems from the concern about climate change to reduce the footprint of agriculture, the expected growth in agricultural demand with population growth and rising incomes, as well as the emergence of the modern bioeconomy, where agricultural commodities serve as feedstocks for fuels, fine chemicals, and medicines.

Traditional labor-intensive agricultural technologies practiced by small farmers tend to differentiate input application within a field and sometimes treat every plant individually. Since the 1940s, however, developments in mechanization, increased labor costs combined with improved varieties, and low-cost chemical inputs led to the emergence of increased farm size and homogeneity in production with the uniform application of inputs at the field level based on average conditions, and thus ignoring micro variability (Sonka, 2016). For example, mechanized application of fertilizer using a conventional tractor would not vary across a field even though an incremental increase in inputs would increase yield in some segments of the field while reducing it in others. Precision technologies require investment in three elements: detection, assessment, and treatment.

Detection of variability within a field for, say, pest infestation or changes in soil quality and slope, has become feasible through alternative means of remote sensing, including satellites, airplanes, and now drones, and light detection and ranging (LIDAR) (Mulla, 2013). Monitoring results using fine-scale, time-dependent mapping of various biophysical conditions that provide an essential input for precision intervention and input application. Detection tools of precision farming allows the identification of plants, and especially livestock, as

individuals and the ability to treat them accordingly. For example, they allow development of a personalized diet or medical treatment to each cow. However, assessment is needed to translate the detection to specialized treatment, as well as to determine the magnitude, timing, and distribution of intervention.

However, the computation of the intervention requires a decision rule that uses both principals of science as well as estimates of effectiveness of different responses under different conditions. Determining these estimates frequently requires advanced statistical techniques as well as availability and reliability of data. The reduction in the cost of computation and the emergence of big data, and new tools like cloud computing as well as machine-learning techniques, expand the range and quality of estimated treatment (Weersink et al., 2018). Farmers may be slow to use precision methods because of the difficulty of applying a prescribed treatment. For example, remote sensing may alert a farmer to a small-scale weed infestation within a certain field, and the appropriate remedy may be known. But the costs of applying treatment with traditional machinery may be prohibitive. However, with the availability of new means (such as drones) to apply treatments, precision treatment becomes more feasible.

Zilberman, Cohen-Vogel, and Reeves (2006) argue that adoption of precision agriculture methods increases variable profits (revenue minus cost of production), but requires additional investment and adoption occurs when the discounted risk-adjusted gain from added variable profit is greater than the investment cost. Precision agriculture, in most cases, tends to reduce variable input use and, in many cases, to increase aggregate output compared to conventional farming. In some cases, the input savings are substantial enough that adoption of precision methods would reduce the output of a field.[2]

---

2   For example, take a field where a portion of the land produces very little output and production requires a certain amount of fertilizer per unit of land. After the adoption of precision technologies, the farmer may not apply any fertilizer to the less productive portion, thus foregoing its small level of output, but will continue to apply input to the productive segments. So overall input use efficiency increases, but total output declines.

Furthermore, precision agriculture may also reduce pollution caused by excessive application of inputs. The average fertilizer use efficiency in North America is estimated at two-thirds. However, precision agriculture may greatly reduce both water quality contamination and greenhouse gas emissions (Weersink et al., 2018). Adoption of precision technologies is likely to increase when (i) the costs of variable inputs, such as fertilizer and water, are increasing, (ii) the price of output is increasing if precision raises output, (iii) stricter environmental regulations are introduced, and (iv) reduction in the cost of or increase in effectiveness of precision technologies. Tozer (2009) suggests that precision agriculture that allows better monitoring is likely to reduce farmers' uncertainty, which suggests that risk-averse farmers are likely to adopt it. Policies that provide credit availability or subsidies for adoption may further enhance the diffusion of precision technologies.

Some of the more recently developed agricultural technologies that have been heavily adopted in California, like IPM and drip irrigation, have strong features of precision technologies. The key feature of IPM is that, instead of a preventive application of pesticides on a pre-determined basis, the application level is adjusted for actual infestation levels or based on observed and forecasted indicators (e.g., humidity, temperature).

Figure 17.3 depicts the evolution of IPM as a concept that was introduced by UC researchers in the 1930s, and its use was enhanced significantly by increased concerns about chemical pesticides with the publication of "Silent Spring." Extension specialists operationalized and implemented this concept through the UC IPM program,, which combined research and extension in the 1970s. The program has grown significantly, and the use of modern information technology has enhanced its impact. The introduction of IPM requires investment in monitoring by scouts or equipment. One of the major contributions of the California Irrigation Management Information System (CIMIS) is actually in pest control. Its network of weather stations throughout the state and historical weather data provide information used for both when and how to intervene. Based on a few case studies, Schatzberg and Zilberman (2016) estimate that adoption of UC IPM suggested management practices contributes between $300-$500 million annually.

Figure 17.3. Timeline: UC IPM

1939	Michelbacher writes "Recommendations for a More Discriminating Use of Pesticides," beginning a concept of IPM
1959	Stern, Smith, van den Bosch, and Hagen outline sustainable pest control systems
1962	Rachel Carson's "Silent Spring" published
1972	Council on Environmental Quality defines IPM
1972	First PCAs licensed
1976	Environmental impact report required for hazardous pesticides
1979	UC IPM founded
1979	Center for Integrated Pest Management initiated
1980	UC IPM first staffed
1980	IPM manuals established
1981	IMPACT system operational
1988	88 percent of growers own IPM manuals
1988	PCA licensing exam study materials published by UC IPM
1988	Farmworker safety training begins
1990	IPM manuals for gardeners published
1994	IPM website launched
2009	Funding for competitive research grants ends

Source: Center for Integrated Pest Management (CIPM)

The adoption of the Gubler-Thomas Powdery Mildew Index (PMI) for preventing powdery mildew outbreaks on grapes is one example of the UC IPM technology that became a standard for managing the most costly disease affecting grapes. Grapes were the highest-value crop in California in 2016, with a farm gate value of about $5.5 billion. Powdery mildew management accounts for the majority of total pesticide applications (around 74 percent of total pounds of active ingredient) by California grape growers and a significant share of total pesticide use in

California agriculture (about 17 percent) (Sambucci et al., 2015). The pecuniary costs of managing powdery mildew depend on various factors such as the location of production and the end-use for the grapes, but these costs typically represent a large share of the total costs of production—in the range of 3–7 percent of the gross value of production in places where powdery mildew pressure is significant (Fuller et al., 2014).

PMI became available to growers in 1996, through a combination of private weather service providers, CIMIS weather station network, and personal weather stations, and is now ubiquitous as a part of any weather service or weather station software. The PMI is a temperature-based forecasting index that predicts the rate of reproduction of powdery mildew spores and recommends the corresponding fungicide spray intervals. In field trials, using the PMI to adjust spray intervals was shown to eliminate two to three applications of fungicides per year, a significant reduction both in the pesticide application costs and in the environmental burden from powdery mildew control (Gubler et al., 1999; Thomas et al., 1994). However, heterogeneity among the producers of grapes in California and the behavioral response to risk by growers came into play once the growers began adopting the index in commercial vineyards.

Recent work on the use of the PMI by grape growers suggests that growers not only adjust the spray intervals, but also the choice and dosage of the pesticide products. However, they may eventually use more sprays or higher dosage over the course of the year than the field trials suggested, and increase their costs of managing powdery mildew as a result (Lybbert et al., 2016; Sambucci and Lybbert, 2016; Sambucci, 2015). While there are no official data on the loss of crop due to outbreaks of powdery mildew, outbreaks are devastating. Outbreaks are most common in vineyards with highly susceptible varieties, such as Chardonnay, and in regions favorable to fungal disease (e.g., the Central Coast). Therefore, an increase in the cost of managing powdery mildew serves as a proxy for an increase in private benefits to growers adopting an improved powdery mildew management strategy.

The adoption of drip and micro-irrigation systems is associated with the increased use of adaptive water application based on monitoring of evapotranspiration (ET), temperature, and soil moisture. More precise application of water, as well as fertilizer and other inputs, contributes significantly to increases in yields in California, water savings, and reduced drainage. The additional income gain to California agriculture associated with adoption of drip and micro-irrigation is estimated to be between $313 and $1,130 million annually (Taylor, Parker, and Zilberman, 2014). In both IPM and precision irrigation, a significant portion of the gains is associated with the use of CIMIS and improved decision rules that are a major component of precision agriculture. It is important to note that UC Extension specialists and researchers contribute significantly to the development of IPM, CIMIS, and irrigation management formulas, which enhances the precision of California agriculture.

U.S. agriculture commonly uses some tools of precision agriculture, such as GPS-based technologies, yield monitors, and variable application rate fertilizer systems. Adoption of these tools had modest impact on farm income. Managerial challenges have limited their impact on productivity, crop biodiversity and farm structure. Furthermore, high capital costs and limited access to high-speed internet in rural regions continue to limit adoption of advanced features of precision agriculture. The rate of adoption of GPS technologies varies among regions and applications, reflecting both the gains from specific applications and socioeconomic factors. One advantage of precision farming is that it can reduce the cost of traceability. Detection of individual units within farms and linking of farming operations to information systems provide a good foundation to the introduction of traceability. As concern about food safety and consumer interest in the production and source of food increase, there is growing value to traceability (Weersink et al., 2018).

One of the major challenges of agriculture is increasing precision of pesticide application. Pesticide residue, which may contaminate water or harm beneficial organisms, tends to increase when pesticide use efficiency is declining. Precision agriculture that monitors pests, like weeds or insects, and applies treatment as needed is a major priority. Weed control is a major area of automation. One approach is the use of co-robots, machines that can augment humans in weeding, and some experiments have shown that they save more than 50 percent of labor (Gallardo and Sauer, 2018). More advanced technologies use "see and shoot" where a robot pulled behind a tractor detects noxious weeds and applies high-precision squirts of herbicide at the weeds, or pulled robots that detect weeds and remove them with a mechanized hand. One application of the see and shoot technology is the LettuceBot that is now used by 10 percent of California lettuce production (Simonite, 2017). Precision methods can play an important role in controlling pests in organic farming systems using permitted chemicals and mechanical approaches. Fennimore et al. (2016) introduced a weed robot that uses sensing technology to detect weeds and then mechanically eliminates them (i.e., a "weed knife").

Many plant metabolism processes depend on environmental factors, such as temperature and day length. For California pistachios, warming winters are threatening a successful, timely exit from dormancy, which is crucial for commercial output. Researchers in UC Cooperative Extension have proposed a solution for this problem: treating dormant trees with a kaolin clay mix, which reflects sunlight and lowers effective temperatures in the tree buds. This approach, generally termed "Micro-Climate Engineering" (Trilnick, Gordon, and Zilberman, 2018), depends on constant weather monitoring. The actual temperature influence on the trees is not the mean winter temperature, but the more elusive metric of chill portions. These portions are accumulated only in hours where temperatures are within a certain range, and stop accumulating when daytime temperatures are too high. Thus, close monitoring of hourly temperatures, especially in the beginning of winter, is required to estimate the eventual chill portion count and set an optimal treatment schedule for orchards. Combining climate change predictions with a model of the pistachio market, Trilnick et al. assess the expected yearly economic gains from the kaolin technology by the year 2030 in the range of $1 billion to $4 billion.

Precision harvesting of fruits and vegetables is a major area of research and development of new technologies motivated by increasing labor costs as California and other states increase the minimum wage and see growing constraints on labor migration. The growing blueberry industry has relied on manual harvesting. Blueberries can be divided into processing and fresh products, where fresh require a higher-quality product regarding firmness, color, and nutritional content. Takeda et al. (2017) suggest that

there are several generations of blueberry harvesters that vary in their precision and ability to protect the quality of the harvested fruit. Automated harvesters are mostly used with processing blueberries, but California continues manual harvesting for its fresh blueberry industry.

However, new technologies that allow more precise discrimination of fruit and avoid catchment damage are being developed and are expected to improve harvesting efficiency by 10–20 times compared to hand-picking. There have been many attempts to automate the harvesting of citrus, cherries, and apples using robotics, but the design of robotics for harvesting systems is challenging because of complex tree structures and inconsistency of fruit size and maturity. Yet, harvesting systems are improving and are likely to be introduced first in fruit for processing and then in fruit for the fresh market (Gallardo and Sauer, 2018).

Mechanized harvesting has made some advances in grape vineyards in California. Growers of premium wine grapes are the most resistant to adopting this practice, partly due to the challenge of operating large machinery on the terrain characteristic of premium grape regions. Most of the grape acreage and production by volume is located in other areas of the state, and there harvesting is almost entirely mechanized. A recent estimate suggests that mechanical harvesting represents 85 percent of wine grapes in the state, and nearly 100 percent of lower to mid-priced grapes (Fichette, 2017). The main concern with mechanized harvesting, as with other mechanized practices in premium vineyards, is the impact of the technology on the quality of grapes and wine.

At a recent information session at the Unified Grape and Wine Symposium, the industry's largest annual event, growers from vineyards of varying price points discussed their experience with mechanization. In addition to mechanized harvesting, other operations such as mechanized pruning and shoot and leaf thinning are gaining momentum. These operations are a tougher sell with the growers of premium grapes partly because cultural practices have an effect lasting for more than one harvest season, unlike a harvester. Growers at Unified shared the belief that while mechanical pruning and harvesting are unattractive techniques, they do not negatively affect the quality of the crop or resulting wine.

Labor shortages, which drive adoption of mechanized practices for all growers, may be particularly costly to growers of premium grapes because it is difficult to schedule management operations or harvesting at preferred times. A mechanical harvester can work through the night with minimal crew, while a grower may be forced to harvest a week earlier or later than preferred based on the availability of a human harvesting crew. A week early or late may be an unacceptable variation in timing for a grower producing grapes for artisanal wine.

Precision agriculture also has major applications in livestock production. There are applications for automation of almost all processes in the dairy industry, from feeding to milking. In most dairies in California, cows are electronically tagged and many aspects of their health are monitored, which allows for personalized treatment regarding nutrition, breeding, and health (Edan, Han, and Kondo, 2009). The most important 21st century innovation in dairy farming is the milking machine. Northern European dairy farms utilize the majority of automatic milking machines, due primarily to high labor costs and weather conditions, but adoption in California is increasing. Research finds that adoption of milking machines reduces labor requirements overall, but shifts labor from milking to other activities and increases the freedom and flexibility of farmers. Adoption requires a minimum herd size to be profitable and the significant equipment costs are covered by labor cost savings, increased yield, and improvements in cow health.

The experience in Europe suggests that more advanced farmers tend to be early adopters and that there is significant peer group learning that benefits the gains from adoption and reduction of risk (in terms of labor availability). Automation and rationalization led to the concentration of production and reduced costs of egg, poultry, and swine sectors, and continues to improve with enhanced monitoring capabilities (Gallardo and Sauer, 2018). Concern for animal welfare is leading to modification of production systems in both swine and poultry sectors. But new precision livestock management technologies that include continuous monitoring of broilers' health through real-time sound and image analysis that can lead to an immediate response, aims to meet improved animal welfare standards and overall productivity (Berckmans, 2014).

Precision agriculture has been heavily integrated into vertical farming systems (farming indoors with multiple layers of production), which can be quite profitable in the production of high-value crops, such as microgreens and lettuce. Two San Francisco Bay Area companies have obtained hundreds of millions in investment and started to sell lettuce and greens in multiple cities, and the industry is set for a major take-off. Vertical farming emphasizes precise application of inputs, including the use of different light colors to affect the growth rate, taste, and appearance of products.

Vertical farming is a high-energy technology, but in locations with low-carbon electricity production, it may reduce greenhouse gases compared to outdoor growing. The technology is in its infancy and has much room for new technologies and interaction with existing ones (e.g., solar). For example, retail supply chains integrate vertical farming to capture consumer preference for freshness and local foods. Vertical farming also plays a role in food retail and distribution, which may lead to integrated food retail and vertical farming hubs for companies like Amazon and Walmart.

PRODUCT SUPPLY CHAIN

Innovations have led to the development of new technologies, but implementation requires commercialization, production, and marketing. A product supply chain is a system of organizations that transform raw inputs to a final product for end-users. In traditional societies, food supply chains were rudimentary, where either farmers consumed food at home or sold it in the market directly to consumers. Farmers or consumers exerted most of the effort in this arrangement. In modern systems, the effort of producing food products and much of food preparation has shifted from the farmer and consumer to the agrifood sector.

Zilberman, Lu, and Reardon (2017) suggest that a simple agricultural supply chain includes input suppliers that provide the inputs to farmers that produce agricultural feedstocks, which is then processed and distributed to wholesalers and retailers. Innovations are new ways of doing things, and may include new products, new production methods, or new locations to produce a product. One of the challenges of an entrepreneur that controls a technology is to design a product supply chain to capture profits adjusted for risk from their innovation.

One of the major features of agricultural food systems is the transition from commodities to differentiated products, and the increased reliance on contracting and vertical integration to capture benefits from new innovations. Contract farming represents a majority of specialty crop production. There has been major consolidation of the poultry and swine sector, either through vertical integration or a contracting relationship between a major corporation and farmers (MacDonald, Korb, and Hoppe, 2013). As production technologies become more science-based, the processors who purchase feedstock from contracted farmers will provide physical inputs, and/or direct production specifications, and monitor farmers' activities.

Over the past 50 years, poultry processors, such as Foster Farms, automated distribution of feed to animals and are producing a diverse set of final poultry products that enhance convenience and nutrition. Despite progress in automation of meat processing, it still heavily relies on physical labor due to a large extent on the inherent biological variation and complexity of animals.

California has been the hub for animal-free meat, an industry that aims to address environmental and animal welfare concerns and ultimately reduce the cost of meat. Animal-free meat consists of animal tissue fabricated using improved molecular biology and tissue engineering technologies. Burgers fabricated by Memphis Meats (San Leandro) and Impossible Foods (Redwood City), companies that rely on UC and Stanford research, are already sold in restaurants. Finless Food (San Francisco) is applying the same concept to seafood. Their workspace and finance, in part, are provided by IndieBio, which is a major seed biotechnology business accelerator.

These companies are part and parcel of the educational-industrial complex as university research, knowledge, and inventions provide the foundations for new enterprises that either result in major companies or they are absorbed by existing agribusinesses. Animal-free meat increases input use efficiency of meat production by reducing significantly the amount of grains, energy, and other inputs needed to produce meat products, thus reducing land use and greenhouse gas emissions associated with livestock and improving food safety (see survey by Bhat and Bhat, 2011).

The value-added of fruits and especially vegetables have benefited significantly from science-based innovations that increase convenience to consumers. A key example is prepackaged salads introduced by Fresh Express. The chief scientist was Jim Lugg, who started as a UC Cooperative Extension specialist. Bruce Church, a major vegetable grower, wanted a technology to lower the instability of lettuce market prices and increase the value of the product by increasing shelf life, increasing the convenience of preparation, and reducing consumer waste. Development of prepackaged salads was built on research from UC Davis, Cornell, and other universities on the atmospheric parameters for extending the shelf life of fruits and vegetables, and adapted the controlled-atmosphere technology developed by Whirlpool for shipping fruit. Lugg and his team, in collaboration with UC scientists and graduates, calibrated the parameters of gases that allowed for preservation of vegetables for more than 10 days.

Pursuing a strategy of "relentless innovation," the team first developed prepackaged lettuce for restaurants, and soon realized that consumers would pay premium prices for prepackaged salads. Bruce Church, Inc., faced a dilemma: vertically integrate their supply chain or establish contractual relationships with suppliers. To achieve economies of scale in processing, Bruce Church, Inc., sold the farm and established contractual relationships with networks of farmers to provide the vegetables to processing facilities around the U.S., and to add salad dressing and other condiments. Today, Fresh Express produces over 400 types of mixed salads. Overall sales of prepackaged salads in 2016 reached $3.7 billion. While iceberg lettuce was a dominant lettuce variety in the 1970s, romaine, kale, spinach, and other leafy green varieties are now more prominent. Furthermore, the introduction of packaged salads reduced uncertainty to farmers because they were assured a price through contracts rather than depending on variable prices in the spot market (Lugg, Shim, and Zilberman, 2017).

Consumers have a choice between eating at restaurants and eating at home. Improvements in storage, as well as increased precision in inventory and temperature control, allow for access to fresh food products throughout the year. Kimes and Laque (2011) surveyed 326 U.S. restaurant chains and found a gradual adoption of electronic ordering by consumers. This technology reduces transaction time and increases sales but may increase peak time load. Restaurant chains, like San Francisco's Eatsa, are introducing a labor-saving, information-intensive innovation. They buy highly processed foods (e.g., pre-washed and pre-cut vegetables and fruit and pre-cut and seasoned meats) assembled by robots to provide customers with a customizable menu of meal options (Gallucci, 2016). U.S. consumers still eat roughly 80 percent of their food at home. Supermarkets, which have introduced automation and precision to their inventory management, are now experimenting with reducing shopping time by nearly eliminating the check-out process.

Amazon is experimenting with using automated monitoring of consumer selection from shelves and charging consumers' accounts. Improved communication technologies, including data storage, and development of computer-aided logistics reduce the cost of shipping. This cost may be further reduced with the adoption of autonomous vehicles. Finally, automation enables expansion of food delivery from restaurants, including new innovations for the provision of on-demand food at different degrees of preparation. Some companies offer subscription meal kits, such as Blue Apron and Sunbasket, with predetermined delivery dates. These companies contract with farmers, maintain their own preparation service, and develop optimized delivery strategies. Recipes are a key asset of these companies, which enable consumers to cook gourmet food at home. These automated and individualized food channels are in their infancy, and are likely to diversify and improve over time. California agriculture and Silicon Valley play a major role in both providing the raw materials as well as the software and hardware used by these companies.

CONCLUSION

The transformation of agricultural food systems has resulted in more diversified food products and more channels that provide food to consumers. The interplay between researchers generating basic knowledge, entrepreneurs creating supply chains to commercialize and scale innovative products, farmers adopting and refining technologies, Cooperative Extension refining practices, and consumers providing feedback have all contributed to this transformation. The ability to address concerns like climate change, a growing population and increasing demand, both in scale and scope, will rely on the ability of agriculture to continue its transformation. This paper shows how precision agricultural technologies addressed certain challenges in California, increased productivity in some crops, and provided new opportunities for growers, processors, and consumers. Generally speaking, all aspects of agriculture, in California and elsewhere, can benefit from this process of translating research to new products and processes.

REFERENCES

Alston, J.M., J.M. Beddow, and P.G. Pardey. 2009. "Agricultural Research, Productivity, and Food Prices in the Long Run." *Science 325*(5945): 1209-1210.

Alston, J.M., M.A. Andersen, J.S. James, and P.G. Pardey. 2010. *Persistence Pays: U.S. Agricultural Productivity Growth and the Benefits from Public R&D Spending.* New York, Springer.

Alston, J.M. and P.G. Pardey. 2008. "Public Funding for Research into Specialty Crops." *HortScience 43*(5): 1461-1470.

Baumgart-Getz, A., L.S. Prokopy, and K. Floress. 2012. "Why Farmers Adopt Best Management Practice in the United States: A Meta-analysis of the Adoption Literature." *Journal of Environmental Management 96*(1): 17-25.

Becker, G.S. 1965. "A Theory of the Allocation of Time." *The Economic Journal,* 75(299): 493-517.

Berckmans, D., 2014. "Precision Livestock Farming Technologies for Welfare Management in Intensive Livestock Systems." *Scientific and Technical Review of the Office International des Epizooties 33*(1): 189-196.

Bhat, Z.F. and H. Bhat. 2011. "Animal-free Meat Biofabrication." *American Journal of Food Technology 6*: 441-459.

Blaustein-Rejto, D. "Don't Count Out Vertical Farms — Indoor Ag Might Use More Energy to Use Less Land, Fertilizer, and Pesticide." *The Breakthrough Institute 30* Jan. 2018. Available at: https://thebreakthrough.org/index.php/voices/vertical-farms-raise-yields-but-what-about-emissions

Chakravorty, U., E. Hochman, C. Umetsu, and D. Zilberman. 2009. "Water Allocation Under Distribution Losses: Comparing Alternative Institutions." *Journal of Economic Dynamics and Control 33*(2): 463-476.

Daberkow, S.G. and W.D. McBride. 2003. "Farm and Operator Characteristics Affecting the Awareness and Adoption of Precision Agriculture Technologies in the U.S." *Precision Agriculture 4*(2): 163-177.

Edan, Y., S. Han, and N. Kondo. 2009. "Automation in Agriculture." In *Springer Handbook of Automation* (pp. 1095-1128). Springer, Berlin, Heidelberg.

Fennimore, S.A., D.C. Slaughter, M.C. Siemens, R.G. Leon, and M.N. Saber. 2016. "Technology for Automation of Weed Control in Specialty Crops." *Weed Technology 30*(4): 823-837.

Fichette, T. 2017. "California Wine Grape Industry Seeks No Touch Vineyard." *Western Farm Press.* February 10, 2017. Available at: http://www.westernfarmpress.com/grapes/california-wine-grape-industry-seeks-no-touch-vineyard

Fuller K.B., J.M. Alston, and O.S. Sambucci. 2014. "The Value of Powdery Mildew Resistance in Grapes: Evidence from California." *Wine Economics and Policy 3*(2): 90-107.

Gallardo, R.K. and J. Sauer. 2018. "Adoption of Labor-saving Technologies in Agriculture." *Annual Review of Resource Economics 10*(1): 185-206.

Gallucci, N. 2016. "Waiter-Less, Cashier-Less Restaurant Is the Stuff of the Future." *Mashable.* Available at: https://mashable.com/2016/12/17/eatsa-waiterless-cashierless-tech-restaurant/#R9Cbei_VksqL.

Graff, G., A. Heiman, and D. Zilberman. 2002. "University Research and Offices of Technology Transfer." *California Management Review 45*(1): 88-115.

Gubler, W.D., M.R. Rademacher, S.J. Vasquez, and C.S. Thomas. 1999. *Control of Powdery Mildew Using the UC Davis Powdery Mildew Risk Index.* APS Net: Plant Pathology Online. http://www.apsnet.org/publications/apsnetfeatures/Pages/UCDavisRisk.aspx.

Hayami, Y. and V.W. Ruttan. 1971. *Agricultural Development: An International Perspective.* Baltimore, Md/London: The Johns Hopkins Press.

Just, D.R., S.A. Wolf, S. Wu, and D. Zilberman. 2002. "Consumption of Economic Information in Agriculture." *American Journal of Agricultural Economics 84*(1): 39-52.

Khanna, M., O.F. Epouhe, and R. Hornbaker;1999. "Site-Specific Crop Management: Adoption Patterns and Incentives." *Review of Agricultural Economics 21*(2): 455-472.

Kimes, S.E. and P.F. Laqué. 2011. "Online, Mobile, and Text Food Ordering in the U.S. Restaurant Industry." *Cornell Hospitality Report 11*:4-15.

King, C.J., 2007. "University Roles in Technological Innovation in California." *Research & Occasional Paper Series*: CSHE. 6.07. Center for Studies in Higher Education.

Klonsky, K., and B. Healy. 2013. *Statistical Review of California's Organic Agriculture, 2009-2012* Agricultural Issues Center University of California.

Lancaster, K. J. 1966. "A New Approach to Consumer Theory." *The Journal of Political Economy* 74(2): 132-157.

Levenstein, H.A. 2003. *Revolution at the Table: The Transformation of the American Diet* (Vol. 7). University of California Press.

Lugg, J., M.E. Shim, and D. Zilberman. 2017. "Establishing Supply Chain for an Innovation: The Case of Prepackaged Salad." *ARE Update* 20(6): 5-8. University of California Giannini Foundation of Agricultural Economics. Available at: https://s.giannini.ucop.edu/uploads/giannini_public/04/ac/04acc853-dd8a-45d6-a4dd-bf2ac9c5f392/v21n1_2.pdf.

Lybbert, T.J., N. Magnan, and W.D. Gubler. 2016. "Multi-Dimensional Responses to Risk Information: How Do Winegrape Growers Respond to Disease Forecasts and to What Environmental Effect?" *American Journal of Agricultural Economics* 98(2): 383–405.

MacDonald, J.M., P. Korb, and R.A. Hoppe. 2013. "Farm Size and the Organization of U.S. Crop Farming." USDA, ERS. Available at: www.ers.usda.gov/publications/erreconomic-researchreport/err-152.aspx.

Meemken, E.M. and M. Qaim. 2018. "Organic Agriculture, Food Security, and the Environment." *Annual Review of Resource Economics* 10: 39-63.

Mulla, D.J., 2013. "Twenty Five Years of Remote Sensing in Precision Agriculture: Key Advances and Remaining Knowledge Gaps." *Biosystems Engineering* 114(4): 358-371.

National Research Council. 1997. *Precision Agriculture in the 21st Century: Geospatial and Information Technologies in Crop Management.* Washington, D.C.: National Academy Press.

Rausser, G., H. Ameden, and R. Stevens, (eds). 2016. *Structuring Public–Private Research Partnerships for Success: Empowering University Partners.* Edward Elgar Publishing.

Rogers, E.M. 2010. *Diffusion of Innovations.* Simon and Schuster.

Sambucci, O. 2015. "Essays on the Economics of Powdery Mildew Management in the California Grape Industry." *Doctoral Dissertation.* Agricultural and Resource Economics, UC Davis.

Sambucci, O and T.J. Lybbert. 2016. "Behavioral Responses to Disease Forecasts: From Precision to Automation in Powdery Mildew Management." *ARE Update* 20(1): 5-8. University of California Giannini Foundation of Agricultural Economics. Available at: https://s.giannini.ucop.edu/uploads/giannini_public/57/a4/57a43d40-0972-40dc-8c8e-4fe5872498fd/v20n1_2.pdf.

Sambucci, O., J.M. Alston, and K. B. Fuller. 2015. "The Costs of Powdery Mildew Management in Grapes and the Value of Resistant Varieties: Evidence from California." Robert Mondavi Center for Wine Economics Working Paper No. 1402. Available at: http://vinecon.ucdavis.edu/publications/CWE1402.pdf.

Schaefer, K.A. 2014. "The Meat Racket: The Secret Takeover of America's Food Business." *American Journal of Agricultural Economics* 96(5): 1507-1508.

Schatzberg, M. and D. Zilberman. 2016. "Valuing the Dissemination of Integrated Pest Management Information in California." *ARE Update* 20(2): 5-8. University of California Giannini Foundation of Agricultural Economics. Available at: https://s.giannini.ucop.edu/uploads/giannini_public/b3/9e/b39eab92-bc4f-43a3-8268-6ff96a57b74f/v20n2_2.pdf.

Schumpeter, J. A. 1934. "The Theory of Economic Development: An inquiry into Profits, Capital, Credit, Interest, and the Business Cycle." Transaction publishers. *Journal of Comparative Research in Anthropology and Sociology.* 2012. 3(2).

Simonite, T. 2017. "Why John Deere Just Spent $305 Million on a Lettuce-Farming Robot." *Wired Magazine.*

Sonka, S. 2016. "Big Data: Fueling the Next Evolution of Agricultural Innovation." *Journal of Innovation Management* 4(1): 114-136.

Sunding, D. and D. Zilberman. 2001. "The Agricultural Innovation Process: Research and Technology Adoption in a Changing Agricultural Sector." *Handbook of Agricultural Economics* 1: 207-261.

Takeda, F., W.Q. Yang, C. Li, A. Freivalds, K. Sung, R. Xu, B. Hu, J. Williamson, and S. Sargent. 2017. "Applying New Technologies to Transform Blueberry Harvesting." *Agronomy7*(2): 33.

Taylor, R., D. Parker, and D. Zilberman, 2014. "Contribution of University of California Cooperative Extension to Drip Irrigation." *ARE Update* 18(2):5-8. University of California Giannini Foundation of Agricultural Economics. Available at: https://s.giannini.ucop.edu/uploads/giannini_public/c3/d4/c3d4e148-59b5-4938-abc1-70beffcba8cc/v18n2_2.pdf.

Tey, Y.S. and M. Brindal. 2012. "Factors Influencing the Adoption of Precision Agricultural Technologies: A Review for Policy Implications." *Precision Agriculture* 13(6):713-730.

Thomas C.S., E.D. Gubler, and G. Leavitt. 1994. "Field Testing of a Powdery Mildew Disease Forecast Model on Grapes in California." *Phytopathology* 84: 1070.

Tozer, P.R. 2009. "Uncertainty and Investment in Precision Agriculture–Is it Worth the Money?" *Agricultural Systems* 100(1-3): 80-87.

USDA. 2017. *Certified Organic Survey 2016 Summary*

Weddle, P.W., S.C. Welter, and D. Thomson. 2009. "History of IPM in California Pears—50 years of Pesticide Use and the Transition to Biologically Intensive IPM." *Pest Management Science* 65(12): 1287-1292.

Weersink, A., E. Fraser, D. Pannell, E. Duncan, and S. Rotz. 2018. "Opportunities and Challenges for Big Data in Agricultural and Environmental Analysis." *Annual Review of Resource Economics* 10: 19-37.

Wolf, S., D. Just, and D. Zilberman. 2001. "Between Data and Decisions: The Organization of Agricultural Economic Information Systems." *Research Policy* 30(1): 121-141.

Wright, B.D., K. Drivas, Z. Lei, and S.A. Merrill. 2014. "Technology Transfer: Industry-funded Academic Inventions Boost Innovation." *Nature 507*(7492): 297-299.

Zilberman, D., D. Cohen-Vogel, and J. Reeves. 2006. "Precision Farming in Cotton.:" *Frontiers in Water Resource Economics*. 255-275. Springer, Boston, MA.

Zilberman, D., J. Zhao, and A. Heiman. 2012. "Adoption versus Adaptation, With Emphasis on Climate Change." *Annual Review of Resource Economics* 4(1): 27-53.

Zilberman, D., L. Lu, and T. Reardon. 2017. "Innovation-Induced Food Supply Chain Design." *Food Policy* Available at: https://scholars.opb.msu.edu/en/publications/innovation-induced-food-supply-chain-design.

CHAPTER 18. SOCIAL VALUE OF THE GIANNINI FOUNDATION

ALEX F. MCCALLA AND GORDON C. RAUSSER

ABSTRACT

The history of the Giannini Foundation of Agricultural Economics (the Foundation) is replete with beneficial contributions to the understanding of contemporary issues facing California agriculture and its environment, as well as providing meaningful solutions to many impeding crises. We argue that the Giannini Foundation is the causal source of what distinguishes the University of California, in the field of agricultural economics, from other land-grant universities. In assessing the social value of the Foundation as an institution, we briefly describe its unique origin with its well-articulated purpose to promote the "economic status of California agriculturalists." Over the course of its history, its commitment to empirical insights, which continue to inform the practical recommendations made by the Foundation's members, underscores a drive towards scientific excellence. Much of its social value stems from the immense human capital that has accumulated across the three university campuses that comprise the Foundation. It is not just that some of the most noted agricultural economists have studied and trained at the Giannini Foundation, but they have created an institution that emphasizes generating improved methodologies for empirical analysis, becoming the nexus for the best conceptual frameworks as well as statistical and econometric methodologies within not only California, but across all land-grant universities throughout the United States.

ABOUT THE AUTHORS

Alex McCalla is an emeritus professor in the Department of Agricultural and Resource Economics at the University of California, Davis. He can be contacted by email at alex@primal.ucdavis.edu. Gordon Rausser is the Robert Sproul Distinguished Professor in the Department of Agricultural and Resource Economics at the University of California, Berkeley. He can be reached by email at rausser@berkeley.edu.

Notes from the authors: We have chosen largely to avoid chronicling which specific members of the Foundation did what and when, and what in our subjective views were the merits of individual contributions. Instead, our focus is on the collective value of the Giannini Foundation for California food and agriculture.

TABLE OF CONTENTS

INTRODUCTION

The Giannini Foundation of Agricultural Economics is nearly 90 years old, having been established as a functioning institution of the University of California at the beginning of the Depression in 1930 following A.P. Giannini's gift of $1.5 million in 1928. The letter from the Bancitaly (later renamed the Bank of America) transmitting the gift, dated Feb. 10, 1928, stated in part:

> *It should be understood that the activities of the Foundation are to be regarded as chiefly: (a) those of research, with the purpose to find the facts and conditions which will promise or threaten to affect the economic status of California agriculturalists; and (b) those of formulating ways and means of enabling the agriculturalists of California to profit from the existence of favorable facts and conditions, and to protect themselves as well as possible from adverse facts and conditions.* (Johnston and McCalla, 2009)

Given this mandate, our purpose in this chapter is to assess the social value of the Foundation. It is clear that the intent was not to just be a passive research organization (finding facts and conditions that affect the well-being of farmers) but also to be an activist in "formulating ways and means of enabling the agriculturalists of California" to profit from favorable events and protect themselves from bad ones. In other words, this chapter evaluates how effective the Foundation has been in providing relevant information and analysis that helped individual agriculturalists do better. We also assess the effectiveness of the Foundation in helping formulate and evaluate policy options and policy performance.

In our assessment, over the almost 90-year history of the Foundation, it is critically important to recognize the evolution of California agriculture over the same period. At the outset of the Foundation, California agriculture in 1930 was just completing a comprehensive transformation from extensive dryland agriculture to intensive irrigated agriculture.

> *After falling in the 1860s and 1870s, the share of intensive crops in the value of total output climbed from less than 4 percent in 1879 to over 20 percent in 1889. By 1909, the intensive share reached nearly one-half, and by 1929, it was almost four-fifths of the total. In terms of the crops*

> *produced—the scale of operations, the quantity and seasonality of the labor demanded, and the types of equipment needed—California agriculture was a very different place than it had been 50 years earlier.* (See Olmstead and Rhode, Chapter 2)

It was also entering the Depression unprepared:

> *Thus California came to the beginning of the decade of the Great Depression with a vastly expanded and as yet unadjusted producing plant, with little experience in meeting Depression conditions and with a comparatively heavy load of debt.* (Johnston and McCalla, 2009)

> *The Depression had hit hard and late in California.* (Johnston and McCalla, 2009)

By 1930, groundwater depletion leading to water shortages was emerging as the dominant threat to the industry as the Depression struck full force. So, the new Foundation came into being in extremely challenging times. After surviving the Depression, California agriculture thrived during WWII and continued to grow in the post-war period so that by the 1960s it was the largest state agricultural sector in the United States.

California agriculture also greatly increased the diversity of commodities produced so that by 1950, the agricultural statistics report claimed California produced more than 200 commodities. That diversity doubled again by 2016 when the same report then boasted that California produced over 400 commodities. It was by then a $50-plus billion per year agricultural industry, the largest in the U.S., producing output with value nearly equal to the sum of the next two largest states: Iowa and Texas.

During this evolution of California agriculture, the overall purpose of the Foundation remained engaged in improving and enhancing the well-being of all participants in California agriculture. However the mechanisms used—human capital development, information collection and distribution, historical and descriptive analysis, applied research, projections and forecasts, and policy prescriptions—continuously adjusted as both California agriculture and the University of California grew and changed.

Initially, the Foundation had 14 founding members at UC Berkeley. Most, if not all, of them had joint appointments with other academic units, including Agricultural Extension. The Foundation had an endowment of $1.5 million, one-third earmarked for building Giannini Hall. It was managed from UC Berkeley. Well over half of early returns from the endowment were invested in the Giannini Foundation Library. In the beginning, the Foundation members were principally agricultural economists focusing on all facets of the markets for California agricultural production and the distribution of food to final consumers. However, with the increasing generation of agricultural production externalities, the expertise of Foundation members expanded to include environmental economists as well. Similarly, the competition for finite resources led to enhanced resource scarcity and as a result the membership was expanded to create focal points for resource economists. As the performance of California agriculture began to depend increasingly on export markets due to increasing globalization, once again Foundation expertise was expanded to include trade and development economists. Finally, given the importance of government intervention and regulation, Foundation members incorporated policy analysts into their membership.

Currently, the Foundation website lists 70 members and associate members. The market value of the endowment in 2017 approached $25 million, generating spendable income of nearly $1 million per year. Expenditures, averaged over the last five years, have been allocated as follows: 43 percent for faculty mini-grants (seed money) to encourage members to initiate innovative research with a broad interpretation of the endowment's focus on California agriculture; 23 percent for graduate student support similarly focused; 15 percent for conferences, seminars, publications, and information services; a declining share of 9 percent for the library; and 10 percent for administration. The faculty mini-grants and graduate student support allows Foundation members to pursue the Foundation mandate addressing problems that matter for which high-quality, nimbly-responsive research might well make a difference. Aside from the focus on California agriculture, the Foundation funding for research and graduate student support is unrestricted.

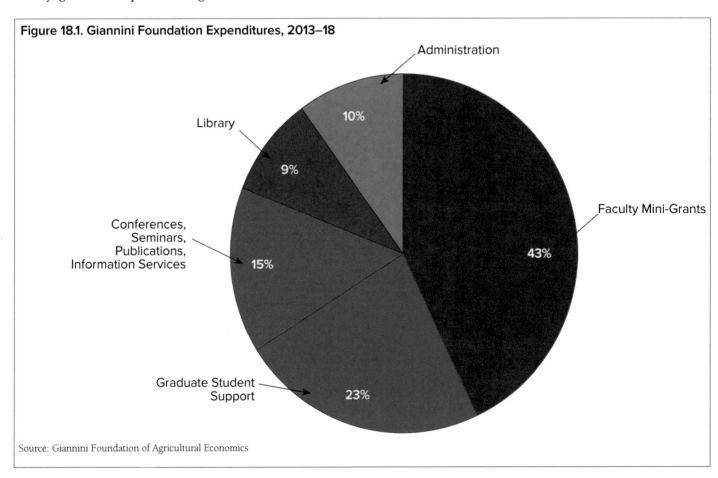

Figure 18.1. Giannini Foundation Expenditures, 2013–18

Administration — 10%

Library — 9%

Conferences, Seminars, Publications, Information Services — 15%

Faculty Mini-Grants — 43%

Graduate Student Support — 23%

Source: Giannini Foundation of Agricultural Economics

GIANNINI FOUNDATION OUTPUT

An early effort, after the establishment of the Foundation, was to invest in the creation and development of a library. The Giannini Foundation Library that received much of the early investment became a world-class library of agricultural economics, second only to the National Agricultural Library's holdings in Washington, D.C. Quoting a report to the UC Board of Regents on April 22, 1966, "The Library, established in 1930, is believed unsurpassed in the world of agricultural economics and related fields, with its collections of approximately 12,000 books, more than 2,000 serials—including 700 periodicals—and a large collection of pamphlets" (Johnston and McCalla, 2009). The library enabled scholars, inside and outside the Foundation, to have the best possible access to a growing body of national and global literature. A library to a social scientist is as important a research tool as an herbarium is to a botanist, soil profiles are to a soil scientist, or a wet lab is to a biochemist. It encouraged research on the cutting edge by allowing access to the best existing knowledge. At its zenith, the Giannini Foundation Library was arguably one of the world's largest collections of agricultural economic information, and contributed to the quality and quantity of research by developing the skills of its users. Its existence was a powerful attractant for new faculty and it was a magnet for graduate students.

Computers, digitization, and the cloud have transformed how information and analytical results are stored. The Giannini Foundation Libraries at UC Berkeley and UC Davis have been mostly digitized. The commitment to ensure a high-quality source of global information endures, but the space required is now only a small fraction of what was formerly required.

Giannini Foundation research has been published in three series: Research Reports 1930–2009, Monographs 1947–2011, and Special Reports 1978–2004. There are 351 Research Reports. The first two in 1930 were entitled "What Determines California Raisin Sales" and "Some Aspects of Shipside Refrigeration at San Francisco." Eight more followed in 1931, addressing issues from factors affecting prices of canned apricots, cling peaches, and

pears to marketing globe artichokes; a summary of the alfalfa industry; collective bargaining in the L.A. milk market; and cooperative marketing of poultry. These reports represented the beginning of an almost 90-year series that, in the 2000s, included analysis of marketing orders and organic crops, GMO traits, GMO rice, horticultural crops, the MBTE ban, and a Hass avocado promotion program.

There are 48 Giannini Foundation Research Monographs, starting in 1947, with the first 17 published in *Hilgardia*, a technical publication of the UC Division of Agriculture and Natural Resources. Monographs are substantial pieces of work, which in more than half the cases, are co-authored by Ph.D. students from UC Berkeley or UC Davis, drawing on their thesis work. The topics covered include input markets such as fertilizer and water, product markets—domestic and international—for annual and perennial crops, livestock production and marketing, and food processing industries. The last Giannini Monograph, *Demand for Food in the United States* (2011), was a tribute to a previous monograph, *Consumer Demand For Food Commodities in the United States* (1971).

Stiffening of merit and promotion processes on each of the three UC campuses where Giannini Foundation members are located (UC Berkeley, UC Davis, and UC Riverside) resulted in a transition to new publication outlets that were more academic, peer-reviewed journals rather than the more service-oriented Giannini publications. This, along with rapidly changing digital information sharing technology, eventually led to discontinuation of regular Giannini Foundation Monographs and Research Reports early in the 21st century.

Many early Research Reports provided price, cost, and market data and analysis while others presented the results of original qualitative and quantitative research. Thus, in 1963, the Foundation separated the two by initiating a third publication series called Information Series, of which this book is a part. This series published useful descriptive analysis, more applied than either the Research Reports or Monographs.

Along the way, the Foundation has sponsored seven periodic Special Reports. The last one in 2004 was written with concerns about the future of California agriculture, provocatively titled "Whither California Agriculture: Up, Down, or Out? Some Thoughts About the Future[1]." It continues to be widely requested. The original publication run of 1,500 copies is long since out of print. It is online at e-scholarship where it has received 1,157 requests since publication in 2004. It received 85 requests in 2017 and early 2018.

In 1997, the Foundation began publishing the *ARE Update* (Update) series. Its articles have included information summaries, topical issue reviews, and applied research summaries. The result is 21 years (volumes) of *ARE Updates*—four issues per year at the start and six per year since 2000—for a total of 114 issues containing more than 400 short articles. The first article in 1997 was "NAFTA: Neither Villain nor Savior" and the first article in 2018 was "Can Micro-Climate Engineering Save California Pistachios?" The Updates are published electronically and in hard copy to a mailing list of 2,248, primarily in California and Washington, D.C., but in other states as well. Over the last 12 years (2005–06 to 2016–17), there have been over 3 million downloads. The number of downloads has grown from less than 160,000 in the first two years to over 400,000 in one year (2012–13), over 300,000 in three separate years, and over 220,000 the remainder of the years.

For the last 10 years, the top 20 articles have attracted 758,880 downloads. The top 10 have attracted over a half million downloads. The top article by Colin Carter, "China's Agriculture: Achievements and Challenges," has been downloaded an impressive 141,201 times. In the top 10, China is a central topic in four articles; strawberries, organic agriculture, and biofuels each are the focus in three articles; and genetically modified (GM) crops in two articles. Eight of the 10 address an international topic. Clearly, *ARE Update* has become the predominant form of providing written knowledge/information by the Giannini Foundation.

---

1 Johnston, W.E., McCalla, A.F. 2004. "Whither California Agriculture: Up, Down or Out? Some Thoughts about the Future." Giannini Foundation Special Report Series 04-1. https://s.giannini.ucop.edu/uploads/giannini_public/43/84/4384fd4a-266c-434a-b85c-83a1ec11e385/escholarship_uc_item_4232w2sr.pdf.

Over its history, the Foundation has sponsored or cosponsored many conferences to highlight issues that were deemed important. During the last 10 years, conference titles have included: Innovation in Agrifood Supply Chains; Water Pricing for a Dry Future; Farm Labor; Biofuels (two); Salinity; Climate Change; Pests, Germs and Seeds; California's Climate Change Policy; and the 75th Anniversary Symposium of the Giannini Foundation. These provide an insight into what the Foundation saw as critical current and future issues.

Foundation members have provided expertise by playing critical roles as UC Cooperative Extension specialists or by providing governmental or public sector service to global institutions, not to mention national, state, and county governments. Foundation members have also lent their expertise to non-governmental organizations (NGOs), including professional associations. The list is varied and includes global institutions such as the World Bank, CGIAR (formerly the Consultative Group for International Agricultural Research), and United Nations agencies like the Food and Agriculture Organization (FAO). In addition, Foundation members have contributed their knowledge to national, state, and local governments through the Council of Economic Advisers within the Executive Office of the President, federal and state departments of agriculture, federal and state environmental protection agencies, state and federal marketing orders, state advisory boards, and as farm advisors at the county level. In terms of impact on NGOs, Foundation members founded the Institute for Policy Reform, and four members provided much of the intellectual leadership for the formation of the International Agricultural Trade Research Consortium (IATRC).

In terms of quantity of output, over 1,000 Ph.D. dissertations have been completed at UC Berkeley, Davis, and Riverside since 1930. Between 40 and 45 percent were international students, approximately 35–40 percent were from U.S. states other than California, and the rest from in-state. More than 40 of these graduates have spent some or all of their careers in the UC system, most as members of the Giannini Foundation. Another 30 have worked in California employed in the state university system, state government, or the private sector. In addition, at UC Davis more than 1,000 Masters of Science degrees have been granted since 1950.

For the quality of output, there are a number of metrics available. The caliber shown is no surprise given the mandate of the Bancitaly letter charge. "The 1928 document called upon the University, in selecting members of the staff of the Giannini Foundation, to appoint 'the most competent persons whose services are available, without restriction as to citizenship or race'" (Johnston and McCalla, 2009). A critically important metric is the National Research Council rankings released in September 2010 which listed UC Berkeley and UC Davis as the top two Ph.D. programs in the country. Another measure is the selection of Foundation members as Fellows of the Agriculture and Applied Economics Association (AAEA). In 1957, the AAEA began granting its highest honor—Fellow—to members. Since then, 251 have been elected (10 were honored the first year and between two and six per year since). Of these, 42 were members of the Giannini Foundation when the honor was granted, 17 percent of the total (Davis, 21; Berkeley, 20; Riverside, 1).

Forty-one (16 percent) of the Fellows received their Ph.D.s while students at UC Berkeley or UC Davis. Given that 13 of the Fellows were members of the Foundation when honored and were homegrown, i.e., had their Ph.D.s from Giannini Foundation departments, the Foundation was involved in shaping 70 AAEA Fellows, nearly 28 percent of the total. The Giannini Foundation currently has about 70 members while the AAEA membership is around 2,500; clearly it is an excellent performance for a small outfit. Eight Foundation members have been elected Fellows of the Western Agricultural Economics Association (WAEA). Foundation members have also been honored as Fellows of other scholarly associations: American Statistical Association, American Association for the Advancement of Science, the American Academy of Arts and Sciences, and the Econometric Society.

Over the course of Foundation history, members have been recipients of many national awards including a multitude of Best Journal Article Awards, Research Discovery Awards, and Publications of Enduring Quality Awards from AAEA. Instructional or teaching awards have also been given to Giannini faculty and graduates. Many of these awards have been documented in detail in *A. P. Giannini and the Giannini Foundation of Agricultural Economics*, published for the 75th Anniversary Symposium in

2005. For UC Davis, much of this information, at least for graduate students, is updated through 2016 in the publication, *UC Davis Agricultural and Resource Economics Ph.D. Program: The First 50 Years*. In addition to the impressive list of elected Fellows of the AAEA, Foundation members have also been elected as president of the AAEA eight times and president of the WAEA 12 times.

Figure 18.2. History of the Giannini Foundation of Agricultural Economics, 1920–2010

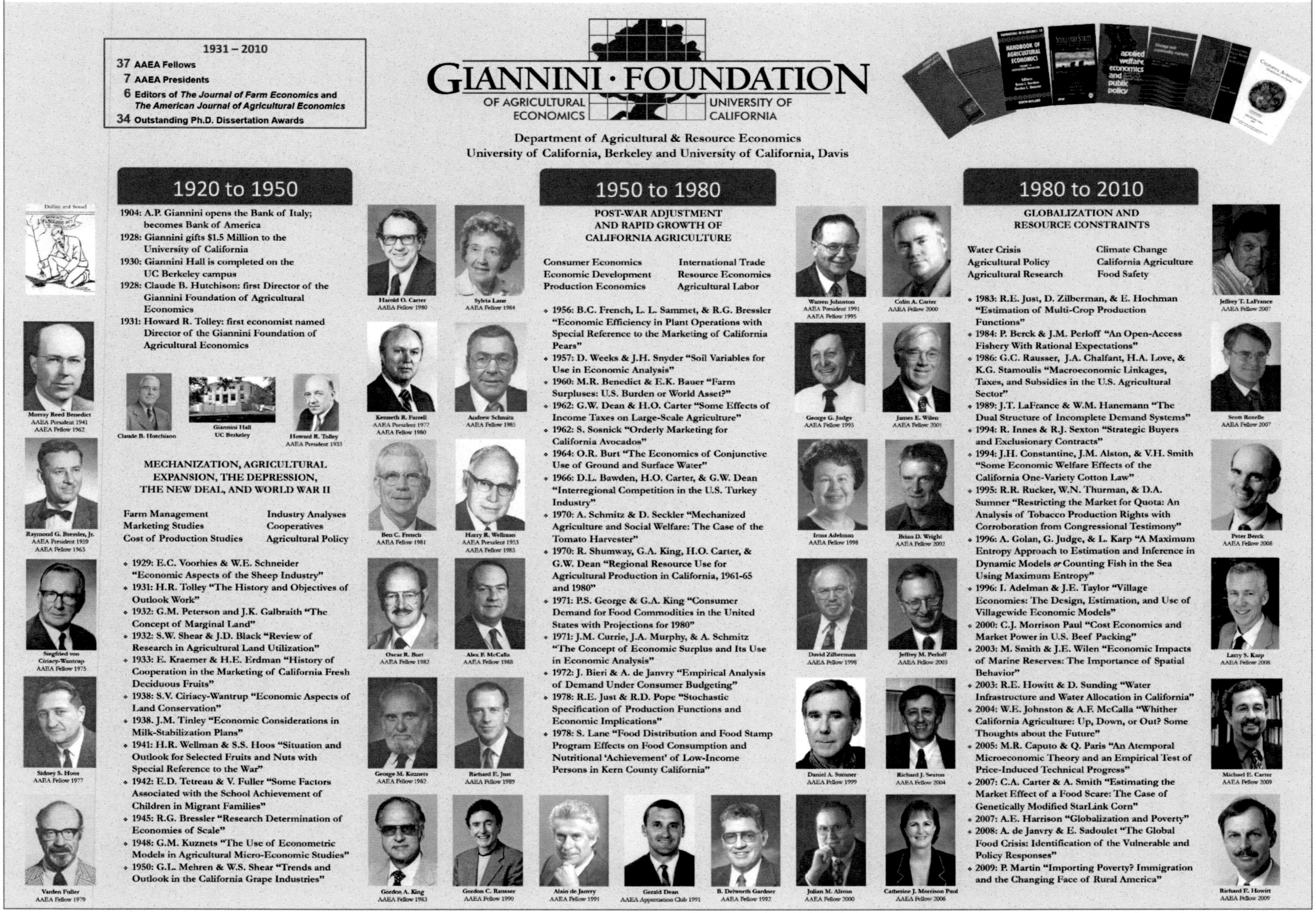

GIANNINI · FOUNDATION

OF AGRICULTURAL ECONOMICS — UNIVERSITY OF CALIFORNIA

Department of Agricultural & Resource Economics
University of California, Berkeley and University of California, Davis

1931 – 2010
- 37 AaEA Fellows
- 7 AAEA Presidents
- 6 Editors of *The Journal of Farm Economics* and *The American Journal of Agricultural Economics*
- 34 Outstanding Ph.D. Dissertation Awards

1920 to 1950

- 1904: A.P. Giannini opens the Bank of Italy; becomes Bank of America
- 1928: Giannini gifts $1.5 Million to the University of California
- 1930: Giannini Hall is completed on the UC Berkeley campus
- 1928: Claude B. Hutchison: first Director of the Giannini Foundation of Agricultural Economics
- 1931: Howard R. Tolley: first economist named Director of the Giannini Foundation of Agricultural Economics

MECHANIZATION, AGRICULTURAL EXPANSION, THE DEPRESSION, THE NEW DEAL, AND WORLD WAR II

Farm Management	Industry Analyses
Marketing Studies	Cooperatives
Cost of Production Studies	Agricultural Policy

- 1929: E.C. Voorhies & W.E. Schneider "Economic Aspects of the Sheep Industry"
- 1931: H.R. Tolley "The History and Objectives of Outlook Work"
- 1932: G.M. Peterson and J.K. Galbraith "The Concept of Marginal Land"
- 1932: S.W. Shear & J.D. Black "Review of Research in Agricultural Land Utilization"
- 1933: E. Kraemer & H.E. Erdman "History of Cooperation in the Marketing of California Fresh Deciduous Fruits"
- 1938: S.V. Ciriacy-Wantrup "Economic Aspects of Land Conservation"
- 1938: J.M. Tinley "Economic Considerations in Milk-Stabilization Plans"
- 1941: H.R. Wellman & S.S. Hoos "Situation and Outlook for Selected Fruits and Nuts with Special Reference to the War"
- 1942: E.D. Tetreau & V. Fuller "Some Factors Associated with the School Achievement of Children in Migrant Families"
- 1945: R.G. Bressler "Research Determination of Economies of Scale"
- 1948: G.M. Kuznets "The Use of Econometric Models in Agricultural Micro-Economic Studies"
- 1950: G.L. Mehren & W.S. Shear "Trends and Outlook in the California Grape Industries"

1950 to 1980

POST-WAR ADJUSTMENT AND RAPID GROWTH OF CALIFORNIA AGRICULTURE

Consumer Economics	International Trade
Economic Development	Resource Economics
Production Economics	Agricultural Labor

- 1956: B.C. French, L.L. Sammet, & R.G. Bressler "Economic Efficiency in Plant Operations with Special Reference to the Marketing of California Pears"
- 1957: D. Weeks & J.H. Snyder "Soil Variables for Use in Economic Analysis"
- 1960: M.R. Benedict & E.K. Bauer "Farm Surpluses: U.S. Burden or World Asset?"
- 1962: G.W. Dean & H.O. Carter "Some Effects of Income Taxes on Large-Scale Agriculture"
- 1962: S. Sosnick "Orderly Marketing for California Avocados"
- 1964: O.R. Burt "The Economics of Conjunctive Use of Ground and Surface Water"
- 1966: D.L. Bawden, H.O. Carter, & G.W. Dean "Interregional Competition in the U.S. Turkey Industry"
- 1970: A. Schmitz & D. Seckler "Mechanized Agriculture and Social Welfare: The Case of the Tomato Harvester"
- 1970: R. Shumway, G.A. King, H.O. Carter, & G.W. Dean "Regional Resource Use for Agricultural Production in California, 1961–65 and 1980"
- 1971: P.S. George & G.A. King "Consumer Demand for Food Commodities in the United States with Projections for 1980"
- 1971: J.M. Currie, J.A. Murphy, & A. Schmitz "The Concept of Economic Surplus and Its Use in Economic Analysis"
- 1972: J. Bieri & A. de Janvry "Empirical Analysis of Demand Under Consumer Budgeting"
- 1978: R.E. Just & R.D. Pope "Stochastic Specification of Production Functions and Economic Implications"
- 1978: S. Lane "Food Distribution and Food Stamp Program Effects on Food Consumption and Nutritional 'Achievement' of Low-Income Persons in Kern County California"

1980 to 2010

GLOBALIZATION AND RESOURCE CONSTRAINTS

Water Crisis	Climate Change
Agricultural Policy	California Agriculture
Agricultural Research	Food Safety

- 1983: R.E. Just, D. Zilberman, & E. Hochman "Estimation of Multi-Crop Production Functions"
- 1984: P. Berck & J.M. Perloff "An Open-Access Fishery With Rational Expectations"
- 1986: G.C. Rausser, J.A. Chalfant, H.A. Love, & K.G. Stamoulis "Macroeconomic Linkages, Taxes, and Subsidies in the U.S. Agricultural Sector"
- 1989: J.T. LaFrance & W.M. Hanemann "The Dual Structure of Incomplete Demand Systems"
- 1994: R. Innes & R.J. Sexton "Strategic Buyers and Exclusionary Contracts"
- 1994: J.H. Constantine, J.M. Alston, & V.H. Smith "Some Economic Welfare Effects of the California One-Variety Cotton Law"
- 1995: R.R. Rucker, W.N. Thurman, & D.A. Sumner "Restricting the Market for Quota: An Analysis of Tobacco Production Rights with Corroboration from Congressional Testimony"
- 1996: A. Golan, G. Judge, & L. Karp "A Maximum Entropy Approach to Estimation and Inference in Dynamic Models or Counting Fish in the Sea Using Maximum Entropy"
- 1996: I. Adelman & J.E. Taylor "Village Economies: The Design, Estimation, and Use of Villagewide Economic Models"
- 2000: C.J. Morrison Paul "Cost Economics and Market Power in U.S. Beef Packing"
- 2003: M. Smith & J.E. Wilen "Economic Impacts of Marine Reserves: The Importance of Spatial Behavior"
- 2003: R.E. Howitt & D. Sunding "Water Infrastructure and Water Allocation in California"
- 2004: W.E. Johnston & A.F. McCalla "Whither California Agriculture: Up, Down, or Out? Some Thoughs about the Future"
- 2005: M.R. Caputo & Q. Paris "An Atemporal Microeconomic Theory and an Empirical Test of Price-Induced Technical Progress"
- 2007: C.A. Carter & A. Smith "Estimating the Market Effect of a Food Scare: The Case of Genetically Modified StarLink Corn"
- 2007: A.E. Harrison "Globalization and Poverty"
- 2008: A. de Janvry & E. Sadoulet "The Global Food Crisis: Identification of the Vulnerable and Policy Responses"
- 2009: P. Martin "Importing Poverty? Immigration and the Changing Face of Rural America"

Photograph captions (AAEA Fellows/Presidents):

Murray Reed Benedict, AAEA President 1941, AAEA Fellow 1962
Raymond G. Bressler, Jr., AAEA President 1959, AAEA Fellow 1963
Siegfried von Ciriacy-Wantrup, AAEA Fellow 1975
Sidney S. Hoos, AAEA Fellow 1977
Varden Fuller, AAEA Fellow 1979

Claude B. Hutchison
Giannini Hall UC Berkeley
Howard R. Tolley, AAEA President 1933

Harold O. Carter, AAEA Fellow 1980
Kenneth R. Farrell, AAEA President 1977, AAEA Fellow 1980
Sylvia Lane, AAEA Fellow 1984
Andrew Schmitz, AAEA Fellow 1983
Ben C. French, AAEA Fellow 1981
Henry R. Wellman, AAEA President 1953, AAEA Fellow 1985
Alex F. McCalla, AAEA Fellow 1988
Oscar R. Burt, AAEA Fellow 1982
Reuben E. Just, AAEA Fellow 1989
George M. Kuznets, AAEA Fellow 1982
Alain de Janvry, AAEA Fellow 1990
Gordon C. Rausser, AAEA Fellow 1990
Gordon A. King, AAEA Fellow 1983
Gerald Dean, AAEA Appreciation Club 1991

Warren Johnston, AAEA Fellow 1995
Colin A. Carter, AAEA Fellow 2000
Irma Adelman, AAEA Fellow 1998
George G. Judge, AAEA Fellow 1995
James E. Wilen, AAEA Fellow 2001
Brian D. Wright, AAEA Fellow 2002
David Zilberman, AAEA Fellow 1998
Jeffrey M. Perloff, AAEA Fellow 2003
Daniel A. Sumner, AAEA Fellow 1999
Richard J. Sexton, AAEA Fellow 2004
B. Delworth Gardner, AAEA Fellow 1992
Julian M. Alston, AAEA Fellow 2000
Catherine J. Morrison Paul, AAEA Fellow 2006

Jeffrey T. LaFrance, AAEA Fellow 2007
Steve Buccola, AAEA Fellow 2007
Peter Berck, AAEA Fellow 2008
Larry S. Karp, AAEA Fellow 2008
Michael E. Carter, AAEA Fellow 2009
Richard E. Howitt, AAEA Fellow 2009

SOCIAL VALUE OF THE GIANNINI FOUNDATION

Historically, developments in agriculture and resource economics have exploited the synergies that exist between science, economic analysis, and practical knowledge of food and agricultural systems. Such synergies were institutionalized by the traditional placement of departments of agricultural economics and their various incarnations within land-grant universities' colleges of agriculture and the national Agricultural Experiment Station system. As experiment station researchers, members of agricultural economics departments are charged explicitly by the Hatch Act with undertaking research that contributes to the continued development and success of agriculture and rural America, including agricultural production, marketing, and management of environmental and natural resources. The Hatch Act of 1887, which established the U.S. Agricultural Experiment Station system, states that the purpose of this system is "to aid in acquiring and diffusing among the people of the United States useful and practical information on subjects connected with agriculture, and to promote scientific investigation and experiments respecting the principles and applications of agricultural science." This institutional structure has facilitated a continuing dialogue regarding the purpose and usefulness of agricultural economic researchers and their respective clientele or stakeholders within agriculture and food systems. This structure has encouraged agricultural economics and related fields, certainly among the Foundation membership, to focus on practical questions, often with immediate implications.

In the context of instruction, the advancement of human capital not only at the undergraduate level, but also at the master's and Ph.D. degree levels, has reflected a number of distinguishing characteristics that differentiate agricultural and resource economics from general economics. Among distinguishing characteristics are: the view that economics and economic analysis are a segment of a larger coordinated social-natural system, the emphasis on integrating economic and scientific modelling, the focus on the importance of time and space in understanding economic phenomenon, the emphasis on identifying the flexibility or inflexibility of factors of production and economic agents, and finally, the recognition of the importance of institutions. In particular, the distinguishing strength of agricultural economics over

the history of the Foundation lies in fusing together institutional and empirical insights with microeconomic theory to capture operational solutions to understanding and interpreting critical policy issues. Given the demands emanating from direct clientele (or stakeholder) interactions, agricultural and resource economic research has naturally gravitated to seeking answers to real-world questions. This underlying philosophy has resulted in contributions to methodologies of measuring economic phenomenon and testing available theoretical constructs.

In this broader setting, throughout the existence of the Foundation, the advancement of knowledge on new frameworks for analytical evaluations of various segments of California food and agriculture has been a principal theme. Armed with empirical data, innovative technical tools, and a well-endowed library, Foundation members have engaged in developing new lenses and analytical paths whenever major challenges have emerged. Generally, they have not followed well-established roads but have blazed their own trails, generating new insights and sustainable methodologies for empirical analysis.

Any assessment of the Foundation must recognize that the members—faculty and Cooperative Extension specialists—have core financial support sourced with instruction on each of the three campuses, and from the Agricultural Experiment Station. This is a common characteristic of land-grant universities covering much of the United States. Any assessment of the incremental value of the Foundation above and beyond these sources of financial support must recognize the complementarities that exist among the three streams of financial support: instruction, experiment station, and the funding from the Foundation.

A hallmark of all of the members of the Foundation and the University of the California system is the fundamental value of academic freedom and the flexibility for agricultural and resource economists to pursue their intellectual curiosity, by focusing on the public interest rather than by administrative directives or the intense interest-group pressures felt by some other land-grant institutions. With respect to both graduate student support and project funding, the Foundation has been instrumental in creating incentives for members to pursue research that may well not only advance the frontiers of knowledge but provide insights for improving public policies, as well as decision-making among California agriculturalists. The degree of academic freedom afforded Foundation membership has been enhanced by the Giannini endowment and the allocation of current funding for supporting the "free choice and passion" of Foundation members and Ph.D. students interested in the welfare of California agriculture, interpreted broadly. The existence of the Foundation within a university system that sets a premium on high-quality research has helped differentiate and ultimately distinguish the contributions of agricultural and resource economists in the state of California from those of other land-grant universities across the United States.

Given the three sources of financial support—instructional, experiment station, and the Foundation—it is the Foundation that has provided incremental value to the land-grant university mandate in the state of California. As noted earlier in this chapter, the agricultural and resource economics departments of UC Berkeley and UC Davis have emerged as the two best in the country, offering instructional and research contributions to the advancement of knowledge. In the case of the Foundation, fulfillment of this commitment began with the establishment of the library, which collected, cataloged, stored, and made available pertinent economic information and analysis. Foundation members have been actively engaged in collecting market price and cost data and making them available to the general public. This has been combined with numerous price and cost publications across the vast majority of the commodities produced and distributed within California food and agriculture. For public policy problems of all forms and shapes, Foundation members have provided not only a retrospective evaluation of policy impacts, which is sometimes required by the underlying legislation, but also a clear delineation of policy incidence (who wins and who loses). Further topics have included: mechanism design; analyzing strategic behavior and which private economic agents can exploit asymmetric information and/or moral hazard; political economics delineating the role of organizational structures, including the emergence of cooperative organizations and interest groups that have a vested interested in directing policies or institutions toward their special interest; and governance structures that delineate who have

access to collective decision-making processes within and across various commodity systems (Rausser, Swinnen, and Zusman, 2011).

Along the historical path of the Foundation, there have been numerous commodity systems analyses for most all of the major products produced by the California food and agricultural system. New methodologies have been developed for evaluating industrial organization and supply chains from one commodity system to another. Diverse forms of quantitative analysis have been applied to California food and agriculture, including various operation research methodologies (dynamic programming, quadratic programming, and linear programming). Much of the initial research on the competitive advantage of California food and agriculture was evaluated by Foundation members utilizing spatial equilibrium, optimal plant location, and time allocation analytical frameworks. This work has extended beyond just production economics and distribution of food products all the way upstream to estimating demand and supply of various inputs, particularly labor.

The emphasis on generating and disseminating improved methodologies for empirical analysis has led Foundation members to be the first economists throughout the UC system who were pioneers in developing econometric methodologies for industry and commodity system analysis. Armed with the underlying data and library resources, Foundation members pioneered the use of econometric analysis to evaluate industry or commodity industrial organization modelling focusing on supply, the marketing chain, and the ultimate consumer demand for various food products produced within the state of California. In other words, Foundation members were the original focal point within the UC system and, for that matter, all land-grant university systems across the United States for empirical analysis using the best statistical and econometric methodologies available. Many of the historic leaders in econometrics, including Lawrence Klein, Zvi Griliches, Yair Mundlak, and Dennis Aigner, honed their skills as students of Giannini Foundation members at Berkeley including, importantly, George Kuznets.

SELECTED EXAMPLES OF GIANNINI FOUNDATION SUPPORT OF CALIFORNIA AGRICULTURE

On numerous occasions, Giannini Foundation members have documented our role in various watershed events since the original A.P. Giannini grant to agricultural economics. Throughout the Foundation's history, members have addressed a number of fundamental questions, such as: Since markets are not perfect, what are the effects of identified imperfections? Which imperfections are important? How might they be mitigated or eliminated? Can the institutional structure be improved and, if so, how? In this section, we have selected a few key watershed events following the establishment of the Giannini Foundation that are indicative of the social value of the Giannini Foundation.[2] In our selection of these events, we have focused on controversial societal issues that have emerged for which the Giannini Foundation research improved our understanding and offered sound analysis and potential prescriptions.

THE GREAT DEPRESSION AND LABOR UNREST

Labor unrest became endemic during the Depression. In 1934, a general strike precipitated by longshoremen closed the Port of San Francisco. Agricultural workers attempted to unionize and strike but were countered by growers who joined forces as the Associated Farmers. A 1939 Senate committee determined that agricultural workers' rights to organize had been violated, but the labor question

dissipated with the onset of the war. Yet, also in 1939, an extraordinarily insightful dissertation supported by the Foundation was completed at UC Berkeley, entitled *The Supply of Agricultural Labor as a Factor in the Evolution of Farm Organization in California*.[3] Varden Fuller's thesis was one of the first empirical studies of agricultural labor by someone who ultimately became a Giannini Foundation member that demonstrated the importance of the supply of seasonal (often immigrant) labor to the agricultural sector.

WORLD WAR II

Without question, another watershed was the economic disruption that took place during World War II. The disruption caused food and labor shortages throughout the United States, necessitating research on price control and self-sufficiency. Even before Pearl Harbor, Foundation members quantified the demand for California products. But perhaps the most lasting legacy of the Foundation on the war-time issue of price controls was by John Kenneth Galbraith, a Ph.D. student at UC Berkeley who was the first agricultural economics lecturer to teach courses at UC Davis. Galbraith credited his time at both Berkeley and Davis with forming the basic themes and ideas behind his important books—*American Capitalism: The Concept of Countervailing Power* (1952) and *The Affluent Society* (1958)—and his war-time role in the Office of Price Administration (OPA). Galbraith based *American Capitalism: The Concept of Countervailing Power* on cooperatives that tried to rebalance the concentration that existed on the buy side of a number of commodity markets for crops produced in California and the marketing order experience for fresh fruits and vegetables.

---

2 For a larger set of events please consult:

Rausser, G. 2009. "The Giannini Foundation and the Welfare of California Agriculturists in a Changing State, Nation, and World." Giannini Foundation 75th Anniversary. https://s.giannini.ucop.edu/uploads/giannini_public/29/45/29453ba7-c473-4c33-a69c-1debb5f319f4/apgiannini-book-contributions-rausser.pdf.

Johnston, W.E., A.F. McCalla. 2004. "Whither California Agriculture: Up, Down or Out? Some Thoughts about the Future." Giannini Foundation Special Report Series 04-1. https://s.giannini.ucop.edu/uploads/giannini_public/43/84/4384fd4a-266c-434a-b85c-83a1ec11e385/escholarship_uc_item_4232w2sr.pdf.

Scheuring A.F. 1995. *Science & Service: A History of the Land-Grant University and Agriculture in California.* Oakland, CA. UC ANR Publications.

---

3 V. Fuller. "The Supply of Agricultural Labor as a Factor in the Evolution of Farm Organization in California".1939.

INTERSTATE COMPETITION

Turning to the decade of the 1950s, competition intensified among various states involved in supplying the major Eastern metropolitan markets. This was especially true in the markets for fresh fruits and vegetables. As the competition from other Western states, Southeastern states, and various geographic locations within the Midwest accelerated, Foundation members assisted California agriculturalists with timely research. Foundation researchers provided practical advice and counsel on establishing a competitive advantage for California producers in their pursuit of growing markets. From the 1950s through the mid-1960s, the increase in interstate competition in the agricultural product and food sectors prompted Giannini Foundation members to study food packing and processing efficiencies, leading to development of several important operational models focused on plant location and optimal raw product assembly. Increasing interstate competition also prompted Giannini Foundation researchers to analyze the optimal distribution of California food products (form, time, and space) under unregulated and regulated conditions. Some Foundation members also integrated economics and engineering science through the application of time and motion studies to improve plant operational efficiencies.

Giannini Foundation members also contributed a significant amount of work on spatial equilibrium models that focused on positioning California to compete with other farm states. Their work on plant location models was designed to determine the optimal location given the trade-off of balancing the cost of distribution with the cost of raw product assembly. At the end of this period, economists within the Foundation began measuring demand elasticities and the implications of such measures on pricing across seasonal periods and different geographical locations, as well as how agriculturists in California should allocate available supply to enhance commercial profits.

BRACEROS AND TOMATOES

As the labor-intensive fruit and vegetable sectors in California agriculture grew, so did the importance of migrant labor. When it became clear that U.S. involvement in World War II would lead to domestic labor shortages, the United States and Mexico negotiated the Bracero (farm-hand) Program to admit temporary migrants to work in the agricultural sector. After the war, agricultural interests succeeded in obtaining repeated extensions of the program until 1964.

Opposition to the program grew from those who claimed that the migrants depressed agricultural wages for U.S. citizens and increased rural poverty. Representatives of tomato farmers claimed that the loss of reasonably priced and available workers would cause the processing tomato industry to move to Mexico where there was no shortage of labor. Instead of disappearing, the value of the industry grew as mechanical tomato harvesters began to replace manual labor. Tomato harvesters had been under development at the University of California for 20 years, and the state Legislature allocated money to speed up this research in anticipation of the end of the Bracero Program. The technology was introduced shortly before the program ended; by the end of the 1960s, nearly all of the tomato harvest was mechanical. The substitution of capital for labor precipitated by the loss of cheap labor has occurred throughout the history of agriculture (and in many other sectors), but seldom has it been as abrupt and obvious as in the case of the tomato harvester and the Bracero Program. The change had profound social effects. The tomato industry thrived but field employment fell by nearly 50 percent. Many small tomato farmers, unable to afford the expensive technology, left the sector—the number of tomato farmers dropped to less than 25 percent of the level in the late 1950s.

Social activists claimed that state support (via UC research) of the tomato harvesting technology handed a windfall to tomato farmers at a great cost to farmworkers and rural communities. Giannini Foundation economists emphasized that this state-funded research was the source for substantial economic return. However, they also recognized that private cost-benefit analysis neglects social costs, particularly those arising from a short-term adjustment of displaced and subsequently unemployed labor.

The fact that the university had financed the research led to more than a decade of litigation over the issue of whether the expenditure of Hatch Act monies (federal government matching funds to support agricultural research) required taking into account the likely social consequences of the supported research. On appeal, the California Supreme Court ruled that it was not practical to determine the effect of university-sponsored research ex ante and that it would be an infringement of academic freedom to require that research be vetted for its potential social consequences. Although the judicial decision was unambiguous, it was followed by many years of public controversy. This controversy continues today as questions about public-private partnerships become increasingly important in university research (Rausser, Ameden, and Stevens, 2016). One of the effects of this controversy is the acknowledgment of the public's legitimate interest in university research. Public interest in university research may seem self-evident but actually represents a major shift in perception. During the first 60 years of the 20th century, the general consensus was that increases in agricultural productivity made possible by university research automatically contributed to the public good. The advent of the tomato harvester and other technological developments made it evident that "progress" creates winners and losers.

The Rise of the United Farm Workers

The social activism behind the political decision to terminate the Bracero Program and the concomitant technological developments that weakened labor's bargaining power were important parts of the social environment that nurtured the United Farm Workers (UFW). This union, formed by Cesar Chavez and Dolores Huerta, began as a worker-rights organization. After a well-publicized, five-year boycott of table grapes that led to union recognition by most major growers and a 40-percent increase in wages, the UFW was able to organize workers in lettuce fields in Salinas and the Imperial Valley.

During the rise of the UFW and its conflict with the Teamsters union, Giannini Foundation members conducted a number of labor productivity studies on California agriculture. They analyzed migrant labor contributions to the agricultural sector and the relative poverty levels of migrant versus domestic laborers. They also analyzed the

effect of legal migrants and the role of the UFW on various socio-economic status measures, including housing, wages, and other forms of compensation. Finally, they conducted a number of studies sponsored by the governor's office on the welfare of California agricultural labor. Giannini Foundation members contributed much of the analysis that informed the California Legislature and the governor's office.

Water

In California resource economics, management of water and water rights intensified in public discourse with the emergence of the California Water Plan in 1957. There is no question that water rights, allocations, and supporting institutions have a material impact on the welfare of California agriculturalists. Plans for water carriers were introduced throughout the first half of the 20th century in the California Water Plan. Members of the Giannini Foundation contributed to the evaluation and design of financial contracts of these state projects. They also provided the economic rationale for conjunctive use of ground and surface water to overcome droughts and instability. Moreover, they introduced pricing and trading schemes that made it possible to capture more value from existing water resources. Among the most significant of these contributions was the first major theoretical and empirical application of conjunctive water use, namely, the joint management of both surface and groundwater (Burt, 1964).

Over the years, a number of crisis events and institutional changes have emerged from California water resource systems, including the so-called 160-acre limitation for access to water-cost subsidies, Kesterson Wildlife Refuge, the drainage crisis, water banks, and the CVPIA (Central Valley Project Improvement Act). In 1985, there was a major drainage problem in California that could not be resolved by the creation of a wetland. Access to federal water was threatened if solutions were not introduced, but the initial proposals were capital-intensive and simply too expensive. The crisis came about very quickly and was a total surprise to some California agriculturalists and most interested parties. In response, Giannini Foundation economists looked at restructuring the kinds of incentives that existed for conservation, changes in land use, and, moreover, implementation of the fundamental notion of option value and the flexibility to wait before making commitments on capital investments. The federal and state governments gathered a drainage task force to assess alternative solutions; the composition of the task force included many Foundation members from UC Davis, Berkeley, and Riverside.[4]

ENVIRONMENT

Another major event was establishment of the U.S. Environmental Protection Agency (EPA). In the early 1970s when the EPA was organized, the agency's founders looked around the country to find the expertise to deal with spatial pollution, air pollution, and land and groundwater pollution and found that agricultural economists were the best equipped to address these critical externality questions. Moreover, a review of all the major grants given by the EPA to academic researchers during the agency's early years would find that almost all went to researchers with formal training in agricultural economics.

Some of the best work on pesticide externalities in the world has been done by Giannini Foundation members. Furthermore, all the work on contingent valuation to determine how society values resources such as Yosemite National Park or Lake Tahoe remaining pristine emerged from some conceptual lenses developed long ago by a Giannini Foundation faculty member (Ciriacy-Wantrup, 1952). A number of current or former Giannini Foundation members became the intellectual leaders in applying these methods.

---

4   In particular, Foundation economists proposed a management solution that included incentives for conservation, changes in land use, and evaporation. This research allowed policy makers additional time to select superior solutions. Subsequently, environmental interest groups pressured the CVPIA to divert water from agriculture to the environment. Giannini Foundation research showed that the costs of diversions would be much smaller if they were combined with water trading, a key component of the CVPIA-motivated Giannini Foundation research. Members of the Foundation helped establish an electronic water system, a mechanism that allowed increased efficiency and water security. More recent Giannini Foundation research has focused on the welfare consequences of reallocating water among urban, agricultural, and environmental uses, particularly the proposed San Diego to Imperial Valley water-transfer transaction.

The Giannini Foundation also conducted important research on pest control, including

(a) the introduction of modern integrated pest management (IPM) and biological control;

(b) the use of modern economics to evaluate health risk and trade-offs with agricultural productivity; and

(c) pesticides as damage-control agents, their potential human health effects, and their substitutability with transgenic seeds.

When the "Big Green" pesticide ban proposal was discussed by legislators in 1991, Giannini Foundation members conducted a study that showed that it would negatively affect low-income consumers. As a result, Giannini Foundation members offered remedies including taxation and pollution regulations (Zilberman et al., 1991). The general public supported these alternative remedies by rejecting the "Big Green" initiative at the polls.

With respect to the proposed phase-out and ban of methylbromide, Foundation researchers showed how a total ban would be costly and counter-productive since scaling back to 25 percent of historical use would preserve 80 percent of the benefits. In the case of invasive species and plant diseases, Foundation research demonstrated how Medflies, Pierce's disease, and white flies may cost billions in damages and how distributional effects are more significant than the aggregate impact. Once again, Foundation researchers offered practical solutions emphasizing the use of monitoring, prevention, and rapid and targeted responses rather than heavy-handed public policies. Finally, to support AB 32[5], the Foundation supported a number of conferences that focused on economic evaluations of proposed Cap-and-Trade Program to control carbon emissions and help reduce the environmentally damaging impacts of global warming. Such assessments helped inform the general public and the ultimate support of AB 32.

---

5   AB 32 or Assembly Bill 32 of 2006 requires California to reduce greenhouse gas emissions to 1990 levels by 2020. This is a reduction approximately 15 percent below emissions expected under a "business-as-usual" scenario.

Farm Financial Crisis

The farm financial crisis of the 1980s began in the Midwest but slowly made its way to California, affecting U.S. agriculture as a whole. Giannini Foundation researchers demonstrated that the major causal forces underlying this financial crisis were sourced with monetary policy, federal fiscal policy, trade flow, and exchange rates. In essence, the monetary policy of the federal reserve in the early 1980s forced interest rates and the relative value of the U.S. dollar to overshoot. The latter phenomenon reduced the export market for agricultural products across the United States, including California, and helped contribute to a dramatic downward spiral in commodity prices. These causal phenomena were almost a complete reversal of what took place over much of the 1970s. The rapid expansion in available debt capital to agriculturalists in the 1970s was asset-collateralization-based. Hence, as inflation began to recede and export markets shrank, the market value of underlying collateralized assets fell dramatically. Debt-service-based finance was relatively uncommon compared to the asset-based financing that took place during much of the 1970s. As a result, the agricultural sector throughout the United States was indeed vulnerable to the effect of reversal of external factors (trade, monetary policy, exchange rates, interest rates) on final market pricing traced all the way upstream to input pricing, particularly land prices. Giannini Foundation members helped to explain the major price bubbles that were taking place in the early 1970s. Foundation members were able to explain the difference between the 1970s and 1980s and the implications for the farm financial crisis of the mid-1980s. This crisis resulted in a bankrupt farm credit system that was resolved by a government bailout. Foundation members helped design the bailout to achieve sustainability and avoid the inherent moral hazard concerns.

Intellectual Property

At the beginning of the genetic-engineering era, the Bayh-Dole Act gave universities the rights to any patents on discoveries financed by federal grants (1980). In the same year, a key Supreme Court decision affirmed that new life-forms were patentable subject matter. Patenting of plants and animals became possible during this period of emerging private spending and stagnant public spending on agricultural research and development. One result is that universities have slowly been pulled into the commercial sector. Universities are generally not accustomed to capturing, let alone fully appreciating, commercial value. Nevertheless, they were given incentives to search for opportunities to realize the commercial value of discoveries that resulted from their scientists' research. This has led to numerous university–private research partnerships that Foundation members have helped to design. In fact, one Foundation member provided the intellectual leadership in the design and establishment of the Berkeley Novartis public-private partnership research agreement supporting research discoveries in plant biotechnology (Rausser, Ameden, and Stevens, 2016). Moreover, Foundation members have been actively involved in structuring patent-pooling arrangements to facilitate access by both the private and the public sector.

The Green Revolution

From the 1970s through the 1990s, the Green Revolution and subsequent increase in productivity in developing countries provided the opportunity to evaluate income versus substitution effects on the global demand for agricultural products produced in California. The indirect effects of the Green Revolution, marked by a notable increase in food production in the Third World because of improved strains of wheat, rice, and maize, not only helped prevent large-scale famine but also made the fundamental study of substitution and income effects possible. The economists of the Giannini Foundation have been actively engaged in demonstrating to California agriculturalists the benefits they derive from the growth of the agricultural sectors in developing countries because of income effects. To be sure, there may be some competitive suffering in the short run due to substitution effects. For example, Chile and Mexico have become more effective competitors for a number of products usually sourced in California. There are, however, complementarities between seasonal supplies from countries that facilitate year-round supplies of fresh fruits and vegetables, making them a regular part of consumers' diets. In the final analysis, major benefits accrue to California agriculturalists as a result of the income effects on demand resulting from economic growth in these countries.

The Green Revolution is usually identified with the CGIAR centers. Various Giannini Foundation members have been actively engaged in the work of CGIAR and the various centers that comprise this global research network, participating as researchers and being involved in its governance. Perhaps more important, however, are the studies and analyses that have been conducted to analyze the economic consequences of new research discoveries and increased productivity of a number of basic crops. For California agriculturalists, much of this research has implications for the short-run substitution effects versus the long-run income effects on export demand for California's higher-quality food products.

GLOBALIZATION

Giannini Foundation members have conducted a large amount of research work on trade liberalization. The focus of this research has been on who wins, who loses, and what the environmental consequences might be from trade liberalization and/or globalization. This Foundation research includes an evaluation of the Uraguay Round of multi-national trade negotiations within the framework of the General Agreement on Tariffs and Trade (the GATT-Uruguay Round) that engaged and brought agriculture into trade negotiations, the North American Free Trade Agreement (NAFTA), and the World Trade Organization (WTO) Doha Round. Topics include: (1) assessment of effects of California's position as the nation's largest exporter of agricultural products; (2) income growth, especially in the Pacific Rim, driving an increased demand for higher-quality food and fiber; (3) international agreements opening more foreign markets to California exports; (4) better access of foreign products to U.S. markets due to the fall in U.S. import barriers; (5) improved assessment of technical trade barriers ,which must be based on scientific evidence; (6) and investments by multinational firms and joint ventures in highly processed products that are changing the form and shape of agricultural trade.

The Giannini Foundation is uniquely well-equipped to evaluate formally the impacts of trade liberalization and globalization on California's agriculturalists based on the intellectual capital of its members. Foundation research has assessed the impact of imperfectly competitive markets and state traders on national and California agricultural

food exports. A few Foundation members helped orchestrate the formation of the International Agricultural Trade Research Consortium (IATRC). Giannini Foundation members have also been involved in trade policy and international trade disputes over invasive species, as well as in leadership of the Agricultural Issues Center. They have analyzed crop-specific effects of trade agreements on segments of California agriculture, such as wine trade and the associated industrial organization of the domestic and international wine markets. What we do know about the international effects of U.S. farm policy has been largely quantified by a few Giannini Foundation members. Finally, Foundation members have conducted analyses that addressed the environmental consequences of globalization.

CHALLENGES

CLIMATE CHANGE

Climate change is real, despite some lingering questions from chronic skeptics, but its speed and consequences remain uncertain. For California agriculture, a probable impact is to alter the seasonal pattern of precipitation to be more rain and less snow. As snow provides a significant share of annual water storage capacity, a permanent reduction of the snowpack would have dire consequences for agriculture, which stills uses almost 80 percent of California's surface water. Also, will rising temperatures render some currently profitable crops non-viable? How will California agriculture adjust? Probably the same way it has for the past 160 years: by changing what it produces, how it produces it, and where it produces it. It will adapt because adaptation is its only choice. But it will also need intellectual capacity and research to continue its never-ending, dynamic adjustment.

TRADE

Globalization has been a continuing challenge to California agriculture over its entire existence. The challenge has been met by research, innovation, productivity enhancement, superior management, and forwarding-looking attention to the demand side of the equation. California agriculture benefits greatly by having in its ever-changing suite of products that people eat more of, particularly as they get richer.

NATURAL RESOURCES

California may be the third largest state in the Union (100 million acres) but the majority of the area is in mountains, forests, and desert. Forty-four million acres are identified as having potential for agriculture. But only 10 million are identified as cropland, and of those, less than 8 million are irrigated. And, these last two numbers are declining. California's population may soon exceed 40 million people, most of whom live in ever-expanding urban areas built almost exclusively on prime agricultural land. Further, rising incomes increase the demand for recreation, water,

land, and environmental conservation. Without doubt, less water and land will be available to agriculture in the future and it will be more expensive. Therefore, cropping patterns are likely to continue to shift towards higher-valued crops, e.g., horticulture, grapes, tree nuts and fruits, and specialty vegetables.

RESOURCE-USE CONFLICTS

Resource-use conflicts clearly will increase in intensity. Multiple demands for water—urban, industrial, agriculture, fisheries, recreation, environmental conservation, energy, and transportation—will press on limited supplies of surface and groundwater. These water supplies are unlikely to expand much and at some point, will necessitate rational management of diminishing groundwater aquifers. Will large concentrations of dairy animals with high demands for water and production of incredible amounts of wastes eventually drive the dairy industry out of California? Other conflicts arising in the management of forests and fisheries inevitably will become more intense with climate change and population growth.

ORGANIC AGRICULTURE

Coevolution of organic and conventional agriculture, along with developments in biology, will continue to offer challenges and opportunities for agriculture. Rapid advancement in precision genetic manipulation for productivity enhancement, management of stresses, and improved nutrition continue to emerge with positive potentials. However, pressure for increased yields has also increased the chemical intensity of conventional agriculture. This has led to concern about increases in toxic chemicals in the food supply, increased negative environmental impacts, and overall concerns about food quality and safety. The rapid rise of the organic movement, the continuing conflicts over GMOs, and the push towards less-intense conservation agriculture are countervailing forces that will make feeding a growing and richer population more challenging.

LABOR

California agriculture has always had intense periodic needs for field operations originally done by farmworkers. The labor supply has always been international, chronologically from China, Japan, India, Philippines, Mexico, and Central America. Mechanization has reduced the demand for labor somewhat; its pace is often accelerated by labor shortages and rising wages. But mechanical harvesting dominates a growing share of the nut industry and more and more of the fruit industry, including perishables such as peaches and boysenberries. Remaining hand operations are in the tree fruit and nut industry in terms of annual pruning and sculpting of nut and fruit trees. It is likely, given the current intense debate on illegal immigrants and California's planned increases in the minimum wage, that further limitations on human labor will occur. What will be next? Could it be robots programmed to precisely trim trees and vines? Could it be soft-handed robots that gently pick the most precious Cabernet Sauvignon grapes and juicy, ripe strawberries? By then, there will be self-driving tractors and trucks. Farmers may well manage their operations electronically from a remote location.

PUBLIC INVESTMENT

Our final challenge is reduced public investment in agricultural research and development, and the potential substitution of public-private research partnership agreements to advance knowledge, discoveries, and commercial value generated by California agriculture. Already, the majority of research and development expenditure for the United States agricultural sector is done in the private sector or by public-private partnerships and this trend is sure to continue. That will leave to Foundation members the task of evaluating the social costs and implementing the needed public-policy analysis. This is what the Giannini Foundation has always done well. The Giannini Foundation research is well positioned to continue to deliver analysis with great social value.

REFERENCES

Burt, O.R. 1964. "The Economics of Conjunctive Use of Ground and Surface Water." *Hilgardia* 36(2): 31-111.

Ciriacy-Wantrup, S. 1952. *Resource Conservation: Economics and Policies*. Berkeley CA: University of California Press.

Fuller, L.V. 1939. *The Supply of Agricultural Labor as a Factor in the Evolution of Farm Organization in California*. Berkeley CA: University of California.

Galbraith, J.K. 1991. *The Affluent Society*. London UK: Penguin Books.

Galbraith, J.K. 2017. *American Capitalism: The Concept of Countervailing Power*. New York NY: Routledge.

Johnston, W.E., and A.F. McCalla. 2004. "Whither California Agriculture: Up, Down or Out? Some Thoughts about the Future." Giannini Foundation Special Report 04-1. Berkeley CA: Giannini Foundation of Agricultural Economics, University of California. Available at: https://s.giannini.ucop.edu/uploads/giannini_public/43/84/4384fd4a-266c-434a-b85c-83a1ec11e385/escholarship_uc_item_4232w2sr.pdf.

Johnston, W.E., and A.F. McCalla, eds. 2009. *A.P. Giannini and the Giannini Foundation of Agricultural Economics*. Davis CA: Giannini Foundation of Agricultural Economics. Available at: http://ageconsearch.umn.edu/bitstream/251962/2/001%20whole%20book.pdf.

McCalla A.F., J.M. Alston, and K.A. Schaefer. 2017. *The UC Davis Agricultural and Resource Economics PhD Program: The First 50 Years*. Davis, CA: Department of Agricultural and Resource Economics, University of California, Davis. Available at: https://50thcelebration.are.ucdavis.edu/uploads/filer_public/ad/7b/ad7b65c9-e82b-409b-9e70-1537b9f8c4bd/the_uc_davis_agricultural_and_resource_economics_phd_program-_the_first_50_years.pdf.

Rausser, G. 2009. "The Giannini Foundation and the Welfare of California Agriculturists in a Changing State, Nation, and World." In W.E. Johnston and A.F. McCalla, eds *A.P. Giannini and the Gianinni Foundation of Agricultural Economics*. Davis CA: Giannini Foundation of Agricultural Economics. Available at: http://ageconsearch.umn.edu/bitstream/251962/2/001%20whole%20book.pdf.

Rausser G., H. Ameden, and R. Stevens. 2016. *Structuring Public-Private Research Partnerships for Success: Empowering University Partners*. Cheltenham UK: Edward Elgar.

Rausser G., J. Swinnen, and P. Zusman. 2011. *Political Power and Economic Policy: Theory, Analysis, and Empirical Applications*. Cambridge UK: Cambridge University Press.

Scheuring A.F., C.O. McCorkle, and J. Lyons. 1995. *Science & Service: A History of the Land Grant University and Agriculture in California*. Oakland CA: University of California Division of Agriculture and Natural Resources.

Zilberman, D., A. Schmitz, G. Casterline, E. Lichtenberg, and J.B. Siebert. 1991. "The Economics of Pesticide Use and Regulation." *Science* 253(5019): 518-522.

Made in the USA
Monee, IL
11 November 2020